A

SHORT HISTORY

OF

OPERA

VOLUME TWO

A
SHORT HISTORY
OF
OPERA

SECOND EDITION

By DONALD JAY GROUT

Given Foundation Professor of Musicology
Cornell University

VOLUME TWO

Columbia University Press
New York and London
1965

CONTENTS

ILLUSTRATIONS

LIST OF ABBREVIATIONS

AfMf	*Archiv für Musikforschung*	MD	*Musica disciplina*
AfMw	*Archiv für Musikwissen-schaft*	Mf	*Musikforschung*
		MfMg	*Monatshefte für Musik-geschichte*
AMZ	*Allgemeine musikalische Zeitung*	MGG	*Musik in Geschichte und Gegenwart*
art.	article	M&L	*Music & Letters*
B&H	Breitkopf & Härtel	MLA Notes	*Music Library Associa-tion Notes*
C.E.	Collected Edition (Gesamtausgabe)		
		MM	*Mercure musical*
C.F.	*Chefs-d'oeuvre de l'opéra français*	MMus	*Modern Music*
		MMR	*Monthly Musical Record*
DdT	*Denkmäler deutscher Tonkunst*	MQ	*Musical Quarterly*
		MR	*Music Review*
DTB	*Denkmäler der Tonkunst in Bayern*	MTNA	*Proceedings of the Music Teachers National Association*
DTOe	*Denkmäler der Tonkunst in Oesterreich*		
		MuG	*Musik und Gesellschaft*
ed.	edition, editor, edited by	mus.	music (by)
EMTA	*Echo Muzyczne, Teatralne i Artystyczne*	NM	*Nuestra musica*
		NOHM	*New Oxford History of Music*
HAM	*Historical Anthology of Music*, Vol. II (Davison and Apel)		
		NZfM	*Neue Zeitschrift für Musik*
		OeM	*Oesterreichische Musik-zeitschrift*
JAMS	*Journal of the American Musicological Society*		
		OHM	*Oxford History of Music*
JMP	*Jahrbuch der Musik-bibliothek Peters*	perf.	performed, performance
		PMA	*Proceedings of the Royal Musical Association* (London)
K	Köchel, *Chronologisch-thematisches Verzeichnis sämtlicher Tonwerke Wolfgang Amade Mozarts*, 3d ed., rev. Einstein		
		RassM	*Rassegna musicale*
		RBM	*Revue belge de musicologie*
		RdM	*Revue de musicologie*
M	*Musica* (Kassel, 1947–)	rev.	revised
MA	*Musical Antiquary*		

RHCM	*Revue d'histoire et de critique musicales* (with No. 10 of Vol. II, 1902, became SIM *Revue musicale*)	SIMG	*Sammelbände der internationalen Musikgesellschaft*
RIdM	*Revue internationale de musique*	STM	*Svensk Tidskrift för Musikforskning*
RM	*Revue musicale* (Paris, 1920–)	SzMw	*Studien zur Musikwissenschaft* (Beihefte der DTOe)
RMI	*Rivista musicale italiana*	VfMw	*Vierteljahrsschrift für Musikwissenschaft*
SB	Schering, *Geschichte der Musik in Beispielen*	ZfMw	*Zeitschrift für Musikwissenschaft*
SchwM	*Schweizerische Musikzeitung*	ZIMG	*Zeitschrift der internationalen Musikgesellschaft*
SIM	Société internationale de musique		

PART 4

THE NINETEENTH CENTURY

(Continued)

CHAPTER 22

THE ROMANTIC OPERA
IN GERMANY[1]

The rise of nationalism in music, one of the outstanding features of the nineteenth century, is nowhere more striking than in the rapid growth of the romantic opera in Germany. Before 1820 German opera was known outside its own country only through *The Magic Flute* and a few Singspiels. A truly national opera came into existence with the performance of Weber's *Freischütz* at Berlin in 1821 and ensuing developments culminated in the world-wide triumph of Wagner's music dramas fifty years later. Since Germany displays more clearly and completely than any other country the effects of the romantic doctrines on opera, it will be convenient to summarize here those features of romanticism which come to light particularly in German opera from 1800 to 1870.

Many of those features are evident also, if to a lesser degree, in other countries. If we were to search for the most general principle of difference between the opera of the eighteenth and that of the nineteenth century, we should probably find it in the contrast between the idea of distinctness on the one hand and that of coalescence on the other. The contrast begins with the relation of the composer to his music. The eighteenth-century composer was a craftsman who stood outside the art works which he created; the nineteenth-century composer thought of

[1] General bibliography: Dent, "The Rise of the Romantic Opera"; Chantavoine and Gaudefroy-Demombynes, *Le Romantisme dans la musique européenne*; Istel, *Die Blütezeit der musikalischen Romantik in Deutschland*, chap. V: Kraus, "Das deutsche Liederspiel in den Jahren 1800–1830"; Goslich, *Beiträge zur Geschichte der deutschen romantischen Oper*; *Almanach der deutschen Musikbücherei auf das Jahr 1924/25*; Schmitz, "Zur Geschichte des Leitmotivs in der romantischen Oper"; Daninger, *Sage und Märchen im Musikdrama*; Ehrenhaus, *Die Operndichtung der deutschen Romantik*; Strunk, *Source Readings*, pp. 782–97.

music rather as a means of self-expression, a projection of his own feelings and ideas. His music has consequently a certain subjective quality which demands that the hearer shall place himself in sympathy with the composer, failing which he may fail to understand the music. Moreover, the music itself is directed more to the listener's emotions and less to his intellect than in the eighteenth century. The horror and rescue operas, the works of Weber, Meyerbeer, Donizetti, Verdi, and Wagner, all make a direct assault on the nerves and feelings of the audience in a manner which to Hasse, Gluck, or Mozart would have been inconceivable. In pursuit of this aim, and emancipated by the authority of individual freedom from the old restrictions, the nineteenth century proceeded to create a new aesthetic and a new set of musical procedures for opera, all of which, as said before, were dominated by the idea of coalescence as against the eighteenth-century idea of distinctness.

Let us look for example at the relation between libretto and music in each of the two periods. We have already seen how in the eighteenth-century opera seria these two elements were harnessd together in a kind of marriage of convenience which, provided certain conventions were observed, left each to a great extent free and unimpeded; the same libretto might receive many different musical settings, and the same music might be used for different words. This conception was no longer prevalent in the nineteenth century even in Italy. Everywhere, and to an increasing degree, the ideal, express or implicit, came to be a complete union of words and music in one perfect whole. But this ideal, especially in Germany, was carried in theory even further to advocate generally the amalgamation of music, poetry, and all the other arts in one supreme art which should be greater than the sum of its individual constituents. The ideal took various and sometimes fantastic forms; thus Schlegel: "The arts should be brought together again, and bridges sought from one to another. Perhaps columns shall come to life as paintings, paintings become poems, poems become music." [2] Poets and

---

[2] Quoted in Adler, *Handbuch* II, 865. Cf. Schelling's well-known definition of architecture as "frozen music" (*Philosophie der Kunst*, pp. 576, 593), and Goethe's similar statement (Eckermann, *Gespräche* I, 261, March 23, 1829). Such conceptions were not peculiar to the nineteenth century. In 1643 Harsdörffer, at the end of his "Spiel von der Welt Eitelkeit" (*Frauenzimmer Gesprechspiele* III. Theil, p. 242), wrote: "Hieraus erhellet wie alle Künste gleichsam also in einer Ketten aneinander hangen / deren ein Glied in das andere geschlossen / und absonderlich zwar ihre volkommene Rundungen / jedoch ohne so dienstliche Stärkleistung / haben. Die Reimkunst ist ein Gemälde / das Gemälde eine ebenstimmige Music / und diese

painters saw in music the ideal toward which the other arts were striving
—immediate in its expression of feeling, limited in its power to depict
the world of objects, but by this very indefiniteness supporting all the
more strongly that flight from the outer to the inner world, toward those
"somber longings, depressions and joyous elation without any recogniz-
able cause" [3] which are typical of certain romantic temperaments. The
arts were united not only in ideal but also in practice : poets and painters
composed music, musicians wrote essays, novels, and poetry. The ultimate stage as far as opera was concerned came with Wagner's theory
and realization of the *Gesamtkunstwerk*, the total, all-inclusive work of
art.

In the librettos of many German romantic operas we find also that
the eighteenth-century distinction between man and nature, and between nature and the supernatural, is broken down. In the eighteenth
century, nature appears in opera only as scenery in the background, and
so the music that depicts nature is of an imitative or descriptive sort,
such as bird-song arias, comparison arias, orchestral storms, and the
like. The supernatural in eighteenth-century opera is either a dramatic
convention (as in Rameau and Gluck) or else a source of farce (Dittersdorf) or pageantry (*The Magic Flute*). But in much German opera of
the nineteenth century, both nature and the supernatural are closely
identified with the moods of man, nature becoming as it were a vast
soundingboard for the murmurs of the unconscious soul, and the "invisible world of spirits" constantly impinging for good or evil on the affairs
of everyday life. The storms in Mozart's *Idomeneo* are only incidental;
the storm in Wagner's *Fliegende Holländer* is the whole mood of the
drama. In Weber's *Freischütz* both the natural background and the
supernatural happenings must be taken seriously or the plot is meaningless; yet here we have scarcely emerged from the fairy-tale stage. In
Tannhäuser and *Lohengrin* the supernatural begins to have symbolic importance. Finally, in the *Ring*, both nature and humanity become ab-

gleichsam eine beseelte Reimkunst." This may be compared with an eighteenth-
century view (Mattheson, *Neueste Untersuchung der Singspiele*, 1744, pp. 86–87)
which notably does not assert the identity of the arts but only their cooperation :
"Meines wenigen Erachtens ist ein gutes Operntheater nichts anders, als eine hohe
Schule vieler schönen Wissenschaften, worinn zusammen und auf einmal Architectur,
Perspective, Mahlerey, Mechanik, Tanzkunst, *Actio oratoria*, Moral, Historie, Poesie,
und vornehmlich Musik, zur Vergnügung und Erbauung vornehmer und ver-
nünftiger Zuschauer, sich aufs angenehmste vereinigen, und immer neue Probe
geben."

[3] Berlioz, program of *Symphonie fantastique*.

sorbed into a supernatural and superhuman realm ruled by transcendent moral forces, so that the whole action takes place on a symbolic, mythical plane.

All this fairy tale, legend, and myth in German romantic opera is national in character, as opposed to the earlier use of Greek mythology, medieval epic, or Roman history. The emphasis on national subject matter in opera followed the movement in literature which had begun in England with the publication of Macpherson's "edition" of Ossian and Percy's *Reliques of Ancient English Poetry* in the 1760s. In Germany Herder's cosmopolitan *Stimmen der Völker in Liedern* (1778–79) was followed in the years 1805–8 by an exclusively German collection, Arnim and Brentano's *Des Knaben Wunderhorn*. Interest in German legends and medieval literature was revived by the brothers Grimm (*Kinder- und Hausmärchen*, 1812–15; *Deutsche Mythologie*, 1835). Folk tales, fairy tales, patriotic odes, historical novels and dramas were produced by many authors. Much of this literature was not only national but also popular, that is, "of the folk." Glorification of "the folk," of humble scenes and pleasures and the instincts of simple people, is common in the early romantic period; and the imprint of these features remained on German opera even after 1830, when new influences were at work in literature.

Turning now to the music of romantic opera, we find likewise a coalescing of formerly distinct factors. Thus in the eighteenth century the functions of voice and orchestra were clearly defined. The orchestra accompanied the singers; it was heard by itself only on specified occasions, as in the overture, the ritornellos, and the ballets, marches, or descriptive pieces. In the nineteenth century the orchestra not only creates moods and provides exotic suggestion but enters intimately into the pattern of the drama itself. Eventually it becomes a continuous web of instrumental sound, thereby freeing the voice for more realistic, varied, and pointed declamation of the text. The overture achieves a close connection, both thematic and structural, with the opera itself. Improvement of the brass and wood-wind instruments, and the introduction of new instruments, make possible an enormously enlarged and variegated color scheme in operatic music. With increasing emphasis on the inner voices and increasing chromaticism in the harmony, the orchestra becomes more and more dominant in the musical texture. Curt Sachs has pointed out how this growth in importance of the orchestra in opera coincides with the rise of non-Italian schools—"the eternal antithesis between the playing North and the singing South." [4] The climax comes with Wagner's music dramas, in which the orchestra develops the entire action in a polyphonic tissue of sound.

Still another contrast between eighteenth- and nineteenth-century opera is seen with respect to musical forms. The older opera consisted of a series of distinct numbers, without thematic interconnection. The tendency throughout the romantic period, as we have already observed, is for the separate numbers to coalesce into larger units, and this process is finally carried to a point where the music flows uninterruptedly from the beginning of an act to the end. This continuity may be simply a matter of concealing the joints, as in late Verdi, or it may be the kind of organic unity in Wagner's music dramas, with a number of musical motifs used continually and systematically throughout a whole act, or a whole opera, or even several different operas. What is true of the form as a whole is true also of the details : distinction between aria and recitative becomes less marked; recitatives, arias, ensembles, and choruses combine freely in large form-complexes. In harmony, the boundaries of tonality become less definite, modulations more frequent and to more distant keys; chromatic alterations, progressions motivated by chromatically moving inner voices, become characteristic. In the later works of Wagner even distinct cadences are avoided, so that the music seems never to come to a full stop but to move on in an endless melody. Finally dissonance, especially in the form of suspension or appoggiatura, takes on new and special importance as a leading means of expression, and the indefinite postponement of its final resolution becomes a symbol of the eternal romantic longing after the unattainable.

The actual historical course of opera in early nineteenth-century Germany was affected by a number of factors which tended to interfere with the steady development of a truly national type. The original inspiration of German romantic opera, both for the poetry and for the music, came from France—in part directly from late eighteenth- and early nineteenth-century opéra comique and in part indirectly through the Singspiel, which, as we have seen, was largely dependent in the beginning on French models. There being no national center of opera in Germany, the Singspiel developed in relatively isolated localities, pre-

[4] "The Road to Major," p. 403.

serving everywhere however two traditional characteristics of the form: the choice, indifferently, of either serious or comic subject matter (or of a mixture of the two) and the use of spoken dialogue. One factor that constantly hampered the growth of a national opera was the rooted public favor for foreign works, or works of essentially foreign cast, so that composers who might otherwise have devoted their full energies to the building of German opera felt often induced to write in imitation of French or Italian models. Beethoven's *Fidelio*, for example, was a French Revolutionary rescue opera; later, it was the French grand opera or the Italian opera of Rossini, Bellini, and Donizetti that offered the fatal attraction to German composers. Nevertheless, the native Singspiel continued to flourish in a modest way, and to make progress during the first two decades of the nineteenth century.

Two general types of libretto are discernible in the Singspiel at the beginning of the century. One type, specializing in familiar, homely scenes and characters idyllically or sentimentally treated, is illustrated in *Die Schweitzerfamilie* ("The Swiss Family"), first given at Vienna in 1809. The music, by Joseph Weigl (1766–1846),[5] has some romantic orchestral coloring and makes use of Swiss themes and of reminiscence motifs. *Die Schweitzerfamilie* continued to be played in Germany and abroad throughout the nineteenth century; one aria was long a favorite showpiece for soprano singers. The other type of Singspiel libretto in the early nineteenth century emphasized legendary or magic elements, strange happenings to men and women living in a "real" world but ever subject to the mysterious intervention of unseen spiritual powers. It was this eminently romantic kind of subject matter that was to furnish the material of German romantic opera.

Romantic motifs came increasingly into the libretto of the Singspiel around the turn of the century, as the mere titles of some works of this time show: *Oberon, Titania, Das Donauweibchen* ("The Nixie"), *Die Geisterinsel* ("The Isle of Spirits"=Shakespeare's "Tempest"), *Der Kobold, Die Sylphen, Der Unsichtbare* ("The Invisible"), and others similar. The first "Faust" opera based on Goethe's poem had appeared in 1797;[6] two works inspired by Mozart's *Magic Flute* were given at Vienna in 1797 and 1798 respectively: *Babilons Piramiden* and *Das Labirint, oder Der Kampf mit den Elementen* ("The Labyrinth; or, The

[5] De Eisner-Eisenhof, "Giuseppe Weigl."
[6] Spitta, "Die älteste Faust-Oper," in his *Zur Musik*, pp. 199–234.

Battle with the Elements"), both on librettos of Schikaneder with music by Peter Winter (1754–1825) [7]—who, however, had had his greatest success with *Das unterbrochene Opferfest* ("The Interrupted Sacrifice") in 1796.

Composers of the other works named above were : Paul Wranitzky (1756–1808; *Oberon*, 1790); Georg Christoph Grosheim [8] (1764–1841; *Titania*, 1792); Ferdinand Kauer (1751–1831; *Das Donauweibchen*, 1798, was very successful and inspired numerous imitations); Friedrich Heinrich Himmel[9] (1765–1814; *Die Sylphen*, 1806, and *Der Kobold*, 1813; but his most popular work was *Fanchon das Leiermädchen*, 1804); and Carl David Eule (1776–1827; *Der Unsichtbare*, 1809). *Die Geisterinsel* was set to music twice in 1798 : by Johann Rudolf Zumsteeg (1760–1802) at Stuttgart and J. F. Reichardt at Berlin.

A decisive stage in the creation of German romantic opera came with two works first performed in 1816 : *Undine*, by E. T. A. Hoffmann at Berlin, and *Faust* by Ludwig Spohr at Prague. Hoffmann (1776–1822),[10] the famous romantic author, is important in the history of German opera for both his writings and his music. In *Undine*, his best opera, the earlier merely fanciful play with fairy elements is given a feeling of human significance, thus achieving some dramatic force in spite of a complex and fantastic plot. The music suffers from some technical faults, but the romantic mood of Weber's *Freischütz* is distinctly foreshadowed, especially in the scenes depicting supernatural beings and in the many folklike melodies and choruses. The more ambitious arias are less successful. Hoffmann shows a sensitiveness for the effect of key contrasts, though the actual results do not always come up to his evident intentions.

Spohr (1784–1859) [11] is now remembered chiefly for his oratorios and violin music, but *Faust* and his other important opera *Jessonda* (1823) are typical of the early romantic musical style. *Faust* makes con-

[7] Frensdorf, *Peter Winter als Opernkomponist*; Moser, *Geschichte der deutschen Musik* II, 5 f.

[8] *Selbstbiographie*, ed. G. Heinrichs.

[9] Odendahl, *Friedrich Heinrich Himmel.*

[10] Hoffmann's literary works are published in an edition by Griesebach; his writings on music separately, ed. Istel. See biography by Kroll; Greeff, *E. T. A. Hoffmann als Musiker und Musikschriftsteller*; Strunk, *Source Readings*, pp. 801–7 (Weber's essay on Hoffmann's *Undine*). The edition of his musical works by G. Becking (1922–23) does not include the operas.

[11] *Selbstbiographie* (to 1838); Wassermann, *Ludwig Spohr als Opernkomponist*; Salburg, *Ludwig Spohr*; Spitta, "Jessonda," in his *Zur Musik*, pp. 237–66.

siderable use of reminiscence motifs, and the idiom, like that of Hoffmann's *Undine*, points toward Weber's *Freischütz*. Spohr's music,
though less masculine and forceful than Weber's, is interesting for its
freedom of key relationships and chromatic progressions;[12] expressive
suspensions and upward-resolving appoggiaturas often suggest the style
of Wagner, although it must be confessed that the romanticism of Spohr
is mostly a matter of such details as these rather than of a fundamentally
new approach. It is somewhat surprising that Spohr was unsympathetic
to the music of Weber and late Beethoven, but he was one of the earliest
champions of Wagner in Germany, and in his own *Kreuzfahrer* ("The
Crusaders," 1845) attempted to write a national romantic opera after
the model of *Der fliegende Holländer* and *Tannhäuser*.

The operatic production of Franz Schubert (1797–1828)[13] extends
from 1814 to 1823 and includes sixteen works (counting those that have
been preserved incomplete), only three of which ever reached performance during the composer's lifetime. These were: the one-act
Singspiel *Die Zwillingsbrüder* ("The Twin Brothers," 1819); the melodrama *Die Zauberharfe* ("The Magic Harp," 1820), Schubert's first big
work for the stage, consisting of choruses and some particularly beautiful
orchestral numbers in a fantastic play by G. E. von Hoffmann; and the
well-known incidental music for Helmine von Chézy's drama *Rosa-
munde von Cypern* (1823). But Schubert's principal dramatic works
were the two large operas *Alfonso und Estrella* (composed 1822, first
performed 1854) and *Fierrabras* (composed 1823, first performed 1897).
Fierrabras has some spoken dialogue, but *Alfonso und Estrella*—exceptionally for German opera in this period—is sung throughout. Schubert
had hoped to see this opera staged at Berlin, but it was rejected because
of the alleged difficulty of the music and because the libretto was found
"unsuitable." The score contains a wealth of arias in great variety, a
large proportion of choruses, and a tremendously big finale—altogether
a work in the grand romantic style, with characteristic Schubertian
harmony and orchestral colors. *Fierrabras* is equally rich in large scene-
complexes with intermingled arias, dramatic accompanied recitatives,
and choruses, and in addition contains many instances of recurring

[12] See for example the passage from the first finale of *Jessonda* quoted in Bücken,
Die Musik des 19. Jahrhunderts, p. 88.

[13] Krott, *Die Singspiele Schuberts*; A. H. King, "Music for the Stage," in *The
Music of Schubert*, ed. G. Abraham; Deutsch, *Schubert: Thematic Catalogue* and
other books on Schubert; M. J. E. Brown, *Schubert: A Critical Biography*.

themes in the orchestra, a device used here with consummate skill and effect. Outstanding numbers in this score are the lovely duet for two sopranos "Weit über Glanz und Erdenschimmer" and the four-part unaccompanied men's chorus "O theures Vaterland" in Act II; the melodrama scene near the end of this act; and the finale-complex at the end of Act I. It is indeed tragic that Schubert never had the opportunity to hear these two operas in the theatre, for he might then have gone on, with that experience as a guide and with the help of better librettos, to adapt his great lyric genius more fully to the practical requirements of the stage [14] and attain in this field the success that always just eluded him.

Two other romantic composers also attempted opera without much success. Mendelssohn's *Hochzeit des Camacho* ("Camacho's Wedding") was withdrawn after a few performances at Berlin in 1827; he composed a half-dozen smaller stage pieces (of which only the one-act Singspiel *Son and Stranger* was published) and left unfinished a large opera, *Loreley*.[15] Schumann's *Genoveva* was performed at Leipzig in 1850 under the composer's direction, but neither then nor since has it obtained enduring public favor.[16] Its libretto is poorly constructed and the music lacks genuine dramatic directness and characterizing power, though there are many beautiful passages (see for example near the beginning of Act IV, Genoveva's recitative and aria from the words "Die letzte Hoffnung schwindet"). Schumann's *Szenen aus Goethes Faust*, for chorus, soloists, and orchestra, is intended for concert performance; it is perhaps, of all *Faust* music, the most appropriate to Goethe's drama and ranks equal with the composer's better-known cantata *Paradise and the Peri*.

Hoffmann and Spohr had prepared the way, but the real founder and hero of German romantic opera was Carl Maria von Weber (1786–1826).[17] Weber's father was a theatre director and the boy was reared in an atmosphere of the stage. His own experience as impresario and

[14] Cf. Liszt's essay on *Alfonso und Estrella*, in his *Gesammelte Schriften* III, 1, pp. 68–78.

[15] Schünemann, "Mendelssohns Jugendopern."

[16] H. Abert, "Robert Schumann's *Genoveva*"; Abraham, "The Dramatic Music," in *Schumann: A Symposium*, chap. vii.

[17] On Weber, see his own writings and the biographies by his son M. M. von Weber (1864), E. Kroll (1934), and H. Schnoor (1953); the best life of Weber in English is L. and R. Stebbins's *Enchanted Wanderer* (1940), which contains a copious and well-organized bibliography; further bibliography in Dünnebeil, *Schrifttum über Carl Maria von Weber* (4th ed., 1957). See further Dünnebeil, *C. M. von Weber, ein Brevier*; thematic catalogue by Jähns. The edition of Weber's works (ed. J. H. Moser) begun in 1926 includes the operas *Das Waldmädchen, Peter Schmoll* (Vol. I); *Rübezahl, Silvana* (Vol. II); *Preciosa* (Vol. III).

conductor at Breslau (1804–6) and Prague (1813–17) gave him a still firmer knowledge of the essentials of dramatic style. At Prague he staged works by Spontini, Méhul, and Cherubini, Grétry's *Richard*, Mozart's *Figaro*, *Don Giovanni*, and *Titus*, Beethoven's *Fidelio*, and other leading operas of the current repertoire. The influence of Weber's principal teacher, the Abbé Vogler, as well as the whole intellectual milieu of his life, inclined him strongly toward romanticism, and in 1814 his settings of ten songs from Körner's *Leyer und Schwert* ("Lyre and Sword") made him the idol of the patriotic youth of Germany. Weber's first extant dramatic work was a Singspiel, *Das stumme Waldmädchen* ("The Dumb Girl of the Forest," 1800), which was not successful; parts of the music were incorporated in *Silvana* (1810, revised 1812). Two comic Singspiels, *Peter Schmoll und seine Nachbarn* ("Peter Schmoll and His Neighbors," 1803) and *Abu Hassan* (1811), and an unfinished romantic work, *Rübezahl* (*ca.* 1805),[18] complete the list of Weber's earlier dramatic compositions. Though he showed in these works an original talent for instrumentation, a gift for comic writing and characterization, and a natural feeling for the quality of German folk melody, there is little in the music to suggest the romantic power later to be unloosed in *Der Freischütz*. *Abu Hassan* may be regarded as a forerunner of *Oberon*, and the medieval-romantic *Silvana* anticipates some features of *Euryanthe*.

Early in the year 1817 Weber, who had just been appointed director of the German opera at Dresden, persuaded his friend Friedrich Kind to write for him a libretto based on a tale by J. A. Apel (1810) and a "romantic tragedy" *Der Freischütz* (1812) by Franz Xavier von Caspar.[19] The legend itself was at least a hundred years older, and some of its motifs belong to still more ancient folklore. The title is difficult to translate : it means literally "The Free Marksman," but the usual English title "The Charmed Bullet" is sufficiently descriptive and certainly more graceful. Weber's music was not completed until 1820, and still another year elapsed before the first performance, at Berlin, on June 18, 1821. The work was fabulously successful from the start and spread like wildfire all over Germany. After its reception in Vienna Weber wrote in his

---

[18] "Rübezahl" is the name of a mountain spirit of the Riesengebirge, a prominent figure in the folklore of Silesia, the subject of many folk tales, plays, and operas. Weber's overture is still occasionally played, in a revised form, under the title "The Ruler of the Spirits."

[19] Mayerhofer, *Abermals vom Freischützen.*

diary, "Greater enthusiasm there cannot be, and I tremble to think of the future, for it is scarcely possible to rise higher than this." [20] His words were unconsciously prophetic, as the fate of *Euryanthe* was to prove; but with *Der Freischütz* he had set German romantic opera on its road and dealt a blow to the century-long Italian reign in the German theatres. The popularity of *Der Freischütz* was due not only to the music but also to the libretto, which, for Germany in the early romantic period, literally had everything.[21] Most of its elements were inherited from the late eighteenth-century Singspiel: a background of nature and a foreground of humble and happy village life; a pure heroine and a well-intentioned but credulous hero; a villain caught in his own trap; the supernatural in many picturesque and shuddery forms; and finally the time-tested figure of the magnanimous prince as righteous judge and father of his people. But though the ingredients were old, the mixture was new. For the first time in opera all these details were convincingly presented as aspects of something important; the trial of marksmanship took on the character of Armageddon, the ultimate battle of good against evil, one sustained by the power of the church and the other aided by the maleficent spirits of ancient heathendom, and the triumph of good was felt as the triumph of the German soul. Thus the national appeal of *Der Freischütz* was not limited to the romantic period but has remained equally strong to this day. "There never was an opera, and there is no likelihood that there ever will be one, so intimately bound up with the loves, feelings, sentiments, emotions, superstitions, social customs, and racial characteristics of a people." [22]

Weber's overture is a model of its kind. Although made up entirely, except for the opening horn theme, of melodies from the opera, it is not a mere medley but a finished composition in symphonic first-movement form. The mysterious last twelve measures of the introduction (diminished sevenths with low clarinets, strings tremolo, pizzicato basses and kettledrums on the afterbeats) are the quintessence of romanticism in music, and so, in a different way, is the clarinet melody in E-flat of the *vivace* movement. The return of the closing triumph theme in C major,

[20] Quoted by Philipp Spitta in his article on Weber in *Grove's Dictionary* (4th ed.) V, 652.

[21] For a synopsis the reader is referred to any opera handbook; many editions of the music do not give the spoken dialogue, which is essential to the understanding of the plot.

[22] Krehbiel, *A Book of Operas*, p. 207.

heralded by a recurrence of the last part of the introduction and three impressive "general pauses," is electrifying. In the larger arias the music of *Der Freischütz* approaches grand opera, and it is natural to find in Caspar's "Der Hölle Netz" (end of Act I) a resemblance to Italian style, or in the opening section of Max's "Durch die Wälder" a mild echo of Méhul. Both this aria and Agathe's "Leise, leise" are complex musical structures, splendidly dramatic and of Beethovenian amplitude. Aennchen's "Kommt ein schlanker Bursch gegangen," with its polacca rhythm, is in keeping with the Singspiel tradition of differentiating the social standing of the characters by means of different musical styles and forms. The contrast between Agathe and Aennchen, mistress and maid, so neatly established in their duet at the beginning of Act II, is confirmed and emphasized in their two following arias.

Parts of the score which did much to endear it to the public were those which glorified the songs and dances of the people : the hunters' and bridesmaids' choruses, the march and waltzes in Act I, and the shorter pieces (lied, romance, cavatina) in popular form. In *Der Freischütz* Weber succeeded as no other composer had done in raising the music of the folk to the dignity of serious opera and combining it skillfully with more pretentious elements. The most celebrated part of the opera has always been the finale of the second act, the "Wolf's Glen" scene, one of the most effective evocations of supernatural thrills ever created for the stage. Among the devices Weber uses may be pointed out the mysterious harmonies (tremolo strings) at the beginning, the monotone choruses of the spirits (note the unison of tenors, altos, and sopranos on a'), the dialogue between the singing Caspar and the speaking Samiel, and the melodrama for the casting of the magic bullets, a Walpurgisnacht of legendary phantoms of the dark forest. The C minor themes of the overture, associated throughout the opera with the demonic powers, are much in evidence. The systematic recurrence of these motifs and others, especially the triumph motif (overture, in E-flat and C major; Agathe's aria, E major; last finale again in C major), contributes much to the feeling of unity which is one of the outstanding qualities of the work. The overture gives the musical plan of the whole as it were in embryo, and the structure thus sketched is fully expanded in the course of the three acts.

Weber's incidental music to P. A. Wolff's play *Preciosa* (adapted from a novel by Cervantes) was composed immediately after *Der*

Freischütz and came sooner to performance (Berlin, March 14, 1821). At about the same time he started, but did not finish, a comic opera on another Spanish subject, *Die drei Pintos* ("The Three Pintos").[23]

Euryanthe was first performed at Vienna October 25, 1823. The source of the plot was a thirteenth-century *fabliau* which had been employed by Boccaccio in the *Decameron* (Day II, Story 9) and Shakespeare in *Cymbeline*; Schlegel had published a version in 1804 under the title "Die Geschichte der tugendsamen Euryanthe von Savoyen" ("The History of the Virtuous Euryanthe of Savoy"). Helmine von Chézy, after many revisions and with considerable help from Weber, produced a libretto. In planning the work Weber, in accordance with his lifelong habit, deliberately tried to correct the faults that critics had found in *Der Freischütz*. The criticisms had been mainly to the effect that the work was deficient in large, highly developed musical forms; that is, that it was too much of a Singspiel and not enough of an opera. Spontini, whose *Olympie* had been thrown into the shade by *Der Freischütz* at Berlin, was particularly bitter, and even Weber's friend, the romantic poet Tieck, was not persuaded. *Euryanthe*, therefore, Weber set to music throughout (it is the only opera of his that does not have spoken dialogue), and on a greater scale than any of his other works. However, he did not wish to make the music dominant as in Italian opera, but conceived rather a kind of Gesamtkunstwerk, "a purely dramatic attempt, aiming to create its effect by means of the combined effects of all the sister arts." [24] Unfortunately the results did not correspond to this ideal, nor did the success of the opera come up to Weber's hopes and expectations. It has never become a public favorite, but its interest for musicians is shown by numerous attempts to promote it in revised forms. There can be no doubt that it includes some of Weber's greatest music (for example, the overture); the arias are broad and powerful,[25] and the way the chorus is used in the drama reminds one of Gluck. Weber's usual skillful handling of the orchestra is evident, as well as the same tasteful use of folklike motifs as in *Der Freischütz*. Contrast of key is used as an aid to characterization, and there is a

[23] It was completed, partly from Weber's sketches and partly from other works of the composer, by Gustave Mahler and performed at Leipzig in 1888.

[24] Quoted in Moser, *Geschichte der deutschen Musik* III, 73, note 1.

[25] See especially Lysiart's aria at the beginning of Act II and Euryanthe's aria with chorus "Zu ihm, und weilet nicht" in Act III.

significant employment of reminiscence motifs. All in all, *Euryanthe* is a grand opera both in form and in loftiness of conception, a landmark in the history of German opera between *Fidelio* and *Lohengrin*, and a work that deserves to be performed more frequently.

Weber's last opera, *Oberon*, was composed to an English libretto by J. F. Planché and first performed under the composer's direction at London, April 12, 1826. The fatigue of the journey and labor of the production hastened Weber's death, which occurred at London on June 4. In some ways *Oberon* was a backward step: the story, a rambling oriental fantasy with numberless scene changes, gave only limited occasion for development of character or genuine human emotion; there were many nonsinging actors, and so much of the action took place in spoken dialogue that the music was reduced almost to an incidental position. Weber intended to rearrange the work for German theatres, and though he did not live long enough to do so, many more or less thoroughgoing revisions and additions have been made (some in accordance with Weber's plan) by later musicians. *Oberon* is historically important chiefly because of its fairy music, such as the opening chorus of Act I, the finales of the second and third acts, and above all the beginning of the overture, with its magic horn call, muted strings, and swift figure in the wood winds. Such music was in the air: Mendelssohn's octet with its scherzo had appeared the year before, and the *Midsummer Night's Dream* overture was composed in the summer of 1826. The more vigorous, ardent, stormy romanticism of Rezia's aria "Ocean, thou mighty monster" (the closing theme of which had appeared in the overture) is also well represented in *Oberon*.

Weber died in mid-career. Had he lived to complete his work, the history of German opera for the next twenty years might have been one of steady development. As it was, although *Der Freischütz* continued its triumphal course, no German work was produced for nearly a generation that could match it either in popularity or in musical worth. The early romantics had created a world of opera in which the lives of simple human beings were felt to be so intertwined with the processes of nature, and both man and nature so informed and governed by all-encompassing spiritual powers, that the three realms seemed as one. This original unity was lost after *Der Freischütz*, with unfortunate results for both libretto and music. Poets and composers began to exploit the supernatural for mere sensation and the human for sentiment or comedy; and periodically they would be distracted by the allurements of grand opera.

If Weber can be said to have had a successor, it was Heinrich Marschner (1795–1861),[26] who first became widely known in 1828 for *Der Vampyr*, an opera now remembered mainly because it was one of Wagner's models for *Der fliegende Holländer* (see especially the ballade in Act III). Marschner's *Templer und Jüdin* ("The Templar and the Jewess," 1829) was adapted from Scott's *Ivanhoe*. His masterpiece, *Hans Heiling* (1833), was on a libretto by Eduard Devrient from a story by Körner, originally intended for Mendelssohn. As the central situation of *Templer und Jüdin* is similar to that of *Lohengrin*, so the figure of Hans Heiling, half man and half earth spirit, in love with a mortal woman, has many points of resemblance to Wagner's Dutchman. Yet in the working out of the story as well as in the music much of the trivial is mingled with the serious. The style for the most part is that of the popular Singspiel, with simple tunes in symmetrical patterns, interspersed with spoken dialogue. Echoes of Weber, Italian opera, and Meyerbeer's *Robert le Diable* are heard. In some respects the music looks ahead to Wagner : the frequent chromatic passing tones in the melody, especially at cadences; the use of modulating sequences; and occasionally a passage of grimly powerful declamation. Many of the choruses are interesting, and the finales of the first and third acts are well constructed. The most original number, and one which shows Marschner's gifts to good advantage, is the melodrama and lied at the beginning of the second scene of Act II.[27] Yet, on the whole, his talent was of second rank, the Biedermeier spirit in music. His later works, in which there are many traces of the fashionable Italian and French opera of the time, contributed nothing to his fame.

Along with the romantic traits of Marschner there lived in German opera a current of sentimental or comic drama, descended from the eighteenth-century Singspiel. A very popular opera was Konradin Kreutzer's (1780–1849)[28] *Nachtlager in Granada* ("The Night-Camp at Granada"), first performed at Vienna in 1834. The libretto, based on

---

[26] Münzer, *Heinrich Marschner*; G. Fischer, *Musik in Hannover* (2d ed.) and *Marschner-Erinnerungen*; Gaartz, *Die Opern Heinrich Marschners*; Gnirs, *Hans Heiling*.

[27] The melody at the words "Sonst bist du verfallen" is the original of Wagner's death-announcement theme in *Die Walküre*.

[28] Riehl, essay in *Musikalische Charakterköpfe* I.

Friedrich Kind's play of the same title, uses the old reliable motif of the good prince in disguise conferring rewards on humble virtue and innocent young love and offers occasion for romances, hunting choruses, a conspirators' chorus, a prayer, airs and ensembles, all somewhat in the manner of Auber and Donizetti—light, sometimes trifling, but on the whole pretty and pleasing music in a harmless way. A more spirited comic vein was worked by Gustav Albert Lortzing (1801–51) [29] in his most successful work, *Zar und Zimmermann* ("Czar and Carpenter," Leipzig, 1837), and especially in *Der Waffenschmied* ("The Armorer," Vienna, 1846). The latter abounds in humorous situations like those of the older Viennese Singspiel, with a fresh, pleasant, often witty melodic style and some ensembles that recall the spirit of Mozart. Most characteristic, however, are the simple songs in folk idiom, reminiscent of the tunes of J. A. Hiller. With *Der Wildschütz* ("The Poacher," 1842) and even more pronouncedly with *Undine* (1845) Lortzing—who in all these works was his own librettist—ventured on the ground of romantic opera, with its supernatural beings and theme of redemption through love. Lortzing was hardly capable of composing music equal to the emotions and characters of this libretto, but his systematic use of recurring motifs and his powers of musical description (especially the water-sprites' music, first heard in Act II, scene 5) are interesting both in themselves and as predecessors of the music of Wagner's *Ring*. Another of Lortzing's comic operas, *Hans Sachs* (1840), is one of the numerous sources of *Die Meistersinger*.

Other composers of German opera toward the middle of the nineteenth century must be only briefly mentioned. Otto Nicolai's (1810–49) [30] *Lustigen Weiber von Windsor* ("The Merry Wives of Windsor," Berlin, 1849) is a fine comic work in which Italian and German characteristics are happily blended. Its sparkling, cosmopolitan style contrasts with the simple homemade quality of another popular contemporary work, *Martha* (1847) by Friedrich von Flotow (1812–83),[31] a sentimental old-fashioned piece which has inexplicably survived while many better operas have been forgotten. An important younger figure of this period

[29] Biographies by Kruse and Killer; *Gesammelte Briefe*, ed. Kruse; Laue, *Die Operndichtung Lortzings*; Burgmüller, *Die Musen darben*.
[30] *Tagebücher* (ed. B. Schröder, 1892; ed. W. Altmann, 1937); Kruse, *Otto Nicolai*; idem, "Otto Nicolai's italienische Opern."
[31] R. Flotow, *Friedrich von Flotow's Leben von seiner Witwe*; Dent, "A Best-Seller in Opera."

was Peter Cornelius (1824–74),[32] disciple of Liszt and champion of Wagner, a poet and composer who wrote his own librettos. His *Barbier von Bagdad* ("The Barber of Bagdad," Weimar, 1858) is a wholly delightful oriental comedy in a sophisticated musical idiom obviously influenced by Wagner, especially with respect to its harmony and melodic line. The rhythms, deriving in part from oriental verse forms, are particularly varied and interesting—for example, the aria "O holdes Bild" (Act II, scene 2) is in alternate 4/4 and 3/4 measures; five-measure phrases are also common throughout the score. Each of the two acts runs continuously, without marked division into numbers. The orchestra has an important role not only in the formal scheme but also in the providing of many humorous details in the accompaniments. A half-dozen recurring motifs are used systematically. *Der Barbier* is not high comedy like *Die Meistersinger* but a farce, cleverly using every resource of music for farcical purposes (see for example the canonic duet "Wenn zum Gebet" in Act I). The freedom of rhythm, the declamatory melodies, the frequent wide intervals and chromatic harmonies often foreshadow the style of Strauss's *Rosenkavalier*. There is also some parody of Italian opera, especially in the sentimental unison love duet "So mag kein anders Wort erklingen" in the second scene of Act II. (This scene is also an unintentional parody of the love duet in the second act of Tristan, with the Barber filling the role of Brangäne.)

During the 1830s and 1840s it seemed almost as if the Italians had been driven from German opera houses only to be replaced by the French. The works of Herold and Adam were particularly popular, while the equally gifted native composers Marschner and Lortzing were often neglected. The situation was saved by Wagner, who after early experiments in the Italian style and that of French grand opera went on to create a new epoch of national German romantic opera in *Der fliegende Holländer*, *Tannhäuser*, and *Lohengrin*.

[32] Complete editions of Cornelius's literary works (4 vols.) and musical works (5 vols., B&H, 1905–6); biographies by M. Hasse and C. M. Cornelius; Hasse, *Peter Cornelius und sein Barbier von Bagdad*.

CHAPTER 23

WAGNER[1]

☙❧

From time to time in the history of music there have been composers whose works summed up the achievement of a whole epoch, making the final synthesis of a style: Palestrina and Bach are the outstanding examples. There have been other composers whose work incorporated not only the end of one style but the beginning of another as well: to this group belong Beethoven and Wagner. Wagner's operas, to and including *Lohengrin*, were the consummation of German romantic opera of the nineteenth century; the later music dramas were in a style which, although retaining many features of what had gone before, nevertheless introduced innovations in both theory and practice. These innovations were not confined to the music but embraced the whole drama, and in working them out Wagner, who perceived all the implications of his ideas and developed them with typical German thoroughness, touched on many issues that were fundamentally involved with nineteenth-century thought. He is the only eminent composer whose writings have been considered important outside the conventional limits of the field of music. For him, indeed, these conventional limits hardly existed; consequently, in order to understand his music, it is necessary to take into account his views on other subjects, including his philosophy of art in general and of the drama in particular. Whether one agrees or disagrees with these views is a question of the same order as whether one likes or dislikes the music: in either case it is desirable to comprehend as well as judge.

[1] Wagner's complete musical works have been published in a Collected Edition by Breitkopf & Härtel. There is as yet no comprehensive bibliography of the enormous Wagner literature. (Oesterlein's *Katalog*, limited to items published during Wagner's lifetime, lists over 10,000 titles.) The primary sources are: Wagner, *Mein Leben*; idem, *Gesammelte Schriften und Dichtungen* (5th ed.); idem, *Briefe in Originalausgaben*; for other principal sources, see Newman's *Life*. The standard

In music, Wagner was for the most part self-taught. During his student days at Leipzig he became acquainted with some of Beethoven's works and heard at the theatre the plays of Schiller and Shakespeare, as well as the operas of Weber and Marschner. He wrote dramas and some instrumental music, including a Symphony in C major which was performed in 1833. During two seasons as chorus trainer at Würzburg (1833–34) he became familiar with many more works of the current opera repertoire and composed his own *Feen* ("The Fairies"), his first completed opera (never performed during Wagner's lifetime). This is a

biography for many years was that of Glasenapp (*Das Leben Richard Wagners*), now superseded by Ernest Newman's *Life of Richard Wagner*. Koch's *Richard Wagner* emphasizes the literary side of Wagner's production; the most popular short German biography is Julius Kapp's (32d ed., 1929); see also W. Jacob, *Taten der Musik*. The "orthodox" Wagner gospel is expounded in the official periodical *Bayreuther Blätter* (from 1878, ed. for many years by Hans von Wolzogen) and in the works of Houston Stewart Chamberlain (*Richard Wagner* and *Das Drama Richard Wagners*. Cf. also his *Grundlagen des neunzehnten Jahrhunderts*). The following books may be found useful: Newman, *The Wagner Operas*; Saitschick, *Götter und Menschen in Richard Wagners Ring*; Mann, "Leiden und Grösse Richard Wagners," in his *Leiden und Grösse der Meister*; A. E. F. Dickinson, *The Musical Design of The Ring*; Hutcheson, *A Musical Guide to the . . . Ring*; Strunk, *Source Readings*, pp. 874–903. Paul Bekker's *Richard Wagner* is diffuse and involved but worth reading for its many insights; a useful new viewpoint is suggested in Joseph Kerman's "Wagner: Thoughts in Season." The most important works dealing specifically with Wagner's music are: Adler, *Richard Wagner, Vorlesungen*; Lorenz, *Das Geheimnis der Form bei Richard Wagner* (4 vols.); Kurth, *Romantische Harmonik und ihre Krise in Wagner's Tristan*; and Westernhagen, *Vom Holländer zum Parsifal*.

A tabular list of Wagner's operas and music dramas is given here:

TITLE	DATE OF COMPOSITION (incl. scoring)	FIRST PERFORMANCE
Die Feen	1833	Munich, 1888
Das Liebesverbot	1835	Magdeburg, 1836
Rienzi	1838–40	Dresden, 1842
Der fliegende Holländer	1841	Dresden, 1843
Tannhäuser	1843–45	Dresden, 1845
Lohengrin	1846–48	Weimar, 1850
Der Ring des Nibelungen	Poem begun 1848, completed 1852	First complete performance, Bayreuth, 1876
I. *Das Rheingold*	1853–54	Munich, 1869
II. *Die Walküre*	1854–56	Munich, 1870
III. *Siegfried*	1856–57, 1864–65, 1869–71	Bayreuth, 1876
IV. *Götterdämmerung*	1869–74	Bayreuth, 1876
Tristan und Isolde	1857–59	Munich, 1865
Die Meistersinger von Nürnberg	1862–67	Munich, 1868
Parsifal	1877–82	Bayreuth, 1882

long work, with the usual subdivision into recitatives, arias, ensembles, and the like. A few traits of the music suggest the later composer of *Rienzi*, but the style on the whole is modeled after Beethoven and Weber. The romantic idiom of the period is handled with great energy, aiming at big theatrical effects by conventional means. There is no technical reason why this opera could not have been performed; it is by no means an inexpert work, only it lacks individuality. Wagner's libretto, based on a fairy tale of Carlo Gozzi, introduces all the fantastic and decorative apparatus of romantic opera in profusion, but without the unifying power of a really significant dramatic idea.

If *Die Feen* may be regarded as an essay in German romantic opera, *Das Liebesverbot* ("The Ban on Love") showed Wagner eagerly assimilating the Italian style. Bellini's *Montecchi e Capuletti* had aroused much enthusiasm at Leipzig in 1834, and Wagner was temporarily in reaction against the alleged heaviness, lack of dramatic life, and unvocal quality of the typical German operas. His libretto for *Das Liebesverbot* was based on Shakespeare's *Measure for Measure*; it is full of comic scenes and has some spoken dialogue. The music is a blend of Auber, Rossini, and Donizetti, with distinct traces of Meyerbeer in the finales, which often seem to strain terribly for effect. The melodies are florid, often with typically Italian cadenzas, and everything is repeated at great length. The best quality of the score is its liveliness and enthusiasm, though even this becomes wearisome after a time. There is not one really distinguished theme in the whole work; the duet in bolero rhythm in the first scene of Act II may be taken as typical of the style (Example 95). Some of the crowd scenes faintly foreshadow the ending of Act II of *Die Meistersinger*; the duet of Isabella and Marianna and the latter's aria in the last act have a sultry erotic quality which looks forward to Richard Strauss. *Das Liebersverbot* was performed only once, and then very badly, at Magdeburg in 1836, with the composer conducting.

From 1837 to 1839 Wagner was music director of the theatre at Riga. Here he began the composition of *Rienzi*, based on Bulwer-Lytton's novel and inspired by a performance of Spontini's *Cortez* which Wagner had witnessed at Berlin in 1836. In the summer of 1839 he went to Paris; the first stage of the trip was the memorable stormy sea voyage to London, the impressions of which later influenced him in the composition of *Der fliegende Holländer* ("The Flying Dutchman"). The two and a half years in Paris were a nightmare of failure, disap-

Das Liebesverbot, Act II, no. 7

EXAMPLE 95   WAGNER

pointment, and poverty. Even the efforts of Meyerbeer on his behalf did not avail to obtain him a hearing. Yet during this time Wagner completed *Rienzi* and wrote *Der fliegende Holländer*, finishing the latter at the suburb of Meudon in August, 1841. At last *Rienzi* was accepted by the Opera at Dresden, where the first performance took place October 20, 1842. Wagner had come from Paris in the summer to supervise the rehearsals. The success of the work was immediate and overwhelming and led to a demand for *Der fliegende Holländer*, which was produced in January, 1843. A month later Wagner was appointed music director for life of the Dresden Opera.

Rienzi, as we have already noted (p. 322), was a grand opera in the fashion of the time, with just enough novelty to make it extremely popular. The reception of *Der fliegende Holländer* was less flattering: in externals this work was less brilliant than *Rienzi*, and its inner dramatic significance went for the most part unperceived. This was not altogether the fault of the audiences, for Wagner himself had not yet perfected his technique. *Der fliegende Holländer* is essentially a German romantic opera in the tradition of *Der Vampyr* or *Hans Heiling* (though without spoken dialogue), and is divided into the customary numbers.

Some of these are quite successful, while others seem mechanical and forced, monotonous in rhythm, and without marked originality of melody or harmony. Wagner took his version of the medieval legend of the Flying Dutchman from a tale by Heinrich Heine, adding features suggested by Marschner's *Vampyr*. As in *Der Freischütz*, nature, animated by supernatural forces, is all-pervasive. This time it is not the forest but the sea : in the storm music, the steersman's song in Act I, and the sailors' choruses in Act III, Wagner set forth with all his power the impressions gathered in the voyage from Riga to London. These portions are not mere musical descriptions of the sea but are filled with symbolic meaning for the human drama. In the story of the redemption of the Dutchman from the curse of immortality by Senta's love Wagner for the first time clearly worked out the idea of salvation through love which became fundamental in his later dramas. It is stated in Senta's Ballad (Act II), the central number of the opera and the one first composed. The ballad, a type of song which in earlier nineteenth-century opera had been as a rule only a set piece, here becomes the pivot of the whole dramatic and musical development, and its traditional two-part form is used to contrast the ideas of curse and salvation. The themes chosen are good examples of Wagner's characteristic procedure of representing basic dramatic ideas by specific musical formulae : the opening motif forming an empty fifth, the stormy chromatics, and the diminished sevenths [2] are set against the calm diatonic major melody of the second section. The ultimate salvation—already prophesied at the end of the overture—is symbolized in the finale of the opera by using the latter theme for an extended plagal cadence in D major. These two themes (or rather theme groups) and their derivatives are used systematically in many other parts of the opera; Wagner has already adopted the device of the reminiscence motif, but has not yet extended it to every portion of the work. The historical interest of *Der fliegende Holländer* lies not so much in this device—which, as we have seen, was not new with Wagner—as in the quality of the themes themselves, in the individuality of their harmonies, and the way they seem to embody the essential dramatic idea, completing its expression and giving it depth and emotional power.

[2] The first motif has an obvious resemblance to the beginning of Beethoven's Ninth Symphony, which Wagner had heard for the first time adequately played by the Paris Conservatoire orchestra under Habeneck. For the orchestration here, as elsewhere in this opera and also in *Tannhäuser*, Wagner had learned much from Berlioz.

Another important number in *Der fliegende Holländer* is the C
minor recitative and aria of the Dutchman in Act I ("Die Frist ist um"),
ending with his pathetic appeal for death ("Ew'ge Vernichtung, nimm
mich auf!") which is echoed mysteriously in E major by the voices of
the unseen crew—a momentary shift of tonality made more striking by
the immediate, implacable return to C minor in the orchestral coda.
The long duet of Senta and the Dutchman in the finale of Act II is the
climax of the drama, but its operatic style is an unfortunate lapse into
an earlier and less individual musical idiom. Of the remaining numbers
it is necessary to mention only the familiar Spinning Song which opens
the second act, with the women's voices in A major offering a pleasant
contrast to the dark colors of Act I and making an ideal prelude to
Senta's Ballad.

In *Tannhäuser* (1845) Wagner aimed to unite the two elements
which he had developed separately in *Der fliegende Holländer* and
Rienzi, to clothe the dramatic idea of redemption in the garments of
grand opera. His poem combined materials from a number of different
sources, treating of the medieval legend of the knight Tannhäuser, who
sojourned with Venus in her magic mountain and later went on a
pilgrimage to Rome to obtain absolution, which was refused him:
"Sooner will this dry staff blossom than your sins be forgiven," he was
told by the Pope. But the staff miraculously blossomed, a sign of God's
mercy. To this story Wagner added the episode of the Song Contest and
the figure of Elizabeth, through whose pure love and intercession the
miracle of salvation was effected. All this is cast in the traditional outlines of an opera with the customary theatrical devices. The division into
numbers is still clear, though with more sweep and less rigidity than in
the earlier works. There are solos (for example, Tannhäuser's song in
praise of Venus, Elizabeth's "Dich, teure Halle," her Prayer, Wolfram's
song to the Evening Star), ensembles (especially the end of Act II),
choruses (for example, the Pilgrims' Choruses for men's voices,[3] a
favorite medium in nineteenth-century opera), the Venusberg ballet,
and the brilliant crowd scene of the Entrance of the Knights and the
Song Contest in Act II. Numbers such as these, treated with Wagner's
mastery of stage effect and in a style that audiences could easily understand, assured the success of *Tannhäuser*, though the new work did
not arouse enthusiasm equal to that which had greeted *Rienzi*. Yet even

[3] Sopranos and altos are added for climactic effect at the end of Act III.

where *Tannhäuser* is most operatic, it does not sacrifice the drama to outward show. The spectacular scenes are connected with the action and have a serious dramatic purpose; indeed, there are few operas in which form and content are so well balanced.

The portions of *Tannhäuser* that listeners failed to comprehend were just those which were most important in Wagner's estimation, and most significant in view of his later development, namely the recitatives, of which Tannhäuser's narrative of his pilgrimage to Rome (Act III) is the principal example. Here is a long solo containing some of the central incidents of the drama; it is certainly not an aria with regular melody and balanced phrases, but neither is it recitative of the neutral, declamatory type found in earlier operas (and elsewhere in Wagner also). It is a melody strictly molded to the text, a semirealistic declamation of the words combined with expression of their content by means of a flexible line supported by an equally important harmonic structure. In addition to providing the harmony, the orchestra has certain musical motifs which, by reason of their character and their association with the text, are heard as a commentary on the words, or as a further and purely musical expression of their meaning (Example 96). This is the style which came to prevail almost exclusively in Wagner's later works, and to which he gave the name *Sprechgesang*, that is, "speech song." It was not entirely new with Wagner—Weber had done something similar in *Euryanthe*—but he used it so extensively, wielded it so effectively, and built it so firmly into his whole theory of the music drama that he perhaps rightly ranks as its discoverer. To the original singers of *Tannhäuser*, as well as to the audience, it was a mystery. Even the famous soprano Wilhelmine Schröder-Devrient, Wagner's staunch friend from the beginning and one from whom he received much inspiration, confessed that she could not make head or tail of her role of Venus; and the tenor Tichatschek, though equally devoted to the composer, had not the slightest perception of his new dramatic aims. Little by little, however, a small section of the Dresden public began to sympathize; this group—which, significantly, included few professional musicians—was the nucleus of the future Wagner cult.

The essential dramatic idea in *Tannhäuser* is, of course, the opposition of the world of sensual ecstasy and the world of ascetic renunciation, the former represented by Venus and her court, the latter by Elizabeth and the Pilgrims. Both Wagner's expansion of the Venusberg ballet for

EXAMPLE 96

Tannhäuser, Act III

WAGNER

(Hör)an! In - brunst im

Strings
p

Her-zen, wie kein Bü - sser noch sie

poco cresc. *(con 8va)*

je_____ ge -fühlt, sucht' ich den Weg nach Rom.

dim. *p* *pp*

the disastrous Paris performances of 1861 and his revision of the last finale to include the actual appearance of Venus served to accentuate the contrast between the two basic ideas of the opera. Wagner's music embodies the character of each of these worlds with an imaginative grasp and intensity of utterance which is more remarkable than anything else in the whole score. His greatness as a composer lies just in this power of evoking in the listener's mind such conceptions, in all their emotional depth and complexity, by means of music in which every detail is consciously or unconsciously directed toward the expressive purpose. In pursuit of his aims, Wagner found it necessary to rely more and more on the resources of harmony and instrumental color; as the aria diminished in importance, the orchestra rose correspondingly. This is evident in *Tannhäuser* both in the thematic importance of the accompaniments and in the separate orchestral pieces. The introduction to the third act, depicting Tannhäuser's pilgrimage, is one of those short symphonic poems of which there were to be more in the later works— Siegfried's Rhine Journey in *Götterdämmerung*, for example, or the Good Friday music in *Parsifal*. The overture to *Tannhäuser* is a complete composition in itself, and, like those of *Der fliegende Holländer* or *Die Meistersinger*, a synopsis of the larger dramatic and musical form to follow.

It has been noted [4] that the first six completed operas of Wagner are grouped in pairs, and that within each pair, each member is in many ways complementary to the other. This is especially noticeable with *Tannhäuser* and *Lohengrin*. The latter was composed in the years 1846–48, though not performed until 1850 at Weimar, under Liszt's direction. Its sources, like those of *Tannhäuser*, are found in folklore and Germanic legend, but the treatment now is considerably different. In *Lohengrin* Wagner is less concerned with the tale itself or the historical setting and more with the timeless significance of the events portrayed. The characters, though adequately depicted as human, are at the same time agents or personifications of forces the conflict of which makes the drama. Thus Lohengrin may be said to represent divine love and its longing for reciprocal love and faith from mankind, while Elsa represents human nature incapable of the necessary unquestioning trust. Whatever meaning one may see in the story, the necessity of some interpretation in the sense suggested is unavoidable. In keeping with

[4] See Chamberlain, *Das Drama Richard Wagners*.

this view of the drama, the musical setting of *Lohengrin* is altogether less spectacular than that of *Tannhäuser*; there are no sensational contrasts, and an extraordinary unity of mood prevails throughout. The system of reminiscence motifs is still further developed, not only in extent but also in the changed function of the motifs themselves : they are no longer used simply to recall earlier scenes and actions but to symbolize situations or abstract ideas. For example, the motif which some analysts label "the forbidden question," first sung by Lohengrin as he lays the command on Elsa never to inquire his name or country, is a complete, periodic, eight-measure theme (Example 97). It recurs, in whole or in

Lohengrin, Act I

EXAMPLE 97   WAGNER

Nie sollst du mich be - fra-gen,   noch Wi - ssens Sor - ge tra-gen, wo-

- her ich kam der Fahrt,   noch wie mein Nam' und Art!

part, wherever throughout the opera the situation touches pointedly on this prohibition : in the introduction to Act II, during the dialogue between Ortrud and Friedrich in the first scene, in the second scene at Ortrud's hypocritical warning to Elsa against the "unknown" knight, at Elsa's sign of doubt in the last scene of the act, and in the closing orchestral cadence; it comes into the duet of Act III, rises to full force as Elsa's fatal question is asked, echoes again at the end of this scene, and is heard once more at Elsa's entrance in the last finale. Other characteristic motifs are used in a similar way. The principle is not yet that of the *Ring*, where the motifs are shorter, essentially harmonic and rhythmic rather than melodic, and employed continuously in a symphonic web; nevertheless, *Lohengrin* carries the practice further than any preceding opera and clearly points the way to Wagner's later style.

From the formal point of view *Lohengrin* has shed many traces of the traditional division into numbers, as well as much of the distinction between aria and recitative. The new free declamation is the normal style in this work, except in a few places like Elsa's "Einsam in trüben Tagen"—and even here the three strophes of the solo are separated by choruses and recitatives—Lohengrin's narrative in Act III, the Bridal Chorus, and the duet following this. The colorful orchestral prelude to Act III is often played as a separate concert number. The prelude to the opera, unlike the overture to *Tannhäuser*, is in one mood and movement, representing (according to Wagner's statement) the descent and return of the Holy Grail, the type of Lohengrin's own mission, as we hear when the same themes and harmonies accompany his narrative in Act III. The A major tonality of the prelude is associated with Lohengrin throughout the opera, just as the key of F-sharp minor is assigned to Ortrud and, as a rule, the flat keys to Elsa. The harmony of *Lohengrin* is remarkably diatonic; there is very little chromaticism of the sort found in the middle section of the Pilgrims' Chorus or the Evening Star aria in *Tannhäuser*. The orchestration likewise contrasts with that of *Tannhäuser*: instead of treating the instruments as a homogeneous group, Wagner by preference divides them into antiphonal choirs, often with the violins subdivided and the wood-wind section expanded so as to make possible a whole chord of three or four tones in a single color. The effect, while less brilliant than in *Tannhäuser*, is at the same time richer and more subtle. Even in the last scene of Act II, showing the dawn of day heralded by trumpet fanfares, and the procession to the minster, the sonority is restrained in comparison with the usual grand-opera treatment of such places.

The skillfully written choruses in *Lohengrin* are an important musical and dramatic factor. For the most part the chorus is treated either as realistically entering into the action, or else as an "articulate spectator" in the manner of Greek tragedy (especially in the second scene of Act I and the finale of Act III). The prominence of the chorus may have been suggested to Wagner by his study of Gluck's *Iphigénie en Aulide*, which he revised for performances at Dresden in 1847.

Lohengrin is generally regarded as the last of the German romantic operas. It has many resemblances to Weber's *Euryanthe*, not only in the plot and characters [5] but also in the continuity of the music, the style of declamation, and the use of recurring motifs. It was Wagner's last dramatic composition for five years, or until he began work on the music

[5] The basic plot—the trial of a wife's love—is common to the two works. The character of Elsa corresponds to Euryanthe, Telramund and Ortrud to Lysiart and Eglantine; the figure of the good king is also in both. Act I of *Lohengrin*, as Bekker points out (*Richard Wagner*, chap. 6), was doubtless also influenced by Marschner's *Templer und Jüdin*.

of *Das Rheingold* in 1853.[6] In 1849, as a result of quarrels with his superiors and a multitude of other difficulties climaxing in his active participation in the revolutionary uprising of May of that year, Wagner was obliged to flee from Dresden. He sought refuge at Weimar with Liszt, who aided him to escape to Switzerland. Settled at Zurich, Wagner found leisure to clarify in his own mind the new ideas on music and the theatre which had already been occupying him at Dresden, and of which some intimations may be found in his earlier operas, *Lohengrin* especially. The result of these cogitations was a series of essays, including the important *Oper und Drama* ("Opera and Drama," published in 1851), a systematic account of the philosophy and technical methods by which all his subsequent works were to be governed. A knowledge of *Oper und Drama* is indispensable for anyone who seriously desires to understand these works—the *Ring, Tristan, Die Meistersinger,* and *Parsifal*—even though Wagner's practice is not always consistent with his theories.[7]

The doctrines of *Oper und Drama* are best exemplified in *Der Ring des Nibelungen* ("The Ring of the Nibelungs"), which consists of four consecutive dramas : *Das Rheingold* ("The Rhine Gold"), shorter than the others, and a prelude to them; *Die Walküre* ("The Valkyrie"); *Siegfried*; and *Götterdämmerung* ("The Twilight of the Gods"). Altogether, the composition of the *Ring* occupied twenty years of Wagner's life. Its subject combines two distinct Germanic myth cycles, the story of Siegfried and that of the downfall of the gods. Wagner in 1848 wrote a drama, *Siegfrieds Tod* ("The Death of Siegfried"), which he expected to set to music at once; but as the subject grew in his mind, he felt the need for another drama to precede this, and wrote *Der junge Siegfried* ("Young Siegfried") in 1851. The work expanded still further : *Die Walküre* was required to lead up to *Der junge Siegfried,* and *Das Rheingold* as a general prelude to the whole. These two poems, in this order, were written in 1852, after which *Der junge Siegfried* and *Siegfrieds Tod* were revised as the present *Siegfried* and *Götterdämmerung* respectively, the whole text being completed by the end of 1852.[8] Mean-

---

[6] The short musical sketches made in 1850 for *Siegfrieds Tod* are similar in style to the *Lohengrin* music. See Newman, *Wagner* II, 159–61.

[7] The English translation of *Oper und Drama* by Edwin Evans is recommended. There is a good summary in G. Abraham, *A Hundred Years of Music*.

[8] On the changes made in the earlier poems, and some resulting inconsistencies in the present text, see Newman, *Wagner* II, chap. 17; on the symbolism, Overhoff, *Richard Wagners germanisch-christlicher Mythos*.

while some sketches for the music had been made; composition was begun in 1853, and by 1857 the setting was completed through the second act of *Siegfried*. After an interim during which he composed *Tristan* and *Die Meistersinger*, Wagner resumed work on the *Ring* in 1865, though *Götterdämmerung* was not finished until nine years later. The first performances of the whole tetralogy took place at Bayreuth in 1876.

The story of the *Ring* is so familiar—or, at least, is so easily accessible in popular books of all sorts, not to mention the scores themselves—that there is no need to recapitulate it here. The material is taken not from history (as in *Rienzi*), or folklore (as in *Die Feen*), or even legend (as in *Der fliegende Holländer* and *Tannhäuser*), but from mythology. The reason is not primarily that the myth is entertaining, but that it is meaningful. According to Wagner the myth presents, in the simplest, most inclusive, and most concentrated form imaginable, the interplay of eternal forces affecting the relation of men to God, to nature, and to each other in society—in other words, living, eternal issues of religious, social, and economic importance, with which it is the duty of art consciously to deal. These issues are set before us in the myth, and consequently in Wagner's *Ring*, by means of symbols, either objects (the Gold, Valhalla, the Sword) or persons (Wotan, Siegfried, Brünnhilde). It is the nature of a symbol to be capable of various interpretations; and although Wagner labored hard, both in the poem itself and in other writings, to make clear his own interpretation of the *Ring*, he did not fully succeed —partly because of some inconsistencies in his thinking and the obscurity of his literary style, but more because the symbols were so ambiguous that it was impossible to make a single definitive explanation of them. Many writers have tried to do so, and have argued vehemently, each according to his own convictions, for or against the doctrines conceived to be embodied in the *Ring*. Still others regard any intentional preaching in art as either of no importance or else downright vicious and inartistic. There is no need at this day to add anything more to the enormous mass of controversial literature about Wagner. It is not within the scope of a book like this to investigate the alleged effects of his teaching, in the *Ring* or elsewhere, on European politics.[9] That he did teach —that his views of art and the theatre impelled him in his operas to

---

[9] An introduction to this subject, with bibliographies, may be found in Viereck's *Metapolitics from the Romantics to Hitler*.

assume the role of prophet as well as musician—is a fact, whether one approves it or not; but all that concerns us here is the consequences of that fact in his art work itself.

It is not easy to dramatize abstractions. In the *Ring*, Wagner felt obliged to introduce some explanatory passages which slow down or interrupt the action of the play—for example, the long dialogue between Wotan and Brünnhilde in the second scene of Act II of *Die Walküre*. For the benefit of opera audiences, who are not particularly interested in metaphysics, these passages are often cut or shortened in performance. The same is true of the many repetitions of the story which occur from time to time, and other apparent digressions. All these matters have their justification, however, in Wagner's theories; moreover, the leisurely pace of the action suggests the tempo of the long medieval epic poems from which the incidents were taken. Another interesting reminiscence of these poetic models is Wagner's employment of *Stabreim*, or alliteration, instead of the more modern device of end rhymes :

> Gab sein Gold mir Macht ohne Mass,
> nun zeug' sein Zauber Tod dem der ihn trägt !
> (As its gold gave me might without measure,
> Now may its magic deal death to him who wears it !)
> *Das Rheingold*, scene 4

The relation of music to drama is one of the subjects on which Wagner discourses in much detail in his writings. The first proposition of *Oper und Drama* is : "The error in opera hitherto consisted in this, that a means of expression (the music) has been made an end, while the end itself (the drama) has been made the means." [10] It does not follow, however, that now poetry is to be made primary and music secondary, but that both are to grow organically out of the necessities of dramatic expression, not being brought together, but existing as two aspects of one and the same thing. Other arts as well (the dance, architecture, painting) are to be included in this union, making the music drama a Gesamtkunstwerk, that is, a composite or total art work. This is not, in Wagner's view, a limitation of any of the arts; on the contrary, only in such a union can the full possibilities of each be realized. The "music of the future," then, will exist not in isolation as heretofore, but as one aspect of the Gesamtkunstwerk, in which situation it will develop new

[10] "Oper und Drama," in *Gesammelte Schriften* III, 231; cf. J. M. Stein, *Richard Wagner and the Synthesis of the Arts*.

technical and expressive resources and will progress beyond the point to which it has now arrived, a point beyond which is cannot substantially progress in any other way.

This view was the consequence of a typical nineteenth-century philosophy. Wagner regarded the history of music as a process of evolution which must inevitably continue in a certain direction. The theory that the line of progress involved the end of music as a separate art and its absorption into a community of the arts is not without analogy to the communistic and socialistic doctrines of the period, with their emphasis on the absorption of the interests of the individual into those of the community as a whole.[11] It is not surprising that some such view of the future of music should have arisen in the second half of the nineteenth century. It is plain enough to us now that the resources of music—that is, of the kind of music which had been growing up since Beethoven—were approaching their utmost limits at this time, and that these limits were in fact reached in the works of Wagner, Brahms, R. Strauss, and Mahler. It has been the mission of twentieth-century composers to recognize this situation and to create new musical styles, much as the composers of the seventeenth century had to do after the culmination of sixteenth-century polyphony in the works of Palestrina, Byrd, and Lassus. In discerning the approaching end of a musical style, therefore, Wagner was right. His error was in postulating the Gesamtkunstwerk as the only possible road for the future.

Wagner held that music in itself was the immediate expression of feeling, but that it could not designate the particular object toward which feeling was directed. Hence, for him the inner action of the drama existed in the music, while the function of word and gesture was to make definite the outer action.[12] This aesthetic is the theoretical basis of many features of the *Ring* and later works. For example, since the inner action is regarded as being always on a plane of feeling where music is appropriate and necessary, there is no spoken dialogue or simple recitative. Moreover, the inner action (unlike the outer) is continuous; hence the music is continuous. (In this theory, intermissions between the acts and the performance of the *Ring* on four separate evenings instead of all at once can only be regarded as one of Wagner's reluctant concessions to human frailty.) Transitions from one scene to the next are made by means of orchestral interludes when necessary, and within each scene the music has a continuity of which the most obvious technical sign is

[11] Cf. Barzun, *Darwin, Marx, Wagner.*

[12] Cf. Schopenhauer, *Die Welt als Wille und Vorstellung* I, Book III, sec. 52; and Vol. II ("Ergänzungen"), chap. 39.

Scene from Weber's *Der Freischütz* (Weimar, 1822); design by Carl Wilhelm
Holdermann, figures by C. A. Schwerdgeburth; aquatint by Holdermann and Carl
Lieber   (*Munich, Theatermuseum*)

Setting for Act III, Scene 1 of the original production of *Die Walküre* (Bayreuth, 1876); design by Joseph Hoffmann   (*Courtesy Archiv des Hauses Wahnfried, Bayreuth*)

Setting for the same scene, Bayreuth, 1960; design by Wolfgang Wagner   (*Courtesy Archiv des Hauses Wahnfried, Bayreuth*)

the avoidance of perfect cadences. Continuity in music, however, is more than avoidance of perfect cadences. It is a result of the musical form as a whole, and since form in Wagner (as in any composer) is partly a function of harmonic procedure, this is an appropriate place to consider these two subjects together.

The statements most frequently made about Wagner's harmony are (1) that it is "full of chromatics" and (2) that the music "continually modulates." Both statements are true but superficial. Much of the chromaticism in the earlier works (for example, in the original version of *Tannhäuser*) is merely an embellishment of the melodic line or occurs incidentally in the course of modulating sequences. Many of the chromatic passages in the *Ring*, such as the magic sleep motif, are found in the midst of long diatonic sections. The impression that Wagner continually modulates is due in part to a short-breathed method of analysis based on a narrow conception of tonality, which tends to see a modulation at every dominant-tonic progression and, preoccupied with such details, overlooks the broader harmonic scheme. A more comprehensive and illuminating view is set forth by Alfred Lorenz in his four studies entitled *Das Geheimnis der Form bei Richard Wagner* ("The Secret of Form in Richard Wagner"). Lorenz, in the enthusiasm of discovery, occasionally strains the facts to make them fit his theory; nevertheless he does succeed in showing that Wagner's music dramas are cast in definite musical forms, and that the formal clarity is evident not only in each work as a whole but also in the constituent sections, down to the smallest. The structure of the music is inseparable from that of the drama, and one of its fundamental elements is the key scheme. *Das Rheingold*, for example, is regarded as a large a–b–a form in D-flat, with an introduction in E-flat (dominant of the dominant); D-flat is also the tonality of the *Ring* as a whole. *Tristan* is likewise in three-part form, Acts I and III corresponding, and Act II being the "b" section—though here the correspondence is one of themes and dramatic action, not of tonality. The three acts of *Die Meistersinger* in the same way make a huge a–a–b form, the first two being equal in length and the third as long as the first two together. These two forms, the *Bogen* (a–b–a, literally "bow") and *Bar* (a–a–b),[13] are frequently exemplified also in the structure of the

---

[13] The Bar, consisting of two *Stollen* (a a) and an *Abgesang* (b), was the favorite form of the German minnesinger. It is well illustrated in both versions of Walther's "Preislied," and explained by Hans Sachs (see *Die Meistersinger*, Act III, sc. 2).

scenes and smaller subdivisions : thus the fifteenth "period" of Act II of *Siegfried* (three measures before "Noch einmal, liebes Vöglein" to change of signature to four sharps "nun sing") is an a–b–a or Bogen in E minor (18 + 30 + 21 measures) and the introduction to Act II of *Die Walküre* is a Bar in A minor (introduction, 14 measures; two *Stollen*, 20 + 19 measures; *Abgesang*, 20 measures). Other form types (strophic, rondo) also appear, and many units are composed of two or more of the basic types in various modifications and combinations.[14] One may not choose to follow Lorenz in every detail, and it would certainly be in order to question some of his interpretations of the basic formal schemes; but taken as a whole, it is impossible in the face of his demonstration not to be convinced of the essential orderliness, at once minute and all-embracing, of the musical cosmos of the *Ring*, as well as of *Tristan*, *Die Meistersinger*, and *Parsifal*. It is an orderliness not derived at second hand from the text but inhering in the musical structure itself. Was Wagner fully aware of it? One is tempted to think not, since he says almost nothing about it in his writings. Yet whether conscious or unconscious, the sheer grasp and creation of such huge and complex organisms is a matter for wonder. It may be unnecessary to remark that the fact (if it is a fact) that Wagner's creative processes were largely instinctive or unconscious does not of itself invalidate any analysis of his music. It is no essential part of a composer's business to be aware, in an analytical sense, of everything he is doing.

Within the larger frameworks of order, and subsidiary to them, take place the various harmonic procedures which have given rise to Wagner's reputation : modulations induced by enharmonic changes in chromatically altered chords and forwarded by modulating sequences; the interchangeable use of major and minor modes and the frequency of the mediants and the flat supertonic as goals of modulation; the determination of chord sequences by chromatic progression of individual voices; the presence of "harmonic parentheses" within a section, related to the tonality of the whole as auxiliary notes or appoggiaturas are related to the fundamental harmony of the chord with which they occur; the systematic treatment of sevenths and even ninths as consonant chords; the resolution of dominants to chords other than the tonic; the

[14] Lorenz's system of analysis cannot be adequately illustrated without going into greater detail than is possible here. See his outline of Act I of *Die Walküre* in Abraham, *A Hundred Years of Music*, Part II, and cf. A. E. F. Dickinson, "The Structural Methods of *The Ring*."

combination of melodies in a contrapuntal tissue; and finally, the frequent suspensions and appoggiaturas in the various melodic lines, which contribute as much as any single factor to the peculiar romantic, Wagnerian, "longing" quality of the harmony—a quality heard in perfection in the prelude to *Tristan und Isolde*.

While the musical forms of Wagner's dramas are determined in part by the harmonic structure, a more obvious role is played by the continuous recurrence and variation of a limited number of distinct musical units generally know as leitmotifs or leading motifs. The term "leitmotif" is not Wagner's but he did use the apparently synonymous word *Hauptmotiv* (principal motif). It seems likely that Wagner suggested this word, as well as the system of analyzing his music dramas in terms of motifs, to Heinrich Porges, whose book on *Tristan und Isolde* written in 1866–77 (though not published before 1902) uses this method. The analysis of Wagner's music in terms of leitmotifs was popularized by Hans von Wolzogen, first editor of the *Bayreuther Blätter* and author of many "guides" to the music dramas.[15]

Different analysts distinguish, and variously name, seventy to two hundred leitmotifs in the *Ring*. Each is regarded as the focal point of expression of a certain dramatic idea, with which it remains associated throughout the tetralogy. The clue to the association of motif and idea is to be found at the first appearance of the former; for example, the Valhalla motif is first heard at the opening of the second scene of *Das Rheingold* as the curtain rises to reveal the castle of Valhalla. Here, as usual at the first statement of a motif, Wagner repeats and spins out the phrase so as to impress it on the memory; moreover, there is a premonition of the Valhalla motif at the end of the preceding scene, where its derivation from the Ring motif is obvious. The motifs are short and of pronounced individual character; they are often suggested by a pictorial image (as the fire motifs), or by association (as the trumpet figure for the sword motif), but each aims to convey not merely a picture but also the essence of the idea for which the visible symbol stands. In this capacity the motifs may recur, not simply as musical labels, but whenever the idea recurs or is suggested in the course of the drama, forming a

[15] See for example his *Thematischer Leitfaden durch die Musik zu Richard Wagners Festspiel Der Ring des Nibelungen* (1876) and later similar works; further in Newman, *Wagner* III, 382–83; cf. also the references in note 1 on page 392. On the earlier history of recurring themes in opera, see G. F. Schmidt, *Die frühdeutsche Oper* II, 255–80; Bücken, *Der heroische Stil in der Oper, passim.*

symphonic web which corresponds in theory, and generally also in fact, to the dramatic web of the action. The connection between the musical forms so evolved and the dramatic forms is thus complete. The motifs may be contrapuntally combined, or varied, developed, and transformed in accordance with the changing fortunes of the idea they represent. Relationship of ideas may be shown by thematic relationships among the motifs (Example 98), though probably some of the resemblances are

EXAMPLE 98   Motifs from the *Ring*

not intentional. Altogether, the statement, recurrence, variation, development, and transformation of the motifs is analogous to the working out of musical material in a symphony.

Since the inner meaning of the drama is found in music, it follows in Wagner's theory that the orchestra is the basic medium rather than the voices. In his phrase, the words "float like a ship on the sea of orchestral harmony." Only rarely are the leitmotifs sung. As a rule, the voice will make a free counterpoint to the instrumental melody. The voice part, however, is always itself melodic, never merely declamatory as in recitativo secco; its line is so arranged as not only to give the correct declamation but also to reproduce the accent, tempo, and inflections appropriate to each character. Textual repetition is avoided. In theory there are to be no ensembles, especially in the old-fashioned sense where some voices are used only to supply a harmonic background; but this rule Wagner relaxed on occasion, as in the finale of Act II of *Götter-dämmerung* or the quintet in *Die Meistersinger*. Of Wagner's genius as an orchestrator there is no need to speak here. His music is the realization of the full, rich, romantic sound ideal of the nineteenth century. Its peculiar texture is determined in large part by the nature of the melodic lines : long phrased, avoiding periodic cadential points (this in contrast to *Lohengrin* and earlier works), so designed that every note tends to move on without ever quite coming to rest.[16] The full resources of symphonic style—counterpoint, orchestral color, and formal structure—are invoked. This in itself was not new in the history of opera, for many earlier composers (for example, Monteverdi in *Orfeo*) had done the same. But Wagner, besides having the immensely developed instrumental resources of the nineteenth century at his disposal, was conscious as no earlier composer had been of the drama as the generating force in the whole plan; and he was original in placing the orchestra at the center, with the essential drama going on in the music, while words and gesture furnished only the outer happenings. From this point of view his music dramas may be regarded as symphonic poems the program of which, instead of being printed and read, is explained and acted out by persons on the stage.

Wagner despised "opera," yet his music dramas have been as popular as any operas. What is the source of their appeal? Primarily, of course, the music itself. Yet there are certain other factors which have at different times made for popular success in opera. One of these factors in the nineteenth century was the appeal to national pride, as in some of Weber's and Verdi's works. Such an appeal is indirectly present in most of Wagner's operas insofar as they are founded on Germanic myths or

---

[16] This is one meaning of Wagner's term "unending melody"; it has other meanings as well. See Lorenz, *Geheimnis der Form* I, 61–70; Kurth, *Romantische Harmonik* (2d ed.), Part 7.

legends; but this kind of nationalism is of little importance, since Wagner thought of his dramas as universal, dealing with what he called the "purely human," not limited to Germans in the sense in which *Der Freischütz* was. Even *Die Meistersinger*, for all its reference to "holy German art," is not narrow in its patriotism or jingoistic in spirit.

Another and more general means of popular appeal in opera is stage spectacle. Wagner availed himself of this resource unstintedly, though always maintaining that every one of his effects grew of necessity out of the drama itself. It would be difficult to think of any beguiling, eye-catching, fanciful, sensational device in the whole history of opera from Monteverdi to Meyerbeer which Wagner did not appropriate and use with expert showmanship somewhere in his works. One has only to look at the poem of the *Ring* to see how prominent is this element; it has a large place also in *Parsifal*. In *Tristan* and *Die Meistersinger*, however, it is less in evidence, for these are dramas of human character and as such appeal directly to fundamental human emotions with less need of spectacular stage effects. This quality of direct, human appeal is heard at only a few places in the *Ring*, as in the love scenes of Siegmund and Sieglinde (*Die Walküre*, Act I), of Siegfried and Brünnhilde (*Siegfried*, Act III), or in the scene of Wotan's farewell to Brünnhilde (*Die Walküre*, Act III); and when Wagner, like Wotan in this scene, put aside his concern with godhood to create the truly memorable characters of Walther, Eva, Hans Sachs, Isolde, and Tristan, he created two works that are likely to outlive all the pageantry and symbolism of the *Ring*.

The poem of *Tristan und Isolde* was begun at Zurich in 1857 and the score finished in 1859. It is often regarded as a monument to Wagner's love for Mathilde Wesendonck, the wife of one of his most devoted friends during his years of exile. Newman sensibly points out, however, that this view probably confuses cause and effect, that Wagner did not compose *Tristan* because he was in love with Mathilde, but rather that he was in love because he was composing *Tristan*. Either way, the matter is not important. In 1857–58 Wagner composed five songs to poems by Mathilde; two of these (*Träume* and *Im Treibhaus*) are made up of thematic material used in *Tristan*, and Wagner later described them as "studies" for the opera. *Tristan* was undertaken at a time when there appeared no prospect of ever bringing the *Ring* to performance, and it was Wagner's hope that a less exacting music drama might have rather better prospects of success. But by now his ideas of what constituted a practicable work had so far outgrown the actual practice of the theatres that *Tristan* for many years could not be produced. After more than seventy rehearsals at Vienna in 1862–63 it was abandoned as impossible. Finally in 1864 the young king Ludwig of Bavaria summoned Wagner to Munich and placed almost unlimited resources at his disposal. After careful preparation, the first performance took place at Munich on June 10, 1865, under the direction of Hans von Bülow.

The legend of Tristan and Isolde is probably of Celtic origin. In the early thirteenth century it was embodied by Gottfried of Strassburg in a long epic poem, which was Wagner's principal source for his drama. Wagner's changes consisted in compressing the action, eliminating non-essential personages (for example, the original second Isolde, "of the white hands"), and simplifying the motives. Some details were doubtless borrowed from other sources : the extinction of the torch in Act II from the story of *Hero and Leander*, the dawning of day at the end of the love scene from Shakespeare's *Romeo and Juliet*, and Tristan's delirium in Act III from Matthew Arnold's poem; the love duet in the second act has some points reminiscent of a dialogue between Faust and Helena in the second part of Goethe's drama and the figure of Brangäne as watcher was perhaps suggested by Goethe's Lynceus.[17] The prominence of the motif of death, the yearning for fulfillment of love in release and annihilation which broods over the whole drama, were at least partly due to Wagner's absorption in the philosophy of Schopenhauer, with whose works he had first become acquainted in 1852.[18] But whatever the contributions of others, *Tristan und Isolde* is Wagner's own. It is owing to him, and to him alone, that this is now one of the great love stories, living in the imagination of millions along with the tales of Romeo and Juliet, Paolo and Francesca, Launcelot and Guinevere.

The peculiar strength of the drama arises from the fact that external events are simplified to the utmost, so that the action is almost all inner, and consequently expressed almost wholly in music. The words themselves often melt into music, losing their very character as intelligible language, nearly superfluous in many places where the plane of expres-

[17] *Faust*, Part II, lines 9372–9418, 11288–11337. These literary derivations are suggested with some diffidence. The torch episode is found in Méhul's *Mélidor et Phrosine*; the watcher is a common figure in German medieval love poems. Cf. Loomis, ed., *The Romance of Tristram and Ysolt by Thomas of Britain*, introduction.

[18] There are echoes here also of Novalis and F. von Schlegel. Cf. Mann, "Leiden und Grösse Richard Wagners," in his *Leiden und Grösse der Meister*, pp. 130–32.

sion is purely that of the emotions—as, for example, in Isolde's "Liebestod" at the end of Act III. "Every theory was quite forgotten," wrote Wagner; "during the working out I myself became aware how far I had outsoared my system." [19]

The three leading ideas of the drama—love, night, and death—are inseparable, but each one in turn is especially emphasized in each of the three acts. The magic potion of Act I is, in Wagner's version, purely a symbol, figuring forth the moment of realization of a love already existing but unacknowledged. Isolde's extinction of the torch is the symbol of Act II; the ecstatic greeting of the lovers leads into the duet "Descend upon us, night of love," followed by the love-death music with the words "O could we but die thus together, endless, never to awaken!" The climax of the whole scene is in the song of Brangäne, off stage: "Lonely I watch in the night; you that are lost in the dream of love, heed the lonely one's call: sorrow comes with awakening. Beware! O beware! For the night soon passes." Few artists have so poignantly expressed what many human beings have experienced, the unutterably sorrowful realization in the midst of happiness that this moment cannot last. There is a comparable passage in the *Arabian Nights*:

Presently one of them arose and set meat before me and I ate and they ate with me; whilst others warmed water and washed my hands and feet and changed my clothes, and others made ready sherbets and gave us to drink; and all gathered round me being full of joy and gladness at my coming. Then they sat down and conversed with me till night-fall, when five of them arose and laid the trays and spread them with flowers and fragrant herbs and fruits, fresh and dried, and confections in profusion. At last they brought out a fine wine-service with rich old wine; and we sat down to drink and some sang songs and others played the lute and psaltery and recorders and other instruments, and the bowl went merrily round. Hereupon such gladness possessed me that I forgot the sorrows of the world one and all and said, "This is indeed life; O sad that 'tis fleeting." [20]

The doom fated from the beginning is fulfilled. Tristan, reproached by King Mark, mortally wounded by Melot, is carried home to his castle of Kareol and dies as Isolde comes to him bringing Mark's forgiveness. The love-death of Isolde herself brings the tragedy to an end.

Volumes could be, and have been, written about the music of *Tristan und Isolde*. The extreme simplification and condensation of the action,

[19] "Zukunftsmusik," in *Gesammelte Schriften* VII, 119.
[20] *Tale of the Third Kalendar* (Burton's translation).

the reduction of the essential characters to only two, and the treatment of these two as bearers of a single all-dominating mood conduce to unity of musical effect and at the same time permit the greatest possible freedom for development of all the musical elements, unchecked by elaborate paraphernalia or the presence of antimusical factors in the libretto. There are comparatively few leitmotifs, and many of the principal ones are so much alike that it is hard to distinguish and label them clearly. The dominant mood is conveyed in a chromatic style of writing which is no longer either a mere decorative adjunct to, or a deliberate contrast with, a fundamentally diatonic idiom, but which is actually the norm, so much so that the few diatonic motifs are felt as deliberate departures, "specters of day" intruding into the all-prevailing night of the love drama. It is impossible here to enter into a comprehensive examination of the technical aspects of this chromaticism;[21] we can only note that history has shown the "*Tristan* style" to be the classical example of the use of a consistent chromatic technique within the limits of the tonal system of the eighteenth and nineteenth centuries. It was not only the climax of all romantic striving in this direction but also the point of departure for Wagner's own later experiments in *Parsifal*, for the more sophisticated, external, ironic chromaticism of Richard Strauss, and for the twelve-tone system of Schoenberg, the conclusion of the whole style. The power of the *Tristan* chromaticism comes from its being founded in tonality. A feature of it is the ambiguity of the chords, the constant, immanent, felt possibility that almost any chord may resolve in almost any one of a dozen different directions. Yet this very ambiguity could not exist except for underlying tonal relations, the general tendencies of certain chord progressions within the tonal system. The continuous conflict between what *might be*, harmonically, and what actually *is*, makes the music apt at suggesting the inner state of mingled insecurity and passionate longing that pervades the drama. This emotional suggestiveness is accompanied throughout by a luxuriance of purely sensuous effect, a reveling in tone qualities and tone combinations as if for their own sake, evident in both the subdued richness of the orchestration and the whole harmonic fabric.

Such matters as these are felt by even the casual listener to *Tristan und Isolde*. What is less obvious, though it may be dimly sensed, is the

---

[21] This task has been performed, with great thoroughness and insight, by E. Kurth in his *Romantische Harmonik und ihre Krise in Wagners Tristan*.

complete formal perfection of the work. Here again the reader must be
referred for details to the epoch-making study of Lorenz.[22] The close
correspondence of Acts I and III, with the resulting Bogen form of the
opera as a whole, has already been mentioned. As to the tonality, Lorenz
holds it to be E major—beginning in the subdominant (A minor) and
ending in the dominant (B major). The tonic itself, in this view, is
almost never sounded, this being at the same time an instance of the
persistent avoidance of resolution in the harmony and a symbol of the
nature of the love of Tristan and Isolde which attains its satisfaction only
in the ideal, not the actual world. The only extended E major portion
of the opera is the scene of Tristan's vision of Isolde in Act III. The
complete first theme as announced in the prelude (measures 1–17) recurs
only three times in the course of the opera, once at the climax of each
act : at the drinking of the potion in Act I, after Mark's question near
the end of Act II, and at Tristan's death in Act III; its function is thus
that of a refrain for the whole work. The continuity and formal sym-
metry, demonstrable in full only by a detailed analysis, are neatly
epitomized by the fact that the opening chromatic motif of the prelude
receives its final resolution in the closing measures of the last act
(Example 99).

Tristan und Isolde

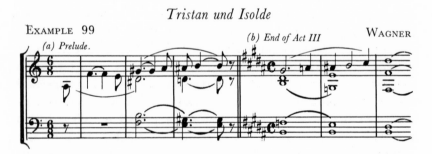

EXAMPLE 99

(a) Prelude.

(b) End of Act III

WAGNER

The score of *Tristan* was completed in 1859. After an unhappy
season in Paris, marked by the scandalous rejection of the revised *Tannhäuser* at the Opéra (March, 1861), Wagner lived for a year and a half
in Vienna. With the failure of prospects for performing *Tristan* there,
his fortunes reached their lowest ebb. His dramatic rescue by the en-
thusiastic King Ludwig of Bavaria brought happier times, but six
months after the successful first performance of *Tristan* Wagner was

[22] *Das Geheimnis der Form*, II.

compelled to leave Munich, owing largely to political jealousies on the part of the king's ministers. He found a home at Hof Triebschen near Lucerne, where he remained from 1866 to 1872. His first wife having died in 1866, he married in 1870 Cosima von Bülow, daughter of Liszt and former wife of Hans von Bülow, the pianist and conductor. Wagner's chief activity in the early years at Triebschen was the composition of *Die Meistersinger*.

Die Meistersinger von Nürnberg ("The Mastersinger of Nuremberg") had been sketched in 1845, as a kind of comic pendant to *Tannhäuser*. Toward the end of 1861 Wagner planned the work anew,[23] writing some parts of the music before the words. The score was completed in 1867 and first performed at Munich in the following year. The story has for historical background the Mastersinger Guilds of sixteenth-century Nuremberg and their song contests, bound about with traditional rules and customs. Wagner not only incorporated many of these points but also borrowed several names and characters of real Mastersingers, notably Hans Sachs, the cobbler-poet-composer who lived 1494–1576.[24] Likewise of historical interest is Wagner's use of an actual Mastersinger melody (the march theme beginning at measure forty-one of the overture), the parody of the Mastersingers' device of *Blumen* or melodic ornaments (literally "flowers") in Beckmesser's songs, and the paraphrase of a poem by the real Hans Sachs (the chorale "Wach' auf !" in Act III). Yet *Die Meistersinger* is not a museum of antiquities but a living, sympathetic re-creation in nineteenth-century terms of an epoch of German musical history, with the literal details of the past illuminated by reference to an ever timely issue, the conflict between tradition and the creative spirit in art. Tradition is represented by the Mastersingers' Guild; the deadly effect of blind adherence to the rules is satirized in the comic figure of Beckmesser, a transparent disguise for the Viennese critic Eduard Hanslick, whose views and influence had made him one of the most persistent and conspicuous of Wagner's opponents. The impetuous, innovating drive of the young artist, impatient of all restraints, is incarnated in the person of Walther von Stolzing, whose conflict with the

[23] On the differences between the two versions, and some minor inconsistencies in the final draft, see Newman, *Wagner* III, 156–64; the various sources of the play are studied in Roethe, "Zum dramatischen Aufbau der Wagnerschen *Meistersinger*." Cf. also Rayner, *Wagner and Die Meistersinger*; H. Thompson, *Wagner and Wagenseil*.

[24] Many of Sachs's melodies may be found in *Das Singebuch des Adam Puschmann*, ed. by G. Münzer, 1906.

Mastersingers is finally resolved by the wisdom of Hans Sachs, the artist grown wise through experience. Sachs shows that neither tradition nor novelty can suffice by itself; they are reconcilable by one who understands the living spirit behind all rules of art and hence realizes that the new must constantly learn from the old, the old constantly absorb the new. It is probably not fanciful to suggest that in Walther and Hans Sachs Wagner has drawn idealized portraits of two aspects of himself, and that the views of Sachs represent his own mature philosophy of art, set forth with deep insight and poetic beauty. One feature of this philosophy is the professed reliance on the judgment of "the people" as final arbiter in artistic matters. *Das Volk* was one of Wagner's most beloved abstractions, one which he always carefully distinguished from *das Publikum*. One is sometimes tempted to believe that the distinction in his mind was simply between those who liked Wagner's music dramas and those who preferred Rossini or Meyerbeer : the former comprising all the unspoiled virtues and sound instincts of the race, while the latter were unhealthy, misled, or corrupt. Yet there is fundamental truth in the doctrine of the sovereignty of the people in art which *Die Meistersinger* proclaims, so long as one understands "the people" in the democratic sense of the word, not as a mob but as bearers of a profound, partly unconscious instinct which—in the long run—is apt to perceive and judge rightly.

In the last analysis, however, *Die Meistersinger* is not to be regarded as a treatise on the philosophy of art; its teachings are of little importance in comparison to the drama and music themselves. It is by far the most human, the most easily accessible, of all Wagner's works. It has every requirement of good comedy : the simple love story of Walther and Eva, the charming scenes of David and the apprentices, the broadly comic strokes of Beckmesser's serenade and his ridiculous attempt to steal Walther's song for the contest. Above all is to be noted the character of Hans Sachs, Wagner's greatest dramatic figure, who surveys the whole drama from the standpoint of one who through suffering has attained resignation, having learned to find joy in the happiness of others and the triumph of principles.

It is interesting to note that, with such a play as this, Wagner was led to compose a score that more nearly approaches the traditional outlines of opera than any of his works since *Tannhäuser*. To be sure, the principle of symphonic development of a set of leitmotifs is maintained, and there is no return to the old-fashioned recitative; but withal there is an amount of formalization of which the listener is, perhaps, hardly aware, since it fits so naturally with the dramatic requirements. Like the Orpheus legend, the *Meistersinger* story is essentially musical in conception. Within its framework fall the four "arias" of Walther, the serenade of Beckmesser, Pogner's "Address," David's song in Act III, and Sachs's two monologues, as well as the formal overture and the chorale at the beginning of Act I. Even more operatic, though no less appropriate, are the apprentices' choruses and the huge final ensemble in Act I, the comic crowd scene at the end of Act II, and the glorified mass finale with a ballet and choruses in Act III. Then, too, there is the quintet in the third act, which is as much pure opera as anything in Donizetti or Verdi: an interpolated number in closed form (a–b–a) and a remote key (G-flat), which does not directly further the action and has only a slight thematic connection with the rest of the work—a number which, in a word, would be out of place in the strict theoretical form of the music drama, but is justifiable here on the same grounds that justify the canonic quartet in *Fidelio* or some of the ensembles of *Don Giovanni*.[25]

It is a sign of Wagner's versatility that, at the same period of his life, he could compose two works which differ so much not only in dramatic plan but also in musical style as do *Die Meistersinger* and *Tristan*. Both the historical background and the nature of the subject matter of *Die Meistersinger* are reflected in the diatonic quality of most of the music, in a certain squareness of rhythmic structure and simplicity of idiom. The chorales, the many melodies of folklike cast, the fugal section and the contrapuntal combination of three principal themes in the overture, as well as the contrapuntal style of the finale and of many other passages—all seem to contain or suggest the very traits and forms that have always been most typical of German music. By contrast the freer, more chromatic individual Wagnerian touch is heard in the love scenes and the monologues of Hans Sachs. The beautiful orchestral prelude to the third act is not only the quintessence of the musical style but also the high point of the drama, the complete, living description of the noble character of Sachs; there is no better example of music as the heart of dramatic life, the true carrier of the inner action of the play.

The essentially musical character of the drama in both *Tristan* and

[25] See above, p. 287.

Die Meistersinger is shown significantly by the fact that in both these works the musical forms are more clear and comprehensive than anywhere else in Wagner. This is, of course, only another way of saying that in these two works we come as close as possible to the ideally perfect union of music and drama within the Wagnerian system. The form type most prevalent in *Die Meistersinger* is, as we have already mentioned, the Bar, of which five examples should be especially noted : (1) Beckmesser's serenade in Act II is a pedantically correct example of two identical Stollen and an Abgesang, the whole being twice repeated to make a song of three strophes. (2) Walther's first song before the Mastersingers, "Am stillen Herd," is a Bar in which the two Stollen are almost, but not quite, identical. (3) Walther's trial song, "So rief der Lenz," is a more extended Bar with two distinct themes in each Stollen, carried on grimly to the end in spite of the uproar of opposition from his audience. (4) In Walther's dream song, the first version of the Prize Song, the two Stollen are not identical, the second being altered so as to cadence in the dominant. (5) In the final version of the Prize Song the melody is further extended and the differences between the two Stollen are likewise greater though still without loss of the essential felt likeness. In addition to many other instances of Bar form, some shorter and some longer than the above, the opera as a whole exemplifies the same structure : anyone who will take the trouble to compare Acts I and II, either with or without the help of Lorenz's outline,[26] will discover that there is a detailed parallelism of the action, and that furthermore in most cases each scene in the second act is a parody of the corresponding scene in Act I—a relationship already foreshadowed by the overture, in which the themes of the middle section parody those of the first. Acts I and II thus form two Stollen, of which Act III is the Abgesang. The whole opera is rounded off by the thematic and tonal correspondence of the beginning and the ending; Lorenz notes that the entire finale, from the entrance of the Mastersingers on, is an expanded and varied reprise of the overture.[27]

The principal events in Wagner's life after *Die Meistersinger* were the completion of the *Ring*, the removal to Bayreuth in 1872, and the first full performance of the *Ring* at the new theatre there in 1876. *Parsifal*, his last music drama, was composed between 1877 and 1882, and first performed at Bayreuth January 13, 1882, exactly a year and

[26] *Das Geheimnis der Form* III, 11–13.
[27] *Ibid.*, p. 171.

one month before Wagner's death. The sources of the *Parsifal* drama are even more varied than those of the earlier works. The convergence of many lines of philosophic thought, the complex and often obscure symbolism of the persons and events, make this the most difficult of all Wagner's music dramas to comprehend, even though the outer action is comparatively simple. The legend of the Holy Grail (already touched upon in *Lohengrin* and some other uncomposed dramatic sketches) is combined with speculations on the role of suffering in human life, and the central idea is again that of redemption—this time not through love, but by the savior Parsifal, the Pure Fool, the one "made wise through pity." The solemnity of this theme, as well as the use of the Christian symbol of the Eucharist, justifies the designation of Parsifal as a "religious festival-play," a character carefully maintained in performances in the present-day opera theatre.

No doubt the complexity of the poem is responsible for the music of *Parsifal* being less clear in formal outlines than that of either *Tristan* or *Die Meistersinger*. There is sufficient resemblance between the first and third acts to delineate a general a–b–a structure, but neither the key scheme nor other details of the various scenes are as amenable to analysis as in the case of the other two works. The music, like that of *Tannhäuser*, depicts different worlds of thought and feeling in sharpest possible contrast; but whereas in *Tannhäuser* there were two such worlds, in *Parsifal* there are three. Least important, being merely a foil for the other two, is the realm of sensual pleasure exemplified in the second act : the Magic Garden and the Flower Maidens of Klingsor's castle, and Kundry as seductress under the power of evil magic. If we compare the music of these scenes with the ebullient eroticism of the Venusberg music or the glowing ardors of the *Siegfried* finale, we may be aware of a slight falling off in Wagner's earlier elemental power, a trifle of oversophistication in the technical means. Not so, however, in the first and third acts. Here are opposed and intermingled the worlds of Amfortas and of the Grail, the agonizing penitent and the mystical heavenly kingdom of pity and peace. The Amfortas music is of the utmost intensity of feeling, expressed in richness of orchestral color, plangency of dissonance, complexity and subtlety of harmonic relationships, and a degree of chromaticism which carries it more than once to the verge of atonality. The Grail music, on the other hand, is diatonic and almost churchlike in style. The very opening theme of the prelude (the Last Supper motif), a single-line melody in free rhythm, is reminiscent of Gregorian chant; the Grail motif is an old Amen formula in use at the Dresden Royal Chapel when Wagner conducted there. One feature of the Grail scenes in *Parsifal* deserves special emphasis, namely the expertness of the choral writing. One does not ordinarily look to opera composers for excellence in a field of composition which has always been chiefly associated with the church, and the peculiar technique of which has not always been grasped by even some of the greatest composers. Wagner's distinguished choral writing in *Lohengrin*, *Die Meistersinger*, and above all in *Parsifal* is therefore of interest;[28] in particular, the closing scenes of Acts I and III of *Parsifal*, with their fine choral effects and the device of separated choirs, with the high and low voices giving an impression in music of actual space and depth, recall the Venetian composers of the later sixteenth century.

In attempting to estimate the significance of Wagner in the history of opera one must first of all acknowledge the man's unswerving idealism and artistic integrity. However open to criticism some aspects of his personal conduct may have been, as an artist he stood uncompromisingly for what he believed to be right. He fought his long battle with such tenacity that his final success left no alternative for future composers but to acknowledge the power of the Wagnerian ideas and methods, whether by imitation, adaptation, or conscious rebellion. His form of the music drama did not, as he had expected, supersede earlier operatic ideals, but certain features of it were of permanent influence. Chief among these was the principle that lay at the basis of the Gesamtkunstwerk idea, namely, that every detail of a work must be connected with the dramatic purpose and serve to further that purpose. Wagner is to be numbered among those opera composers who have seriously maintained the dignity of drama in their works. In addition, many of his procedures left their mark on the next generation or two of composers, for example, the parallel position of voice and orchestra, the orchestral continuity, and the symphonic treatment of leitmotifs. Other matters, however, were less capable of being imitated. Wagner's use of Nordic mythology as subject matter, and his symbolism, were so individual that most attempts to copy them resulted only in unintended parody. The qualities of his

---

[28] It is not always remembered that Wagner greatly admired the music of Palestrina and had made an arrangement of his *Stabat Mater* for a concert in 1848.

poetry, though appropriate enough in connection with his own music, are not those of the highest literary art. Likewise the structure of aesthetic, economic, historical, and other doctrines by which Wagner sought to give theoretical support to his artistic aims can no longer be defended, though a knowledge of it is none the less valuable for the sake of the light it sheds on his own artistic practice.

In the last analysis, the important thing about Wagner is his music. It would not have been his wish to be remembered primarily as a musician, but the world has so chosen, and the world in this case has probably understood the genius better than he understood himself. The quality of Wagner's music that has been the cause of its great popularity has been equally the cause of the severest attacks upon it by musicians, namely, that it is not pure, absolute, spontaneous music, created for music's sake and existing in a realm governed only by the laws of sound, rhythm, and musical form. Wagner is not, like Bach or Mozart, a musician's musician. There is about him in music, as in literature and philosophy, something of the nature of an amateur, though on a gigantic scale and an intellectual level which make the word seem ridiculous.[29] For him no art was self-sustaining. Music, like poetry and gesture, was but one means to a comprehensive end which can perhaps best be defined as "great theatre." Granted this end (which may or may not be conceived as a limitation), it is hardly possible to deny the adequacy of Wagner's music in relation to it. Not only does the music possess sensuous beauty. It can suggest, depict, characterize a universe of the most diverse objects and ideas. Above all is its power—by whatever aesthetic theory one seeks to explain it—of embodying or evoking feeling, with a purity, fullness, and intensity surely not surpassed in the music of any other composer. Such emotion is justified by the grandiose intellectual conceptions with which it is connected and by the monumental proportions of the musical forms in which it is expressed. In this monumental quality, as well as in the characteristic moods, aspirations, and technical methods of his music, Wagner is fully representative of the time in which he lived.

By 1900 the Wagner cult had reached unbelievable proportions, but since then the tide has ebbed. Neither the modes of feeling he projected, nor the musical idiom in which he spoke, nor the ideas he sought to

[29] Mann, *Leiden and Grösse*, p. 104 *et passim*.

propagate by means of his magic arts can evoke now the vehement response they did around the turn of the century. Wagner the man and artist, no longer an object of passionate loyalty or passionate loathing, has become simply one of the great composers of the past. Dusk falls on the gods; their works, for a little while, live after them.

CHAPTER 24

THE LATER
NINETEENTH CENTURY

FRANCE.[1] The state of musical taste in Paris (that is to say, in France) from 1840 to 1870 is sufficiently illustrated by three facts : the adoration of Meyerbeer, the neglect of Berlioz, and the craze for Offenbach. The disaster of the Franco-Prussian War was a salutary shock to both public and musicians. The rise of a new school and a new spirit in French music began when the Société Nationale de Musique was founded, with the device *Ars gallica*. Undiscriminating acceptance of incongruous musical styles on the one hand and a frivolous addiction to the trivialities of operetta on the other were succeeded by a strenuous effort to restore in modern terms the great musical individuality which had belonged to France in the sixteenth, seventeenth, and eighteenth centuries. The range of activity was widened. Whereas before 1870 composers had centered nearly all their efforts on opera, now choral, symphonic, and chamber music began to be undertaken; higher standards of musical education were introduced, and a more cultivated and exacting public gradually came into being. This renewal of national musical life made the opera more vital, original, and adventurous. And although the highest rewards of popular success still went to those composers who were able and willing to bend their talents to the public fancy, nevertheless

[1] *Almanach des Spectacles*, Paris, 1874–1913; *Cinquante Ans de musique française*, ed. Rohozinski; Bruneau, *La Musique française*; Rolland, *Musiciens d'aujourd'hui*; Seré, *Musiciens français d'aujourd'hui* (contains excellent bibliographical lists); E. B. Hill, *Modern French Music*; Coeuroy, *La Musique française moderne;* Jullien, *Musiciens d'aujourd'hui*, 2 vols. (1892–94); Tiersot, *Un Demisiècle de musique française* [1870–1917]; Aubry, *La Musique française d'aujourd'hui*; M. Cooper, "Opera, 1890–1910," in *French Music: From the Death of Berlioz to the Death of Fauré*, chap. v.

the best work found hearing and appreciation; there were no scandals like those of the Second Empire, when *Tannhäuser* was hissed off the stage and *Les Troyens* closed after only twenty-one performances. It is worth remarking that almost every important new operatic work in Paris after 1870 was produced not at the Opéra but at the more enterprising and progressive Opéra-comique. The old distinction between the forms of opera and opéra comique had practically disappeared by the end of the nineteenth century, for the latter had by then largely abandoned the traditional spoken dialogue; so the repertoire of the two theatres contrasted simply as large-scale, established, conventional works in the one, and new, often experimental works in the other—alternating, of course, with the light, operetta-like pieces, which continued to flourish. Composers of serious operas that should have been produced at the Paris Opéra frequently had recourse also to the Théâtre de la Monnaie at Brussels for the first performances; and Monte Carlo was the scene of some notable premières. How little the term "opéra comique" in this period had to do with "comic" opera will be realized by recalling that Bizet's *Carmen*, Delibes's *Lakmé*, Lalo's *Roi d'Ys*, Massenet's *Manon*, Bruneau's *Attacque du moulin*, D'Indy's *Fervaal*, Charpentier's *Louise*, and Debussy's *Pelléas et Mélisande* were all staged at the Théâtre de l'Opéra-comique in Paris.

One of the first new operas of distinction to be produced was Georges Bizet's (1838–75) [2] *Carmen* in 1875. *Carmen* was not altogether a failure at first, but its full success in France did not begin until some eight years after the composer's death. It stands today as the most popular and vital French opera of the later nineteenth century. Its Spanish subject was a reflection of the exotic trend in French music which had begun a generation earlier with David; but more important than this feature was the realism with which scenes and characters were depicted, a realism which the librettists had somewhat toned down from Mérimée's original story (especially with respect to Carmen herself), but which still was strong enough to scandalize Paris in the seventies. The tragic ending of this opéra comique was also a novelty. As to the music, Bizet had formed his style from many sources. Probably the least important feature is the mild Spanish local color evident in such numbers as the Habañera, the Toreador Song, and the seguidilla "Près des remparts de Séville"

---

[2] Biographies by W. Dean (1948) and M. Curtiss (1958); special Bizet number of RdM (November, 1938); Istel, *Bizet und Carmen*.

(Act I). Many of the choruses and ensembles are in characteristic operetta style. Fundamental, however, is the firm, concise, and exact musical expression of every situation in terms of which only a French composer would be capable: the typical Gallic union of economy of material, perfect grasp of means, vivid orchestral color, and an electric vitality and rhythmic verve, together with an objective, cool, yet passionate sensualism. This opera contains some spoken dialogue and is otherwise divided into the conventional arias, ensembles, and other numbers. So far as Bizet was concerned, Wagner's music dramas and theories might never have existed. The occasional repetition of certain motifs is of no more significance in *Carmen* than in Verdi's *Rigoletto* a quarter of a century earlier. The whole structure and aesthetic of *Carmen* was such that Nietzsche, after he had turned against Wagner, might point to it as the ideal opera according to the principles of a properly "Mediterraneanized" European art.[3] It is hard to imagine what was in the minds of those contemporary critics who found the music untuneful, lacking in definite outlines, and overpowered by a too rich orchestration—charges, in a word, of Wagnerianism, such as had been leveled earlier at Gounod. But "Wagnerian" was a convenient word in France at this time for damning anything a critic disliked or could not understand. The styles of Gounod and Bizet do, indeed, have much in common, but the affinity is more apparent in Bizet's earlier operas *Les Pêcheurs de perles* ("The Pearl Fishers," 1863) and *Djamileh* (1872). But these works have less musical individuality and interest than *Carmen*; in fact, the only other compositions of Bizet that compare with this opera are his incidental music to Daudet's play *L'Arlésienne* (1872) and his early Symphony in C (1855).

The slight exotic flavor of *Carmen* and *Les Pêcheurs de perles* is found again in *Lakmé* (1883), the best opera of Léo Delibes (1836–91),[4] which has a Hindu locale and a tragic plot faintly reminiscent of Meyerbeer's *Africaine* and more than faintly foreshadowing Puccini's *Butterfly*. Delibes's music is elegant, graceful, and well orchestrated but lacks the intense quality of Bizet's. In *Lakmé* the oriental perfume is blended with an otherwise conventional idiom. Delibes's amusing and tuneful opéra comique *Le Roi l'a dit* ("The King Said So," 1873) is still remembered; a more serious work, *Jean de Nivelle* (1880), was almost equally

---

[3] "Der Fall Wagner," ¶ 3; "Jenseits von Gut und Böse," Part VIII *passim*.
[4] Biography by H. de Curzon.

successful at first but has not remained in the repertoire. On the whole, Delibes excelled as a composer of ballets, his best works in this form being *La Source* (1866), *Coppélia* (1870), and *Sylvia* (1876).

A more substantial figure than Delibes in French nineteenth-century opera was Ernest Reyer (1823–1909).[5] Reyer belongs with those composers whose music often compels more respect for its intentions than admiration for its actual sound. He had "genius without talent," [6] that is, lofty and ideal conceptions without the technique for realizing them fully in an attractive musical form. This incapacity may have been due in part to his defective early training, but it was also a matter of temperament; as a critic he was a despiser of mere prettiness, a rebel against the superficial judgments of the Paris public,[7] and an early defender of Berlioz and Wagner. Reyer was influenced by the fashionable orientalism in his choice of subjects, as seen in his symphonic ode *Sélam* (1850) and the ballet-pantomime *Sacountala* (1858). His first important operatic work, *La Statue* (1861), is also an oriental story. A similar background is found in his last opera, *Salammbô* (1890), taken with few alterations from Flaubert's novel and treated in an austere oratorio-like style, yet with a grandeur of line recalling the spirit of Berlioz's *Troyens*; the plot in general and the closing scene in particular are reminiscent of Verdi's *Aida*. The most successful of Reyer's operas was *Sigurd* (composed in the 1870s, first performed 1884); the subject is almost identical with that of Wagner's *Siegfried* (Act III) and *Götterdämmerung*, with a touch of *Tannhäuser* in the shape of a seductive ballet, with a wordless chorus of elves, in Act II. But the resemblance to Wagner is only skin-deep, even in the libretto : Sigurd talks in the accents of Quinault's Renaud rather than like the great blond lad of the *Ring*; and the rest of the personages likewise somehow seem more Gallic than Teutonic. In the music there is no sign whatever of Wagner; on the contrary, we find the old separate numbers of grand opera, a distinctly periodic melody, and very little chromaticism. There is some recurrence of motifs, but this is not a distinctly Wagnerian trait. The musical style is serious and even has a certain nobility; its model, clearly enough, is *Les Troyens*.

Parisian journalists had been crying "Wolf ! wolf !" for years before any serious reflection of Wagner's ideas or musical style became

[5] See his *Notes de musique* and *Quarante Ans de musique*; also biography by De Curzon and the same author's *Légende de Sigurd*.

[6] Alfred Bruneau, quoted in Combarieu, *Histoire* III, 389.

[7] See Lavignac, *Encyclopédie*, Part I, Vol. III, pp. 1727–28.

apparent in French music. The bitterness of the Franco-Prussian War, aggravated by Wagner's silly gibes in his playlet *Eine Kapitulation*, delayed his acceptance still longer. Yet by the early eighties apparently all was forgiven, and Wagner became the rage in Paris for some ten or twelve years.

From 1885 Wagner's work acted directly or indirectly on the whole of artistic thought, even on religious and intellectual thought of the most distinguished people of Paris. . . . Writers not only discussed musical subjects, but judged painting, literature, and philosophy, from a Wagnerian point of view. . . . The whole universe was seen and judged by the thought of Bayreuth.[8]

A remarkable evidence of this enthusiasm was the flourishing periodical *La Revue Wagneriénne* (1885–88), contributors to which included Verlaine, Mallarmé, Huysmans, and practically every other important writer in Paris (Baudelaire had been converted already in 1861). One effect of all this was to introduce the subject of music to many people who would not otherwise have taken an interest in it; another was to stimulate symphonic composition. In opera, the risks involved in the magic garden of Wagnerism were so patent that the composers for the most part withstood temptation, though not always without effort. It is sometimes difficult to decide what is to be called imitation of Wagner and what is simply acceptance of new ideas, such as the abolition of formal separate arias and recitatives. Taken altogether, however, the direct influence of Wagner on French opera, in both literary and musical treatment, is seen most strongly in works by three composers : Chabrier, D'Indy, and Chausson.[9]

Emanuel Chabrier (1841–94)[10] was one of the foremost composers of the new movement in France, as well as a pianist of exceptional ability. At first sight he seems an unlikely person to be an apostle of Wagner, for the pieces by which he is best known (the orchestral rhapsody *España* and the *Bourrée Fantasque*) show him as a composer of typical Gallic vivacity, wit, and rhythmic exuberance. It is these qualities which are uppermost in his first important comic opera, *L'Etoile* ("The Star," 1877),[11] and in his best-known stage work, *Le Roi*

[8] Rolland, *Musicians of Today*, p. 253.

[9] Cf. D'Indy, *Richard Wagner et son influence sur l'art musical français.*

[10] See Hill, *Modern French Music*, chap. IV, and studies by Martineau and Servières.

[11] This work was produced in the United States as *The Merry Monarch* and elsewhere under various titles. See Loewenberg, *Annals.*

malgré lui ("The King in Spite of Himself," 1887), harmonically one of the most original opéras comiques of this period. But in 1879 Chabrier heard a performance of *Tristan und Isolde* at Munich which made a strong impression on him, reinforced by his experience shortly afterwards in directing rehearsals of *Lohengrin* and *Tristan* for performances at Paris. His opera *Gwendoline* (first performed at Brussels in 1886) is obviously influenced by Wagnerian elements : the libretto brings echoes of *Der fliegende Holländer*, of the Valhalla mythology, and above all of *Tristan*, even to a love duet in the second act and a love-death at the end of the third. The form is a compromise between continuous drama and the older number opera. The music shows more than a trace of Wagner in its systematic use of leitmotifs, chromatics, chords of the seventh and ninth, and the characteristic appoggiaturas and suspensions. However, this must not be taken to mean that it is a mere copy of Wagner's idiom. Chabrier had an individual harmonic style, one quite advanced for his time, as well as a genuine and sometimes profound gift of serious expressiveness. The most interesting portions of *Gwendoline* are the Spinning Song in Act I, which incorporates an air from Moore's *Irish Melodies*, the love duet (strongly reminiscent of *Tristan*), and the orchestral prelude to Act II, the style of which has been well described as one of the links between Wagner and Debussy.[12] The skillful voice writing and the highly poetic orchestration of this opera should also be noted. But the uneven quality of the music as a whole, together with a rather dull and awkwardly proportioned libretto, have worked against its success. In his unfinished opera *Briséis* (Act I performed 1899) Chabrier demonstrated even more daring harmonies than in *Gwendoline*.

Somewhat similar in subject matter to *Gwendoline*, and likewise tinctured with Wagnerian conceptions, is César Franck's (1822–90)[13] only important opera, *Hulda*, composed in 1882–85 and first performed in 1894. But the most thorough and at the same time the most personal adaptation of Wagner's methods to French opera was brought about by Franck's pupil Vincent d'Indy (1851–1931)[14] in his *Fervaal* (1897) and *L'Etranger* ("The Stranger," 1903). Like Wagner, D'Indy wrote his own

[12] Abraham, *A Hundred Years of Music*.

[13] Biographies by D'Indy and L. Vallas; Van den Borren, *L'Oeuvre dramatique de César Franck*; see also the bio-bibliography by Lynn.

[14] Vallas, *Vincent d'Indy*; also the following special studies : Bréville, *Fervaal*; Calvocoressi, *L'Etranger*; Destranges, *Le Chant de la cloche*; *idem*, *Fervaal*; *idem*, *L'Etranger*. See also D'Indy's *Wagner et son influence sur l'art musical français*.

librettos. The background of *Fervaal* is vaguely mythological, and the action in both operas is treated as symbolic of broad moral issues—the conflict between pagan religion and sacrificial love in *Fervaal* and the expiation of unlawful love through death in *L'Etranger*. But whereas Wagner's symbolism is nearly always in practice wielded for theatrical effect, D'Indy's evident purpose is to make art a vehicle for essentially religious teachings and to use every possible artistic means toward this end. The almost medieval combination of this austere ideal with a catholic breadth of resource, welded into unity by superb technical skill, is the clue to D'Indy's style.[15] It explains how he was able to take over many features of Wagner's music dramas without sacrificing his own individuality : pseudo mythology, symbolism, continuity of the music, harmonic sophistication, the symphonic orchestral texture with cyclical recurrence of motifs, free arioso treatment of the voice line, Wagnerian instrumental sonorities, even (in the love music of the first and third acts of *Fervaal*) actual reminiscenes of *Tristan*. Indebtedness to Wagner is much less apparent in *L'Etranger* than in the earlier opera. The strange suggestiveness of the musical landscape in the introduction to Act II of *Fervaal* and the somber, mysterious poetry of the following scene are especially noteworthy. The third scene of Act II of *L'Etranger* is remarkable for imaginative and pictorial power (Example 100). As in his dramatic choral works, *Le Chant de la cloche* ("The Song of the Bell," 1879–83) and *La Légende de St. Christophe* (composed 1908–15), in the operas too D'Indy introduces choral treatments of Gregorian melodies, notably the "Pange lingua" in the transcendently beautiful closing scene of *Fervaal*.[16] That neither of these operas has become popular may be owing in part to the unusual character of their librettos but more to the music, which lacks the simple, salient, easily perceived qualities necessary for success on the stage. One cannot help feeling that, for the theatre, the music has many of the defects of Wagner without the latter's compelling emotional power. Yet *Fervaal* in particular deserves respect as one of the outstanding French operas of the later nineteenth century in the noble tradition of Berlioz's *Troyens*.

The influence of Wagner is still noticeable in *Le Roi Arthus* by Ernest Chausson (1855–99), first performed in 1903. It is a not very

[15] See Rolland, chapter on D'Indy in *Musiciens d'aujourd'hui*.

[16] Cf. also the quotation of the intonation of the "Credo" in Act II, sc. 1 of the same opera; and in the finale of Bruneau's *Messidor* (also 1897), the plainsong passage from the Litany.

L'Etranger, Act II, sc. 3

EXAMPLE 100

D'INDY

(*Example 100 continued*)

Si - nis - tre

mer   aux co - lè - res   char - meu - ses;

O

successful mixture of old grand-opera formal elements with the new Wagnerian idiom, including the inevitable Tristanesque love duet in Act I. Neither libretto nor music offers any passages of real distinction; indeed, the composer himself regarded *Le Roi Arthus* as only an experiment. This is perhaps the final word for all the attempts by French composers to assimilate Wagner's methods in the nineteenth century, since no consistent or historically important school grew out of them. Along with these experiments the natural line of French lyric opera in descent from Gounod continued to flourish. We now turn our attention to the composers of this distinctively national group.

The first is Camille Saint-Saëns (1835–1921),[17] whose *Princesse jaune* ("The Yellow Princess," 1872) set the fashion for Japanese subjects in comic opera. Saint-Saëns's most famous dramatic work is the biblical *Samson et Dalila* (1877), half opera and half oratorio, like Liszt's *Legende von der heiligen Elisabeth* or D'Indy's *St. Christophe*. Saint-Saëns was not by nature a dramatic composer, but his technical facility and knowledge of many different musical styles enabled him to construct smooth and competent, if not exciting, works in dramatic form. Of his sixteen stage works the most successful (next to *Samson et Dalila*) were *Henri VIII* (1883), *Ascanio* (1890), and the opéra comique *Phryné* (1893). Another composer of conservative national tendency was Edouard Lalo (1823–92)[18] with *Le Roi d'Ys* (1888), based on a Breton legend. The music of this opera is original in style, of remarkable rhythmic vitality, varied in color, and admirably adapted to the stage— qualities that have assured its survival to the present day. Three other French composers of the late nineteenth century should be mentioned in passing, though their work is less important than that of Saint-Saëns or Lalo : Emile Paladilhe (1844–1926; *Patriel*, 1886); Benjamin Godard (1849–95), a composer of facile and pleasing melodies whose *Jocelyn* (1888) was long remembered because of one number, the "Berceuse"; and Isidore De Lara (1858–1935), English by birth and residence but most of whose operas, including the successful *Messaline* (1899), were written to French texts and produced in France.

The outstanding French opera composer of this era was Jules Massenet (1842–1912),[19] an exceptionally productive worker whose

[17] Biographies by Langlois and Chantavoine; see also the composer's own writings, especially *Portraits et souvenirs*; Du Tillet, "A propos du drame lyrique."
[18] Biography by G. Servières.
[19] Biographies by L. Schneider and Bruneau; Massenet, *Mes Souvenirs*.

music is marked by characteristic French traits that we have already noticed in earlier composers such as Monsigny, Auber, Thomas (Massenet's teacher), and Gounod. First among these is the quality of the melody. Massenet's melody is of a highly personal sort : lyrical, tender, penetrating, sweetly sensuous, rounded in contours, exact but never violent in interpreting the text, sentimental, often melancholy, sometimes a little vulgar, and always charming. This melody determines the whole texture. The harmonic background is sketched with delicacy and a fine sense of instrumental color, and every detail of the score shows smooth craftsmanship. With no commitment to particular theories of opera, Wagnerian or otherwise, Massenet within the limits of his own style never hesitated to make use of any new device that had proved effective or popular, so that his works are not free of eclecticism and mirror in their own way most of the successive operatic tendencies of his lifetime. The subjects and their treatment also show the composer's sensitiveness to popular taste. Thus *Le Roi de Lahore* (1877) is an oriental story, *Le Cid* (1885) is in the manner of grand opera, *Esclarmonde* (1889) is Wagnerian, *La Navarraise* (1894) shows the influence of Italian *verismo*, and *Cendrillon* (1899) recalls Humperdinck's *Hänsel und Gretel*; but *Le Jongleur de Notre Dame* (1902) is a miracle play for which there could have been no public demand, but which the composer treated with special affection and thereby produced one of his best operas. The suspicion sometimes arises that Massenet's choice of subjects, as well as his use of certain fashionable musical devices, was motivated by a desire to give his audiences what he knew they wanted rather than by any inner impulsion. But there is no sacrifice of musical individuality in all this; and in the case of a composer whose instincts were so completely of the theatre, who always succeeded in achieving so neatly and spontaneously just the effect he intended, it seems a little ungracious to insist too strongly on an issue of artistic sincerity. Massenet excelled in the musical depiction of passionate love, and most of his best works are notable for their heroines—unforgettable ladies all, of doubtful virtue perhaps, but indubitably alive and vivid. To this gallery belong Salomé in *Hérodiade* (1881), the heroines of *Manon* (1884), *Thaïs* (1894), *Sapho* (1897), and Charlotte in *Werther* (1892). With these works should also be mentioned *Thérèse* (1907), one of the last operas of Massenet to obtain general success.

Massenet traveled the main highway of French tradition in opera and his natural gifts so corresponded to the tastes of his day that success seemed to come almost without effort. Nor was his style without influence, direct or indirect, on later French composers. But he was the last to produce operas so easily. Changing musical idioms and new literary movements had their effect on the next generation, giving its work a less assured, more experimental character. One of these literary movements was that known as "naturalism."

The word "naturalism" and the related word "realism," however useful they may be in the study of literature or the graphic arts, are exceedingly vague when applied to music. Unless they refer to the unimportant practice of imitating everyday sounds by voices or instruments in a musical composition (as, for example, the bleating of sheep in Strauss's *Don Quixote*), it is difficult to see what meaning they can have that is related directly to music itself. What some writers call "realistic" or "naturalistic" music is simply, in effect, a certain kind of program music; the realism is deduced not from the music but from an extra-musical fact (such as a title) about the composition in question. When we speak of realistic or naturalistic opera, therefore, we have reference primarily to the libretto; we mean that the opera presents persons, scenes, events, and conversations that are recognizably similar to the common daily experience of its audience, and that these things are treated seriously, as becomes matters of real moment, not with persiflage or fantasy as in an operetta. It goes without saying that such tendencies in late nineteenth-century opera grew out of earlier tendencies in literature. Thus Bizet's *Carmen*, the first important realistic opera in France and one of the principal sources of the Italian verismo, was based on Mérimée's story. The chief disciples of realism in later nineteenth-century French literature were Guy de Maupassant (1850–93) and Emile Zola (1840–1902). The latter found a musical interpreter in Alfred Bruneau (1857–1934),[20] Massenet's pupil, the librettos of whose principal operas were either adapted from Zola's books or written especially for the composer by Zola himself; to the former group belong *Le Rêve* ("The Dream," 1891) and *L'Attacque du moulin* ("The Attack on the Mill," 1893); to the latter *Messidor* (1897), *L'Ouragan* ("The Hurricane," 1901), and *L'Enfant roi* ("The Child King," 1905). These works were concerned with current social and economic problems, pre-

---

[20] Boschot, *La Vie et les œuvres d'Alfred Bruneau*; see also Bruneau's own writings.

sented in compact, tense situations with symbolical overtones, and in prose instead of the customary verse. Unfortunately, the rhythm of Zola's prose did not always inspire Bruneau to achieve correspondingly flexible rhythms in the music; the melodic line is declamatory rather than lyrical, but the regular pattern of accentuation indicated by the bar lines becomes monotonous. The music is austere; it is especially apt in the creation of moods through reiterated motifs, but with all its evident sincerity and undoubted dramatic power, the important quality of sensuous charm is often lacking. Nevertheless, Bruneau is significant as a forerunner of some later experiments in harmony and as an independent, healthy force in the growth of modern French opera, counterbalancing to some extent the Wagnerian tendencies of D'Indy and the hedonism of Massenet.

A fuller measure of success in the field of operatic naturalism was granted to another pupil of Massenet, Gustave Charpentier (1860–1956).[21] The "musical novel" *Louise* (1900) is his only important opera, a strange but successful combination of several distinct elements. In scene, characters, and plot *Louise* is realistic; Charpentier, writing his own libretto, has almost gone out of his way to introduce such homely details as a bourgeois family supper, the reading of a newspaper, and a scene in a dressmaking shop; many of the minor personages are obviously taken "from life," and sing in a marked Parisian dialect. The melodramatic closing scene recalls the mood of the Italian verismo composers. Charpentier, like Bruneau, touches occasionally on social questions: the issue of free love, the obligations of children to their parents, the miseries of poverty. But along with realism there is symbolism, especially in the weird figure of the Noctambulist, personification of "the pleasure of Paris." Paris itself is, as Bruneau remarked,[22] the real hero of this opera. Behind the action is the presence of the great city, seductive, mysterious, and fatal, enveloping persons and events in an atmosphere of poetry like that of the forest in Weber's *Freischütz*. Its hymn is the ensemble of street cries, running like a refrain through the first scene of Act II and echoing elsewhere throughout the opera. To realism and symbolism is added yet a third factor: sentiment. The dialogue between Louise and her father in Act I is of a convincing tenderness, while the love music of Act III, with the often-heard "Depuis le jour,"

[21] Delmas, *Gustave Charpentier et le lyrisme français*; Himonet, *Louise*.
[22] *La Musique française*, p. 154.

is not only a fine scene of passion but also one of the few of its kind in late nineteenth-century French opera that never reminds us of *Tristan und Isolde*—or hardly ever. It was the achievement of Charpentier to take all this realism, symbolism, and sentiment, holding together only with difficulty in the libretto itself, and mold them into one powerful whole by means of music. The score reminds one in many ways of Massenet: there is the same spontaneity and abundance of ideas, the same simple and economical texture, obtaining the maximum effect with the smallest apparent effort. The harmonic idiom is more advanced than Massenet's but less daring than Bruneau's. The orchestral music is continuous, serving as background for spoken as well as sung passages, and is organized by recurring motifs. A number of standard operatic devices are cleverly adapted to the libretto: Julien's serenade with accompaniment of a guitar, the ensemble of working girls in Act II (where the tattoo of the sewing machine replaces the whirr of the old romantic spinning wheel), and the ballet-like scene where Louise is crowned as the Muse of Montmartre in Act III. On the whole, it will be seen that when this opera is cited as an example of naturalism the word needs to be taken with some qualifications. In any case, it is not the naturalism that has caused it to survive, for this was but a passing fashion. *Louise* remains in the repertoire for the same reason as other successful operas: because it has melodious and moving music wedded to a libretto that permits the music to operate as an effective partner in the projection of the drama.

Fashions in opera might come and go, but the operetta and kindred forms went their way unperturbed. The line of French light opera, established in the nineteenth century by Auber, Adam, and Offenbach, was continued after 1870 by Charles Lecocq (1832–1918),[23] whose best work was *La Fille de Madame Angot* (1872); Jean-Robert Planquette (1848–1903), whose sentimental and still popular *Cloches de Corneville* ("The Bells of Corneville") came out in 1877; Edmond Audran (1840–1901) with *La Mascotte* (1880); and Louis Varney (1844–1908) with *Les Mousquetaires au couvent* ("The Musketeers in the Convent," 1880). Somewhat later began the long series of popular operas and operettas by André Messager (1853–1929),[24] distinguished conductor and facile composer in a straightforward, attractively melodious vein (*La Basoche*, 1890; *Les P'tites Michu*, 1897; *Monsieur Beaucaire*, 1919). At the beginning of the twentieth century appeared the operettas of Claude Terrasse (1867–1923), including *Le Sire de Vargy* (1903) and *Monsieur de la Palisse* (1904).

[23] Louis Schneider, *Hervé. Charles Lecocq.*
[24] Biographies by Augé-Laribé and H. Février.

ITALY. As Italians in the eighteenth century would have nothing to do with Gluck, so in the nineteenth they cared little for Wagner. It was not until the eighties that even *Lohengrin* began to be accepted. With the exception of Boito, no important out-and-out Wagner disciples appeared in Italy. There was considerable talk about Wagner and considerable skepticism as to the future of Italian opera, but the only result of any consequence was to call forth a vigorous national reaction of which the greatest monument is Verdi's *Otello*. Italian opera was too secure in its tradition and methods, too deeply rooted in the national life, to be susceptible to radical experiments, especially experiments resulting from aesthetic theories of a sort in which Italians were temperamentally uninterested. A mild influence of German romanticism, but hardly more, may be found in a few Italian opera composers of the late nineteenth century. Alfredo Catalani (1854–93) [25] is the most distinguished of this group; his principal operas were *Loreley* (1890; a revision of his *Elda* which had appeared in 1880), *Dejanice* (1883), and *La Wally* (1892). Catalani has a refined melodic style, nearly always free of exaggerated pathos, with interesting harmonies and a good balance of interest between voice and orchestra. Along with traces of Tristanesque chromaticism are experiments in harmony and texture that anticipate some of the favorite devices of Puccini. The robust rhythms are notable, especially in the choruses and dances of *La Wally*. Unfortunately, Catalani appeared at a time when the Italian public was being seduced by Mascagni and Leoncavallo, so that his reserved and aristocratic music was drowned by the bellow of verismo. Some influence of Wagner seems to be present in the harmonies and the important position of the orchestra in the operas of Antonio Smareglia (1854–1929),[26] whose chief work, *Nozze istriane* ("Istrian Wedding"), was performed in 1895; but Smareglia lacked the convincing popular touch in his melodies and his operas were not greatly successful. Alberto Franchetti (1860–1942) has been called "the Meyerbeer of Italy" because of his fondness for massive scenic effects, but his music, on the whole, is undistinguished; his principal operas were *Cristoforo Colombo* (1892) and *Germania* (1902). None of these composers was attracted by the verismo movement of the 1890s, which was the popular trend in Italy at that time.

[25] See biography by C. Gatti and articles by J. W. Klein.
[26] See biographical studies by Nacamuli and A. and M. Smareglia.

The most explosive reaction against Wagner was launched with the performance of *Cavalleria rusticana* ("Rustic Chivalry") by Pietro Mascagni (1863–1945) [27] in 1890 and *I pagliacci* ("The Clowns") by Ruggiero Leoncavallo (1858–1919) two years later. Neither composer was ever able to duplicate the fantastic success these two works achieved, though Mascagni approached it with *L'amico Fritz* (1891) and *Iris* (1898), while Leoncavallo's *Zaza* (1900) became fairly widely known. But *Cavalleria* and *Pagliacci*, now usually given on the same evening as a double bill, are the classics of verismo, or "realism." [28] This typically Italian movement resembles the French naturalism in the use of scenes and characters from common life; but the French naturalists used these materials as a means for the development of more general ideas and feelings, idealizing both scene and music, whereas the goal of the Italian realists was simply to present a vivid, melodramatic plot, to arouse sensation by violent contrasts, to paint a cross section of life without concerning themselves with any general significance the action might have. Verismo is to naturalism what the "shocker" is to the realistic novel, and the music corresponds to this conception. It aims simply and directly at the expression of intense passion through melodic or declamatory phrases of the solo voices, to which the orchestra contributes sensational harmonies. Choral or instrumental interludes serve only to establish a mood which is to be rent asunder in the next scene. Everything is so arranged that the moments of excitement follow one another in swift climactic succession. It cannot be denied that there was plenty of precedent in Donizetti and the earlier works of Verdi for melodramatic situations in opera; but by comparison the action of the veristic operas takes place as in an atmosphere from which the nitrogen has been withdrawn, so that everything burns with a fierce, unnatural flame, and moreover quickly burns out. The brevity of these works is due not so much to concentration as to rapid exhaustion of the material. Much the same is true of the verismo movement as a whole, historically considered. It flared like a meteor across the operatic sky of the 1890s, but by the end of the century it was practically dead, though its influence can occasionally be detected in some later operas.

The leading figure in Italian opera of the late nineteenth and the

---

[27] Studies by De Donno; biography by Jeri (1945); *Mascagni parla* (reminiscences, 1945).

[28] See Rinaldi, *Musica e verismo*.

early twentieth century was Giacomo Puccini (1858–1924),[29] who resembles Massenet in his position of mediator between two eras, as well as in many features of his musical style. Puccini's rise to fame began with his third opera, *Manon Lescaut* (1893), which is less effective dramatically than Massenet's opera on the same subject (1884) but rather superior in musical interest—this despite occasional reminiscences of *Tristan*, which few composers in the nineties seemed able to escape. Puccini's world-wide reputation rests chiefly on his next three works: *La Bohème* (1896), *Tosca* (1900), and *Madama Butterfly* (1904). *La Bohème* is a sentimental opera with dramatic touches of realism, on a libretto adapted from Henri Murger's *Scènes de la vie de Bohème* ("Scenes of Bohemian Life"), which had been dramatized in 1849 under the title *La Vie de Bohème*; *Tosca*, taken from Victorien Sardou's drama of the same name (1887), is "a prolonged orgy of lust and crime" made endurable by the beauty of the music; and *Madama Butterfly* is a tale of love and heartbreak in an exotic Japanese setting. The outstanding musical characteristic of Puccini in all these operas is the "sensuous warmth and melting radiance of the vocal line." [30] It is like Massenet without Massenet's urbanity: naked emotion crying out, and persuading the listener's feeling by its very urgency. For illustrations the reader need only recall the aria "Che gelida manina" and the ensuing duet in the first scene of *La Bohème*, the closing scene of the same work, or the familiar arias "Vissi d'arte" in *Tosca* and "Un bel dì" in *Butterfly*. The history of this type of melody is instructive. It will be remembered that in Verdi we encountered from time to time a melodic phrase of peculiar poignancy which seemed to gather up the whole feeling of a scene in a pure and concentrated moment of expression, such as the "Amami, Alfredo" in *La traviata* (Example 93), the recitative "E tu, come sei pallida" of *Otello* (Example 94), or the kiss motif from the same work. Later composers, perceiving that the high points of effectiveness in Verdi were marked by phrases of this sort, naturally became ambitious to write operas which should consist entirely (or as nearly so as possible) of such melodic high points, just as the verismo composers had tried to write operas consisting entirely of melodramatic shocks. Both

[29] Studies by Carner and Sartori; *Carteggi Pucciniani*, ed. Gara; *Giacomo Puccini* (symposium), ed. Sartori; Ricci, *Puccini interprete di se stesso*. For bibliography, see Marino, "Giacomo Puccini: A Check List."

[30] Carner, *Puccini*, p. 273; the entire section is an excellent analysis of the composer's melodic and general musical style.

tendencies are evidence of satiety of sensation. These melodic phrases in Verdi are of the sort sometimes described as "pregnant"; their effect depends on the prevalence of a less heated manner of expression elsewhere in the opera, so that they stand out by contrast. But in Puccini we have, as an apparent ideal if not always an actuality, what may be called a kind of perpetual pregnancy in the melody, whether this is sung or entrusted to the orchestra as a background for vocal recitative. The musical utterance is kept at high tension, almost without repose, as though it were to be feared that if the audiences were not continually excited they would go to sleep. This tendency toward compression of language, this nervous stretto of musical style, is characteristic of the *fin de siècle* period.

The sort of melody we have been describing runs through all of Puccini's works. In his earliest and latest operas it tends to be organized in balanced phrases, but in those of the middle period it becomes a freer line, often embodying a set of recurring motifs. These motifs of Puccini, admirably dramatic in conception, are used either simply for recalling earlier moments in the opera or, by reiteration, for establishing a mood, but they do not serve as generating themes for musical development.

Puccini's music was enriched by the composer's constant interest in the new harmonic developments of his time; he was always eager to put current discoveries to use in opera. One example of striking harmonic treatment is the series of three major triads (B-flat, A-flat, E-natural) which opens *Tosca* and is associated throughout the opera with the villainous Scarpia (Example 101). The harmonic tension of the augmented fourth outlined by the first and third chords of this progression

Tosca, the "Scarpia" chords

EXAMPLE 101

is by itself sufficient for Puccini's purpose; he has created his atmosphere with three strokes, and the chord series has no further use but to be repeated intact whenever the dramatic situation requires it. One common trait of Puccini's, found in all his operas from the early *Edgar* (1889) down to his last works, is the "side-slipping" of chords (Example 102);

EXAMPLE 102   *Madama Butterfly*, Act II   PUCCINI

doubtless this device was learned from Verdi (compare the passage "Oh! come è dolce" in the duet at the end of Act I of *Otello*) or Catalani, but it is based on a practice common in much non-European music and one going back in Western musical history to medieval organum and fauxbourdon. Its usual purpose in Puccini is to break a melodic line into a number of parallel strands, like breaking up a beam of light by a prism into parallel bands of color. In a sense it is a complementary effect to that of intensifying a melody by duplication at the unison and octaves—an effect dear to all Italian composers of the nineteenth century and one to which Puccini also frequently resorted. Parallel duplication of the melodic line at the fifth is used to good purpose in the introduction to scene 3 of *La Bohême* to suggest the bleakness of a cold winter dawn; at the third and fifth, in the introduction to the second scene of the same opera, for depicting the lively, crowded street scene (a passage which may or may not have been in the back of Stravinsky's mind when he wrote the music for the first scene of *Petrouchka*); and parallelism of the same sort, extended sometimes to chords of the seventh and ninth (as with Debussy), is found at many places in the later operas.

The most original places in Puccini, however, are not dependent on any single device; take for example the opening scene of Act III of *Tosca*, with its broad unison melody in the horns, the delicate descending parallel triads over a double pedal in the bass, the Lydian melody of the shepherd boy, and the faint background of bells, with the veiled, intruding threat of the three Scarpia chords from time to time—an inimitably beautiful and suggestive passage, technically perhaps owing something to both Verdi and Debussy, but nevertheless thoroughly individual.

An important source of color effects in Puccini's music is the use of exotic materials. Exoticism in Puccini was more than a mere borrowing of certain details but rather extended into the very fabric of his melody, harmony, rhythm, and instrumentation.[31] It is naturally most in evidence in the works on oriental subjects, *Madama Butterfly* and *Turandot* (1926). *Turandot*, based on a comedy of the eighteenth-century Carlo Gozzi and completed after Puccini's death by Franco Alfano, shows side by side harmonic experimentation (for example, the bitonality at the opening of Acts I and II), the utmost development of Puccinian lyric melody, and the most brilliant orchestration of any of his operas.

Puccini did not escape the influence of verismo, but the realism of his operas is always tempered by, or blended with, romantic and exotic elements. In *La Bohême*, common scenes and characters are invested with a romantic halo; the repulsive melodrama of *Tosca* is glorified by the music; and the few realistic details in *Madama Butterfly* are unimportant. A less convincing attempt to blend realism and romance is found in *La fanciulla del West* ("The Girl of the Golden West"), taken from a play by David Belasco and first performed at the Metropolitan Opera House in 1910. Though enthusiastically received by the first American audiences, *La fanciulla* did not attain as wide or enduring popularity as the preceding works. The next opera, *La rondine* ("The Swallow," 1917), was even less successful. A return was made, however, with the *trittico*, or triptych, of one-act operas performed at the Metropolitan in December, 1918 : *Il tabarro* ("The Cloak"), a veristic melodrama; *Suor Angelica* ("Sister Angelica"), a miracle play; and *Gianni Schicchi*, the most popular of the three, a delightful comedy in the spirit of eighteenth-century opera buffa. Puccini's comic skill, evidenced also in some parts of *La Bohême* and *Turandot*, is here seen at its most spontaneous, incorporating smoothly all the characteristic harmonic devices of his later period. Only the occasional intrusion of sentimental melodies in the old vein breaks the unity of effect.

Puccini was not one of the great composers, but within his own limits

[31] See Carner's essay, with musical examples, "The Exotic Element in Puccini."

—of which he was perfectly aware—he worked honorably and with mastery of his technique. Bill Nye remarked of Wagner's music that it "is better than it sounds"; Puccini's music, on the contrary, often sounds better than it is, owing to the perfect adjustment of means to ends. He had the prime requisite for an opera composer, an instinct for the theatre; to that he added the Italian gift of knowing how to write effectively for singers, an unusually keen ear for new harmonic and instrumental colors, a receptive mind to musical progress, and a poetic imagination excelling in the evocation of dreamlike, fantastic moods. Even *Turandot*, for all its venturesome harmonies, is a romantic work, an escape into the exotic in both the dramatic and the musical sense.

A younger contemporary of Puccini was Umberto Giordano (1867–1948),[32] whose *Andrea Chénier* (1896) is like a rescue opera of the French Revolution period without the rescue; both plot and music show the influence of verismo in the exaggerated emphasis on effect at all costs (Example 103). Apart from its undoubted dramatic qualities, the score offers little of interest; the harmonies are heavy and old-fashioned and there are few notable lyric passages in the voice parts, though some local color is provided by the use of revolutionary songs ("Ça ira," "La Carmagnole," "La Marseillaise"). *Fedora* (1898) and *Siberia* (1903) are in the same style, with Russian instead of French background. In *Madame Sans-Gêne* (New York, 1915) the composer's theatrical talents are applied to a vivacious and tuneful comedy drama. Of Giordano's later operas, *La cena delle beffe* ("The Feast of Jests," 1924), a lurid four-act melodrama, has been the most successful. None of these are of great significance musically; they are the work of a gifted but not profound composer operating within the traditional Italian framework and skillfully adapting it to the current practice of orchestral continuity. A similar but less conspicuous position must be assigned to Francesco Cilèa (1866–1950),[33] who was, incidentally, one of the first Italian composers of this period to have occupied himself much with music in other forms than opera. His *Adriana Lecouvreur* (1902), based on a libretto by Scribe, is an involved drama of the age of Louis XV with expertly contrived music of a lyrical-tragic sort obviously influenced by Puccini, unadventurous harmonically or rhythmically but good theatre and effective for the singers.

[32] Biography by Cellamare (1949).
[33] Biography by T. d'Amico (1960); see also Pilati, "Francesco Cilèa."

Andrea Chénier, sc. 2

EXAMPLE 103

GIORDANO

GERMANY.[34] Wagner affected the course of lyric drama like a new planet hurled into a solar system. The center of the operatic universe shifted; all the old balances were disturbed; regroupings took place, accompanied by erratic movements. These consequences were least marked in Italy, more so in France, and most of all, naturally, in Germany. Yet even there they did not appear quickly; established traditions —romantic opera in the manner of Marschner and grand opera on the model of Meyerbeer—were still strong. Max Bruch's (1838–1920) [35] *Loreley* (1863), on a libretto originally written for Mendelssohn, was a

[34] General bibliography: Schiedermair, *Die deutsche Oper*; R. Louis, *Die deutsche Musik der Gegenwart* (1909); Istel, "German Opera Since Richard Wagner"; *idem, Die moderne Oper* (2d ed., 1923); *Monographien moderner Musiker*, ed. Segnitz; Moser, *Geschichte der deutschen Musik* III 351–451, *passim*; Kroyer, "Die circumpolare Oper."

[35] Biography by F. Gysi (1922).

romantic opera, conventional in form though with some progressive traits in the musical style; Karl Goldmark's (1830–1915) [36] *Königin von Saba* ("The Queen of Sheba," 1875), one of the favorite German works of the later nineteenth century, is an agreeable but old-fashioned grand opera, complete with set numbers, ballets, pageantry, and some conventional strokes of oriental color. Goldmark had accepted Wagner as far as *Tannhäuser*, but was evidently not acquainted with, or at any rate not at all influenced by, the later style of *Tristan* and the *Ring*.

Some typically Wagnerian subject matter had come into German opera independently of Wagner : thus Karl Mangold (1813–89) had produced a *Tanhäuser* in 1846 and Heinrich Dorn (1804–92) [37] a *Nibelungen* in 1854, both composed without knowledge of Wagner's corresponding works; Dorn's opera, indeed, was seriously regarded for a time as rivaling Wagner's *Ring*. One of the first composers in whom the direct influence of Wagner can be seen was Franz von Holstein (1826–78),[38] poet and composer whose "grand opera" *Der Haideschacht* (1868) was based on Hoffmann's tale *Die Bergwerke zu Falun* ("The Mines at Falun"); but Holstein resented being known as a mere epigone of Wagner and in fact demonstrated considerable independence in his *Hochländer* ("The Highlanders") of 1876, a historical grand opera in the tradition of Meyerbeer, which incidentally uses some Scottish melodies. Wagnerian ideas in subject matter and treatment, use of leitmotifs, importance of the orchestra, and attempted musical continuity—all modified, however, by some compromises with older operatic forms—are evident in *Iwein* (1879) and *Gudrun* (1882) by August Klughardt (1847–1902),[39] in *Gudrun* (1884) by Felix Draeseke (1835–1913),[40] *Kunihild* (also 1884) by Cyrill Kistler (1848–1907), *Wieland der Schmied* (1880, rev. 1894) by Max Zenger (1837–1911), and *Kudrun* (1896) by the Swiss Hans Huber (1852–1921).[41] But some of these composers later managed to shake off the Wagnerian influence and develop along lines more congenial to their own temperaments—Kistler, for example, toward operas of a simple popular style, Zenger (especially in his last opera, *Eros und Psyche*, 1901) toward the classical ideal of Gluck,

---

[36] Goldmark, *Erinnerungen*; biography by L. Koch.
[37] Dorn, *Aus meinem Leben*; Rauh, *Heinrich Dorn als Opernkomponist*.
[38] Biography by G. Glaser.
[39] Biography by L. Gerlach.
[40] Biography by E. Röder.
[41] Biography by E. Refardt (1944).

and Huber, with moderate success, toward romantic opera (*Die schöne Bellinda*, 1916).

The Wagnerian school toward the end of the century is represented by Felix von Weingartner (1863–1942)[42] with *Sakuntala* (1884), *Genesius* (1892), and the trilogy *Orestes* (1902), as well as many later dramatic works in various styles; Heinrich Zöllner (1854–1941) with *Faust* (1887); and especially August Bungert (1845–1915),[43] whose *Homerische Welt* ("The Homeric World"), consisting of two cycles of six operas in all, was the most ambitious musico-dramatic undertaking since the *Ring* but nevertheless failed to make its way with the public because of appallingly uninteresting music. These composers for the most part followed Wagner in writing their own librettos. Among other Wagnerian works of this period may be mentioned some early operas by other composers who subsequently developed a more personal style: Kienzl's *Urvasi* (1886), Schillings's *Ingwelde* (1894), R. Strauss's *Guntram* (1894), Pfitzner's *Armer Heinrich* (1896), and D'Albert's *Kain* (1900).

The inevitable consequence of all this imitation of Wagner was a reaction. Both public and composers, growing tired of repetitions of a style in which Wagner had already said the final word, were ready for something new, and ways out were sought in three directions: comic opera, popular opera ("Volksoper"), and fairy-tale opera ("Märchenoper"). An outstanding work in the comic genre was *Der Widerspenstigen Zähmung* ("The Taming of the Shrew," 1874) by Hermann Goetz (1840–76),[44] an opera which, like Cornelius's *Barbier von Bagdad*, has never had the wide success it merits by the cleverness of its libretto and the Mozartean humor of its music. A later, more sophisticated school of comic opera, going back for musical inspiration to *Der Barbier* or Wagner's *Meistersinger*, is represented by the celebrated but seldom performed *Corregidor* (1896) of Hugo Wolf (1860–1903).[45] Based on a story by P. A. de Alarcón, *Der Corregidor* is in many respects an inspired attempt to create a gay, original German comic opera "without the gloomy, world-redeeming ghost of a Schopenhaurian philosopher in

---

[42] See Weingartner's own writings, especially *Lebenserinnerungen* and *Die Lehre von der Wiedergeburt des musikalischen Dramas* (1895).

[43] Biography by M. Chop (1903).

[44] Biographies by Kreuzhage and Kruse.

[45] Biographies by Decsey, Walker, and Von Graedener-Hattingberg; Hellmer, *Der Corregidor*.

the background." [46] This laudable intention was frustrated by Wolf's long-standing admiration for Wagner's music: the orchestra of *Der Corregidor* is as heavily polyphonic as that of *Die Meistersinger*, and the music is full of leitmotifs—a style completely unsuited to Wolf's libretto. Moreover Wolf, like Schubert and Schumann, was not at home in the theatre: his invention seems to have been paralyzed by the requirements of the stage; the music goes from one song to the next like a Liederspiel; neither persons nor situations are adequately characterized. This composer, "who could be so dramatic in the lied, here in the drama remained above all a lyricist." [47] *Der Corregidor*, though not lacking in finely wrought details,[48] was a failure as an opera. Another Spanish subject, from Lope de Vega, was treated by Anton Urspruch (1850–1907) in his comic opera *Das Unmöglichste von allem* ("The Most Impossible of All," 1897), with light parlando dialogue and intricate contrapuntal ensembles derived from the style of Mozart. A more spirited and dramatic composer in this field was the Austrian Emil Nikolaus von Reznicek (1860–1945),[49] whose *Donna Diana* (1894; another Spanish subject) gave promise of a future that was not realized in his next few operas; but with *Ritter Blaubart* ("Knight Bluebeard," 1920), "an eclectic score embodying elements of Italian cantilena style and the technique of French impressionism," [50] he renewed his reputation.

One of the best German comic operas of the late nineteenth century was D'Albert's *Abreise* ("The Departure," 1898), a fine example of swift-moving dialogue with a tuneful, spontaneous, and deftly orchestrated score, somewhat reminiscent of Cornelius. More in the *Meistersinger* idiom were Blech's comic operas *Das war ich* ("That Was I," 1902) and the more ambitious *Versiegelt* ("Sealed," 1908); but these, like Wolf's *Corregidor*, suffered from the music being, as a rule, too heavy and polyphonic for the simple librettos. Two other similar comic operas of this period were Schillings's *Pfeifertag* ("The Parliament of Pipers," 1899) and R. Strauss's *Feuersnot* ("The Fire Famine," 1901),

---

[46] Letter of Wolf to Grohe, 1890. See Istel, "German Opera Since Wagner," pp. 278–79.

[47] Moser, *Geschichte der deutschen Musik* III, 397.

[48] For instance: the duet "In solchen Abendfeierstunden," Act II; Frasquita's "In dem Schatten meiner Locken" (Act I), a charming song taken from Wolf's earlier *Spanisches Liederbuch*; Luka's monologue (Act III, sc. 3), the most nearly dramatic music in the opera.

[49] Studies by Chop and Specht.

[50] Slonimsky, *Music Since 1900*.

the latter an extraordinary combination of humor, eroticism, and auto-biography, with music which shows the composer in transition from his early Wagnerian style to that of *Salome* and *Elektra*. On the whole, however, German comic opera of this type in the late nineteenth and the early twentieth century is disappointing. No unified or generally accepted tradition was evolved, and individual works of talent remained isolated experiments which their composers seemed unable to repeat.

It was otherwise with the *Volksoper*. Two works of this class in the late nineteenth century were Ignaz Brüll's (1846–1907) *Das goldene Kreuz* ("The Golden Cross," 1875), a pleasant comedy with music slightly reminiscent of Auber; and the popular *Trompeter von Säckingen* (1884) by the Alsatian Viktor Nessler (1841–90), with men's choruses, airs, and dances all in a simple, tuneful style. Even more successful was *Der Evangelimann* (1895) by the Austrian Wilhelm Kienzl (1857–1941).[51] The personage of the "Evangelimann" has no English equivalent; he is a wandering mendicant who receives alms in return for reading and telling stories from the Scriptures. Kienzl's appeal is founded on the application of Wagnerian techniques to nonheroic subjects, but much of his musical material has a distinctly folklike flavor (Example 104). *Der Evangelimann* is, in fact, a kind of anthology of popular dance and song types, together with sentimental melodies in the vein of Nessler and amusing reminiscences of *Lohengrin, Tristan, Die Meistersinger,* and *Hänsel und Gretel*— all attached to a libretto of the most flagrantly melodramatic-romantic sort. Its popularity in Germany and Austria may be judged by the fact that *Der Evangelimann* had over 5,300 performances in the first forty years of its existence. Closely related to Kienzl's work is that of another Austrian, Julius Bittner (1874–1939),[52] whose operas (to his own texts) are based on a folklike type of melody, alternating closed numbers with declamatory passages and combining sentiment with humor. *Die rote Gred* ("Red-headed Gred," 1907) and *Der Musikant* ("The Musician," 1910) show his characteristic style in purest form; *Der Bergsee* ("The Mountain Lake," 1911) has curious post-Wagnerian reminiscences. *Das höllisch Gold* ("The Infernal Gold," 1916), a humorous miracle play, was his most varied and most popular work. Likewise in the field of people's opera must be noted the

---

[51] Two *Festschriften* (1917, 1937) have been dedicated to Kienzl; see his auto-biography and other writings; essay by Morold in Segnitz's *Monographien* III; selections from the autobiography and letters in *Kienzl-Rosegger,* ed. H. Sittner.

[52] Biography by R. Specht.

Der Evangelimann, Act I

EXAMPLE 104

KIENZL

O Zit-ter-bart, o Zit-ter-bart, o Franz Xa-ve-rius Zit-ter-bart! Du

trifst ja nicht den La-den mehr; die Ku-gel ist für dich zu schwer.

Viennese Richard Heuberger (1850–1914) with *Barfüssele* (1905) and the Czech Karel Weis (1862–1944) with *Der polnische Jude* (1901), both works popular in their day. Finally may be mentioned the Viennese operetta, which flourished in the early twentieth century with new hits by Franz Lehár [53] (1870–1948; *Die lustige Witwe*, "The Merry Widow," 1905), Oscar Straus [54] (1870–1954; *Ein Walzertraum*, "A Waltz Dream," 1907; *Der tapfere Soldat*, "The Chocolate Soldier," 1908), and Leo Fall (1873–1925; *Die Dollarprinzessin*, "The Dollar Princess," 1907).

The way of recourse to the *Märchenoper* as a means of escape from wholesale imitation of Wagner—in effect, a return to one kind of subject matter that had been current in the early romantic era—was discovered almost inadvertently. Alexander Ritter (1833–96),[55] a disciple of Liszt and composer of a number of historically important symphonic poems, had produced at Munich in 1885 a fairy-tale opera, *Der faule Hans* ("Lazy Hans"), which, although it had only a moderate success, is of interest as being a forerunner of a most important fairy-tale opera which came out in 1893: Engelbert Humperdinck's (1854–1921)[56] *Hänsel*

---

[53] Biographies by Czech (1957) and Peteani.

[54] Grun, *Prince of Vienna* (1955).

[55] Biography by Von Hausegger (1907).

[56] Biography by Besch; Kuhlmann, *Stil und Form in der Musik von Humperdincks Hänsel und Gretel.*

und Gretel. Humperdinck first wrote this music for a play for his sister's children to perform at home; made into a full opera, it caught the public fancy to such a degree as to start a whole new school in Germany. People turned with relief from the misty depths of mythology to the homely, familiar, enchanted world of the fairy tale, to subjects like those which their grandparents had enjoyed in the days of Marschner and Lortzing. The transition was made easier because Humperdinck kept up an appearance of loyalty to Wagner: the music of *Hänsel und Gretel* is, in fact, a peculiar mixture of German folk melody and Wagnerian polyphony. Perhaps the texture is too complicated for the subject matter, but if this be a fault, it is one easy to forgive in view of the many musical beauties and the heartfelt, simple emotion of the work. The music brings together many qualities rooted in the affections of Germans over generations: the songs and dances of the children, the idyllic forest scenes, just enough of the supernatural (but with a comic touch), and the chorale-like feeling of the "Evening blessing" melody, which recurs in the finale to the words

> When past bearing is our grief,
> God himself will send relief.

Among the many fairy-tale operas in neo-Wagnerian style that followed *Hänsel und Gretel* were Humperdinck's *Königskinder* ("The Royal Children"), first composed in 1898 as incidental music to a play made into an opera ten years later; Zöllner's best opera, *Die versunkene Glocke* ("The Sunken Bell"), in 1899; *Lobetanz* (1898) by Ludwig Thuille (1861–1907),[57] *Illsebill* (1903) by Friedrich Klose (1862–1942),[58] *Rübezahl* (1904) by Hans Sommer (1837–1922),[59] and two works by Humperdinck's pupil Leo Blech (871–1958):[60] *Alpenkönig und Menschenfeind* ("Alpine King and Man's Enemy," 1903; revised in 1917 under the title of *Rappelkopf*) and *Aschenbrödel* ("Cinderella," 1905). Here in varying degrees the post-Wagnerian musical idiom was adapted to popular subjects. To this group of composers belongs also Richard Wagner's son Siegfried Wagner (1869–1930),[61] another pupil of

---

[57] Biography by Munter (1923).   [58] Biography by Knappe (1921).
[59] Biography by E. Valentin (1939).
[60] W. Jacob, ed., *Leo Blech: Ein Brevier* (1931).
[61] See S. Wagner, *Erinnerungen*; letters, ed. Rebois; Glasenapp, *Siegfried Wagner und seine Kunst*; Du Moulin-Eckart, *Wahnfried*; other studies by Pretzsch and Daube. (*Der Bärenhäuter* is untranslatable. The story on which it is based will be found under the title "Des Teufels russiger Bruder" in Grimm, *Kinder- und Haus-Märchen* [Berlin, 1815] II, 100–105.)

Humperdinck, whose *Bärenhäuter* (1899) was the first and best of a long series of fairy-tale operas to his own texts which attempt to combine legend, symbolism, and humor in a popular style. None of the later works, however, attained the lasting success of *Hänsel und Gretel*, which remains the classic example of late nineteenth-century German *Märchenoper* as well as a perennial source of pleasure for children of all ages.

CHAPTER 25

NATIONALISM AND OPERA

The nineteenth century saw the rise of independent schools of composition in many countries that had previously been tributary to the chief musical nations of Europe or, like Spain and England, had been for a long time only on the periphery of the main developments. In the growth of musical nationalism opera played a leading part, since the use of characteristic national subjects, often from patriotic motives, stimulated composers to seek an equally characteristic national expression in their music. National operas, as a rule, were not exportable; only exceptionally (as in the case of some Russian operas) did these works make their way into foreign countries. The national schools are important in the history of nineteenth-century opera, however, and it is the purpose of the present chapter to give a survey of their development.

Russia.[1] Native opera began to appear in Russia before the end of the eighteenth century. It had been preceded, as in the countries of western Europe, by various types of drama that used music in incidental

---

[1] Bibliography: (1) General histories of Russian music: Asaf'ev, *Russkaia muzyka ot nachala XIX stoletiia*; Akademiia Nauk, Institut istorii iskusstv, *Istoriia russkoĭ muzyki*; Keldysh, *Istoriia russkoĭ muzyki*, Vols. II and III; Livanova, *Ocherki i materialy po istorii muzykal'noĭ kultury*; Calvocoressi and Abraham, *Masters of Russian Music*; Abraham, *Studies in Russian Music*; idem, *On Russian Music*. (2) General works on Russian opera: Bernandt, *Slovar' oper*; Cheshikhin, *Istoriia russkoĭ opery*; Druskin, *Voprosy muzykal'noĭ dramaturgii opery*; Iarustovskiĭ, *Dramaturgiia russkoĭ opernoĭ klassiki*; Asaf'ev, *Izbrannye trudy*; Newmarch, *The Russian Opera*. See also articles in *Sovetskaia muzyka*. (3) For the period before Glinka: Findeisen, *Ocherki po istorii muzyki v Rossii . . . do kontsa XVIII veka*; idem, "The Earliest Russian Operas"; Ginzburg, *Russkiĭ muzykal'nyĭ teatr 1700–1835*; Rabinovich, *Russkaia opera do Glinki*; Livanova, *Russkaia muzykal'naia kul'tura XVIII veka*; Gozenpud, *Muzykal'nyĭ teatr v Rosii*; Lehmann, *Russlands Oper und Singspiel in der zweiten Hälfte des 18. Jahrhunderts*; Seaman, "The National Element in Early Russian Opera"; Selden, "Early Roots of Russian Opera"; Mooser, *Opéras . . . joués en Russie durant le 18e siècle*. See also in bibliography, titles under Berkov (1950) and Druskin (1956).

fashion : religious mystery plays, going back to the sixteenth century or earlier, as well as school dramas and court pageants in the seventeenth and eighteenth centuries. When the first public theatre was opened at St. Petersburg in 1703 its offerings consisted for the most part of foreign plays which occasionally used incidental music. The record of Italian opera at the Russian court begins in 1731; under Catherine the Great (reigned 1762–96) St. Petersburg became as much of a cosmopolitan center for opera as London, with Galuppi, Paisiello, Cimarosa, Salieri, and others in residence for varying lengths of time, while many other Italians, as well as the leading composers of the French opéra comique and German Singspiel, were represented in the repertoires. During the last quarter of the century nearly 350 operas had their premieres in Russia, over thirty new ones coming out in the year 1778 alone. Most of the operas by foreign composers that were performed in Russia were sung in the original languages, and even some by Russian composers had foreign-language librettos; thus Dmitri Bortniansky (1751–1825), who during his years of study in Italy had produced Italian operas, after his return to St. Petersburg in 1779 wrote comic operas to French librettos.

Nevertheless, by the 1770s operas with original Russian texts began to appear; musical scores of about thirty such works before 1800 have been preserved, and librettos of forty more. Most of them are comic and some are satirical, while sentimental or fairy-tale elements begin to appear toward the end of the century; the usual form is spoken dialogue alternating with solo airs and ensembles. The plots typically introduce characteristic Russian scenes and persons and the music may draw on popular folk melodies. In one early comic opera entitled *The Miller-Magician, Deceiver and Matchmaker* (Moscow, 1779), all the songs were set to popular tunes, in the manner of the earliest French operas comiques. More often, however, the composers incorporated folk song into their own more sophisticated style which they had learned from Western examples or training. The leading composer of Russian opera before 1800 was Evstigney Ipatovich Fomin (1761–1800), who produced a half-dozen comic operas at St. Petersburg between 1786 and 1800; his *The Coachmen* (1787) had a score entirely based on folk material and including choruses in which the composer attempted to transcribe the authentic polyphony of Russian folk song.

Russian opera was thus well under way by the end of the eighteenth century. Under Alexander I (reigned 1801–25) the great upsurge of national sentiment, imbued in Russia as elsewhere with the spirit of Byronesque romanticism, wonderfully encouraged the production of national opera. Curiously, one of the principal composers of Russian opera in the early nineteenth century was a versatile Neapolitan, Catterino Cavos (1775–1840), who came to St. Petersburg in 1799 and remained for the rest of his life. He composed, to Russian, French, or Italian texts, over forty operas; among those on Russian themes and in the Russian language were *Ilya the Hero* (1807), *The Firebird* (1822), and *Ivan Susanin* (1815), his best work and one that remained a model of musical nationalism until Glinka's opera on the same subject replaced it twenty years later. Among the native-born composers of the early and middle nineteenth century was Alexey Nikolayevich Verstovsky (1799–1862), whose chief operas, *The Tomb of Askold* [2] (Moscow, 1835) and *Thunder* (Moscow, 1857), held the stage in Russia into the twentieth century.

An important milestone in the history of Russian opera was the performance in 1836 at St. Petersburg of *A Life for the Tsar* (now known under its original title, *Ivan Susanin*) by Mikhail Ivanovich Glinka (1804–57).[3] Although it has sometimes been regarded as the very foundation and source of Russian national opera, *A Life for the Tsar* owed its reputation in this respect more to its plot and its immense and long-continued popularity in Russia than to any consistent, strongly pronounced national qualities in the music, which indeed sounds for the most part as much French or Italian as Russian. Quotations from folk song occur in the opening of Susanin's aria No. 3 and in the accompaniments to Susanin's last two solo passages at the end of Act IV, and the choral theme of the epilogue so took hold on popular fancy as to become almost a second national anthem; but, with few exceptions, melodies such as that of the Bridal Chorus in Act III (Example 105) represent Glinka's nearest approach in this score to a genuinely national idiom. Compensation may be found for the undistinguished quality of much of the music in the clear and varied orchestration, which was a model for all the later Russian nationalists, including Rimsky-Korsakov.

---

[2] Given at New York in 1869, the first Russian opera in America.

[3] Akademiia Nauk, Institut istorii iskusstv, *Pamiati Glinki, 1857–1957: Issledovaniia i materialy*; Glinka, *Literaturnoe nasledie*; *idem, Zapiski*; see also titles in bibliography under Livanova (1950), Stasov (1953, 1955), Dmitriev (1957), and Protopopov (1961). Biographies in English by Calvocoressi (1911) and Montagu-Nathan (1916).

EXAMPLE 105

A *Life for the Tsar*, Act III

GLINKA

Moreover, in the extensive use of recurring motifs Glinka was far in advance of any opera composer before Wagner. The Polish soldiers, for example, are characterized by themes in the national dance rhythms of polonaise and mazurka, which, first heard in the ball scene of Act II, recur in Act III at the entrance of the Poles, and the mazurka rhythm again at their appearance in Act IV. The quasi-folk-song theme of the opening chorus is used as a leitmotif of Russian heroism, sung by the hero Susanin in Act III as he defies the Polish conspirators; and the opposing national motifs are again contrasted in the orchestral introduction to the epilogue. Susanin's last aria (Act IV) is to a large extent made up of previously heard themes, the recurrences here producing a purposeful dramatic effect. The theme of the final chorus, repeated again and again with cumulative power, has been subtly prepared by two or three statements earlier in the opera. This brilliant epilogue is not only the climax of patriotic emotion but also a fine example of the highly colored mass effects of sound and spectacle so beloved in Russian opera.

Although *A Life for the Tsar* was more popular, the significant musical foundations for the future were laid in Glinka's second and last opera, *Ruslan and Ludmila* (1842). The libretto is a fantastic and incoherent fairy tale adapted from a poem of Pushkin; the music, in spite of some traces of Weber, is more original than that of Glinka's earlier opera, and the musical characterizations more definite. The system of recurring motifs is abandoned; almost the only trace of it is the recurrent descending whole-tone scale associated with the wicked magician Chernomor (Example 106)—said to be the earliest use of the whole-tone scale in European music. At least five distinct styles or procedures characteristic of later Russian music appear in *Ruslan and Ludmila*: (1) the heroic, broad, solemn, declamatory style, with modal suggestions and archaic effect (introduction and song of the Bard, Act·I);

EXAMPLE 106   *Ruslan and Ludmila*, Act IV

GLINKA

(2) the Russian lyrical style, with expressive melodic lines of a folkish cast, delicately colored harmony featuring the lowered sixth or raised fifth, and chromatically moving inner voices (Fina's ballad and Ruslan's first aria in Act II); (3) depiction of fantastic occurrences by means of unusual harmonies, such as whole-tone passages or chord progressions pivoting about one note (scene of Ludmila's abduction, toward the end of Act I); (4) oriental atmosphere, sometimes using genuine oriental themes (Persian chorus at opening of Act III), sometimes original melodies (Ratmir's romance, Act V), but always characterized by fanciful arabesque figures in the accompaniment and a languorous harmony and orchestration; (5) the vividly colored choruses and dances, with glittering instrumentation and often daring harmonies (chorus in honor of Lel, finale of Act I; Chernomor's march and following dances,

especially the *lezginka*, finale of Act IV)— models for such scenes in Borodin's *Prince Igor*, Rimsky-Korsakov's *Sadko*, and even Stravinsky's *Sacre du Printemps*.

The first important Russian opera after *Ruslan and Ludmila* was Alexander Sergeyevich Dargomyzhsky's (1813–69)[4] *Russalka* (1856), likewise on a text from Pushkin and somewhat similar in subject to Glinka's work. Musically, however, it was inferior to *Ruslan*; its best feature was the realistic declamation of the recitative, which Dargomyzhsky proceeded to develop to the highest degree in his last opera, *The Stone Guest*. This work (a setting of Pushkin's Don Juan drama) was completed after Dargomyzhsky's death by Cui, orchestrated by Rimsky-Korsakov, and first performed in 1872. It is no masterpiece and never had a popular success, but it was influential on later Russian opera because of the composer's attempt to write the entire work (except for some songs near the beginning of Act II) in a melodic recitative, a vocal line which should be in every detail the equivalent of the words. The result, though accurate in declamation and dramatic in places, lacks sharp characterization or melodic interest, and there is no compensation for the melodic poverty in the orchestral part, which is conceived as accompaniment rather than a continuous symphonic tissue. In his repudiation of set musical forms and his high respect for the words, Dargomyzhsky may have been influenced to a slight degree by Wagner's theories, though there is no trace of Wagner in the musical substance itself. Harmonically, some interest attaches to Dargomyzhsky's use of whole-tone scale fragments as motifs for the Statue and some passages constructed entirely on this scale.

Dargomyzhsky had arrived in his own way at certain features of the Wagnerian music drama; but the most explicit and self-conscious disciple of Wagner in Russia was Alexander Nikolayevich Serov (1820–71). His first opera, *Judith* (1863), shows the composer's admiration for all the methods of grand opera of the Meyerbeer and early Wagner type. In his third and last opera, *The Power of Evil* (completed by N. T. Soloviev and first produced in 1871), Serov aimed "to embody the Wagnerian theories in a music drama written in Russian, on a Russian subject," and to keep "more closely than has yet been done [*sic*] to the forms of Russian popular music, as preserved unchanged in our folk-

---

[4] See studies by Pekelis (1951) and Serov (1953).

songs." [5] The result, however, was a disappointing hybrid, full of striking but superficial effects. Serov's operas won little regard from musicians but were nevertheless popular enough with the public to remain in the repertoire of Russian opera companies until the First World War.

From about the middle of the nineteenth century, Russian musicians were divided into two groups. In one were the professional, foreign-trained, and officially supported composers who were not primarily interested in musical nationalism but wished to see Russian musical life develop along the same lines as in western Europe, particularly Germany. The head of this school was Anton Rubinstein (1829–94), the famous pianist, founder and first director of the Imperial Conservatory at St. Petersburg. Of Rubinstein's nineteen operas (eight on Russian and eleven on German texts), *The Demon* (1875) had a considerable success both in Russia and abroad. Its libretto strongly recalls Wagner's *Fliegende Holländer*, but the forms are conventional and the musical style is that of pre-Wagnerian romanticism mingled with some oriental elements. Musically more interesting, though less popular, was *The Merchant Kalashnikov* (1880). Rubinstein's biblical operas, or rather stage oratorios (for example, *The Maccabees,* 1875), are remembered now only for a few separate numbers.

The leading composer of the nonnationalist school was Piotr Ilyich Tchaikovsky (1840–93),[6] in whom Slavic temperament and German training were leavened by lyrical genius and a lively appreciation of Italian opera and French ballet. Reckoned by bulk, if not also by musical excellence, Tchaikovsky's achievement is as important in the field of opera as in that of the symphony. After two early works in which he experimented with the then fashionable nationalism—*The Guardsman* (1874) and *Vakula the Smith* (1876; in a revised version as *The Little Slippers*, 1887)—Tchaikovsky produced his masterpiece, *Eugen Onegin*, at Moscow in 1879. In both the libretto (after Pushkin) and the musical style this is an old-fashioned romantic opera, but the music is in Tchaikovsky's happiest vein, with graceful melodies, expressive har-

---

[5] Quoted in Newmarch, *The Russian Opera*, p. 157.
[6] Iarustovskiĭ, *Opernaia dramaturgiia Chaĭkovskogo*; *Muzykal'noe nasledie Chaĭkovskogo*; biographies in English by Newmarch and E. Evans; *Diaries* in English translation; Abraham, ed., *Tchaikovsky: A Symposium*; Bowen and Von Meck, "*Beloved Friend*"; Zagiba, *Tschaikovskij*; see also titles in bibliography under Al'shvang, Berliand-Chernaia, Iakovlev.

monies, transparent and imaginative orchestration—true and living in expression without the hysterical emotionalism of some of the later symphonic works. The character of the heroine, Tatiana, is delineated with especial sympathy, and that of Onegin himself is scarcely less vivid. The ballet music (particularly the waltz in Act II) is tuneful and charming, as are also the choruses in Act I. Tchaikovsky's next three operas were in a more heavily dramatic style. *The Maid of Orleans* (1881, libretto after Schiller) was less successful than *Mazeppa* (1884, from a poem of Pushkin), which contains two of the composer's finest dramatic moments: the monologue of Kochubey and the extremely pathetic final scene. *The Enchantress* (1887) had such a disappointing reception that Tchaikovsky returned to his more characteristic lyrical style for his last two operatic works: *The Queen of Spades* (1890), his most popular opera next to *Onegin*, and *Iolanthe* (1892). In *The Queen of Spades*, based on a melodramatic tale of Pushkin, Tchaikovsky attained a more nearly perfect balance than in any of his other operas between dramatic declamation, lyrical expressiveness, and divertissement music (see especially the ballets in Act II).

The struggle for Russian national music, begun by Glinka and Dargomyzhsky, was carried on after 1860 by a group of five composers :[7] Balakirev, Cui, Mussorgsky, Borodin, and Rimsky-Korsakov. All were amateurs; only Rimsky-Korsakov—and he only at a comparatively late stage of his career—ever had a thorough conventional technical training in composition. Balakirev wrote no operas. César Antonovich Cui (1835–1918)[8] wrote ten, but most of them are not Russian in subject, none are Russian in musical style, and, with the possible exception of *William Ratcliffe* (1869), they are unimportant from any point of view. The Russian national opera in its highest development, therefore, is the work of the remaining three composers of the "mighty five."

The lack of the usual technical musical education (which meant, at this time, a German conservatory training) had the advantage of turning the nationalist composers to the resources of their own country for dramatic and musical material, and to their own instincts and national traditions for the means of shaping this material into operatic form. These conditions were especially important for Modest Petrovich

[7] Livanova, *Stasov i russkaia klassicheskaia opera.*
[8] Cui, *Izbrannye stat'i* (1952). The composer's *Musique en Russie* (1880) is the source of many errors concerning the Russian national school.

Mussorgsky (1839–81),[9] the most original of the group, who in *Boris Godunov* (St. Petersburg, 1874) created one of the great masterpieces of nineteenth-century opera, a monument of much that is most typical in Russian musical drama and at the same time an absolutely personal, inimitable work. *Boris* was first composed in 1868–69 and rewritten in 1871–72. In 1896 Rimsky-Korsakov prepared a thoroughly revised version, with "corrections" of the harmony, improvements in the orchestration, a different order of scenes, and many cuts; the deleted portions were restored in a second revision (1908), and in this form the opera made its way into the repertoire of all foreign opera houses. After the revolution of 1918 the composer's own score was revived for performances in Russia, and this original version was published in 1928.

The libretto of *Boris Godunov* was prepared by Mussorgsky himself, using as sources Pushkin's drama of the same title and N. M. Karamzin's *History of the Russian Empire*. The character of the half-mad emperor Boris (reigned 1598–1605), especially as sung and acted by Feodor Chaliapin, is one of the most vivid in all opera. An equally potent force in the action is the cruel, anonymous mass of the Russian people—a force visibly present in the mighty crowd scenes but also invisibly working like the relentless pressure of Fate at every step toward the catastrophe of the drama. With grim poetic vision Mussorgsky set this primeval force in the closing scene of the opera [10] over against the figure of the Idiot Boy, who, left alone at the last on a darkened stage, keens his lament : "Weep, ye people; soon the foe shall come, soon the gloom shall fall; woe to our land; weep, Russian folk, weep, hungry folk !" One senses in such scenes the influence of the democratic ideals prevalent in Russia during the sixties and seventies in the period after the liberation of the serfs under Alexander II, ideals so eloquently expounded in the writings of Tolstoy. In comparison to the elemental power of most of Mussorgsky's opera, the love episode (Act III) seems both dramatically and musically a pale diversion—as does most of the love interest in Russian opera generally. In form, *Boris Godunov* is a series of detached scenes rather than a coherently developed plot, thus

[9] Biography by Calvocoressi (1956); Leyda and Bertensson, *The Musorgsky Reader*; Godet, *En Marge de Boris Godounof*; Abraham, "Moussorgsky's *Boris* and Pushkin's"; Hoffmann-Erbrecht, "Grundlagen der Melodiebildung bei Mussorgski"; cf. also Szabolcsi, *Bausteine zu einer Geschichte der Melodie*.

[10] References are to Mussorgsky's 1874 version, piano-vocal score published by J. & W. Chester, Ltd., London, cop. 1926.

illustrating the Russian habit, in both musical and literary creation (compare Tolstoy's *War and Peace*), of complete absorption in the present moment, leaving the total impression to be achieved by the cumulative impact of many separate effects.

A striking feature of Mussorgsky's music is the way in which, in the declamation, the melodic line always manages to convey the emotion of the text in the most direct, compressed, and forcible manner imaginable. Perhaps the best examples of this are the two most familiar scenes of the opera, the last part of Act II (including the "clock scene") and the farewell and death of Boris in Act IV. Here Mussorgsky realized the ideal of dramatic, semimelodic recitative which Glinka had foreshadowed in *Ruslan and Ludmila* and which Dargomyzhsky had sought in *The Stone Guest*. Much of the same gloomy power, though with less violence, is displayed in the monastery scene at the beginning of Act I. A more songful idiom, equally characteristic of the composer, is heard in the first part of the Inn scene (Act I, scene 2). Still more characteristic are the children's songs in the first part of Act II—examples of a psychological insight and musical style in which Mussorgsky is almost unique, and which he had demonstrated in his song cycle *The Nursery* (composed 1870–72). It is to be noted that in all these songs, whether declamatory or lyrical, the melodic line is the guiding factor. It is a style of melody which, with its peculiar intervals (especially the falling fourth at cadences), monotonous reiteration of patterns, irregularity of phrase structure, and archaic, modal basis, has grown most intimately out of Russian folk song. To this melodic line the harmony is generally a mere added support, but it likewise is of a strongly personal type, blended of modal feeling, impressionistic—often childlike—fondness for the mere sound of certain combinations, an unconventional harmonic training, and (one suspects) the happy outcome of improvisation at the piano. While the harmony remains consonant and tonal, nevertheless any effort to analyze a typical passage of Mussorgsky according to textbook principles will show how completely foreign his methods were to the conventional practice of the nineteenth century. Not unrelated to the naïveté of his harmonies is Mussorgsky's reveling in raw, massive color effects. This trait is seen most clearly in the great crowd scene of the coronation, the orchestral introduction of which is also an example of the Russian mannerism of alternating chords pivoting on one common tone (in this case A-flat^7 and D^7 on the common tone G-flat = F-sharp).

The chorus itself in this scene is built on the same traditional tune that Beethoven used in his second "Razumovsky" Quartet.

Of Mussorgsky's other operas the principal one is *Khovantchina*, a "people's drama" upon which he worked devotedly but spasmodically from 1873 until the end of his life, but which was left unfinished after all; completed and orchestrated by Rimsky-Korsakov, it was performed at St. Petersburg in 1886. Mussorgsky here took for his subject the conflict of the old feudal regime and the sect of the Old Believers with the new Western tendencies in Russia during the first years after the accession of Peter the Great (1689). Both libretto and music are as intensely national as in *Boris*, but the drama moves less vigorously and the musical style in general is less well sustained. Nevertheless the best numbers—including the prelude, the crowd scenes, Shaklovity's aria in Act III, and especially some of the choruses of the Old Believers where Mussorgsky seems to have distilled the very spirit of ancient Russian church style—are equal to anything elsewhere in his works.

Mussorgsky's cardinal aim was realistic expression at all costs : truth before beauty, melodic recitative "*true to life* and not melodic in the classical sense . . . a sort of melody created by [human] speech . . . intelligently justified melody" [11] (Example 107). To this end, he avoided conventional formulae, evolving a style as restrained, economical, and incapable of successful imitation as that of Debussy. By temperament, Mussorgsky was inclined to depict predominantly that side of the Russian character which gives itself over to gloom and mysticism, to the emotions of violence, brutality, and madness which predominate in *Boris Godunov* and *Khovantchina*. A different, though no less normal, aspect of the national personality comes to life in *Prince Igor*, the opera by Alexander Porfirievich Borodin (1833–87) [12] first performed at St. Petersburg in 1890. The libretto is by the composer, after a plan by Stasov; the score, unfinished at Borodin's death, was completed by Glazounov and Rimsky-Korsakov and orchestrated by the latter. The story is taken from a medieval Russian epic (apparently genuine, though long suspected to be an eighteenth-century forgery), but the central plot is of little importance except to give occasion for the many episodic scenes which make up most of the opera. Some of these scenes are comic, others

[11] Letter to Stasov, December 25, 1876 (*The Musorgsky Reader*, p. 353).

[12] Biographies by Dianin (Russian; 2d ed., 1960) and Abraham (English, 1927); Habets, *Borodin and Liszt*.

EXAMPLE 107

MUSSORGSKY

are love scenes, but a large place is also reserved for spectacle, dances, and choruses (for example, the well-known Polovtsian ballets in Act II). The musical ancestor of *Prince Igor* is Glinka's *Ruslan and Ludmila*, and its principal descendant is Rimsky-Korsakov's *Sadko*. The style of *Prince Igor* is predominantly lyric, with many of the arias in conventional Italian forms; there is some arioso writing, but little dramatic recitative in the manner of Dargomyzhsky. Indeed, the music is not dramatic at all in the sense in which *Boris Godunov* is dramatic; it does not so much embody a drama as present a series of musical tableaux to accompany and complete the stage pictures. In technical details also it is less unconventional than Mussorgsky; the most original portions are the oriental scenes, for which Borodin evolved an idiom partly based on Central Asiatic themes but fundamentally an outgrowth of his eighteen-year-long absorption in the subject and his study of all available musical and historical material. His ancestry (he was the illegitimate son of a Caucasian prince) may also have given him a particular bent toward this style which, with its persistent rhythmic patterns, chromatic intervals, and melodic arabesques, dominates the second and third acts of the opera. *Prince Igor*, like *Boris Godunov*, makes some use of recurring motifs, but a more important source of unity is the derivation, unobtrusive but unmistakable, of many of the themes of Acts II and III from phrases in the melody of the first Polovtsian chorus.[13]

If *Boris Godunov* represents a darkly fanatical aspect of the Russian character and *Prince Igor* a cheerful, hearty one, then the picture is completed by Nikolay Andreyevich Rimsky-Korsakov (1844–1908),[14] whose most characteristic operas reflect a fairy-tale world of fantasy, romance, and innocent humor. This individual musical and dramatic style of Rimsky-Korsakov was not arrived at without some experimentation, and even after it had been achieved, he still continued to experiment. His first two operas, *The Maid of Pskov* (1873), and *May Night* (1880), showed the influence of Dargomyzhsky and Glinka. *The Snow Maiden* (1882) was more spontaneous and original, based on a fairy legend with vaguely symbolic touches. *Mlada* (1892), in which some

[13] Abraham, *Studies in Russian Music*, pp. 132–41.
[14] N. A. Rimskiĭ-Korsakov, *Letopis' moeĭ muzykal'noĭ zhizni* (7th ed., 1955); English (from the 5th ed., 1935) as *My Musical Life* (New York, 1942); A. N. Rimskiĭ-Korsakov, *N. A. Rimskiĭ-Korsakov: Zhizn' i tvorchestvo*; see other titles in bibliography under Gozenpud (1957), Iastrebtsev, and USSR, Tsentral'nyĭ gosudarstvennyĭ literaturnyĭ arkhiv (1951); Abraham, *Rimsky-Korsakov*.

traces of Wagner may be seen, was adapted from a libretto which was to have been collectively composed by Cui, Mussorgsky, Rimsky-Korsakov, and Borodin twenty years before (this joint undertaking was never completed). *Christmas Eve* (1895) was, like *May Night*, taken from a story by N. V. Gogol (1809–52). Both these works are village tales, with love stories and comic-supernatural additions; the subject of *Christmas Eve* is the same as that of Tchaikovsky's *Vakula the Smith*. In 1898 appeared Rimsky-Korsakov's masterpiece, *Sadko*,[15] an "opera legend," a typical combination of the epic and fantastic in a libretto adapted jointly by the composer and V. I. Bielsky from an eleventh-century legend and drawing much of the musical material from Rimsky-Korsakov's symphonic poem of the same title (1867, with revisions in 1869 and 1891). Then followed several experimental works: *Mozart and Salieri, Boyarinya Vera Sheloga* (both 1898), and *The Czar's Bride* (1899), the last a real tragedy with arias and concerted numbers in the old Italian style, "the old operatic convention of the first half of the nineteenth century decked out with Wagnerian leit-motives and Dargomizhskian 'melodic recitative' and mildly flavoured here and there with the Russian folk-idiom."[16] *Czar Saltan* (1900), another fairy tale, returned to distinctive national traits in both libretto and music. *Servilia* (1902) and *Pan Voyevode* (1904) were unsuccessful essays in more dramatic plots with Wagnerian influence in the music. *Kaschey the Immortal* (1902) was also Wagnerian in technique, with declamatory lines and constant use of lietmotifs, as well as in the redemption idea woven into the legendary story; the music represents Rimsky-Korsakov's extreme excursion in the direction of chromaticism and dissonance. The last two operas were, with *Sadko*, the most important: *The Legend of the Invisible City of Kitezh* (1907) and *The Golden Cockerel* (1909). *Kitezh* has been called "the Russian Parsifal" because of its mystical and symbolical story, based on two ancient legends. But beyond an evident aspiration to combine features of pagan pantheism and orthodox Christianity in the figure of the heroine Fevronya, the symbolism is vague and not of fundamental importance. *The Golden Cockerel*, from a humorous-fantastic tale of Pushkin, is more objective and ironic, even satirical, but equally unclear as to the detailed application of its moral.

Other than a gradual growth in complexity of idiom and an in-

---

[15] See monograph by Tsukkerman (1936).
[16] Abraham, *Studies in Russian Music*, p. 248.

creasing skill in the fabrication of piquant harmonic and coloristic effects, there is little that can be called an evolution in Rimsky-Korsakov's musical style through these fifteen operas—nothing remotely comparable to the change in Wagner from *Die Feen* to *Parsifal*. Rimsky-Korsakov was a lyrical and pictorial composer, resembling Mendelssohn in exquisiteness of detail as well as in the absence of strongly emotional and dramatic qualities. The realism of Mussorgsky was not for him : art, he once said, was "essentially the most enchanting and intoxicating of lies" [17]—a statement that doubtless explains much in his own music. The dramatic force of the last act of *The Maid of Pskov* and the serious musical characterization of Fevronya in *Kitezh* are exceptional in his work; his original, personal contribution lies in another realm.

[He] must be granted the quite peculiar power of evoking a fantastic world entirely his own, half-real, half-supernatural, a world as limited, as distinctive and as delightful as the world of the Grimms' fairy-tales or as Alice's Wonderland. It is a world in which the commonplace and matter-of-fact are inextricably confused with the fantastic, naivete with sophistication, the romantic with the humorous, and beauty with absurdity. He was not its inventor, of course; he owed it in the first place to Pushkin and Gogol. But he gave it a queer touch of his own, linking it with Slavonic antiquity and hinting at pantheistic symbolism, which makes it peculiarly his. And musically, of course, he reigns in it undisputed. He invented the perfect music for such a fantastic world : music insubstantial when it was matched with unreal things, deliciously lyrical when it touched reality, in both cases coloured from the most superb palette musician has ever held.[18]

For Rimsky-Korsakov an opera was primarily a musical rather than a dramatic-literary work; hence the importance of musical design, which frequently dominates both the poetry and the scenic plan (for example, the rondo form in the fourth tableau of *Sadko*). Along with this there is usually a definite association of certain keys with certain moods and, in most of the operas, a consistent use of recurring motifs. These are not, as in Wagner, the material out of which a symphonic fabric is developed but are rather melodic fragments (sometimes only a phrase from a large theme) or even inconspicuous harmonic progressions, woven into the opera in a kind of mosaic pattern; they are as often given to the voices as to the orchestra. In the harmony, two distinct idioms are usually found in each opera : one chromatic, fanciful, cunningly contrived, for the

---

[17] Quoted in Calvocoressi and Abraham, *Masters of Russian Music*, p. 411.
[18] Ibid., p. 422. Quoted by permission of the publisher.

EXAMPLE 108   *Sadko*, sc. 2   RIMSKY-KORSAKOV

(Example 108 continued)

imaginary scenes and characters (Example 108); and the other diatonic, solid, often modal, for the "real" world. The vocal parts, as usual in Russian opera, alternate between melodic recitative and closed aria-like forms. In his lyrical melodies, Rimsky-Korsakov owes much to the model of Glinka; his own melodies are elegant and graceful, though marked by certain persistently recurring formulae. An important factor in his style is the extensive use of folk tunes, and of original tunes of folk-song type; the source or inspiration for many of these was his own collection of Russian folk songs, made in 1876. Church melodies are also occasionally used, notably in *Kitezh*. The oriental idiom, however, is much less extensive and less significant in Rimsky-Korsakov's music than in that of either Balakirev or Borodin. Like all Russian opera composers, he excelled in the depiction of crowd scenes, especially in *The Maid of Pskov* (Act II), *Sadko*, *Kitezh* (Act II and finale), and the humorous ensembles in *May Night*, *Christmas Eve*, and *Sadko*. Above all, of course, he is distinguished for his mastery of orchestral effects, a virtuosity in the treatment of instrumental color such as few composers in history have equaled.

A number of minor Russian opera composers of the late nineteenth- and early twentieth-century period can be only briefly mentioned. Eduard Napravnik (1839–1916), as conductor of the St. Petersburg Opera from 1869, was influential in bringing out the works of the native school; the most successful of his own operas was *Dubrovsky* (1895). A pupil of Rimsky-Korsakov, but influenced in opera by Tchaikovsky, was Anton Stepanovich Arensky (1861–1906; *Raphael*, 1894). Also under the influence of Tchaikovsky were the operatic works of Sergey Vassilievich Gulak-Artemovsky (1813–73), whose *Zaporozhets za Dunayem* ("A aninov (1864–1956), and Mikhail Mikhailovich Ippolitov-Ivanov (1859–1935). Sergey Ivanovich Taneyev (1856–1918) produced an *Orestes* trilogy (1895) in severe contrapuntal style with admixtures of Rubinstein and Tchaikovsky. The impressionist movement was reflected in Russian opera in the works of Vladimir Ivanovich Rebikov (1866–1920).

Early composers of opera in the Ukraine [20] were Semyon Stepanovich Gulak-Artemovsky (1813–73), whose *Zaporozhets za Dunayem* ("A

---

[19] Boelza, S. V. *Rakhmaninov i russkaia opera* (1947).

[20] Arkhymovych, *Ukraïns'ka klasychna opera*; Dovzhenko, *Narysy z istorii ykraïns'koï radians'koi muzyky*. Music in *Ukrainskaia klassicheskaia muzyka* (*Antologiia klassicheskoi muzyki narodov SSSR* [Moscow, Muzgiz, 1955], Vyp. 1).

Cossack Beyond the Danube," 1863), in spoken dialogue with simply harmonized songs and choruses, was long popular; and Pyotor Petrovich Sokalsky (1832–87) [21] with *Mazeppa* (1859), *Maiskaya noch* ("May Night," 1863), and *Obsada Dubno* ("The Siege of Dubno," 1878). The chief creator of Ukrainian national opera was Nikolai Vitalievich Lissenko (1842–1912), who used folk melodies in most of his works. His principal opera was *Taras Bulba* (1890); another work, *Natalka-Poltavka* ("Natalie from Poltava," 1890), was also popular, and he wrote two operas on librettos adapted from Gogol: *Rizdviana Nich* ("Christmas Night," 1882) and *Utoplena* (from "May Night," 1885).[22]

POLAND. The early history of opera in Poland [23] is similar to that in Russia, except that the importation of Italian operas began as early as 1628; the first regular court opera was organized five years later and presented a dozen Italian operas and ballets before 1646. A public opera theatre was constructed at Warsaw in 1724, but the opere serie of Hasse and other Italian composers failed to win a large following; after 1765, however, a repertoire of French opéra comique and Italian opera (sometimes in Polish translation) in the renamed "National Public Theatre" proved more attractive. The influence of an intense national spirit was evident in Polish opera from the 1770s onward. As in Russia, the first operas in Poland on national themes were in the form of spoken dialogue with songs interspersed. The earliest of such works was *Nedza uszczesliwiona* ("Misery Made Happy") by Mathias Kamienski (1734–1821), produced at Warsaw in 1778. Another notable early Polish opera was Jan Stefani's (1746–1829) [24] *Cracovians and Mountaineers* (1794); this remained popular to the end

[21] Biography by Karysheva (1959).

[22] On opera in some of the other nations of the Soviet Union, see Tigranov, *Armianskŭ muzykal'nyĭ teatr* (1960); Kulikovich, *Belaruskaia savetskaia opera* (1957).

[23] Bibliography: (1) General works on the history of Polish music: Jachimecki, *Historia Muzyki polskiej w zarysie*; idem, *Muzyka polska*; Reiss, *Najpiekniejsza ze wsystkich jest muzyka polska*; Opieński, *La Muusikue polonaise*. (2) General histories of opera in Poland: Karasowski, *Rys historyczny opery polskiej*; *Muzyka*, tom 10 ("Opera: Monografia zbiorowa," ed. M. Gliński; Reiss, *Muzyka w Krakowie w XIX wieku*; Michaowski, *Opery polskie* (catalogue and chronology, 1788-1953); Glowacki, "The History of Polish Opera." (3) On the period before Moniuszko: Bernacki, *Teatr, dramat i muzyka za Stanislawa Augusta*; Zetowski, "Teoria polskiej opery narodowej z końca XVIII i poczatku XIX wieku"; Wierzbicka, *Zróda do historii teatru warszawskiego od roku 1762 do roku 1833*; Opieński, "Les Premiers Opéras polonais"; Golos, "Italian Baroque Opera in Seventeenth-Century Poland."

[24] See in bibliography, articles by Karasowski (1857), Niewiadomski (1931), and Stromenger (1946).

of the nineteenth century and has been revived several times since, while some of its melodies (using Polish dance rhythms) have passed into the realm of national folk song. A prolific if not especially distinguished composer was Joseph Xaver Elsner (1768–1854),[25] Chopin's teacher, whose *King Lokietek* (1818) was a rescue opera with a libretto reminiscent of *Les Deux Journées*. An influential personage in the early nineteenth century was Karol Kurpinski (1785–1857)[26] with *Jadwiga* (1814), a historical opera on an original Polish libretto, and *Zabobon* (1816; also known by an alternative title, *The New Cracovians*), a work in popular style that was quite successful.

The definitive creation of a Polish national school of opera, however, is due to Stanislaw Moniuszko (1819–72),[27] whose famous *Halka*—first produced at Vilna privately in 1847, then publicly in 1854, and in its final version in four acts at Warsaw in 1858—has remained a staple of the Polish opera theatre to this day. Curiously, the music of *Halka* does not sound markedly "Polish," at least to a foreigner. The style is rather that of early nineteenth-century romanticism, remarkable for lyric grace of melody, with expressive but unsensational harmonies and transparent instrumentation; yet *Halka*, for all its disarming naïveté, is not devoid of real dramatic force. The conventional recitative-aria form of Moniuszko's operas is modified by the use of transitional passages and recurring themes. Other works, similar in style to *Halka*, include *The Raftsman* (1858), the comedy *The Countess* (1860), and especially the semicomic opera *The Haunted Manor* (1865), next to *Halka* his best and most popular work and one that makes considerable use of recurring motifs.

Owing to unfavorable political conditions, the promising work begun by Moniuszko did not come to complete fruition in the latter part of the nineteenth century. One of the principal composers in this period was Wladislaw Zelenski (1837–1921)[28] with *Konrad Wallenrod* (1885), a grand opera on a historical subject; *Goplana* (1896), a romantic fairy-tale opera with lyrical melodies and delicate orchestral colors; and *An Old Fairy Tale* (*Stara baśń*, 1907), in which the influence of both Weber

[25] Biography by Nowak-Romanowicz (1957).
[26] Biography by Pomorska (1948); Reiss, "Koryfeusz muzyki polskiej."
[27] Biographies by Walicki (1873), Jachimecki (1921), and Opieński (1924); see also articles listed under Karasowski, Poźniak, and Rudziński.
[28] Biographies by Szopski (1928) and Jachimecki (1952); see also Paderewski, "*Konrad Wallenrod*"; Niewiadomski, "W Zeleński i jego *Goplana*."

and Wagner is conspicuous. Others who came to a greater or lesser degee under the Wagnerian spell were Sigismund Noskowski[29] (1846–1909; *Livia Quintilla*, 1898); Henryk Jarecki (1846–1918; *Powrót taty*, "The Father's Return," 1897); Roman Statkowski (1860–1925), whose *Filenis* (1904) won the prize in an international competition, and whose style in this and his other opera *Maria* (1906) was somewhere between pre-Wagnerian and the music drama; Ignace Jan Paderewski (1860–1941), more celebrated as a pianist than for his one opera, *Manru* (1901);[30] and Miecyslaw Soltys (1863–1929; *Panie Kochanku*, 1924). A new generation of more progressive tendencies began to be heard from after the restoration of Polish independence in 1919.

CZECHOSLOVAKIA.[31] The father of Bohemian music was Bedřich Smetana (1824–84),[32] whose first great success came in 1866 with *The Bartered Bride*. This melodious comic opera, so permeated with the rhythms and spirit of national music, has become famous all over the world. Two other comic operas of Smetana, *The Kiss* (1876) and *The Secret* (1878), showed advances in technical skill and were almost as successful in the composer's own country as *The Bartered Bride*. Smetana's serious operas, especially *Dalibor* (1868) and *Libussa* (composed 1872, performed 1881), were attacked by patriotic critics because of their use of certain procedures associated with Wagner, such as leit-motifs and the declamatory character of the vocal parts. But the alleged Wagnerisms hardly ever penetrated to the substance of the music, which remained stoutly individual. The leader of the next generation of Bohemian composers, Antonin Dvořák (1841–1904),[33] was primarily a symphonic rather than a dramatic musician, though several of his ten operas were successful at Prague. *The Cunning Peasant* (1878) was

[29] Chybiński, "Zygmunt Noskowski."

[30] Essay on *Manru* by Niewiadomski (1901).

[31] Bibliography: (1) General music histories: Hostinský, *Die Musik in Böhmen*; Soubies, *Histoire de la musique en Bohême*; Helfert, *Geschichte der Musik in der tschechoslovakischen Republik*; Nejedlý, *Dějiny opery Národniko divadla*. (2) General works on opera: Teuber, *Geschichte des Prager Theaters*; Hnilička, *Kontury vývoje hudby poklasické v Čechách*; Boelza, *Cheshskaia opernaia klassika*; Hoza, *Opera na Slovensku*. Principal composers before Smetana were: František Skroup (1801–62), František Skuherský (1830–92), Karel Sebor (1845–1903), Karel Bendl (1838–97), and Vilém Blodek (1834–74); for others, see Adler, *Handbuch* II, 925.

[32] Pražák, *Smetanovy zpěvohry*; Nejedlý, *Bedřich Smetana*; idem, *Zpěvohry Smetanovy*; *Smetana in Briefen*; Abraham, "The Genesis of *The Bartered Bride*."

[33] Šourek, *Život a dilo Antonína Dvořáka*; see also studies in English by Fischl (ed.), Robertson, and Šourek; Clapham, "The Operas of Antonín Dvořák."

inspired by Smetana's *Bartered Bride*. *The Devil and Kate* (1899) was Dvořák's most popular work in the comic style. In serious opera, he underwent the influence first of Meyerbeer and then of Wagner; the height of his achievement in this field was attained in a late work, *Rusalka* (1901), the libretto of which was well adapted to his lyrical powers. A third figure in Bohemian music was Zdenko Fibich (1850–1900),[34] a prolific composer who, more internationally minded than either Smetana or Dvořák, came fully under the influence of romanticism and the Wagnerian music drama. He was noted especially for the classical trilogy *Hippodameia* (1890–91), set entirely as a melodrama—that is, orchestral music accompanying or alternating with a spoken text—a form established by the eighteenth-century Bohemian composer Georg Benda. Fibich's best opera was *Sarka* (1897), based on a story from Czech mythology.

Other composers of this generation were Adalbert Hřimalý (1842–1908; *The Enchanted Prince*, 1872), Joseph Nešvera (1842–1914; *Woodland Air*, 1897), and Hanuš Trneček (1858–1914).

An important Bohemian composer of the late nineteenth century was Joseph Bohuslav Foerster (1859–1951),[35] whose most successful operas were *Eva* (1889) and *Jessika* (1905). Four pupils of Fibich also made their mark in Bohemian opera: Karel Kovařovic (1862–1920; *On the Old Bleaching Ground*, 1901), Karel Weis (1862–1944), Antonín Horák (1875–1910), and Otakar Ostrčil (1879–1935; *The Bud*, 1911). An influential composer and teacher was Vitězlav Novák (1870–1949),[36] with four operas of which the most important was *The Imp of Zvikov* (1915).

HUNGARY. The founder of opera in Hungary [37] was Ferenc Erkel (1810–93), whose *Hunyady László* (1844) holds the same position in its

[34] Rektorys, ed., *Zdeněk Fibich*.

[35] See J. B. Foerster: *Jeho životní pouť a tvorba* (1949); Foerster, *Der Pilger* (memoirs, first publ. in Czech, 1947).

[36] Stěpán, *Novák a Suk*; see also Newmarch, "New Works in Czechoslovakia" (1931).

[37] Bibliography: Eősze, *Az opera útja* (Budapest, 1960), pp. 465–96; Abrányi, *Erkel Ferenc élete és müködése*; Bónis, *Mosonyi Mihály*; articles in the series *Zenetudományi tanulmányok*, Vol. II, 1954 (*Erkel Ferenc és Bartók Béla emlékére*), on Erkel by I. Barna (pp. 175–218) and J. Maróthy (pp. 25–174); Vol. IV, 1955 (*A magyar zene történetéből*), on Erkel by Barna (pp. 211–72; continuation of the essay in Vol. II); and Vol. IX, 1961 (*Az opera történetéből*), on Erkel by Somfai (pp. 81–158) and on Mosonyi by Bónis (pp. 169–96; also in German: "Die ungarischen Opern M. Mosonyi's," *Studia musicologica* II [1962] 139–88).

country as do *A Life for the Tsar* in Russia and *Halka* in Poland; and Erkel's other operas were almost equally popular, especially *Bánk-Ban* (1861). Another important national composer was Mihály Mosonyi (1814–70), whose chief opera, *Szép Ilonka* ("Fair Ilonka"), was produced in 1861. Others of the early nationalist group were Andreas Bartay (1798–1856), whose *Csel* ("The Trick," 1839) was the first original Hungarian comic opera; and August von Adelburg (1830–73), with the successful opera *Zrinyi* in 1868. Later nationalists included Jenö Hubay (1858–1937), a celebrated violinist and prolific composer whose principal opera, *A Cremonai hegedis* ("The Violin Maker of Cremona," 1894), is still given; and Ede Poldini (1869–1957) with the comic opera *A csavargó és királylány* ("The Vagabond and the Princess," 1903). The works of Odön Mihalovich (1842–1929) were Germanic and Wagnerian in musical style, even when on Hungarian librettos (*Toldi szerelme*, "Toldi's Love," 1893), and a pronounced flavor of German romanticism is heard in the operas of Géza Zichy (1849–1924),[38] whose most ambitious undertaking was a trilogy on the life of Rákóczi (produced at Budapest 1905–12). A similarly international romantic style is characteristic of the music of the noted pianist-composer Ernst von Dohnányi (1877–1960) in his opera *A Vajda tornya* ("The Tower of the Voyvod"), produced at Budapest in 1922.

The principal opera composers of Rumania were : Liubicz Skibinski (*Verfel cu Dor*, 1879); Edoardo Caudella (1841–1923; *Petru Raresch*, 1900); Georg Kosmovici (*Marioara*, 1904); Theodor von Flondor (d. 1908; *Mosul Ciorkârlan*, 1901) : Sabin Dragoi (b. 1894); a pupil of Dvořák and Janáček, with sophisticated modern use of Rumanian folk song in *Napasta* (1928); and Georges Enesco (1881–1955), with one opera, *Oedipe* (Paris, 1936).

Croatian opera is represented by Vatroslav Lisinski (1819–54; *Ljubav i Zloba*, 1846); Ivan Zajc (Giovanni von Zaytz, 1831–1914; *Nikola Subič Zrinski*, 1876); Franz Vilhar (1852–1928; *Smiljana*, 1897); Peter Konjović (b. 1882; *Koštana*, 1931); Krešimir Baranović (b. 1894; *Striženo-Košeno*, 1932); and Jakov Gotovac (b. 1895; *Morana*, 1930).

In Serbia the only opera composers of importance were Davorin Jenko (1835–1914),[39] whose many works for the theatre include the first Serbian comic opera, *Vračara* ("The Enchantress," 1882); and Alexander Savine (1881–1949; *Xenia*, 1919). Bulgarian opera has two composers : Georgi Atanasov (1881–1931), a pupil of Mascagni (*Borislav*, 1911), and Pantcho

[38] Autobiography (*Aus meinem Leben*).
[39] Cvetko, *Davorin Jenko: Doba, življenje, delo.*

Vladigerov (b. 1899), with the nationalist opera *Tsar Kaloyan* (1936). A nationalist of Greece was Manolis Kalomiris (1883–1962), whose *Protomastoros* ("The Master Builder," 1916) was the first opera by a Greek on a Greek subject; his later works include *Mother's Ring* (1917) and a festival opera with choruses on a historical subject, *Constantine Paleologos*—the last Byzantine emperor, who ruled from 1448 to 1453—first performed in the theatre of Herod Atticus at Athens in the summer of 1962.

The first Turkish operas, *Tas Babek* and *Kerem*, by Ahmed Adnan Saygun (b. 1907), were produced at Ankara in 1934 and 1957 respectively.

GERMANIC, SCANDINAVIAN, AND BALTIC COUNTRIES. On the whole, opera found no very congenial ground in these countries, but there are sporadic examples, of which some of the most important will be mentioned.

The earliest Dutch opera, *De triomferende min* ("Love's Triumph") by Carolus Hacquart (*ca.* 1649-*ca.* 1730), was published in 1680, but its first performance took place only in 1920 at Arnhem. During the nineteenth century, when the Netherlands was largely under the musical domination of Germany, a few national operas were produced. Among composers of this period [40] were Richard Hol (1825–1904; *Floris V*, 1892); Cornelis van der Linden (1839–1918; *Leiden ontzet*, "The Relief of Leiden," 1893); Henri Brandts-Buys (1850–1905; *Albrecht Beiling*, 1881); Karl Dibbern (b. 1855; *Odja*, 1901); Emile van Brucken-Fock (1857–1944; *Seleneia*, 1895); Cornelis Dopper (1870–1939; *Het Eerekruis*, "The Cross of Honor," 1903); and Charles Grelinger (b. 1873), with the successful opera *Op Hoop van Zegen* ("On Board the 'Hope of Blessing,'" 1907). Jan Brandts-Buys (1868–1933) was more German than Dutch (*Die drei Schneider*, Dresden, 1916), but national traits appeared in the realistic-satiric operas of Hol's pupil Johan Wagenaar (1862–1941); his *Doge van Venetie* (1904) and *De Cid* (1916) are serious operas.

Flemish [41] opera composers of the nineteenth and early twentieth centuries were: Joseph Mertens (1834–1901; *De zwaarte Kapitein*, 1877); Peter Benoit (1834–1901; *Le Roi des Aulnes*, 1859; *Isa*, 1867); Jan Blockx (1851–1912;[42] *De Herbergprinses*, 1896; *De Bruid der Zee*, 1901); Paul Gilson (1865–1942; *Prinses Zonneschijn*, 1903); and Auguste de Boeck (1865–1937; *La Route d'Emeraude*, 1921).

Denmark, like Holland, has been to a large extent a musical province of Germany. The German composer Franz Gläser (1798–1861) wrote three operas to Danish texts. The earliest national opera composers were Johan

[40] Reeser, *Een Eeuw nederlandse Muziek*; Bottenheim, *De Opera in Nederland*; Dresden, *Het Muziekleven in Nederland sinds 1880.*

[41] Closson, ed., *La Musique en Belgique*; Corbet, ed., *De vlaamse Muziek sedert Benoit.*

[42] Biography by Frank Blockx (1943).

Hartmann (1805–1900; *Liden Kirsten*, 1846); Henrik Rung (1807–71; *Stormen paa København*, 1845); Siegfried Saloman (1816–99; *Diamantkorset*, 1847); and Peter Arnold Heise (1830–79; *Drot og Marsk*, 1878). Four operas by Peter Erasmus Lange-Müller (1850–1926) were produced at Copenhagen (*Spanske Studenter*, 1883). One of the most successful Danish comic operas was Carl August Nielsen's (1865–1931)[43] *Maskarade* (1906). The most prolific Danish opera composer was August Enna (1860–1939; *Hexen*, 1892; *The Match Girl*, 1897).

The first Norwegian opera [44] was *A Mountain Adventure* by Waldemar Thrane (1790–1828), which was published by 1824 but not performed on the stage until 1850. Twenty years later came *Junkeren og Flubergrosen* ("The Knight and the Fluberg Sprite") by Martin Andreas Udbye (1820–99), and in 1894 the first of Johannes Haarklou's (1847–1925) five operas, *Fra gamle Dage* ("Of Olden Days"). Ole Olsen (1850–1927) wrote four operas, of which *Lajla* was performed at Christiania in 1908. Gerhard Schjelderup (1859–1933), though of Norwegian birth, composed most of his operas to German texts; the same is true of Sigwardt Aspestrand (1856–1941). Catherinus Elling (1858–1942) wrote one opera, *Kosakkerne* (1897).

Sweden from the seventeenth century had been in touch with the general development of opera in Europe.[45] Italian, French, and German subjects and musical styles, as might be expected, dominated Swedish opera houses in the late eighteenth and early nineteenth centuries. The earliest attempt at a Swedish historical subject was made by Carl Stenborg with *Konung Gustaf Adolphs Jagt* ("King Gustavus Adolphus's Hunting Party") in 1777, a "comedy mingled with songs," imitated from Collet's *opéra comique La Partie de chasse de Henri IV*, part of which had been used by Weisse and Hiller for their popular Singspiel *Die Jagd* in 1770.[46] The first grand opera in Swedish was *Thetis och Pelée* (1773), by the Italian composer Francesco Antonio Uttini (1723–95). Swedish opera composers in the early and middle nineteenth century included Franz Berwald (1796–1868),[47] J. N. Ahlström (1805–57), Adolf Lindblad (1891–78), and Johan August Södermann (1832–76). Some German composers in this period also occasionally wrote operas to Swedish texts. A more definitely national type of Swedish opera, using native legends and folk melodies, appeared toward the end of the nineteenth century with the works of Ivar Hallström (1826–1901; *Den Bergtagna*, "The Mountain Ghost," 1874). Nationalism was temporarily pushed aside by the desire to emulate the Wagnerian music drama, as in the earlier operas of Andreas

---

[43] Biographies of Nielsen by T. Meyer and L. Dolleris.
[44] Kindem, *Den norske Operas Historie*; Benestad, *Waldemar Thrane*.
[45] See Moberg, "Essais d'opéras en Suède," in *Mélanges de musicologie*, pp 123–32; Engländer, *Joseph Martin Kraus*; Sundström, "Franz Berwalds Operor."
[46] See Lindström, "Vårt första nationella Sångspel."
[47] Biography by R. Layton (1957).

Hallén (1846–1925; *Harald Viking*, Leipzig, 1881), though more independent traits are evident in his *Waldemar's Treasure*, written for the opening of the new Stockholm Opera in 1899. A Wagner propagandist in Sweden was Richard Henneberg (1853–1925), who wrote a comic opera, *Drottningen's Pilgrimage*, in 1882. A combination of the Wagner style with national melodies is found in the operas of Wilhelm Stenhammar (1871–1927; *Tirfing*, 1898; *Das Fest auf Solhaug*, Stuttgart, 1899). A more decisive step toward national opera, though still on a Wagnerian basis, was *Arnljot* (1910), by Olof Wilhelm Peterson-Berger (1867–1942).[48] Natanaël Berg (1879–1957) and Kurt Atterberg (b. 1887) were distinguished chiefly in the field of the symphony, though both produced operas. A notable opera composer of their generation was Ture Rangström (1884–1947; *Kronbruden*, "The Crown Bride"; Stuttgart, 1919, and in Swedish at Stockholm from 1922; based on Strindberg's drama).

In Finland there was no national opera before the twentieth century. *Kung Carls Jakt* ("King Charles's Hunting Party") by Fredrik Pacius (1809–91), performed at Helsinki in 1852 and sometimes called the "first Finnish opera," was by a German-born composer and on a Swedish text.[49] The first opera composed to Finnish words was Oskar Merikanto's (1868–1924)[50] *Pohjan Neiti* ("The Maid of Bothnia"), performed at Viipuri in 1908. Merikanto's subsequent works (*Elinan Surma*, "Elina's Death," 1910; *Regina von Emmeritz*, 1920) were somewhat influenced by Italian verismo methods. Other composers of this period were Erkki Gustaf Melartin (1875–1937; *Aino*, 1909) and Selim Palmgren (1878–1951; *Daniel Hjort*, 1910, on a Swedish text). A more distinctly national style, with folk melodies and recitative rhythms adapted to the Finnish language, was exemplified by Armas Launis (1884–1959; *Seitsemän veljestä*, "The Seven Brothers," 1913; *Kullervo*, 1917). Another Finnish folk-song scholar, Ilmari Krohn (1867–1960), produced the opera *Tuhotulva* ("The Deluge") at Helsinki in 1928. Important Finnish operas by Leevi Madetoja (1887–1947), a pupil of D'Indy, are *Pohjalaisia* ("The East Bothnians," 1924) and *Juha* (1935).

A few national operas were produced in the smaller Baltic states after the First World War. In Latvia an opera company was organized at Riga in 1919. National composers include Alfreds Kalnins (1879–1951; *Banuta*, 1920; *Dzimtenes Atmoda*, "The Nation's Awakening," 1933, a historical opera); Jāzeps Mediņš (1877–1947; *Vaidelote*, "The Virgin," 1927); Jānis Mediņš (b. 1890; *Uguns un Nakts*, "Fire and Night," 1921); and Jānis Kalnins (b. 1904; *Hamlet*, 1936). A Lithuanian opera house was opened at Kaunas toward the end of 1920 and the first Lithuanian opera, *Birute*, by Petrauskas Miskas, was performed in 1921. Another Lithuanian composer is Jurgio Karnavičius (b. 1885; *Grazina*, 1933). Estonian operas

---

[48] Biography by Carlberg (1950).
[49] See Loewenberg, *Annals*.
[50] Biography by Suomalainen (1950).

have been composed by Arthur Lemba (b. 1885; *Armastus ja Surm*, "Love and Death," Tallinn, 1931; *Elga*, 1934).

JAPAN. The development of modern opera in Japan [51] (as distinct from that nation's traditional musical-dramatic forms, the *nō* and *kabuki*) followed a course similar in many respects to that in the countries of eastern Europe. Apparently the first Western opera to be staged in Japan was Gounod's *Faust* (Act I only) at Tokyo in 1894. Gluck's *Orfeo*, in Japanese translation and with a Japanese cast, was heard at Tokyo in 1903. The first opera by a Japanese composer was *Hagoromo* ("Magic Clothes of an Angel," 1906), based on a national legend and set to music by Kōsuke Komatsu (b. 1884). Subsequent composers aimed to amalgamate the tradition of Japanese musical drama with that of Western opera. Representative works in this line are: *Kurofune* ("Black Ships," 1940) by Kōsaku Yamada (b. 1886); *Yūzuru* ("Crane of Twilight") by Ikuma Dan (b. 1924), first produced at Tokyo in 1952 and known in the West from performances at Zurich in 1957; and *Shuzenji-monogatari* ("A Tale at Shuzenji"; Tokyo, 1954, and Los Angeles, 1962) by Osamu Shimizu (b. 1911). The libretto of *Kurofune* uses a national historical subject; that of *Yūzuru* is based on a national folk tale, while *Shuzenji-monogatari* simply takes over a *kabuki* drama without altering so much as a word. In these and other modern operas, national subjects—and to a certain extent also national musical materials—are blended with various Western musical styles from Puccini to the most advanced contemporary idioms.

SPAIN, PORTUGAL, AND LATIN AMERICA. [52] With the disappearance of the old tonadilla in the first half of the nineteenth century, Spanish national opera went into an eclipse from which it did not emerge until about 1850. The first signs of reaction against the reign of Italian opera and French opéra comique in Spanish theatres appeared in the works of a resident Italian composer, Basilio Basili, who in the late thirties and early forties brought out at Madrid a number of comic operas in Span-

---

[51] For the information here presented I am indebted to the courtesy of Professor Kōzo Hattori of the University of Arts, Tokyo.

[52] See Chase, *The Music of Spain*, for a survey of this subject, with bibliographies. Further consult: Lavignac, *Encyclopédie*, Part I, Vol. IV, pp. 2290–2351, 2470–84; Salazar, *La música contemporánea en España*; music dictionaries of Saldoni and Pedrell and the "Espasa" encyclopedia; Trend, *A Picture of Modern Spain*; Peña y Goñi, *La ópera española*; Subirá, *Historia y anecdotario del Teatro Real*; *idem, El Teatro del Real Palacio*; Muñoz, *Historia de la zarzuela*. See also titles under early Spanish opera (above, p. 268).

ish. The first of these (1837) was labeled a *zarzuela-comedia*, thus reviving the ancient Spanish designation. Within a decade the new zarzuela was flourishing, in a form derived from the eighteenth-century tonadilla, using music of a light, popular, national style with admixture of some French and Italian elements. Many of the early librettos were from French sources—an instance of the influence which France has constantly exerted on the growth of national Spanish music. The leading composer of this first period of the revival was Francisco Asenjo Barbieri (1823–94), who produced over seventy zarzuelas between 1850 and 1880, including the classic work of this type, *Pan y toros* ("Bread and Bulls," 1864). This and other zarzuelas of Barbieri were long popular and have been influential on the development of national music in both Spain and South America. The principal contemporaries of Barbieri were Rafael José María Hernándo (1822–88), Joaquín Gaztambide (1822–70), Cristóbal Oudrid y Segura (1829–77), and Emilio Arrieta y Corera (1823–94).

Two distinct types of zarzuela developed at Madrid, corresponding to the two types of French opéra comique that evolved during the nineteenth century. On the one hand was the *genero chico*—comic, popular, informal, often quite ephemeral pieces in one act, which were produced in immense numbers throughout the century and indeed have continued up to the present day. The other type was the *zarzuela grande*, usually in three acts, which might be on a serious subject and even in some cases approach the scale and style of grand opera. Most composers of the later nineteenth century wrote zarzuelas of both kinds. Some of the most popular works of the genero chico were *La gran vía* ("The Great Road," 1886) by Federico Chueca (1846–1908), in collaboration with Joaquín Valverde (1846–1910); *La viejecita* ("The Old Woman," 1897) by Manuel Fernández-Caballero (1835–1906); *La bruja* ("The Witch," 1887) and *La revoltosa* ("The Revolutionary Girl," 1897) by Ruperto Chapí y Lorente (1851–1909); and above all *La verbena de la paloma* ("The Festival of Our Lady of the Dove," 1894) by Tomas Bretón y Hernández (1850–1923).[53]

Along with the rise of the popular zarzuela came a growing desire for a national serious opera in Spain. Spanish composers of the earlier nineteenth century had rarely used Spanish texts or national subjects, and their music seldom had anything differentiating it from the contempo-

[53] Biography by Salcedo.

rary Italian style. A solitary early crusader for Spanish opera was Joaquín Espín y Guillén (1812–81), one act of whose *Padilla, o el Asedio de Medina* ("Padilla; or, The Siege of Medina") was performed at Madrid in 1845. Later in the century, however, the zarzuela composers interested themselves in the task of creating a more permanent and artistic form of national lyric drama than could be made of the pieces in the *genero chico* to which they owed their popular success. Barbieri had definite ideas on the subject; Arrieta, who had composed a number of Italian operas, expanded his two-act zarzuela *Marina* into a three-act Spanish opera with recitatives (1871). Chapí wrote several serious zarzuelas (*La tempestad*, "The Storm," 1882; *Curro Vargas*, 1898) as well as operas (*Margarita la Tornera*, 1909), but his genius was for the comic rather than the serious. Bretón, who had also written Italian operas, composed a Spanish opera, *La Dolores*, in 1895. Still another composer of this period was Emilio Serrano y Ruiz (1850–1939), with the operas *Irene de Otranto* in 1891 and *Gonzalo de Cordoba* (to his own text) in 1898.

The honorable title of "father of modern Spanish music" belongs to Felipe Pedrell (1841–1922),[54] distinguished scholar, composer of operas and symphonic and choral works, and teacher or mentor of most of the Spanish composers of the following generation. Pedrell combined a deep feeling for the qualities of Spanish folk song and the great Spanish music of the past with a romantic-mystical temperament which led him frequently into paths where the general public could not follow. He was a greater idealist than composer, and his beneficent influence on Spanish music is out of all proportion to the very slight outward success of his own works. He was dubbed "the Spanish Wagner"; his most successful opera, *La Celestina* (1904), was called "the Spanish *Tristan*." These expressions exaggerate the resemblance of his work to Wagner's. That there was some influence is unquestionable, but the examples of Glinka, Mussorgsky, and the other Russian opera composers were at least equally potent. As a matter of fact, if comparisons must be made, the composer whom Pedrell most closely resembles is D'Indy. The likeness is one of both temperament and musical style : each was irresistibly drawn into the orbit of Wagner; each, being an ardent nationalist and an artist of high ethical purpose, adapted the technique of the music

[54] Studies by Tebaldini, Curzon, and Istel; Pedrell, *Jornadas de arte*; catalogue by Reiff.

drama for his own aims; and each succeeded in being individual in spite of this debt. D'Indy was a better technician than Pedrell and was more at home in the realm of purely musical expression; Pedrell, on the other hand, drew his musical idiom from more varied sources.

The most important of Pedrell's ten operas is *Los Pirineos* ("The Pyrenees"), a trilogy in three acts with prologue, composed to a Catalan text of Victor Balaguer in 1890–91 and first performed in Italian translation at Barcelona in 1902.[55] The poem offers a number of effective

EXAMPLE 109   *Los Pirineos*, Act II   PEDRELL

scenes, but on the whole its nature is more that of an epic than of a dramatic work. Pedrell's setting is unified by the use of leitmotifs. An idea of his style may be gained from Example 109, part of the Funeral March in the second act. The orchestra has a much less conspicuous posi-

[55] *Los Pireneos* is itself the first opera of a larger trilogy, of which *La Celestina* is the second number; the third, *Raymond Lully*, was not completed.

tion than in Wagner, and the voice parts are nearly always melodic. An important proportion of the score is given to set pieces, which appear in great variety. The composer's scholarly conscience is shown in his evident care to reproduce as authentically as possible the oriental idiom in the solos of the heroine, "Moon-Ray"; the scene of the Love Court in Act I offers modern adaptations of trouvère and troubadour art forms—*tenso*, *lai*, and *sirventes*. There are quotations from plainsong and from sixteenth-century Spanish church composers, and the excellent choral writing throughout the opera should be especially mentioned. The prologue in particular should make a very effective concert number for a choral society.

It is too much to claim that Pedrell is to be numbered among the greatest opera composers. His dramatic sense often failed him. Too many pages of *Les Pirineos* are thin in inspiration, repetitious, and lacking in rhythmic vitality and variety. But, out of a sincere artist's soul, enough moments of greatness have emerged to make this work an honor to its composer and country and to entitle it to at least an occasional performance, even if in a shortened version.

The national spirit which Pedrell did so much to inspire achieved world-wide recognition in the piano music of two of his pupils, Isaac Albéniz (1860–1909)[56] and Enrique Granados (1867–1916).[57] Both these composers essayed opera, but without important results. Albéniz, apparently under a mistaken notion of his own gifts, and also instigated by a wealthy English patron who fancied himself a dramatic author, devoted several years to writing operas in a heavy, pseudo-Wagnerian style but finally obtained a moderate success with a comic work, *Pepita Jiménez* (1896). Granados, like many of his contemporaries, was interested in trying to re-create the spirit of Madrid as typified in Goya, and the music of his principal opera, *Goyescas* (New York, 1916), was expanded from a series of piano pieces of the same title. The plot of this opera has a strong tinge of Italian verismo.

In addition to his influence on what may be called the main stream of modern Spanish opera, Pedrell is also the founder of the regional school of Catalonia. The leading figure in this school is Jaime Pahissa (b. 1880), with *La presó de Lleida* ("The Prison of Lérida," 1906; rewritten in 1928 as the three-act opera *La Princesa Margarida*) and *Gala Placidia* (1913).

[56] Laplane, *Albeniz*; Collet, *Albeniz et Granados*.
[57] Studies by Boladeres Ibern and Subirá.

Other Catalan composers are Enric Morera [58] (1865–1942; *Emporium*, 1906), Juan Lamote de Grignon (1872–1949; *Hesperia*, 1907), and Joan Manén (b. 1883; *Acté*, 1903). Independent regional development is characteristic of Spanish music, but the only extensive regional opera outside Catalonia is found in the Basque country. The oustanding composer here was José María Usandizaga (1887–1915) with the nationalistic *Mendi-Mendyian* (1910) and the successful Puccinian melodramatic opera *Las golondrinas* ("The Swallows," 1914). Another Basque composer is Jesús Guridi (b. 1886), whose national folk opera *Mirentxu* (1910) was followed in 1920 by a more ambitious work with some Wagnerian traits, *Amaya*, and a successful zarzuela, *El Caserio* ("The Hamlet"), in 1926.

The early history of dramatic music in Portugal [59] is similar to that of Spain, except that there was no distinct national form of as great importance as the tonadilla. The first opera in Portuguese was *La vida do grande D. Quixote de la Mancha* (1733) by Antonio José da Silva (1705–39), an isolated attempt which led to nothing. Italian opera came to Portugal as early as 1682, but its flourishing period began only about 1720. Of the Portuguese composers who devoted themselves to writing in the Italian style, the chief was Marcos Antonio Portugal (1762–1830), whose thirty-five operas were widely performed in Europe in the late eighteenth and early nineteenth centuries. He was also the composer of twenty-one comic operas to Portuguese texts. Italian and French opera continued to dominate the Portuguese stage throughout the nineteenth century; Miguel Pereira's (1843–1901) opera *Eurico* (1870), with Italian text arranged from a Portuguese novel, is typical of this tendency. Native composers only occasionally adopted their own language or musical idiom, except for comic pieces. In this genre, however, there were successful works by Antonio Luiz Miró (d. 1853; *A marqueza*, 1848); Guilherme Cossoul (1828–80; *A cisterna do diablo*, "The Devil's Cistern," 1850); Francisco Alves Rente (1851–91; *Verde gaio*, "Light Yellow," 1876); and Domingo Cyriaco de Cardoso (1846–1900; *O burro do Senhor Alcaide*, "The Mayor's Donkey," 1891). An outstanding nationalist composer was Alfredo Keil (1850–1907), of whose serious Portuguese operas *Serrana* (1899) was most frequently performed. The principal later composer of operas in Portugal was Rui Coelho (b. 1891; *Belkiss*, 1938).

[58] Biography by Iglesias.

[59] Bibliography: Luper, "The Music of Portugal," in Chase, *Music of Spain*, chap. XVIII; Vieira, *Diccionario biographico de musicos portuguezes*; Fonseco Benevides, *O real theatro de S. Carlos de Lisboa*; Lavignac, *Encyclopédie*, Part I, Vol. IV, pp. 2422–35, 2447–57.

Opera in Latin America [60] has been for the most part an offshoot of Italian and Spanish opera. In the colonial period the missionaries promoted plays with music, and at larger centers (for example, Lima) there were performances of the works of Calderón and other Spanish dramatists with music. The earliest extant opera in the New World seems to have been *La purpúra de la rosa* by Tomás de Torrejón y Velasco, performed at Lima in 1701. An Italian opera, *La Partenope*, with music by Manuel Zumaya, was produced at Mexico City in 1711. A few tonadillas were brought from Spain to the American colonies in the eighteenth century, but regular seasons of opera did not begin before the second quarter of the nineteenth century. Brazil had a national opera company from 1857, and the most famous Latin American opera composer of the nineteenth century, Antonio Carlos Gomes (1836–96),[61] was a Brazilian who studied in Italy and produced at Milan in 1870 his masterpiece, *Il Guarnay*, a work still given in Brazil and Italy. Although Gomes chose national subjects for some of his operas and endeavored also to introduce national elements in his music, he was too strongly inclined to the Italian style to be entirely successful. A like inclination is evident in the music of Henrique Eulalio Gurjão (1833–85), whose best-known opera was *Idalia* (1881). Leopoldo Miguez (1850–1902) was influenced by Wagner in *Os Saldunes* (1901). Even the so-called nationalist composer Alberto Nepomuceno (1864–1920) did not develop an independent musical style in his operas.

[60] Chase, *A Guide to the Music of Latin America*, 2d ed. (1962); publications of the Pan American Union, Washington, D.C. Periodicals: *Handbook of Latin American Studies*; *Boletín latino-americano de música*; *Rivista brasileira de música*; special number of RM, February-March, 1940 ("La Musique dans les pays latins"). Slonimsky, *Music of Latin America*; Chase, *The Music of Spain*; idem, articles with bibliographies in *Harvard Dictionary of Music* (by countries); Alfredo Fiorda Kelley, *Cronología de las óperas . . . etc. cantados en Buenos Aires* [1825–1933]; Acquarone, *História de la música brasileira*; Corrêa de Azevedo, *150 anos de música no Brasil (1800–1950)*; Ayesterán, *Crónica de una temporada musical en el Montevideo de 1830*; Abascal Brunet, *Apuntes para la historia del teatro en Chile*; Abascal Brunet and Pereira Salas, *Pepe Vila* [1861–1936]: *La zarzuela chica en Chile*; Pereira Salas, *História de la música en Chile*; Salas and Feo Calcaño, *Sesquicentenario de la opera en Caracas . . . ciento años de opera 1808–1958*; R. Stevenson, "Opera Beginnings in the New World"; idem, *The Music of Peru*; Sixto Prieto, "El Perú en la música escénica" (bibliography of scores and librettos of operas, ballets, etc., the subjects of which relate to Peru); Saldívar, *História de la música en México*; Stevenson, *Music in Mexico*; Romero, *La ópera en Yucatán*; Maria y Campos, *Una temporada de opera italiana en Oaxaca* [1874–75]; Tolón and González, *Operas cubanas y sus autores*; Sáez, *El teatro en Puerto Rico*.

[61] Studies by Seidl, Marchant, and Andrade; Corrêa de Azevedo, "Carlos Gomes"; biography by Gomes Vaz de Carvalho (3d ed., 1946).

In Argentina the Italian influence was even stronger, though national subjects were occasionally used, as in *La indígena* (1862) by Vinceslao Fumi (1823–80) and in *Pampa* (1897) and *Yupansky* (1899) by Arturo Berutti (1862–1938). Justin Clérice (1863–1908), a native of Argentina, won recognition in Europe for his French comic operas and ballets.

Early Mexican composers of Italian operas were Luis Baca (1826–55), Cenobio Paniagua (1821–82; *Catalina di Guisa*, 1864), and Melesio Morales (1838–1908), whose principal works were *Ildegonda* (1866), *Cleopatra* (1891), and *Anita*, a one-act opera in verismo style (never performed). German romanticism is characteristic of the music of Ricardo Castro (1864–1907) in *La Légende de Rudel*, though national themes had appeared in his earlier *Atzimba*. A distinguished national opera on an Aztec subject, using popular melodies, was *Guatimotzín* (1871) by Aniceto Ortega (1823–75). A recent national historical opera in Mexico was *Tata Vasco* by Miguel Bernal Jiménez (b. 1910), pre-sented at Morelia in 1941, which includes many choral scenes and draws musical material from diverse sources including Gregorian chant and Indian melodies.[62]

Most of the favorite Spanish zarzuelas were brought to the New World and inspired similar works by local composers in all Latin American countries. Thus the Venezuelan José Angel Montero (1839–81) produced fifteen zarzuelas as well as an opera, *Virginia* (1873). In Colombia, zarzuelas and similar pieces were composed by Juan Crisós-tomo Osorio y Ricaurte (1863–87) and Santos Cifuentes (1870–1932); in Mexico there was a popular comic opera, *Keofar* (1893), by Felipe Villanueva (1862–93). Other Latin American opera composers in this period were: in Colombia, Augusto Azzali (*Lhidiac*, 1893) and José María Ponce de León (1846–82; *Ester*; *Florinda*); in Peru, Daniel Alomias Robles (1871–1942; *Illa-Cori*) and Teodoro Valcárcel (1900–1942; *Suray-Surita*, ballet opera); in Chile, Eleodoro Ortíz de Zarate (1865–1953; *La fioraia di Lugano*, 1895, with Italian text); and in Cuba, Eduardo Sanches de Fuentes (1874–1944; *Dolorosa*, 1910; *Kabelia*, 1942).[63]

The twentieth-century national musical renaissance in Latin

[62] See Stevenson, *Music in Mexico*, chap. IV and pp. 262–64; Barros Sierra, "*Tata Vasco* y su partitura."
[63] See Chase, "Some Notes on Afro-Cuban Music and Dancing."

America did not bring forth operas comparable in either number or importance to the music produced in other forms. In Argentina, where there was more native opera than anywhere else, the Italian influence was still predominant. This is especially the case with Ettore Panizza (b. 1875), whose works include *Il fidanzato del mare* ("The Bridegroom of the Sea," 1897), *Medio evo latino* (1900; three one-act operas, each placed in a different Latin country and a different medieval century), *Aurora* (1908, commissioned for the opening of the new Teatro Colón at Buenos Aires), and *Bisanzio* (1939). Alfredo Schiuma's (b. 1885) Italian opera *Tabaré* (1925), closely patterned after Verdi's *Forza del destino*, was very successful; another highly praised work of Schiuma is *Las Vírgenes del sol* (1939).[64] A more definitely national group is represented by Felipe Boero (1884–1958) with his folk opera *El matrero* ("The Rogue," 1929). Others in this group are Pascal de Rogatis (b. 1881; *Huémac*, 1916; *La novia del hereje*, "The Heretic's Bride," 1935), Raul Espoile (b. 1889; *La ciudad roja*, "The Red City," 1938), and Enrique Casella (b. 1891; *La tapera*, "The Ruin").

In Brazil the new nationalism was evident in the works of Oscar Lorenzo Fernandez (1897–1948; *Malazarte*, 1941), Francisco Mignone (b. 1897), and Comargo Guarnieri (b. 1907; one-act comic opera *Pedro Malazarte*, 1942). Heitor Villa-Lobos (1887–1959), the most famous of recent South American composers, wrote four operas but only one (*Izaht*, composed 1912–14) was ever performed—in 1940 in a concert version and in 1958 at Rio de Janeiro on the stage.

THE BRITISH ISLES [65] AND THE UNITED STATES. Little need be added to what has already been written about English opera in the nineteenth century.[66] It was a time when serious opera was universally understood to mean Italian opera, that "exotic and irrational entertainment" which the British had been patronizing ever since the days of Dr. Johnson.[67] Almost the only English musical stage works to have any success at all in the nineteenth century were those of the light variety, by such composers as Balfe, Wallace, Benedict, and (later) Sullivan. The Carl Rosa Opera Company, beginning in 1875, commissioned a few English works, including some from Arthur Goring Thomas (1850–92), whose *Esmeralda*

[64] Ferrari Nicolay, "En torno a *Las Vírgenes*."

[65] Walker, *History of Music in England*; E. W. White, *The Rise of English Opera*.

[66] See above, p. 338.

[67] Cf. Mapleson, *Memoirs*; Carlyle, "The Opera."

and *Nadeshda* were given at London in 1883 and 1885 respectively. The current vogue for Wagner—signalized by the establishment of a London branch of the Wagner Society which published a periodical entitled *Meister* from 1888 to 1895, and furthered by the circumstance that most of the leading English composers of the generation of the 1840s and 1850s received their training in Germany—was reflected in the numerous English operas on national historical or "Nordic" legendary subjects and in a musical style obviously inspired from Bayreuth. Perhaps the most zealous English disciple of Wagner was Frederick Corder (1852–1932; *Nordisca*, 1887, and *Ossian*, 1905). Sullivan's *Ivanhoe* made a great stir at its first production in 1891 but has fortunately long since disappeared from the stage. Other operas of a German-romantic cast were produced in England (and in some instances also in Germany) by Sir Frederic Cowen (1852–1935),[68] Sir Alexander Campbell Mackenzie (1847–1935), and Sir Charles Villiers Stanford (1852–1924).[69] Cowen's *Pauline* (1876) was commissioned by the Carl Rosa company; his *Thorgrim* and two others of similar titles were produced at London in the 1890s. Mackenzie's *Colomba*, first heard at London in 1883, was later produced in Germany; his most successful opera was *The Cricket on the Hearth*, composed around 1900 and first performed in 1914. Stanford attempted to create an English *Meistersinger* in *The Canterbury Pilgrims* (1884), but was better known for his comic opera *Shamus O'Brien* (1896); his *Much Ado about Nothing* made a favorable impression at its first performance in 1901 and was revived in 1935.

The revival of Celtic literature in the late nineteenth and early twentieth centuries led to a number of operas on Celtic legends. Most notable among these was Josef Holbrooke's (1878–1958)[70] mythological Welsh trilogy *The Cauldron of Anwen*, broadly conceived along Wagnerian lines and written in a neoromantic musical style strongly influenced by Wagner. Welsh subjects also attracted Joseph Parry (1841–1903), Granville Bantock (1868–1946; *Caedmar*, 1892; *The Seal Woman*, 1924), and George Lloyd (b. 1913). Scottish stories or legends were used by Hamish MacCunn (1868–1916) in *Jeanie Deans* (from Scott's *Heart of Midlothian*; performed at Edinburgh in 1894)

[68] See his memoirs, *My Art and My Friends.*
[69] On Stanford, see Fuller-Maitland, *The Music of Parry and Stanford*, chap. 9, and biography by H. P. Greene.
[70] Biography by G. Lowe (1920); see also the symposium *Josef Holbrooke* (1937).

and *Diarmid* (London, 1897), as well as in *Quentin Durward* by Alick Maclean (Newcastle-on-Tyne, 1920); and Irish subjects appear with Robert O'Dwyer's (1862–1949) *Eithne*, on a Gaelic text (Dublin, 1910), and Geoffrey Palmer's (b. 1882) *Sruth na Maoile* ("The Sea of Moyle"; Dublin, 1923).

English operetta and light opera of this period were represented by Alfred Cellier (1844–91); Edward Soloman (1853–95); George H. Clutsam (1866–1951); Sidney Jones (1861–1946; *The Geisha*, 1896); Sir Edward German (1862–1936; *Merrie England*, 1902); Ivan Caryll (1861–1921; *The Duchess of Dantzic*, 1903); Edward Naylor (1867–1934; *The Angelus*, 1909); and Hubert Bath (1883–1945; *Bubbles*, 1923). Later comic operas by English composers were Lord Berners's (1883–1950) *Carosse du Saint-Sacrement* (Paris, 1921) and Arthur Benjamin's (1893–1960) *The Devil Take Her* (1932)—both witty one-act pieces in a fluent modern style.

The early history of opera in the United States [71] is similar to that in the other nations of the Western Hemisphere. It begins in colonial times with the importation of comic operas from Europe (in this case English ballad opera instead of the Spanish zarzuela); during the nineteenth and early twentieth centuries fashion favors successively Italian opera, French grand opera, or German music drama. Tentative and unsuccessful efforts are made by native composers to imitate the musical style currently in vogue, sometimes applying it to "American" subjects, the Indians and the Puritan colonists being the two commonest sources of material for librettos. Prizes are offered and awarded; new operas by American composers are produced with fanfare, given a few performances, then shelved and forgotten. A few experimental works on a small scale are produced, but the American public shows little interest in them, preferring to hear *Il barbiere di Siviglia*, *Il Trovatore*, *Les Huguenots*, or *Die Walküre* in sumptuous settings and sung by expensive foreign stars. In a word, American opera remains, until well into the twentieth century, simply a longed-for but unrealized ideal.

It is possible that the first opera performance in the United States took place as early as 1703, but the earliest date which can yet be substantiated is 1735, when *Flora; or, Hob in the Well*, a ballad opera, was presented at Charleston, South Carolina. *The Beggar's Opera* and

---

[71] General bibliography: *Dictionary of American Biography*; histories of American music by Ritter (to 1880), Howard, and Chase; Hipsher, *American Opera*; Ewen, *Complete Book of the American Musical Theater*; memoirs by Mapleson, Gatti-Casazza; other studies by Mattfeld, Kolodin, Moore, Carson, Gagey, R. Davis.

several similar works were played in New York in 1750–51, and a like repertoire was heard in Annapolis and Upper Marlborough, Maryland, in 1752. In the same year ballad operas were given at Williamsburg, Virginia. Philadelphia followed two years later. All during the latter half of the eighteenth century there were seasons of opera, fairly regularly at New York and sporadically at other places; the total number in proportion to the population was actually greater than at any period since. Most of the works so presented were English comic operas (Shield, Storace, Dibdin, and others), but there were also a few French opéras comiques (Grétry, Monsigny, Philidor), usually in translation and with the music more or less extensively altered and adapted by English and American arrangers, besides many pantomimes and ballets. French opera, both grand and comic, flourished at New Orleans from 1791 until the Civil War and even afterwards. The first season of regular Italian opera in New York was in 1825. From that time on, the uneven career of foreign opera in the United States becomes too complicated to follow here even in outline, the more since our chief concern is not with "opera in America" but "American opera."

The known American operas of the eighteenth century have been thoroughly studied by Oscar G. T. Sonneck.[72] Many of these were of the type of *The Beggar's Opera*, with characters and dialects appropriate to the American locale. Toward the end of the century there were imitations and adaptations of popular plays, such as *The Archers* (1796), with music by the English-born composer Benjamin Carr (1768–1831), inspired by Schiller's *Tell*; in 1797 there was a melodrama, *Ariadne Abandoned*, probably imitated from Benda. Still other "operas" were on patriotic themes, with battle scenes and allegorical tableaux. None of these pieces had continuous music; most, in fact, were merely plays with incidental songs. The composers (or arrangers) included Francis Hopkinson (1737–91; *The Temple of Minerva*, 1781), James Hewitt (1770–1827; *Tammany*, 1794), and Victor Pelissier, a native of France who came to America around 1792 and produced several plays with music, among them *Edwin and Angelina; or, The Banditti* at New York in 1796. In 1808 an "operatic melo-drame" by J. N. Barker entitled *The*

---

[72] "Early American Operas," in his *Miscellaneous Studies*, pp. 16–92. See also Sonneck's *Bibliography of Early Secular American Music*; *Early Concert Life in America*; *Early Opera in America*; and further, Wegelin, *Micah Hawkins*; idem, *Early American Plays*; Seilhamer, *History of the American Theatre*; Mates, *The American Musical Stage before 1800*.

Indian Princess was performed at Philadelphia; like the earlier examples mentioned, this was a play (the first extant one on the popular story of Pocahontas and Captain John Smith) with extensive musical numbers composed by John Bray (1782–1822), including descriptive instrumental pieces, songs, and choruses.[73] A similar work, *The Enterprise*, with music by Arthur Clifton (b. *ca.* 1784), was given at Baltimore in 1822.[74] These are but two examples of many such homemade semi-operatic entertainments that dot the history of the American stage in the early part of the nineteenth century.

The first publicly performed opera with continuous music by a native American composer was *Leonora* by William Henry Fry (1813–64),[75] given at Philadelphia in 1845 and in a revised version at New York in 1858—a work of considerable competence and musical interest, modeled on the styles of Donizetti and Meyerbeer. Fry's next opera, *Notre-Dame de Paris*, was given at Philadelphia in 1864. Another American composer of this period was George Frederick Bristow (1825–98), whose *Rip Van Winkle* (New York, 1855) was arranged from Irving's tale with added love scenes and other episodes. This opera has some spoken dialogue; the music is conventional and undistinguished, a lame imitation of the fashionable European light-opera style.

Of the many German-descended or German-trained American composers in the later nineteenth century, the most important in the field of opera was Walter Damrosch (1862–1950),[76] whose first success with *The Scarlet Letter* (1896) was hardly equaled by his two later works, *Cyrano* (1913) and *The Man without a Country* (1937). Damrosch's music is pleasantly put together and technically well fashioned, but does not depart from the style of late nineteenth-century German romanticism. A rather more original score, though one still strongly suggestive of Wagner, is John Knowles Paine's (1839–1906) *Azara*, published in 1901 but performed only in concert version (1907). The operas of George Whitefield Chadwick (1854–1931)[77] attracted little attention outside his native Boston, but those of his pupils Converse, Hadley, and Parker (see below, p. 533) were more widely recognized.

[73] See Hitchcock, "An Early American Melodrama."
[74] Gettel, "Arthur Clifton's *Enterprise*."
[75] Biography by W. T. Upton (1954).
[76] Autobiography, *My Musical Life.*
[77] Yellin, "The Life and Operatic Works of George Whitefield Chadwick."

Dependence of American composers on foreign (usually German) models in the nineteenth century, and lack of any sustained movement toward a national musical style, are painfully illustrated in the operas above mentioned and those of lesser composers of the same period. Two early opera composers of German birth were Eduard de Sobolewski (1808–72; *Mohega*, Milwaukee, 1859) and Johann Heinrich Bonawitz (1839–1917; *Ostrolenka*, Philadelphia, 1875). With this group may also be listed the Americans Frederick Grant Gleason (1848–1903; *Otho Visconti*, Chicago, 1907) and Louis Adolphe Coerne (1870–1922), of whose three operas only *Zenobia* was ever performed (at Bremen, 1905; the first opera by an American composer to be staged in Europe). To the same generation as Coerne belong Arthur Finley Nevin (1871–1943; *Poia*, Berlin, 1910; *The Daughter of the Forest*, Chicago, 1918), Joseph Carl Breil (1870–1926; *The Legend*, New York, 1919), and John Adam Hugo (1873–1945; *The Temple Dancer*, New York, 1919).

American operetta and comic opera may be traced from the works of the German-born Julius Eichberg (1824–93; *The Doctor of Alcantara*, Boston, 1862) through Dudley Buck (1839–1909; *Deseret*, New York, 1880), Edgar Stillman Kelley (1857–1944; *Puritania*, Boston, 1892), and John Philip Sousa (1854–1932; *El Capitan*, Boston, 1896) to Reginald De Koven (1859–1920; *Robin Hood*, Chicago, 1890) and Victor Herbert (1859–1924; *Babes in Toyland*, 1903). Both De Koven and Herbert attempted grand opera, but without much success (De Koven's *The Canterbury Pilgrims*, New York, 1917, and *Rip van Winkle*, Chicago, 1920; Herbert's *Natoma*, Philadelphia, 1911, and *Madeleine*, New York, 1914).

In light opera and musical comedy [78] after the First World War the two leading figures were Jerome Kern (1885–1945; *Sally*, 1920) and George Gershwin (1898–1937;[79] *Of Thee I Sing*, 1931). Each of these composers has written one distinguished work in more serious style : Kern's *Show Boat* (1927) and Gershwin's *Porgy and Bess* (1935); both works have become practically American folk operas. Notable musical comedies of later vintage were Rodgers and Hammerstein's *Oklahoma!* (1943) and *South Pacific* (1949) and Lerner and Loewe's *My Fair Lady* (1956; from Shaw's *Pygmalion*).

[78] C. Smith, *Musical Comedy in America*; S. Green, *The World of Musical Comedy*.
[79] Biographies by Armitage and Ewen; Durham, *Du Bose Heyward*.

PART 5

*THE
TWENTIETH
CENTURY*

CHAPTER 26

OLD BOTTLES AND
NEW WINE

The most radical influence on musical style in the first fifteen years of
the present century was impressionism, which originated in France with
Debussy and made itself felt nearly everywhere gradually from 1900 on.
Another source of change was the development of the post-Wagnerian
late romantic style in Germany and Austria, evident in Mahler, early
Schoenberg, and Richard Strauss. A third set of influences came from
composers who carried on with the national movements already begun
in the nineteenth century. The effects of these forces appeared in varying degrees and combinations, but underlying all change was the
conservative power of tradition, still inescapable and still respected:
progress, not revolution, was the ruling ideal, and even "advanced"
experiments soon slipped into the central current of evolution without
causing too much disturbance.

IMPRESSIONISM AND THE FRENCH SCENE. The most important
French opera of the early twentieth century was *Pelléas et Mélisande* by
Claude Debussy (1862–1918),[1] on a text by Maurice Maeterlinck. It is
Debussy's only work for the stage, with the exception of the miracle
drama *Le Martyre de Saint-Sébastien* (1911, based on D'Annunzio's
play) and an early cantata, *L'Enfant prodigue*, which has sometimes
been given in operatic form. The first sketches for *Pelléas et Mélisande*
are dated 1893, and Debussy revised the score continually. The first
performance took place at the Opéra-Comique on April 30, 1902—

[1] Biographies by Vallas and Lockspeiser; Debussy's essays, published under the
title *Monsieur Croche, anti-dilettante*; studies of *Pelléas et Mélisande* by Gilman,
Maurice Emmanuel, and Van Ackere.

"one of the three or four red-letter days in the history of our lyric stage," as Romain Rolland said.[2]

It is customary, and in the main correct, to regard *Pelléas et Mélisande* as a monument to French operatic reaction from Wagner; but this opera is at the same time a focal point of French dramatic music, gathering up many essential national traits and giving them exceptionally clear and perfect expression, though colored by the individual genius of Debussy. The personal qualities of the music are so salient that they tend to usurp attention, and it is therefore well to emphasize that *Pelléas* is characteristic not only of Debussy but also of France.

Four things have marked French opera from the beginning of its history. First is the belief that an opera is fundamentally a drama in words to which music has been added; from this doctrine comes the insistence on clear and realistic declamation of the text. Both the contemporary admiration for Lully's recitative and Rousseau's later objections to it as "mannered" came from the same interest in the text as basic to the drama and hence to the opera. In no other country has so much attention been given to this issue. The flourishing of the opéra comique with its spoken dialogue was a constant witness that the French were willing to do without music rather than let it interfere with the understanding of the words. *Pelléas et Mélisande* conforms to this ideal. It is one of the rare instances of a long play, not expressly made for music, being turned into an opera with practically no rearranging.[3] In most places the music is no more than an iridescent veil covering the text : the orchestral background is shadowy, evanescent, almost a suggestion of sound rather than sound itself; and the voice part, with its independence of the bar line, narrow range, small intervals, and frequent chanting on one tone, adheres as closely as possible to the melody of French speech. Only in a few places, as in Mélisande's song at the beginning of Act III or in the love duet in Act IV, scene 4, does the melody become really lyric. How typical this narrow melodic line is of French music may be realized by comparing the contours of French folk-song melodies with those of German or English folk songs, the

---

[2] *Musiciens d'aujourd'hui*, essay on Debussy.

[3] The following scenes in the play are omitted in the opera : Act I, sc. 1; Act II, sc. 4; Act III, sc. 1; and Act V, sc. 1. There are many other small omissions ranging from a single phrase to a dozen lines, and numerous alterations in wording. Some words have been added : see especially Act III, sc. 1 of the opera.

instrumental themes of Saint-Saëns or César Franck with those of a German like Richard Strauss, or French nineteenth-century recitative in general with the wide-ranging arioso of Verdi or Wagner. The use of the Wagnerian type of melody with French words, such as we find in the operas of Chabrier and D'Indy (and, to a lesser extent, in Bruneau and Charpentier), was soon felt to be unnatural. In the return to a more natural declamation and in the damping of orchestral sonorities, therefore, Debussy was in accord not only with the traditional French practice but with an even more ancient ideal, that of the early Florentine founders of opera, Peri, Caccini, and Gagliano.

The second historical feature of French opera is its tendency to center the musical interest not in the continuous orchestra or in the solo aria but in the divertissements, that is, interludes in the action where music might be enjoyed without the attention being divided by the necessity of following the drama at the same time. In early French opera and through the nineteenth century the common form of divertissement was the ballet with choruses. There are no ballets in *Pelléas*, and only one quite brief chorus, but the function of the divertissement is fulfilled by the orchestral preludes and the interludes which are played for changes of scene. Here, and here only, music has the foreground and the full symphonic resources are employed. But the interludes are not independent of the action; rather, they resume in wordless and concentrated form what has just passed and by gradual transition prepare for what is to come. Thus Debussy combines the Lullian form of opera with the nineteenth-century practice of treating every detail as a means toward the central dramatic purpose.

Still another constant feature of French opera has been the deliberate choice of measured, objective, well-proportioned, and rational dramatic actions. The French have not been misled, except momentarily, either by the desire to be forceful at any cost or by the attractions of metaphysical speculation. Not that French opera is as direct and uninhibited in its approach as the Italian; but the French prefer to suggest a hidden meaning by subtle juxtaposition of facts, trusting to stimulate the imagination rather than overwhelm it with exhaustive details, as Wagner tends to do. Now the quintessence of this indirect, suggestive method in literature is found in the movement known as symbolism, of which Maeterlinck's five-act drama *Pelléas et Mélisande* (1892) is an outstanding example. The story is purposely vague and seems slight indeed when reduced to a bare summary. But the whole effect is in the manner, not the matter. As Edmund Gosse has said :

Maeterlinck is exclusively occupied in revealing, or indicating, the mystery which lies, only just out of sight, beneath the surface of ordinary life. In order to produce this effect of the mysterious he aims at an extreme simplicity of diction, and a symbolism so realistic as to be almost bare. He allows life itself to astonish us by its strangeness, by its inexplicable elements. Many of his plays are really highly pathetic records of unseen emotion; they are occupied with the spiritual adventures of souls, and the ordinary facts of time and space have no influence upon the movements of the characters. We know not who these orphan princesses, these blind persons, these pale Arthurian knights, these aged guardians of desolate castles, may be; we are not informed whence they come, nor whither they go; there is nothing concrete or circumstantial about them. Their life is intense and consistent, but it is wholly of a spiritual character; they are mysterious with the mystery of the movements of a soul.[4]

Debussy's music perfectly supports the mysterious, spiritual character of the drama, doing everything by understatement and whispered suggestion. The full orchestra is hardly ever heard outside the interludes. Instrumental doubling is avoided; solo timbres and small combinations are the rule, while the strings are often muted and divided. There are only four fortissimos in the whole score. Debussy's almost excessive "genius for good taste"[5] is apparent if we contrast the wild greeting of the lovers in the second act of *Tristan* with the meeting of Pelléas and Mélisande in Act IV (Example 110), or the touching scene of Mélisande's death in Act V with Isolde's Liebstod.

However, soft music is not of necessity better than loud music; restraint is of no artistic value unless we are made aware that there is something to be restrained. And here we come to the fourth and last quality characteristic of French opera, which Debussy carries to the ultimate degree, namely a capacity for the appreciation of the most refined and complex sensory stimuli. In the quality of its acceptances as well as of its refusals, French opera has always tended to be aristocratic. The style of musical impressionism which *Pelléas et Mélisande* exemplifies is essentially one of aristocratic sensualism, treating sounds as of primary value for themselves irrespective of accepted grammatical forms, and creating moods by reiterated minute impacts of motifs,

[4] "Maeterlinck," in *Encyclopædia Britannica* (11th ed.) XVII, 299a. Quoted by permission.
[5] Rolland, *Musiciens d'aujourd'hui.*

Pelléas et Mélisande, Act IV, sc. 4

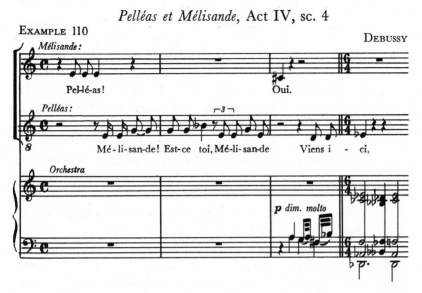

harmonies, and timbres. These elements in *Pelléas* sounded so completely unprecedented in themselves, and so completely detached from the familiar system of musical progressions, that audiences were at first bewildered; but they soon learned to associate the musical moods with those of the poetry and discovered a marvellous correspondence between the two. For as Maeterlinck's drama moved in a realm outside ordinary time and space, so Debussy's music moved in a realm outside the then known tonal system; lacking any strong formal associations within the field of music itself, his harmonies were irresistibly attracted to the similarly free images of the poet. Never was a happier marriage of music and verse. The technical methods of Debussy are familiar to all students of music and may be only briefly indicated here.[6] Modal, whole-tone, or pentatonic melodies and harmonies suggest the far-off, dreamlike character of the play. The free enchainment of seventh and ninth chords, often in organum-like parallel movement, and the blurring of tonality by complex harmonic relationships are also typical. Certain motifs recur and are transformed and harmonically varied, but they are not treated in the continuous symphonic manner of Wagner. D'Indy has well expressed their function by the term "pivot themes."[7]

[6] See further M. Emmanuel, *Pelléas et Mélisande*, pp. 97–114 *et passim*.
[7] *Richard Wagner et son influence sur l'art musical français*, p. 81.

The influence of Wagner on Debussy is felt chiefly in a negative fashion, that is, by the care Debussy took to avoid writing like Wagner. In those days it was not easy. Debussy complained of his first draft of the duet in Act IV that "the ghost of old Klingsor, alias R. Wagner, keeps peeping out." [8] But the final score cannot be said to owe anything to Wagner beyond the orchestral continuity, the use of recurring motifs, and the exclusion of all merely ornamental details; in technique, idiom, feeling, and declamation it is Debussy's own. Whatever he had learned from *Tristan* or from Mussorgsky's *Boris Godunov*, from Massenet, Grieg, or from oriental music had been completely assimilated. So peculiarly was the musical style fitted to Maeterlinck's drama that it is no wonder Debussy was never able to find another suitable libretto. *Pelléas et Mélisande*, like *Fidelio*, remains an isolated masterpiece of its composer in the field of opera.

The next notable French opera of the twentieth century was Paul Dukas's (1865–1935) [9] *Ariane et Barbe-Bleue* ("Ariadne and Blue-beard," 1907)—like *Pelléas*, the composer's only opera and likewise on a symbolist drama by Maeterlinck. The influence of Debussy is apparent in the declamation and in some details of the harmony, but the recitative is less supple and poetic than Debussy's. The orchestration is sonorous, using the brasses with brilliant effect, and the musical style on the whole is anything but impressionistic. Dukas was a composer of great technical attainment whose strong point was the development of ideas in large symphonic forms. Unfortunately, his themes are too often undistinguished in themselves, and their development marked less by inspiration than by system and perseverance; for example, the constant practice of repeating the exposition of a theme immediately in a new key (compare the exposition in the first movement of César Franck's symphony) becomes almost a mannerism. Dukas's harmony is subtle, but here again one sometimes feels the absence of any compelling musical or dramatic reason for some of his complicated chord progressions. Another defect is the excessive reliance on the augmented triad in association with the whole-tone scale, a device which has lost the attraction of novelty since 1907. So much must be stated by way of negative criticism of *Ariane et Barbe-Bleue*; on the other hand, its many excellences must be empha-

---

[8] Letter to Chausson, quoted in Abraham, *A Hundred Years of Music*, p. 278.

[9] Studies by Samazeuilh and Favre; special Dukas number of RM, May–June, 1936.

sized. The work is less an opera than a huge symphony with the addition of choruses (essential to the drama, not mere embellishments) and solo voices. Cyclical recurrence and transformation of themes are used to create an architectural structure of grand proportions. The large coda that forms the end of Act III is particularly impressive, summing up with Beethovenian finality all the principal themes of the opera and rounding off the whole with the theme which was first heard in the opening measures of the prelude to Act I. Among the many fine details of the score is the song of the "five daughters of Orlamonde," a folk-songlike melody from which many of the motifs of the opera are derived (Example 111). Altogether, *Ariane et Barbe-Bleue* is the most important French lyric drama of the early twentieth century next to *Pelléas et Mélisande*—important, that is, if measured in terms of artistic qualities rather than popular following. It is none the less significant musically for lacking those traits that made the success of Massenet and Charpentier.

Several more operas of this period merit special mention, each being in its own way a distinctive contribution. Déodat de Séverac's (1873–1921) [10] *Cœur du moulin* ("The Heart of the Mill," 1909), a simple and poignant love story in a pastoral setting, has a musical score in which the influence of Debussy is modified by an original gift for direct, spontaneous expression and a charming regional flavor of southern France, evident especially in the choruses. Although its individual features were acclaimed by critics, *Le Cœur du moulin* has not had any popular success. Better known are the two operas of Maurice Ravel (1875–1937).[11] *L'Heure espagnole* ("The Spanish Hour," 1911), a one-act opera buffa based on the comedy of Franc-Nohain, is a tour de force of rhythm and orchestration, varied and witty in declamation, with a libretto in which the art of the *double-entendre* is carried to a height worthy of Favart. The vocal lines are suggestive of Richard Strauss, while under them the orchestra carries on a suite of Spanish dances ending with a mock-grand "scena and habañera." The scene being laid in a clockmaker's shop gives occasion for many charming and clever sound effects, among which the cuckoo motif is, of course, prominent. The strength of this opera is in just those qualities which Dukas's *Ariane*

[10] Biography by B. Selva (1930).
[11] Roland-Manuel, *Maurice Ravel et son œuvre dramatique*; special numbers of RM (April, 1925; December, 1938).

Ariane et Barbe-Bleue, Act I

EXAMPLE 111

DUKAS

lacks, namely piquant details and a sense of lightness, gaiety, and improvisation. Ravel's "lyrical fantasy" *L'Enfant et les sortilèges* ("The Child and the Sorceries"), on a libretto by Colette, was first performed at Monte Carlo in 1925. It is a charming score, one worthy of the composer of *Ma Mère l'Oye*, lighter in texture than *L'Heure espagnole* but equally rich in ingenious orchestral and vocal effects.

Le Pays ("The Country," 1912), by J. Guy Ropartz (1864–1955),[12] is a soundly dramatic and well-proportioned score with symphonic treatment of the orchestra, original in inspiration and evidencing the sound classical training its composer received from César Franck. One can detect in it a modified Wagnerianism in the melody and harmony, as well as the then fashionable obsession with the sound of the augmented fifth chord. A special position must be assigned to the operas of Gabriel-Urbain Fauré (1845–1924),[13] the most important of which are *Prométhée* (1900) and *Pénélope* (1913). The latter particularly is a beautiful example of the composer's exquisite harmonic style, which lends to the classical subject matter an appropriate atmosphere of repose and remoteness, evoking the feeling of the antique world as no more common idiom could. From the viewpoint of theatrical effectiveness, *Pénélope* is perhaps too refined; the slow tempo of the action (in Acts I and II especially) emphasizes the statuesque quality which is both the greatest musical beauty and the most serious dramatic weakness of this opera.

In sum, the dominant tendency of late nineteenth- and early twentieth-century French opera was idealistic; the noble, if somewhat vague, striving of *Fervaal* and *L'Etranger*, the mood of meditation on destiny in *Pelléas* and *Ariane*, the naïve religious faith of *Le Jongleur de Notre Dame*, the moral earnestness of *Le Cœur du moulin* and *Le Pays*, the serene, contemplative beauty of *Pénélope*—all show this. Even the so-called naturalistic operas of Bruneau and Charpentier used realism largely as a means of calling forth idealistic sentiment. Thus motivated, composers sought to bring into the theatre the finest and most comprehensive resources of a highly developed musical art—resources enriched after 1900 by the new techniques of impressionism—aspiring toward universality of expression, freely using any and all means to which they found themselves attracted. Viewed from a later age, theirs seems an

[12] Biographies by Lamy (1948) and Kornprobst (1949).
[13] Biographies by Koechlin and N. Suckling; special number of RM (October, 1922).

art of leisure and luxury, such as is possible only in a time of prosperity and peace. But leisure gave time for the unfolding of ideals, while luxury provided the material means for their realization on a scale which we have not seen since and probably shall not in the near future.

Among the minor composers of serious opera in this period were Gabriel Pierné (1863–1937; *La Fille de Tabarin*, 1901), Alexandre Georges (1850–1938; *Charlotte Corday*, 1901), Xavier Leroux (1863–1919; *La Reine Fiamette*, 1903, influenced by Puccini and Massenet; *Le Chemineau*, 1907), Henri Février (1875–1957; *Monna Vanna*, 1909), and Jean Noguès (1875–1932), whose *Quo Vadis* (1909) is a mild blend of Massenet and Fauré. Distinguished especially for works in a lighter vein were the Venezuelan-French Reynaldo Hahn (1875–1947; *La Carmélite*, 1902) and Camille Erlanger (1863–1919; *Le Juif polonais*, 1900; *Aphrodite*, 1906). More individual in style was Raoul Laparra (1876–1943) with his operas on Spanish subjects, the most popular being *La Habanera* (1908) and *L'Illustre Fregona* (1931). The music of Ernest Bloch's (1880–1959) *Macbeth* (1910), strongly influenced by Debussy, has declamatory vocal lines, much parallelism in the orchestral texture, and a monotonously constant use of the augmented 5–7 chord, which seems to have fascinated opera composers of this period as much as the diminished seventh had fascinated their predecessors a hundred years earlier. *Macbeth* was severely criticized on account of its "modernistic" harmonies and rhythms and soon dropped out of the repertoire, but has been occasionally revived. Sylvio Lazzari (1857–1944) with *La Lépreuse* (1912) and Louis Aubert (b. 1877) with *La Forêt bleue* (Geneva, 1913) had no great success, but Henri Rabaud's (1873–1949) oriental opéra comique *Mârouf, savetier de Caire* ("Marouf, Cobbler of Cairo," 1914), a witty, brilliantly scored work, has become a favorite both in Paris and abroad. It is undoubtedly one of the finest modern comic operas, a worthy descendant of the long French line of works in this style and on similar subjects. Another oriental opera was Gabriel Dupont's (1878–1914) *Antar*, finished in 1914 but not performed until 1921. The Belgian Albert Dupuis (b. 1877; *La Passion*, Monte Carlo, 1916) in his operas reverted to the style of Massenet.

It must be remembered that throughout the period we have been considering the semidramatic form of the ballet occupied much of the attention of French composers. Lalo's *Namouna* (1882) never received the recognition it merited, but in the early twentieth century the performances of such works as Florent Schmitt's mimodrama *La Tragédie de Salomé* (1907), Ravel's *Daphnis et Chloé* (1912), and Stravinsky's *Firebird, Petrouchka*, and *The Ceremonial of Spring* (1910, 1911, and 1913 respectively) were important musical events.

Impressionism made its mark in Germany with Franz Schreker

(1878–1934),[14] whose first opera, Der ferne Klang ("The Distant Tone"), was composed in 1903–9, though not performed until 1912. The first notable feature of Schreker's music is the harmony, which basically is like that of Debussy (seventh and ninth chords as consonant units; free use, singly or in combination, of chromatic alteration, pedal points, and organum-like parallel progressions; treatment of sensuous effect as an end in itself). But it is the Debussy of L'Après-midi, the Nocturnes, and La Mer rather than of the subdued Pelléas et Mélisande who is Schreker's model. His texture is exceedingly full, often having complicated decorative rhythmic motifs within the beat, or making use of several separated tone masses (as in the opening of Act II of Der ferne Klang). All this is, of course, supported by an orchestration of corresponding richness, in which harps, muted strings and horns, glissandi, tremolos, and similar effects are prominent. The feeling of tone impressions (Klang) in Schreker's operas is so strong as to lead naturally to a symbolism in which sounds become the embodiment of ideal, mystic forces. There are other signs of the late romantic period as well: occasional Straussian storm and stress in the harmony, reminiscences of Verdi in a melodic line, and traces of Puccini's declamation and orchestral treatment.

The whole, nevertheless, is not mere patchwork but an original and very effective theatrical style which made Schreker, during the years of the First World War and the decade after, one of the most highly regarded opera composers in Germany. His librettos (written by himself) have been criticized for awkwardness of language and for their preoccupation with sex in exaggerated, pathological forms. Die Gezeichneten ("The Stigmatized Ones," 1918), a Renaissance subject, has this feature to an extreme degree. His chief work, Der Schatzgräber ("The Treasure Digger," 1920), shows a tendency toward more triadic harmony, with much parallelism, and a somewhat less complicated texture. The leitmotif system is much less prominent here than in his earlier works, and in Irrelohe (1924) it is abandoned altogether. Meanwhile Das Spielwerk und die Prinzessin ("The Playthings and the Princess"), considerably revised in 1920 from the original version of 1913, experimented with pandiatonicism and other new harmonic devices.

THE ITALIAN TRADITIONS. Opera in Italy during the early 1900s

[14] Studies by Bekker, Kapp, and R. S. Hoffmann; also numerous articles in Anbruch (see especially Jahrg. II, VI, X).

continued without any noticeable break along the lines already drawn before the turn of the century. The leading composer at this time was Puccini, whose work has already been dealt with.[15] Along with the passing of the fashion for verismo, more and more Italian composers began to take interest in other forms of composition as well as opera, and to become more susceptible to the influence of current tendencies from abroad. It was a period of internationalism, even a certain amount of eclecticism. After Wagner came Strauss, Debussy, and Stravinsky in turn to stamp their impress, more or less distinctly, on Italian composers. Interest was aroused in symphonic and chamber music, as evidenced in the output of such men as Giuseppe Martucci (1856–1909) and Giovanni Sgambati (1841–1914), while an important renewal of church music was led by Don Lorenzo Perosi (1872–1956) and Enrico Bossi (1861–1925).

Aside from the opera composers already mentioned, three names deserve particular notice in the early twentieth-century period. A quite popular figure was the German-Italian Ermanno Wolf-Ferrari (1876–1948),[16] whose special talent was for comedy on librettos either adapted from the eighteenth-century Goldoni or of a similar type. These include *Le donne curiose* ("The Curious Ladies," Munich, 1903) and *Il segreto di Susanna* ("The Secret of Suzanne," Munich, 1909), his most famous work. His only tragic opera, an experiment with some of the methods of verismo, was *I gioielli della Madonna* ("The Jewels of the Madonna," Berlin, 1911), a work strongly suggestive of Donizetti with modern trimmings in harmony and rhythm. The Serenade in Act II, perhaps the best-known number in the opera, is a good illustration of the vivacity and rather superficial harmonic cleverness of the style. One of the last composers of the verismo school, whose work is full of the old traditional Italian opera devices, was Mascagni's pupil Riccardo Zandonai (1883–1944);[17] his most important opera is *Francesca da Rimini* (1914), based on D'Annunzio's tragedy of the same name, a smoothly contrived score with a pleasant tincture of late romantic harmony.

The decline of verismo and the effort to combine some of its features with the neoromantic or exotic type of opera found in Puccini, Giordano, and others is one symptom of a new spirit in Italian musical life.

[15] See above, pp. 441–45.

[16] Biographies by De Rensis and Grisson; Pfannkuch, "Das Opernschaffen Ermanno Wolf-Ferraris."

[17] Bonajuti Tarquini, *Riccardo Zandonai, nel ricordo dei suoi intimi.*

Particular evidence is found in the operas of Italo Montemezzi (1875–1952),[18] especially *L'amore dei tre rè* ("The Love of the Three Kings," 1913) and *La nave* ("The Ship," 1918), where the influence of both Wagner and Debussy is blended with a native Italian lyricism to produce music sound in workmanship, rich in instrumental color, conservative in idiom though not merely imitative, and of enduring beauty. *L'amore dei tre rè* is one of the best Italian tragic operas since Verdi's *Otello*. Notable is the refinement of style : chromaticism is handled with intelligence and restraint, intensifying the expression of feeling by the very refusal to dwell on obvious tricks of theatrical effect. There are memorable moments of classic breadth, as at the end of the love duet in Act II (Example 112). The voice line is an admirable adjustment of vocal melody to a continuous symphonic texture; recurring motifs and a carefully worked out key scheme make a formal whole of satisfying proportions. Altogether this opera, with its night-shrouded castle, its lovers swooning in sensual ecstasy, and the tragic figure of the blind Archibaldo, with its music which seems from beginning to end one low cry of voluptuous pain, of delicately scented agony and hopeless fatalism, is an appropriate work with which to close our contemplation of the course of Italian opera at the end of the romantic period : the ripe fruit of a dying age, the sunset of a long and glorious day.

Some less well-known Italian composers of opera in the twentieth century may be mentioned here. Ottorino Respighi (1879–1936),[19] especially noted for his symphonic poems, wrote a number of operas in a neoromantic idiom strongly influenced by impressionism : the comic colorful *Belfagor* (1923), *La campana sommersa* ("The Sunken Bell," 1927), the spectacular biblical ballet *Belkis* (1930), the mystery play *Maria Egiziaca* (1932), and *La fiamma* ("The Flame," 1934), with a sumptuous orchestral texture. Riccardo Pick-Mangiagalli (1882–1949) had some operas performed successfully at Rome, and his *Ospite inatteso* ("The Unexpected Guest," 1931) was the first opera to have a world premiere by radio. The operas of Felice Lattuada (1882–1962) were conventional in the main. Operas by Mario Castelnuovo-Tedesco (b. 1895) include *La mandragola* (1926) and some later works in miniature style. Adriano Lualdi (b. 1885) wrote his most popular opera, *La figlia del rè* ("The King's Daughter"), in 1922. One of the most prolific Italian composers was Lodovico Rocca (b. 1895), whose works include *Il dibuc* (1934) and *L'uragano* (1952).

[18] Tretti and Fiumi, eds., *Omaggio a Italo Montemezzi*.
[19] Biography by E. Respighi (1954).

EXAMPLE 112 · *L'amore dei tre rè*, Act II · MONTEMEZZI

While the Wagnerian movement found some echo in Italy, the influence of verismo in turn was felt in Germany. Its methods are evident in *Tiefland* ("The Lowlands," 1903) by Eugen d'Albert (1864–1932),[20] first produced at Prague in 1903, the most successful of this composer's twenty operas. *Tiefland* is a brutally realistic drama in an effective musical setting that combines Italian-style recitative with Wagnerian harmonies and recurrent motifs in the manner of Puccini. Another popular veristic opera in Germany was *Mona Lisa* (1915) by Max von Schillings (1868–1933),[21] murder and melodrama against a Renaissance background, with a modern frame of prologue and epilogue; the music lies strongly under the influence of Puccini in melody and instrumentation and apparently also of early Debussy in the harmony, and there is some tendency toward separate musical numbers instead of the symphonic continuity of Von Schillings's earlier operas, although recurring motifs are still present. Still another German opera of the realist school was Wolfgang von Waltershausen's (1882–1954)[22] *Oberst Chabert* (1912), written in a nonmelodic declamatory style with the dramatic situations underlined by rapidly fluctuating harmonies in which the constant alternation of two triads at the interval of an augmented fourth has the effect of a persistently recurring motif.

POST-WAGNER AND ANTI-WAGNER IN GERMAN OPERA. A certain eclectic tendency, not unlike that found in Italy, is manifest in German opera of the early twentieth century. The influences of impressionism and verismo already noted in the work of some German composers are combined with other features inherited from the post-Wagnerian and late romantic style. Representative of a more purely German tradition— though explicitly conservative and romantic—was Hans Pfitzner (1869–1949),[23] in whose works a musical language deriving fundamentally from Wagner came to be modified by more diatonic melody, asceticism of feeling, long dwelling on mystical, subjective moods, and frequently

---

[20] E. Schmitz, "Eugen d'Albert als Opernkomponist."

[21] Biography by W. Raupp.

[22] See Waltershausen's writings on music, listed in the bibliography; Sailer, "Waltershausen und die Oper."

[23] Biographies and studies by Dent, Abendroth (1935; the basic biography), Valentin, Müller-Blattau, Rutz; Riezler, *Hans Pfitzner und die deutsche Bühne*; Halusa, "Pfitzners musikdramatisches Schaffen"; Bahle, *Hans Pfitzner und der geniale Mensch*; studies of separate operas by R. Louis (*Die Rose vom Liebesgarten*, 1901), Hirtler, and Berrsche (*Der arme Heinrich*). See also Pfitzner's writings listed in the bibliography.

dissonant contrapuntal texture with long-breathed melodic lines (Example 113). Pfitzner's *Armer Heinrich* of 1896 had a pronounced

Palestrina, Prelude

success, surpassed only by that of his masterpiece, the "musical legend" *Palestrina* in 1917. The latter is a version of Baini's romantic but unfounded story of the way Palestrina "rescued" polyphonic church music by composing his "Pope Marcellus" Mass for the Council of Trent;

musical motifs from the Mass are incorporated in Pfitzner's score. It does not require any great penetration to perceive that Pfitzner (who in this one instance was his own librettist) has treated the legend with reference to his own position as defender of the ancient, good tradition of music against the modernists and Philistines. This implication, not unrelated to the dramatic idea of Wagner's *Meistersinger*, was doubtless responsible in part for the favor *Palestrina* enjoyed for a time with the German public, a favor which died out after a couple of decades and which never found much echo in other countries. A more advanced harmonic style and partial return to the form of separate numbers was apparent in Pfitzner's later opera, *Das Herz* ("The Heart," 1931).

Contemporary with Pfitzner was the Viennese Alexander von Zemlinsky (1872–1942); [24] of the six operas of his that were produced between 1897 and 1933 the most successful was *Es war einmal* ("Once upon a Time," 1900), but his influence has also been felt through the work of two of his distinguished pupils, Arnold Schoenberg and Erich Korngold. Another Viennese composer of this generation was Franz Schmidt (1874–1939),[25] a pupil of Bruckner and esteemed in Austria as a symphonist, who had some success with the first of his two operas, *Notre Dame* (composed 1902–4, first performed 1914). Other contemporaries whose work for the theatre was mostly conservative in musical style include: Paul Graener (1872–1944; *Friedemann Bach*, 1931), Max Ettinger (1874–1951; *Frühlings Erwachen*, 1928), Joseph Haas [26] (1879–1960; *Tobias Wunderlich*, 1937), Julius Weismann (1879–1950; *Leonce und Lena*, 1925), Walter Braunfels (1882–1954; *Die Vögel*, 1920), and Paul von Klenau (1883–1946; *Rembrandt van Rijn*, 1937).

A solitary and enigmatic figure in music of the early twentieth century was Ferruccio Busoni (1866–1924).[27] Of mixed German and Italian ancestry, one of the foremost concert pianists of his day, a scholar and philosopher, he reminds one of an artist of the Renaissance in the breadth of his outlook. His aesthetic views, which involved rejection of Wagner and adherence to the operatic ideals of Mozart, made him an important early protagonist of the neoclassic movement. His first opera, *Die Brautwahl* ("The Bridal Choice," 1912), revives the classical principle of set numbers, though the libretto and music still retain many

[24] See special number of *Der Auftakt* (Prague, 1921).
[25] Biography by A. Liess (1951).
[26] Biography by K. Laux (1954).
[27] Biographies by Dent (1933), Guerrini (1944), and Giazotto (1947); Bekker, *Klang und Eros*; Gatti, "The Stage Works of Ferruccio Busoni"; writings of Busoni and "Nota bio-bibliografica."

romantic traits. The one-act *Arlecchino* (1917) is an ironical comedy making use of the old commedia dell' arte masks and including some spoken dialogue. The score of *Turandot* (two acts; first performed on the same program with *Arlecchino*) was arranged from earlier incidental music to Gozzi's play. *Doktor Faust*, completed by Busoni's disciple Philipp Jarnach and produced posthumously in 1925, is the composer's principal opera and one of the most significant musical treatments of this subject in the twentieth century. Busoni (here as always his own librettist) went back not to Goethe but to the medieval version of the Faust legend, adapting it to his own mystical and symbolical intentions. The score is cast in large musical forms, skillfully using both conventional set numbers and complex polyphony, the whole worked out with uncompromising idealism and making exceptional demands on an audience's attention. It may be true, as Professor Dent has said, that "one cannot apply to *Doctor Faust* the ordinary standards of operatic criticism. It moves on a plane of spiritual experience far beyond that of even the greatest of musical works for the stage";[28] but, like many another high plane of "spiritual experience," this one is sometimes dull for outsiders. Despite moments of dramatic force and musical beauty, the general style of *Doktor Faust* is so compressed, so complex in both its dramatic and harmonic implications, and so rooted fundamentally in the late German romantic sound-world that the opera is unlikely ever to become a permanent work in the repertoire.

We have traced hitherto the different movements in Germany that may be understood as being, in one way or another, attempts to break away from the potent spell of Wagner : in the fairy-tale opera, by the choice of a different kind of subject matter while retaining to varying degrees the Wagnerian idiom, the technique of leitmotifs, and the general idea of the Gesamtkunstwerk; in the Volksoper, by radical simplicity of both subject matter and music; in the "realistic" operas of D'Albert and others, by returning to dramas of uncomplicated human passion without metaphysical implications in a musical style influenced by the methods of Italian verismo; and in the operas of some other composers (notably Schreker), by infusing into the Wagnerian form some of the methods of French impressionism. After the first decade of the twentieth century there becomes evident a rather general antiromantic

[28] *Ferruccio Busoni*, p. 304.

tendency, evidenced by changing ideals as to both the form and the content of opera : in form, a movement of return to the eighteenth-century principle of separate musical numbers, with the device of recurring motifs playing only a subordinate role (as in the later works of Von Schillings, Pfitzner, and Schreker); in content, by a return to purely human drama—historical or other—and a musical idiom emphasizing melody, clarity of texture, basically diatonic harmony, and formal structure governed by purely musical principles. This general neoclassic tendency is of course subject to all sorts of exceptions and modifications in individual cases, and after 1920 it finds itself in competition with more radical movements which it will be our business to describe in the next chapter; nevertheless, it persists until well along in the twentieth century. Its chief representative is Richard Strauss (1864–1949),[29] whose work is an epitome of the movement from post-Wagner to anti-Wagner in Germany.

Strauss had already produced two operas—*Guntram* (1894) and *Feuersnot* (1901)—and most of his symphonic poems before he attracted the horrified attention of the entire operatic world with *Salome* in 1905. Oscar Wilde's drama, originally written in French, translated into German by Hedwig Lachmann, and then considerably compressed and revised by Strauss himself, formed the libretto. Its peculiar blend of oriental, sensuous, decadent luxuriance was perfectly captured in the music, which describes the necrophilic ecstasy of Salome as vividly as Wagner had once described the agonies of the suffering Amfortas. The final scene of *Salome* was one of the first—perhaps the very first—in which the suggestive power of music had been successfully applied to such a subject, yet it is only one instance of Strauss's amazing skill in musical characterization. Formally, *Salome* is in the Wagnerian style : the orchestra is dominant, the music is continuous throughout the one act, there is a system of leitmotifs, the texture is uniformly thick and polyphonic, the rhythms are nonperiodic, and the voice parts are mostly of an arioso character. Strauss's mastery of orchestral effect, the individuality and variety of his instrumental coloring, are as evident in the operas as in the symphonic poems. His harmony, which sounded so daring and dissonant at the turn of the century, is no longer novel, but

[29] Bibliography: Krause, *Richard Strauss: Gestalt und Werk*; Trenner, ed., *Richard Strauss: Dokumente seines Lebens und Schaffens*; R. Strauss, *Betrachtungen und Erinnerungen*; correspondence (see bibliography); Schuh, *Über Opern von Richard Strauss*.

just for this reason we can now better appreciate how appropriate it is for the dramatic purposes. Technically it may be regarded as a continuation of Wagner, with progressions generally conditioned by chromatic voice leading but less bound up with romantic expressiveness, more remote and sudden in its modulations, and much more dissonant. It it a kind of harmony which assumes a familiarity with Wagner on the listener's part, and which as it were telescopes the characteristic Wagner progressions in a manner analogous to the treatment of a fugue subject in stretto. (We have already noticed a similar evolution from the Verdi melodic style in Puccini's operas.) The melodies in *Salome* are of two sorts : either declamatory, with many unusual intervals rising out of the harmonic progressions, or else long-sustained, impassioned outpourings, marked by a very wide range and wide leaps. Strauss has managed to combine the characteristics of the music drama with the striking dramatic quality of Italian verismo and also to introduce some features of grand opera (for example, the Dance of the Seven Veils).

The characteristics of *Salome* are pushed even further in *Elektra* (1909), the first opera Strauss wrote in collaboration with his principal librettist, the Austrian poet and dramatist Hugo von Hofmannsthal (1874–1929). In *Elektra* the central passion is the heroine's insane thirst for vengeance on the murderers of her father, and here again Strauss has matched the somber horrors of the libretto with music of fearful dissonance, lurid melodramatic power, and a harmonic idiom in which for long stretches polytonality is the normal state. Perhaps the most noticeable feature of the score is the contrast between this dissonant idiom and the occasional stretches of lush, late-romantic sentimentality, with cloying sevenths, ninths, chromatic alterations, and suspensions. Whatever the composer's intentions may have been, these portions give the final dreadful touch of spiritual abnormality to the whole action; they are like something familiar suddenly seen in a ghastly, strange light.

With *Der Rosenkavalier* ("The Rose-Bearer," 1911), a "comedy for music," Strauss and Hofmannsthal achieved an enduring success not equaled by any of their other joint creations. This romantic comedy of Viennese life around the time of Maria Theresa—the mid-eighteenth century—forms a perfect libretto, with humor, farce, sentiment, swiftly moving action, variety of scenes, and superb characterizations. The music is as varied as the drama. In some portions it is no less complex (though considerably less dissonant) than that of *Salome* and *Elektra*.

The erotic quality of the love music in the first part of Act I is equal to Strauss's best in this vein. For the most part, however, the style of *Der Rosenkavalier* is more simple and tuneful than that of his earlier operas. The famous waltzes are anachronistic; the waltzes of Schubert, Lanner, and J. Strauss, which these imitate, were not, of course, a feature of eighteenth-century Vienna. But this is of little importance, and it is still less important that Strauss has seen fit to decorate the waltz themes with some of his own harmonic twists. The best musical characterizations are those of the Princess, a figure of mingled humor, wisdom, and pathos, and her country cousin Baron Ochs, a type of comic boor drawn, at Strauss's insistence, rather more coarsely than Hofmannsthal would have preferred. Sophie and Octavian, the young lovers, are by comparison colorless; their music is that of situations and sentiment rather than of personalities, and any possible realism in their relationship is prevented by making Octavian's part a *Hosenrolle*, a "trouser role"— that is, a man's part sung by a woman, like Mozart's Cherubino. The scene of their first meeting and the presentation of the silver rose thus moves in an atmosphere of ideal, magical, passionless beauty, unsurpassed anywhere in the whole realm of opera. It is remarkable that here Strauss writes in an almost purely diatonic idiom, even emphasizing the triads by outlining them in the melodies; one of the composer's happiest inspirations, the theme of the silver rose (high, dissonant appoggiatura triads with celesta, flutes, harps, and three solo violins), tinkles against this background.

The ensembles of *Der Rosenkavalier* are virtuoso creations, particularly the scene of the levee in Act I : a dissolution and at the same time an apotheosis of the eighteenth-century opera buffa ensemble, bringing together all the elements of this form in seeming confusion and yet with a curious illusion of realism; the introduction of a stylized Italian tenor aria, a veritable interpolated number in this scene, is accomplished in the spirit of sporting with the formal technique. The first two-thirds of Act III forms another long ensemble of broad farcical nature with elements of the old Viennese popular theatre, laid on musically with a rather heavy hand, but of an irresistible comic dash which can only be compared to the ending of the second act of *Die Meistersinger* or the finale of *Falstaff*. After all this hurly-burly follows one of those transformations of mood which are so characteristic of *Der Rosenkavalier*. The trio for three soprano voices (Sophie, the Princess,

Octavian) is another superlative number, a melting baroque texture of long-spun, interweaving lines above simple diatonic harmonies. The long decrescendo continues: the last song is a duet in G major, two strophes of a lyric melody in thirds and sixths, in the style of the old German Singspiel. The themes of the silver rose and the lovers' first meeting sound once more. The opera closes with a pantomime of the Princess's little Negro pageboy, to the same music which was heard at his first appearance near the beginning of Act I. This masterly finale was largely shaped by Strauss's requirements. Hofmannsthal at one time feared it would be feeble in effect, but Strauss wrote: "It is at the conclusion that a musician, if he has any ideas at all, can achieve his best and supreme effects—so you may safely leave this for me to judge . . . from the Baron's exit onwards, I'll *guarantee* that, provided you undertake to guarantee the rest of the work." [30]

Der Rosenkavalier was hardly finished before Strausss and Hofmannsthal were at work on their next collaborative effort, *Ariadne auf Naxos* (1912), designed as a pendant to a German version of Molière's *Bourgeois Gentilhomme*. This one-act piece is a profoundly poetic, sensitive treatment of the myth of Ariadne and Bacchus, in form and spirit suggesting the pastorales and ballets of Lully and Molière, which were likewise usually enclosed within a comedy;[31] and like those models, it introduces comic-satirical elements through personages borrowed from the Italian commedia dell' arte. Strauss's music continues the trend toward diatonicism and simplicity already evident in *Der Rosenkavalier*; harmonically, it starts from the point which the composer had reached in the silver-rose scene of the earlier opera and becomes progressively less and less chromatic. The trio in scene 3 for three sopranos is similar to the trio in the last act of *Der Rosenkavalier* and is likewise followed by a simple folklike song. A new element is the light, swift, parlando style of the comic scenes and of the prologue, which was added in 1916 when *Ariadne* was taken out of its original setting in the Molière play. One role, that of Zerbinetta, is especially written for a high coloratura soprano. The leitmotif technique is used to a slight extent, but the

[30] Letter of September 12(?), 1910. Quoted by permission from E. Oser's translation in *A Working Friendship*, pp. 67–68.

[31] The analogy will be seen most clearly by comparison with the following works of Molière: *La Princesse d'Elide* (1664), *Psyché* (a *tragédie–ballet*, 1671), the pastorale in *La Comtesse d'Escarbagnas* (1671), and the pastoral *intermèdes* in *Georges Dandin* (1668) and *Le Malade imaginaire* (1673), music by M. A. Charpentier.

Sketch by Leo Pasetti for the production of Strauss's *Salome* at Munich in 1923   (*Munich, Theatermuseum*)

Scene from the original production of Orff's *Oedipus der Tyrann* (Stuttgart, 1959); design by Caspar Neher, staging by Günther Rennert

orchestra (only thirty-six players) is subordinated to the voices, and there is a distinct tendency toward division into separate numbers.

Ariadne auf Naxos was the definitive stage of Strauss's conversion to a Mozartean style, an intimate opera in which the musical idiom is refined to classic purity in comparison with the earlier works. From this point on, Strauss remained musically conservative. He had summed up in his own career the transition from Wagnerian music drama to the new anti-Wagnerian opera. But the flame of inspiration no longer burned quite so steadily; moreover, Strauss's later operas, while no less perfect in construction and technical realization than his earlier ones, fell coldly on the ears of a changed postwar world, a world which could only hear his music as something out of a vanished and irrecoverable past. This historical misfortune has deprived the opera-going public, especially outside Germany, of acquaintance with some works that well deserve to be better known.

One of these is *Die Frau ohne Schatten* ("The Woman without a Shadow"), composed during the years of the First World War on a libretto by Hofmannsthal based on one of his prose tales, and first performed at Vienna in 1919. *Die Frau ohne Schatten* is a weightily symbolic drama with a complex score of grandiose proportions, embodying contrasting musical styles and rich in orchestral effects. On a more intimate scale is *Intermezzo* (1924), a "middle-class comedy with symphonic interludes" on a libretto by the composer in an autobiographical vein reminiscent of the *Sinfonia domestica*, and a real virtuoso piece for the soprano. With *Die ägyptische Helena* (1928, revised version 1933) Strauss and Hofmannsthal returned, not altogether successfully, to the realm of mythology. The best of their postwar operas was the "lyrical comedy" *Arabella*, similar in atmosphere and general sound to *Der Rosenkavalier*, with a plot verging on operetta but handled with delicacy and spontaneous lyric warmth, a happy blending of Strauss's full orchestral sonorities and fine details of chamber music style. *Die schweigsame Frau* ("The Silent Woman," 1935), on a libretto by Stefan Zweig after Ben Jonson, is a comedy including some spoken dialogue, recitatives, lyric passages, and many ensembles, with a few musical quotations from older composers and Strauss himself. *Friedenstag* ("Day of Peace," 1938) is an exceptional one-act work in subject, style, and spirit. Its author, Josef Gregor, also delivered the librettos of Strauss's next two operas, both on mythological themes: *Daphne* (1938), a "bucolic tragedy," and *Die Liebe der Danae* ("The Love of Danae"), a "merry mythological tale" composed in 1938–40 but not performed until 1952.

Strauss's last opera, *Capriccio* (1942), is a one-act "conversation piece for music" on a libretto by Clemens Krauss—"no work for the public, only a fine dish for connoisseurs," the composer said. With only a pretext of a plot, *Capriccio* revolves about a discussion (which never reaches a positive conclusion) of certain "theoretical questions of art," especially the relation of words, music, and staging in opera; yet for all the lack of dramatic movement, the personages are no mere shadows, but fully drawn human characters. The scene is laid in Paris at the time of the Gluck-Piccinni quarrel, which gives Strauss occasion to quote now and then a musical phrase from operas by these two composers. *Capriccio* completes a cycle which *Ariadne* began. Appropriately to its period, the score is of a stylized rococo quality and is held throughout in the mood of chamber music. A full orchestra is required but is used for the most part only in small combinations; the sonority of the string sextet, first heard in the introduction, runs like a thread through the opera. The words are made to come clearly through the polyphonic orchestral texture,[32] being conveyed in lifelike dialogue and broadly designed ensembles; the principal aria, a number of central importance in the score, is a lyrical setting of a sonnet translated from Ronsard's *Continuation des Amours* (Paris, 1555; see Example 114). Altogether, *Capriccio* must be regarded as among the very best of Strauss's operas, the musical testament of an artist in the matured wisdom of age: in this, as in other respects, a worthy companion to Verdi's *Falstaff*.

OTHER COUNTRIES. The sources of the main stream of operatic production in the early part of the twentieth century were still the three countries Italy, France, and Germany. At the same time, the nationalist movement continued more or less vigorously in other lands, although as time went on the earlier marked national quality of the music tended to become somewhat overlaid by foreign elements and thus more nearly approach a common international style. In addition, a few composers of this period brought out operas which, while not distinctively national or otherwise outstanding, deserve to be at least mentioned.

The two principal Polish opera composers of the early twentieth century were Ludomir Różycki (1883–1953) and Karol Szymanowski

---

[32] Always an important consideration with Strauss; cf. his prefaces to this opera and *Intermezzo*.

Capriccio, sc. 6 ("The Sonnet")

EXAMPLE 114

R. STRAUSS

Allegro moderato ♩ = 108

Kein An - dres, das ich so wie dich be - gehr - te, und käm' von

(5 + 5 measures, then:)

Ve - nus mir ein An - ge - bot. Dein Au - ge beut

mir himm - lisch-sü - sse Not, und wenn ein Auf-schlag al - le

(*Example 114 continued*)

Qual ver- mehr - te, ein andrer Won-ne mir und Lust _____

_____ ge - währ - te, zwei Schlä-ge sind dann Le - ben o - der

dim.

Tod. Und trüg ich's fünf-mal-hun - dert-tau-send Jah- re,

p   *p*

(1882–1937).[33] Różycki, though regarded in Poland as a nationalist composer, had absorbed Western influences from Germany. His works include *Eros and Psyche* (1917), the comic opera *Casanova* (1923), *Beatrice Cenci* (1927), and *Madame Walewska* (composed 1945), as well as a successful ballet, *Pan Twardowski* (1921). Szymanowski, the leading Polish composer of this period, worked primarily in symphonic and choral forms and wrote only two operas. *Hagith* (composed 1912–14) was influenced in subject matter and construction by Strauss's *Elektra* and in harmony largely by the music of Ravel. Particularly important is Szymanowski's *Król Roger* ("King Roger," 1926), a monumental dramatic work on a libretto somewhat similar to Schreker's *Der ferne Klang*. The music is harmonically rich in a neoimpressionistic idiom, with national influences in the melody; the solo lines range freely from declamatory-arioso phrases to ample melodic arches. The choral writing is particularly effective; some of the choral sonorities are derived from Russian Church style, with full texture, doubling of the parts, and parallel movement of the voices (Example 115). The ballets in Act II introduce oriental motifs.

A group of composers who for the most part came to recognition only after the establishment of Polish independence in 1919 includes Henryk Melcer (1869–1928; *Marja*, 1904); Emil Mlynarski (1870-1935; *Summer Night*, 1924); Henryk Opienski (1870–1942; *Jacob the Lutenist*, 1927); Tadeusz Joteyko (1872–1932; *Zygmund August*, 1925); Felix Nowowiejski (1877–1946; *Baltic Legend*, 1924);[34] and Adam Tadeusz Wieniawski (1879–1950; *Megae*, 1912).

The most famous Hungarian opera of the twentieth century is *Duke Bluebeard's Castle* by Béla Bartók (1881–1945),[35] composed in 1911 and first performed at Budapest in 1918—"the first genuinely Hungarian and at the same time modern opera." [36] The libretto by Béla Balász, inspired by Maeterlinck's version of the ancient tale and first published in 1910 as a "mystery play," involves only two characters and

[33] On Różycki, see biography by Wieniawski; also articles by Chybiński and Różycki in bibliography. The standard biography of Szymanowski is by Łobaczewska (1950); other biographies by Jachimecki (1927) and Golachowski (1956); see also in bibliography articles by Jachimecki and Iwaszkiewicz.

[34] Kamienski, "Legenda bałtyku."

[35] Biographies by H. Stevens and S. Moreux; *Béla Bartók: A Memorial Review*; Kroó, *Bartók Béla szinpadi müvei* (the chapter on *Duke Bluebeard's Castle*, in English translation, appeared in *Studia Musicologica* I [1961] 251–340); Lendvai, "A kékszakállu herceg vára" (important musical analysis).

[36] Kroó, "Duke Bluebeard's Castle," p. 340.

EXAMPLE 115

SZYMANOWSKI

(*Example 115 continued*)

(Example 115 continued)

contains hardly any external action; the inner, symbolic drama proceeds with the opening, one after another, of the seven doors that give on the hall of Blubeard's castle. Bartók's music, like Debussy's for *Pelléas*, seems a perfect and inimitable embodiment of the mysterious text. The music flows unbrokenly throughout the single act, its continuity emphasized by recurrence of "pivot" motifs and themes. The orchestral color and harmony, impressionistic in essence but stamped everywhere with Bartók's individuality, supports a vocal line consisting for the most part of irregular declamatory phrases whose melodic and rhythmic outlines derive from Hungarian folk song (Example 116).

Equally imbued with Hungarian national feeling though far less radical in musical idiom than *Bluebeard* are the stage works of Zoltán Kodály (b. 1882),[37] which combine spoken dialogue with songs and choruses either borrowed from or composed in the style of folk music: *Háry János* (1926), on the adventures of a comic character from national folklore; the ballad opera *Székely fonó* ("The Spinning-Room," 1932, revised from the original version of 1924); and *Czinka Panna*, composed for a national centennial celebration and produced at Budapest in 1948.

A notable figure in Spanish opera of the early twentieth century was Manuel de Falla (1876–1946)[38] although, like Szymanowski, Bartók, and Kodály, he worked mainly in other forms of composition. His principal opera is the charming little marionette piece *El retablo di Maese Pedro* ("Master Peter's Puppet Show," 1923), for three singing parts and an orchestra of twenty-five players, on an episode from *Don Quixote*, using a boy soprano as narrator and in a musical style that cleverly combines archaic features with modern harmonies in an austere but appropriate texture. Falla's earlier opera, *La vida breve* ("Life Is Short"), composed in 1905 and first performed in 1913, is less notable for its dramatic qualities than for the ballets in Act II; Falla's other ballets, *El amor brujo* and *El sombrero de tres picos*, are important works in this form.

During the last twenty years of his life Falla was continually occupied with what he intended to be his masterwork, *La Atlántida*. Although this vast "scenic cantata" was left unfinished, the music was put together from the composer's sketches by his devoted pupil Ernesto Halffter (b. 1905); it is as yet uncertain how much of the music as published is

[37] Biography by Eősze.
[38] Biography by Pahissa; V. S. Viu, "The Mystery of . . . *La Atlántida*."

(*Example 116 continued*)

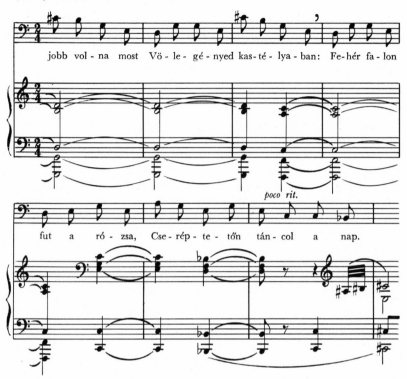

jobb vol - na most Vö - le - gé - nyed kas-té - lya - ban: Fe-hér fa - lon

fut a ró - zsa, Cse - rép - te - tőn tán - col a nap.

actually the work of Falla and how much that of Halffter. Portions of *La Atlántida* were performed in public for the first time, without staging, at Barcelona on November 24, 1961. The first stage production (with the words in Italian translation) took place at La Scala on June 18, 1962, and a concert version (incomplete) was given at New York on September 29 and 30, 1962.

The text of *La Atlántida* is taken from an epic poem (1878) by Mossén Jacinto Verdaguer. Within a framework of half-pagan, half-Christian mythology it ranges from the remote geological past over the legendary history of the Spanish peninsula, recounting the exploits of Hercules, the Gardens of the Hesperides, the opening of the Straits of Gibraltar, the destruction of Atlantis, the founding of Cadiz and Barcelona, and culminating with a prophetic vision of Columbus's voyages and the establishment of a Spanish empire in America. In form as well as in some aspects of the subject, the work is reminiscent of Milhaud's *Christophe Colomb*. *Atlántida* is a monumental combination of oratorio and opera, some three hours in length, requiring for full performance a narrator, a dozen soloists, two choruses, and a huge orchestra. The music has extraordinary variety and breadth; the style in general is markedly different from that of Falla's earlier works and has an austere, archaic grandeur (especially in the many choral portions) that recalls the spirit of the great sixteenth-century Spanish church composers.

Some other continental European composers of opera in the first part of the twentieth century will be briefly noticed here. In Spain, the disciples of Pedrell include Angel Barrios (b. 1882) and Conrado del Campo y Zabaleta (1879–1953) with a jointly composed opera, *El Avapiés* (1919; the title is the name of a quarter in Madrid), and Amadeo Vives (1871–1932), composer of the "lyric eclogue" *Maruxa* (1914) and the popular comic opera *Doña Francisquita* (1923). Joaquín Turina (1882–1949) composed the operas *Margot* (1914) and *Jardín de oriente* (1923). A notable composer of Holland was Willem Pijper (1894–1947), whose only completed opera, *Halewijn*, was given at Amsterdam in 1933. In Switzerland Othmar Schoeck (1886–1957), distinguished especially as a writer of songs, produced a number of operas, the most successful of which was *Penthesilea* (1927).

The situation in England in the early part of the twentieth century is interesting because of the contrast between the work of continentally oriented composers and the efforts of others to create a viable opera of distinctly English character. To the former group belongs the only (so far) successful woman opera composer, Dame Ethel Smyth (1858–1944).[39] Following two early operas brought out in Germany, her principal stage work, *The Wreckers*, written originally on a French libretto, was produced in a German translation (as *Strandrecht*) at Leipzig in 1906 and finally played in English at London in 1909; it has been revived there with success since 1939. Her next opera was a comedy, *The Boatswain's Mate*, which had a fair success in England; two further one-act operas appeared in 1923 and 1925.

A virtual expatriate was Frederick Delius (1862–1934);[40] born in England of German parentage, he lived most of his life abroad—first in Florida, then for a period of study in Leipzig, and from 1888 in France.

[39] Biography by C. St. John (1959); see also the composer's own writings, especially her memoirs (*Impressions That Remained*); Capell, "Dame Ethel Smyth's Operas at Covent Garden" (1923).

[40] Biography by Heseltine; Hutchings, "Delius's Operas."

Three of his six operas came to performance, all first in Germany. The best known of them, *A Village Romeo and Juliet* (1907), might from the story almost have been entitled "A Village Tristan and Isolde." It is full of lovely music in a late romantic style—rich in texture, chromatic, with long expressive lines for the solo voices and some fine choral scenes. Celtic folk-song idiom is apparent in some places, for example in Vreli's song at the opening of scene 4; the familiar orchestral selection *The Walk to the Paradise Garden* (from the end of scene 5) is typical of the style.

Among other early twentieth-century composers of serious opera in English were John Edmund Barkworth (1858–1921; *Romeo and Juliet*, 1916) and Ernest Bryson (1867–1942; *The Leper's Flute*, 1926). Philip Napier Miles (1865–1935),[41] active promoter of opera in England, composed *Westward Ho!* (1913) and *Markheim* (1924). Well constructed and worked out though conservative in musical style were the operas of Nicholas Comyn Gatty (1874–1946): *Greysteel* (1906), *Duke or Devil* (1909), the romantic Shakespearean *Tempest* (1920), and the charming fairy opera *Prince Ferelon* (1921). Sir Eugene Goossens (1893–1958) had some success with his two operas on texts by Arnold Bennett : *Judith* (1929) and *Don Juan de Mañera* (1937). Others in this period were Sir Donald Francis Tovey (1875–1940; *The Bride of Dionysus*, 1932), Colin Macleod Campbell (1890–1953; *Thais and Talmaae*, 1921), and Lawrance Arthur Collingwood (b. 1887; *Macbeth*, 1934). The only one of Albert Coates's (1882–1953) three operas to be produced in England was *Pickwick* (1936).

About 1908 Rutland Boughton (1878–1960),[42] an ardent disciple of Wagner's theories and himself a composer of frankly romantic tendencies, conceived the idea of founding an English equivalent of Bayreuth. One outcome of this project was the establishment of the Glastonbury Festival in 1914 and the production there in 1916 of Boughton's *The Round Table*, designed to be the first music drama in an Arthurian tetralogy. (*The Birth of Arthur*, the prologue, had been heard earlier, with a piano substituting for the orchestra.) Boughton completed the tetralogy, but only the second number (*The Lily Maid*) was performed, in 1934, and the entire cycle still awaits production.

[41] Colles, "Philip Napier Miles."
[42] See Boughton's own writings listed in bibliography; Hurd, *Immortal Hour*; Antcliffe, "A British School of Music-Drama."

Meanwhile, the composer had achieved an unexpected success with a less ambitious but appealing opera, *The Immortal Hour* (1914).

The two leading English composers of the early twentieth century, Gustav Holst (1874–1934)[43] and Ralph Vaughan Williams (1872–1958),[44] made significant contributions to opera. Holst's *Savitri* (composed 1908, performed 1916) is a chamber opera of exquisite tenderness and simple emotion, in a musical style that suggests the Eastern setting of the story without attempting literal imitation of Hindu melodies; it contains some beautiful writing for women's chorus. Holst's principal opera, the one-act comedy *The Perfect Fool*, had successful performances at Covent Garden in 1923; the music shows the composer fully emancipated from the neo-Wagnerian tendencies of his earlier dramatic works. *At the Boar's Head* (1925) is a Shakespearean intermezzo with words from *Henry IV*, a jolly work made up largely of traditional English tunes, somewhat in the manner of ballad opera. The influence of these works is not to be reckoned so much by their outward success as by the fact that they represent the serious, original, and uncompromising efforts of a first-rank English composer in the restricted and rather thankless field of native opera. Much the same may be said of Vaughan Williams's dramatic works. *The Shepherds of the Delectable Mountains*, a pastoral episode after Bunyan, has been frequently revived in England since its first performance in 1922. *Hugh the Drover; or, Love in the Stocks* (1924) is a ballad-type opera with continuous music, containing allusions to a number of traditional tunes without direct quotation, and as thoroughly English in spirit as anything of Gilbert and Sullivan. *Sir John in Love* (1929), based on Shakespeare's *Merry Wives of Windsor*, is the composer's biggest work for the stage (four acts); the music is similar to that of *Hugh the Drover*, but more highly developed both formally and harmonically—a truly English *Falstaff* not unworthy of comparison with Verdi's Italian one. The Gilbert and Sullivan tradition lives on in *The Poisoned Kiss* (1936), a tuneful comic opera with spoken dialogue. *Riders to the Sea* (1937) is a restrained but moving setting (in one act) of Synge's play, the vocal parts in flexibly declaimed melodies and the harmonies in neomodal style with much parallel chord progression, the whole having a subdued

---

[43] Biography by Imogen Holst; *idem, The Music of Gustav Holst.*

[44] Howes, *The Music of Ralph Vaughan Williams*; see also Gordon, "Folklore in Modern English Opera."

intensity of feeling that accords well with the peculiar atmosphere of the drama.

German influences were still preponderant in American music at the beginning of the twentieth century, but by this time composers were more thoroughly trained, more ambitious, versatile, and productive, and were speaking a more authoritative musical language. Nevertheless it is worth remarking that neither of the two leading figures in this generation, Charles Martin Loeffler and Edward MacDowell, wrote an opera. The principal composers who did write for the theatre were three pupils of Chadwick : Frederick Shepherd Converse (1871–1940), Henry Hadley (1871–1937),[45] and Horatio Parker (1863–1919).[46] Converse's *The Pipe of Desire* (Boston, 1906) was the first American opera to be presented at the Metropolitan (1910)—a pleasant, tuneful score showing some influence of impressionism. Another opera, *The Sacrifice*, was given at Boston in 1911. Hadley's chief successes, in a sound conservative style, were *Azora, Daughter of Montezuma* (Chicago, 1917) and *Cleopatra's Night* (New York, 1920).

Parker's two prize-winning operas, *Mona* (New York, 1912) and *Fairyland* (Los Angeles, 1915), are regarded by many as significant American operas that have been unjustly ignored. The neglect is certainly not due to any technical shortcomings in the scores, which are sound in craftsmanship, large in conception, distinguished in musical ideas, and well planned for theatrical effect. But the librettos are sadly old-fashioned : *Mona*, a sufficiently good drama in essence, is markedly in the romantic style of its day, with a scene laid in ancient Britain and the whole obviously owing much to *Tristan und Isolde*. *Fairyland* is one of those combinations of whimsy, symbolism, and vague pantheistic aspiration such as are found in the fairy operas of Rimsky-Korsakov or in Converse's *Pipe of Desire*; and Parker's music is likewise typical of the late romantic period. *Mona* is a slightly modernized *Tristan*, with the same sort of continuous symphonic structure, system of leitmotifs, opulent harmony, chromatic melody, and avoidance of cadences that characterize its model; *Fairyland* is somewhat lighter in texture and more diatonic in harmony—Wagner leavened by a dash of

---

[45] See biography by Boardman and monograph by Berthoud.

[46] Chadwick, *Horatio Parker*; D. S. Smith, "A Study of Horatio Parker"; memoir by Semler.

late Strauss. Musically, the gravest accusation that can be made against either opera is that the same things had been said before; and it may be regretted that these works had the misfortune to come at a moment when tastes in musical matters were on the verge of radical change.

Of later American operas in conservative style, designed for full-scale production, the most successful were two by Deems Taylor (b. 1885):[47] *The King's Henchman* (New York, 1927) and *Peter Ibbetson* (New York, 1931), smooth, expert works in a mild late-romantic style with modern trimmings, well molded to the taste of that large majority of the opera-going public who are pleased with expressive melodies and sensuous harmonies that pleasantly stimulate without disturbing. Other American operas at the Metropolitan have been less enthusiastically received—for example, Richard Hageman's (b. 1882) *Caponsacchi* (1937, after a first performance in German translation at Freiburg in 1932). Among American operas that have been produced under respectable auspices and gone their way without leaving a mark may be mentioned Ernest Carter's (1866–1953) *The White Bird* (Chicago, 1924) and John Laurence Seymour's (b. 1893) prize-winning *In the Pasha's Garden* (New York, 1935).[48]

National scenes and subjects, as might be expected, have been frequently tried. Charles Wakefield Cadman's (1881–1946) *The Robin Woman (Shanewis)*, given at the Metropolitan in 1918, uses a number of authentic Indian tunes and has an attractive, if superficial, melodic vein, but is slight in substance and awkward in dramatic details. The same composer's *A Witch of Salem* (Chicago, 1926) had a fair number of performances. An important American historical opera was *Merry Mount* by Howard Hanson (b. 1896),[49] commissioned by the Metropolitan and produced there in 1934. The score incorporates many ballets and choruses in a wild, implausible story of Puritan New England. It may be the extravagance of the libretto which has interfered with the full success of *Merry Mount*, or it may be a somewhat stiff, oratorio-like, undramatic quality and the generally static harmonic and melodic style of much of the music. Yet there is considerable variety of idiom: the

---

[47] See study by J. T. Howard.

[48] For fuller lists see Hipsher, *American Opera*; Howard, *Our Contemporary Composers*.

[49] See study by Tuthill (1936).

love strains of Bradford's aria "Rise up, my love" with the following duet, and the "Walpurgisnacht" ballets in Act II are particularly remarkable; and the work as a whole is able, serious, and uncompromising—a compliment of the sort that opera audiences do not always seem to appreciate.

CHAPTER 27

TRADITION AND
RENEWAL:
THE RECENT PAST[1]

Of all musical forms, opera is the most immediately sensitive to changes in political, economic, social, and general cultural conditions. Its very nature as a complex and costly public spectacle largely dependent on official patronage or private subsidy makes it especially vulnerable to political dictates and economic vicissitudes: its subject matter reflects, positively or negatively, current human preoccupations; its form, content, and idiom are all affected by changing ideals of dramatic and musical style. Two world wars, a world-wide economic depression, and the emergence of political systems committed to strict control of art in the interest of the state have been the salient external factors in the first half of the twentieth century. Widespread emigration of authors and composers in the 1930s affected the development of opera in the United States and elsewhere. The passionately felt need of the artist to come to grips in contemporary terms with contemporary issues stimulated new uses of traditional techniques and experiments with new dramatic and musical means. Technological developments also played a part: radio, television, and the long-playing phonograph record immensely increased

[1] General bibliography: K. H. Wörner, *Neue Musik in der Entscheidung*; Collaer, *La Musique moderne*; Slonimsky, *Music Since 1900*; Machlis, *Introduction to Contemporary Music*; *Oper im XX. Jahrhundert* (*Musik der Zeit*, Heft 6); *Opera Annual*, ed. H. Rosenthal (1954 and following years). See also bibliography, including articles in current periodicals and the section "Current Chronicle" in MQ (April, 1948, and following issues). On opera in the United States, see especially the files of *Opera News* (1936+) and *American Composers Alliance Bulletin* (1938, 1952+); Heinsheimer, "Opera in America Today" (MQ, 1951).

the actual and potential audience, bringing the traditional repertoire and style of opera within everyone's reach and making it possible, to some extent at least, for the public to become acquainted with newer developments. As a result opera has become of interest to a larger number of people than ever before in its history. Free pursuit of the new, together with an enlarged and diverse public, accounts for an unprecedented diversity of operatic styles in our time—the "polyphonic" or "many-voiced century," as one writer has called it.[2]

As in all periods, the subject matter of twentieth-century opera has been drawn variously from imagined dramatic interactions of human personalities, from history, myth, legend, or folklore, or from the circumstances of contemporary life; treatment has been serious or light, earnest or satirical or playful, as of timeless significance or as applicable peculiarly to the present moment. The aims have been equally varied : mere amusement or entertainment (whether of a general public or of special groups, as for example opera for children); instruction and conversion —that is, propaganda; comedy with contemporary social application; or high tragedy in the Aristotelian sense: "the imitation of an action that is serious and also, as having magnitude, complete in itself . . . with incidents arousing pity and fear, wherewith to accomplish its catharsis of such emotions" [3]—this kind of drama, inviting the audience as it does to contemplate heroic greatness of deed or character, being in some instances more or less overtly directed toward confirmation of religious faith.

We may recall that the twentieth century inherited, along with the timeless and unchanging line of light or "entertainment" opera, two fundamentally contrasting conceptions of serious musical drama. Stated in simplest terms, these were : (1) the Wagnerian drama of ideas, with personages primarily symbolical and with music in a continuous orchestral texture organized by means of leitmotifs, the vocal lines being of declamatory or arioso character; and (2) the Verdian drama of typical human beings in psychological interaction, with music in the form of distinct numbers connected by recitatives and a texture of emotionally expressive vocal melody sustained by orchestral accompaniment. By and large, composers at the beginning of the twentieth century adhered to one or the other of these two basic conceptions, even if with compromises

[2] K. Honolka, *Das vielstimmige Jahrhundert* (1960).
[3] Aristotle, *Poetics*, chap. vi (1449b20), Bywater's translation.

or modifications: Strauss in *Salome* and *Electra* (and later in *Die Frau ohne Schatten*) was in the line of descent from Wagner, as was essentially also Debussy in *Pelléas et Mélisande* despite its un-Wagnerian harmonies and dynamics; on the other hand, Puccini and the composers of the verismo school descended (in both senses of the word) from Verdi. Meanwhile, a new conception was growing up, or rather an old one was being revived: the eighteenth-century classical idea of an opera as primarily a musical entity, with poetry "the obedient daughter of music," as Mozart had expressed it. This new-old conception involved, as a rule, the use of distinct musical numbers in definite form, objectivity of expression, and a tendency to let the music develop in its own way, following the dramatic action in broad lines but not attempting to mirror it in detail. This conception of opera, an early example of which is Strauss's *Ariadne*, has influenced many twentieth-century composers —Falla, Ravel and most of the French, some Germans (notably Hindemith), and Stravinsky, especially in *The Rake's Progress*.

One development that attracted much attention in the 1920s and 1930s was the opera of social protest, conspicuous first in Germany and later in the United States. To be sure, the theme of social protest had occurred in opera before, but now it became explicit and central instead of only incidental.

Another phenomenon of the period since 1920 has been the tendency to combine the traditional form of opera with certain features of the oratorio, such as a narrator or a contemplative or didactic chorus. Introduction of oratorio-like elements has occurred typically in large-scale works on historical or legendary subjects, such as Stravinsky's *Oedipus rex*, Milhaud's *Christophe Colomb*, Hindemith's *Mathis der Maler*, Egk's *Columbus*, Schoenberg's *Moses und Aron*, and Orff's *Antigonae*. A like infiltration of oratorio or cantata technique is found in some stage works of smaller scale, such as Falla's *Retablo de Maese Pedro*, Vaughan Williams's *Pilgrim's Progress*, and Britten's *Rape of Lucretia*. Forerunners of the opera-oratorio may be found in Wagner's *Parsifal* and Pfitzner's *Palestrina*, but the combination is especially characteristic of the mid-twentieth century.

Likewise characteristic of this period is the importance of ballet, especially ballet with dramatic elements (Bartók, Stravinsky, Prokofiev) and the incorporation of choreographic (often also choral) spectacle in opera (as in many of the works mentioned above), or even a fusion of opera and ballet as in Casella's "choreographic comedy" *La giara* (1924) or Henze's *Boulevard Solitude* (1952). Still another feature of the twentieth century is the unprecedented extent to which composers have worked in smaller forms—"chamber" or "workshop" opera, requiring few performers, sometimes written specifically for amateurs or for children. This movement, the result of special conditions, has been particularly prominent in England and the United States, but is not by any means confined to those countries. Finally may be mentioned the rise of opera for the new media of radio and television and the writing of incidental music for films as well as for stage plays.

No single one of the typical twentieth-century operatic phenomena (except for the use of radio or television) can be called completely "new." What is new, as has already been said, is the unprecedented diversity of operatic styles existing in one and the same period. In part, of course, that diversity is an illusion caused by our nearness to events, our lack of historical perspective; but even discounting this (insofar as possible) the diversity remains. We shall try to cope with it by making a division into six general headings (determined chiefly by considerations of musical style) and mentioning some representative works under each. But the reader must be warned at the outset that our categories have been selected only for convenience in ordering the material and do not claim to be rigid or mutually exclusive. Some composers and some works might equally well be placed under a different heading or under more than one. Above all, denominations like traditional, popular, national, progressive, experimental, and the like imply no judgment as to aesthetic value : there are, of course, better and worse works within each category; but no one category is inherently or necessarily superior to another.

1. THE TRADITION

Despite many well-publicized experiments and new departures, a large proportion of operas produced after 1920—including some of the best as well as most popular works of this period—kept recognizably close to traditional forms and subjects and avoided any radical departure from accepted musical styles. In the favorable environment of Italy the tradition was carried on by Franco Alfano (1876–1954),[4] the choice of

[4] *Cinquanta anni di opera e balletto in Italia* (1954); Gatti, "Franco Alfano"; *idem*, "Recent Italian Operas"; Della Corte, *Ritratto di Franco Alfano*.

whom to complete the unfinished score of Puccini's *Turandot* was symbolical of his intermediary position in the history of Italian opera. Alfano had become known as early as 1904 for his *Risurrezione* ("Resurrection"); his most significant later works were *La leggenda di Sakuntala* (1921), a heavily tragic work of grand-opera proportions, and the one-act neo-Puccinian lyrical comedy *Madonna Imperia* (1927), whose vocal lines, alternating smoothly between melodic phrases and a lively, expressive arioso, are supported by luscious harmonies in impressionistic orchestral colors—a perfect match for the refinedly voluptuous text. Alfano's *L'ultimo Lord* (1930), a vivacious comic work, and *Il dottor Antonio* (1949) continued in the same essentially conservative style.

The operas of Ildebrando Pizzetti (b. 1880) [5] are somewhat less conservative in their harmonies than those of Alfano. They have a continuous full-bodied orchestral texture in a mosaic of recurring motifs, are primarily lyrical in expression with flexible speechlike vocal melodies, and are characterized by extensive dramatic use of choruses in a sensitive polyphonic style inspired by classical Italian models. The most important of Pizzetti's early operas, and one of his best scores, was *Fedra* (1915), on a text by Gabriele D'Annunzio. A group of works to his own librettos comprised *Debora e Jaele* (1922), *Fra Gherardo* (1928), and *Lo straniero* ("The Stranger," 1930). Pizzetti's later operas include *Orséolo* (1935), *Vanna Lupa* (1949), *Ifigenia* (first given in radio broadcast, 1950), *Cagliostro* (1953), *La figlia di Iorio*, a "pastoral tragedy" by D'Annunzio (1954), and *Assassinio nella cattedrale* ("Murder in the Cathedral," 1958), based on a translation of T. S. Eliot's play.

In France, conditions after the First World War were less favorable than in Italy for new serious operas in styles so closely related to tradition as were those of Alfano and Pizzetti. Paris, the principal and virtually the only important operatic center, readily accepted new pieces in the lighter forms, but the public for serious opera either remained content with the standard old repertoire or centered its attention on composers of distinctly "modern" tendencies. Thus a quite exceptional event was the production in 1939 of Henri Sauguet's (b. 1901) *Chartreuse de Parme*, a work conforming in every external detail to the pattern of nineteenth-century singers' opera and couched in a simple—though far

[5] Biography by Gatti; La Morgia, ed., *La città dannunziana di Ildebrando Pizzetti*.

from unsophisticated—musical idiom that might have traced its lineage from Satie.

One of the outstanding French operas of the mid-twentieth century was *Les Dialogues des Carmélites* by Francis Poulenc (1899–1963),[6] performed at Milan in January, 1957, and at Paris in June of the same year. In contrast to the composer's earlier satirical, surrealist comic opera *Les Mamelles de Tirésias* ("The Breasts of Tiresias," 1947) and his later tense monodrama *La Voix humaine* ("The Human Voice," 1959), the *Carmélites* presents no ostentatiously novel features either in subject, form, or musical idiom. The theme of its libretto—written by Georges Bernanos after a novella by Gertrude von Le Fort—is the conquest of fear by divine grace. The central personage is a timorous young Carmelite nun caught in the religious persecutions under the Reign of Terror; the drama, developed with fine psychological perception and excellent balance between inner and outer action, had obvious and terrible implications for conditions in France in the 1940s, but its topical features are less important than its universal significance. The latter is powerfully communicated by Poulenc's music, selflessly devoted to the text and bound with it in a union no less perfect than that which Debussy had accomplished in *Pelléas*. These two operas are alike furthermore in the way they achieve profoundly dramatic results through restraint in the use of resources. Like Debussy, Poulenc connects the scenes within each act by means of instrumental interludes and makes unobtrusive use of recurring themes. The vocal solo lines, cast for the most part in quasi-melodic declamation (see Example 117), are kept in clear relief above the continuous, ever-changing, but always lucid and evocative orchestral sonorities. The chorus, used only sparingly throughout most of the opera, comes into the foreground at the dramatic, moving final scene. Altogether, *Les Dialogues des Carmélites* takes a worthy and, one may hope, a permanently honored place in the history of French opera.

In the German-speaking countries the composer who probably best represents the continuing central tradition in opera is an Austrian, Gottfried von Einem (b. 1918).[7] In his music often piercing harmonic

[6] Hell, *Francis Poulenc*; Poulenc, *Entretiens avec Claude Rostand*; *idem*, "Comment j'ai composé les *Dialogues des Carmélites*"; La Maestre, "Francis Poulenc und seine Bernanos-Oper."

[7] Rutz, *Neue Oper: Gottfried Einem und seine Oper Dantons Tod*; Von Einem, "*Der Prozess*"; Graf, "*Der Prozess* von Gottfried von Einem"; analysis of *Der Prozess* by W. Reich in MQ XL (1954) 62–76.

EXAMPLE 117

POULENC

dissonances and sharp variegated rhythms are contained within an essentially tonal and romantic framework of expression with singable melodic lines, the whole enlivened by original thematic ideas and handled with a natural flair for stage effect. Von Einem's output for the theatre hitherto includes, in addition to ballets, the two operas *Dantons Tod* ("The Death of Danton," 1947), on a libretto adapted from Georg Büchner's drama, an immediately appealing work especially notable for its tumultuous crowd scenes, and *Der Prozess* ("The Trial," 1953), based on Franz Kafka's novel, a score in which each scene constitutes a musical unit with its own characteristic rhythms, its own singing (or speaking) style, instrumental color, and formal pattern.

Another opera composer to be noted here is Werner Egk (b. 1901), like Von Einem primarily a musician of the theatre. His *Columbus*, originally written for radio broadcast in 1933 and frequently performed since on German stages in a revised version, is a rather static combination of opera and epic; a later and possibly better mixture of these elements is found in *Irische Legende* (1955). Most memorable of Egk's operas is *Peer Gynt* (1938), a straightforward human drama with a musical score of considerable variety, color, and melodic interest. Rudolf Wagner-Régeny (b. 1903) is known chiefly through *Der Günstling* ("The Favorite," 1935) and *Die Bürger von Calais* ("The Citizens of Calais," 1939). A favorite composer in Switzerland is Heinrich Sutermeister (b. 1910), who combines a pleasing melodic style with good feeling for the theatre, exemplified in the tragic operas *Romeo und Julia* (1940) and *Raskolnikoff* (1948; after Dostoyevsky), as well as in various short works of lighter character, written for the radio and later revised for regular theatre performance.

In England and the United States the ultraconservative style in opera has been illustrated in mid-century by two competent large-scale works, both launched under favorable official auspices: *Troilus and Cressida* (London, 1954) by Sir William Walton (b. 1902) [8] and *Vanessa* (New York, 1958) by Samuel Barber (b. 1910). More varied and adventurous, though still not involving any radical break with tradition, has been the work of two composers whose interest centers largely in the musical theatre: Benjamin Britten (b. 1913) [9] in England and Gian

[8] Reizenstein, "Walton's *Troilus and Cressida*."

[9] D. Mitchell and H. Keller, eds., *Benjamin Britten*; E. W. White, *Benjamin Britten*; *Benjamin Britten: Das Opernwerk* (*Musik der Zeit*, Heft 11, 1955); Britten and others, *The Rape of Lucretia: A Symposium*; numerous articles in *Tempo* and other periodicals (see bibliography).

Carlo Menotti (b. 1911) in the United States. Significantly, a considerable proportion of their output has been in the form of chamber opera.

Britten's most important large operas are *Peter Grimes* (1945) and *A Midsummer Night's Dream* (1960). The former is an admirably constructed drama, with music in separate numbers linked by orchestral interludes and a few recurring themes, in an idiom permeated with the spirit of English folk song while unobtrusively incorporating individual traits of color, rhythm, and harmony. An outstanding feature is the sensitive declamation of the text; the expertly handled choral sonorities play an important part in creating the stark dramatic atmosphere of the work. *Peter Grimes* seems to be well established in the repertoire. *A Midsummer Night's Dream* is a less successful score despite some beautiful numbers—the duets in Act I, the comic rehearsal of the rustics in the first scene of Act II, and the ensemble for six boys at the end of the same act, for example. But some mannerisms, such as glissandi in the double-basses and ostinato techniques generally, are overworked, and a certain monotony of effect results from the prevailing color of high voices; in particular, the countertenor role of Oberon is dramatically unconvincing. Britten's operas for smaller performing groups include the tragic *Rape of Lucretia* (1946), which uses a commentative "chorus" consisting of two solo voices; the comic *Albert Herring* (1947); and an unusual work, *The Turn of the Screw* (1954), a dramatization of Henry James's tale with music in the form of fourteen variations on a tone row —which, however, is treated as a theme rather than by the usual twelve-tone techniques of construction and moreover is so conceived and harmonized as to produce an effect not far removed from conventional tonality. The music successfully captures the supernatural mood of the story, but the dramatic material is perhaps too subtle to be effectively projected in the theatre. Wholly delightful are Britten's operas for children, *The Little Sweep* (1949) and *Noye's Fludde* (1958). All in all, there can be no question as to Britten's signal importance in contemporary English opera or his significance as an original, skillful, and idealistic composer adapting himself without sacrifice of integrity to the practical conditions of his place and time.

Other British composers of opera are : Arthur Benjamin (1893–1960; *A Tale of Two Cities*, 1953); Alan Dudley Bush (b. 1900; *Wat Tyler*, 1952); Lennox Berkeley (b. 1903; *Nelson*, 1951); and Michael Tippett (b.

1905), whose *Midsummer Marriage* (1955) is a significant and original work.

Menotti is a born theatre composer of the order of Puccini and the verismo school. His musical style is eclectic, drawing upon heterogeneous elements with a single eye to dramatic effect, of which he is an unerring master. He writes his own librettos. Conspicuous among his many successful works for the stage are *The Medium* (1946), an unashamed melodrama perfectly matched by equally melodramatic music; a short comic opera, *The Telephone* (1947); and *The Consul* (1950), a compelling treatment of the tragedy of homeless persons in an indifferent world. *Amahl and the Night Visitors*, originally produced on television in 1951, is on the way to becoming a popular classic. It is not necessary to make extravagant claims for Menotti's musical originality in order to recognize that he is one of the very few serious opera composers on the contemporary American scene who thoroughly understand the requirements of the theatre and are making a consistent, sincere attempt to reach the large opera-loving public; his success is a testimonial to the continuing validity of a long and respectable operatic tradition.

Another well-established American composer of serious opera is Douglas Moore (b. 1893). In *The Devil and Daniel Webster* (1939) and later in *Giants in the Earth* (1951) and *The Ballad of Baby Doe* (1956), Moore combined distinctively American subject matter and musical idiom with good theatrical craftsmanship. More recent works are *Gallantry*, a "soap opera" (1958), and *The Wings of the Dove* (1961).

The marked rise of local opera groups, both amateur and professional, and the generally increased opportunities for performance of new works in the United States have encouraged the production of operas by American composers, especially since the end of the Second World War. Undoubtedly the most flourishing branch of the musical theatre in this country is still musical comedy, and no work has yet risen to challenge the secure place of *Porgy and Bess* in the history of American opera. Among the more or less successful newer works outside the musical comedy class may be listed : *The Warrior* (1947) and *The Veil* (1950) by Bernard Rogers (b. 1893); *The Trial of Lucullus* (1947) by Roger Sessions (b. 1896); *The Tender Land* (1954) by Aaron Copland (b. 1900); *The Mighty Casey* (1953) by William Schuman (b. 1910); *The Ruby* (1955) and *The Trial at Rouen* (1956) by Norman Dello Joio (b. 1913); *The Crucible* (1961) by Robert Ward (b. 1917); *Good Soldier Schweik* (1958) by the talented American-born Czech composer Robert Kurka (1921–57); *The Wife of Martin Guerre*

(1956) by William Bergsma (b. 1921); *The Jumping Frog of Calaveras County* (1950) by Lukas Foss (b. 1922); *Susannah* (1955) and *Wuthering Heights* (1959) by Carlisle Floyd (b. 1926); [10] and operas by Hugo Weisgall (b. 1912), including *The Tenor* (1952), *The Stronger* (1952), and *Six Characters in Search of an Author* (1959, after Pirandello). [11]

2. COMIC OPERA

"Comic opera," in the twentieth century as in earlier periods, is a designation embracing many different types. At one end of the scale are frankly popular works—musical comedies, operettas, and the like—that seek to entertain a large public by means of (1) music in a style familiar enough to be enjoyed without much effort or close attention but containing some novelty in details; and (2) a dramatic content uncomplicated, superficial (in the sense of carrying no "message"), humorous or sentimental or both, and possibly enlivened by reference to current foibles or topics in the news. Other kinds of comic opera may be distinguished by music in a more advanced style, greater sophistication of plot and subtlety of characterization, or evidence of some aim (for example, satire) in addition to that of entertainment. Most successful writers of light popular works produce nothing of significance outside that special field. Examples of more sophisticated kinds of comic opera, however, have come from nearly every composer for the theatre in the present century, including some who are equally competent in the "serious" realm—Alfano, Poulenc, Britten, and Menotti, for instance, as we have already seen.

Among the composers of comic opera in France during the interwar years were Charles Levadé (1869–1948; *La Rôtisserie de la Reine Pédauque*, 1920; *La Peau de Chagrin*, 1929), Marcel Samuel-Rousseau (1882–1955; *Le Bon Roi Dagobert*, 1927), and especially Jacques Ibert (1890–1962). Ibert's *Angélique* (1927) is a one-act farce with spoken dialogue, the music scintillating and epigrammatic, using polytonal chords, dance rhythms, and conventional melodies dressed up with dissonant harmonies—a twentieth-century revival of the old spirit of the Paris vaudevilles. Later operatic works of Ibert include *Le Roi d'Yvetot* (1930), *L'Aiglon* and *Les Petites Cardinal* (1937 and 1938, both in collaboration with Honegger), and a radio opera, *Barbe-Bleue* (1943). Other notable French comic operas were Sauguet's *Le Plumet*

10 See articles by Eyer and Sabin.
11 Rochberg, "Hugo Weisgall."

du colonel (1924), Milhaud's three "opéras minutes" (1927), and Honegger's *Les Adventures du Roi Pausole* (1930).

The comic spirit in French opera was characterized by a peculiar national combination of sophistication and spontaneity. In Germany and Italy it was more typically connected with self-consciously "advanced" musical and literary movements. One conspicuous "hit" in Germany was *Jonny spielt auf* ("Johnny Strikes Up," 1927) by Ernst Krenek (b. 1900) [12]—a combination of fantasy and gross realism set to exuberant rhythms and catchy tunes in jazz style with just enough dissonance to give the impression of daring "modernism." Considerable variety of mood was achieved within this general idiom, from the gaudily vulgar strains of a restaurant orchestra to romantic expressiveness and the final apotheosis of Johnny, the Negro band leader, symbol of the vigorous optimistic new world "conquering Europe with the dance." Krenek intended *Jonny* to be taken seriously, but audiences for the most part regarded it as a comedy or satire, and—whether or not owing to this misunderstanding—it had a brilliant though short-lived success.

The comic operas of Paul Hindemith (1895–1963) [13] well illustrate the satirical tendencies fashionable in Germany during the late 1920s. *Hin und Zurück* ("There and Back," 1927) is a one-act tour de force in which the second half reverses the action of the first, so that at the end the situation is exactly the same as at the beginning; the music correspondingly reverses the order of its themes and movements, though without going into the intricacies of strict retrograde canon. The work is scored for an orchestra of seven wind instruments and two pianos; the music, in various styles by turns but unified in effect nevertheless, is decidedly clever and successful in performance. *Neues vom Tage* (1929; revised 1954), the last opera of Hindemith to be produced in Germany before the war, is a longer work, a witty revue about a married couple who, through their efforts to obtain evidence for a divorce, become "the news of the day," with characters so firmly established in the minds of their public that they no longer have any right of private action and cannot even drop their divorce proceedings although they wish to. On this plot are strung several amusing episodes, including a chorus of stenographers to the rhythmic accompaniment of clacking typewriters and a bathroom scene. The music, like most of Hindemith's in this

[12] See the composer's books *Music Here and Now* and *Zur Sprache gebracht*.
[13] Biography by H. Strobel (3d ed., 1948); Hindemith, *A Composer's World*.

period, is linear in texture and strongly rhythmic, well suited to the lively action. There is, of course, a jazz scene, and the final chorus is a fugue. One of Hindemith's most charming stage works is a children's opera, *Wir bauen eine Stadt* ("We Build a Town"), in straightforward simple melodic style, first performed at Oxford in 1931.

Comedy on contemporary subject matter was not a prominent feature of Italian opera under the Fascist government. Composers rather sought material in the safe and distant past, producing such works as the *Tre commedie goldoniane* (1926) of G. F. Malipiero (b. 1882),[14] three short comedies after Goldoni in concentrated musical settings, for the most part in lively *parlando* recitative over continuous orchestra; and *La donna serpente* (1932) by Alfredo Casella (1883–1947),[15] based on a tale by Carlo Gozzi. These are excellent examples of the Italian neoclassical movement, which also inspired the subjects and musical treatment of some other operas by the same two composers—for example, Malipiero's trilogy *L'Orfeide* (1925), his operas *Antonio e Cleopatra* (1938) and *Ecuba* (1941), and Casella's *Favola d'Orfeo* (1932).

Comic operas of a more robust and popular character were appearing around this time in Czechoslovakia. *Schwanda the Bagpiper* by Jaromir Weinberger (b. 1896), first performed at Prague in 1927, is doubtless the most widely known of these. Boshuslav Martinů (1890–1959),[16] a native of Czechoslovakia who from 1923 lived in Paris and later in the United States, has been heard mainly in symphonic and chamber compositions; but he also wrote twelve operas, including *Comedy on the Bridge* (1937) and others both comic and serious which still remain little known.

More recent comic operas by some of the composers above mentioned include Sauguet's *La Gageure imprévue* ("The Unexpected Wager," 1944) and G. F. Malipiero's *I capricci di Callot* ("The Caprices of Callot," 1942) and *Venere prigionera* ("Venus Imprisoned," 1957). Interesting experiments in form as well as in subject matter and musical idiom have been tried by younger composers since the 1940s. Particular mention may be made of Riccardo Malipiero (b. 1914; nephew of G. F.

---

[14] Bontempelli, *Gian Francesco Malipiero*; Gatti, ed., *L'opera di Gian Francesco Malipiero*.

[15] D'Amico and Gatti, eds., *Alfredo Casella*; see also the composer's memoirs, *I segreti della giara*.

[16] Safránek, "Bohuslav Martinů und das musikalische Theater."

Malipiero) [17] in Italy, with *Minnie la candida* (1942), *La donna è mobile* ("Woman Is Fickle," 1954), and a bitterly satirical television opera, *Battono alla porta* ("They Beat on the Door," 1961), which introduces electronic effects. Equally adventurous works, in different directions, have appeared in other countries. Comic opera, being by nature less subject than serious opera to the drag of tradition, continues in the twentieth century to be what it has always been, a congenial soil for the sprouting of new ideas.

3. POLITICAL OPERA

In the seventeenth and eighteenth centuries operas were used in schools for teaching moral and religious doctrines; in the twentieth century in like manner operas were used for teaching left-wing political doctrines. In both cases the method was to clothe the teachings in easily understood, popularly accessible music. The principal twentieth-century examples stemmed from the "epic theatre" movement in Germany, headed by Bertolt Brecht (1898–1956).[18] Foremost among them were two settings of Brecht's librettos by Kurt Weill (1900–1950): *Die Dreigroschenoper* ("The Threepenny Opera," 1928) and *Aufstieg und Fall der Stadt Mahogonny* ("The Rise and Fall of the City of Mahogany," 1927; extended version, 1930), both of which remain popular in spite of political changes that have made many parts of their original librettos outdated. (A revised "Americanized" text for *The Threepenny Opera* was provided by Marc Blitzstein in 1952.) Similar in political aim were Weill's school opera *Der Jasager* ("The One Who Consents," 1930) and a larger work, *Die Bürgschaft* ("The Surety," 1932), his last opera to be presented in Germany before the coming of the Nazi regime. Weill later had a second career in the United States as composer of operas and musical comedies, including *Knickerbocker Holiday* (1938), *Street Scene* (1947), and the "folk opera" *Down in the Valley* (1938).

Other works of Brecht in musical settings were *Die Massnahme* (1930) with music by Hanns Eisler (1898–1962) and *Das Verhör des Lukullus* ("The Trial of Lucullus") by Paul Dessau (b. 1894), first given in East Germany in 1951 and revived after 1959. Conspicuous among

[17] Sartori, *Riccardo Malipiero*.

[18] See, in addition to Brecht's own writings: Shumacher, *Die dramatischen Versuche Bertolt Brechts*; Hartung, "Zur epischen Oper Brechts und Weills"; Drew, "Topicality and the Universal"; articles in *The Score*, No. 23 (July, 1958).

recent politically slanted works was *Intoleranza 1960* by the Italian composer Luigi Nono (b. 1924), first performed at Venice in 1961. It is a "scenic action" on a libretto which, while incorporating Communist quotations and slogans, is nevertheless conceived as a protest against authoritarianism rather than as party-line propaganda; the music, typically for Nono, effectively uses various novel sound effects and is in an "advanced" style markedly incongruous with the officially sponsored ideals of Moscow.

Satire of less doctrinaire stripe flourished in some of the early stage works of Krenek : *Der Sprung über den Schatten* ("The Leap over the Shadow," 1924), a farce operetta of variegated musical styles; *Zwingburg* ("Dungeon Castle," 1924); and three short pieces from 1928, including *Schwergewicht* ("Heavyweight"), a satire on the glorification of prominent athletes.

The opera of social protest with music in popular style reechoed in the United States, chiefly with Marc Blitzstein's (b. 1905) *The Cradle Will Rock* (1937), in which spoken dialogue alternates with recitatives and songs in a cultured and clever jazz idiom. Blitzstein's *No for an Answer* (1941) is similar in aim and general musical style, though with a wider range of expression, and includes some fine choral portions.

The political right produced no important operatic propaganda, with the possible exception of a couple of works from Italy. Casella's *Il deserto tentato* ("The Conquest of the Desert," 1937), a "mystery in one act" inspired by Mussolini's Ethiopian adventure, aimed to reflect the "poetic exaltation of the civilizing mission of a great nation" in music of rather simple oratorio-like style with massive choral sections. Malipiero's *Giulio Cesare* (1936), based on Shakespeare's play, was also conceived at least in part as a gesture of acclaim to Mussolini.

4. SOVIET RUSSIA[19] AND EASTERN EUROPE

In the Soviet Union the all-reaching power of the state has been exerted, especially since about 1930, in favor of certain kinds of music and opera. This influence, together with the manner in which the

[19] Bibliography : *Sovetskaia opera: Sbornik kriticheskikh statei* (1953); Kulikovich, *Sovetskaia opera na sluzhbe partii i pravitel'stva* (1955); articles in *Sovetskaia muzyka, passim*; Abraham, *Eight Soviet Composers*; Laux, *Die Musik in Russland und der Sowjetunion* (*II. Teil*); Moisenco, *Realist Music*; Olkhovsky, *Music under the Soviets*; Polyakova, *Soviet Music*.

musical life of the country is organized, has tended to produce a body of Soviet music cut off from, and apparently largely indifferent to, the various contemporary "advanced" currents in western Europe and the Americas. The officially accepted ideals require, among other things, that music should be treated as the possession of the entire people and not only of a musical elite; that its material should be sought in, or shaped by, the music of the people of its own country or region; that it should emphasize melody and be written in a style not too difficult for general comprehension; that it should be "optimistic" in spirit and that its subject matter—where a text is involved—should affirm socialist ideals. This policy naturally encouraged production of a great many symphonic poems, ballets, choruses, and operas distinguished rather for massive size and sound political intentions than for musical vitality. On the other hand, official policy aimed to stimulate the development of popular and especially of regional musical life within the Soviet Union and thus to enrich the musical language of the country from genuine Eastern folkloristic sources. Among the many non-Russian national operas performed since 1930 may be mentioned : Reinhold Glière's (1875–1956) *Shah-Senem* (1934), based on Caucasian legends and including musical elements from Caucasian and Iranian sources; Sergey Vassilenko's (1872–1956) *Buran* (1939), with colors and rhythms derived from national Uzbek music; operas in the Tatar language by Nazib Zhiganov (b. 1911), particularly *Jalil* (1957); *Aïchurek* (1939) by Aldylas Moldybaev (b. 1906), based on a Kirghizian epic poem and using national melodies; and operas by two leading composers from the Ukraine, Boris Liatoshinsky (b. 1895; *Schors,* 1938) and Y. S. Meitus (b. 1903; *The Young Guard,* 1950).

A work long regarded as a model for Soviet opera was *The Quiet Don* by Ivan Dzerzhinsky (b. 1909), first performed at Leningrad in 1935 and subsequently with great success all over the country. This work appears to hold a position in the history of Soviet opera comparable to that of Moniuszko's *Halka* in Poland or Erkel's *Hunyady László* in Hungary : its patriotic subject is treated in accordance with Dzerzhinsky's conviction that "everything that is lived by the people" can be expressed in opera but that this must be done "in artistically generalized, typified figures, avoiding the pitfalls of naturalism";[20] the music is

---

[20] Symposium on Soviet opera in *Sovetskaia muzyka* (May, 1939), quoted in Abraham, *Eight Soviet Composers,* p. 82.

technically naïve, simple in texture, predominantly lyric, containing many melodies that suggest folk song without actual citation, and having a few "modern" touches of harmony and rhythm. A similar work, once even more highly regarded by Soviet critics, was Dzerzhinsky's second opera, *Virgin Soil Upturned* (1937). Dzerzhinsky was representative of a trend in the 1930s toward the "song opera," of which one of the best examples was *Into the Storm* (1939) by Tikhon Khrennikov (b. 1913). The "song opera" as a type, however, was subject to certain inherent weaknesses, principally the lack of clear, individual characterization through recitatives and ensembles and the general absence of sharply defined dramatic contrasts.

Stalin's pointed approval of *The Quiet Don* was timed so as to coincide with a blast of official wrath at *Lady Macbeth of Mtzensk* by Dmitri Shostakovich (b. 1906).[21] When this opera was first presented at Moscow in 1934 it won praise at home and soon made its way abroad; two years later, an article in *Pravda* denounced it as "confusion instead of natural human music," unmelodic, fidgety, and neurasthenic, and moreover bad in that it tried to present a wicked and degenerate heroine as a sympathetic character. It is hard to say how much of the story, in Shostakovich's treatment, was intended as satire and how much as mere pornography and perversion. The music is brutal, lusty, vivid in the suggestion of cruelty and horror, full of driving rhythm and willful dissonance. As in other works of his early period, Shostakovich excels in two idioms : a nervously energetic presto, thin textured, tonally erratic, and rhythmically irregular; and a long-spun adagio, mounting with clashing contrapuntal lines to sonorous climaxes. There are some fine choral scenes (particularly in the last act), and some of the aria melodies are related to folk-song idiom, though the solo lines for the most part are declamatory and interwoven with the orchestral texture.

Needless to say, *Lady Macbeth* promptly disappeared from the Soviet theatres. The early wholesale condemnation of the opera gave way to a more discriminating evaluation by later Soviet critics, especially since a marked change in Shostakovich's style was signalized in his Fifth Symphony (1937)—a change that mirrored the transition from the revolutionary and experimental period in Soviet music to a period of stricter control under party directives. Similar but less acute crises of policy occurred afterwards, notably in 1948 when criticism of V. I. Muradeli's

[21] Biographies by Martynov and Rabinovich (1959).

(b. 1908) opera *The Great Friendship* caused it to be withdrawn and brought forth an official decree warning against "formalism" and "anti-popular" tendencies in Soviet music.[22] Objections were made also to K. Dankevich's (b. 1905) historical opera *Bogdan Khmelnitzky* when it came out in 1951, but a new version two years later was more favorably received. The decree was rescinded in 1958, and Shostakovich's revision of *Lady Macbeth*, under the title *Katerina Izmailova*, was staged in 1962. The new version made few changes in the libretto; when the opera was given at London in 1963 (its first performance in the West) critical opinion of the musical revisions was generally favorable.

Other notable operas by Soviet composers are Dzerzhinsky's *Fate of a Man* (1962), Khrennikov's *Mother* (1958, based on a novel by M. Gorky), Dmitry Kabalevsky's (b. 1904) *The Family of Taras* (1947, after B. Gorbatov's story *The Unvanquished*), and Y. A. Shaporin's (b. 1889) *The Decembrists* (1953).

The outstanding name among the composers of Soviet Russia, however, is that of Sergey Prokofiev (1891–1953).[23] Neither his life nor his music can be called typical for a Soviet composer: from 1918 to 1933 he lived abroad, chiefly at Paris; an early opera, *The Gambler*, composed in 1915–17, was first performed (in a revised version) at Brussels in 1929. *The Love for Three Oranges* (Chicago, 1921) has a merrily lunatic plot based on a fantastic tale by Gozzi, well suited to Prokofiev's sharp rhythmic style of this period and to his talents for humor and grotesquerie. Choruses, external to the action, intervene capriciously; the solo parts make a mosaic of detached phrases over sparse but colorful orchestration; the only extended tunes are the well-known orchestral March and Scherzo.

Prokofiev's next opera was *The Flaming Angel* (composed 1919–27; concert performance 1954; first stage performance, Venice, 1955). Another fantastic libretto—this time a tragedy, laid in Germany of the sixteenth century, full of superstition, evil magic, ecstatic visions, hallucination, and horror—gave occasion for a complex but theatrically effective score, with arioso vocal lines over rather heavy orchestral

---

[22] A translation of the statement issued by the Central Committee of the Communist Party is printed in Olkhovsky, *Music under the Soviets*, pp. 280–85.

[23] *Autobiography* (2d ed., 1961); Nest'ev, *Prokof'ev* (1957; English translation, 1960); R. Jahn, "Vom *Spieler* zur *Erzählung vom wahren Menschen.*" See also articles by D. Mitchell (on *The Love for Three Oranges*) and Swarsenski (on *The Flaming Angel*).

accompaniment and some impressive choral scenes forming the climax of the last act. *The Flaming Angel*, being sadly deficient in optimistic proletarian spirit, has been welcomed only in the decadent West.

Returned to Russia, Prokofiev began the long and difficult process of adapting his earlier pungent, ironic, often dissonant style to the requirements of his own country. He busied himself with ballets and other semidramatic compositions (including *Lieutenant Kije*, the "symphonic tale" *Peter and the Wolf*, and the cantata *Alexander Nevsky*) and finally a new opera, *Semyon Kotko* (1940), based on scenes from the life of a hero of the Revolution of 1918. Here the composer's typical declamatory prose style was relieved by some tuneful episodes, but both libretto (written, as usual, by Prokofiev himself) and music were adversely criticized; *Semyon* was soon withdrawn, but was revived in a concert performance in 1957 and on the stage at Perm and Leningrad in 1960. Another opera on a contemporary subject, *The Story of a Real Man*, was withdrawn after a private performance in 1948; its first public performance occurred at Moscow in 1960.

More successful was the comic opera *The Duenna*,[24] composed in 1939–40, performed at Leningrad in 1946, and revived at Moscow in 1959. The libretto, adapted from Sheridan's play, gave Prokofiev ample scope for comedy and satire as well as for lyrical expression, providing likewise "an opportunity to introduce many formal vocal numbers— serenades, ariettas, duets, quartets and large ensembles—without interrupting the action." [25] These "formal vocal numbers" are scattered throughout the score; many of them alternate kaleidoscopically with fragments of dialogue in short tuneful phrases or strict recitative, all held together by a continuous pulsatile accompaniment with countermelodies and mildly dissonant harmonies. The whole spirit and structure of the work, as well as the plot and characters, make it a charming modern descendant of the classical *opera buffa*.

In 1955 at Leningrad occurred the premiere of Prokofiev's operatic masterpiece, *War and Peace*. Based on Tolstoy's novel and composed largely under the patriotic emotions of the war years (a partial performance of the first version took place in 1946), this is a historical grand opera of heroic proportions, consisting in its final form of thirteen scenes and a choral prologue. The epic range of incidents and emotions

[24] The Russian title is *Betrothal in a Monastery*.
[25] The composer, quoted in Nest'ev (1960), p. 323.

EXAMPLE 118   *War and Peace*, Act I, sc. 1   PROKOFIEV

is matched by music of corresponding variety and convincing dramatic power. As in his previous operas, Prokofiev makes some use of recurrent themes as a unifying device, and in the vocal writing maintains a balance between flexible declamation and lyrical closed forms, both solo and ensemble (see Example 118). Choruses naturally contribute to the grandeur of the whole, though not so conspicuously as to overshadow the individual characters. The score is particularly rich in expressive (not sentimental) melodies, and the distinctly national character of the melodic writing is unmistakable; the harmonic style is tonal, prevailingly diatonic and consonant, but with a quality of originality that reminds one of Mussorgsky. More than any of his other works for the theatre, *War and Peace* places Prokofiev in the great tradition of Russian opera : profoundly national in inspiration and musical style but also profoundly human and therefore transcending national limitations.

Leoš Janáček (1854–1928),[26] the leading composer in Czechoslovakia in the first quarter of the twentieth century, may be called a nationalist in the sense that all his operas were written to texts in his own language and his melodic idiom was one that grew organically out of the rhythms and inflections of national speech and folk song. But his style, particularly in the late works, was so individual and his genius for dramatic characterization so exceptional as to make him a figure of more than national importance. His most famous opera, *Jenufa* (Czech title : *Her Foster Daughter*), produced at Brno in 1904 but ignored elsewhere until after the performance at Prague in 1916, already has passages showing distinctive shapes and concise rhythms rising out of speech intonation, along with expansive melodies of a more conventionally romantic sort. Greater concentration of both drama and music is found in the beautifully poetic, moving *Katya Kabanova* (1921)—a work equally remarkable for sensitive characterizations, fine orchestral colorings, and an indescribable poignancy of expression in the melodic outlines (see Example 119)—one of the masterpieces of twentieth-century opera.

Tender and strange, blended of humor and pity, is *The Sly Vixen*

---

[26] J. Vogel, *Leoš Janáček, dramatik; idem, Leoš Janáček: Leben und Werk*; Brod, *Leoš Janáček*; Holländer, "Leoš Janáček in seinen Opern"; Racek, "Der Dramatiker Janáček"; Shawe-Taylor, "The Operas of Leoš Janáček." Published correspondence: in Czech, Prague, 1950, 1951; in German and English translations, 1955 (see bibliography).

EXAMPLE 119   *Katya Kabanova*, Act III

(Example 119 continued)

(*Example 119 continued*)

(1924), a work which may be regarded as complementary to *Katya* and is even more original in style—this despite some impressionistic influences in the harmony and orchestration. *The Makropulos Case* (1926) shows Janáček on the way to the final stage of his style, reached in the *Glagolitic Mass* of 1927 and the opera *The House of the Dead*, composed in 1928 and first performed in 1930. *The House of the Dead* has no plot, properly speaking; its scenes are taken from Dostoyevsky's memoirs of his prison life in Siberia. The music is intensely concentrated, stark, primitive, violent, with rough harmonies and raw orchestral colors—a grim finale for a composer whose four greatest operas were all written after the age of sixty-five.

Other Czechoslovak composers of opera include Otakar Zich (1879–1934; *Guilt*, 1922); Rudolf Karel (1880–1945), the last pupil of Dvořák (*Godmother's Death*, 1933); Jaroslav Křička (b. 1882; *White Ghost*, 1929); Alois Haba (b. 1893; *Die Mutter*, 1931, and later operas using quarter-tones); and Eugen Suchon (b. 1908; *The Whirlpool*, 1949).[27]

The leading Polish opera composer of the mid-twentieth century is Tadeusz Szeligowsky (b. 1896), whose *Bunt Żakow* ("The Revolt of the

[27] Clapham, *"The Whirlpool."*

Zaks")[28] was produced at Warsaw in 1951 and shortly thereafter at other Polish cities and at Moscow. Its plot is based on an occurrence at the University of Cracow in 1549: the "Zaks"—students of peasant birth who received their education in return for performing menial duties—rebelled because of ill treatment and left the university and the town in a body. A love story and some comic episodes are added to make up the libretto, but the main emphasis is on the stirring choral scenes. Szeligowsky's music, though harmonically conservative, is very well adapted to the requirements of the theatre. Many of the tunes and rhythms have a definite national folk character; in keeping with the historical background are some stylized or literal references to Polish poetry and music of the sixteenth century.

5. THE NEW LINES

The music of most of the operas considered hitherto in this chapter has been "conservative" in the sense of being attached to a continuing tradition—introducing new elements of course, but not too abruptly, and not being especially concerned with any fundamental change in the established musical order. But the first half of the twentieth century was —or at any rate so it appears to us now—anything but conservative in music. The composers whose names dominate that period were innovators, many of them self-consciously so, and some to such a degree as to be quite incomprehensible to the vast majority of the music-consuming public. To be sure, most of their music sounds less radical to us than it did to their immediate contemporaries; but the gap between the twentieth-century composer and the public is still wide, and nowhere wider, probably, than in opera. In the eighteenth century everyone wanted to hear new operas; now most people prefer to hear old ones. The only radically new opera of the last fifty years to come anywhere near general public acceptance is Berg's *Wozzeck*, which dates from 1925.

Roughly speaking, the development of Western musical style since 1915 may be summarized as follows: A period lasting until about 1930 was marked by diverse experiments with all the elements of composition, including rhythm but especially looking toward either a radical extension of the classical concept of tonality or the complete transcendence of that concept. After about 1930 two main directions are discernible: (1) Reconciliation with tonality in a modern musical idiom, moderation of

[28] Lissa, "Pierwsza opera w Polsce Ludowej. (*Bunt żaków*)."

extreme dissonance, maintenance of communication, and in general some degree of attachment to tradition. The composers who followed this direction sought inspiration largely from preromantic Western art music. (2) Replacement of tonality by other systems of order, typically some form of organization stemming from principles developed by Schoenberg in the 1920s. Composers who followed this direction generally retained some elements of traditional music, though in the more extreme manifestations connection with the past, as well as the idea of music as a sensuous language of communication, seems to have disappeared. Of course the two tendencies which we have thus artificially distinguished interacted in practice and moreover were accompanied by various experiments in timbre, rhythm, and form and by occasional exotic influences. Most recently, the rise of electronic music has opened a completely new field, one whose special possibilities for opera have barely begun to be explored.

The combination of drama and choreography, so typical in the history of French opera, is illustrated in an important opera-ballet, *Padmâvati* by Albert Roussel (1869–1937),[29] produced at Paris in 1923. *Padmâvati* is a large work, scenically splendid, with fascinating rhythms and beautiful choral writing. Roussel's complex, highly refined harmonic style incorporates Hindu scales and melodic formulas so perfectly as to make the exotic quality an inherent part of the music, not a mere external adornment. In the same way, within a smaller framework, Roussel uses Greek scales in the one-act lyric opera *La Naissance de la lyre* (1925), on a libretto adapted by Théodore Reinach from Sophocles' *Ichneutai*.

A major composer of French opera was the Swiss Arthur Honegger (1892–1955),[30] whose output includes many ballets and much music for films as well as operas. *Judith* (1926), rewritten as an opera from the incidental music to René Morax's biblical drama produced in 1925, has the characteristic traits of Honegger's style at this period: fervid declamatory phrases in incisive rhythms over percussive harmonies the progressions of which are actuated by contrapuntal, chromatically moving lines generally in contrary motion, with much use of ostinato figures. The chorus functions chiefly as a background for the soloists'

[29] Special issue of RM (1929); biography by Basil Deane (1961).
[30] Biographies by Delannoy and Tappolet.

singing, except in the last scene, with its strong closing fugue "Gloire au dieu tout puissant Jehovah des armées." Honegger's *Antigone* (1927), to a text by Jean Cocteau "freely adapted from Sophocles," is a concentrated, continuous symphonic setting of the drama without word repetitions, arias, ballets, or any other diversionary matter. The vocal lines are constantly in a type of recitative analogous to that of Lully (that is, deriving its pace, accent, and contour immediately and in detail from the words), but of course much more varied in rhythm and melodic pattern than Lully's. An unusual feature of the declamation is the placing of first syllables on the accented beat instead of treating them in the usual way as anacruses, resulting in a singular vehemence of expression (Example 120). The orchestral part is dissonant and percussive;

Antigone, SC. 4

EXAMPLE 120   HONEGGER

la   jus - ti - ce   non plus n'im-po - se   pas   des   lois   de   ce

gen-re et   je   ne croy-ais   pas   que   ton   de-cret put fai- re pré-va-loir   le

ca-pri-ce d'un homme sur la ré-gle des im-mor-tels sur ces lois qui ne sont pas é-crites

the effect is altogether stark, quite in keeping with the grim, swift-moving text.

Honegger is especially notable as a composer of the typical twentieth-century combination form of opera-oratorio. His *King David* (1921) is a work of this type, as are also, in different ways, the "stage oratorio" *Cris du monde* (1931) and the "dramatic legend" *Nicolas de Flue* (1941). Most important in this category, however, is *Jeanne d'Arc au bûcher* (1938), on a text by Paul Claudel. As in all his serious dramatic works, Honegger here is concerned with basic social and moral conflicts of man in the modern world, dramatized in historic-legendary characters of heroic stature. Like a medieval cathedral, *Jeanne d'Arc* unites sacred and secular, great and small, ascetic and sensuous, the solemn and the grotesque, profundity and naïveté, in one vast structure of poetic and musical architecture: solos, choruses, and ballets, Gregorian chants, dance tunes, medieval and modern folk songs, mingle in the complex, highly colored, music of Honegger; five speaking and five solo parts, a mixed chorus, and a children's chorus are required in addition to a full orchestra.

A minor but far from negligible French opera composer was Honegger's pupil Marcel Delannoy (1898–1962), whose most successful stage work, *Le Poirier de Misère* ("Misère's Peartree," 1927), is a "Flemish legend" set to music in the restless, dissonant style of the time.

The dramatic works of Darius Milhaud (b. 1892),[31] most prolific of all twentieth-century French composers, divide naturally into three groups: (1) opera-oratorios: a trilogy, *Orestie* (composed 1913–24), consisting of the operas *Agamemnon* (1927), *Les Choéphores* ("The Libation-Bearers"; 1919 in concert form, 1935 on the stage), and *Les Euménides* (1927); *Christophe Colomb* (1930); and *David* (1954). (2) Short operas, surrealistic, ironic, comic, or satirical, all composed 1924–26: *Les Malheurs d'Orphée* (1926); the opéra-bouffe *Esther de Carpentras* (1938); *Le Pauvre Matelot* (1927); three "opéras minutes," each ten to fifteen minutes long: *L'Enlèvement d'Europe* (1927), *L'Abandon d'Ariane* (1928), and *La Délivrance de Thésée* (1928); and *Fiesta* (1958). (3) The heroic operas *Maximilien* (1932), *Médée* (1939), and *Bolivar* (1950). To the foregoing may be added an early opera, *La Brebis égarée* ("The Lost Lamb"; composed 1910–15, performed 1923), the scenic cantata *La Sagesse* (1945), and the mystery play *Le Jeu de Robin et Marion* (1951), besides ballets and incidental music to plays.

Le Pauvre Matelot, Milhaud's first big success, is a setting of a short three-act play by Jean Cocteau about a sailor who, returning home rich after an absence of many years, decides to test his wife's fidelity by telling her he is a rich friend of her husband who, he says, is about to return home in utter poverty; the wife, not recognizing him, murders the supposed stranger in order to get his money for her husband. The peculiar unreality of Cocteau's text is heightened by Milhaud's music, which is in a half-serious, ironic manner, constantly tuneful with sophisticated dissonant harmonies (see Example 121). Similar musical procedures, in a more mocking spirit, are evident in the three *opéras minutes*, parodies of Greek myths in the fashion of the old Théâtre de la Foire. *Esther de Carpentras*, a modern, lightly satirical version of the biblical Esther

[31] Studies by Collaer and G. Beck; Milhaud, *Notes sans musique*; Rostand, "The Operas of Darius Milhaud."

(Example 121 continued)

story, is especially remarkable for the comic ensembles of Act I and the vivid crowd scenes of Act II.

Of the operas of the *Orestie* trilogy (the dramas of Aeschylus in translation by Paul Claudel) only *Les Euménides* is set entirely to music. All three include massive choral portions, constantly polytonal in a dissonant texture of blended ostinato figures; extremely sonorous and effective are the places in *Les Choéphores* where the chorus instead of singing speaks in powerful rhythmic measures sustained by a large battery of percussion.

Similar technical procedures mark *Christophe Colomb*. Its two acts and twenty-seven scenes call for ten principal soloists, thirty-five other solo parts, three speaking parts, a chorus, and an orchestra reinforced by a special percussion section. Claudel's drama is conceived in epic-allegorical form, with a Narrator and other external personages, presented in a series of tableaux which are explained, commented on, and connected by choral and spoken interludes with percussion accompaniment. The mystical interpretation of Christopher Columbus is always at the forefront as the various scenes in his career unfold. The climax of Act I is the scene of the mutiny on board Columbus's ship; this act ends with a gigantic setting (in Latin) of the Sanctus. Part II finally takes us back to the Inn at Valladolid, the exact point at which the action began after the prologue, and there is an epilogue ending with a choral Alleluia.

Much of the music is in planar polytonal harmony, that is, with free dissonance arising from superposing motifs (often chord streams) in different tonalities, though as a rule no one motif is completely in a single key. The usual method of construction, except in the longest scenes, is to introduce one theme, establish it by ostinato-like repetition, then add successively one, two, or more themes, each of which is also usually treated in ostinato fashion. Of course the various planes of harmony are kept distinct to some degree by contrasting timbres; and there is compensation for the static harmonic effect produced by constant complex dissonance in the variety and vitality of Milhaud's rhythmic patterns as well as in the monumental impression produced by this type of musical construction. Moreover, when the long-continued dissonance finally resolves to a simple chord at the end of a section, the intensity of the resolution is magnified. An example of this is the mutiny scene in Act I, where after a climax of four tonalities in the chorus and four in the orchestra (a total of seven different keys at once, one being reduplicated), the whole resolves on a closing climactic triad of B-flat major.

Milhaud applied similar techniques to *Maximilien*, a historical opera based on a drama by Franz Werfel. Here, however, the degree of stylization surpasses that of any previous works : action, melodies, rhythms, all are ritualistic; even church hymns and military marches are indicated in formal, antirealistic outline as parts of a tonal design rather than representations of actual happenings. But in *Médée* there is less of the monumental, less dissonance, more lyricism, and more interest in the individual figures of the drama. The restrained dramatic force of the scene of the preparation of the enchantments is remarkable. Most expressive are the slow, melismatic, long lines in the soprano role of the suffering Creusa, innocent victim of Medea's cruelty. *Bolivar*, with *Christophe Colomb* and *Maximilien*, completes a trilogy of operas on Latin American subjects; like *Médée*, it concentrates on characterizing the persons of the drama, and continues the composer's gradual trend away from the revolutionary character of his earlier works. *David* was commissioned to celebrate the 3,000th anniversary of Jerusalem as the capital of David's kingdom; its music seems like a final summing-up of Milhaud's operatic development, a synthesis in which all elements of his style appear, now transfigured and calm within the broad framework of this festival opera-oratorio.

Hindemith, like Milhaud, began as an iconoclast and later modified his style, softening harmonic asperities and clarifying tonal relationships. Several large works of his dating from the 1920s were issued later in revised versions which incorporated such changes. Among them was the opera *Cardillac* [32] (1926; revised 1952), on an excellent tragic libretto by Ferdinand Lyon. No opera of this period more clearly exemplifies the classical principle of separate musical numbers; each number, moreover, is constructed according to purely musical laws, the themes being straightforwardly developed in the manner of a concerto, undeflected by any attempt to illustrate mere details of the text: music and drama run parallel but without interpenetration. The "absolute," instrumental character of the music is reinforced by the prevailing texture, highly rhythmic and contrapuntal; the voice is treated in the late baroque manner as one melodic line among concertizing instruments. In addition to this characteristic linear style, two other idioms are occasionally used: a kind of accompanied recitative in which the vocal declamation is set against a single rhapsodic line in the orchestra; and a quieter, chordal, neoromantic style which foreshadows some aspects of Hindemith's later development (for example, the recitative and aria "Die Zeit vergeht" in Act I, scene 2). The chorus writing is vigorous, idiomatic, and effective, especially in the closing scene.

Mathis der Maler ("Matthias the Painter," 1938) is an opera-oratorio with a libretto by the composer on the subject of Matthias Grünewald, the sixteenth-century German painter—a long, complex work holding much the same position in Hindemith's dramatic production as *Christophe Colomb* in Milhaud's and embracing a great variety of musical styles, among which suggestions of medieval modality are prominent. The most familiar portions of *Mathis* are those arranged by the composer as an orchestral suite, which is frequently heard in concert programs.

[32] Willms, *Führer zur Oper Cardillac.*

The neobaroque trend in Hindemith's music culminates in *Die Harmonie der Welt* ("The Harmony of the Universe," 1957).[33] Like *Mathis*, this is an opera-oratorio, but on an even greater scale : there are eleven solo roles in addition to choruses, and a full orchestra is supplemented by a second orchestra on the stage; many of the sets require a divided stage. Each of the fourteen scenes in the five acts represents an episode in the life and philosophy of the astronomer Johannes Kepler, the title of whose treatise *Harmonices mundi* (1619) Hindemith adopted for his opera. The drama of *Mathis der Maler* had dealt with the position of the artist in society; *Die Harmonie der Welt* was conceived rather as an exemplification of Hindemith's views— going back to medieval teachings—of the order in a work of music as being symbolical of an all-embracing order in the physical and spiritual universe. Consequently, the events and characters have a symbolic function as well as a dramatic one, and this entails both a certain static quality in the development of the drama and an occasional impression that some of the persons are more like allegorical figures than real human beings. This monumental, oratorio-like character of *Die Harmonie der Welt*, in addition to the enormous resources required for its presentation, will doubtless prevent it from ever becoming fixed in the operatic repertoire—which is a misfortune. A richly polyphonic orchestral texture is the basis of the musical structure. As in many twentieth-century operas, classical instrumental forms play a large role in the musical development. Examples are : the "scherzo" in 7/8 time in Act II; the "variations on an old war song" in Act V; and especially the closing scene, reminiscent of the grandiose finales in baroque opera, which introduces the earth, sun, and planets (each represented by the personage who was its mystical incarnation in the drama) in a magnificent apotheosis, to a sonorous, orchestral-choral passacaglia on a theme made up of the following tones :

Tones of passacaglia theme from *Die Harmonie der Welt*
EXAMPLE 122   HINDEMITH

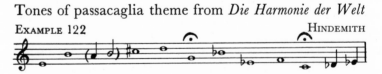

Another important work of the opera-oratorio type was Igor

33 Briner, "Eine Bekenntnisoper Paul Hindemith."

Stravinsky's (b. 1882) [34] *Oedipus rex* ("Oedipus the King"), performed first in concert form in 1927 and the next year on the stage. Its Latin text is a translation of Cocteau's French version of Sophocles. *Oedipus rex* is more oratorio than opera : all the "action" is narrated between the several "scenes," which consist of stark, blocklike solo and choral numbers that magically convey the feeling of the ancient tragedy, antique, impersonal, yet eternally significant. An earlier one-act opera of Stravinsky, *Mavra* (1922), is a short comic piece, stylized almost to the point of burlesque, with puppetlike characters, the action running from beginning to end as it were in a single breath of swift song over continuous music, eccentrically rhythmic and brilliantly scored for a small group of solo instruments.

Stravinsky's only full-length opera is *The Rake's Progress* (1951), on a libretto by W. H. Auden and Chester Kallman, inspired by Hogarth's prints of the same title. This work, like everything else of Stravinsky's, has been so much written about that little need be said here. It is the most thorough example in modern times of a return to classical opera. Not only does it consist of separate solo (or ensemble) vocal numbers with accompaniment by a small orchestra; its whole texture, the harmonic and melodic idiom of the music itself, are neo-Mozartean. A harpsichord accompanies the recitatives; there is a closing "moral," as in *Don Giovanni*; and the mingled tone of spoofing and sentiment throughout is reminiscent of *Figaro* or *Così fan tutte*. Part of the charm of *The Rake's Progress*, of course, comes from our being kept constantly aware that its eighteenth-century costume is a disguise which only half conceals the sophisticated complexity of the drama and music—a mask which can be enjoyed for its own inanimate beauty but which at the same time shields the oversensitive spectator from direct contact with the emotions of laughter and pity, thereby allowing him to enjoy those emotions behind an unmoving mask of his own. But the disguise is forgotten when we come to the dialogue between Tom and Nick in Act III and the pathetic closing scenes in Bedlam, including Anne's tender farewell lullaby (Example 123).

[34] Wade, "A Selected Bibliography of Igor Stravinsky"; Stravinsky, *Poetics*; *idem, Memories and Commentaries*; Stravinsky and Craft, *Conversations*; *idem, Expositions and Developments*; Ramuz, *Souvenirs*; Vlad, *Strawinsky*; Morton, "Stravinsky," in *Encyclopédie de musique* (Fasquelle, 1961); Stravinsky, "On *Oedipus rex*"; Goldovsky, "*Mavra*"; articles on *The Rake's Progress* by White, C. Mason, Schuh, Kerman, Craft, and D. Cooke.

The Rake's Progress, Act III

EXAMPLE 123

STRAVINSKY

Gent - ly, lit - tle boat, A - cross the o - cean float, the crys - tal waves di - vi - ding: the sun __ in the west Is go - ing to rest Glide, glide, glide, to - ward the is - lands of the Blest.

We turn now to some operas based on an aesthetic of drama and a musical style fundamentally different from those so far considered. The expressionist movement in the early part of the twentieth century was reflected in opera most clearly in the works of Arnold Schoenberg (1874–1951) [35] and his pupil, Alban Berg (1885–1935).[36] Schoenberg's *Erwartung* ("Expectation") and *Die glückliche Hand* ("The Lucky Hand") were composed in 1909 and 1913 respectively, though not performed until 1924. Both call for a large orchestra, usually subdivided with only a few instruments playing at one time, and both are in the dissonant, thick Schoenbergian harmonic style of the prewar period. The voice lines are wide in range, with large, ultraexpressive intervals, occasionally going over into *Sprechstimme*—that is, a kind of vocal utterance halfway between speaking and singing, with exactly notated rhythm but only approximately notated pitch. Both dramas are essentially subjective, the outward scenery and action being symbolical; both are, in scale, rather cantatas than operas. *Erwartung* is a monodrama : a woman seeking her lover finds only his dead body, over which she sings a long monologue, a modernistic Liebestod. *Die glückliche Hand* has three soloists with a chorus of twelve voices, and uses colors symbolically in scenery, costumes, and lighting. Schoenberg's later one-act comic opera, *Von Heute auf Morgen* ("From Today until Tomorrow," 1930), is completely in the twelve-tone technique, with distinct recitatives and arias, thus following the general trend of the postwar period toward the number opera. Of the three works, *Erwartung* is the most successful; in both dramatic technique and musical style it may be regarded as a foretaste of Berg's *Wozzeck*.

Schoenberg's one large work for the theatre is *Moses und Aron*, of which he wrote the entire libretto and had composed the music of the first two acts by 1932 (only a few sketches exist for the music of Act III); a radio performance was given in 1954 and the first stage performance in 1957. *Moses und Aron* is an opera-oratorio in which Schoenberg has

[35] Biography by Stuckenschmidt; Wörner, *Gotteswort und Magie*; *idem*, "Arnold Schoenberg and the Theater"; Keller, "Schoenberg's *Moses and Aron*"; Babbitt, "An Introduction to the Music [of *Moses und Aron*]," in brochure accompanying the recording of the opera Columbia K3L-241; Keller, "Schoenberg's Comic Opera [*Von Heute auf Morgen*]."

[36] Biographies and studies by Reich and Redlich; Leibowitz, "Alban Berg et l'essence de l'opéra"; Reich, "A Guide to *Wozzeck*"; Kerman, "Terror and Self-Pity"; Jouve, *Wozzeck ou le nouvel opéra*; Perle, "The Music of *Lulu*"; *idem*, "*Lulu*: The Formal Design."

taken the biblical material for dramatic presentation of the tragic abyss (tragic, because unbridgeable by good will) that lies between wisdom and action: Moses, the philosopher-lawgiver, cannot communicate his vision; Aron, the man of action, can only misunderstand and falsify it. Schoenberg's profound drama is united to a musical score of fearful difficulty (he himself doubted whether a performance would actually be possible), towering in conception, masterly in realization, and of over-whelming dramatic effect. Within the unity imposed by consistent use of a single tone row is endless variety of expression and sound, from the (symbolical) Sprechstimme of Moses' role to the gorgeous oriental colors and wild dance rhythms in the scene of the worship of the Golden Calf. *Moses und Aron*, though unfinished—and its very incompleteness may also be symbolic—is one of the great works of twentieth-century opera, and one that will remain significant for many generations.

In contrast to the oratorio-like character of so many contemporary operas, those of Berg are pure theatre. *Wozzeck*, composed between 1914 and 1922 and first performed at Berlin in 1925, is based on a "dramatic fragment" by Georg Büchner (1813–37), the original twenty-five scenes being reduced by Berg to fifteen and grouped in three acts of five scenes each. Wozzeck, the hero, is a representative of what he himself calls "Wir arme Leut'" ("We poor folk"), tormented by circumstances, suffering but unconscious of guilt, finally murdering his mistress and drowning himself, driven always by forces he never thinks of questioning or resisting. Despite the date of Büchner's drama, *Wozzeck* is thoroughly typical of the postwar period in Germany; its atmosphere seems as though infected by the morbid, bitter, neurotic mood of that time. Yet it is not merely topical: Wozzeck is a universal figure, symbol of the oppressed and, in a larger sense, of man in his naked helplessness before blind powers that care nothing about his fate. Since the expressionist technique makes every external object a projection of Wozzeck's own soul, the scenes, characters, and events of the opera have an unearthly quality, like a nightmarish puppet show; and Berg's music belongs to this nightmare world as surely as Debussy's belongs to the dream world of *Pelléas et Mélisande*. The harmonic style of *Wozzeck* is in most places atonal, full of strange, wonderful color effects (for example, the scene of Wozzeck's suicide) and distorted reminiscences of the normal "waking" world (for example, the "folk song" in Act I, the caricature of the *Rosenkavalier* waltzes in Act II). The vocal lines, mostly in sharply

pointed declamation with abrupt wide intervals, alternate between
ordinary speech, Sprechstimme, and song. There are a few recurring
motifs, notably Wozzeck's "Wir arme Leut'" (see Example 124), but

EXAMPLE 124   *Wozzeck*, Act I, sc. 1

BERG

the chief means of unity is the organization of each act and scene in set
musical forms derived from classical patterns. But these patterns reveal
themselves only on analysis; it is no part of the composer's intention
that the auditor should perceive them, unless subliminally. Sometimes
they have a direct dramatic function: there is a grim fitness, for
example, in the choice of the learned passacaglia form for the scene
(Act I, scene 4) where Wozzeck submits himself to a doctor as a subject
for scientific experiments. The scenes within each act are connected by
orchestral interludes; the longest of these, in Act III, recapitulates the

themes of the entire drama in climax before leading into the brief coda-like final scene. *Wozzeck* provoked a riot at the first performance; now that the sound of the music has become more familiar, it has come to be generally recognized not only as a powerful drama in music but also as one of the few really successful operas in a fully modern style.

Berg's second opera, *Lulu*, was completed in substance before the composer's death, but the orchestration had been finished only through the first two acts and a small part of the third. The first two acts, and two fragments of the third, were performed in 1937 and there have been frequent revivals since. The libretto is taken, with some cuts, from two plays by Frank Wedekind. The central personage, Lulu, is conceived as the incarnation of the "primal woman-spirit," and the drama is concerned with the fatal effects of her attraction for various lovers, finally ending with her own doom. Although externally occupied with the most realistic details, the work is not essentially realistic but rather expressionistic, sometimes grotesquely and extravagantly so. As drama, the subject is too specialized to have the same elemental human appeal that *Wozzeck* has; and it is probably this defect, as much as the notorious complexity of the music, that has kept *Lulu* from becoming as popular as Berg's earlier opera. Notwithstanding the complexity, however, *Lulu* is marvellously effective in the theatre. The changing flow of the drama and the intensity of its emotional expression are always controlled by the composer's intellectual power in wielding musical forms. Certain motifs, harmonies, tone series, and combinations are associated with particular characters and scenes. The opera is not, as has often been stated, based throughout on a single tone row, but its felt musical unity is the result of interconnections among the different formal elements. Such subtle relationships are no more consciously grasped by the audience than are the comparable relationships in *Wozzeck*; but the formal unity and the dramatic import of both works can be sensed in the theatre without a knowledge of their technical construction.

Within the general orbit of the Schoenbergian musical style was *Alkestis* (1924) by Egon Wellesz (b. 1885),[37] a one-act setting of a text by Hofmannsthal (after Euripides) in a series of broad tableux in a rather austere, monolithic idiom. The important position of the chorus in this work was even more emphasized in Wellesz's *Die Bakchantinnen*

[37] Beer, "Egon Wellesz und die Oper"; Redlich, "Egon Wellesz."

(1931). Likewise of the same Central European school were two operas of Ernst Krenek: *Das Leben des Orest* ("The Life of Orestes," 1930), a half-satirical treatment of the Orestes myth cycle; and the large historical opera *Karl V* (1938), Krenek's most important work for the theatre, remarkable for nobility of style well suited to the grandeur of the subject. Krenek's *Pallas Athene weint* ("Pallas Athene Weeps," 1955) presents scenes of the war between Athens and Sparta with application to the modern issue of how to defend freedom without succumbing to tyranny; the music is based on an adaptation of the twelve-tone technique. A somewhat similar technique is used in *The Bell Tower* (Urbana, 1957), an expertly wrought, dramatically and musically satisfying setting of a libretto by the composer based on the story by Herman Melville.

Since 1940 an increasing number of composers in every country have adopted some form of twelve-tone technique, either using it as the basis of all their writing or blending or combining it with other techniques and styles. The leading composer of this school in Germany, Wolfgang Fortner (b. 1907), is distinguished for symphonic and choral works as well as operas; his principal opera is *Die Bluthochzeit* ("Blood Wedding," 1957), a melodious, clean-textured setting of García Lorca's tragedy *Bodas de sangre*.

Among many other composers in postwar Germany, two have attracted particular notice for their operas. The Swiss-born Rolf Liebermann (b. 1910) [38] in *Lenore 40/45* (1952) and *Penelope* (1954) has juxtaposed contrasting musical styles for novel treatment, half realistic and half fantastic-satirical, of contemporary subject matter. His *School for Wives* (1955) is a witty modern version, with music in tonal style, of Molière's comedy. Hans Werner Henze (b. 1926) in *Boulevard Solitude* (1952) presented a realistic adaptation of the *Manon Lescaut* story in which each of the separate scenes is accompanied by a stylized modern dance. Henze, one of the most active younger German composers for the theatre, next produced *Ein Landarzt* ("A Country Doctor," 1953), based on Kafka's story, with music in a style deriving from Berg's *Lulu*; and *König Hirsch* ("King Stag," 1956), a fairy-tale opera with a long, elaborate, and variegated score. *Der Prinz von Homburg* (1960), adapted from Kleist's drama, is a full-scale grand opera with choruses, but its carefully constructed music fails to avoid monotony.

[38] R. Klein, "Rolf Liebermann als dramatischer Komponist"; Glanville-Hicks, "Some Reflections on Opera."

One of the most successful strict applications of twelve-tone technique to opera is heard in *Il prigionero* ("The Prisoner," 1950) by Luigi Dallapiccola (b. 1904) [39]—successful, because the technical method is perfectly absorbed into the musical content: gradations of dissonance, all the subtle sonorities, function for expressive ends, and the solo parts are conceived, in the good Italian tradition, as singing human voices rather than abstract contrapuntal lines. Four soloists, a large orchestra (including saxophones, vibraphone, and other "extra" wood winds and percussion), with brass, bells, and organ and large and small choruses onstage, make up the performing forces. There are four scenes, with a prologue and two choral interludes on Latin liturgical texts. The drama centers around the condition of a Prisoner tortured by hope, "the ultimate torture," but destined never in this world to escape; this Prisoner (nameless, like all the other characters) is the type of modern man. Dallapiccola's thought was occupied with the same theme of imprisonment and escape in his *Canti di prigionia* ("Songs of the Prison," 1941) and *Canti di liberazione* ("Songs of Liberation," 1955). The music of *Il prigionero* makes use at times of fixed forms, and often approaches the effect of conventional tonality (especially in the second choral interlude). An idea of the style can be obtained from a portion of the second "ricercare" from scene 3, based on a recurrent motif associated with the ironic word "fratello" ("brother") by which his jailers always address the Prisoner (Example 125).

6. SOME EXPERIMENTS

In the course of the general tendency toward sophistication or massiveness in opera music of the 1930s, a move in the opposite direction, toward radical simplification, was undertaken by Carl Orff (b. 1895).[40] The resulting works aroused more comment, favorable or otherwise, than any other operas of the time—to begin with, because none were operas in the traditional sense of the word, and none were so called in their titles. The *Carmina burana* (1937), *Catulli carmina* (1943), and *Trionfo di Afrodite* (1953) are essentially combinations of cantata and

[39] Vlad, "Dallapiccola 1948–1955"; Nathan, "The Twelve-Tone Compositions of Luigi Dallapiccola"; Dallapiccola, "The Genesis of the *Canti di prigionia*."

[40] Liess, *Carl Orff*; Kiekert, *Die musikalische Form in den Werken Carl Orff's*; Helm, "Carl Orff"; W. Keller, *Karl Orff's Antigonae*; Stäblein, "Schöpferische Tonalität."

EXAMPLE 125   *Il prigionero*, SC. 3

♩ = 38–40   DALLAPICCOLA

The Prisoner (quasi senza fiato)

Non reg - go.   Sor - pre-so qui, la

not-te,   e - vi-tar non po-tre-i nuo-via-tro-ci sup - pli - zi.

Che   fa - re?   Ri - tor - na - re nel-la mia

cel - la scu-ra ad a-spet-ta-re an-co-ra e sem-pre in-va-no?

ballet; so also, but in a different manner and with greater use of spoken dialogue, are *Die Bernauerin* (1947) and *Astutuli* (1953). More like operas in the ordinary sense are *Der Mond* ("The Moon," 1939) and *Die Kluge* ("The Wise Woman," 1943), though it would perhaps be more accurate to designate these as "folk-plays with music." The typical idiom in *Die Kluge* is a narrow-ranged, strongly accented melody with many repeated notes and with the phrases reiterated over and over in ostinato fashion; this melody is accompanied by the simplest possible harmonies, statically persistent, from a small orchestra with emphasis on percussion instruments and percussive rhythmic sound.

This type of percussive-ostinato background, with still further simplification of harmony and melody, is applied to a totally different kind of dramatic material in Orff's two operas *Antigonae* (1949) and *Oedipus der Tyrann* (1959), both settings of Hölderlin's translations from Sophocles. In these, there are five gradations of vocal delivery for both soloists and chorus : (1) ordinary speech; (2) rhythmic semi-speech (similar to Berg's Sprechstimme); (3) a form of stylized speech consisting of rhythmic chanting centered on one tone but punctuated by melodic deflections to nearby tones or occasional wide leaps; (4) the same, but expanding into a longer quasi-melodic chant; and (5) a combination of (3) or (4) with sweeping stepwise fast impassioned melismatic outbursts, characteristically placed at the beginning of a phrase (Example 126). The voices may be either unaccompanied or accompanied by ostinato rhythmic patterns in many different combinations of percussion, either without fixed pitch or in static harmonies. The chorus constantly participates in the action and each scene is in a clearly outlined musical form. No description can do more than suggest the unique effects produced by the composer's peculiar choice of means. Music, reduced nearly to the primal elements of rhythm and single tones, enters into a union with language that conjures up for the imagination a far-off mythical stage in the history of human speech when word and tone were still one and unseparated. The variety of sounds and the varying degrees of dramatic tension that Orff manages to achieve within his self-imposed musical limitations are remarkable; nevertheless, the very intensity of the idiom tends to limit the length of time within which it can be effective, and for this reason perhaps *Oedipus*, being shorter than *Antigonae*, is the more successful of the two works.

EXAMPLE 126 *Oedipus der Tyrann* ORFF

Orff's is certainly the most significant "experiment" in the musical theatre of the twentieth century. Some others that have attracted attention, but that have not—or not yet—led to any important consequences, include the two operas on texts of Gertrude Stein composed by Virgil Thomson (b. 1896):[41] *Four Saints in Three Acts* (1934) and

[41] Hoover and Cage, *Virgil Thomson*; Helm, "Virgil Thomson's *Four Saints in Three Acts.*"

The Sly Vixen, Act III

EXAMPLE 127

JANÁČEK

Jak je les di - vu - krás - ný!

Až ru - sal - ky přij - dou za - se do - mů,

do svých let - ních sí - del,

(Example 127 continued)

(*Example 127 continued*)

The Mother of Us All (1947), both in a sophisticatedly simple musical style with sensitive word-setting; Max Brand's [42] *Maschinist Hopkins* (1929), climax in opera of the "motoristic" era of the 1920s, an expressionistic work with mechanical sound effects, dissonant percussive harmonies, and some numbers in jazz style; and Louis Gruenberg's (b. 1884) *The Emperor Jones* (1933), based on Eugene O'Neill's play and exploiting a neoprimitive orchestra with drum rhythms and choral interludes. A momentary sensation in Europe was George Antheil's (1900–1959) satirical jazz opera *Transatlantic* (1930). More recent novelties were Boris Blacher's (b. 1903) *Abstract Opera No. 1* (Frankfurt, 1953), on a text of meaningless syllables with music in lightly satirical vein; and *Aniara* (1959), by the Swedish composer Karl-Birger Blomdahl (b. 1916), in which the characteristic unearthly sound of

---

[42] Brand, "'Mechanische' Musik und das Problem der Oper"; articles in *Signale für die musikalische Welt*, 1929, 1930.

electronic music is applied to a drama on a space ship out of control, falling endlessly into the interstellar depths.

Here our survey of the history of opera ends. It is sad to think that so much beauty lies buried in the silence of the past, that all these things which so mightily pleased our forefathers have become old things of yesterday. The operas of the past can live now, with their movement and color and sound, for the most part only in our imagination, as we are able to cast ourselves back for a moment to the times when they were part of the life of men now passed away, "faded into impalpability through death, through absence, through change of manners." [43] But earth remains and ancient beauty comes again in new forms. "Here in these woods," sings Janáček's Forester (see Example 127), "life renews itself, and the nightingales return with each returning Spring to find their nests, and Love . . . always the same : where then was parting, now is meeting." [44]

[43] Joyce's *Ulysses*, ninth episode.
[44] Paraphrase of Max Brod's German version of Janáček's text.

BIBLIOGRAPHY

I

BIBLIOGRAPHIES, LEXICONS, GUIDES, HISTORIES, COLLECTED ESSAYS, AND OTHER GENERAL WORKS

Abbiati, Franco. Storia della musica. Milan, A. Garzanti, 1953–54. 5 vols.

Aber, Adolf. Die Musik im Schauspiel, Geschichtliches und Aesthetisches. Leipzig, M. Beck, 1926.

Abert, Anna Amalie. Die Oper : Von den Anfangen bis zum Beginn des 19. Jahrhunderts. Cologne, 1953.

—— "Wort und Ton," in Gesellschaft für Musikforschung: Bericht über den internationalen . . . Kongress Hamburg 1956 (Kassel, [etc.] Bärenreiter, 1957) 43–46.

Abert, Anna Amalie, and Hans Ehinger. "Oper," MGG X, 1–75.

Abert, Hermann. Gesammelte Schriften und Vorträge. Halle an der Saale, M. Niemeyer, 1929.

—— Grundprobleme der Operngeschichte. Leipzig, B&H, 1926.

Abry, Emile. Histoire illustrée de la littérature française . . . par E. Abry, C. Audic, P. Crouzet. Paris, Didier, 1935. New ed.

Ademollo, Alessandro. Bibliografia della cronistoria teatrale italiana. Milan, Ricordi, 1888.

Adler, Guido. Handbuch der Musikgeschichte unter Mitwirkung von Fachgenossen. Frankfurt/M., Frankfurter Verlags-Anstalt, 1924.

Albinati, Giuseppe. Piccolo dizionario di opere teatrali, oratori, cantati, ecc. Milan, Ricordi, 1913.

Altmann, Wilhelm. Führer durch die einaktigen Opern, Operetten und Singspiele des Verlages Ed. Bote und G. Bock. Berlin, Bote & Bock, 1919.

—— Katalog der seit 1861 in den Handel gekommenen theatralischen Musik (Opern, Operetten, Possen, Musik zu Schauspielen, usw) : Ein musikbibliographischer Versuch. Wolfenbüttel, Verlag für musikalische Kultur und Wissenschaft, 1935.

Ambros, August Wilhelm. Geschichte der Musik, Band IV. Leipzig, Leuchart, 1909. 3d ed., rev. and enl. by Hugo Leichtentritt.

Andeutungen zur Geschichte der Oper. Marienwerder, A. Baumann, 1845. "Besonderer Abdruck aus dem ersten Hefte des Archivs für vaterländische Interessen pro 1845."

Appia, Adolphe. Die Musik und die Inscenierung : Aus dem Französischen übersetzt. Munich, Bruckmann, 1899.

Apthorp, William Foster. The Opera Past and Present. London, John Murray, 1901.

Arnals, Alexander d'. Der Operndarsteller : Lehrgang zur musikalischen Darstellung in der Oper. Berlin, Bote & Bock, [1932].

Arundell, Dennis. "Operatic Ignorance," PMA LI (1924–25) 73–96.

Associazione dei musicologi italiana. Bolletino : Catalogo delle opere musicali sino ai primi decenni del secolo XIX, Parma, 1910–11.
Catalogues of music collections by cities, under each city by libraries, under each library by forms and media, e.g., "opere teatrali."

Aubin, Léon. Le Drame lyrique : Histoire de la musique dramatique en France. [Tours, Edition de l' "Echo littéraire et artistique"], 1908.

Auden, W. H. "Quelques réflexions sur la musique et sur l'opéra," in Encyclopédie de la musique (Paris, Fasquelle, [cop. 1958]) I, 93–100.

—— "Some Reflections on Opera as a Medium," Tempo No. 2 (Summer, 1951) 6–10.

Austin, Cecil. "Cinema Music," M&L V (1924) 177–91.

Balanchine, George. Balanchine's Complete Stories of the Great Ballets. Edited by Francis Mason. Garden City, N.Y., Doubleday & Co., 1954.

Barrenechea, Maríano Antonío. Historia estética de la música, con dos estudios mas sobre consideraciones historicas y tecnicas acerca del canto y la obra maestra del teatro melodramatico. Buenos Aires, Editorial Claridad, 1941.

Bauer, Rudolf. Oper und Operette : Ein Führer durch die Welt der Musikbühne. Berlin, Deutsche Buch-Gemeinschaft, [1959].

Bekker, Paul. Klang und Eros. Stuttgart and Berlin, Deutsche Verlags-Anstalt, 1922.

—— Kritische Zeitbilder. Berlin, Schuster & Loeffler, 1921.

—— Das Operntheater. Leipzig, Quelle & Meyer, 1931.

—— Wandlungen der Oper. Zurich and Leipzig, Orell Füssli, [1934]. Translated as : The Changing Opera. [New York], W. W. Norton, [1935].

Beloch, Julius. "La populazione d'Italia nei secoli XVI, XVII e XVIII," Bulletin de l'Institut international de statistique III (1888) 1–42.

Bernet Kempers, Karel P. De Italiaansche Opera, haar Ontstaan en Ontwikkeling van Peri tot Puccini. Amsterdam, H. J. Paris, 1929.

Bertrand, Paul. "Pure Music and Dramatic Music," MQ IX (1923) 545–55.

Bethléem, Abbé L., and others. Les Opéras, les opéras-comiques et les opérettes. Paris, Editions de la Revue des lectures, 1926.

Biancolli, Louis, and Robert Bagar, eds. The Victor Book of Operas. New York, Simon & Schuster, 1953. Newly rev. ed.

Bie, Oskar. Die Oper. Berlin, S. Fischer, 1913.

Biehle, Herbert. Musikgeschichte der Stadt Bautzen. Berlin Dissertation, 1923.

Blaze de Bury, Yetta. "The French Opera," *Nineteenth Century* (1890) No. 2, 39–53.

Böhme, Franz Magnus. Geschichte des Tanzes in Deutschland. Leipzig, B&H, 1886. 2 vols.

Boll, André. La Grande Pitié du théâtre lyrique. Paris, Editions France Empire, 1946.

Bollert, Werner. Aufsätze zur Musikgeschichte. Bottrop, Postberg, 1938.

Bologna. Liceo musicale. Biblioteca. Catalogo della biblioteca del Liceo musicale di Bologna, compilato da Gaetano Gaspari. Bologna, Libreria romagnoli dell' acqua, 1890–1905. 4 vols.

Bonaccorsi, Alfredo. "L'opera in musica," RMI XXXVI (1929) 594–99.

Bonaventura, Arnaldo. L'opera italiana. Florence, Novissima enciclopedia monografia illustrata, [1928].

—— Saggio storico sul teatro musicale italiano. Leghorn, R. Giusti, 1913.

Boston Public Library. Allen A. Brown Collection. A Catalogue of the Allen A. Brown Collection of Books Relating to the Stage. Boston, 1919.

—— Catalogue of the Allen A. Brown Collection of Music. Boston, 1910–16. 4 vols.

Botstiber, Hugo. Geschichte der Ouvertüre und der freien Orchesterformen. Leipzig, B&H, 1913.

Brandl, Willy. Der Weg der Oper. Stuttgart, Curt E. Schwab, 1949.

British Museum. Department of Manuscripts. Catalogue of Manuscript Music in the British Museum, by Augustus Hughes-Hughes. London, 1906–9. 3 vols.

—— Department of Printed Books. Catalogue of Printed Music Published between 1487 and 1800 Now in the British Museum, by W. Barclay Squire. [London], 1912. 2 vols. The Second Supplement (1940) lists all acquisitions from 1912 to 1940 and makes corrections of the 1912 catalogue.

—— Department of Printed Books. King's Music Library. Catalogue of the King's Music Library, by William Barclay Squire. London, 1927–29. 3 vols.

Brockway, Wallace, and Herbert Weinstock. The Opera : A History of Its Creation and Performance, 1600–1941. New York, Simon & Schuster, 1941. 2d ed. : New York, Pantheon, 1962.

Bruneau, Alfred. La Musique française : Rapport sur la musique en France du XIIIe au XXe siècles; la musique à Paris en 1900. Paris, E. Fasquelle, 1901.

Brussels. Bibliothèque royale de Belgique. Catalogue de la bibliothèque de F. J. Fétis acquise par l'état belge. Ghent, J. S. Van Doosselaere; Brussels, C. Muquardt : Paris, Firmin-Didot, 1877.

—— Conservatoire royal de musique. Bibliothèque. Catalogue de la bibliothèque du Conservatoire royal de musique de Bruxelles . . . par Alfred Wotquenne. Brussels, J.-J. Coosemans, 1898– . 4 vols. Annexe[s]

I, Brussels, O. Schepens, 1901, contains : Libretti d'opéras et d'oratorios italiens du XVIIe siècle.

Bücken, Ernst. Der heroische Stil in der Oper. Leipzig, Kistner & Siegel, 1924.

Bulthaupt, Heinrich Alfred. Dramaturgie der Oper. Leipzig, B&H, 1887. 2 vols.

Burian, Karel Vladimir. Die Oper : Ihre Geschichte in Wort und Bild. [Prague], Artia, 1961.

Bustico, Guido. Bibliografia delle storie e cronistorie dei teatri italiani. Milan, Bollettino bibliografico musicale, 1929.

Cambridge University. Fitzwilliam Museum. Library. Catalogue of the Music in the Fitzwilliam Museum, Cambridge, by J. A. Fuller-Maitland. London, C. J. Clay, 1893.

Canal, Pietro. Dalla musica in Mantova. Venice, Presso la segreteria del R. Istituto, 1881.

Capell, Richard. Opera. London, E. Benn, [1930].

Capri, Antonio. Il melodramma dalle origini ai nostri giorni. Modena, Guanda, 1938.

Carducci, Edgardo. "The Tenor Voice in Europe," M&L XI (1930) 318–23.

Challis, Bennett. "The Techniques of Operatic Acting," MQ XIII (1927) 630–45.

Chavarri, Eduardo López. Historia de la música. Barcelona, Imprenta elzeviriana, 1929. 3d ed.

Cheney, Sheldon. The Theatre. New York, Longmans, Green, 1929.

Child, Harold. "Some Thoughts on Opera Libretto," M&L II (1921) 244–53.

Chouquet, Gustave. Histoire de la musique dramatique en France. Paris, Firmin-Didot, 1873.

Chrysander, Friedrich. "Ueber die Unsittlichkeiten in unseren Operntexten," AMZ XIV (1879) 257–59, 273–74, 305–8.

Clément, Félix. Dictionnaire des opéras (dictionnaire lyrique), rev. et mis à jour par Arthur Pougin. Paris, Larousse, [1905].

Closson, Hermann. Musique et drame. Brussels, [Institut national belge de radiodiffusion], 1939.

Combarieu, Jules. Histoire de la musique. Paris, A. Colin, 1920. 3d ed. 3 vols.

—— "Histoire du théâtre lyrique." RHCM VII (1907) 581–97; VIII (1908) 1–594 passim; IX (1909) passim; X (1910) passim.

Cone, Edward T. "Music : A View from Delft," MQ XLVII (1961) 439–53.

Corbet, August. Het Muziekdrama in de XVIe en XVIIe Eeuwen in Italie gezien in het Licht van H. Wölfflin's Kunstgeschichtliche Grundbegriffen: Ein Bijdrage tot de Theorie van het Parallelisme in de Kunst. Antwerp, De Sikkel, 1936.

Covent Garden Opera Series. London, Boosey & Hawkes, 1947(?)– .

Cross, Milton. Complete Stories of the Great Operas. Garden City, N.Y., Doubleday & Co., 1955.

Crowell's Handbook of World Opera. Compiled by Frank Ledlie Moore. New York, Thomas Y. Crowell Co., [1961].

Curzon, Henri de. L'Evolution lyrique au théâtre dans les differents pays : Tableau chronologique. Paris, Fortin, 1908.

Czech, Stan. Das Operettenbuch. Stuttgart, Muth, 1960. 4th ed.

Czerny, Peter, ed. Opernbuch. Berlin, Henschelverlag, [1961]. 5th ed.

Damerini, Adelmo, and Gino Roncaglia, eds. Musicisti della scuola emiliano. Siena, Accademia Musicale Chigiana, 1956.

Dassori, Carlo. Opere e operisti (dizionario lirico 1541–1902) : Elenco nominativo universale dei maestri compositori di opere teatrali, col prospetto cronologico dei lori principali lavori e catalogo alfabetico generale delle opere . . . coll' indicazione di data e di luogo della prima rappresentazione, avuto speciale reguardo al repertorio italiano. Genoa, R. Istituto sordomuti, 1903.

Davey, Henry. History of English Music. London, Curwen, [1921]. 2d ed., revised.

Decugis, Nicole, and Suzanne Reymond. Le Décor de théâtre en France du moyen âge à 1925. Paris, Compagnie Française des Arts Graphiques, 1953.

Deditius, Annemarie. Theorien über die Verbindung von Poesie und Musik. Liegnitz, Seyffarth, 1918.

Della Corte, Andrea. Drammi per musica dal Rinuccini allo Zeno. Turin, Unione Tipografico-Editrice Torinese, [1958]. 2 vols.

—— Il libretto e il melodramma. Turin, A. Viretto, [1951].

—— La "poesia per musica" ed il libretto d'opera. Introduzione a una storia dell' opera. Turin, Gheroni, 1950.

—— "Questioni melodrammaliturgiche in un saggio sul libretto," Collectanea historiae musicae II (1956) 127–34.

—— Tre secoli di opera italiana. Turin, Arione, [1938].

Denkmäler des Theaters : Inszenierung, Dekoration, Kostüm des Theaters. Vienna, Nationalbibliothek; Munich, R. Piper, [1925?–30]. In twelve parts; plates (some colored) in portfolios, with explanatory text laid in. Also published as : Monumenta scenica : The Art of the Theatre. London, Batsford, 1925–31.

Dent, Edward J. "The Nomenclature of Opera," M&L XXV (1944) 132–40, 213–26.

—— Opera. New York, Penguin Books, [1940].

—— "The Translation of Operas," PMA LXI (1934–35) 81–104.

Dilla, Geraldine P. "Music Drama : An Art Form in Four Dimensions," MQ X (1924) 492–99.

Doisy, Marcel. Musique et drame. Paris, A. Flament, [1949].

Dubech, Lucien, J. de Montbrial, and Hélène Horn-Monval. Histoire générale illustrée du théâtre. Paris, Librairie de France, 1931–34. 5 vols.

Dumesnil, René. Histoire illustré du théâtre lyrique. Paris, Plon, [1953].

—— L'Opéra et l'opéra-comique. Paris, Presses Universitaires de France, 1947. 2d ed.

Edwards, [Henry] Sutherland. History of the Opera from Monteverdi to Donizetti. London, W. H. Allen, 1862. 2d ed.

Eichborn, Hermann. Die Trompete in alter und neuer Zeit. Leipzig, B&H, 1881.

Einstein, Alfred. Essays on Music. New York, W. W. Norton, [1956].

—— "German Opera, Past and Present," MMus XI, No. 2 (January–February, 1934) 65–72.

—— "The Mortality of Opera," M&L XXII (1941) 358–66.

Elson, Arthur. A Critical History of Opera : Giving an Account of the Rise and Progress of the Different Schools, with a Description of the Master Works in Each. Boston, L. C. Page, 1901.

Elson, Louis C. "Atrocities and Humors of Opera," MQ VI (1920) 206–13.

Enciclopedia della spettacolo. Rome, Casa Editrice Le Machere, 1954– . 5 vols. to 1960.

Euting, Ernst. Zur Geschichte der Blasinstrumente im 16. und 17. Jahrhundert. Berlin, A. Schulze, 1899.

Ewen, David. Encyclopedia of the Opera. New York, A. A. Wyn, [1955].

Falconi, Dino, and Angelo Frattini. Guida alla rivista e all' operetta. Milan, Academia, [1953].

Ferand, Ernst. Die Improvisation in der Musik. Zurich, Rhein-Verlag, [1938].

Fink, Gottfried Wilhelm. Wesen und Geschichte der Oper : Ein Handbuch für alle Freunde der Tonkunst. Leipzig, G. Wigand, 1838.

Foss, Hubert J. The Heritage of Music. Vol. III. London, Oxford University Press, 1951.

Frankenfelder, August. Historische Elemente in der Oper und ihre ästhetische Bedeutung. Würzburg, Becker, 1896.

Freedley, George, and John A. Reeves. A History of the Theatre. New York, Crown Publishers, [1941].

Fürst, Leonhard. Der musikalische Ausdruck der Körperbewegung in der Opernmusik. Miesbach, Mayr, 1932.

Galli, Amintore. Estetica della musica ossia del bello nella musica sacra, teatrale, e da concerto in ordine alla sua storia. Turin, Bocca, 1899.

Galloway, W. Johnson. The Operatic Problem. London, Long, 1902.

Gavazzeni, Gianandrea. La morte dell' opera. [Milan], Meridiana, [1954].

—— La musica e il teatro. [Pisa], Nistri-Lischi, [1954].

—— "La poesia dell' opera in musica," RassM XI (1938) 137–62.

Gedenkschrift für Hermann Abert. Halle an der Saale, M. Niemeyer, 1928.

Geisenheyner, Max. Kulturgeschichte des Theaters : Volk und Drama. Berlin, Safari-Verlag, 1951.

Gilder, Rosamond, and George Freedley. Theatre Collections in Libraries and Museums : An International Handbook. New York, Theatre Arts, 1936.

Ginisty, Paul. Le Melodrama. Paris, L. Michaud, [1910].

Gloggner, Carl. "Oper und Gesangskunst," Musikalisches Wochenblatt I (1870) 65–67, 81–82, 97–98, 113–14.

Goddard, Joseph. The Rise and Development of Opera. London, W. Reeves, 1912.

Götze, Willibald. Studien zur Formbildung der Oper. Frankfurt/M., Brönner, 1935.

Goldschmidt, Hugo. "Zur Geschichte der Arien- und Symphonie-Formen," MfMg XXXIII (1901) 61–70.

Goode, Gerald. The Book of Ballets. New York, Crown Publishers, [1939].

Grand-Carteret, John. "Les Titres illustrés et l'image au service de la musique," RMI V (1898) 1–63, 225–80; VI (1899) 289–329; IX (1902) 557–635; XI (1904) 1–23, 191–227.

Grégoir, Edouard. Des Gloires de l'opéra et la musique à Paris. Brussels, Schott, 1878. 3 vols.

—— Littérature musicale. Brussels, Schott, 1872–76. 4 vols.

—— Panthéon musical populaire. Brussels, Schott, 1876–77. 6 vols.

Gregor, Hans. Die Welt der Oper—die Oper der Welt. Berlin, Bote & Bock, [1931].

Gregor, Joseph. Kulturgeschichte der Oper : Ihre Verbindung mit dem Leben, den Werken des Geistes und der Politik. Vienna, Gallus Verlag; Zurich, Scientia Verlag, [1950]. 2d ed.

—— Weltgeschichte des Theaters. [Zurich], Phaidon, [1933].

Griggs, John C. "The Influence of Comedy upon Operatic Form," MQ III (1917) 552–61.

Grove, Sir George. Dictionary of Music and Musicians. Edited by Eric Blom. London, Macmillan, 1954. 5th ed. 9 vols. Supplementary Volume. New York, St. Martin's Press, 1961.

Grün, Bernard. Kulturgeschichte der Operette. Munich, Langen, Müller, [1961].

Gundry, Inglis. "The Nature of Opera as a Composite Art," PMA LXXIII (1946–47) 25–33.

Haas, Robert M. Afführungspraxis der Musik. Wildpark-Potsdam, Athenaion, [1931].

Hagemann, Carl. Oper und Szene : Aufsätze zur Regie des musikalischen Dramas. Berlin, Schuster & Loeffler, 1905.

Hansemann, Marlise. Der Klavier-Auszug von den Anfängen bis Weber. Borna, Meyen, 1943.

Hartnoll, Phyllis, ed. The Oxford Companion to the Theatre. London, New York, Oxford University Press, 1957. 2d ed. See especially the articles "Incidental Music" (E. Blom) and "Opera" (A. Loewenberg).

Hatton, A. P. "Personality in Opera," M&L XII (1931) 164–69.

Hausswald, Günter. Das neue Opernbuch. Berlin, Henschelverlag, 1957. 7th ed.

Haweis, Hugh Reginald. Music and Morals. New York, Harper, 1872.

Hédouin, Pierre. Mosaique : Peintres—musiciens— . . . à partir du 15e siècle jusqu'à nos jours. Paris, Heugel, 1856.

Heinrich, Viktor. Komik und Humor in der Musik. Vienna Dissertation, 1931.

Heseltine, Philip. "The Scope of Opera," M&L I (1920) 230–33.

Hirsch, Franz. Die Oper und der Literaturgeist : Ein Wort zu Operntextreform. Leipzig, Voigt, 1868.

Hirsch, Paul. Katalog der Musikbibliothek Paul Hirsch . . . Band II : Opern-Partituren. Berlin, Breslauer, 1930.

Hope-Wallace, Philip. A Picture History of Opera. New York, Macmillan, [1959].

Horowicz, Bronislaw. Le Théâtre d'opera : Histoire—réalisations scéniques —possibilités. Paris, Editions de Flore, 1946.

Hostomská, Anna. Opera. Prague, Státní nakladatelství krásné literatury, hubdy a umění, 1958. 3d ed.

Howes, Frank. A Key to Opera. London and Glasgow, Blackie, [1939].

—— "Professor Wellesz on Opera," M&L XV (1934) 120–27.

Hussey, Dyneley. Euridice; or, The Nature of Opera. London, K. Paul, 1929.

—— Some Composers of Opera. London, New York, Toronto, Oxford University Press, 1952.

Istel, Edgar. Das Buch der Oper. Berlin, M. Hesse, [1920]. 2d ed.

—— Die komische Oper : Eine historisch-ästhetische Studie. Stuttgart, C. Grüninger, [1906].

—— Das Libretto : Wesen, Aufbau und Wirkung des Opernbuchs. Berlin and Leipzig, Schuster & Loeffler, 1914. Translated (revised) as : The Art of Writing Opera Librettos. New York, G. Schirmer, [1922].

—— Revolution und Oper. Regensburg, G. Bosse, 1919.

Jansen, Lothar. Studien zur Entwicklungsgeschichte der Oper in Italien, Frankreich, und Deutschland. Bonn Dissertation, 1914.

Junk, Victor. Die Bedeutung der Schlusskadenz im Musikdrama. Leipzig, L. Doblinger, [1926].

Kapp, Julius. Das Opernbuch : Eine Geschichte der Oper und ein musikalisch-dramatischer Führer. Leipzig, Hesse & Becker Verlag, 1941. New ed.

Karstädt, Georg. "Zur Geschichte des Zinken und seiner Verwendung in der Musik des 16.–18. Jahrhunderts," AfMf II (1937) 385–432.

Keller, Otto. Die Operette in ihrer geschichtlichen Entwicklung. Vienna, Stein-Verlag, 1926.

Keppler, Philip, Jr. "Some Comments on Musical Quotation," MQ XLII (1956) 473–85.

Kerman, Joseph. Opera as Drama. New York, Alfred A. Knopf, 1956.

Kinsky, Georg. [Geschichte der Musik in Bildern.] A History of Music in Pictures. London, J. M. Dent, [1937].

Kirby, Percival R. "The Kettle-drums : An Historical Survey," M&L IX (1928) 34–43.

Klein, Herman. The Golden Age of Opera. London, George Routledge, 1933.

Klob, Karl Maria. Die Oper von Gluck bis Wagner. Ulm, H. Kerler, 1913.

Kobbé, Gustav. Kobbé's Complete Opera Book. Edited and revised by the Earl of Harewood. New York, G. P. Putnam's Sons, [1954].

Köhler, Louis. Die Melodie der Sprache in ihrer Anwendung besonders auf das Lied und die Oper. Leipzig, Weber, 1853.

Krause, Ernst. Briefe über die Oper : Die Erneuerung der Musikbühne. [Dresden], VVB Verlag, Dresdner Verlag, [1951].

—— Oper von A–Z : Ein Handbuch. Leipzig, B&H, 1961.

Kraussold, Max. Geist und Stoff der Operndichtung : Eine Dramaturgie in Umrissen. Leipzig, Strache, 1931.

Krehbiel, Henry Edward. A Book of Operas. New York, Macmillan, 1928. 2 vols. in one, combining "A Book of Operas" and "A Second Book of Operas."

[Kretzschmar, Hermann.] Festschrift Hermann Kretzschmar zum 70. Geburtstag. Leipzig, Peters, 1918.

—— "Für und gegen die Oper," JMP XX (1913) 59–70.

—— Gesammelte Aufsätze über Musik und anderes. Leipzig, F. W. Grunow, 1910–[11]. 2 vols.

—— Geschichte der Oper. Leipzig, B&H, 1919.

—— Geschichte des neuen deutschen Liedes. I. Teil : von Albert bis Zelter. Leipzig, B&H, 1911.

Krieger, Ludwig. Die sozialische Lage der Theatermusiker. Heidelberg, Schulze, 1913.

Kunath, Martin. "Die Charakterologie der stimmlichen Einheiten in der Oper," ZfMw VIII (1925–26) 403–10.

—— Die Oper als literarische Form. Leipzig Dissertation, 1925.

Lajarte, Théodore de. Bibliothèque musicale du théâtre de l'opéra. Paris, Librairie des bibliophiles, 1878. 2 vols.

—— Curiosités de l'opéra. Paris, Calmann Lévy, 1883.

La Laurencie, Lionel de. Inventaire critique du fonds Blancheton de la Bibliothèque du Conservatoire de Paris. Paris, E. Droz, 1930–31. 2 vols.

Lang, Paul Henry. Music in Western Civilization. New York, W. W. Norton, [1941].

Lavignac, Alexandre Jean Albert, ed. Encyclopédie de la musique et Dictionnaire du Conservatoire. Première Partie : Histoire de la musique. Paris, Delagrave, 1913–22. 5 vols.

Leibowitz, René. Histoire de l'opéra. [Paris], Buchet-Chastel, Corrêa, [1957].

Leichtentritt, Hugo. Music, History, and Ideas. Cambridge, Mass., Harvard University Press, 1938.

Leti, Giuseppe, and Louis Lachat. L'Esotérisme à la scène : La Flûte enchantée, Parsifal, Faust. Annecy, L. Dépollier, 1935.

Lindner, Ernst Otto. Zur Tonkunst : Abhandlungen. Berlin, I. Guttentag, 1864.

Loewenberg, Alfred, compiler. Annals of Opera, 1597–1940 : Compiled from the Original Sources. Geneva, Societas Bibliographica, [1955]. 2d ed. 2 vols.

López Chavarri. See Chavarri, Eduardo López.

Loschelder, Josef. Die Oper als Kunstform. Vienna, A. Schroll, [1941].

Luciani, Sebastiano Arturo. La rinascità del dramma : Saggio sul teatro di musica. Rome, Ausonia, 1922.

MacFarren, Sir George Alexander. "The Lyrical Drama," PMA VI (1880) 125–40.

McSpadden, Joseph W. Operas and Musical Comedies. New York, Thomas Y. Crowell Co., [1954]. Enlarged ed.

Madrid. Biblioteca nacional. Departamento de manuscritos. Catálogo de las piezas de teatro. Madrid, Blass, 1934–35. 2 vols.

Manferrari, Umberto. Dizionario universale delle opere melodrammatiche. Florence, Sansoni Antiquariato, 1954–55. 3 vols.

Manners, Charles. "The Financial Problems of National Opera," M&L VII (1926) 93–105.

Mantzius, Karl. A History of Theatrical Art in Ancient and Modern Times. London, Duckworth, 1903–21. 6 vols.

Martens, Frederick Herman. A Thousand and One Nights of Opera. New York, D. Appleton, [1926].

Matthews, Brander. "The Conventions of the Music Drama," MQ V (1919) 255–63.

Mayer, Anton. Die Oper : Eine Anleitung zu ihrem Verständnis. Berlin, K. Wolff, [1935].

Mayer, Ernesto Rodolfo. "Verso quali mète è diretta l' 'opera'?" RMI XLII (1938) 363–67.

Maylender, Michele. Storia delle accademie d'Italia. Bologna, L. Cappelli, [1926–30]. 5 vols.

Mayor, A. Hyatt, Mercedes Viale, A. della Corte, and A. G. Bragaglia. Tempi e aspetti della scenografia. [Turin, Edizioni Radio Italiani, 1954.]

Mengelberg, Curt Rudolf. "Das Musikdrama als Kunstform," Die Musik XIII (1913–14) 288–99.

Mercure de France. Paris. 1672–1820.

Mila, Massimo. "Il concetto di musica drammatica," RassM IV (1931) 98–106.

Monaldi, Gino. Cantanti evirati celebri del teatro italiano. Rome, Ausonia, 1920.

Moser, Hans Joachim. Geschichte der deutschen Musik. Stuttgart and Berlin, J. G. Cotta, 1920–24. 3 vols.

Die Musik in Geschichte und Gegenwart. Edited by Friedrich Blume. Kassel & Basel, Bärenreiter, 1949–

Musik und Bild : Festschrift Max Seiffert. Kassel, Bärenreiter, 1938.

Napoli-Signorelli, Pietro. Storia critica dei teatri antichi e moderni. Naples, V. Orsino, 1787–90. 6 vols. A later ed., 1813, 10 vols.

Navarra, Ugo. Nel tricentenario del teatro lirico 1637–1937 : Grande inchiesta particolare sulle condizioni odierne della scena melodrammatica. Milan, Alba, 1937.

Neitzel, Otto. Der Führer durch die Oper des Theaters der Gegenwart. Leipzig, A. G. Liebeskind, 1890–98. 3 vols.

Newman, Ernest. More Stories of Famous Operas. New York, Alfred A. Knopf, 1943.

—— Seventeen Famous Operas. New York, Alfred A. Knopf, 1955.

—— Stories of the Great Operas and Their Composers. New York, Garden City Publishing Company, [1928]. 3 vols. in one.

New York Public Library. The Development of Scenic Art and Stage Machinery : A List of References in the New York Public Library. New York, 1920.

—— Stage Scenery : A List of References to Illustrations Since 1900 in the New York Public Library. Compiled by William Burt Gamble. New York, [New York Public Library] 1917.

Nicoll, Allardyce. The Development of the Theatre. New York, Harcourt, Brace, 1958. 4th ed.

—— A History of English Drama, 1660–1900. Cambridge, The University Press, 1952–59. 6 vols.

Niecks, Frederick. "Historical Sketch of the Overture," SIMG VII (1905–6) 386–90.

Ollone, Max d'. Le Théâtre lyrique et le public. Paris & Geneva, La Palatine, [1955].

O'Neill, Norman. "Music to Stage Plays," PMA XXXVII (1911) 85–102.

"Opera," in Enciclopedia universal ilustrada europea-americana ("Espasa") XXI, 1297–1300; XXXIX, 1360–94.

Pankratova, V. A., ed. Opernye libretto : Kratkoe izlozhenie soderzhaniia oper. Moscow, Gos. muz. izd-vo, 1962.

Pannain, Guido. L'Opera e le opere ed altri scritti di letteratura musicale. Milan, Edizioni Curci, 1958.

Paoli, Domenico de. L'opera italiana dalle origini all' opera verista. Rome, Studium, [1955].

Paris. Bibliothèque nationale. Département des imprimés. Catalogue du fonds de musique de la Bibliothèque nationale, par J. Ecorcheville. Paris, 1910–14. 8 vols.

—— Conservatoire national de musique et de déclamation. Bibliothèque. Catalogue bibliographique . . . avec notices et reproductions musicales des principaux ouvrages de la réserve, par J. B. Weckerlin. Paris, Firmin-Didot, 1885.

Pastor, Ludwig, Freiherr von. The History of the Popes, from the Close of the Middle Ages. Vols. 29, 30, 31. London, Kegan Paul, 1938–40.

Peltz, Mary Ellis. The Metropolitan Opera Guide. New York, The Modern Library, [1939].

Percival, Robert. "Can Opera Be Made to Pay?" M&L VII (1926) 114–19.

[Pereira Peixoto d'Almeida Carvalhaes, Manoel.] Catálogo da importante biblioteca que pertencen ao . . . erudito e bibliofilo ilustre Manuel de Carvalhaes . . . organisado par Augusta Sâ da Costa. Lisbon, 1928.

Petit, Henri. "Défense de l'opéra-comique," L'Information musicale II (1942) Nos. 76 and 77.

Petzoldt, Richard. Die Oper in ihrer Zeit. Leipzig, VEB B&H, 1956.

Peyser, Herbert F. "Some Observations on Translation," MQ VIII (1922) 353–71.

Pizzetti, Ildebrando. Musica e dramma. Rome, Edizioni della Bussola, [1945].

Pols, André M. Trilogie van de Hartstocht : Don Giovanni, Tristan en Eroos, Pelléas. Antwerp, Die Poorte, 1952.

Polyphonie. Premier cahier (1947–48) : Le Théâtre musical.

Prod'homme, Jacques Gabriel. "Etat alphabétique sommaire des archives de l'opéra," RdM XIV (1933) 193–205.

—— L'Opéra (1669–1925). Paris, Delagrave, 1925.

—— "Two Hundred and Fifty Years of the Opéra (1669–1919)," MQ V (1919) 513–37.

Pulver, Jeffrey. "The Intermezzi of the Opera," PMA XLIII (1916–17) 139–63.

Raabe, Peter. Kulturwille im deutschen Musikleben. Regensburg, G. Bosse, [1936].

Rabich, Ernst. Die Entwicklung der Oper. Langensalza, Beyer, 1926.

Radford, Maisie. "A Comparative Study of Indigenous Forms of Opera," M&L VII (1926) 106–13.

Reclams Opern- und Operettenführer. Stuttgart, Reclam-Verlag, [1956].

Refardt, Edgar. Verzeichnis der Aufsätze zur Musik in den nichtmusikalischen Zeitschriften der Universitätsbibliothek Basel abgeschlossen auf den 1. Januar 1924. Leipzig, B&H, 1925.

Renner, Hans. Die Wunderwelt der Oper : Der grosse Führer durch die Oper und die klassische Operette. Berlin, Vier Falken Verlag, [1938].

Riemann, Hugo. Handbuch der Musikgeschichte. 2d ed. Leipzig, B&H, 1919–22. 2 vols. in 5 parts.

—— Opern-Handbuch : Repertorium der dramatisch-musikalischen Litteratur. Leipzig, H. Seemann Nachfolger, [published in parts; 1881–1900?].

Rinaldi, Mario. L'opera in musica : Saggio estetico. Rome, "Novissima," [1934].

Rolandi, Ulderigo. Il libretto per musica attraverso i tempi. Rome, Edizioni dell' Ateneo, 1951.

Rolland, Romain. "Les Maîtres de l'opéra : Recueil de musique inédite du XVIIe et du XVIIIe siècle," RHCM III (1903) 40–41, 178–79.

—— Musiciens d'autrefois. Paris, Hachette, 1924. 9th ed. Translated as : Some Musicians of Former Days. London, K. Paul, 1915.

Roncaglia, Gino. Invito all' opera. Milan, Tarantola, 1954. 2d ed.

Rosenfeld, Paul. Discoveries of a Music Critic. New York, Harcourt, Brace, [1936].

Ross, Anne, ed. The Opera Directory. New York, Sterling Publishing Co., 1961.

Rossi-Doria, Gastone. "Opera," in Enciclopedia italiana XXV (1935) 390–404.

Rubsamen, Walter. "Political and Ideological Censorship of Opera," in Papers of the American Musicological Society, Annual Meeting, 1941 . . . Edited by Gustave Reese (Printed by the Society [cop. 1946]) 30–42.

Sadler's Wells Opera Books. London, John Lane, 1945– .

Salvioli, Giovanni. Bibliografia universale del teatro drammatico italiano. Volume primo. Venice, [1894–]1903. A-Czarina only; no more published.

Sauerlandt, Max. Die Musik in fünf Jahrhunderten der europäischen Malerei etwa 1450 bis etwa 1850. Leipzig, Langewiesche Verlag, 1922.

Schaal, Richard. "Die vor 1801 gedruckten Libretti des Theatermuseums München," Mf X (1957) 388–96, 487–97; XI (1958) 54–69, 168–77, 321–36, 462–77; XII (1959) 60–75, 161–77, 299–306, 454–61; XIII (1960) 38–46, 164–72, 299–306, 441–48; XIV (1961) 36–43, 166–83.

Schering, Arnold. Aufführungspraxis alter Musik. Leipzig, Quelle & Meyer, 1931.

—— Geschichte des Instrumentalkonzerts. Leipzig, B&H, 1927, 2d ed.

—— Geschichte des Oratoriums. Leipzig, B&H, [1911].

—— Musikgeschichte Leipzigs. Leipzig, Kistner & Siegel, 1926. 3 vols.

Schiedermair, Ludwig. "Ueber den Stand der Operngeschichte," in International Music Society, Second Congress Report (Leipzig, B&H, 1907) 212–16.

Schladebach, Julius. "Geschichte der Oper bis auf Gluck," Die Wissenschaft im 19. Jahrhundert I (1856) 361.

Schletterer, Hans Michael. Die Entstehung der Oper. Nördlingen, C. H. Beck, 1873.

—— Zur Geschichte dramatischer Musik und Poesie in Deutschland. Augsburg, Schlosser, 1863.

Schmitz, Eugen. Geschichte der weltlichen Solo–Kantate. Leipzig, B&H, 1914.

Scholz, János, ed. Baroque and Romantic Stage Design. New York, Beechhurst Press, [1955]. New ed.

Schünemann, Georg. Geschichte der deutschen Schulmusik. Leipzig, Kistner & Siegel, 1928.

Schuré, Edouard. Le Drame musicale. Paris, Didier, 1886. 2 vols.

Schwanbeck, Gisela. Bibliographie der deutschsprachigen Hochschulschriften zur Theaterwissenschaft von 1885 bis 1952. Berlin, Gesellschaft für Theatergeschichte, 1956.

Scuola veneziana, La (secoli XVI–XVIII), note e documenti. Siena, Libreria editrice Ticci, 1941.

Sear, H. G. "Operatic Mortality," M&L XXI (1940) 60–74.

Searle, Humphrey. Ballet Music: An Introduction. London, Cassell, [1958].

Sedwick, B. Frank. "Opera Errors," JAMS VII (1954) 48–51.

Seltsam, William H., compiler. Metropolitan Opera Annals : A Chronicle of Artists and Performances. New York, H. W. Wilson Co., in Association with the Metropolitan Opera Guild, Inc., 1947.

Serov, Aleksandr Nikolaevich. Aufsätze zur Musikgeschichte. Berlin, Aufbau-Verlag, 1955.

Skraup, Siegmund. Die Oper als lebendiges Theater. Berlin, Henschel-Verlag, 1956. 3d ed.

Small, Herbert F. "On Opera," MQ IV (1918) 37–49.

Solvay, Lucien. L'Evolution théatrale. Brussels and Paris, G. van Oest, 1922. 2 vols.

Sonneck, Oscar George Theodore. Miscellaneous Studies in the History of Music. New York, Macmillan, 1921. Contains "*Caractacus* Not Arne's *Caractacus*," "Ciampi's *Bertoldo, Bertoldino e Cacasenno* and Favart's *Ninette à la cour:* A Contribution to the History of the Pasticcio," "A Description of Alessandro Striggio and Francesco Corteggia's Intermedi : *Psyche and Amor*, 1565," "Early American Opera," and "A Preface."

—— "Noch etwas über Opernlexika," *Die Musik* XIII (1913–14) Qt. 4, 140–43.

—— *See also* United States Library of Congress.

Statisticus [pseud.]. "Notes sur l'histoire de l'Opéra," RHCM III (1903) 277–79.

Steger, Hellmuth, and Karl Howe. Operettenführer, von Offenbach bis zum Musical. Frankfurt/M., Hamburg, Fischer, 1958.

Steidel, Max. Oper und Drama. Karlsruhe, G. Braun, 1923.

Stieger, Franz. "Opernkomponistinnen," *Die Musik* XIII (1913–14) Qt. 4, 270–71.

Storck, Karl G. L. Das Opernbuch : Ein Führer durch den Spielplan der deutschen Opernbühnen. Stuttgart, Muth, [1949]. 45th ed.

[Strangways, A. H. Fox.] "Opera and the Musician," M&L XIII (1932) 119–25.

Streatfeild, Richard Alexander. The Opera. London, G. Routledge, 1925. 5th ed.

Struck, Gustav. "Die Wende zur Literatur-Oper : Zur 50 Wiederkehr der *Salome*-Uraufführung," M IX (1955) 589–94.

Strunk, Oliver, ed. Source Readings in Music History. New York, W. W. Norton, 1950.

Szabolcsi, Bence, and Dénes Bartha, eds. Az opera történetéből. Budapest, Akadémiai Kiadó, 1961. Series : Zenetudományi tanulmányok, IX.

Ternant, Andrew de. "French Opera Libretti," M&L XI (1930) 172–76.

Theatrical Designs from the Baroque through Neo-Classicism : Unpublished Material from American Private Collections. New York, H. Bittner, 1940. 3 vols.

Thrane, Carl. Danske Komponister. Copenhagen, Forlagsbureaunet, 1875.

Tiersot, Julien. "Lettres de musiciens écrites en francais du XVe au XXe siècle," RMI XVII (1910)–XXI (1914); XXIII (1916); XXIX (1922)–XXX (1923); XXXIII (1926)–XXXIV (1927); XXXVI (1929)–XXXVIII (1931), *passim*.

Tiraboschi, Girolamo. Storia della letteratura italiana. Rome, L. P. Salvioni, 1782–97. 10 vols.

Tittmann, Julius. Kleine Schriften zur deutschen Literatur und Kulturgeschichte. Göttingen, Dieterischen Buchhandlung, 1847.

Tommasini, Vincenzo. "Del drama lirico," RMI XXXIX (1932) 73–113.

Tonelli, Luigi. Il teatro italiano dalle origini ai giorni nostri. Milan, Modernissima, 1924.

Torrefranca, Fausto. "L'officina dell' opera," RassM III (1930) 136–46.

—— "Opera as a 'Spectacle for the Eye,' " MQ I (1915) 436–52.

Touchard-Lafosse, G. Chroniques secrètes et galantes de l'opéra depuis 1667 jusqu'en 1845. Paris, Lachapelle, 1846. 4 vols.

Tovey, Donald Francis. Essays in Musical Analysis, III : The Concerto. London, Oxford University Press, 1936.

Towers, John. Dictionary-Catalogue of Operas and Operettas Which Have Been Performed on the Public Stage. Morgantown, W. Va., Acme, [1910].

Toye, Francis. "Is Musical Reservation Justifiable?" MQ I (1915) 118–28.

Turin. Biblioteca civica. Sezione teatrale. [Letteratura drammatica. Turin, G. B. Vassallo, 1912, 1911. 2 vols.]

United States Library of Congress. Division of Music. Catalogue of Opera Librettos Printed before 1800. Prepared by Oscar George Theodore Sonneck. Washington, Government Printing Office, 1914. 2 vols.

—— Dramatic Music (Class M 1500, 1510, 1520) : Catalogue of Full Scores. Compiled by E. G. T. Sonneck. Washington, Government Printing Office, 1908.

Upton, George Putnam. The Standard Light Operas. Chicago, A. C. McClurg, 1902.

—— The Standard Operas. Chicago, A. C. McClurg, 1928. New ed.

Vaillat, Léandre. Ballets de l'Opéra de Paris (ballets dans les opéras—

nouveaux ballets). Paris, Compagnie Française des Arts Graphiques, 1947.

Valentin, Erich. "Dichtung und Oper : Eine Untersuchung des Stilproblems der Oper," AfMf III (1938) 138–79.

Vatielli, Francesco. "Operisti-librettisti dei secoli XVII e XVIII," RMI XLIII (1939) 1–16, 315–32, 605–21.

Vetter, Walther. Mythos—Melos—Musica : Ausgewählte Aufsätze zur Musikgeschichte. Leipzig, Deutscher Verlag für Musik, 1957.

Vogel, Emil. Bibliothek der gedruckten weltlichen Vokalmusik Italiens aus den Jahren 1500–1700. Berlin, A. Haack, 1892. New ed. (A. Einstein) serially in MLA Notes, 2d ser. II, No. 3 (June, 1945) to V, No. 4 (September, 1948).

Walker, Ernest. A History of Music in England. 3d ed., revised by J. A. Westrup. Oxford, Clarendon Press, 1952.

Weigl, Bruno. Die Geschichte des Walzers nebst einem Anhang über die moderne Operette. Langensalza, Beyer, 1910.

Wellesz, Egon. Essays on Opera. Translated . . . by Patricia Kean. London, Dennis Dobson, [1950].

Westrup, Jack A. "The Nature of Recitative," Proceedings of the British Academy XLII (1956) 27–43.

Wichmann, Heinz. Der neue Opernführer, mit einem Anhang, Klassische Operetten. Berlin, P. Franke, 1943.

Wiese, Berthold. Geschichte der italienischen Litteratur. Leipzig and Vienna, Bibliographisches Institut, [1898–]1899. Fourth to fifteenth centuries by Wiese; sixteenth century to present by E. Pèrcopo.

Wolff, Hellmuth Christian. "Orpheus als Opernthema," Musica XV (1961) 423–25.

Wossidlo, Walter. Opern-Bibliothek : Populärer Führer durch Poesie und Musik. Leipzig, Rühle & Wendling, [1919?].

Zenetudományi tanulmányok. Series of collections of musicological essays; Budapest, Hungarian Academy of Sciences, 1953–62. 10 vols., each with separate title. Articles on the history of opera in Vol. II (Erkel Ferenc és Bartók Béla emlékére, 1954); Vol. IV (A magyar zene történetéből, 1955); Vol. V (Mozart emlékére, 1957); and Vol. IX (Az opera történetéből, 1961).

Zingel, Hans Joachim. "Studien zur Geschichte des Harfenspiels in klassischer und romantischer Zeit," AfMf II (1937) 455–65.

Zopff, Hermann. Grundzüge einer Theorie der Oper. Leipzig, Arnold, 1868.

II

MUSIC AND DRAMA TO THE END OF THE SIXTEENTH CENTURY

Adam de la Halle. Le Jeu de Robin et de Marion. Précédé du Jeu du Pèlerin. Edité par Kenneth Varty. [Transcriptions musicales d'Eric Hill.] London, Harrap, [1960].

—— Œuvres complètes du trouvère Adam de la Halle, poésies et musique: Publiées . . . par E. de Coussemaker. Paris, A. Durand & Pedone-Lauriel, 1872.

Alaleona, Domenico. "Su Emilio de' Cavalieri," La nouva musica, Nos. 113–14 (1905) 35–38, 47–50.

Albrecht, Otto E. Four Latin Plays of St. Nicholas from the 12th Century Fleury Play-Book : Text and Commentary, with a Study of the Music of the Plays, and of the Sources and Iconography of the Legends. Philadelphia, University of Pennsylvania Press; London, Oxford University Press, 1935.

Anglès, Higini. La música a Catalunya fins al segle XIII. Barcelona, Institut d'Estudis Catalans : Biblioteca de Catalunya, 1935.

Anthon, Carl Gustav. Music and Musicians in Northern Italy during the Sixteenth Century. Harvard Dissertation, 1943.

Anticlo, ——. "Gli spiriti della musica nella tragedia greca," RMI XX (1913) 821–87.

Aristotle. Aristotle's Treatise on Poetry. Translated . . . by Thomas Twining. London, Payne and Son [etc.], 1789.

Augé-Chiquet, Mathieu. La Vie, les idées et l'œuvre de Baïf. Paris [etc.], Edouard Privat Hachette, 1909.

Bacot, Jacques, tr. and ed. Représentations théâtrales dans les monastères du Tibet : Trois mystères tibetains. Paris, Bossard, 1921.

Ballard, William J. The Sources, Development and Culmination of the Dramatic Madrigal. Ann Arbor, University Microfilms, 1958.

Bartholomaeis, Vincenzo de, ed. Laude drammatiche e rappresentazioni sacre. Florence, Le Monnier, 1943. 3 vols.

Bartsch, Karl. Romances et pastourelles françaises des XIIe et XIIIe siècles. Leipzig, F. Vogel, 1870.

Becherini, Bianca. "La musica nelle 'Sacre rappresentazioni' Fiorentine," RMI LIII (1951) 193–241.

Bohn, [Emil?]. "Theophilus : Niederdeutsches Schauspiel aus einer Handschrift des 15. Jahrhunderts," MfMg IX (1877) 3–4. Music, pp. 24–25.

Bonaventura, Arnoldo. "Le maggiolate," RMI XXIV (1917) 272–99.

Bonfantini, Mario, ed. Le sacre rappresentazioni italiane : Raccolta di testi dal secolo XIII al secolo XVI. [Milan], Bompiani, [1942].

Bowles, Edmund A. "The Role of Musical Instruments in Medieval Sacred Drama," MQ XLV (1959) 67–84.

Brandsetter, Renward. "Musik und Gesang beiden Luzerner Osterspielen," Der Geschichtsfreund XL (1885) 145–68.

Brinkmann, Hennig. Zum Ursprung des liturgischen Spieles. Bonn, F. Cohen, 1929.

Brown, Howard Mayer. Music in the French Secular Theater, 1400–1550. Cambridge, Mass., Harvard University Press, 1963.

Brownlow, Jane. "The Bardi Coterie," PMA XXII (1896) 111–27.

Bukofzer, Manfred. "The *Book of the Courtier* on Music," MTNA XXXVIII (1944) 230–35.

Burckhardt, Jakob. The Civilization of the Period of the Renaissance in Italy. London, C. K. Paul, 1878. 2 vols.

Camillucci, Guido. "*L'Amfiparnaso,* comedia harmonica," RMI LIII (1951) 42–60.

Casella, Alfredo, ed. *La favola di Orfeo,* opera in un atto di Messer Angelo Ambrogini detto "Poliziano." Milan, Carisch, [1934].

Castiglione, Baldassare, conte. Il libro del cortegiano. Florence, Heredi di Philippo di Giunta, 1528. Translated by Thomas Hoby as : The Courtier. [New York], The National Alumni, [1907].

Chailley, Jacques. "Le Drame liturgique médiéval à St.-Martial de Limoges," *Revue d'histoire du théâtre* VII (1955) 127–44.

—— "La Nature musicale du *Jeu de Robin et Marion,*" in *Mélanges d'histoire du théâtre du moyen-âge et de la renaissance, offerts à Gustave Cohen* . . . (Paris, Librairie Nizet, 1950) 111–17.

Chambers, E. K. The Medieval Stage. London, Oxford University Press, 1903. 2 vols.

Chrysander, Friedrich. "Ludovico Zacconi als Lehrer des Kunstgesanges," VfMw VII (1891) 337–96; IX (1893) 249–310; X (1894) 531–67.

Civita, A. Ottavio Rinuccini e il sorgere del melodramma in Italia. Mantua, Manuzio, 1900.

Clément, Félix. "Liturgie, musique et drama du moyen âge," *Annales archéologiques* VII (1847) 303–20; VIII (1848) 36–48, 77–87, 304–11; IX (1849) 27–40, 162–74; X (1850) 154–60; XI (1851) 6–15.

Cohen, Gustave. Histoire de la mise en scène dans le théâtre réligieux français du moyen âge. Paris, Champion, 1926. New ed.

Cohen, Gustave, ed. Anthologie du drame liturgique en France au moyen-âge : Textes originaux accompagnés de traductions. Paris, Les Editions du Cerf, 1955.

—— Recueil de farces françaises inédites du XVe siècle. Cambridge, Mass., Mediæval Academy of America, 1949.

Colomb de Batines. Bibliografia delle antiche rappresentazioni italiane sacre e profane, stampate nei secoli XV e XVI. Florence, Società tip., 1852. Additions by E. Narducci in *Il bibliofilo* III (1882) 73–74, 87–88.

Comte, Charles, and Paul Laumonier. "Ronsard et les musiciens du XVIe siècle," *Revue d'histoire littéraire de la France* VII (1900) 341–81.

Corbin, Solange. "Le Manuscrit 201 d'Orléans : Drames liturgiques dits de Fleury," *Romania* LXXIV (1953) 1–43.

Coussemaker, Edmond de. Drames liturgiques du moyen âge. Rennes, H. Vatar, 1860; Paris, Lib. archéologique de V. Didron, 1861.

Crocker, Eunice. The Instrumental Ensemble Canzona. Radcliffe Dissertation, 1943.

D'Ancona, Alessandro. Origini del teatro italiano. Turin, E. Loescher, 1891. 2d ed. 2 vols.

—— Sacre rappresentazioni dei secoli XIV, XV e XVI. Florence, Successori Le Monnier, 1872. 3 vols.

Dent, Edward J. "The *Amfiparnaso* of Orazio Vecchi," MMR XXXVI (1906) 50–52, 74–75.

—— "Notes on the *Amfiparnaso* of Orazio Vecchi," SIMG XII (1910–11) 330–47.

De Vito, M. S. L'origine del dramma liturgico. Milan, Dante Alighieri, [1939?].

Donovan, Richard B. The Liturgical Drama in Medieval Spain. Toronto, Pontifical Institute of Musical Studies, 1958.

"Early Elizabethan Stage Music," MA I (1909–10) 30–40; IV (1912–13) 112–17.

Einstein, Alfred. "Firenze prima della monodia," RassM VII (1934) 253.

—— "The Greghesca and the Giustiniana of the Sixteenth Century," *Journal of Renaissance and Baroque Music* I (1946) 19–32.

—— The Italian Madrigal. Princeton, Princeton University Press, 1949. 3 vols.

—— "Die mehrstimmige weltliche Musik von 1450–1600," in Adler, *Handbuch der Musikgeschichte* (Frankfurt/M., Frankfurter Verlags-Anstalt, 1924) 358–73.

[Eitner, Robert.] "Die Quellen zur Entstehung der Oper," MfMg XIII (1881) 10–15, 21–28.

Ellinwood, Leonard. "The *Conductus*," MQ XXVII (1941) 165–204.

Engel, Hans. "Nochmals die Intermedien von Florenz 1589," in *Festschrift Max Schneider zum 80. Geburtstage* (Leipzig, Deutscher Verlag für Musik, [1955]) 71–86.

Fano, Fabio, ed. La camerata fiorentina : Vincenzo Galilei. Milan, Ricordi, 1934. (Istituzioni e monumenti dell' arte musicale italiana, Vol. IV.)

Flecha, Mateo. Las Ensaladas (Praga, 1581). Transcripción y estudio por Higinio Anglès. . . . Barcelona, Diputación Provincial de Barcelona : Biblioteca Central, 1954.

Flemming, Willi. Geschichte des Jesuitentheaters in den Landen deutscher Zunge. Berlin, Gesellschaft für Theatergeschichte, 1923.

Frati, Lodovico. "Musica e balli alla corte dei Pico della Mirandola," RMI XXV (1918) 249–58.

—— "Torquato Tasso in musica," RMI XXX (1923) 389–400.

Fremy, Edouard. Origines de l'Académie française : L'Académie des derniers Valois. Paris, E. Leroux, [1887].

Frere, Walter Howard, ed. The Winchester Troper, from Mss. of the Xth and XIth Centuries, with Other Documents Illustrating the History of Tropes in England and France. London, [Printed for the Henry Bradshaw Society by Harrison and Sons], 1894.

Galilei, Vincenzo. Dialogo della musica antica, et della moderna. Fiorenza, G. Marescotti, 1581. Facsimile reprint, Rome, R. Accademia d'Italia, 1934.

[Galluzzi, Riguccio.] Istoria del granducato di Toscana sotto il governo della casa Medici. Florence, Stamperia di R. del Vivo, 1781. 5 vols. New ed., Florence, 1822. 11 vols.

Gandolfi, Riccardo. "Appunti di storia musicale : Cristofano Malvezzi— Emilio de' Cavalieri," *Rassegna nazionale* XV (November, 1893) 297–306.

Gautier, Léon. Histoire de la poésie liturgique au moyen âge : Les tropes. Paris, V. Palmé, 1886.

Gégou, Fabienne. "Fragments de drame liturgique (?) découvert dans le manuscrit La Vallière de la Bibliothèque Nationale," RdM XLV (1960) 76–83.

Gérold, Théodore. La Musique au moyen âge. Paris, Champion, 1932.

Ghisi, Federico. Alle fonti della monodia : Due nuovi brani della *Dafne*; il *Fuggilotio musicale* di G. Caccini. Milan, Bocca, 1940.

—— "Un Aspect inédit des intermèdes de 1589 à la cour medicéenne et le développement de courses masquées et des ballets équestres durant les premières décades du XVIIe siècle," in *Les Fêtes de la Renaissance* (Paris, Centre National de la Recherche Scientifique, 1956) 145–52.

—— I canti carnascialeschi nelle fonti musicali del XV e XVI secolo. Florence-Rome, L. S. Olschki, 1937.

—— "An Early 17th Century MS with Unpublished Italian Monodic Music by Peri, Caccini, and Marco da Gagliano," *Acta musicologica* XX (1948) 46–60.

—— Feste musicali della Firenze Medicea. Florence, Vallecchi, 1939.

Glareanus, Henricus. Dodecachordon. Leipzig, B&H, 1888. Translated and transcribed by Peter Bohn. Originally published 1547.

Goldschmidt, Hugo. "Verzierungen, Veränderungen und Passaggien im 16. und 17. Jahrhundert," MfMg XXIII (1891) 111–26.

Greenberg, Noah, ed. The Play of Daniel [Br. Mus. Egerton 2615]. New York, Oxford University Press, 1959.

Greulich, Martin. Beiträge zur Geschichte des Streichinstrumentenspiels im 16. Jahrhundert. Saalfeld, Günther, [1934?].

Guy, Henri. Bibliographie critique du trouvère Adan de la Hale. Paris, A. Fontemoing, [1900].

—— Essai sur la vie et les œuvres littéraires du trouvère Adan de le Hale. Paris, Hachette, 1898.

Hamilton, Edith. "The Greek Chorus, Fifteen or Fifty?" *Theatre Arts Monthly* XVII (1933) 459.

Handschin, Jacques. "Das Weinachts-Mysterium von Rouen als musikgeschichtliche Quelle," *Acta musicologica* VII (1935) 97–110.

Hartmann, Arnold, Jr. "Battista Guarini and *Il pastor fido*," MQ XXXIX (1953) 415–25.

Henderson, William James. Some Forerunners of the Italian Opera. London, John Murray, 1911.

Hoepffner, Ernest. "Les Intermèdes musicaux dans le *Jeu provençal de*

Sainte Agnès," in *Mélanges d'histoire du théâtre du moyen-âge et de la renaissance, offerts à Gustave Cohen* ... (Paris, Librairie Nizet, 1950) 97–104.

Hoffmann von Fallersleben, August Heinrich. In dulci jubilo . . . ein Beitrag zur Geschichte der deutschen Poesie. Hanover, C. Rümpler, 1854.

Hol, Joan C. "*L'Amfiparnaso* e *Le veglie di Siena*," RMI XL (1936) 3–22.

—— "Horatio Vecchi et l'évolution créatrice," in *Gedenkboek Dr. D. F. Scheurleer* (The Hague, Nijhoff, 1925) 159–67.

—— Horatio Vecchi's weltliche Werke. Leipzig, Heitz, 1934.

—— "*Le veglie di Siena* de Horatio Vecchi," RMI XLIII (1939) 17–34.

"*Hortus musarum* de Pierre Phalèse, deuxième partie (1553)," in *Chansons au luth et airs de cour français du XVIe siècle* (Paris, E. Droz, 1934).

Hughes, Dom Anselm, ed. Early Medieval Music up to 1300. London, New York, Toronto, Oxford University Press, 1954. (NOHM, Vol. II.)

Ingegneri, Angelo. Della poesia rappresentativa e del modo di rappresentare le favole sceniche. Ferrara, V. Baldini, 1598.

Jeppesen, Knud, ed. Die Mehrstimmige italienische Laude um 1500. Leipzig, B&H; Copenhagen, Levin & Munksgaard, 1935.

Jubinal, Achille, ed. Mystères inédits du quinzième siècle. Paris, Téchener, 1837. 2 vols.

Kaff, Ludwig. Mittelalterliche Oster- und Passionsspiele aus Oberösterreich im Spiegel musikwissenschaftlicher Betrachtung. Linz, Oberösterreich Landesverlag, in Komm., 1956.

Kinkeldey, Otto. "Luzzasco Luzzaschi's Solo-Madrigale mit Klavierbegleitung," SIMG IX (1907–8) 538–65.

—— Orgel und Klavier in der Musik des 16. Jahrhunderts. Leipzig, B&H, 1910.

Kirby, Percival R. "A 13th Century Ballad Opera," M&L XI (1930) 163–71.

Kretzenbacher, Leopold. Frühbarockes Weihnachtsspiel in Kärnten und Steiermark : Klagenfurter und Grazer Weihnachtsspieltexte des frühen 17. Jahrhundert als kulturhistorische Denkmäler der Gegenreformation in Innerösterreich. Klagenfurt, Geschichtsverein für Kärnten, 1952.

Krieg, Eduard. Das lateinische Osterspiel von Tours. [With Anhang : "Das lateinische Osterspiel aus der Handschrift 927 (Ff. 1–8) der Stadtbibliothek von Tours."] Würzburg, Triltsch, 1956.

Kroyer, Theodor. Anfänge der Chromatik im italienischen Madrigal des XVI. Jahrhunderts. Leipzig, B&H, 1902.

Kühl, Gustav. "Die Bordesholmer Marienklage, herausgegeben und eingeleitet," *Jahrbuch des Vereins für niederdeutsche Sprachforschung* XXIV (1898) 1–75 and Musikbeilage of 14 pages.

Kuhn, Max. Die Verzierungskunst in der Gesangs-Musik des 16.–17. Jahrhunderts (1535–1650). Leipzig, B&H, 1902.

Lach, Robert. "Das mittelaltleriche Musikdrama im Spiegel der Kunstge-schichte," in *Festschrift Adolph Koczirz* (Vienna, Strache, [1930]) 17–20.

Lacroix, Paul. Ballets et mascarades de cour, de Henri III à Louis XIV (1581–1652). Geneva, J. Gay, 1868–70. 6 vols.

Landi, Antonio. Il commodo, commedia d'Antonio Landi con i suoi inter-medi [etc.]. Florence, I. Giunti, 1566. The intermedi are by G. B. Strozzi the elder. Earlier ed. 1539.

Lavoix, Henri. "Les Opéras madrigalesques," *Revue et gazette musicale* XLIV (1877) 307–9, 323–24, 331–32.

Lebègue, Raymond. Le Mystère des Actes des Apôtres. Paris, Champion, 1929.

——— "Les Représentations dramatiques à la cour des Valois," in *Les Fêtes de la Renaissance* (Paris, Centre National de la Recherche Scientifique, 1956) 85–91.

Liliencron, Rochus, Freiherr von. "Die Chorgesänge des lateinischen-deutschen Schuldramas im 16. Jahrhundert," VfMw VI (1890) 309–87.

Lipphardt, Walther. Die Weisen der lateinischen Osterspiele des 12. und 13. Jahrhunderts. Kassel, Bärenreiter, [1948].

Liuzzi, Fernando. "Drammi musicali dei secoli XI–XIV," *Studi medievali, nuova serie* III (1930) 82–109.

——— "L'espressione musicale nel dramma liturgico," *Studi medievali, nuova serie* II (1929) 74–109.

Lozzi, C. "La musica e specialmente il melodramma alla Corte Medicea," RMI IX (1902) 297–338.

Lucianus Samosatensis. Lucian; with an English Translation by A. M. Harmon. London, W. Heinemann; New York, Macmillan, 1913–36. Contains "On the Dance," V, 209–89.

Lupo, Bettina. "Scene e persone musicale dell' *Amfiparnaso*," RassM XI (1938) 445–59.

Marsan, Jules. La Pastorale dramatique en France à la fin du XVIe et au commencement du XVIIe siècle. Paris, Hachette, 1905.

Martin, Henriette. "La 'Camerata' du Comte Bardi et la musique floren-tine du XVIe siècle," RdM XIII (1932) 63–74, 152–61, 227–34; XIV (1933) 92–100, 141–51.

Modena. Accademia di Scienze, Lettere ed Arti in Modena. Orazio Vecchi, precursore del melodramma (1550–1605) nel IV centenario della nascità. Contributi di studio raccolti dalla Accademia di Scienze, Lettere ed Arti di Modena. Modena, 1950.

Mone, Franz Joseph, ed. Altdeutsche Schauspiele. Quedlinburg and Leip-zig, G. Basse, 1841.

——— Schauspiele des Mittelalters. Karlsruhe, C. Macklot, 1846. 2 vols.

Morphy, G., compiler. Les Luthistes espagnoles du XVIe siècle. Leipzig, B&H, 1902. 2 vols.

Mountford, J. F. "Greek Music in the Papyri and Inscriptions," in J.

Powell and E. Barber, *New Chapters in the History of Greek Literature, Second Series* (London, Oxford University Press, 1929) 146–83.

Musique et poésie au XVIe siècle. Paris. Editions du Centre National de la Recherche Scientifique, [1954].

Nagel, Willibald. "Die Chöre aus *Philargyrus* von Petrus Dasypodius," MfMg XXI (1889) 109–12.

—— "Die Musik in den schweitzerischen Dramen des 16. Jahrhunderts," MfMg XXII (1890) 67–83.

Neri, Achille. "Gli intermezzi del *Pastor fido*," *Giornale storico della letteratura italiana* XI (1888) 405–15.

Nolhac, Pierre, and Angelo Solerti. Il viaggio in Italia di Enrico III, re di Francia, e le feste a Venezia, Ferrara, Mantova, e Torino. Turin, L. Roux, 1890.

Orel, Alfred. "Die Weisen im 'Wiener-Passionsspiel' aus dem 13. Jahrhundert," *Mitteilungen des Vereins für Geschichte der Stadt Wien* VI (1926) 72–95.

Palisca, Claude V. "Girolamo Mei : Mentor to the Florentine Camerata," MQ XL (1954) 1–20.

—— "Vincenzo Galilei and Some Links between 'Pseudo-Monody' and Monody," MQ XLVI (1960) 344–60.

Palisca, Claude V., ed. Girolamo Mei (1519–1594) :· Letters on Ancient and Modern Music to Vincenzo Galilei and Giovanni Bardi. A Study with Annotated Texts. [Rome], American Institute of Musicology, 1960.

Pedrell, Felipe. "*La Festa d'Elche* ou le drame lyrique liturgique La Mort et l'assomption de la Vierge," SIMG II (1900–1901) 203–52.

Perinello, C. "L' *Amfiparnaso* di Horatio Vecchi," RMI XLI (1937) 1–23.

Phalèse. *See* Hortus musarum.

Pirrotta, Nino. "Temperaments and Tendencies in the Florentine Camerata," MQ XL (1954) 169–89. Originally published in Italian in *Le manifestazioni culturali dell' Accademia Nazionale di Santa Cecilia.* Rome, 1953.

—— "Tragédie et comédie dans la 'Camerata fiorentina,' " in *Musique et poésie au XVIe siècle* (Paris, Editions du Centre National de la Recherche Scientifique, 1954) 287–97.

Poliziano, Angelo Ambrogini, known as. Le stanze, l'Orfeo e le rime. Florence, G. Barbèra, 1863.

—— Orfeo. *See* Casella, Alfredo.

Prunières, Henry. "Ronsard et les fêtes de cour," RM V (May, 1924) 27–44.

Quittard, Henri. "L' *Hortus musarum* de 1552–53 et les arrangements de pièces polyphoniques pour voix seule et luth," SIMG VIII (1906–7) 254–85.

—— "Le Théorbe comme instrument d'accompagnement," *Bulletin français de la SIM.* (1910) 221–37, 362–84.

Reese, Gustave. Music in the Middle Ages. New York, W. W. Norton, [1940].

—— Music in the Renaissance. New York, W. W. Norton, 1954.

Refardt, Edgar. "Die Musik der Basler Volksschauspiele des 16. Jahrhunderts," AfMw III (1921) 199.

Reinach, Théodore. La Musique grècque. Paris, Payot, 1926.

Rolandi, Ulderico. "Didascalie sceniche in un libretto dell' Euridice del Rinuccini (1600)," RMI XXXIII (1926) 21–27.

Rolland, Romain. "Les Origines de l'opéra et les travaux de M. Angelo Solerti," RHCM III (1903) 127–29, 280–82.

Roncaglia, Gino. "Gli elementi precursori del melodramma nell' opera di Orazio Vecchi : Attuazioni e limiti," RMI LV (1953) 251–56.

—— "Orazio Vecchi, precursore drammatico ed umorista," RMI LI (1949) 265–73.

Ronga, Luigi. "Lettura storica dell' Amfiparnaso," RassM XXIII (1953) 101–15.

[Rossi, Bastiano de'.] Descrizione dell' apparato e degli intermedi fatti per la commedia rappresentata in Firenze nelle nozze de' serenissimi Don Ferdinando Medici, e Madama Cristina di Loreno, gran duchi di Toscana. Florence, A. Padouani, 1589.

Rothschild, James, Baron de, ed. Le Mistère du Viel Testament. Paris, Firmin-Didot, 1878–91. 6 vols.

Rubsamen, Walter. Literary Sources of Secular Music in Italy (ca. 1500). Berkeley and Los Angeles, University of California Press, 1943.

Sachs, Curt. Die Musik der Antike. Potsdam, Athenaion, [1928].

Sacre rappresentazioni nel manoscritto 201 della Bibliothèque municipale di Orléans. Ed. fototipica. Testi e musiche trascritti e commentati da Giampiero Tintori. Precede uno studio di Raffaello Monterosso. Cremona, Athenaeum Cremonense, 1958.

Schering, Arnold. "Zur Geschichte des begleiteten Sologesangs im 16. Jahrhundert," ZIMG XIII (1911–12) 190–96.

Schlitzer, Franco. "A Letter from Cesti to Salvator Rosa," MMR LXXXIV (1954) 150–52.

Schneider, Max. Die Anfänge des Basso Continuo und seiner Bezifferung. Leipzig, B&H, 1918.

—— "Zur Geschichte des begleiteten Sologesangs," Festschrift Hermann Kretzschmar zum 70. Geburtstage überreicht von Kollegen, Schülern, und Freunden (Leipzig, C. F. Peters, 1918) 138–40.

Schoenemann, Otto. "Der Sündenfall und Marienklage : Zwei niederdeutsche Schauspiele," MfMg VII (1875) 129–39, 145–57.

Schrade, Leo. "Les Fêtes du mariage de Francesco dei Medici et de Bianca Cappello [1579]," in Les Fêtes de la Renaissance (Paris, Editions du Centre National de la Recherche Scientifique, 1956) 107–31.

—— La Représentation d' Edipo Tiranno au Teatro Olimpico (Vicenze

1585). Paris, Editions du Centre National de la Recherche Scientifique, 1960.

Schuler, Ernst August. Die Musik der Osterfeiern, Osterspiele und Passionen des Mittelalters. Kassel & Basel, Bärenreiter, [1951].

Schwietering, Julius. "Ueber den liturgischen Ursprung des mittelalterlichen geistlichen Spiels," Zeitschrift für deutsche Altertum LXII (1925) 1–20.

Sievers, Heinrich. Die lateinischen liturgischen Osterspiele der Stiftskirche St. Blasien zu Braunschweig. Wolfenbüttel, Georg Kallmeyer, 1936.

Silbert, Doris. "Francesca Caccini, Called La Cecchina," MQ XXXII (1946) 50–62.

Smits van Waesberghe, Jos. "A Dutch Easter Play," MD VII (1953) 15–37.

—— Muziek en drama in de Middeleeuwen. Amsterdam, Bigot & Van Rossum, 1942.

Smoldon, William L. "The Easter Sepulchre Music-Drama," M&L XXVII (1946) 1–17.

—— "Medieval Church Drama and the Use of Musical Instruments," The Musical Times CIII, No. 1438 (December, 1962) 836–40.

—— "The Music of the Medieval Church Drama," MQ XLVIII (1962) 476–97.

Solerti, Angelo. Gli albori del melodramma. Milan; R. Sandron, [1905]. 3 vols.

—— "Laura Guidiccioni ed Emilio de' Cavalieri : I primi tentativi del melodramma," RMI IX (1902) 797–829.

—— "Precedenti del melodramma," RMI X (1903) 207–33, 466–84.

—— "Primi saggi del melodramma giocoso," RMI XII (1905) 814–38; XIII (1906) 91–112.

—— Vita di Torquato Tasso. Turin, Rome, E. Loescher, 1895. 3 vols.

Solerti, Angelo, ed. Ferrara e la corte Estense nella seconda metà del secolo decimosesto : I discorsi di Annibale Romei, gentiluomo ferrarese. Città di Castello, S. Lapi, 1891.

Solerti, Angelo, compiler and ed. Le origini del melodramma : Testimonianze dei contemporanei. Turin, Fratelli Bocca, 1903.

Sonneck, Oscar George Theodore. "A Description of Alessandro Striggio and Francesco Corteccia's Intermedi Psyche and Amore, 1565," MA III (1911) 40.

Sternfeld, Frederick W. "Le Symbolisme musical dans quelques pièces de Shakespeare présentées à la cour d'Angleterre," in Les Fêtes de la Renaissance (Paris, Editions du Centre National de la Recherche Scientifique, 1956) 319–33.

Stevens, John. "Music in Mediæval Drama," PMA LXXXIV (1957–58) 81–95.

Stratman, Carl J. Bibliography of Medieval Drama. Berkeley and Los Angeles, University of California Press, 1954.

Symonds, John Addington. The Renaissance in Italy : Italian Literature. New York, Henry Holt, 1882. 2 vols.

Tasso, Torquato. Opere. Pisa, Capuro, 1821–32. 33 vols.

Teatro italiano antico. Milan, 1808–12. 10 vols.

Thomas, L. P. "Les Strophes et la composition du Sponsus," *Romania* LV (1929) 45–112.

—— "La Versification et les leçons douteuses du Sponsus," *Romania* LIII (1927) 43–81.

Tiby, Ottavio. La musica bizantina, teoria e storia. Milan, Fratelli Bocca, 1938.

Tiersot, Julien. "Ronsard et la musique de son temps," SIMG IV (1902–3) 70–142.

Tirabassi, M. A. "Introduction à l'étude de la parabole des vierges sages et des vierges folles," *Annales de la Société R. d' archéologie de Bruxelles* XXXII (1926) 15.

Toffani, Giuseppe, ed. Storia letteraria d'Italia : Il Cinquecento. Milan, Vallardi, 1929. 3d ed.

Trend, John Brande. "The Mystery of Elche," M&L I (1920) 145–57.

Turrini, G. "De Vlaamsche Componist Giovanni Nasco te Verona (1547–1551)," *Tijdschrift der Vereeniging voor Nederl. Muziekgeschiedenis* XIV, No. 3 (1935) 132–59; XV, No. 2 (1937) 84–93. Also in Italian, *Note d'archivio* XIV (1937) 180–225.

Tutti i trionfi, carri, mascherate, o Cante carnascialeschi andati per Firenze dal tempo del magnifico Lorenzo de' Medici fino all' anno 1559. Cosmopoli [i.e., Lucca], 1750. 2d ed.

Ursprung, Otto. "Das Sponsus-Spiel," AfMf III (1938) 80–95, 180–92.

Vecchi, Giuseppe. Uffici drammatici padovani. Florence, L. S. Olschki, 1954.

Vecchi, Orazio. L'Amfiparnaso. Trascrizione e interpretazione di Bonaventura Somma. Rome, De Santis, [1953].

Vicentino, Nicola. L'antica musica ridotta alla moderna prattica. Rome, A. Barre, 1555.

Walker, D. P. "Musical Humanism in the 16th and Early 17th Centuries," MR II (1941) 1–13, 111–21, 220–27, 288–308; III (1942) 55–71.

—— Der musikalische Humanismus in 16. und frühen 17. Jahrhunderts. Kassel & Basel, Bärenreiter, 1949.

—— "La Musique des intermèdes florentins de 1589 et l'humanisme," in *Les Fêtes de la Renaissance* (Paris, Editions du Centre National de la Recherche Scientifique, 1956) 133–44.

Weakland, Rembert. "The Rhythmic Modes and Medieval Latin Drama," JAMS XIV (1961) 131–46.

Wessely, Carl. Antike Reste griechischer Musik. [Vienna, 1891.]

Yates, Frances A. "Dramatic Religious Processions in Paris in the Late Sixteenth Century," *Annales musicologiques* II (1954) 215–70.

—— The French Academies of the Sixteenth Century. [London], Warburg Institute, University of London, 1947.

—— "Poésie et musique pour les magnificences du mariage du Duc de Joyeuse, Paris, 1581," in *Musique et poésie au XVIe siècle* (Paris, Editions du Centre National de la Recherche Scientifique, 1954) 248.

Young, Karl. The Drama of the Medieval Church. Oxford, Clarendon Press, 1933. 2 vols.

Zarlino, Gioseffo. Le istituzioni harmoniche. Venetia, [Pietro da Fino?], 1558.

III

SEVENTEENTH CENTURY

Abert, Anna Amalie. Claudio Monteverdi und das musikalische Drama. Lippstadt, Kistner & Siegel, 1954.

—— "Schauspiel und Opernlibretto im italienischen Barock," Mf II (1949) 133–41.

Adel, Kurt. Das Jesuitendrama in Oesterreich. Vienna, Bergland-Verlag, [1957].

Ademollo, Alessandro. La bell' Adriana ed altre virtuose del suo tempo alla corte di Mantova : Contributo de documenti per la storia della musica in Italia nel primo quarto del Seicento. Città di Castello, Lapi, 1888.

—— I primi fasti del teatro di via della Pergola in Firenze (1657–1661). Milan, Ricordi, [etc., 1885].

—— I teatri di Roma nel secolo decimosettimo. Rome, L. Pasqualucci, 1888.

Adler, Guido. "Einleitung [to Cesti's *Pomo d'oro*]," DTOe, Jahrg. III, Part 2 (1896) v–xxvi.

—— "Die Kaiser Ferdinand III., Leopold I., Joseph I. und Karl VI. als Tonsetzer und Förderer der Musik," VfMw VIII (1892) 252–74.

Alaleona, Domenico. Studi su la storia dell' oratorio musicale in Italia. Turin, Bocca, 1908.

Aldrich, Putnam C. The Principal Agréments of the Seventeenth and Eighteenth Centuries : A Study in Musical Ornamentation. Harvard Dissertation, 1942.

Allacci, Leone. Drammaturgia . . . accresciuta e continuata fino all' anno MDCCLV. Venice, G. Pasquali, 1755. First published Rome, 1666.

Allam, Edward. "Alessandro Stradella," PMA LXXX (1954) 29–42.

Amour, L. Maurice. "Les Musiciens de Corneille, 1650–1699," RdM XXXVII (1955) 43–75.

Apel, Willi. "Anent a Ritornello in Monteverdi's *Orfeo*," MD V (1951) 213–22.

Arger, Jane. Les Agréments et le rhythme : Leur représentation graphique dans la musique vocale française du XVIIe siècle. Paris, Rouart, Lerolle, [pref. 1917].

Arger, Jane. "Le Rôle expressif des 'agréments' dans l'école vocale française de 1680 à 1760," RdM I (1917–19) 215–26.

Arnheim, Amalie. "Ein Beitrag zur Geschichte des einstimmigen weltlichen Kunstliedes in Frankreich im 17. Jahrhundert," SIMG X (1908–9) 399–421.

Arnold, Frank T. The Art of Accompaniment from a Thorough-Bass as Practiced in the XVIIth and XVIIIth Centuries. London, Oxford University Press, 1931.

Arundell, Dennis. The Critic at the Opera. London, Benn, 1957.

—— Henry Purcell. London, Oxford University Press, 1927.

Bannard, Yorke. "Music of the Commonwealth," M&L III (1922) 394–401.

Barclay Squire. See Squire, W. Barclay.

Barthélemy, Maurice. André Campra, sa vie et son oeuvre (1660–1744). Paris, Picard, 1957.

—— "La Musique dramatique à Versailles de 1660 à 1715," XVIIe siècle No. 34 (March, 1957) 7–18.

—— "Les Opéras de Marin Marais," RBM VII (1953) 136–46.

—— "L'Orchestre et l'orchestration des oeuvres de Campra," RM No. sp. 226 (1955) 97–104.

Bartmuss, Arwed Waldemar. Die Hamburger Barockoper und ihre Bedeutung für die Entwicklung der deutschen Dichtung und der deutschen Bühne. Jena Dissertation, 1925.

Bauer, Anton. Opern und Operetten in Wien : Verzeichnis ihrer Erstaufführungen in der Zeit von 1629 bis zur Gegenwart. Graz, Cologne, Vienna, Hermann Böhlaus Nachfolge, 1955.

Baxter, William Hubbard, Jr. Agostino Steffani : A Study of the Man and His Work. University of Rochester Dissertation, 1957. 2 vols.

Beare, Mary. The German Popular Play Atis and the Venetian Opera : A Study of the Conversion of Operas into Popular Plays, 1675–1722. Cambridge, University Press, 1938.

Beaujoyeulx, Baltasar de. Balet comique de la royne, faict aux nopces de Monsieur le Duc de Ioyeuse & madamoyselle de Vaudemont sa soeur. Paris, LeRoy, Ballard & Patisson, 1682.

Becker, Heinz. "[Review of :] Hellmuth Christian Wolff : Die Barockoper in Hamburg (1678–1738)," Mf XIII (1960) 211–14.

Benham, Evelyn. "A Musical Monopolist [J. B. Lully]," M&L IX (1928) 249–54.

Benvenuti, Giacomo. "Il manoscritto veneziano della Incoronazione di Poppea," RMI XLI (1937) 176–84.

Berend, Fritz. Nicolaus Adam Strungk. Hanover, E. Homann, [1915].

Bergmans, Paul. "Une Collection de livrets d'opéras italiens (1669–1710)," SIMG XII (1910–11) 221–34.

Bernhard, Christoph. Die Kompositionslehre Heinrich Schützens in der

Fassung seines Schülers Christoph Bernhard. Edited with an introduction by J. M. Müller-Blattau. Leipzig, B&H, 1926.

Bertolotti, Antonio. Artisti francesi in Roma nei secoli XV, XVI e XVII. Mantua, Mondovi, 1894.

—— Musici alla corte dei Gonzaga in Mantova dal secolo XV al XVII: Notizie e documenti raccolti negli Archivi Mantovani. Milan, Ricordi, [1890].

Bicknell, Joan Colleen. Interdependence of Word and Tone in the Dramatic Music of Henry Purcell. Stanford University Dissertation, 1960.

Bittrich, Gerhard. Ein deutsches Opernballett des siebzehnten Jahrhunderts: Ein Beitrag zur Frühgeschichte der deutschen Oper. Leipzig, Frommhold & Wendler, 1931.

Blaze, [François Henri Joseph], called Castil-Blaze. L'Académie impériale de musique... de 1645 à 1855. Paris, Castil-Blaze, 1855.

—— Chapelle-musique des rois de France. Paris, Paulin, 1832.

—— De l'opéra en France. Paris, Janet et Cotelle, 1820.

—— L'Opéra-Italien de 1548 à 1856. Paris, Castil-Blaze, 1856.

Blümml, Emil Karl, and Gustav Gugitz. Alt-Wiener Thespiskarren: Die Frühzeit der Wiener Vorstadtbühnen. Vienna, A. Schroll, 1925.

Böhme, Erdmann Werner. "Die frühdeutsche Oper in Altenburg," *Jahrbuch der Theaterfreunde für Altenburg und Umkreis* (1930) 53 ff.

—— Die frühdeutsche Oper in Thüringen. Stadtroda in Thuringia, Richter, 1931.

—— Musik und Oper am Hofe Christians von Sachsen-Eisenberg (1677–1707). Stadtroda in Thuringia, Richter, [1930]. First published in *Mitteilungen des Geschichts- und Altertumsvereins zu Eisenberg in Thüringen*, 41. und 42. Heft (8. Band, 1. und 2. Heft, 1930).

—— "Zur Vorgeschichte der Barockoper in Altenburg," *Jahrbuch der Theaterfreunde für Altenburg und Umkreis* (1931).

Böttger, Friedrich. Die "Comédie-Ballet" von Molière-Lully. Berlin, Funk, 1931.

Boislisle, Arthur Michel de. "Les Débuts de l'opéra français à Paris," *Mémoires de la Société de l'histoire de Paris* II (1876) 172 ff.

Bonaventura, Arnaldo. "Una celebre cantante livornese del Settecento," *Musica d'oggi* VI (1924) 255–58.

Borcherdt, Hans Heinrich. "Beiträge zur Geschichte der Oper und des Schauspiels in Schlesien bis zum Jahre 1740," *Zeitschrift für die Geschichte Schlesiens* XLIII (1909) 217 ff.

Borrel, Eugène. L'Interprétation de la musique française (de Lully à la révolution). Paris, F. Alcan, 1924.

—— "L'Interprétation de l'ancien récitatif français," RdM XII (1931) 13–21.

—— Jean-Baptiste Lully: Le cadre, la vie, la personnalité, le rayonnement, les oeuvres, bibliographie. Paris, La Colombe, 1949.

Borrel, Eugène. "Les Notes inégales dans l'ancienne musique française," RdM XII (1931) 278–89.

―― "Remarques sur l'histoire de la musique au théâtre en France au XVIIe siècle," RdM XXXIX (1957) 56–60.

Borren, Charles van den. *Il ritorno d'Ulisse in patria* du Claudio Monteverdi. Brussels, Weissenbruch, 1925.

Bowden, William R. The English Dramatic Lyric, 1603–42 : A Study in Stuart Dramatic Technique. New Haven, Yale University Press, 1951.

Bragaglia, Anton Giulio. "Celebrazioni Marchigiane : Giacomo Torelli da Fano," *Il giornale di politica e di letteratura* X (1934) 331–62; XI (1935) 69–80.

Bricqueville, Eugène de. Le Livret d'opéra français de Lully à Gluck. Brussels, 1888.

Briganti, Francesco. Gio. Andrea Angelini-Bontempi (1624–1705) musicista, letterato, architetto : Perugia-Dresda. Florence, L.S. Olschki, 1956.

Bukofzer, Manfred F. Music in the Baroque Era. New York, W. W. Norton, 1947.

Caccini, Giulio. Le nuove musiche : Riproduzione dell' edizione dell' 1601. Rome, Raccolte Claudio Monteverdi (R. Mezzetti), 1930.

Calmus, Georgy. "Drei satirisch-kritische Aufsätze von Addison über die italienische Oper in England," SIMG IX (1907–8) 131–45, 448.

Cametti, Alberto. "Alcuni documenti inediti su la vita di Luigi Rossi," SIMG XIV (1912–13) 1–26.

―― Christina di Svezia, l'arte musicale e gli spettacoli teatrali in Roma. Rome, Tipografia Romano Mezzetti, 1931.

―― Il teatro di Tordinona, poi di Apollo. Tivoli, A. Chicca, 1939.

Capri, Antonio. Il Seicento musicale in Europa. Milan, Hoepli, 1933.

Carfagno, Simon A. The Life and Dramatic Music of Stefano Landi with a Transliteration and Orchestration of the Opera *Sant' Alessio*. University of California, Los Angeles Dissertation, 1960. 2 vols. in 4.

Carlez, Jules. Pierre et Thomas Corneille librettistes. N.p., n.d.

―― La *Sémiramis* de Destouches. Caen, H. Delesques, 1892.

Castil-Blaze. *See* Blaze.

Catelani, Angelo. Delle opere di Alessandro Stradella esistente nel l'archivio musicale della R. Biblioteca Palatina di Modena. Modena, C. Vincenzi, 1866.

Cavalli, Francesco. Venti arie tratte dai drami musicali di Francesco Cavalli. Vienna-Trieste, Verlag Schmiedel (Mozarthaus), 1909.

Celani, Enrico. "Canzoni musicale del secolo XVII," RMI XII (1905) 109–50.

Champigneulle, Bernard. "L'Influence de Lully hors de France," RM XXII (February–March, 1946) 26–35.

Chevaillier, Lucien. "Le Récit chez Monteverdi," RHCM X (1910) 284–94.

Chrysander, Friedrich. "Eine englische Serenata von J. Sigismund Kusser um 1710," AMZ XIV (1879) 408–12, 417–22.

—— "Die Feier des zweihundertjährigen Bestandes der Oper in Hamburg," AMZ XIII (1878) 113–15, 129–32, 145–48.

—— "Geschichte der Braunschweig-Wolfenbüttelschen Capelle und Oper vom XVI. bis zum XVIII. Jahrhundert," *Jahrbücher für musikalische Wissenschaft* I (1863) 147–286.

—— ["Geschichte der Hamburger Oper"], AMZ XII–XV (1877–80):
"Die erste Periode," AMZ XII (1877) 369–486 *passim*
"Die zweite Periode," AMZ XIII (1878) 289–442 *passim*
". . . unter . . . J. S. Kusser 1693–1696," AMZ XIV (1879) 385–408 *passim*
". . . vom Abgange Kusser's bis zum Tode Schott's," AMZ XIV (1879) 433–534 *passim*
". . . unter der Direction von Reinhard Keiser (1703–1706)," AMZ XV (1880) 17–87 *passim*.

Clark, George Norman. The Seventeenth Century. Oxford, Clarendon Press, 1929.

Clarke, Henry Leland. "Cambert, Lully, and Blow." Unpublished essay.

—— Dr. John Blow (1649–1708), Last Composer of an Era. Harvard Dissertation, 1947.

Collaer, Paul. "L'orchestra di Claudio Monteverdi," *Musica* II (Florence, 1943) 86–104.

[Conti, Armand de Bourbon, prince de.] Traité de la comédie et des spectacles selon la tradition de l'église, tirée des conciles & des saints pères. Paris, L. Billaine, 1669.

Coradini, Francesco. Antonio Maria Abbatini e d. Lorenzo Abbatini: Notizie biografiche. Arezzo, Scuola tipografica aretina, 1922.

—— "P. Antonio Cesti: Nuove notizie biografiche," RMI XXX (1923) 371–88.

Coryate, Thomas. Coryat's Crudities . . . New York, Macmillan, 1905. Originally published 1611.

Cousser, Jean Sigismond. Composition de musique, suivant la méthode françoise . . . Stoutgard, 1684.

Crocioni, Giovanni. L'Alidoro o dei primordi del melodramma. Bologna, L. Parma, 1938.

Crussard, Claude. "Marc-Antoine Charpentier théoricien," RdM XXVII (2e–3e trimestre 1945) 49–68.

—— Un Musicien français oublié, Marc-Antoine Charpentier. Paris, Floury, 1945.

Cummings, William H. "Matthew Locke, Composer for the Church and Theatre," SIMG XIII (1911–12) 120–26.

Cutts, John. "Le Rôle de la musique dans les masques de Ben Jonson et notammement dans *Oberon* (1610–1611)," in *Les Fêtes de la Renaissance* (Paris, Editions du Centre National de la Recherche Scientifique, 1956) 285–303.

Davari, Stefano. "Notizie biografiche del distinto maestro di musica

Claudio Monteverdi," *Atti e memorie della R. Accademia Virgiliana di Mantova* X (1884–85) 79–183.

De Angelis, Alberto. "Il teatro farnese di Parma," RMI XLIII (1939) 364–82.

Dedekind, Constantin Christian. Heilige Arbeit über Freud und Leid der alten und neuen Zeit in Music-bekwehmen Schau-Spielen (9) ahngewendet. Dresden, 1676.

—— Neue geistliche Schauspiele (5) bekwehmet zur Musik. [Dresden], 1670.

Deierkauf-Holsboer, S. Wilma. Le Théâtre du Marais. II : Le Berceau de L'Opéra et de la Comédie-française, 1648–1673. Paris, Nizet, 1958.

DeLage, Joseph O., Jr. The Overture in Seventeenth-Century Italian Opera. Ann Arbor, University Microfilms, 1961.

Della Corte, Andrea. "*La forza d'amor paterno* di Alessandro Stradella," *Musica d'oggi* XIII (1931) 389–94.

—— "Tragico e comico nell' opera veneziana della seconda parte del Seicento," RassM XI (1938) 325–33.

Demarquez, Suzanne. Purcell : La Vie, l'oeuvre, discographe. Paris, La Colombe, [1951].

Demuth, Norman. "A Musical Backwater," MQ XL (1954) 533–47.

Denizard, Marie. "La Famille française de Lully," MM VIII, No. 5 (1912) 1–14.

Dent, Edward J. "The Baroque Opera," MA I (1909–10) 93–107.

—— Foundations of English Opera. Cambridge (England), University Press, 1928.

—— "Italian Chamber Cantatas," MA II (1911) 142–53, 185–99.

—— "The Musical Interpretation of Shakespeare on the Modern Stage," MQ II (1916) 523–37.

De' Paoli, Domenico. Claudio Monteverdi. Milan, Hoepli, 1945.

De Rensis, Raffaello. Ercole Bernabei. Rome, tip. Sociale, 1920.

—— "Un musicista diplomatico del Settecento : Agostino Steffani," *Musica d'oggi* III, No. 5 (May, 1921) 129–32.

"Documents historiques : Les origines de l'opéra en France," RHCM VIII (1908) 562–64.

Doebner, Richard, ed. Briefe der Königin Sophie Charlotte von Preussen und der Kurfürstin Sophie von Hannover an hannoversche Diplomaten. Leipzig, S. Hirzel, 1905.

Doni, Giovanni Battista. Compendio del trattato de' generi de' modi della mvsica. Rome, A. Fei, 1635.

Abstract of a larger work which was never published. Portions of this work are quoted in Solerti's *Origini* under the title "Trattato della musica scenica."

—— Lyra Barberina ΑΜΦΙΧΟΡΔΟΣ : Accedunt eiusdem opera, pleaque nondum edita ad veterem musicam illustrandam pertinentia. Florentiae typis Caesareis, 1763. 2 vols.

Ducharte, Pierre-Louis. La Commedia dell' arte et ses enfants. Paris, Editions d' "Art et Industrie," 1955.

Du Gérard, N. B. Tables alphabetique & chronologique de pieces representées sur l'ancien Theatre italien, depuis son etablissement jusqu'en 1697. Paris, Prault, 1750.

Dupré, Henri. Purcell. Paris, Alcan, 1927. Translated, New York, Alfred A. Knopf, 1928.

Ecorcheville, Jules. "Corneille et la musique," *Courrier musical* IX (1906) 405–12, 438–49. Also separate : Paris, Fortin, 1906.

—— De Lulli à Rameau, 1690–1730 : L'esthétique musicale. Paris, Fortin, 1906.

—— "Lully gentilhomme et sa descendance," MM VII, No. 5 (1911) 1–19; No. 6, pp. 1–27; No. 7, pp. 36–52.

Ehrichs, Alfred. Giulio Caccini. Leipzig, Hesse & Becker, 1908.

Einstein, Alfred. "Agostino Steffani," *Kirchenmusikalisches Jahrbuch* XXIII (1910) 1–36.

—— "Agostino Steffani," *Neue Musik-Zeitung* XLIX (1928) 316–19.

—— "Ein Bericht über den Turiner Mordanfall auf Alessandro Stradella," in *Festschrift Adolf Sandberger* (Munich, Zierfuss, 1918) 135–37.

Eitner, Robert. "Johann Philipp Krieger," MfMg XXIX (1897) 114–17.

Eitner, Robert, ed. "Das älteste bekannte deutsche Singspiel, *Seelewig*, von S. G. Staden, 1644," MfMg XIII (1881) 53—147.

Engelke, Bernhard. Musik und Musiker am Gottorfer Hofe. Band 1. Die Zeit der englischen Komödianten (1590–1627). Breslau, Hirt, 1930.

Engländer, Richard. "Il *Paride* in musica (1662) di G. A. Bontempi," *Note d'archivio* XVII (1940) 39–53.

—— "Zur Frage der *Dafne* (1671) von G. A. Bontempi und M. G. Peranda," *Acta musicologica* XIII (1941) 59–77.

Enzinger, Moriz. Die Entwicklung des Wiener Theaters vom 16. zum 19. Jahrhundert. Berlin, Gesellschaft für Theatergeschichte, 1918–19. 2 vols.

Eppelsheim, Jürgen. Das Orchester in den Werken Jean-Baptiste Lullys. Tutzing, H. Schneider, 1961.

Epstein, Peter. "Dichtung und Musik in Monteverdi's *Lamento d'Arianna*," ZfMw X (1927–28) 216–22.

—— "Zur Rhythmisierung eines Ritornells von Monteverdi," AfMw VIII (1926) 416–19.

Evans, Herbert Arthur, ed. English Masques. London, Glasgow, Blackie & Son, 1897.

Evans, Willa McClung. Ben Jonson and Elizabethan Music. Lancaster, Pa., Lancaster Press, 1929.

Evelyn, John. Diary. London, J. M. Dent, 1907. 2 vols.

Fassini, Sesto. "Gli albori del melodramma italiano a Londra," *Giornale storico della letteratura italiana* LX (1912) 340–76.

Fellerer, Karl Gustav. Beiträge zur Musikgeschichte Freisings. Freising, Freising. Tagbl., 1926.

Fetting, Hugo. Die Geschichte der Deutschen Staatsoper. Berlin, Henschel, 1955.

Finney, Gretchen Ludke. "Chorus in *Samson Agonistes*," *Publications of the Modern Language Association of America* LVIII (1943) 649–64.

—— "*Comus*, Dramma per Musica," *Studies in Philology* XXXVII (1940) 483–500; also separate.

Flemming, Willi, ed. Die Oper. Leipzig, Reclam, 1933.

Flood, W. H. Grattan. "Quelques Précisions nouvelles sur Cambert et Grabu à Londres," RM IX (August, 1928) 351–61.

Florence, Italy. R. Istituto musicale. Atti dell' accademia del R. Istituto musicale di Firenze, Anno XXXIII : Commemorazione della riforma melodrammatica. Florence, Galletti e Cocci, 1895.

Fogaccia, Piero. Giovanni Legrenzi. Bergamo, Edizioni Orobiche, [1954].

Forsyth, Cecil. Music and Nationalism : A Study of English Opera. London, Macmillan, 1911.

Fortune, Nigel. "Italian Secular Monody from 1600 to 1635 : An Introductory Survey," MQ XXXIX (1953) 171–95.

—— "Italian 17th-Century Singing," M&L XXXV (1954) 206–19.

Frati, Lodovico. "Per la storia della musica in Bologna nel secolo XVII," RMI XXXII (1925) 544–65.

Freund, Hans, and Wilhelm Reinking. Musikalisches Theater in Hamburg: Versuch über die Dramaturgie der Oper. Hamburg, Hans Christians, 1938.

Friess, Hermann. 300 Jahr Münchener Oper. [Munich, im Auftrag der Intendanz der Bayerischen Staatsoper, s.d.]

Fürstenau, Moritz. "Die Oper *Antiope* und die Bestellungen des Kurfürstlich Sächsischen Vicekapellmeisters Nicolaus Adam Strunck und des Hofpoeten Stefano Pallavicini," MfMg XIII (1881) 1–6.

—— "Eine theologische Zeitschrift des 17. Jahrhunderts über Castraten und Oper : Johann Samuel Adami," *Musikalisches Wochenblatt* I (1870) 241–43.

—— Zur Geschichte der Musik und des Theaters am Hofe zu Dresden. Dresden, R. Kuntze, 1861–62. 2 parts.

Gaspari, Gaetano. "Dei musicisti Bolognesi al XVII secolo e delle loro opere a stampa," *Atti e memorie della R. R. Deputazione di storia patria per le provincie dell' Emilia, Nuova serie* III (1878) 1–24.

Gastoué, Amadée. "Les Notes inédites du Marquis de Paulmy sur les oeuvres lyriques françaises (1655–1775)," RdM Série spéciale, No. 1 (1943) 1–7.

Geffcken, Johannes. "Die ältesten Hamburgischen Opern," *Zeitschrift des Vereines für Hamburgische Geschichte* III (1851) 34–55.

Gentili, Alberto. "Alessandro Stradella," in *Miscellanea della Facoltà di*

Lettere e Filosofia, Serie Prima (Turin, R. Università di Torino, 1936) 155–76.

Gérold, Théodore. L'Art du chant en France au XVIIe siècle. Strasbourg, G. Fischbach, 1921.

Ghisi, Federico. Del *Fuggilotio musicale* di Giulio Romano (Caccini): Saggio critico. Rome, De Santis, 1934.

Ghislanzoni, Alberto. Luigi Rossi (Aloysius de Rubeis), biografia e analisi delle composizioni. Milan-Rome, Fratelli Bocca, [cop. 1954].

Giazotto, Remo. Il melodramma a Genova nei secoli 17 & 18 : Con gli elenchi completi dei titoli, dei musicisti, dei poeti e degli attori di quei componomenti rappresentati fra il 1652 e il 1771 ai teatre detti "Del Falcone" e "Da S. Agostino." Genoa, A cura dell' ente del Teatro Carlo Felice, 1941.

—— Vita di Alessandro Stradella. [Milan], Curci, [1962]. 2 vols.

Goldschmidt, Hugo. "Cavalli als dramatischer Komponist," MfMg XXV (1893) 45–48, 53–58, 61–111.

—— "Claudio Monteverdi's Oper : *Il ritorno d'Ulisse in patria*," SIMG IX (1907–8) 570–92.

—— "Francesco Provenzale als Dramatiker," SIMG VII (1905–6) 608–34.

—— "Die Instrumentalbegleitung der italienischen Musikdramen in der ersten Hälfte des XVII. Jahrhunderts," MfMg XXVII (1895) 52–62.

—— Die italienische Gesangsmethode des XVII. Jahrhunderts und ihre Bedeutung für die Gegenwart. Breslau, Schlesische Buchdruckerei, 1890. 2d ed., Breslau, S. Schottlaender, 1892.

—— Die Lehre von der vokalen Ornamentik, erster Band : Das 17. und 18. Jahrhundert bis in die Zeit Glucks. Charlottenburg, P. Lehsten, 1907.

—— "Monteverdi's *Ritorno d'Ulisse*," SIMG IV (1902–3) 671–76.

—— Studien zur Geschichte der italienischen Oper im 17. Jahrhundert. Leipzig, B&H, 1901–4. 2 vols. Review by R. Rolland, RHCM II (1902) 20–29.

Gołos, Jerzy. "Italian Baroque Opera in Seventeenth-Century Poland," *The Polish Review* VIII, No. 2 (Spring, 1963) 67–75.

Gombosi, Otto. "Some Musical Aspects of the English Court Masque," JAMS I, No. 3 (1948) 3–19.

Grattan Flood. *See* Flood, William Henry Grattan.

Gray, Alan. "Purcell's Dramatic Music," PMA XLIII (1916–17) 51–62.

Groppo, Antonio. Catalogo di tutti i drammi per musica recitati ne' teatri di Venezia dall' anno 1637 sin all' anno presente 1745. Venice, A. Groppo, [1745?].

Gros, Etienne. Philippe Quinault. Paris, E. Champion, 1926.

Grout, Donald Jay. "The Chorus in Early Opera," in *Festschrift Friedrich Blume* (Kassel, Bärenreiter, 1963) [151]–161.

—— "German Baroque Opera," MQ XXXII (1946) 574–87.

—— "The Music of the Italian Theatre at Paris, 1682–1697," in *Papers of the American Musicological Society, Annual Meeting, 1941 ... Edited by Gustave Reese* (Printed by the Society [cop. 1946]) 158–70.

Grout, Donald Jay. "Seventeenth Century Parodies of French Opera," MQ XXVII (1941) 211–19, 514–26.

—— "Some Forerunners of the Lully Opera," M&L XXII (1941) 1–25.

Haar, James. "Astral Music in Seventeenth-Century Nuremberg: The *Tugendsterne* of Harsdörffer and Staden," MD XVI (1962) 175–89.

Haas, Robert M. "Beitrag zur Geschichte der Oper in Prag und Dresden," *Neues Archiv für Sächsische Geschichte und Altertumskunde* XXXVII (1916) 68–96.

—— "Gioseppe Zamponis *Ulisse nell' isola di Circe*," ZfMw III (1920–21) 385–405.

—— Die Musik des Barocks. Potsdam, Athenaion, [1934].

—— "Zur Neuausgabe von Claudio Monteverdis *Il ritorno d'Ulisse in Patria*," SzMw IX (1922) 3–42.

Hadamowsky, Franz. Barocktheater am Wiener Kaiserhof: Mit einem Spielplan (1625–1740). Vienna, Sexl, 1955. Reprinted from *Jahrbuch der Gesellschaft für Wiener Theaterforschung*, 1951–52.

Hampe, Theodor. Die Entwicklung des Theaterwesens in Nürnberg von der 2. Hälfte des 15. Jahrhunderts bis 1806. Nuremberg, J. L. Schrag, 1900.

[Harsdörffer, Georg Philipp.] Frauenzimmer Gesprechspiele so bey ehrund tugendliebenden Gesellschaften mit nutzlicher Ergetzlichkeit beliebet und geübet werden mögen. Nuremberg, W. Endtern, 1643–57. 8 vols.

Hartmann, Fritz. Sechs Bücher Braunschweigischer Theatergeschichte. Wolfenbüttel, J. Zwissler, 1905.

[Hawkins, John?] Memoirs of the Life of Sig. Agostino Steffani. [London? 17—.]

Herford, Charles. "Jonson," in *Dictionary of National Biography* X (1917) 1069–79.

Hess, Heinz. Zur Geschichte des musikalischen Dramas im Seicento: Die Opern Alessandro Stradellas. Leipzig, B&H, 1906.

Heuss, Alfred. Die Instrumental-Stücke des *Orfeo* und die venetianischen Opern-Sinfonien. Leipzig, B&H, 1903. (Both parts of this work were published independently in SIMG IV.)

Hjelmborg, Bjørn. "Aspects of the Aria in the Early Operas of Francesco Cavalli," in *Natalicia musicologica Knud Jeppesen* (Copenhagen, W. Hansen, 1962) 173–98.

—— "Une Partition de Cavalli," *Acta musicologica* XVI–XVII (1944–45) 39–54.

Holland, A. K. Henry Purcell: The English Musical Tradition. London, Penguin Books, 1949.

Holst, Imogen. Henry Purcell: The Story of His Life and Work. London, Boosey & Hawkes, 1961.

Holst, Imogen, ed. Henry Purcell, 1659–1695 : Essays on His Music. London, Oxford University Press, 1959.

Huber, Wolfgang. Das Textbuch der frühdeutschen Oper : Untersuchung über literarische Voraussetzung, stoffliche Grundlagen und Quellen. Munich Dissertation, 1957.

[Hunold, Christian Friedrich.] Die allerneueste Art, zur reinen und galanten Poesie zu gelangen. Hamburg, G. Liebernickel, 1707.

—— "Gesellschaftliche Verhältnisse in der Oper zu Anfang des achtzehnten Jahrhunderts," AMZ [New Series] XV (1880) 753–58, 769–73, 785–90.

—— Theatralische, galante und geistliche Gedichte. Hamburg, G. Liebernickel, 1706.

Ingram, R. W. "Operatic Tendencies in Stuart Drama," MQ XLIV (1958) 489–502.

Jander, Owen H. A Catalogue of the Manuscripts of Compositions by Alessandro Stradella Found in European and American Libraries. Wellesley, Mass., Wellesley College, 1962. Rev. ed.

Kellner, Altman. Musikgeschichte des Stiftes Kremsmünster. Kassel & Basel, Bärenreiter, 1956.

Kiesewetter, R[aphael] G[eorg], Edler von Wiesenbrunn. Schicksale und Beschaffenheit des weltlichen Gesanges. Leipzig, B&H, 1841.

Klages, Richard. Johann Wolfgang Franck. Hamburg, 1937.

Kleefeld, Wilhelm. "Hessens Beziehungen zur alten deutschen Oper," Vom Rhein: Monatsschrift des Altertumsvereins für die Stadt Worms IV (1905) 15.

—— "Das Orchester der Hamburger Oper 1678–1738," SIMG I (1899–1900) 219–89.

Klein, Herman. "The Vienna Hofoper," M&L XIV (1933) 239–46.

Köchel, Ludwig, Ritter von. Johann Josef Fux. Vienna, A. Hölder, 1872.

—— Die kaiserliche Hofmusikkapelle in Wien von 1543 bis 1867. Vienna, Beck, 1869.

Kramer, Margarete. Beiträge zu einer Geschichte des Affektenbegriffes in der Musik von 1550–1700. Halle Dissertation, 1924.

Kreidler, Walter. Heinrich Schütz und der Stile concitato von Claudio Monteverdi. Kassel, Bärenreiter, 1934.

Křenek, Ernst. "Zur musikalischen Bearbeitung von Monteverdis Poppea," SchwM LXXVI (1936) 545–55.

Kretzschmar, Hermann. "Beiträge zur Geschichte der venetianischen Oper," JMP XIV (1907) 71–81; XVII (1910) 61–71; XVIII (1911) 49–61.

—— "Einige Bemerkungen über den Vortrag alter Musik," JMP VII (1900) 53–68.

—— "Monteverdi's Incoronazione di Poppea," VfMw X (1894) 483–530.

—— "Die venetianische Oper und die Werke Cavalli's und Cesti's," VfMw VIII (1892) 1–76.

Kutscher, Artur. Vom Salzburger Barocktheater zu den Salzburger Fest-spielen. Düsseldorf, Pflugscher-Verlag, 1939.

La Laurencie, Lionel de. "André Campra, musicien profane : Notes bio-graphiques," *Année musicale* III (1913) 153–205.

——"Une Convention commerciale entre Lully, Quinault et Ballard en 1680," RdM II (1920–21) 176–82.

—— Les Créateurs de l'opéra français. Paris, F. Alcan, 1930. New ed.

—— Lully. Paris, F. Alcan, 1911.

—— "Notes sur la jeunesse d'André Campra," SIMG X (1908–9) 159–258. Also separate : Leipzig, B&H, 1909.

—— "L'Opéra français au XVIIe siècle : La musique," RM VI (January, 1925) 26–43.

—— "Un Opéra inédit de M.-A. Charpentier : *La Descente d'Orphée aux enfers*," RdM X (1929) 184–93.

—— "L'*Orfeo nell' inferni* d'André Campra," RdM IX (1928) 129–33.

—— "Les Pastorales en musique au XVIIe siècle en France avant Lully et leur influence sur l'opéra," in *International Musical Society, 4th Congress Report* (London, Novello, 1912) 139–46.

Lang, Paul Henry. The Literary Aspects of the History of the Opera in France. Cornell Dissertation, 1935.

La Roche, Charles. Antonio Bertali als Opern- und Oratorienkomponist. Vienna Dissertation, 1919.

La Tour, Georges Imbart de. "La Mise en scène d' *Hippolyte et Aricie*," MM IV (1908) 247–71.

Lawrence, William John. The Elizabethan Playhouse and Other Studies. Philadelphia, J. B. Lippincott, 1912.

—— "The English Theatre Orchestra: Its Rise and Early Characteristics," MQ III (1917) 9–27.

—— "Foreign Singers and Musicians at the Court of Charles II," MQ IX (1923) 217–25.

—— "Notes on a Collection of Masque Music," M&L III (1922) 49–58.

[Le Cerf de la Viéville, Jean Laurent, seigneur de Freneuse.] Comparaison de la musique italienne et de la musique françoise. Brussels, F. Foppens, 1704–6. 3 vols. Also forms Vols. 2–4 of Jacques Bonnet's Histoire de la musique et de ses effets. Amsterdam, J. Royer, 17—.

[Leclercq, Louis.] Les Décors, les costumes, et la mise en scène au XVIIe siècle, 1615–1680, par Ludovic Celler [pseud.]. Paris, Liepmannssohn & Dufour, 1869.

Leichtentritt, Hugo. "On the Prologue in Early Opera," MTNA XXXI (1936) 292–99.

Lengl, Georg. Die Genesis der Oper. Munich, Mössl, 1936.

[Le Prévost d'Exmes, François.] Lully, musicien. [Paris, 1779.]

LeRoux, Maurice. Claudio Monteverdi. [Paris], Editions du Coudrier, [1951].

Levinson, André. "Notes sur le ballet au XVIIe siècle : Les danseurs de Lully," RM VI (January, 1925) 44-55.

Lieboldt, J. "Der Verbleib der alten Hamburger Operndekoration *Der Tempel Salomonis*," *Mitteilungen des Vereins für Hamburgische Geschichte* XIII (1890) 128-29.

[Limojon de St. Didier, Alexandre Toussaint.] La Ville et la république de Venise. Paris, G. de Luyne, 1680. Translated as : The City and Republick of Venice. London, C. Brome, 1699.

Lindner, Ernst Otto. Die erste stehende deutsche Oper. Berlin, Schlesinger, 1855. 2 vols.

Liuzzi, Fernando. I musicisti in Francia. Vol. I : Dalle origini al secolo XVII. Rome, Edizioni d'Arte Dansei, 1946.

Loschelder, Josef. "Aus Düsseldorfs italienischer Zeit : Römische Quellen zu Agostino Steffanis Leben," in Karl Gustav Fellerer, ed., *Beiträge zur Musikgeschichte der Stadt Düsseldorf* (Cologne & Krefeld, Staufen-Verlag, 1952) 17-53.

Lote, Georges. "La Déclamation du vers français à la fin du XVIIe siècle," *Revue de phonétique* II (1912) 313-63.

Lugli, A. Il melodramma, l'ultima geniale creazione del rinascimento. Milan, A. Ballardi, 1921.

Lully et l'opéra français. RM, numéro spécial, Vol. VI (January, 1925).

McManaway, J. G. "Songs and Masques in *The Tempest*," in *Luttrell Society Reprints*, No. 14 (1953) 71-96.

McMullen, Edward Wallace. The Earliest Operatic Adaptations of Shakespeare. Columbia Dissertation (A.M.), 1939.

Maione, Italo. "Tasso-Monteverdi : *Il combattimento di Tancredi e Clorinda*," RassM III (1930) 206-15.

Malipiero, Gian Francesco. Claudio Monteverdi. Milan, Treves, 1929.

—— "Claudio Monteverdi of Cremona," MQ XVIII (1932) 383-96.

Manifold, John Streeter. The Music in English Drama from Shakespeare to Purcell. London, Rockliff, [1956].

Mantica, Francesco, ed. Prime fioriture del melodramma italiano. Rome, Casa editrice Claudio Monteverdi, 1912-30. 2 vols.

Mariani, Valerio. "Ricordando Sabbatini e Torelli scenografi marchigiani," *Rassegna Marchigiana* XII (1934) 193-207.

Mark, Jeffrey. "Dryden and the Beginnings of Opera in England," M&L V (1924) 247-52.

—— "The Jonsonian Masque," M&L III (1922) 358-71.

Masson, Paul-Marie. "*Les Fêtes vénitiennes* de Campra," RdM XIII (1932) 127-46, 214-26.

—— "Lullistes et Ramistes," *L'Anée musicale* I (1911) 187-211.

Maugars, André. "Response faite à un curieux sur le sentiment de la musique d'Italie, écrite à Rome le premier octobre 1639 . . . in deutscher Uebersetzung mitgetheilt von W. J. von Wasialewski," MfMg X (1878) 1-9, 17-23.

Maxton, Willy. Johann Theile. Tübingen Dissertation, 1927.

Meer, J. H. van der. Johann Josef Fux als Opernkomponist. Bilthoven, A. B. Creyghton, 1961. 3 vols. plus music supplement.

Menantes, pseud. *See* Hunold, Christian Friedrich.

Ménestrier, Claude François. Des Ballets anciens et modernes. Paris, R. Guignard, 1682.

Menke, Werner. Das Vokalwerk Georg Philipp Telemanns : Uberlieferung und Zeitfolge. Kassel, Bärenreiter, 1942.

Mercure françois, Le. Paris, J. Richer, 1612–48. 25 vols.

Mersenne, Marin. Harmonie universelle. Paris, S. Cramoisy, 1636–37.

Mielsch, Rudolf. "*Dafne,* die erste deutsche Oper," *Die Musik* XIX (May, 1927) 586–91.

Mies, Paul. "Ueber die Behandlung der Frage im 17. und 18. Jahrhundert," ZfMw IV (1921–22) 286–304.

Mila, Massimo. "Jacopo Peri," RassM VI (1933) 214–27.

Moberg, Carl Allan. "Un Compositeur oublié de l'école de Lully : Jean Desfontaines," RdM X (1929) 5–9.

Molmenti, P[ompeo] G[herardo]. La storia di Venezia nella vita privata dalle origini alla caduta della repubblica. Bergamo, Istituto italiano d'arti grafiche, 1905–8. 3 vols.

Monaldi, Gino. I teatri di Roma negli ultimi tre secoli. Naples, R. Ricciardi, 1928.

[Monteverdi, Claudio.] *See* special number of RassM II (October, 1929).

Moore, Robert Etheridge. Henry Purcell and the Restoration Theatre. London, Heinemann, [1961].

—— "The Music to *Macbeth,*" MQ XLVII (1961) 22–40.

Morgan [Sydney (Owenson)], Lady. The Life and Times of Salvator Rosa. London, 1824. 2 vols.

Muffat, Georg. Suavioris harmoniae instrumentalis hyporchematicae florilegium I. Augustae Vindelicorum, Typis Jacobi Koppmayr, 1695. Reprinted in DTOe, Vol. 2.

—— Florilegium secundum. Passovii, Typis Georgij Adam Höller, 1698. Reprinted in DTOe, Vol. 4.

Nagel, Willibald. "Daniel Purcell," MfMg XXX (1898) 47–53.

Nagler, A. M. "Lullys Opernbühne," in *Kleine Schriften der Gesellschaft für Theatergeschichte,* Heft 17 (Berlin, 1960) 9–26.

Narciss, Georg Adolf. Studien zu den Frauenzimmergesprächspielen Georg Philipp Harsdörfers. Leipzig, H. Eichblatt, 1928.

Naylor, Edward Woodall. "Music and Shakespeare," MA I (1909–10) 129–48.

—— Shakespeare and Music. London, J. M. Dent, [1931].

Nef, Karl. Zur Geschichte der deutschen Instrumentalmusik in der 2. Hälfte des 17. Jahrhunderts. Leipzig, B&H, 1902.

—— "Zur Instrumentation im 17. Jahrhundert," JMP XXXV (1929) 33–42.

Neisser, Arthur. *Servio Tullio,* eine Oper aus dem Jahre 1685 von Agostino Steffani. Leipzig, C. G. Röder, 1902.

Nettl, Paul. "Beitrag zur Geschichte des deutschen Singballets," ZfMw VI (1923–24) 608–20.

—— "Exzerpte aus der Raudnitzer Textbüchersammlung," SzMw VII (1920) 143–44.

—— "Zur Geschichte der kaiserlichen Hofkapelle von 1636–1680," SzMw XVI (1929) 70–85; XVII (1930) 95–104; XVIII (1931) 23–35; XIX (1932) 33–40.

Neuhaus, Max. "Antonio Draghi," SzMw I (1913) 104–92.

Neumann, Friedrich-Heinrich. Die Aesthetik des Rezitativs : Zur Theorie des Rezitativs im 17. und 18. Jahrhundert. Strasbourg, Heitz, 1962.

Nicoll, Allardyce. "Italian Opera in England : The First Five Years," *Anglia* XLVI (1922) 257–81.

Nietan, Hanns. Die Buffoszenen der spätvenezianischen Oper (1680 bis 1710). Halle Dissertation, 1925.

Noack, Friedrich. "Die Musik zu der molièreschen Komödie *Monsieur de Pourceaugnac* von Jean Baptiste de Lully," in *Festschrift für Johannes Wolf* (Berlin, Breslauer, 1929) 139–47.

Nodot, ——. "Le Triomphe de Lully aux Champs-Elysées," RM VI (January, 1925) 89–106. First printing of Bibliothèque de l'Arsenal MS 6.542, pp. 260 ff.

Norman, Gertrude. A Consideration of Seicento Opera with Particular Reference to the Rise of the Neapolitan School. Columbia Dissertation (A. M.), 1937.

Noyes, Robert Gale. Ben Jonson on the English Stage, 1660–1776. Cambridge, Mass., Harvard University Press, 1935.

—— "Contemporary Musical Settings of the Songs in Restoration Dramatic Operas," *Harvard Studies and Notes in Philology and Literature* XX (1938) 99–121.

Nuitter. *See* Truinet.

Nungezer, Edwin. Dictionary of Actors and Other Persons Associated with the Public Representations of Plays in England before 1642. New Haven, Yale University Press; London, Oxford University Press, 1929.

Oliver, A. Richard. "Molière's Contribution to the Lyric Stage," MQ XXXIII (1947) 350–64.

O'Neill, Norman. "Music to Stage Plays in England," SIMG XIII (1911–12) 321–28.

Opel, Julius Otto. "Die erste Jahrzehnte der Oper in Leipzig," *Neues Archiv für sächsische Geschichte und Altertumskunde* V (1884) 116–141.

Osthoff, Wolfgang. Das dramatische Spätwerk Claudio Monteverdis. Tutzing, Hans Schneider, 1960.

—— "Neue Beobachtungen zu Quellen und Geschichte von Monteverdis *Incoronazione di Poppea,*" Mf XI (1958) 129–38.

Osthoff, Wolfgang. "Die venezianische und neapolitanische Fassung von Monteverdis *Incoronazione di Poppea*," *Acta musicologica* XXVI (1954) 88–113.

—— "Zu den Quellen von Monteverdis *Ritorno di Ulisse in Patria*," *Studien zur Musikwissenschaft*, XXIII (1956) 67–78.

Ottzen, Curt. Telemann als Opernkomponist. Berlin, E. Ebering, 1902. 2 vols. See review by Oskar Fleischer, ZIMG III, 497.

Pannain, Guido. "Studi monteverdiani," RassM XXVIII (1958) 7–15, 97–108, 187–95, 281–92; XXIX (1959) 42–50, 95–105, 234–46, 310–21; XXX (1960) 24–32, 230–40, 312–24; XXXI (1961) 14–26.

Paoli, Domenico de. Monteverdi. Milan, Hoepli, 1945.

Paoli, Rodolfo. "Difesa del primo melodramma," RassM XX (1950) 93–100.

Parry, Sir C[harles] Hubert H[astings]. The Music of the Seventeenth Century. London, Oxford University Press, 1938. 2d ed. (OHM, Vol. III.)

—— "The Significance of Monteverde," PMA XLII (1915–16) 51–67.

Passuth, Laszlo. Monteverdi : Der Roman eines grossen Musikers. Vienna-Berlin-Stuttgart, Paul Neff Verlag, 1959.

Pepys, Samuel. The Diary of Samuel Pepys. London, G. Bell; New York, Harcourt, Brace, 1924–26. 8 vols.

Perrault, Charles. Les Hommes illustres qui ont paru en France pendant ce siècle. Paris. A. Dezallier, 1696.

Piccioli, Giuseppe. Composizioni di antichi autori bolognesi. Bologna, Bongiovanni, 1933.

Pirchan, Emil, Alexander Witeschnik, and Otto Fritz. 300 Jahre Wiener Operntheater : Werk und Werden. Vienna, Fortuna Verlag, [1953].

Pirro, André. Schütz. Paris, F. Alcan, 1913.

Pirrotta, Nino. " 'Commedia dell' Arte' and Opera," MQ XLI (1955) 305–24.

Policastro, Guglielmo. "Musica e teatro nel Seicento nella provincia di Catania," RMI LV (1953) 109–48.

—— "I teatri dell '600 in Catania," RMI LIV (1952) 207–17, 316–28.

Pougin, Arthur. "L'Orchestre de Lully," Le Ménestrel LXII (1896) 44–45, 59–60, 67–68, 76, 83–84, 91–92, 99–100.

—— "Les Origines de l'opéra français : Cambert et Lully," Revue d'art dramatique Année 6, tome XXI (1891) 129–55.

—— Les Vrais Créateurs de l'opéra français, Perrin et Cambert. Paris, Charvay, 1881.

Prendergast, Arthur H. "The Masque of the Seventeenth Century," PMA XXIII (1897) 113–31.

Pribram, Alfred Francis. Materialen zur Geschichte der Preise und Löhne in Oesterreich. Band I. Vienna, C. Ueberreuter, 1938.

Prod'homme, Jacques Gabriel. "The Economic Status of Musicians in France until the French Revolution," MQ XVI (1930) 83–100.

—— "Pierre Corneille et l'opéra français," ZIMG VII (1905–6) 416–21.

Prota-Giurleo, U. Francesco Cirillo e l'introduzione del melodramma a Napoli. Grumo Nevano, A cura del Comune, 1952.

Prunières, Henry. "L'Académie royale de musique et de danse," RM VI (January, 1925) 3–25.

—— Le Ballet de cour en France avant Benserade et Lully. Paris, H. Laurens, 1914.

—— Cavalli et l'opéra vénitien au XVIIIe siècle. Paris, Rieder, [1931].

—— Claudio Monteverdi. Paris, F. Alcan, 1924.

—— "De l'interpretation des agréments du chant aux XVIIe et XVIIIe siècles," RM XIII (May, 1932) 329–44.

—— "Jean de Cambefort," Année musicale II (1912) 205–26.

—— "La Jeunesse de Lully (1632–62)," MM V (1909) 234–42, 329–53.

—— "Lecerf de la Viéville et l'esthétique musicale classique au XVIIe siècle," MM IV (1908) 619–54.

—— "Lettres et autographes de Lully," MM VIII (1912) 19–20.

—— "I libretti dell' opera veneziana nel secolo XVII," RassM III (1930) 441–48.

—— Lully. Paris, H. Laurens, 1909.

—— "Lully and the Académie de Musique et de Danse," MQ XI (1925) 528–46.

—— "Lully, fils de meunier," MM VIII (1912) 57–61.

—— "Monteverdi's Venetian Operas," MQ X (1924) 178–92.

—— "Les Musiciens du Cardinal Antonio Barberini," in Mélanges de musicologie (Paris, Droz, 1933) 117–22.

—— "Notes sur la vie de Luigi Rossi (1598–1653)," SIMG XII (1910–11) 12–16.

—— "Notes sur les origines de l'ouverture française," SIMG XII (1910–11) 565–85.

—— "Notes sur une partition faussement attribuée à Cavalli : L'Eritrea (1686)," RMI XXVII (1920) 267–73.

—— L'Opéra italien en France avant Lulli. Paris, E. Champion, 1913. Review by R. Rolland, MM X, No. 5 (1914) 6–15.

—— "Les Premières Ballets de Lully," RM XII (June, 1931) 1–17.

—— "Recherches sur les années de jeunesse de J. B. Lully," RMI XVII (1910) 646–54.

—— "Les Représentations du Palazzo l'Atlante à Rome (1642) d'après des documents inédits," SIMG XIV (1912–13) 218–26.

—— La Vie et l'œuvre de Claudio Monteverdi. Paris, Librairie de France, 1926. 2d ed., 1931. Translated as : Monteverdi : His Life and Works. London, J. M. Dent, 1926.

—— La Vie illustre et libertine de Jean-Baptiste Lully. Paris, Plon-Nourrit, [1929].

Purcell's The Fairy Queen, as Presented at the Royal Opera House, Covent Garden : A Photographic Record by Edward Mandinian with Preface to the Original Text, a Preface by Prof. E. J. Dent, and Articles by Constant Lambert and Michael Ayrton. London, John Lehmann, 1948.

Pure, Michel de. Idée des spectacles anciens et nouveaux. Paris, M. Brunet, 1668.

Quinault, Philippe. Théâtre. Paris, Compagnie des Libraires, 1739. 5 vols.

Quittard, Henri. "L'Orchestre de l' *Orfeo*," RHCM VII (1907) 380–89, 412–18.

Radet, Edmond. Lully, homme d'affaires, propriétaire et musicien. Paris, L. Allison, [1891].

Rau, Carl August. Loreto Vittori. Munich, Verlag für moderne Musik, [1916].

Redlich, Hans Ferdinand. Claudio Monteverdi, Leben und Werk. Olten, Verlag Otto Walter AG, 1949. Translated as : Claudio Monteverdi : Life and Works. London, New York, Toronto, Oxford University Press, 1952.

—— "Monteverdi-Renaissance," *Atlantis* VIII (1936) 768.

—— "Notationsprobleme in Cl. Monteverdis *Incoronazione di Poppea*," *Acta musicologica* X (1938) 129–32.

—— "Sull' edizione moderna delle opere di Claudio Monteverdi," RassM VIII (1935) 23–41.

—— "Zur Bearbeitung von Monteverdis *Orfeo*," SchwM LXXVI (1936) 37–42, 74–80.

Reiner, Stuart. "Collaboration in *Chi soffre speri*," MR XXII (1961) 265–82.

Rendell, E. D. "Some Notes on Purcell's Dramatic Music, with Especial Reference to the *Fairy Queen*," M&L I (1920) 135–44.

Reuter, Fritz. "Die Entwicklung der Leipziger, insbesondere italienischen Oper bis zum siebenjährigen Krieg," ZfMw V (1922–23) 1–16.

—— Die Geschichte der deutschen Oper in Leipzig am Ende des 17. und am Anfang des 18. Jahrhunderts (1693–1720). Leipzig Dissertation, 1923.

Reyher, Paul. Les Masques anglais. Paris, Hachette, 1909.

Ricci, Corrado. Vita barocca. Milan, L. F. Cogliati, 1904.

Ricci, Vittorio. "Un melodramma ignoto della prima metà dell '600 : *Celio di Baccio Baglioni e di Niccolò Sapiti*," RMI XXXII (1925) 51–79.

Richard, Pierre. "Stradella et les Contarini : Episode des moeurs vénitiennes au XVIIe siècle," *Le Ménestrel* XXXII (1864–65), XXXIII (1865–66), *passim*.

Riedel, Emil. Schuldrama und Theater. Hamburg, L. Voss, 1885.

Riemann, Hugo. "*Basso ostinato* und *Basso* quasi *ostinato*: Eine Anregung," in *Festschrift Liliencron* (Leipzig, B&H, 1910) 193–202.

Ritscher, Hugo. Die musikalische Deklamation in Lully's Opernrezitativen. Berlin Dissertation, 1925.

Ritter, A. G. "Die musikalischen Chöre des Chr. Th. Walliser zur Tragödie *Andromeda*," MfMg I (1869) 134–41.

Rokseth, Yvonne. "Antonia Bembo, Composer to Louis XIV," MQ XXIII (1937) 147–67.

Rolandi, Ulderico. "*Il Ciclope*: Dramma harmonica con musica di D. Lorenzo Ratti (Roma : 1628)," *Note d'archivio* X (1933) 253–60.

Rolland, Romain. "Notes sur l' *Orfeo* de Luigi Rossi et sur les musiciens italiens à Paris, sous Mazarin," RHCM I (1901) 225–36, 363–72.

—— "L'Opéra populaire à Venise : Francesco Cavalli," MM II, No. 1 (1906) 61–70, 151–60.

—— Les Origines du théâtre lyrique moderne : Histoire de l'opéra en Europe avant Lully et Scarlatti. Paris, E. Thorin, 1895. New ed. Paris, E. de Boccard, 1931.

—— "La Première Représentation du *San Alessio* de Stefano Landi en 1632, à Rome, d'après le journal manuscrit de Jean Jacques Bouchard," RHCM II (1902) 29–36, 74–75.

—— "La Représentation d' *Orféo* à Paris et l'opposition religieuse et politique à l'opéra," RHCM I (1901) 10–17.

Rommel, Otto. Die Alt-Wiener Volkskomödie : Ihre Geschichte vom barocken Welt-Theater bis zum Tode Nestroys. Vienna, Schroll, [1952].

Roncaglia, Gino. Le composizioni di Alessandro Stradella esistenti presso la R. Biblioteca Estense di Modena. Milan, Bocca, 1942.

—— La rivoluzione musicale italiana (secolo XVII). Milan, G. Bolla, 1928.

—— "Il *Trespolo tutore* di Alessandro Stradella, 'la prima opera buffa,'" RMI LVI (1954) 326–32.

R[onga], L[uigi]. "Su Monteverdi e sull' opera italiana del Seicento," RMI LVII (1955) 140–50.

Rotondi, Joseph E. Literary and Musical Aspects of Roman Opera, 1600–1650. Ann Arbor, University Microfilms, 1959.

Rudhart, Franz Michael. Geschichte der Oper am Hofe zu München . . . Erster Theil : Die italienische Oper von 1654–1787. Freising, F. Datterer, 1865.

Sabbatini, Nicola. Pratica di fabricar scene, e machine ne' teatri. Ravenna, Pietro de Paoli, 1638. New ed. German ed. as : Anleitung Dekorationen und Theatermaschinen herzustellen. Weimar, Gesellschaft der Bibliophilen, 1926. Ed. by Willi Flemming.

Sachs, Curt. "Die Ansbacher Hofkapelle unter Markgraf Johann Friedrich (1672–86)," SIMG XI (1909–10) 105–37.

[Salvioli, Giovanni.] I teatri musicali di Venezia nel secolo XVII. Milan, Ricordi, [1879].

Salza, Abd-el-kader. "Drammi inediti di Giulio Rospigliosi," RMI XIV (1907) 473–508.

Sandberger, Adolf. "Beziehungen der Königin Christine von Schweden zur italienischen Oper und Musik, insbesondere zu M. A. Cesti : Mit einem Anhang über Cestis Innsbrucker Aufenthalt," *Bulletin de la Société union musicologique* V (1925) 121–73.

Sandberger, Adolf. "Zur Geschichte der Oper in Nürnberg in der 2. Hälfte des 17. und zu Anfang des 18. Jahrhunderts," AfMw I (1918) 84–107.

—— "Zur venezianischen Oper," JMP XXXI (1924) 61–70; XXXII (1925) 53–63.

Sartori, Claudio. Monteverdi. Brescia, La Scuola, 1953.

Savaron, Jean. Traitté contre les masques. Paris, Perier, 1611. 3d ed.

Saviotti, Alfredo. "Feste e spettacoli nel Seicento," Giornale storico della letteratura italiana XLI (1903) 542–77.

Schering, Arnold. "Zur Geschichte des italienischen Oratoriums im 17. Jahrhundert," JMP X (1903) 31–44.

Scheurleer, D. F. "Ein Marionetten-Theater te Amsterdam 1696," Tijdschrift der Vereeniging voor Noord Nederlands Muziekgeschiedenis IX, No. 3 (1912) 147–53.

Schiedermair, Ludwig. "Die Anfänge der Münchener Oper," SIMG V (1903–4) 442–68.

—— "Briefe Johann Philipp Käfers," in Festschrift Adolf Sandberger (Munich, Zierfuss, 1918) 121–28.

—— Die deutsche Oper : Grundzüge ihres Werdens und Wesens. Bonn, Berlin, Ferd. Dümmlers Verlag, 1943. 3d ed.

—— "Die Oper an den badischen Höfen des 17. und 18. Jahrhunderts," SIMG XIV (1912–13) 191–207, 369–449, 510–50.

Schild, M. Die Musikdramen Ottavio Rinuccinis. Würzburg, Mayr, 1933.

Schletterer, Hans Michael. Vorgeschichte und erste Versuche der französischen Oper. Berlin, R. Damköhler, 1885. (Vol. III of his Studien zur Geschichte der französischen Musik.)

Schlitzer, Franco. Intorno alla Dori di Antonio Cesti. Florence, Edizioni Sansoni Antiquariato, 1957.

Schmidt, Günther. Die Musik am Hofe der Markgrafen von Brandenburg-Ansbach vom ausgehenden Mittelalter bis 1806. Kassel, Bärenreiter, 1956.

Schmidt, Gustav Friedrich. "Die älteste deutsche Oper in Leipzig am Ende des 17. und Anfang des 18. Jahrhunderts," in Festschrift Adolf Sandberger (Munich, Zierfuss, 1918) 209–57.

—— Die frühdeutsche Oper und die musikdramatische Kunst Georg Caspar Schürmann's. Regensburg, G. Bosse, 1933. 2 vols.

—— "Johann Wolfgang Francks Singspiel Die drey Töchter Cecrops," AfMf IV (1939) 257–316.

—— Neue Beiträge zur Geschichte der Musik und des Theaters am Herzoglichen Hofe zu Braunschweig-Wolfenbüttel. Munich, W. Berntheisel, 1929.

—— "Zur Geschichte, Dramaturgie und Statistik der frühdeutschen Oper (1627–1750)," ZfMw V (1922–23) 582–97, 642–65; VI (1923–24) 129–57, 496–530.

Schmidt, Immanuel. "Ueber Ben Jonson's Maskenspiele," Archiv für das Studium der neueren Sprachen XXVII (1860) 55–90.

Schmitz, Arnold. "Monodien der Kölner Jesuiten aus der ersten Hälfte des 17. Jahrhunderts," ZfMw IV (1921–22) 266–85.

Schmitz, Eugen. "Antonio Brunelli als Monodist," ZIMG XI (1909–10) 383–86.

—— "Zur Frühgeschichte der lyrischen Monodie Italiens im 17. Jahrhundert," JMP XVIII (1911) 35–48.

—— "Zur Geschichte des italienischen Continuo-Madrigals im 17. Jahrhundert," SIMG XI (1909–10) 509–28.

—— "Zur musikgeschichtlichen Bedeutung der Harsdörfferschen 'Frauenzimmergesprächspiele,'" in Festschrift . . . Liliencron (Leipzig, B&H, 1910) 254–77.

Schneider, Constantin. "Franz Heinrich von Biber als Opernkomponist," AfMw VIII (1926) 281–347.

Schneider, Louis. Un Précurseur de la musique italienne aux XVIe et XVIIe siècles : Claudio Monteverdi. Paris, Perrin, 1921.

Das Schönbrunner Schlosstheater : Beiträge. Vienna, Bundesministerium für Unterricht im H. Baur-Verlag, 1947.

Scholes, Percy. The Puritans and Music in England and New England. London, Oxford University Press, 1934.

Scholz, Hans. Johann Sigismund Kusser. Leipzig, Röder, 1911.

Schrade, Leo. Monteverdi, Creator of Modern Music. New York, W. W. Norton, 1950.

Schreiber, Irmtraud. Dichtung und Musik der deutschen Opernarien 1680–1700. Bottrop i. W., Postberg, 1934.

Schulze, Walter. Die Quellen der Hamburger Oper (1678–1738). Hamburg-Oldenburg, G. Stalling, 1938.

Settecento italiano, Il. Milan-Rome, Bestetti & Tumminelli, 1932. 2 vols.

Sietz, Reinhold. Henry Purcell, Zeit—Leben—Werk. Leipzig, B&H, 1955.

Silin, Charles I. Benserade and His Ballets de Cour. Baltimore, Johns Hopkins Press, 1940.

Sittard, Josef. Zur Geschichte der Musik und des Theaters am württembergischen Hofe. Stuttgart, W. Kohlhammer, 1890–91. 2 vols.

Solerti, Angelo. "Un balletto musicato da Claudio Monteverdi," RMI XI (1904) 24–34.

—— "Feste musicale alla Corte di Savoia nella prima metà del secolo XVII," RMI XI (1904) 675–724.

—— "Lettere inedite sulla musica di Pietro della Valle a G.B. Doni ed una veglia drammatica-musicale del medesimo," RMI XII (1905) 271–338.

—— Musica, ballo e drammatica alla corte Medicea dal 1600 al 1637. Florence, R. Bemporad, 1905.

—— "I rappresentazioni musicali di Venezia dal 1571 al 1605," RMI IX (1902) 503–58.

—— "Un viaggio in Francia di Giulio Caccini," RMI X (1903) 707–11.

Sonneck, Oscar George Theodore. "*Dafne*, the First Opera," SIMG XV (1913–14) 102–10.

Speer, Daniel. Grund-richtiger, kurtz, leicht und nöthiger Unterricht der musikalischen Kunst. Ulm, G. W. Kühnen, 1687.

Spink, Ian. "Playford's 'Directions for Singing after the Italian Manner,' " MMR LXXXIX (1959) 130–35.

Spitz, Charlotte. "Eine anonyme italienische Oper um die Wende des 17. zum 18. Jahrhundert," ZfMw II (1919–20) 232–35.

—— "Die Entwickelung des 'stilo recitativo,' " AfMw III (1921) 237–44.

Squire, William Barclay. "J. W. Franck in England," MA III (1911–12) 181–90.

—— "The Music of Shadwell's *Tempest*," MQ VII (1921) 565–78.

—— "An Opera under Innocent X," in *Gedenkboek . . . Scheurleer* (The Hague, Nijhoff, 1925) 65–71.

—— "Purcell's Dramatic Music," SIMG V (1903–4) 489–564.

Stanley, Albert Augustus. "Cesti's *Il Pomo d'Oro*," MTNA I (1906) 139–49.

Stefan, Paul. Die Wiener Oper : Ihre Geschichte von den Anfängen bis in der neueste Zeit. Vienna, Augartenverlag, 1932.

Stenhouse, May. The Character of the Opera Libretto according to Quinault. Columbia Dissertation (A.M.), 1920.

Storz, Walter. Der Aufbau der Tänze in den Opern und Balletts Lully's vom musikalischen Standpunkte aus betrachtet. Göttingen, Dieterischen Universitäts-Buchdruckerei, 1928.

Swalin, Benjamin F. "Purcell's Masque in *Timon of Athens*," in *Papers of the American Musicological Society, Annual Meeting, 1941 . . . Edited by Gustave Reese* (Printed by the Society [cop. 1946]) 112–24.

Swanepoel, Pieter. Das dramatische Schaffen Henry Purcells. Vienna Dissertation, 1926.

Taubert, Otto. "*Daphne*, das erste deutsche Operntextbuch," in *Programm des Gymnasiums zu Torgau* (Torgau, Fr. Lebinsky, 1879).

Tessier, André. "Berain, créateur du pays d'opéra," RM VI (January, 1925) 56–73.

—— "Les Deux Styles de Monteverdi," RM III, No. 8 (June, 1922) 223–54.

—— "Giacomo Torelli a Parigi e la messa in scena delle *Nozze di Peleo e Teti* di Carlo Caproli," RassM I (1928) 573–90.

—— "L'*Orontée* de Lorenzani et l'*Orontea* du Padre Cesti," RM IX, No. 8 (1928) 169–86.

—— "Quelques notes sur Jean Desfontaines," RdM X (1929) 9–16.

—— "Robert Cambert à Londres," RM IV (December, 1927) 101–22.

Teutsche Arien, welche auf dem Kayserlich-privilegierten Wienerischen Theatro in unterschiedlich producirten Comoedien, deren Titeln hier jedesmahl beygerucket, gesungen worden : Codex MS 12706–12709 der Wiener Nationalbibliothek. Vienna, E. Strache, 1930.

Thorp, Willard, ed. Songs from the Restoration Theatre. Princeton, Princeton University Press, 1934.

Tiby, Ottavio. L'incoronazione di Poppea di Claudio Monteverdi. Florence, A. Vallechi, 1937.

Tiersot, Julien. "Les Choeurs d' Esther de Moreau," RHCM III (1903) 35–40.

—— "La Musique des comédies de Molière à la Comédie-française," livre, [1922].

—— "La Musique des comédies de Molière à la Comédie-française," RdM VI (1922) 20–28.

Tintelnot, Hans. Die Entwicklungsgeschichte der barocken Bühnendekoration in ihren Wechselbeziehungen zur bildenden Kunst. Berlin, Mann, 1938.

Tirabassi, Antonio. "The Oldest Opera : Belli's Orfeo Dolente," MQ XXV (1939) 26–33.

Toni, Alceo. "Sul basso continuo e l'interpretazione della musica antica," RMI XXVI (1919) 229–64.

Torchi, Luigi. "L'accompagnamento degli istrumenti nei melodrammi italiani della prima metà del Seicento," RMI I (1894) 7–38; II (1895) 666–71.

—— "Canzoni ed arie italiane ad una voce nel secolo XVII," RMI I (1894) 581–656.

Torrefranca, Fausto. "Il 'grande stregone' Giacomo Torelli e la scenografia del Seicento," Scenario III (1934) 473–80.

—— "La prima opera francese in Italia? (l'Armida di Lulli, Roma 1690)," in Festschrift für Johannes Wolf (Berlin, Breslauer, 1929) 191–97.

Torri, Luigi. "Il primo melodramma a Torino," RMI XXVI (1919) 1–35.

Trenkle, J. B. "Ueber süddeutsche geistliche Schulkomödien," Freiburger Diöcesan-archiv II (1866) 131–76.

[Truinet, Charles Louis Etienne, and A. E. Roquet (Thoinan).] Les Origines de l'opéra français. Paris, Plon-Nourrit, 1886.

Tufts, George. "Ballad Opera : A List and Some Notes," MA IV (1912–13) 61–86.

Untersteiner, Alfredo. "Agostino Steffani," RMI XIV (1907) 509–34.

Ursprung, Otto. "Ueber die Aufführung von Monteverdis Combattimento und von Peris Euridice durch das musikwissenschaftliche Seminar der Universität München," ZfMw XVI (1934) 188–90.

Vallas, Léon. Un Siècle de musique et de théâtre à Lyon (1688–1789). Lyon, P. Masson, 1932.

Vogel, Emil. "Claudio Monteverdi : Leben, Werken im Lichte der zeitgenössischen Kritik," VfMw III (1887) 315–450.

—— "Marco da Gagliano," VfMw V (1889) 396–442, 509–68.

Wagner, Rudolf. "Beiträge zur Lebensgeschichte Johann Philipp Kriegers und seines Schülers Nikolaus Deinl," ZfMw VIII (1925–26) 146–60.

Wallaschek, Richard. Das K. k. Hofoperntheater. Vienna, Gesellschaft für vervielfältigende Kunst, 1909.

Waltershausen, Hermann Wolfgang Karl Sartorius, Freiherr (von). *Orpheus und Eurydike:* Eine operndramaturgische Studie. Munich, Drei Masken, 1923.

Ward, Charles. *"The Tempest:* A Restoration Opera," *ELH Journal of English Literary History* XIII, No. 2 (June, 1946) 119–30.

Weaver, Robert Lamar. Florentine Comic Operas of the Seventeenth Century. Ann Arbor, University Microfilms, 1958.

—— "Sixteenth-Century Instrumentation," MQ XLVII (1961) 363–78.

Weilen, Alexander von. Geschichte des Wiener Theaterwesens von den ältesten Zeiten bis zu den Anfängen der Hoftheater. Vienna, Gesellschaft für vervielfältigende Kunst, 1899.

——Zur Wiener Theatergeschichte: Die vom Jahre 1629 bis zum Jahre 1740 am Wiener Hofe zur Aufführung gelangten Werke theatralischen Charakters und Oratorien. Vienna, A. Hölder, 1901.
An important supplement to Köchel's *Kaiserliche Hofmusikkapelle;* see corrections in Nettl, "Exzerpte aus der Raudnitzer Textbüchersammlung," SzMw VII (1920) 143–44.

Wellesz, Egon. "Die Aussetzung des Basso Continuo in der italienischen Oper," in *International Musical Society, Fourth Congress Report* (London, Novello, 1912) 282–85.

—— Der Beginn des musikalischen Barock und die Anfänge der Oper in Wien. Vienna and Leipzig, Wiener literarische Anstalt, 1922.

—— "Cavalli und der Stil der venetianischen Oper von 1640–1660," SzMw I (1913).

—— "Einige handschriftliche Libretti aus der Frühzeit der Wiener Oper," ZfMw I (1918–19) 278–81.

—— "Die Opern und Oratorien in Wien von 1660–1708," SzMw VI (1919) 5–138.

—— "Zwei Studien zur Geschichte der Oper im 17. Jahrhundert," SIMG XV (1913) 124–54.

Werckmeister, Andreas. Der edlen Music-Kunst Würde, Gebrauch und Missbrauch. Frankfurt, Calvisius, 1691.

Werner, Arno. "Briefe von J. W. Franck, die Hamburger Oper betreffend," SIMG VII (1905–6) 125–28.

Werner, Theodor Wilhelm. "Agostino Steffanis Operntheater in Hannover," AfMf III (1938) 65–79.

Westrup, Jack Allan. "The Cadence in Baroque Recitative," in *Natalicia musicologica Knud Jeppesen* (Copenhagen, W. Hansen, 1962) 243–52.

—— "Monteverdi and the Orchestra," M&L XXI (1940) 230–45.

—— "Monteverdi's *Lamento d'Arianna,*" MR I (1940) 144–54.

—— "The Originality of Monteverde," PMA LX (1933–34) 1–25.

—— Purcell. London, J. M. Dent; New York, E. P. Dutton, [1937]. New York, Pellegrini & Cudahy, 1949.

—— "Two First Performances : Monteverdi's *Orfeo* and Mozart's *La Clemenza di Tito*," M&L XXXIX (1958) 327–35.

White, Eric Walter. The Rise of English Opera. London, John Lehmann, 1951.

Wiedemann, Carla. Leben und Wirken des Johann Philipp Förtsch, 1652–1732. Kassel & Basel, Bärenreiter, 1955.

Wiel, Taddeo. I codici musicali contariniani del secolo XVII nella R. Biblioteca di S. Marco in Venezia. Venice, F. Ongania, 1888.

—— "Francesco Cavalli," MA IV (1912–13) 1–19.

Wiley, W. L. The Early Public Theatre in France. Cambridge, Mass., Harvard University Press, 1960.

Winterfeld, Carl von. Johannes Gabrieli und sein Zeitalter. Berlin, Schlesinger, 1834. 3 vols.

Witeschnik, Alexander. Wiener Opernkunst : Von den Anfängen bis zu Karajan. Vienna, Buchgemeinschaft Donauland, [1961].

Wolff, Hellmuth Christian. Die Barockoper in Hamburg (1678–1738). Wolfenbüttel, Möseler, 1957. 2 vols.

—— Die venezianische Oper in der zweiten Hälfte des 17. Jahrhunderts. Berlin, Elsner, 1937.

Worsthorne, Simon Towneley. "Some Early Venetian Opera Productions," M&L XXX (1949) 146–51.

—— Venetian Opera in the Seventeenth Century. Oxford, Clarendon Press, 1954.

—— "Venetian Theatres : 1637–1700," M&L XXIX (1948) 263–75.

Wotquenne, Alfred. Etude bibliographique sur le compositeur napolitain Luigi Rossi. Brussels, Coosemans, 1909.

Zelle, Friedrich. Johann Philipp Förtsch. Berlin, R. Gaertner, 1893.

—— Johann Theile und Nikolaus Adam Strungk. Berlin, R. Gaertner, 1891.

—— Johann Wolfgang Franck. Berlin, R. Gaertner, 1889.

Zenger, Max. Geschichte der Münchner Oper. Munich, Verlag für praktische Kunstwissenschaft, Dr. F. X. Weizinger & Co., 1923.

Zucker, Paul. Die Theaterdekoration des Barok. Berlin, R. Kaemmerer, 1925.

IV

EIGHTEENTH CENTURY

Abert, Anna Amalie. Christoph Willibald Gluck. Munich, Bong, [1960].

—— "Der Geschmackswandel auf der Opernbühne, am Alkestis-Stoff dargestellt," Mf VI (1953) 214–35.

Abert, Hermann. "Die dramatische Musik," in *Herzog Karl Eugen von Württemberg und seine Zeit* I (Esslingen a. N., 1907) 555–611.

—— "Glucks Alkestis im Stuttgarter Landestheater," ZfMw VI (1923–24) 353–61.

Abert, Hermann. "Gluck und unsere Zeit," *Die Musik* XIII (1913–14) Qt. 4, 3–9.

—— "Händel als Dramatiker," in *Haendelfestspiele (Göttingen, 1922)*. Göttingen, Turm-Verlag, 1922.

—— "Herzog Karl von Württemberg und die Musik," in *Süddeutsche Monatshefte* V (1908) Band 1, 548–54.

—— "Johann Christian Bach's italienische Opern und ihr Einfluss auf Mozart," ZfMw I (1918–19) 313–28.

—— "Mozart and Gluck." M&L X (1929) 256–65.

—— Niccolo Jommelli als Opernkomponist, mit einer Biographie. Halle an der Saale, M. Niemeyer, 1908.

—— W. A. Mozart. Neubearb. und erweiterte Ausg. von Otto Jahns *Mozart*, hrsg. von Anna Amalie Abert. Leipzig, B&H, 1956. 7th ed. 2 vols.

—— "Zur Geschichte der Oper in Württemberg," in *III. Kongress der Internationalen Musikgesellschaft . . . Bericht* (Vienna, Artaria; Leipzig, B&H, 1909) 186–93.

Abraham, Gerald. "The Operas," in *The Mozart Companion,* ed. H. C. Robbins Landon and Donald Mitchell (London, Rockliff; New York, Oxford University Press, [1956]) 283–323.

Abraham, Gerald, ed. Handel : A Symposium. London, New York, Toronto, Oxford University Press, 1954.

Achenwall, Max. Studien über die komische Oper in Frankreich im 18. Jahrhundert und ihre Beziehungen zu Molière. Eilenburg, Offenhauer, 1912.

Adimari, Lodovico. "Satira quarta : Contro alcuni vizi delle donne, e particolamente contro le cantatrice," in *Satire del marchese Lodovico Adimari* (London, Si vende in Livorno presso T. Masi e comp., 1788) 183–253.

Ahnell, Emil Gustave. The Concept of Tonality in the Operas of Jean-Philippe Rameau. Ann Arbor, University Microfilms, 1957.

Albert, Maurice. Les Théâtres de la foire (1660–1789). Paris, Hachette, 1900.

—— Les Théâtres des boulevards (1789–1848). [Paris?], Lecène et Oudin, 1902.

Alfieri, Pietro. Notizie biografiche di Niccolò Jommelli di Aversa. Rome, Tip. delle belle arte, 1845.

Algarotti, Francesco, conte. Saggio sopra l'opera in musica. Leghorn, Coltellini, 1763.

Allorto, Riccardo. "Stefano Arteaga e *Le rivoluzioni del teatro musicale italiano*," RMI LII (1950) 124–47.

Altmann, Charlotte. Der französische Einfluss auf die Textbücher der klassischen Wiener Operette. Vienna Dissertation, 1935.

Anderson, Emily, ed. The Letters of Mozart and His Family Chronologically Arranged, Translated and Edited with an Introduction, Notes and Indices . . . with Extracts from the Letters of Constanze Mozart to

Johann Anton André Translated and Edited by C. B. Oldman. London, Macmillan, 1938. 3 vols., paged continuously.

Anecdotes dramatiques : Contenant toutes les pièces de théâtre . . . joués à Paris . . . jusqu'à l'année 1775. Paris, Duchesne, 1775. 3 vols.

Anheisser, Siegfried. Für den deutschen Mozart. Emsdetten i. Westf., H. & J. Lechte, 1938.

—— "Die unbekannte Urfassung von Mozarts Figaro," ZfMw XV (1932–33) 301–17.

Arend, Max. "Gluck, der Reformator des Tanzes," Die Musik XIII (1913–14) Qt. 4, 16–22.

—— Gluck, eine Biographie. Berlin, Schuster & Loeffler, 1921.

—— "Die Ouvertüren zu Glucks Cythère assiégée," ZfMw IV (1921–22) 94–95.

—— "Die unter Gluck's Mitwirkung, verschollene älteste deutsche Übersetzung der Iphigenia auf Tauris," ZIMG VII (1905–6) 261–67.

Armitage-Smith, J. N. A. "The Plot of The Magic Flute," M&L XXXV (1954) 36–39.

Arnaldi, Enea, conte. Idea di un teatro nelle principali sue parte simile a' teatri antichi. Vicenza, A. Veronese, 1762.

Arnheim, Amalie. "Le Devin du village von Jean-Jacques Rousseau und die Parodie Les Amours de Bastien et Bastienne," SIMG IV (1902–3) 686–727.

Arnoldson, Mrs. Louise Parkinson. Sedaine et les musiciens de son temps. Paris, l'Entente linotypiste, 1934.

Arteaga, Stefano. Le rivoluzioni del teatro musicale italiano, dalla sua origine fino al presente. Venice, C. Palese, 1785. 2d ed. 3 vols.

Asenjo y Barbieri, Francisco. Cancionero musical de los siglos XV y XVI. Madrid, Tip. de los huérfanos, [1890].

Aubignac, François Hédelin, abbé d'. La Pratique du théâtre. Amsterdam, J. F. Bernard, 1715. New ed. Alger, J. Carbonel, 1927.

Auriac, Eugène d'. Théâtre de la foire : Recueil de pièces représentées aux foires St.-Germain et St.-Laurent, précédé d'une essai historique sur les spectacles forains. Paris, Garnier frères, 1878.

Babbitt, Irving. Rousseau and Romanticism. Boston and New York, Houghton Mifflin, 1919.

Babcock, Robert W. "Francis Coleman's 'Register of Operas,' 1712–1734," M&L XXIV (1943) 155–58. Supplemented and corrected in a letter by O. E. Deutsch, ibid. XXV (1944) 126.

Bacher, Otto. "Die deutschen Erstaufführungen von Mozarts Don Giovanni," Jahrbuch des Freien deutschen Hochstifts Frankfurt a. M. (1926) 338–79. Also separately reprinted.

—— "Ein Frankfurter Szene zu Glucks Don Juan," ZfMw VII (1924–25) 570–74.

—— "Frankfurts musikalische Bühnengeschichte im 18. Jahrhundert.

Theil I. Die Zeit der Wandertruppen (1700–1786)," *Archiv für Frankfurts Geschichte und Kunst* (1925) 133–206.

Bacher, Otto. Die Geschichte der Frankfurter Oper im 18. Jahrhundert. Frankfurt/M., Englert und Schlosser, 1926.

—— "Ein Mozartfund," ZfMw VIII (1925–26) 226–30.

—— "Zur Geschichte der Oper auf Frankfurter Boden im 18. Jahrhundert," ZfMw VIII (1925–26) 93–102.

Barberet, Vincent. Lesage et le théâtre de la foire. Nancy, 1887.

Barberio, Francesco. "Disavventure di Paisiello," RMI XXIII (1916) 534–58.

—— "Giovanni Paisiello tra le ire di un copista e di un innovatore," RMI XXII (1915) 301–18.

—— "Lettere inedite di Paisiello [1792–1812]," RMI XXIV (1917) 173–88.

—— "I primi dieci anni di vita artistica di Paisiello," RMI XXIX (1922) 264–76.

Barbieri, Francisco. *See* Asenjo y Barbieri.

Barclay Squire. *See* Squire, William Barclay.

Bardi-Poswiansky, Benno. Der tolle Kapellmeister : Heitere Oper in 3 Akten mit Benutzung Reinhard Keiserscher Melodien. Textbuch. Berlin, Revo-Verlag, [1929].

Baroni, Jole Maria. "La lirica musicale di Pietro Metastasio," RMI XII (1905) 383–406.

Bartha, Dénes, and László Somfai. Haydn als Opernkapellmeister : Die Haydn-Dokumente der Esterházy-Opernsammlung. Mainz, Schott's Söhne, 1960.

Bateson, F. W. English Comic Drama, 1700–1750. Oxford, Clarendon Press, 1929.

Bauer, Anton. Das Theater in der Josefstadt zu Wien. Vienna and Munich, Manutiuspresse, 1957.

Beau, A. Eduard. "Die Musik im Werk des Gil Vicente," *Volkstum und Kultur der Romanen* IX (1936) 177–201.

Beaulieu, Henri. Les Théâtres du boulevard de Crime . . . de Nicolet à Déjazet (1752–1862). Paris, H. Daragon, 1905.

Beaumarchais, Pierre Augustin, Caron de. Théâtre : Lettres relatives à son théâtre. Texte établi et annoté par Maurice Allem et Paul-Courant. [Paris, Librairie Gallimard, 1957.]

Beck, Paul. "Oberschwäbische Volkstheater im 18. Jahrhundert," *Alemannia* XX (1892) 73–97.

Beer, Otto Fritz. Mozart und das Wiener Singspiel. Vienna Dissertation, 1932.

Behrend, William. "Weyse und Kuhlau : Studie zur Geschichte der dänischen Musik," *Die Musik* III, No. 22 (1904) 272–86.

Bekker, Paul. "Glucks *Alkeste* auf der Bühne," ZfMw I (1918–19) 193–96.

Bellaigue, Camille. "Les Epoques de la musique : L'opéra-comique," *Revue des deux mondes* (1905) No. 5, 177–210.

—— "Les Epoques de la musique : L'opéra mélodique—Mozart," *Revue des deux mondes* (1901) No. 6, 885–907.

—— "Les Epoques de la musique : L'opéra récitatif," *Revue des deux mondes* (1900) No. 6, 608–38.

Belluci la Salandra, Mario. Opere teatrali serie e buffe di Nicolò Piccinni. Rome, Edizioni Psalterium, 1935. For corrections, etc., see *Note d'archivio* XIII (1936) 55–58.

—— Saggio cronologico delle opere teatrali di Gaetano Latilla. Bari, 1935. Separate from "*Japigia,*" *Rivista di arch., storica e arte.*

—— Triade musicale bitontina: . . . Logroscino, Traetta, Planelli. Bitonto, A. Amendolagene, 1935.

[Benjamin, Lewis Saul.] Life and Letters of John Gay . . . by Lewis Melville [pseud.]. London, D. O'Connor, 1921.

Benn, Frederick Christopher. Mozart on the Stage. London, Ernest Benn Ltd., 1946.

Bérard, Jean Antoine. L'Art du chant. Paris, Dessait & Saillant, 1755.

Berger, Arthur V. "*The Beggar's Opera,* the Burlesque, and Italian Opera," M&L XVII (1936) 93–105.

Berthier, Paul. Réflexions sur l'art et la vie de Jean-Philippe Rameau, 1683–1764. Paris, Picard et Cie., 1957.

Beyle, Henri. Vies de Haydn, de Mozart et de Métastase. Paris, H. Champion, 1914. Text established and annotated by Daniel Muller, preface by Romain Rolland.

Bitter, Christof. Wandlungen in den Inszenierungsformen des *Don Giovanni* von 1787 bis 1928 : Zur Problematik des musikalischen Theaters in Deutschland. Regensburg, G. Bosse, 1961.

Bitter, Karl Hermann. Mozart's *Don Juan* und Gluck's *Iphigenia in Tauris:* Ein Versuch neuer Uebersetzungen. Berlin, F. Schneider, 1866.

Blom, Eric. "The Problem of *Don Giovanni,*" M&L XIII (1932) 381–90.

Blondel, S. "Les Castrats," *La Chronique musicale* IX (1875) 241–50.

Boas, Hans. "Lorenzo da Ponte als Wiener Theaterdichter," SIMG XV (1913–14) 325–38.

[Bobillier, Marie.] "Grétry, sa vie et ses œuvres," in *Mémoires couronnés et autres mémoires publiés par l'Académie royale . . . de Belgique,* Tome XXXVI, 1884.

Bötcher, Elmar. Goethes Singspiele *Erwin und Elmire* und *Claudine von Villa Bella* und die "opera buffa." Marburg, Elwert, 1912.

Bollert, Werner. Die Buffoopern Baldassare Galuppis. Bottrop, Postberg, 1935.

—— "Giuseppe Petrosellini quale librettista di opere," RMI XLIII (1939) 531–38.

—— "Tre opere di Galuppi, Haydn e Paisiello sul' *Mondo della luna* di Goldoni," *Musica d'oggi* XXI (1939) 265–70.

Bolte, Johannes. Die Singspiele der englischen Komödianten und ihrer Nachfolger in Deutschland, Holland und Skandinavia. Hamburg and Leipzig, L. Voss, 1893.

Bonnet, George Edgar. Philidor et l'évolution de la musique française au XVIIIe siècle. Paris, Delagrave, 1921.

[Bonnet, Jacques.] Histoire de la musique, et de ses effets. Paris, J. Cochart, 1715.

Borcherdt, Hans Heinrich. "Geschichte der italienischen Oper in Breslau," Zeitschrift für die Geschichte Schlesiens XLIV (1910) 18 ff.

Borland, John E. "French Opera before 1750," PMA XXXIII (1907) 133–57.

Borrel, Eugène. "Notes sur l'orchestration de l'opéra Jephte de Montéclair (1733) et de la symphonie des Elémens de J. F. Rebel (1737)," RM No. sp. 226 (1955) 105–16.

—— "Un Paradoxe musical au XVIIIe siècle," in Mélanges de musicologie (Paris, Droz, 1933) 217–21.

Borren, Charles van den. Alessandro Scarlatti et l'esthétique de l'opéra napolitain. Paris, Editions de la Renaissance d'occident, 1921.

—— "Roma centro musicale del Settecento," RMI XXXI (1924) 69–71.

Bourdelot, Pierre. See Bonnet, Jacques.

Boyer, Noël. La Guerre des bouffons et la musique française (1752–1754) suivi de : Le Mal des chèvres. . . . Paris, Les Editions de la Nouvelle France, [1945].

Bragard, Roger. "Li Voyedje di Tchaufontaine," in Mélanges Ernest Closson (Brussels, Société Belge de Musicologie, 1948) 48–59.

Braun, Lisbeth. "Die Balletkomposition von Joseph Starzer," SzMw XIII (1926) 38–56.

Breitholtz, Lennart. Studier i operan Gustaf Wasa. Uppsala, Lundequistska Bokhandeln, [1954].

Brenet, Michel, pseud. See Bobillier, Marie.

Breydert, Frédéric M. Le Génie créateur de W. A. Mozart : Essai sur l'instauration musicale des personnages dans Les Noces de Figaro, Don Juan, La Flute enchantée. Paris, Editions Alsatia, 1956.

Briquet, Marie. "L'Alceste de E.-J. Floquet," Mélanges d'histoire et d'esthétique musicales offerts à Paul-Marie Masson II (Paris, 1955) 19–29.

Brosses, Charles de. Lettres familières sur l'Italie. Paris, Firmin-Didot, 1931.

Brown, John. Letters on the Italian Opera. London, T. Cadell, 1791. 2d ed.

Brück, Paul. "Glucks Orpheus und Euridike," AfMw VII (1925) 436–76.

Brückner, Fritz. Georg Benda und das deutsche Singspiel. Leipzig, B&H, 1904. Also SIMG V (1903–4) 571–621.

—— "Zum Thema 'Georg Benda und das Monodram,' " SIMG VI (1904–5) 496–500.

Brüggemann, Fritz. Bänkelgesang und Singspiel vor Goethe. Leipzig, Reclam, 1937.

Bruger, Hans. Glucks dramatische Instrumentationskunst und ihre geschichtlichen Grundlagen. Teil 1 : Glucks italienischen Werke (einschliesslich der Wiener Reformopern). Heidelberg Dissertation, 1922.

Brukner, Fr. Die Zauberflöte: Unbekannte Handschriften und seltene Drucke aus der Frühzeit Mozarts Oper. Vienna, Gilhofer & Rauschburg, 1934.

Bruyère, André. "Les Muses galantes," RM No. 218 (1952) 5–31.

Bruyr, José. Grétry. Paris, Rieder, [1931].

Burney, Charles. A General History of Music from the Earliest Ages to the Present Period. London, Printed for the Author, 1776. Also : 2d ed., with critical and historical notes by Frank Mercer. London, Foulis; New York, Harcourt, Brace, 1935.

—— Memoirs of the Life and Writings of the Abate Metastasio; in Which Are Incorporated Translations of His Principal Letters. London, G. G. and J. Robinson, 1796. 3 vols.

—— The Present State of Music in France and Italy. London, T. Becket, 1771.

—— The Present State of Music in Germany, the Netherlands, and United Provinces. London, T. Becket, 1773. 2 vols.

Burt, Nathaniel. "Opera in Arcadia," MQ XLI (1955) 145–70.

Burton, Humphrey. "Les Académies de musique en France au XVIIIe siècle," RdM XXXVII (1955) 122–47.

Busi, Leonida. Benedetto Marcello. Bologna, N. Zanichelli, 1884.

Bustico, Guido. "Gli spettacoli musicali al 'Teatro Novo' di Novara (1779–1873)," RMI XXV (1918) 84–103, 202–48; "Nuovo contributo," RMI XXVI (1919) 615–52.

—— Pier Alessandro Guglielmi, musicista. Massa, Medici, 1898.

Cahn-Speyer, Rudolf. Franz Seydelmann als dramatischer Komponist. Leipzig, B&H, 1909.

Callegari, Matelda. "Il melodramma e Pietro Metastasio," RMI XXVI (1919) 518–44; XXVII (1920) 31–59, 458–76.

Calmus, Georgy. "Die Beggar's Opera von Gay und Pepusch," SIMG VIII (1906–7) 286–335.

—— Die ersten deutschen Singspiele von Standfuss und Hiller. Leipzig, B&H, 1908.

—— Zwei Opernburlesken aus der Rokokozeit. Berlin, Liepmannssohn, 1912. Contents : Télémaque (Lesage), The Beggar's Opera (Gay and Pepusch).

Cametti, Alberto. "Critiche e satire teatrali romane del '700," RMI IX (1902) 1–35.

—— "Leonardo Vinci e i suoi drammi in musica al Teatro delle Dame 1724–30," Musica d'oggi VI (1924) 297–99.

Cametti, Alberto. "Saggio cronologico delle opere teatrali (1754–1794) di Nicolò Piccinni," RMI VIII (1901) 75–100.

Campardon, Emile. L'Académie royale de musique au XVIIIe siècle. Paris, Berger-Levrault, 1884. 2 vols.

—— Les Comédiens du roi de la troupe italienne. Paris, Berger-Levrault, 1880. 2 vols.

—— Les Spectacles des foires . . . depuis 1595 jusqu'à 1791. Paris, Berger-Levrault, 1877. 2 vols.

Cannon, Beekman C. Johann Mattheson, Spectator in Music. New Haven, Yale University Press, 1947.

Capri, Antonio. Il Settecento musicale in Europa. Milan, Hoepli, 1936.

Carey, Clive. "The Problem of Don Giovanni Again," M&L XIV (1933) 30–35.

Carlez, Jules. Un Opéra biblique au XVIIIe siècle. Caen, Le Blanc-Hardel, 1879.

Carmena y Millán, Luis. Crónica de la ópera italiana en Madrid desde el año 1738 hasta nuestros dias. Madrid, M. Minuesa de los Rios, 1878.

Carmody, Francis J. Le Repertoire de l'opéra-comique en vaudevilles de 1708 à 1764. Berkeley, California, University of California Press, 1933.

Carreras y Bulbena, José Rafael. Domenech Terradellas. Barcelona, F. X. Altés, 1908.

Carroll, Charles Michael. François-André Danican-Philidor : His Life and Dramatic Art. Ann Arbor, University Microfilms, 1960. 2 vols.

Casavola, Franco. Tommaso Traetta di Bitonto (1727–1779) : La vita e le opere. Bari, Società di Storia Patria per la Puglia, 1957.

Celani, Enrico. "Musica e musicisti in Roma (1750–1850)," RMI XVIII (1911) 1–63; XX (1913) 33–88.

Cesari, Gaetano, and others. Antonio Bartolomeo Bruni, musicista cuneese (1751–1821). Turin, S. Lattes, 1931.

Chailly, Luciano. Il matrimonio segreto, guida musicale. [Milan], Istituto d'Alta Cultura, [1949].

Chantavoine, Jean. Mozart dans Mozart. Paris, Desclée de Brouwer, [1948].

Chatfield-Taylor, H. C. Goldoni : A Biography. New York, Duffield, 1913.

Chrysander, Friedrich. "Adonis: Oper von Reinhard Keiser," AMZ XIII (1878) 65–70, 81–87, 97–101.

—— "Der erste Entwurf der Bassarie 'Nasce al bosco' in Händel's Oper Ezio (1732)," AMZ XIV (1879) 641–46.

—— G. F. Händel. Leipzig, B&H, 1858–67. 3 vols.

—— "Mattheson's Verzeichniss Hamburgischer Opern von 1678 bis 1728, gedruckt im Musikalischen Patrioten, mit seinen handschriftlichen Fortsetzungen bis 1751, nebst Zusätzen und Berichtigungen," AMZ XII (1877) 198–282, passim.

—— "Musik und Theater in Mecklenburg," Archiv für Landeskunde in *den Grossherzogthümern Mecklenburg* IV (1854) 105–25, 258–80, 346–79.

—— "Neue Beiträge zur mecklenburgischen Musikgeschichte," *Archiv für Landeskunde in den Grossherzogthümern Mecklenburg* VI (1856) 666–82.

—— "Die Oper *Don Giovanni* von Gazzaniga und von Mozart," VfMw IV (1888) 351–435.

—— "Reinhard Keiser," in *Allgemeine deutsche Biographie* XV (1882) 540–51.

[Cimarosa, Domenico.] Per il bicentenario della nascità di Domenico Cimarosa. Aversa, A cura del Comitato per le Celebrazioni, 1949. Contains "Annali delle opere," pp. 73–148 by F. Schlitzer and other essays.

Clercx, Suzanne. Grétry, 1741–1813. Brussels, Editions La Renaissance du Livre, [1944].

Clive, Geoffrey. "The Demonic in Mozart," M&L XXXVII (1956) 1–13.

Cohen, Hermann. Die dramatische Idee in Mozarts Operntexten. Berlin, Cassirer, 1916.

Combarieu, Jules. "J.-J. Rousseau et le mélodrame," RHCM I (1901) 273–77.

—— "L'Opéra-comique d'hier et d'aujourd'hui," (RHCM VII (1907) 549–63.

Confalonieri, Giulio. "Nota su *Varrone e Perrica* di Alessandro Scarlatti," *Accademia musicale chigiana* XIV (1957) 39–49.

Conrad, Leopold. Mozarts Dramaturgie der Oper. Würzburg, Triltsch, 1943.

[Contant d'Orville, André Guillaume.] Histoire de l'opéra bouffon. Amsterdam and Paris, Grangé, 1768. 2 vols.

Cooper, Martin. Gluck. New York, Oxford University Press, 1935.

—— Opéra comique. New York, Chanticleer Press, [1949].

Coopersmith, J[acob] M[aurice]. [1.] An Investigation of Georg Friedrich Händel's Orchestral Style. [2.] A Thematic Index of the Printed Works of Händel. Harvard Dissertation, 1932. 12 vols.

—— "The Libretto of Handel's *Jupiter in Argos*," M&L XVII (1936) 289–96.

Corder, Frederick. "The Works of Sir Henry Bishop," MQ IV (1918) 78–97.

Cortese, Nino. "Un' autobiografia inedita di Giovanni Paisiello," RassM III (1930) 123–35. Following is Paisiello's autobiography.

Cotarelo y Mori, Emilio. Historia de la zarzuela o sea El drama lírico en España, desde su origen a fines del siglo XIX. Madrid, Tipografía de Archivos, 1934.

—— Orígenes y establecimento de la ópera en España hasta 1800. Madrid, Tip. de la "Revista de arch.," [etc.], 1917.

Cotarelo y Mori, Emilio, ed. Colección de entremeses, loas, bailes, jácaras y mojingangas desde fines del siglo XVI á medíados del XVII. Madrid, Bailly-Baillière, 1911.

Croce, Benedetto. I teatri di Napoli, secolo XV–XVIII. Naples, L. Pierro, 1891. New ed., 1916.

Crowder, C. Fairfax. "Neglected Treasures in Handel's Operas," M&L II (1921) 135–48.

Cucuel, Georges. Les Créateurs de l'opéra-comique français. Paris, F. Alcan, 1914.

—— "La Critique musicale dans les 'revues' du XVIIIe siècle," L'Année musicale II (1912) 127–203.

—— "Giacomo Casanova e la musica," RMI XXXVI (1929) 446–65.

—— "Notes sur la comédie italienne de 1717 à 1789," SIMG XV (1913–14) 154–66.

—— "Les Opéras de Gluck dans les parodies du XVIIIe siècle," RM III (1922) No. 5, 201–21; No. 6, 51–68.

—— "Sources et documents pour servir à l'histoire de l'opéra-comique en France," L'Année musicale III (1913) 247–82.

Cummings, William H. "The Lord Chamberlain and Opera in London, 1700 to 1741," PMA XL (1914) 37–72.

Curiel, Carlo Leone. Il teatro S. Pietro di Trieste, 1690–1801. [Milan], Archetipographia di Milano, 1937.

Curzon, Henri de. Grétry. Paris, Laurens, [1907].

Dacier, Emile. "Les Caractères de la danse: Histoire d'un divertissement pendant la première moitié du XVIIIe siècle," RHCM V (1905) 324–35, 365–67.

—— "Une Danseuse française à Londres au début du XVIIIe siècle," MM III (1907) 437–63, 746–65.

—— "L'Opéra au XVIIIe siècle : Les premières représentations du Dardanus de Rameau," RHCM III (1903) 163–73.

Dahms, Walter. "The 'Gallant' Style of Music," MQ XI (1925) 356–72.

Dahnk-Baroffio, Emilie. "Nicola Hayms Anteil an Händels Rodelinde-Libretto," Mf VII (1954) 295–300.

Dallapiccola, Luigi. "Notes on the Statue Scene in Don Giovanni," Music Survey III (1950) 89–97.

Damerini, Adelmo. "Un precursore italiano di Gluck : Tommaso Traetta," Il pianoforte (July, 1927).

—— "Tommaso Traetta : Cenni biografici," Bollettino bibliografico musicale II (July, 1927) 1–13.

D'Angeli, Andrea. Benedetto Marcello, vita e opere. Milan, Fratelli Bocca, 1940.

—— Commemorazione di Gio. Batta. Pergolesi. Padua, L. Penada, 1936.

Da Ponte, Lorenzo. Memorie. New York, Lorenzo e Carlo Da Ponte, 1823. 2 vols. Translated, with introduction and notes, by L. A. Sheppard, Boston, Houghton Mifflin, 1929. Translated by Elisabeth Abbott, edited and annotated by Arthur Livingston, Philadelphia, J. B. Lippincott, 1929. Other editions : Bari, G. Laterza, 1918 (Italian); Paris, Henri Jonquières, 1931 (French; includes previously unpublished letters to Casanova; preface and notes by Raoul Vèze).

—— Storia compendiosa della vita di Lorenzo Da Ponte scritta di lui medesimo. New York, Riley, 1807.

D'Arienzo, Nicola. "Le origini dell' opera comica," RMI II (1895) 597–628; IV (1897) 421–59; VI (1899) 473–95; VII (1900) 1–33.

Dean, Winton. Handel's Dramatic Oratorios and Masques. London, New York, Oxford University Press, 1959.

—— "The Libretto of The Secret Marriage," Music Survey III (1950) 33–38.

De Angelis, Alberto. Il teatro Alibert o delle Dame nella Roma papale. Tivoli, A. Chicca, [1951].

De' Calsabigi, Ranieri. "Dissertazione . . . su le poesie drammatiche del Sig. Abate Pietro Metastasio," in Poesie del Signor Abate Pietro Metastasio (Paris, Vedova Quillan, 1755–69) I, xix–cciv.

—— Risposta . . . alla critica ragionatissima delle poesie drammatiche del C. de' Calsabigi, fatta del baccelliere D. Stefan Arteaga. Venice, Curti, 1790.

Decker, Herbert. Dramaturgie und Szene der Zauberflöte. Regensburg, G. Bosse, [1950].

De Dominicis, Giulia. "Roma centro musicale nel Settecento," RMI XXX (1923) 511–28.

Degey, Maurice. Les Echos imprévus de la mort de Grétry. Liége, Editions de la Vie wallonne, 1938.

Della Corte, Andrea. "Appunti sull' estetica musicale di Pietro Metastasio," RMI XXVIII (1921) 94–119.

—— Baldassare Galuppi : Profilo critico. Siena, 1948.

—— "Cimarosa nel '99 e nella fortuna postuma," RassM IX (1936) 280–83.

—— Figuras y motivas de lo opera bufa italiano. Buenos Aires, La revista de musica, 1928.

—— Gluck e i suoi tempi. Florence, G. C. Sansoni, 1948.

—— "Nel II centenario della morte di Pergolesi : Il geloso schernito e Il maestro di musica," RassM IX (1936) 202–8.

—— "Notizie di Gaetano Pugnani musicista torinese (1731–1798)," Rassegna mensile municipale "Torino" (1931) 26–39.

—— L'opera comica italiana nel 1700. Bari, G. Laterza, 1923. 2 vols.

—— Paisiello : Con una tavola tematica. L'estetica musicale di P. Metastasio. Turin, Fratelli Bocca, 1922.

—— Piccinni (Settecento italiano) : Con frammenti musicali inediti e due ritratti. Bari, G. Laterza, 1928.

—— "Tetide in Sciro, l'opera di Domenico Scarlatti ritrovata," RassM XXVII (1957) 281–89.

—— Tutto il teatro di Mozart. [Turin], Edizioni Radio Italiana, [1957].

Della Corte, Andrea, ed. Canto e bel canto (Tosi e Mancini). Turin, G. B. Paravia, [1933].

Della Torre, Arnaldo. Saggio di una bibliografia delle opere intorno a Carlo Goldoni (1793–1907). Florence, Alfani e Venturi, 1908.

Demarquez, Suzanne. "Un Voyageur français et la musique italienne au XVIIIe siècle," RM, numéro spécial, "La Musique dans les pays Latins" (February–March, 1940) 125–33.

De Napoli, Giuseppe. "Niccolò Piccinni nel secondo centenario della nascita," RMI XXXV (1928) 209–18.

Dennis, John. An Essay on the Opera's after the Italian Manner, Which Are About to Be Established on the English Stage : With Some Reflections on the Damage Which They May Bring to the Publick. . . . London, J. Nutt, 1706.

Dent, Edward J. Alessandro Scarlatti : His Life and Works. New Impression, with Preface and Additional Notes by Frank Walker. London, Edward Arnold, [1960]. First published 1905.

—— "Alessandro Scarlatti," PMA XXX (1904) 75–90.

—— "Emanuel Schikaneder," M&L XXXVII (1956) 14–21.

—— "Ensembles and Finales in 18th Century Italian Opera," SIMG XI (1909–10) 543–69; XII (1910–11) 112–38.

—— "Giuseppe Maria Buini," SIMG XIII (1911–12) 329–36.

—— Handel. London, Duckworth, [1934].

—— "Handel on the Stage," M&L XVI (1935) 174–87.

—— "Italian Opera in the Eighteenth Century, and Its Influence on the Music of the Classical Period," SIMG XIV (1912–13) 500–509.

—— "Leonardo Leo," SIMG VIII (1906–7) 550–66.

—— Mozart's Operas : A Critical Study. London, Chatto & Windus; New York, McBride, Nast, 1913. 2d ed., New York, Oxford University Press, 1947.

—— Mozart's Opera The Magic Flute: Its History and Interpretation. Cambridge, W. Heffer, 1911.

—— "Notes on Leonardo Vinci," MA IV (1912–13) 193–201.

—— "The Operas of Alessandro Scarlatti," SIMG IV (1902–3) 143–56.

—— "A Pastoral Opera [La fede riconosciuta, 1710] by Alessandro Scarlatti," MR XII (1951) 7–14.

De' Paoli, Domenico. "Diane ed Endimione di Alessandro Scarlatti," RassM XIII (1940) 139–46.

De Rensis, Raffaello. Musica italiana in Francia : La riforma intitolata a Gluck. Rome, Casa editrice "Musica," 1916.

Desastre, Jean. Carlo Broschi : Kuriose Abenteuer eines Sopranisten. Zurich, Bürdecke & Herwig, 1903.

[Desboulmiers, Jean Auguste Julien.] Histoire anecdotique et raisonée du théâtre italien, depuis son rétablissement en France jusqu'à l'année 1769. Paris, Lacombe, 1769. 7 vols.

—— Histoire du théâtre de l'opéra-comique. Paris, Lacombe, 1769. 2 vols.

Desessarts, Nicolas Toussaint Lemoyne. Les Trois Théâtres de Paris, ou abrégé historique de l'établissement de la Comédie Françoise, de la Comédie Italienne & de l'Opéra. Paris, Lacombe, 1777.

Desnoiresterres, Gustave. Gluck et Piccinni, 1774–1800. Paris, Didier, 1875. 2d ed.

Deutsch, Otto Erich. Das Freihaustheater auf der Wieden, 1787–1801. Vienna-Leipzig, Deutsche Verlag für Jugend und Volk Gesellschaft, [1937].

—— Handel : A Documentary Biography. London, A. & C. Black; New York, W. W. Norton, 1955.

—— Mozart und die Wiener Logen : Zur Geschichte seiner Freimaurer-Kompositionen. Vienna, Wiener Freimaurer-Zeitung, 1932.

Diderot, Denis. Le Neveu de Rameau : Satyre publiée pour la première fois sur le manuscrit original autographe. Paris, Plon, Nourrit, 1891.

Dietz, Max. Geschichte des musikalischen Dramas in Frankreich während der Revolution bis zum Directorium (1787 bis 1795). Vienna, Groscher & Blaha, 1885. 2d ed., Leipzig, B&H, 1893.

Di Giacomo, Salvatore. Il conservatorio dei poveri di Gesu Cristo e quello di S. M. di Loreto. Palermo, Sandron, 1928.

—— Il conservatorio di Sant' Onofrio a Capuana e quello di S. M. della Pietà dei Turchini. Naples, Sandron, 1924.

[Ditters] von Dittersdorf, Karl. Karl von Dittersdorfs Lebensbeschreibung: Seinem Sohne in die Feder diktiert. Leipzig, B&H, 1801. Translated as: The Autobiography of Karl von Dittersdorf. London, R. Bentley, 1896. Modern German editions : Leipzig, Reclam, 1909 (Istel); Regensburg, G. Bosse, [ca. 1940] (E. Schmitz); Leipzig, Staackmann, 1940 (Loets).

Donath, Gustav. "Florian Gassmann als Opernkomponist," SzMw II (1914) 34–211.

Doran, John. "Mann" and Manners at the Court of Florence, 1740–1786: Founded on the Letters of Horace Mann to Horace Walpole. London, R. Bentley, 1876. 2 vols.

Downes, Edward O. D. "The Neapolitan Tradition in Opera," in International Musicological Society, Report of the Eighth Congress, New York 1961 (Kassel, [etc.], Bärenreiter, 1961) I, 277–84.

—— The Operas of Johann Christian Bach as a Reflection of the Dominant Trends in Opera Seria 1750–1780. Harvard Dissertation, 1958.

—— "Secco Recitative in Early Classical Opera Seria (1720–80)," JAMS XIV (1961) 50–69.

Draper, John W. Eighteenth Century English Aesthetics : A Bibliography. Heidelberg, C. Winter, 1931.

Druilhe, Paule. Monsigny. Paris, La Colombe, [1955].

DuBos, Jean Baptiste. Critical Reflections on Poetry, Painting and Music. London, J. Nourse, 1748. 3 vols. Translated from the French 5th ed. Originally published anonymously, Paris, 1719.

Ducannès-Duval, G. "L'Opéra à Bordeaux en 1784," RdM XXI (1937) 82–83.

Dumesnil, René. Le *Don Juan* de Mozart. Paris, Editions musicales de la librairie de France, 1927; Paris, Editions d'histoire et d'art, Plon, [1955].

—— "Le Livret et les personnages de *Don Giovanni*," RM No. 4 (February, 1927) 118–28.

Ebert, Alfred. Attilio Ariosti in Berlin (1697–1703). Leipzig, Giesecke & Devrient, 1905.

Eckermann, Johann Peter. Gespräche mit Goethe. Berlin, Bong, [1916]. 2 vols.

Edgar, Clifford B. "Mozart's Early Efforts in Opera," PMA XXXII (1906) 45–58.

—— "A Résumé of Mozart's Early Operas," ZIMG VII (1905–6) 460–64.

Einstein, Alfred. "Concerning Some Recitatives in *Don Giovanni*," M&L XIX (1938) 417–25.

—— "Das erste Libretto des *Don Giovanni*," *Acta musicologica* IX (1937) 149–50.

—— "The First Performance of Mozart's *Entführung* in London," MR VII (1946) 154–60.

—— Gluck. London, Dent; New York, E. P. Dutton, [1936].

—— Gluck : Sein Leben, seine Werke. Zurich & Stuttgart, Pan-Verlag, [1954]. English translation : London, J. M. Dent & Son; New York, E. P. Dutton & Co., [1954].

—— "Mozart e Tarchi : Un episodio della storia delle *Nozze di Figaro*," RassM VIII (1935) 269–72.

—— "Mozart et l'opéra-bouffe à Salzburg," RdM XXI (1937) 1–4.

—— Mozart, His Character, His Work. New York and London, Oxford University Press, 1945.

—— "Ein Schüler Gluck's," *Acta musicologica* X (1938) 48–50.

—— "Die Text-Vorlage zu Mozart's *Zaide*," *Acta musicologica* VIII (1936) 30–37.

—— "Eine unbekannte Arie der Marcelline," ZfMw XIII (1930–31) 200–205.

Eisenschmidt, Joachim. Die szenische Darstellung der Opern Georg Friedrich Händels auf der Londoner Bühne seiner Zeit. Wolfenbüttel and Berlin, Kallmeyer, 1940.

Eitner, Robert. "Benedetto Marcello," MfMg XXIII (1891) 187–94, 197–211.

—— "Die deutsche komische Oper," MfMg XXIV (1892) 37–92.

—— "Der Generalbass des 18. Jahrhunderts," MfMg XII (1880) 151–54.

Ellinger, Georg. "Händel's *Admet* und seine Quelle," VfMw I (1885) 201–24.

Engel, Carl. "A Note on Domenico Cimarosa's *Il matrimonio segreto*," MQ XXXIII (1947) 201–6.

Engel, Gustav. "Eine mathematisch-harmonische Analyse des *Don Giovanni* von Mozart," VfMw III (1887) 491–560.

Engel, Hans. "Die Finali der Mozartschen Opern," *Mozart-Jahrbuch 1954* (1955) 113–34.

—— "Richard Wagners Stellung zu Mozart," in *Festschrift Wilhelm Fischer* (Innsbruck, 1956) 39–48.

Engelke, Bernhard. "Aus den entscheidenden Entwicklungsjahren der Opéra-comique," in *Festschrift Arnold Schering* (Berlin, A. Glas, 1937) 51–60.

Engländer, Richard. "Domenico Fischietti als Buffokomponist in Dresden," ZfMw II (1919–20) 321–52, 399–442.

—— "Dresden und die deutsche Oper im letzten Drittel des 18. Jahrhunderts," ZfMw III (1920–21) 1–21.

—— "Das Ende der *opera seria* in Dresden : Naumanns *Clemenza di Tito* 1769," *Neues Archiv für Sächsische Geschichte und Altertumskunde* XXXIX (1918) 311–29.

—— "Glucks *Cinesi* und *Orfano della China*," *Gluck-Jahrbuch* I (1913) 54–81.

—— "Gluck und der Norden," *Acta musicologica* XXIV (1952) 62–83.

—— Johann Gottlieb Naumann als Opernkomponist. Leipzig, B&H, 1922.

—— Joseph Martin Kraus und die Gustavianische Oper. Uppsala, Almqvist & Wiksell; Leipzig, O. Harrassowitz, [1943].

—— "Die Opern Joseph Schusters," ZfMw X (1927–28) 257–91.

—— "The Sketches for *The Magic Flute* at Upsala," MQ XXVII (1941) 343–55.

—— "Zur Musikgeschichte Dresdens gegen 1800," ZfMw IV (1921–22) 199–241.

—— "Zur Psychologie des Gustavianischen Opernrepertoires," in *Natalicia musicologica Knud Jeppesen* (Copenhagen, W. Hansen, 1962) 267–82.

Epstein, Th. *Don Giovanni* von Mozart. Frankfurt/M., Offenbach/M., Andre, 1870.

Fabbri, Mario. Alessandro Scarlatti e il principe Ferdinando de' Medici. Florence, L. S. Olschki, 1961.

Färber, Sigfrid. Das Regensburger Fürstlich Thurn und Taxissche Hoftheater und seine Oper 1760–1786. [Regensburg], Pustet, 1936.

Fassini, Sesto. "Il melodramma italiano a Londra ai tempi del Rolli," RMI XIX (1912) 35–74, 575–636.

—— Il melodramma italiano a Londra nella prima metà del Settecento. Turin, Bocca, 1914.

Faustini-Fasini, Eugenio. "Gli astri maggiori del 'bel canto' Napoletano," *Note d'archivio* XII (1935) 297–316.

—— "Documenti paisielliani inediti," *Note d'archivio* XIII (1936) 105–27.

—— G. B. Pergolesi attraverso i suoi biografi e le sue opere. Milan, Ricordi, 1900.

Faustini-Fasini, Eugenio. "Leonardo Leo e la sua famiglia," *Note d'archivio* XIV (1937) 11–18.

—— Opere teatrali, oratori e cantate di Giovanni Paisiello (1764–1808): Saggio storico-cronologico. Bari, Laterza, 1940.

Favart, Charles Simon. Mémoires et correspondances littéraires, dramatiques et anecdotiques. Paris, L. Collin, 1808. 3 vols.

—— Théâtre. Paris, DuChesne, 1763–[77]. 10 vols.

Fedeli, Vito. "Dal *Cavaliere Ergasto* alla *Molinarella*," RMI XVIII (1911) 357–81.

—— "La *Molinarella* di Piccinni," SIMG XIII (1911–12) 302–21, 507.

—— "Un' opera sconosciuta di Pergolesi?" SIMG XII (1910–11) 139–50.

Fehr, Max. Apostolo Zeno, 1668–1750, und seine Reform des Operntextes. Zurich, A. Tschopp, 1912.

—— "Pergolesi und Zeno," SIMG XV (1913–14) 166–68.

—— "Zeno, Pergolesi und Jommelli," ZfMw I (1918–19) 281–87.

Fellerer, Karl Gustav. "Max von Droste-Hülshoff," AfMf II (1937) 160–72.

—— "Mozart und Händel," *Mozart-Jahrbuch 1953* (1954) 47–55.

Fellmann, Hans Georg. Die Böhmsche Theatergruppe und ihre Zeit. Leipzig, L. Voss, 1928.

Fellowes, E. H. "The Philidor Manuscripts," M&L XII (1931) 116–29.

Festschrift zur Händel-Ehrung der Deutschen Demokratischen Republik 1959. Leipzig, Deutsche Verlag für Musik, [1959].

Fischer, Georg. Musik in Hannover. Hanover, Hahn, 1903. 2d enlarged edition of his Opern und Concerte im Hoftheater zu Hannover bis 1866.

Fischer, Wilhelm. " 'Der, welcher wandelt diese Strasse voll beschwerden,' " *Mozart-Jahrbuch 1950* (1951) 41–48.

—— "Piccinni, Gluck und Mozart," *Mozart-Jahrbuch 1953* (1954) 9–14.

Fiske, Roger. "The Operas of Stephen Storace," PMA LXXXVI (1959–60) 29–44.

—— "A Score for *The Duenna*," M&L XLII (1961) 132–41.

Fitzlyon, April. The Libertine Librettist : A Biography of Mozart's Librettist Lorenzo da Ponte. London, J. Calder, [1955].

Flögel, Bruno. "Studien zur Arientechnik in den Opern Händels," *Händel-Jahrbuch* II (1929) 50–156.

Flood, W. H. Grattan. "The *Beggar's Opera* and Its Composers," M&L III (1922) 402–6.

Florimo, Francesco. La scuola musicale di Napoli e i suoi conservatori. Naples, V. Morano, 1880–82. 4 vols. 2d ed.

Flower, Newman. George Frideric Handel : His Personality and His Times. New and revised ed. London, Cassell, 1959.

Fondi, Enrico. La vita e l'opera letteraria del musicista Benedetto Marcello. Rome, W. Modes, 1909.

Font, Auguste. Favart, l'opéra-comique et la comédie-vaudeville aux XVIIe et XVIIIe siècles. Paris, Fischbacher, 1894.

Fontana, Francesco. "Vita di Benedetto Marcello," in *Estro poetico-armonico parafrasi sopra le primi venticinque salmi, poesia di Girolamo*

Asconio Giustiniani, musica di Benedetto Marcello (Venice, Sebastiano Valle, 1803), I, 1–48.

Franklin, Benjamin. "The Ephemera : An Emblem of Human Life," in *The Writings of Benjamin Franklin*, edited by Albert Henry Smith (New York, Macmillan, 1907) VII, 206–9.

Frati, Lodovico. "Antonio Bernacchi e la sua scuola di canto," RMI XXIX (1922) 443–91.

—— "Attilio Ottavio Ariosti," RMI XXXIII (1926) 551–57.

—— "Un impresario teatrale del Settecento e la sua biblioteca," RMI XVIII (1911) 64–84.

—— "Metastasio e Farinelli," RMI XX (1913) 1–30.

—— "Musicisti e cantanti bolognesi del Settecento," RMI XXI (1914) 189–202.

—— "Satire di musicisti," RMI XXII (1915) 560–66.

Freisauff, Rudolf von. Mozart's *Don Juan*, 1787–1887. Salzburg, H. Kerber, 1887.

Friedländer, Max. Das deutsche Lied im 18. Jahrhundert. Stuttgart and Berlin, Cotta, 1902. 3 parts in 2 vols.

Friedrich, Götz. Die humanistische Idee der *Zauberflöte* : Ein Beitrag zur Dramaturgie der Oper. Hrsg. vom Ministerium für Kultur, Hauptabteilung künstlerische Lehranstalten. Dresden, VEB Verlag der Kunst, 1954.

Fuchs, Albert. "Wieland et l'esthétique de l'opéra," *Revue de littérature comparée* X (1930) 608–33.

Fuchs, Marianne. Die Entwicklung des Finales in der italienischen Opera Buffa vor Mozart. Vienna Dissertation, 1932.

Fürstenau, Moritz. "Maria Antonia Walpurgis, Kurfürstin von Sachsen: Eine biografische Skizze," MfMg XI (1879) 167–81.

—— "Zur Don Juan-Literatur," MfMg II (1870) 41–47.

Fuller-Maitland, John Alexander. The Age of Bach and Handel. Oxford, Clarendon Press, 1902. 2d ed., London, Oxford University Press, 1931. (OHM, Vol. IV.)

Gagey, Edmond M. Ballad Opera. New York, Columbia University Press, 1937.

Gardien, Jacques. Jean-Philippe Rameau. Paris, La Colombe, 1949.

Gastoué, Amadée. "Gossec et Gluck à l'opéra de Paris : Le ballet final d'*Iphigénie en Tauride*," RDM XVI (1935) 87–99.

—— "Nicolò Piccinni et ses opéras à Paris," *Note d'archivio* XIII (1936) 52–54.

Gay, John. The Beggar's Opera. London, De la Mare Press, 1905.

Gaye, Phoebe Fenwick. John Gay : His Place in the 18th Century. London, Collins, 1938.

Geiringer, Karl. The Bach Family : Seven Generations of Creative Genius. New York, Oxford University Press, 1954.

—— Haydn : A Creative Life in Music. New York, W. W. Norton, 1946.

Geiringer, Karl. "Haydn as an Opera Composer," PMA LXVI (1939–40) 23–30.

—— Joseph Haydn : Der schöpferische Werdegang eines Meisters der Klassik. Mainz, B. Schott's Söhne, 1959.

Genest, Emile. L'Opéra-comique connu et inconnu. Paris, Fischbacher, 1925.

Gentili, Alberto. "La raccolta Mauro Foà nella Biblioteca Nazionale di Torino," RMI XXXIV (1927) 356–68.

Georges, Horst. Das Klangsymbol des Todes im dramatischen Werk Mozarts. Wolfenbüttel-Berlin, G. Kallmeyer, 1937.

—— "Mozart—oder : Die Zeitlosigkeit der Oper," *Hamburger Jahrbuch für Theater und Musik 1951*, 77–83.

Georgiades, Thrasybulos. "Aus der Musiksprache des Mozart-Theaters," *Mozart-Jahrbuch 1950* (1951) 76–98.

Gerber, Rudolf. Christoph Willibald Gluck. Potsdam, Athenaion, [1950].

—— Der Operntypus Johann Adolf Hasses und seine textlichen Grundlage. Leipzig, Kistner & Siegel, 1925.

Geulette, Thomas Simon. Notes et souvenirs sur le théâtre-italien au XVIIIe siècle. Paris, E. Praz, 1938.

Gherardi, Evaristo, compiler. Le Théâtre italien de Gherardi. Amsterdam, M. C. le Cene, 1721. 6 vols. 5th ed.

Giazotto, Remo. "Apostolo Zeno [,] Pietro Metastasio e la critica del Settecento," RMI XLVIII (1946) 324–60; XLIX (1947) 46–56; L (1948) 39–65, 248–58; LI (1949) 43–66, 130–61.

—— Poesia melodrammatica e pensiero critico nel Settecento. Milan, Fratelli Bocca, [1952].

Giraldi, Romolo. Giovanni Battista Pergolese. Rome, Laziale, 1936.

Girdlestone, Cuthbert. Jean-Philippe Rameau : His Life and Work. London, Cassel & Co., [1957].

Gluck, Christoph Willibald, Ritter von. Collected Correspondence and Papers. Edited by Hedwig and E. H. Mueller von Asow, translated by Stewart Thomson. London, Barrie and Rockliff, [1962].

—— "Correspondance inédite," MM X, No. 11 (1914) 1–16.

—— "Vier Gluck-Briefe," *Die Musik* XIII (1913–14) Qt. 4, 10–15.

Gluck-Jahrbuch. Jahrgang I–IV (1913, 1915, 1917, 1918). Leipzig, B&H. Ed. by H. Abert.

Gmeyner, Alice. Die Opern M. A. Caldaras. Vienna Dissertation, 1935.

Die Göttinger Händel-Festspiele (Festschrift). Göttingen, Göttinger Händelgesellschaft, 1953.

Goldoni, Carlo. Mémoires. Paris, Veuve Duchesne, 1787. 3 vols. Translated as : Memoirs of Goldoni. London, H. Colburn, 1814. 2 vols.

Goldschmidt, Hugo. "Das Cembalo im Orchester der italienischen Oper der zweiten Hälfte des 18. Jahrhunderts," in *Festschrift Liliencron* (Leipzig, B&H, 1910) 87–92.

—— Die Musikästhetik des 18. Jahrhunderts und ihre Beziehungen zu seinen Kunstschaffen. Zurich, Rascher, 1915. *See also* review by A. Schering, ZfMw I (1918–19) 298–308.

—— "Die Reform der italienischen Oper des 18. Jahrhunderts und ihre Beziehungen zur musikalischen Aesthetik," in *III. Kongress der Internationalen Musikgesellschaft . . . Bericht* (Vienna, Artaria; Leipzig, B&H, 1909) 196–207.

Gómez, Julio. "Don Blas de Laserna : Un capítolo de la historia del teatro lirico español," *Archivo y museo al ayuntamicuto de Madrid* (1925–26).

Gonzales Ruiz, Nicolas. La caramba (vida alegre y muerte ejemplar de una tonadillera del siglo XVIII). [Madrid, Ediciones Morata, 1944.]

Gottsched, Johann Christoph. Nöthiger Vorrath zur Geschichte der deutschen dramatischen Dichtkunst oder Verzeichniss aller deutschen Trauer- Lust- und Sing-Spiele, die im Druck erschienen von 1450 bis zur Hälfte des jetzigen Jahrhunderts. Leipzig, J. M. Teubner, 1757–65. 2 vols.

—— Versuch einer kritischen Dichtkunst vor die Deutschen. Leipzig, B. C. Breitkopf, 1730. 2d ed., 1737.

Goudar, Ange. Le Brigandage de la musique italienne. 1777.

[Goudar, Mme. Sara.] De Venise, remarques sur la musique & la danse. Venice, C. Palese, 1773.

Gounod, Charles François. Mozart's *Don Giovanni:* A Commentary. London, R. Cocks, 1895. Translated from the 3d French ed.

Grannis, Valleria Belt. Dramatic Parody in Eighteenth Century France. New York, Institute of French Studies, 1931.

Grasberger, Franz. "Zur Symbolik der *Zauberflöte,*" in *Bericht über den internationalen musikwissenschaftlichen Kongress Wien, Mozartjahr 1956* (Graz, Böhlaus, 1958) 249–52.

Grattan Flood. *See* Flood, William Henry Grattan.

Graves, Richard. "The Comic Operas of Stephen Storace," *The Musical Times* XCV (October, 1954).

—— "English Comic Opera : 1760–1800," MMR LXXXVII (1957) 208–15.

Greither, Aloys. Die sieben grossen Opern Mozarts : Versuche über das Verhältnis der Texte zur Musik. Heidelberg, Verlag Lambert Schneider, 1956.

Grétry, André Ernest Modeste. Mémoires, ou essais sur la musique. Paris, Imprimerie de la république, [1797]. 3 vols. First published 1789.

—— Oeuvres complètes : Réflexions d'un solitaire. Brussels-Paris, Von Oest, 1919–22. 4 vols.

Grimm, Friedrich Melchior, Freiherr von. Correspondance littéraire, philosophique et critique. Paris, Garnier, 1877–82. 16 vols. Contains "Lettre sur Omphale," XVI, 287–309.

—— Le Petit Prophète de Boemischbroda. Paris, 1753.

—— "Poëme lyrique," in *Encyclopédie ou Dictionnaire raisonné . .* (Neuchâtel, S. Faulche, 1765) XII, 822–36.

[Grosley, Pierre Jean.] New Observations on Italy and Its Inhabitants. London, L. Davis & C. Reymers, 1769. 2 vols.

Grout, Donald J. The Origins of the Opéra-comique. Harvard Dissertation, 1939.

Grüel, C. Aufschlüsse über die Bedeutung des angeblich Schikaneder'schen Textes zu Mozart's *Zauberflöte*. Magdeburg, Creutz, 1868.

Güttler, Hermann. Königsbergs Musikkultur im 18. Jahrhundert. Kassel, Bärenreiter, [1929].

Guiet, René. L'Evolution d'un genre : Le livret d'opéra en France de Gluck à la révolution (1774–1793). Northampton, Mass., Smith College, Dept. of Modern Languages, 1936.

Guingené, Pierre Louis. Notice sur la vie et les ouvrages de Nicolas Piccini. Paris, Panckoucke, [1801].

Haas, Robert M. Gluck und Durazzo im Burgtheater. Zurich, Amalthea, 1925.

—— "Josse de Villeneuves Brief über den Mechanismus der italienischen Oper von 1756," ZfMw VII (1924–25) 129–63.

—— "Die Musik in der Wiener deutscher Stegreifkomödie," SzMw XII (1925) 1–64.

—— "Teutsche Comedie Arien," ZfMw III (1920–21) 405–15.

—— "Die Wiener Ballet-Pantomime im 18. Jahrhundert und Glucks *Don Juan*," SzMw X (1923) 3–36.

—— "Der Wiener Bühnentanz von 1740 bis 1767," JMP XLIV (1937) 77–93.

——"Wiener deutsche Parodieopern um 1730," ZfMw VIII (1925–26) 201–25.

—— Die Wiener Oper. Vienna-Budapest, Eligius, 1926.

—— Wolfgang Amadeus Mozart. Potsdam, Akademische Verlagsgesellschaft Athenaion, 1950. 2d ed.

Haberl, Franz X. "Johann Mattheson : Biographische Skizze," *Caecilien Kalender* (1885) 53–60.

Haböck, Franz. Die Gesangskunst der Kastraten : Erster Notenbuch A. Die Kunst des Cavaliere Carlo Broschi Farinelli. B. Farinellis berühmte Arien. Vienna, Universal, [1923].

—— Die Kastraten und ihre Gesangskunst. Stuttgart, Deutsche Verlags-Anstalt, 1927.

Händel-Festspiele . . . 1922 : Veranstaltet vom Universitätsbund. Göttingen, W. H. Lange, 1922.

Händel-Jahrbuch. Leipzig, B&H, 1928–.

Hagen, Oskar. "Die Bearbeitung der Händelschen *Rodelinde* und ihre Uraufführung am 26. Juni 1920 in Göttingen," ZfMw II (1919–20) 725–32.

Halle. Stadtarchiv. Georg Friedrich Händel, Abstammung und Jugendwelt. Halle, Gebauer-Schwetschke, 1935.

Hamilton, Mrs. Mary (Neal). Music in Eighteenth Century Spain. Urbana, The University of Illinois, 1937.

Harich, J. "Das Repertoire des Opernkapellmeisters Joseph Haydn in Esterháza (1780–1790)," The Haydn Yearbook I (1962) 9–110.

Hastings, Margaret. "Gluck's Alceste," M&L XXXVI (1955) 41–54.

Hauger, George. "William Shield," M&L XXXI (1950) 337–42.

Hawkins, John. A General History of the Science and Practice of Music. London, T. Payne, 1776. 5 vols.

Hédouin, Pierre. Richard Coeur-de-Lion de Grétry. Boulogne, Birlé-Morel, 1842.

Heger, Theodore E. The Function and Type of Music in the English Dramatic Theater of the Early 18th Century. Michigan A.M. Dissertation, 1939.

Heinichen, Johann David. Der General-Bass in der Composition. Dresden, bey dem Autor, 1728. A revised ed. of his Neu erfundene und gründliche Anweisung (Hamburg, B. Schiller, 1711).

Heinse, Wilhelm. Hildegard von Hohenthal. Berlin, Vossischen Buchhandlung, 1795–96. 3 vols.

Helfert, W. "Zur Geschichte des Wiener Singspiels," ZfMw V (1922–23) 194–209.

Henderson, William James. "A Note on Floridity," MQ II (1916) 339–48.

Heriot, Angus. The Castrati in Opera. London, Secker & Warburg, 1956.

Heulhard, Arthur. La Foire Saint-Laurent : Son histoire et ses spectacles. Paris, A. Lemerre, 1878.

—— Jean Monnet. Paris, A. Lemerre, 1884.

Heuss, Alfred. "Carl Heinrich Graun's Montezuma," ZIMG VI (1904–5) 71–75.

—— "Das dämonische Element in Mozarts Werken," ZIMG VII (1906) 175–86.

—— "Gluck als Musikdramatiker," ZIMG XV (1913–14) 274–91.

—— "Graun's Montezuma und seine Herausgabe durch Albert Mayer-Reinach," MfMg XXXVII (1905) 67–71.

—— "Mozarts Idomeneo als Quelle für Don Giovanni and Die Zauberflöte," ZfMw XIII (1930–31) 177–99.

—— "Zu Umlauf's Singspiel : Die Bergknappen," ZIMG XIII (1911–12) 164–71.

Hiller, Johann Adam. Johann Adam Hiller. Leipzig. C. F. W. Siegel, [1915].

Hiltebrandt, Philipp. Preussen und die römische Kurie. Berlin, Bath, 1910. Vol. I : Die vorfriderizianische Zeit (1625–1740).

Hinrichsen, Max, ed. Ninth Music Book, Containing John Gay and the Ballad Opera [The Beggar's Opera] by Geoffrey Handley-Taylor and Frank Granville Barker. . . . London & New York, Hinrichsen Edition, [1957].

Hirsch, R. Mozart's *Schauspieldirektor:* Musikalische Reminiscenzen. Leipzig, Matthis, 1859.

Hirschberg, Eugen. Die Enzyklopädisten und die französische Oper im 18. Jahrhundert. Leipzig, B&H, 1903. *See also* review by A. Heuss, ZIMG V (1903–4) 280–87.

Hirschfeld, Robert. "Mozart's *Zaide* in der Wiener Hofoper," ZIMG IV (1902–3) 66–71.

Hirzel, Bruno. "Operatic Italy in 1770—by an Eyewitness," MTNA V (1910) 219–31.

Hitzig, Wilhelm. Georg Friedrich Händel, 1685–1759 : Sein Leben in Bildern. Leipzig, Bibliographisches Institut, [1935].

Hocquard, Jean Victor. "III. Le Pensée dramatique de Mozart," in *La Pensée de Mozart* (Paris, Editions du Seuil, [1958]) 341–566.

Hodermann, Richard. Georg Benda. Coburg, H. Wechsung, 1895.

—— Geschichte des Gothaischen Hoftheaters 1725–1779. Hamburg, L. Voss, 1894.

Höffding, Harold. Jean Jacques Rousseau and His Philosophy. New Haven, Yale University Press; London, Oxford University Press, 1930. Translated from the 2d Danish ed.

Högg, Margarete. Die Gesangskunst der Faustina Hasse und das Sängerinnenwesen ihrer Zeit in Deutschland. Königsbrück i. Sa., Pabst, 1931.

Hoffman, Ernst Theodor Amadeus. "Don Giovanni : A Marvelous Adventure Which Befell a Traveling Enthusiast." Translated by Abram Loft. MQ XXXI (1945) 504–16.

Hoffmann von Fallersleben, August Heinrich. Unsere volkstümlichen Lieder. Leipzig, W. Engelmann, 1900. 4th ed.

Holl, Karl. Carl Ditters von Dittersdorfs Opern für das wiederhergestellte Johannisberger Theater. Heidelberg, C. Winter, 1913.

Holmes, William C. "Pamela Transformed," MQ XXXVIII (1952) 581–94.

Holzer, Ludmilla. "Die komische Opern Glucks," SzMw XIII (1926) 3–37.

Hopkinson, Cecil. A Bibliography of the Works of C. W. von Gluck, 1714–1787. London, Printed for the Author, 1959.

Hucke, Helmuth. "Die beiden Fassungen der Oper *Didone abbandonata* von Domenico Sarri," in *Gesellschaft für Musikforschung: Bericht über den internationalen . . . Kongress Hamburg 1956* (Kassel, [etc.], Bärenreiter, 1957) 113–17.

—— "La *Didona abbandonata* di Domenico Sarri nella stesura del 1724 e nella revisione di 1730," *Gazzetta musicale di Napoli* (1956) No. 11–12.

—— "Die neapolitanische Tradition in der Oper," in *International Musicological Society, Report of the Eighth Congress, New York 1961* (Kassel, [etc.], Bärenreiter, 1961) I, 253–77.

Hueber, Kurt. "Gli ultimi anni di Giovanni Bononcini : Notizie e documenti inediti," *Atti e memorie della Accademia di Scienze, Lettere e Arti di Modena*, Ser. 5, XII (1954) 3–21.

Hughes, Charles W. "John Christopher Pepusch," MQ XXXI (1945) 54–70.

Hughes, Spike [i.e., Patrick Cairns Hughes]. Famous Mozart Operas : An Analytical Guide for the Opera-Goer and Armchair Listener. London, Hale, 1957.

Hussey, Dyneley. "Casanova and *Don Giovanni*," M&L VIII (1927) 470–72.

Hutchings, A. J. B. "The Unexpected in Mozart," M&L XX (1939) 21–31.

Iacuzzi, Alfred. The European Vogue of Favart : The Diffusion of the Opéra-Comique. New York, Institute of French Studies, 1932.

Irving, William Henry. John Gay, Favorite of Poets. Durham, N.C., Duke University Press, 1940.

Iselin, Isaak. Pariser Tagebuch 1752. Basel, Benno Schwabe, 1919.

Istel, Edgar. "Einiges über Georg Benda's 'akkompagnierte' Monodramen," SIMG VI (1904–5) 179–82.

—— Die Entstehung des deutschen Melodramas. Berlin, Schuster & Loeffler, 1906.

—— "Gluck's Dramaturgy," MQ XVII (1931) 227–33.

—— "Mozart's *Magic Flute* and Freemasonry," MQ XIII (1927) 510–27.

—— Studien zur Geschichte des Melodrams. I. Jean Jacques Rousseau als Komponist seiner lyrischen Szene *Pygmalion*. Leipzig, B&H, 1901. Continued in *Annals de la Société Jean Jacques Rousseau* I (1905) 141–72; II (1906); III (1907) 119–55.

Jacobs, Reginald. Covent Garden, Its Romance and History. London, Simpkin, 1913.

Jäger, Erich. "Gluck und Goethe," *Die Musik* XIII (1913–14) Qt. 4, 131–39.

Jahn, Otto. W. A. Mozart. Translated as : Life of Mozart. London, Novello, Ewer, 1882. 3 vols. (From the 2d German ed., 1867.) *See also* Abert, Hermann.

Jansen, Albert. Jean-Jacques Rousseau als Musiker. Berlin, Reimer, 1884.

Janz, Curt Paul. "Kierkegaard und das Musikalische, dargestellt an seiner Auffassung von Mozarts *Don Juan*," Mf X (1957) 364–81.

Japy, André. L'Opéra royal de Versailles. [Versailles], Comité National pour la Sauvegarde du Château de Versailles, 1958.

Jenny, Ernst. "Das alte Basler Theater auf dem Blömlein," *Basler Jahrbuch* (1908) 1–68.

Jersild, Jorgen. "Le Ballet d'action italien du 18e siècle au Danemark," *Acta musicologica* XIV (1942) 74–93.

Johnson, Harold Edgar. Iphigenia in Tauris as the Subject for French Opera. Cornell A.M. Thesis, 1939.

Jouve, Pierre Jean. Le Don Juan de Mozart. Freiburg, Librairie de l'Université, 1942. Translated as : Mozart's Don Juan. London, Stuart, 1957.

Jullien, Adolphe. La Cour et l'opéra sous Louis XVI. Paris, Didier, 1878.

—— La Ville et la cour au XVIIIe siècle. Paris, E. Rouveyre, 1881.

Jungk, Klaus. Tonbildliches und Tonsymbolisches in Mozarts Opern. Berlin, Triltsch & Huther, 1938.

Junk, Victor. Goethe's Fortsetzung der *Zauberflöte*. Berlin, Duncker, 1899.

Junker, Hermann. "Zwei 'Griselda'-Opern," in *Festschrift Adolf Sandberger* (Munich, Zierfuss, 1918) 51–64.

Kaestner, Erwin. Das Opernproblem und seine Lösung bei Mozart. Jena, Neuenhahn, 1932.

Kaestner, Rudolf. Johann Heinrich Rolle. Kassel, Bärenreiter, 1932.

Kalbeck, Max. "Zu Scheidemantels *Don Juan*-Uebersetzung," *Die Musik* XIII (1913–14) Qt. 4, 67–72.

Kapp, Julius. Geschichte der Staatsoper Berlin. Berlin, M. Hesse, 1937. New ed., 1942.

—— 185 Jahre Staatsoper. Berlin, Atlantic-Verlag, 1928.

—— 200 Jahre Staatsoper im Bild. Berlin, M. Hesse, 1942.

Kaul, Oskar. Geschichte der Würzburger Hofmusik im 18. Jahrhundert. Würzburg, Becker, 1924.

—— "Die musikdramatischen Werke des Würzburgischen Hofkapellmeisters Georg Franz Wassmuth," ZfMw VII (1924–25) 390–408, 478–500.

Keller, Hans. "The *Entführung*'s 'Vaudeville,'" MR XVII (1956) 304–13.

Keller, Otto. "Gluck-Bibliographie," *Die Musik* XIII (1913–14) Qt. 4, 23–37, 85–91.

—— Wolfgang Amadeus Mozart : Bibliographie und Ikonographie. Berlin, Gebrüder Paetel, 1927.

Kelly, Michael. Reminiscences of the King's Theatre. London, H. Colburn, 1826. 2 vols.

Kerchove, Arnold de. "Méditations sur le Don Juan de Mozart," *Cahiers du sud* XLIII (1956) No. 336.

Kidson, Frank. *The Beggar's Opera,* Its Predecessors and Successors. Cambridge, The University Press, 1922.

Kierkegaard, Søren. Either/Or, a Fragment of Life . . . Volume One, translated by David F. Swenson and Lillian Marvin Swenson. Princeton, Princeton University Press; London, Humphrey Milford, Oxford University Press, 1944.
Contains : "The Immediate Stages of the Erotic or The Musical Erotic," pp. 35–110.

Killer, Hermann. Die Tenorpartien in Mozarts Opern. Kassel, Bärenreiter, 1929.

King, Alexander Hyatt. Mozart in Retrospect : Studies in Criticism and Bibliography. London, New York, Toronto, Oxford University Press, 1955.

Kinsky, Georg. "Glucks Reisen nach Paris," ZfMw VIII (1925–26) 551–66.

Kirby, F. E. "Herder and Opera," JAMS XV (1962) 316–29.

Kirkpatrick, Ralph. Domenico Scarlatti. Princeton, Princeton University Press, 1953.

Kisch, Eve. "Rameau and Rousseau," M&L XXII (1941) 97–114.

Kitzig, Berthold. "Briefe Carl Heinrich Grauns," ZfMw IX (1926–27) 385–405.

Kleefeld, Wilhelm. Landgraf Ernst Ludwig von Hessen-Darmstadt und die deutsche Oper. Berlin, Hofmann, 1904.

Klein, Rudolf. "Die Tonarten des *Don Giovanni*," OeM XI (1956) 259–60.

Kling, H. "Caron de Beaumarchais et la musique," RMI VII (1900) 673–97.

Klob, Karl Maria. Beiträge zur Geschichte der deutschen komischen Oper. Berlin, "Harmonie," [1903].

Kloiber, Rudolf. Die dramatischen Ballette von Christian Cannabich. Munich Dissertation, 1927.

Knapp, J. Merrill. "A Forgotten Chapter in English Eighteenth-Century Opera," M&L XLII (1961) 4–16.

—— "Handel, the Royal Academy of Music, and Its First Opera Season in London (1720)," MQ XLV (1959) 145–67.

Köchel, Ludwig, Ritter von. Chronologisch-thematisches Verzeichnis sämtlicher Tonwerke Wolfgang Amade Mozarts. Ann Arbor, J. W. Edwards, 1947. 3d ed., revised and with a Supplement by Alfred Einstein.

Komorzyński, Egon von. Emmanuel Schikaneder. Berlin, B. Behr, 1901.

—— Emmanuel Schikaneder : Ein Beitrag zur Geschichte des deutschen Theaters. Vienna, Doblinger, [1951].

—— Mozart : Sendung und Schicksal. Vienna, Kremayr & Scheriau, [1955]. 2d ed.

—— Pamina, Mozarts letzte Liebe. Berlin, Max Hesse, [1941].

—— "Streit um den Text der *Zauberflöte*," *Alt-Wiener Kalender* (1922) 79–105.

—— "Das Urbild der *Zauberflöte*," *Mozart-Jahrbuch 1952* (1953) 101–9.

—— "*Die Zauberflöte*: Entstehung und Bedeutung des Kunstwerks," *Neues Mozart-Jahrbuch* I (1941) 147–74.

—— "*Die Zauberflöte* und *Dschinnistan*," *Mozart-Jahrbuch 1954* (1955) 177–94.

—— "*Zauberflöte* und *Oberon*," *Mozart-Jahrbuch 1953* (1954) 150–61.

Krause, Christian Gottfried. Abhandlung von der musikalischen Poesie. Berlin, J. F. Voss, 1752.

Krauss, Rudolf. Das Stuttgarter Hoftheater von den ältesten Zeiten bis zur Gegenwart. Stuttgart, J. B. Metzler, 1908.

—— "Das Theater," in *Herzog Karl Eugen von Württemberg und seine Zeit* (Esslingen a. N., 1907) I, 481–554.

Krebs, Carl. Dittersdorfiana. Berlin, Gebrüder Paetel, 1900.

Krehbiel, Henry. Music and Manners in the Classical Period. New York, Scribner, 1899.

Kretzschmar, Hermann. "Allgemeines und Besonderes zur Affektenlehre," JMP XVIII (1911) 63–77; XIX (1912) 65–78.

Kretzschmar, Hermann. "Aus Deutschlands italienischer Zeit," JMP VIII (1901) 45–61.

—— "Die *Correspondance littéraire* als musikgeschichtliche Quelle," JMP X (1903) 77–92; also in his *Gesammelte Aufsätze* II, 210–25.

—— "Hasse über Mozart," ZIMG III (1901–2) 263–65.

—— "Mozart in der Geschichte der Oper," JMP XII (1905) 53–71.

—— "Zum Verständnis Glucks," JMP X (1903) 61–76.

—— "Zwei Opern Nicolo Logroscinos," JMP XV (1908) 47–68.

Krogh, Torben Thorberg. "Reinhard Keiser in Kopenhagen," in *Musikwissenschaftliche Beiträge: Festschrift für Johannes Wolf* (Berlin, Breslauer, 1929).

—— Zur Geschichte des dänischen Singspiels im 18. Jahrhundert. Copenhagen, Levin & Munksgaard, 1924.

Krone, Walter. Wenzel Müller. Berlin, Ebering, 1906.

Kufferath, Maurice. *La Flûte enchantée* de Mozart. Paris, Fischbacher, 1914.

Kurth, Ernst. "Die Jugendopern Glucks bis *Orfeo*," SzMw I (1913) 193–277.

Lach, Robert. "Sebastian Sailers *Schöpfung* in der Musik," *Akademie der Wissenschaften in Wien, Denkschriften*, 60. Band, 1. Abhandlung (1917).

Lafont du Cujala. "Réflexions sur l'état actuel de la musique dramatique en France," *Mercure de France* (February, 1782) 38–44.

Lalande, Joseph Jérôme Lefrançais de. Voyage d'un françois en Italie, fait dans les années 1765 & 1766. A Venise, et se trouve à Paris chez Desaint, 1769. 8 vols.

La Laurencie, Lionel de. "Deux Imitateurs français des bouffons : Blavet et Dauvergne," *Année musicale* II (1912) 65–125.

—— "Un Emule de Lully : Pierre Gautier de Marseille," SIMG XIII (1911–12) 39–69, 400.

—— "La Grande Saison italienne de 1752 : Les bouffons," MM VIII, No. 6 (1912) 18–33; Nos. 7–8, pp. 13–22. Also separate as : Les Bouffons (1752–1754). Paris, Publications de la Revue SIM, 1912.

—— "Leclair; une assertion de Fétis; Jean-Marie Leclair l'ainé à l'orchestre de l'Opéra," RHCM IV (1904) 496–503.

—— "Un Musicien dramatique du XVIIIe siècle français : Pierre Guedron," RMI XXIX (1922) 445–72.

—— "Un Musicien italien en France à la fin du XVIIIe siècle," RdM XII (1931) 268–77.

—— *Orphée* de Gluck : Etude et analyse. Paris, Mellottée, 1934.

—— "Quelques documents sur Jean-Philippe Rameau et sa famille," MM III (1907) 541–614.

—— Rameau, biographie critique. Paris, Laurens, [1908].

—— "Rameau et les clarinettes," MM IX, No. 2 (1913) 27–28.

—— "Rameau et son gendre," MM VII, No. 2 (1911) 12–23.

Laloy, Louis. "Les Idées de Jean-Philippe Rameau sur la musique," MM III (1907) 1144–59.

Landon, H. C. Robbins. "Haydn's Marionette Operas," *The Haydn Year-book* I (1962) 111–97.

Lang, Paul Henry. "Handel—Churchman or Dramatist?" in *Festschrift Friedrich Blume* (Kassel, Bärenreiter, 1963) [214]–220.

—— "Haydn and the Opera," MQ XVIII (1932) 274–81.

Langlois, Rose-Marie. L'Opéra de Versailles. Paris, P. Horay, 1958.

[Lardin, Jules.] *Zémire et Azor* par Grétry : Quelques questions à propos de la nouvelle falsification de cet opéra. Paris, Moëssard et Jousset, 1846.

La Rotella, Pasquale. Niccolo Piccinni. Bari, Cressati, 1928.

Larsen, Jens Peter. Die Haydn-Ueberlieferungen. Copenhagen, Munksgaard, 1939.

La Salandra. *See* Belluci La Salandra.

Lauppert, Albert von. Die Musikästhetik Wilhelm Heinses : Zugleich eine Quellenstudie zur Hildegard von Hohenthal. Greifswald, J. Abel, 1912.

Lawner, George. Form and Drama in the Operas of Joseph Haydn. University of Chicago Dissertation, 1959.

Lawrence, William John. "Early Irish Ballad Opera and Comic Opera," MQ VIII (1922) 397–412.

—— "The Early Years of the First English Opera House," MQ VII (1921) 104–17.

—— "Marionette Operas," MQ X (1924) 236–43.

[Le Blond, Gaspard Michel, ed.] Mémoires pour servir à l'histoire de la révolution opérée dans la musique par M. le Chevalier Gluck. Naples and Paris, Bailly, 1781.

Leclerc, Hélène. "*Les Indes galantes* (1735–1952) : Les sources de l'opéra-ballet, l'exotisme orientalisant, les conditions matérielles du spectacle," *Revue d'histoire du théâtre* V (1953) 259–85.

Lee, Vernon, pseud. *See* Paget, Violet.

Leerink, Hans. Joseph Haydn : Een Leven vol Muziek. Amsterdam, A. & G. Strengholt, [1949].

Lehner, Walter. "Franz Xaver Süssmayr als Opernkomponist," SzMw XVIII (1931) 66–96.

Leichtentritt, Hugo. Händel. Stuttgart-Berlin, Deutsche Verlags-Anstalt, 1924.

—— "Handel's Harmonic Art," MQ XXI (1935) 208–23.

—— Reinhard Keiser in seinen Opern. Berlin, Tessarotypie-Actien-Gesellschaft, 1901.

Leist, Friedrich. "Geschichte des Theaters in Bamberg bis zum Jahre 1862," *Berichte des historischen Vereins zu Bamberg* LV (1893) 1–283.

Lejeune, Caroline. "Opera in the Eighteenth Century," PMA XLIX (1922–23) 1–20.

Lenzewsky, Gustav. "Friedrich der Grosse als Komponist des Singspiels *Il Re Pastore*," *Schriften des Vereins für die Geschichte Berlins* XXIX (1912) 20.

Leo, Giacomo. Leonardo Leo, celebre musicista del secolo XVIII, ed il suo omonimo Leonardo Leo di Corrado : Nota storica. Naples, Cozzolino, 1901.

Leo, Giacomo. Leonardo Leo . . . e le sue opere musicali. Naples, Melfi & Joele, 1905.

[Léris, Antoine de.] Dictionnaire portatif des théâtres. Paris, C. A. Jombert, 1754. Another ed., 1763.

Lert, Ernst. Mozart auf dem Theater. Berlin, Schuster & Loeffler, 1918.

Le Sage, Alain René. Le Théâtre de la foire ou l'Opéra-comique. Paris, P. Gandouin, 1724–37. 10 vols.

Leux, Irmgard. Christian Gottlob Neefe. Leipzig, Kistner & Siegel, 1925.

—— "Ueber die 'verschollene' Händel-Oper *Hermann von Balcke*," AfMw VIII (1926) 441–51.

Levallois, Andrée, and Anne Souriau. "Caractérologie musicale (les personnages du *Don Juan* de Mozart)," *Revue d'esthétique* VII (1954) 157–82.

Levarie, Siegmund. Mozart's *Le Nozze di Figaro* : A Critical Analysis. Chicago, University of Chicago Press, 1952.

Lincoln, Stoddard. "The First Setting of Congreve's *Semele*," M&L XLIV (1963) 103–17.

Livermore, Ann Lapraik. "*The Magic Flute* and Calderón," M&L XXXVI (1955) 7–16.

—— "The Spanish Dramatists and Their Use of Music," M&L XXV (1944) 140–49.

Livingston, Arthur. Lorenzo da Ponte in America. Philadelphia, Lippincott, 1930.

Lockwood, Elisabeth M. "Some Old-Fashioned Music," M&L XII (1931) 262–70.

Loehner, Ermanno von. "Carlo Goldoni e le sue memorie," *Archivio veneto* XXIII (1881) 45–65; XXIV (1882) 5–27.

Loewenberg, Alfred. "*Bastien and Bastienne* Once More," M&L XXV (1924) 176–81.

—— "Gluck's *Orfeo* on the Stage," MQ XXVI (1940) 311–39.

—— "Lorenzo da Ponte in London," MR IV (1943) 171–89.

—— "Paisiello's and Rossini's *Barbiere di Siviglia*," M&L XX (1939) 157–67.

Loft, Abram. "The Comic Servant in Mozart's Operas," MQ XXXII (1946) 376–89.

The London Stage, 1660–1800. Carbondale, Southern Illinois University Press, 1960–62. Part II : 1700–29, ed. by Emmett L. Avery, 2 vols. Part III : 1729–47, ed. by Arthur H. Scouten, 2 vols. Part IV : 1747–76, ed. by George W. Stone, 3 vols.

Long des Clavières, P. "Lettres inédites de A. E. M. Grétry," RMI XXI (1914) 699–727.

—— "Les *Réflexions d'un solitaire* par A. E. M. Grétry," RMI XXVI (1919) 565–614.

Lorenz, Alfred Ottokar. Alessandro Scarlatti's Jugendoper. Augsburg, Benno Filser, 1927. 2 vols.

—— "Alessandro Scarlattis Opern und Wien," ZfMw IX (1926–27) 86–89.

—— "Das Finale in Mozarts Meisteropern," Die Musik XIX (June, 1927) 621–32.

Lowens, Irving. "The Touch-Stone (1728): A Neglected View of London Opera," MQ XLV (1959) 325–42.

Lozzi, C. "Brigida Banti, regina del teatro lirico nel secolo XVIII," RMI XI (1904) 64–76.

Luciani, Sebastiano Arturo. "Domenico Scarlatti," RassM XI (1938) 460–72; XII (1939) 20–31, 61–74.

Lüthge, Kurt. Die deutsche Spieloper. Brunswick, W. Piepenschneider, 1924.

Luin, E. J. "Giovanni Ferrandini e l'apertura del Teatro Residenziale a Monaco nel 1745," RMI XXXIX (1932) 561–66.

—— "Mozarts Opern in Skandinavien," in Bericht über den internationalen musikwissenschaftlichen Kongress Wien, Mozartjahr 1956 (Graz, Böhlaus, 1958) 387–96.

Lutze, G. Aus Sonderhausens Vergangenheit. III. Band. Sonderhausen, Fr. Aug. Eupel, 1919.

Mably, Gabriel Bonnot de. Lettres à Madame la Marquise de P . . . sur l'opéra. Paris, Didot, 1741.

McClure, Theron Reading. A Reconstruction of Theatrical and Musical Practice in the Production of Italian Opera in the Eighteenth Century. Ann Arbor, University Microfilms, 1956.

Maddalena, E. "Libretti del Goldoni e d'altri," RMI VII (1900) 739–45.

Magni-Dufflocq, Enrico. "Domenico Cimarosa, note biografiche," Bollettino bibliografico musicale V (1930) 5–15.

Maier, Johann Christoph. Beschreibung von Venedig. Leipzig, J. A. Barth, 1795. 4 vols. 2d ed.

[Mainwaring, John.] Memoirs of the Life of the Late George Frederic Handel. London, R. & J. Dodsley, 1760.

Malherbe, Charles Théodore. "Un Précurseur de Gluck: Le comte Algarotti," RHCM II (1902) 369–74, 414–23.

Malignon, Jean. Rameau. [Paris], Editions du Seuil, [1960].

[Marcello, Benedetto.] Il teatro alla moda, osia metodo sicuro, e facile per ben comporre, & esequire l'Opere Italiane in Musica all' uso moderno. [Venice], Borghi di Belisania per A. Licante, [ca. 1720]. Among the numerous later editions the following may be cited: Venice, Tip. dell' Ancora, 1887; Milan, Bottega di Poesia, 1927; French translation ("Le Théâtre à la mode au XVIIIe siècle") Paris, Fischbacher, 1890; German translation ("Das Theater nach der Mode") Munich and Berlin, G. Müller, [1917]; English translation: MQ XXXIV (1948) 371–403; XXXV (1949) 85–105.

Marchesan, Angelo. Della vita e delle opere di Lorenzo Da Ponte. Treviso, Turazza, 1900.

Marmontel, Jean François. Elémens de littérature. [Paris, Née de la Rochelle], 1787. 6 vols.

Marpurg, Friedrich Wilhelm. Anleitung zur Musik überhaupt und zur Singkunst besonders. Berlin, A. Wever, 1763.

—— Historisch-kritische Beiträge zur Aufnahme der Musik. Berlin, G. A. Lange, 1754–62. 5 vols.

Martens, Heinrich. Das Melodram. Berlin, Vieweg, 1932. (Music.)

Martienssen, C. A. "Holger Danske, Oper von Fr. L. Ae. Kunzen," ZIMG XIII (1911–12) 225–32.

Marx, Adolf Bernhard. Gluck und die Oper. Berlin, O. Janke, 1863. 2 vols.

Mason, James Frederick. The Melodrama in France from the Revolution to the Beginning of Romantic Drama. Johns Hopkins Dissertation, 1911. Chapter I published: Baltimore, J. H. Furst, 1912.

Masson, Paul-Marie. "Les Deux Versions du Dardanus de Rameau," Acta musicologica XXVI (1954) 36–48.

—— "Les Idées de Rousseau sur la musique," SIM Revue musical VIII, No. 6 (1912), 1–17; Nos. 7–8, pp. 23–32.

—— "La Lettre sur Omphale (1752)," RdM XXVII (1945) 1–19.

—— "Musique italienne et musique française," RMI XIX (1912) 519–45.

—— L'Opéra de Rameau. Paris, Laurens, 1930.

—— "Rameau and Wagner," MQ XXV (1939) 466–78.

Mattei, Saverio. Memorie per servire alla vita di Metastasio. Colle, A. M. Martini, 1785.

Mattheson, [Johann]. Grundlage einer Ehrenpforte. Hamburg, In Verlegung des Verfassers, 1740. New ed., Berlin, L. Liepmannssohn, 1910.

—— Mithridat, wider den Gift einer welschen Satyre, genannt: La musica. Hamburg, Geissler, 1749.

—— Der musikalische Patriot. Hamburg, 1728.

—— Das neu-eröffnete Orchestre. Hamburg, B. Schillers Wittwe, 1713.

—— Die neueste Untersuchung der Singspiele. Hamburg, C. Herold, 1744.

—— Der vollkommene Capellmeister. Hamburg, C. Herold, 1739.

Maurer, Julius. Anton Schweitzer als dramatischer Komponist. Leipzig, B&H, 1912.

Mayer-Reinach, Albert. "Carl Heinrich Graun als Opernkomponist," SIMG I (1899–1900) 446–529.

—— "Zur Herausgabe des Montezuma von Carl Heinrich Graun in den Denkmälern deutscher Tonkunst," MfMg XXXVII (1905) 20–31.

Meinardus, Ludwig. "Johann Mattheson und seine Verdienste um die deutsche Tonkunst," in Waldersee, Sammlung musikalischer Vorträge (Leipzig, B&H, 1879–98) I, 215–72.

Meissner, August Gottlieb. Bruchstücke zur Biographie J. G. Naumann's. Prague, K. Barth, 1803–4. 2 vols.

Melville, Lewis, pseud. *See* Benjamin, Lewis Saul.

Mennicke, Karl. Hasse und die Brüder Graun als Sinfoniker. Leipzig, B&H, 1906.

—— "Johann Adolph Hasse : Eine biographische Skizze," SIMG V (1903–4) 230–44, 469–75.

Merbach, Paul Alfred. "Das Repertoire der Hamburger Oper 1718–1750," AfMw VI (1924) 354–72.

Merlo, Johann. "Zur Geschichte des Kölner Theaters im 18. und 19. Jahrhundert," *Annalen des historischen Vereins für den Niederrhein* L (1890) 145–219.

Metastasio, Pietro. Dramas and Other Poems. Translated from the Italian by John Hoole. London, Otridge, 1800.

—— Lettere. Florence, Della rosa, 1787–89. 4 vols.

—— Lettere disperse e inedite, Vol. I. Bologna, N. Zanichelli, 1883.

—— Opere. Padua, G. Foglierini, 1811–12. 17 vols.

—— *See also* Burney, *Memoirs.*

Meyer, Ralph. Die Behandlung des Rezitatives in Glucks italienischen Reformopern. Leipzig, B&H, 1919.

Migot, Georges. Jean-Philippe Rameau et le génie de la musique française. Paris, Delagrave, 1930.

Milizia, Francesco. Trattato completo, formale e materiale del teatro. Venice, Pasquali, 1794.

Minor, Jakob. Christian Felix Weisse. Innsbruck, Wagner, 1880.

Mirow, Franz. Zwischenaktsmusik und Bühnenmusik des deutschen Theaters in der klassischen Zeit. Berlin, Gesellschaft für Theatergeschichte, 1927.

Misson, Maximilien. A New Voyage to Italy. London, R. Bonwicke, 1714. 2 vols.

Mitjana y Gordón, Rafael. Histoire du développement du théâtre dramatique et musical en Espagne des origines au commencement du XIXe siècle. Uppsala, Almqvist & Wiksell, 1906.

Mizler [von Kolof], Lorenz [Christoph]. Neu eröffnete musikalische Bibliothek. Leipzig, Im Verlag des Verfassers, 1739–54. 4 vols.

Mohr, Albert Richard. Frankfurter Theaterleben im 18. Jahrhundert. Frankfurt/M., W. Kramer, 1940.

Moller, Johannes. Cimbria literata. Havniae, G. E. Kisel, 1744. 3 vols.

Mondolfi, A. "Cimarosa copista di Handel," *Gazzetta musicale di Napoli* (1956) No. 7–8.

Mondolfi, Anna, and Helmut Hucke. "Neapel," in MGG IX, 1307–42.

Monnet, Jean. Mémoires. Paris, Louis-Michaud, [1884].

Monnier, Philippe. Venise au XVIIIe siècle. Paris, Perrin, 1907. Translated as : Venice in the Eighteenth Century. London, Chatto & Windus, 1910.

Montagu, Lady Mary [Pierrepont] Wortley. The Letters and Works of Lady Mary Wortley Montagu, London, Bickers, [1861]. 2 vols.

—— Letters to and from Pope. In Alexander Pope, *Works* (London, Longman, 1847) VII, 27–119.

Mooser, R. Aloys. "Un Musicien espagnol en Russie à la fin du XVIIIe siècle," RMI XL (1936) 432–49.

Morenz, Siegfried. *Die Zauberflöte:* Eine Studie zum Lebenszusammenhang Aegypten—Antike—Abendland. Münster & Cologne, Böhlau-Verlag, 1952.

Mortari, Virgilio. "L' *Oca del Cairo* di W. A. Mozart," RMI XL (1936) 477–81.

Moser, Hans Joachim. Christoph Willibald Gluck. Stuttgart, Cotta, 1940.

[Mozart, Wolfgang.] Ausstellung die Zauberflöte : Mozarthaus, Katalog. Salzburg, Mozarteum, 1928.

Mozart : Briefe und Aufzeichnungen. Gesamtausgabe, hrsg. von der Internationale Stiftung Mozarteum, Salzburg; gesammelt und erläutert von Wilhelm A. Bauer und Otto Erich Deutsch. Band I : 1755–1776. Kassel, [etc.], Bärenreiter, 1962.

Mozart, die Dokumente seines Lebens. Gesammelt und erläutert von Otto Erich Deutsch. In : Mozart, *Neue Ausgabe sämtlicher Werke*, Serie 10, Werkgruppe 34. Kassel, Bärenreiter, 1955.

Mozart in Italia : I viaggi, a cura di Guglielmo Barblan, con scritti di G. Barblan [and others]. Le lettere, a cura di Andrea della Corte. [Milan], Ricordi, [1956].

Mozart-Jahrbuch, ed. Abert. Munich, Drei Masken, 1923–29. 3 vols. (suspended 1925–28).

—— hrsg. von der Internationalen Stiftung Mozarteum. Salzburg, 1951– . Articles relevant to opera will be found separately listed under the following authors : Engel, Fellerer, Fischer, Georgiades, Komorzynski, Orel, Schmid, and Zingerle.

Mozart operái. Budapest, 1956.

Mozart und seine Welt in zeitgenössischen Bildern. In : Mozart, *Neue Ausgabe sämtlicher Werke*, Serie 10, Werkgruppe 32. Kassel, Bärenreiter, 1955.

Müller, Erich H. "Isaak Iselins *Pariser Tagebuch* als musikgeschichtliche Quelle," ZfMw VII (1924–25) 545–52.

Müller-Blattau, Joseph M. Georg Friedrich Händel : Der Wille zur Vollendung. Mainz, Schott, [1959].

—— "Gluck und die deutsche Dichtung," JMP XLV (1938) 30–52.

Müller-Hartmann, Robert. "Wieland's and Gluck's Versions of the *Alkestis*," *Journal of the Warburg Institute* II (October, 1938) 176–77.

Muratori, Lodovico Antonio. Della perfetta poesia italiana, spiegata e dimostrata con varie osservazioni. Venice, S. Colete, 1724. Contains: Lib. III, Cap. V (Vol. II, pp. 30–45) "De' difetti, che possono osservarsi ne' moderni Drammi." Refutation of Muratori's criticisms is undertaken by Johann Mattheson in his *Nueste Untersuchung der Sing-spiele*.

Musatti, Cesare. "Drammi musicali di Goldoni e d' altri tratti dalle sue commedie," *Ateneo Veneto* XXI (1898) 51–60. Also separate : Venice, Fratelli Visentini, 1898.

Myers, Robert Manson. "Mrs. Delany : An Eighteenth-Century Handelian," MQ XXXII (1946) 12–36.

Nagel, Willibald. "Deutsche Musiker des 18. Jahrhunderts im Verkehr mit J. Fr. A. v. Uffenbach," SIMG XIII (1911–12) 69–106.

—— "Das Leben Christoph Graupner's," SIMG X (1908–9) 568–612.

Negri, Francesco. La vita di Apostolo Zeno. Venice, Alvisopoli, 1816.

Nettl, Paul. "Casanova and Music," MQ XV (1929) 212–32.

—— "An English Musician at the Court of Charles VI," MQ XXVIII (1942) 318–28.

—— Mozart and Masonry. New York, Philosophical Library, [1957].

—— "Mozart, Casanova, Don Giovanni," SchwM XCVI (1956) 60–65.

—— Musik und Freimaurerei : Mozart und die königliche Kunst. [Esslingen], Bechtle Verlag, [1956].

Neues Mozart-Jahrbuch : Im Auftrage des Zentralinstituts für Mozartforschung am Mozarteum Salzburg, hrsg. von Erich Valentin. Regensburg, G. Bosse, 1941–43. 3 Jahrgänge.

Newman, Ernest. Gluck and the Opera. London, B. Dobell, 1895.

Nicolai, Paul. Der Ariadne-Stoff in der Entwicklungsgeschichte der deutschen Oper. Viersen, J. H. Meyer, 1919.

Niggli, Arnold. "Faustina Bordoni-Hasse," in Waldersee, *Sammlung musikalischer Vorträge* (Leipzig, B&H, 1879–98) II, 261–318.

Nin [y Castellano], J[oachin]. Sept Chansons picaresques espagnoles anciennes, librement harmonisées et précédées d'une étude sur les classiques espagnols du chant. Paris, M. Eschig, 1926.

—— Septs Chants lyriques espagnols anciens, librement harmonisés et précédés d'une étude sur les classiques espagnols du chant. Paris, M. Eschig, 1926.

Noack, Friedrich. "Die Opern von Christoph Graupner in Darmstadt," in *Bericht über den I. Musikwissenschaftlichen Kongress der Deutschen Musikgesellschaft* (Leipzig, B&H, 1926) 252–59.

Nohl, Ludwig. *Die Zauberflöte:* Betrachtungen über Bedeutung der dramatischen Musik in der Geschichte des menschlichen Geistes. Frankfurt/M., Schneider, 1862.

Nouveau Théâtre italien, Le. Paris, Briasson, 1733–1753. New ed.

Nowak, Leopold. Joseph Haydn : Leben, Bedeutung und Werk. Zurich, Leipzig, Vienna, Amalthea-Verlag, [1959]. 2d ed.

Nuovo, Antonio. Tommaso Traetta. Bitonto, A. Amendolagine, 1938.

Oliver, Alfred Richard. The Encyclopedists as Critics of Music. New York, Columbia University Press, 1947.

Olivier, Jean Jacques (pseud.). Les Comédiens français dans les cours d'Allemagne au XVIIIe siècle. Paris, Société française d'imprimerie et de libraire, 1901–5. Series 1–4.

Orel, Alfred. Goethe als Operndirektor. Bregenz, E. Russ, 1949.

—— "Die Legende um Mozarts *Bastien und Bastienne*," SchwM No. 91 (1951) 137–43.

—— "Mozart auf Goethes Bühne," *Mozart-Jahrbuch 1953* (1954) 85–94.

"Origen y progressos de las tonadillas que se cantan en los Coliseos de esta Corte," *Memorial literario, instructivo y curioso de la corte de Madrid* XII (1787) 169–80.

[Origny, Abraham Jean Baptiste Antoine d'.] Annales du théâtre-italien. Paris, Duchesne, 1788. 3 vols.

Orlandini, Giuseppe. "Domenico Cimarosa e la musica nella seconda civiltà latina," *Rivista bolognese* II [?] (1868) 933–47, 1005–24.

[Paget, Violet.] Studies of the Eighteenth Century in Italy. London, W. Satchell, 1880. "By Vernon Lee" (pseud.).

Pahlen, Kurt. Das Rezitativ bei Mozart. Vienna Dissertation, 1929.

Paisiello, Cavalier Giovanni. "Saggio del corso dei travagli musicali del cavaliere Giovanni Paisiello," RassM III (1930) 124–35.

[Parfaict, François.] Dictionnaire des théâtres de Paris. Paris, Lambert, 1756. 7 vols.

—— Histoire de l'ancien théâtre italien depuis son origine en France, jusqu'à sa suppression en l'année 1697. Paris, Lambert, 1753.

—— Mémoires pour servir à l'histoire des spectacles de la foire. Paris, Briasson, 1743.

Parini, Giuseppe. "La evirazione (La musica) [Ode]," in *Le odi, il giorno e poesie minore, con note di Guido Mazzoni* (Florence, Barbèra, 1947) 50–57.

Parisini, G. Musica e balli in Faenza nel 1745. Faenza, Lega, 1935.

Parodies du nouveau théâtre italien . . . avec les airs gravés, Les. Paris, Briasson, 1738. New ed.

Parolari, Cornelio. "Giambattista Velluti," RMI XXXIX (1932) 263–98.

Pascazio, Nicola. L'uomo Piccini e la querelle célèbre. Bari, Laterza, 1951.

Pastore, Giuseppe A. Leonardo Leo. Galatina (Lecce), Editore Pajano, 1957.

Pauly, Reinhard G. "Alessandro Scarlatti's *Tigrane*," M&L XXXV (1954) 339–46.

—— "Benedetto Marcello's Satire on Early 18th-Century Opera," MQ XXXIV (1948) 222–33.

Paumgartner, Bernhard. "Die beiden Fassungen des *Idomeneo*: Ein Beitrag zur Dramaturgie Mozarts," M IX (1955) 423–29.

—— Mozart. Freiburg & Zurich, Atlantis-Verlag, [1958]. 5th ed.

Pavan, Giuseppe. Contributo alla storia del teatro musicale; il dramma più musicato; l'*Artaserse* del Metastasio. Cittadella, Tip. Sociale, 1917.

Pearce, Charles E. "Polly Peachum" : The Story of *Polly* and *The Beggar's Opera*. London, S. Paul, [1923].

Pedrell, Felipe. "L'Eglogue *La Forêt sans amour* de Lope de Vega, et la musique et les musiciens du théâtre de Calderón," SIMG XI (1909–10) 55–104.

—— Teatro lírico español anterior al siglo XIX. La Coruña, Berea, [1897–]1898. 5 vols.

Peiser, Karl. Johann Adam Hiller. Leipzig, Gebrüder Hug, 1894.

Pelicelli, Nestore. "Musicisti in Parma nel secolo XVIII : La musica alla corte di Parma nel 1700," *Note d'archivio* XI (1934); XII (1935) 27–42, 82–92.

Pellisson, Maurice. Les Comédies-ballets de Molière. Paris, Hachette, 1914.

Pfeiffer, Konrad. Von Mozarts göttlichem Genius : Eine Kunstbetrachtung auf der Grundlage der Schopenhauerschen Philosophie. Berlin, Verlag Walter de Gruyter & Co., 1956. 3d ed.

Pierre, Constant. Les Hymnes et chansons de la révolution : Aperçu général et catalogue avec notes historiques, analytiques et bibliographiques. Paris, Imprimerie nationale, 1904.

Pincherle, Marc. "Antonio Vivaldi : Essai biographique," RdM XI (1930) 161–70, 265–81.

—— Vivaldi. Paris, Editions Le Bon Plaiser, Librairie Plon, [1955]. Translated as : Vivaldi : Genius of the Baroque. New York, W. W. Norton, [1957].

Piovano, Francesco. "A propos d'une recente biographie de Léonard Leo," SIMG VIII (1906–7) 70–95, 336.

—— "Baldassare Galuppi : Note bio-bibliografiche," RMI XIII (1906) 676–726; XIV (1907) 333–65; XV (1908) 233–74.

—— "Elenco cronologico delle opere (1757–1802) di Pietro Guglielmi," RMI XII (1905) 407–46.

—— "Notizie storico-bibliografiche sulle opere di Pietro Guglielmi (Guglielmini) con appendice su Pietro Guglielmi," RMI XVI (1909) 243–70, 475–505, 785–820; XVII (1910) 59–90, 376–414, 554–89, 822–77. This is about the son, Pietro Carlo Guglielmi, 1763–1817.

—— "Un Opéra inconnu de Gluck," SIMG IX (1907–8) 231–81, 448.

Pirro, André. Descartes et la musique. Paris, Fischbacher, 1907.

Pirrotta, Nino. "Falsirena e la più antica delle cavatine," *Collectanea historiae musicae* II (1957) 355–66.

Pistorelli, L. "Due melodrammi inediti di Apostolo Zeno," RMI III (1896) 261–74.

—— "I melodrammi giocosi del Casti," RMI II (1895) 36–56, 449–72; IV (1897) 631–71.

Piton, Alexis. "Les Origines du mélodrame français à la fin du XVIIIe siècle," *Revue d'histoire littéraire* (1911) 256–96.

Planelli, Antonio. Dell' opera in musica. Naples, D. Campo, 1772.

Plümicke, Carl Martin. Entwurf einer Theatergeschichte von Berlin. Berlin and Stettin, F. Nicolai, 1781.

Pohl, Karl Ferdinand. Joseph Haydn. Leipzig, B&H, 1878–1927. 3 vols. in 2.

Poladian, Sirvart. Handel as an Opera Composer. Ann Arbor, University Microfilms, 1958.

Polko, Elise. Die Bettler-Oper. Hanover, Rümpler, 1863. 3 vols.

Pompeati, Arturo. "Il Parini e la musica," RMI XXXVI (1929) 556–74.

Potter, John. The Theatrical Review; or, New Companion to the Playhouse; Containing a Critical and Historical Account of Every Tragedy, Comedy, Opera, Farce &c Exhibited at the Theatres during the Last Season. London, S. Crowder, 1772. 2 vols.

Pougin, Arthur. "Bernardo Mengozzi," RMI XXV (1918) 176–201, 323–44.

—— Un Directeur d'opéra au dix-huitième siècle; l'opéra sous l'ancien régime; l'opéra sous la révolution. Paris, Fischbacher, 1914.

—— Jean-Jacques Rousseau musicien. Paris, Fischbacher, 1901.

—— Madame Favart, étude théâtrale, 1727–1772. Paris, Fischbacher, 1912.

—— Molière et l'opéra-comique. Paris, J. Baur, 1882.

—— Monsigny et son temps. Paris, Fischbacher, 1908.

—— Musiciens français du XVIIIe siècle : Dezèdes. Paris, N. Chaix, 1862.

—— L'Opéra-comique pendant la révolution de 1788 à 1801. Paris, A. Savine, 1891.

Powers, Harold S. "Il Serse trasformato," MQ XLVII (1961) 481–92; XLVIII (1962) 73–92.

Preibisch, Walter. "Quellenstudien zu Mozart's Entführung aus dem Serail: Ein Beitrag zur Geschichte der Türkenoper," SIMG X (1908–9) 430–76.

Prochazka, R. Mozart in Prag. Prague, G. Neugebauer, 1899.

Prod'homme, Jacques Gabriel. "Austro-German Musicians in France in the Eighteenth Century," MQ XV (1929) 171–95.

—— "Les Dernières Représentations du Devin du village (mai–juin 1829)," RM VII (August, 1926) 118–25.

—— "Deux Collaborateurs italiens de Gluck : Raniero de Calzabigi e Giuseppe D'Affligio," RMI XXIII (1916) 33–65, 201–18.

—— "A French Maecenas of the Time of Louis XV : M. de la Pouplinière," MQ X (1924) 511–31.

—— Gluck. Paris, Société d'Editions Françaises et Internationales, 1948.

—— "Gluck's French Collaborators," MQ III (1917) 249–71.

—— "Lettres de Gluck et à propos de Gluck (1776–1787)," ZIMG XIII (1911–12) 257–65.

—— "Marie Fel (1713–1794)," SIMG IV (1902–3) 485–518.

—— "La Musique à Paris de 1753 à 1757, d'après un manuscrit de la Bibliothèque de Munich," SIMG VI (1904–5) 568–87.

—— "Notes sur deux librettistes français de Gluck : Du Roullet et Moline (d'après des documents inédits)," ZIMG VII (1905-6) 12-15.

—— "*Le Page inconstant:* Ballet anacréontique . . . sur la musique de Mozart," RdM XVI (1935) 205-12.

—— "A Pastel by La Tour : Marie Fel," MQ IX (1923) 482-507.

—— "Pierre de Jélyotte (1713-1797)," SIMG III (1901-2) 686-717.

—— "Rosalie Levasseur, Ambassadress of Opera," MQ II (1916) 210-43.

Prota-Giurleo, Ulisse. Alessandro Scarlatti, "il Palermitano" (la patria & la famiglia). Naples, L'autore, 1926.

—— La grande orchestra del Teatro S. Carlo nel Settecento (da documenti inediti). Naples, L'autore, 1927.

—— Musicanti napoletani alla corte di Portogallo nel 700. Naples, Elzevira, 1925.

—— Nicola Logroscino, "il dio dell' opera buffa." Naples, L'autore, 1927.

—— "Sacchini fra Piccinisti e Gluckisti," *Gazzetta musicale di Napoli* (1957) Nos. 4 and 5.

Provenzal, Dino. La vita e le opere di Lodovico Adimari. Rocca S. Casciano, L. Cappelli, 1902.

Prunières, Henry. "Défense et illustration de l'Opéra-comique," RM XIV (November, 1933) 243-47.

Pupino-Carbonelli, Giuseppe. Paisiello. Naples, Tocco, 1908.

Puttman, Max. "Zur Geschichte der deutschen komischen Oper von ihren Anfängen bis Dittersdorf," *Die Musik* III (1903-4) Qt. 4, 334-49, 416-28.

Quadrio, Francesco Saverio, abate. Della storia e della ragione d'ogni poesia. Bologna, F. Pisarri, 1739-49. 4 vols.

Quantz, Johann Joachim. Versuch einer Anweisung die Flöte traversiere zu spielen. Leipzig, C. F. Kahnt, 1906. Originally published Berlin, J. F. Voss, 1752.

Quittard, Henri. "Les Années de jeunesse de J. P. Rameau," RHCM II (1902) 61-63, 100-14, 152-70, 208-18.

—— "*Le Bucheron,* opéra comique de Philidor," RHCM VII (1907) 421-24.

—— "*Ernelinde,* de Philidor," RHCM VII (1907) 469-74.

—— "La Première Comédie française en musique," *Bulletin français de la SIM* IV (1908) 378-96, 497-537.

—— "*Le Sorcier,* opéra comique de Philidor," RHCM VII (1907) 537-41.

Raab, Leopold. Wenzel Müller. Boden bei Wien, Verein der N.-Oe. Landesfreunde in Boden, 1928.

Rabany, Charles. Carlo Goldoni : Le théâtre et la vie en Italie au XVIIIe siècle. Paris, Berger-Levrault, 1896.

Raccolta di melodrammi giocosi scritti nel secolo XVIII. Milan, Soc. tip. dei classici italiani, 1826.

Raccolta di melodrammi serj scritti nel secolo XVIII. Milan, Soc. tip. dei classici italiani, 1822. 2 vols.

Radiciotti, Giuseppe. "L'arte di G. B. Pergolesi," RMI XVII (1910) 916–25.

—— Pergolesi. Milan, Fratelli Treves, [1935]. German edition : Giovanni Battista Pergolesi : Leben und Werk. [Enlarged and rev. by Antoine E. Cherbuliez.] Zurich, Pan-Verlag, [1954].

Raeburn, Christopher. "Figaro in Wien," OeM XII (1957) 273–77.

—— "Die textlichen Quellen des Schauspieldirektors," OeM XIII (1958) 4–10.

—— "Das Zeitmass in Mozarts Opern," OeM XII (1957) 329–33.

Raeburn, Michael, and Christopher Raeburn. "Mozart Manuscripts in Florence," M&L XL (1959) 334–40.

Raeli, V. "The Bi-Centenary of Tommaso Traetta," The Chesterian VIII (1926–27) 217–23.

—— "Tommaso Traetta," Rivista nazionale di musica (March, 1927).

[Raguenet, François.] Défense du parallèle des Italiens et des François en ce qui regarde la musique et l'opéra. Paris, C. Barben, 1705.

—— Paralele des Italiens et des François en ce qui regarde la musique et les opéras. Paris, J. Moreau, 1602 [i.e., 1702]. Translated as : A Comparison between the French and Italian Musick and Opera's . . . to Which Is Added a Critical Discourse upon Opera's in England. London, W. Lewis, 1709. German translation with notes in Mattheson's Critica Musica (Hamburg, 1722).

Rauber, A. Die Don Juan Sage im Lichte biologischer Forschung. Leipzig, Georgi, 1898.

Redlich, Hans F. "Handel's Agrippina (1709) : Problems of a Practical Edition," MR XII (1951) 15–23.

—— "L'oca del Cairo," MR II (1941) 122–31.

Reichardt, Johann Friedrich. Ueber die deutsche comische Oper. Hamburg, C. E. Bohn, 1774.

Reichel, Eugen. "Gottsched und Johann Adolph Scheibe," SIMG II (1900–1901) 654–68.

Reiff, A. "Die Anfänge der Oper in Spanien, mit Textproben," Spanien, Zeitschrift für Auslandskunde Jahrgang I, Heft 3 (1919).

Reimers, Dagmar. Geschichte des Rigaer deutschen Theaters von 1782–1822. Poznan, A. Meyer, 1942.

[Rémond de Saintmard, Toussaint.] Reflexions sur l'opéra. The Hague, J. Neaulme, 1741.

"Revue der Revueen : Zum 200. Geburtstag von Chr. W. Gluck," Die Musik XIII (1913–14) Qt. 4, 223–27, 276–78.

Riccoboni, Luigi. Reflexions historiques et critiques sur les differens théâtres de l'Europe. Paris, J. Guérin, 1738.

Richebourg, Louisette. Contribution à l'histoire de la "Querelle des Bouffons." Paris, Nizet, 1937.

Riedinger, Lothar. "Karl von Dittersdorf als Opernkomponist," SzMw II (1914) 212–349.

Riess, Otto. "Johann Abraham Peter Schulz' Leben," SIMG XV (1913–14) 169–270.

Rinaldi, Mario. Antonio Vivaldi. Milan, Istituto d'alta cultura, [1943].

Rivalta, Camillo. Giuseppe Sarti. Faenza, F. Lega, 1928.

Roberti, Giuseppe. "La musica in Italia nel secolo XVIII secondo le impressioni di viaggiatori stranieri," RMI VII (1900) 698–729; VIII (1901) 519–59.

Robinson, Percy. Handel and His Orbit. London, Sheratt & Hughes, 1908.

—— "Handel up to 1720 : A New Chronology," M&L XX (1939) 55–63.

Rockstro, William Smyth. The Life of George Frederick Handel. London, Macmillan, 1883.

Rogers, Francis. "Handel and Five Prima Donnas," MQ XXIX (1943) 214–24.

—— "The Male Soprano," MQ V (1919) 413–25.

—— "Sophie Arnould (1740–1803)," MQ VI (1920) 57–61.

Rognoni, Luigi. Un' opera incompiuta di Mozart : L' oca del Cairo; a proposito di una ricostruzione. Milan, Bocca, 1937.

Rolandi, Ulderico. Il librettista del Matrimonio segreto: Giovanni Bertati. Trieste, C. Reali, 1926.

Rolland, Romain. "L'Autobiographie d'un illustre oublié : Telemann," in Voyage musical au pays du passé (Paris, Eduard-Joseph, 1919).

—— "Le Dernier Opéra de Gluck : Echo et Narcisse (1779)," RHCM III (1903) 212–15.

—— "Gluck, une révolution dramatique," Revue de Paris (1904) No. 3, 736–72.

—— Haendel. [New ed.] Paris, Michel, [1951].

—— "Métastase, précurseur de Gluck," MM VIII, No. 4 (1912) 1–10.

Roncaglia, Gino. Il melodioso Settecento italiano. Milan, Hoepli, 1935. Contains examples of music by Galuppi, Paisiello, Cimarosa, A. M. Bononcini, and T. Giordani.

Ronga, Luigi. "Scarlatti fra due epoche," Musicista VII (1940) 57–61.

Rosa, Salvator. "La musica," in Mattheson, Mithridat (Hamburg, Geissler, 1749) i–lvi, with German translation.

Roscoe, P. C. "Arne and The Guardian Outwitted," M&L XXIV (1943) 237–45.

Rosenfeld, Ernst. Johann Baptist Schenk als Opernkomponist. Vienna Dissertation, 1921.

Rosenthal, Harold. Two Centuries of Opera at Covent Garden. London, Putnam, 1958.

Rosenthal, Karl. "Ueber Volksformen bei Mozart : Ein Beitrag zur Entwicklung der Vokalformen von 1760 bis 1790," SzMw XIV (1927) 5–32.

Ross, Erwin. Deutsche und italienische Gesangsmethode : Erläutert auf Grund ihrer geschichtlichen Gegensätzlichkeit im achtzehnten Jahrhundert. Kassel, Bärenreiter, 1928.

Rossell, Denton. The Formal Construction of Mozart's Operatic Ensembles and Finales. Ann Arbor, University Microfilms, 1956. 2 vols.

Roth, Hermann. "Händels Ballettmusiken," *Neue Musik-Zeitung* XLIX (1928) 245–52.

—— "Händels Ballettoper *Ariodante:* Zur deutscher Uraufführung," ZfMw IX (1926–27) 159–67.

—— "Zur Karlsruher Einrichtung von Händels *Tamerlan*," ZfMw V (1922–23) 380–82.

Rousseau, Jean Jacques. Dictionnaire de musique. Amsterdam, M. M. Rey, 1768. Vol. II, Amsterdam, M. M. Rey, 1779. Translated as : A Complete Dictionary of Music. London, J. Murray, 1779.

—— Lettre à Mr. d'Alembert sur les spectacles. Ed. critique par Max Fuchs. Geneva, Droz; Lille, Giard, 1948.

—— Œuvres complètes. Paris, P. Dupont, 1823–26. 25 vols. Contains "Confessions," Vols. 14–16; writings on music, Vols. 11–13.

Roustan, Marius. Les Philosophes et la société française au XVIIIe siècle. Paris, Hachette, 1911.

Rowell, Lewis E., Jr. Four Operas of Antonio Vivaldi. University of Rochester Dissertation, 1958.

Rubsamen, Walter. "Mr. Seedo, Ballad Opera, and the Singspiel," in *Miscelánea en homenaje a Mons. Higinio Anglés* (Barcelona, Consejo Superior de Investigaciones Cientificas, 1958–61) II, 776–809. Also separate.

Rückert, Heinz. "Das musikalische Theater ruft nach Händel," *Händel-Jahrbuch* VIII (1956) 57–61.

Russo, Joseph Louis. Lorenzo da Ponte, Poet and Adventurer. New York, Columbia University Press, 1922.

Russo, Luigi. Metastasio. Bari, G. Laterza, 1921.

Sacchi, Giovenale. Vita del cavaliere Don Carlo Broschi. Vinegia, Coleti, 1784.

Sachs, Curt. Musik und Oper am kurbrandenburgischen Hofe. Berlin, J. Bard, 1910.

Sage, Jack. "Calderón e la música teatral," *Bulletin hispanique* LVIII (1956) 275–300.

Saint-Evremond, Charles de Marguetel de St. Denis, Seigneur de. Œuvres meslées. London, Tonson, 1709. 3 vols. 2d ed. Contains "Sur les opera," II, 214–22; "Les Opera, comedie," II, 223–92; "A Monsieur Lulli," III, 106–7.

Saint-Foix, Georges de. "Autour de Paisiello," RMI XLVIII (1946) 243–50.

—— "La Conclusion de l'ouverture de *Don Juan*," RdM V (1924) 169–72.

—— "Le Livret de *Così fan tutte*," RdM XI (1930) 43–97.

—— "Les Maîtres de l'opéra bouffe dans la musique de chambre à Londres," RMI XXXI (1924) 507–26.

—— "Sammartini et les chanteurs de son temps," RMI XLIII (1939) 357–63.

—— "Le Théâtre à Salzbourg en 1779–80," RdM XVI (1935) 193–204.

Salazar, Adolfo. Juan del Encina y la música en el primitivo teatro español. Mexico, D.F., 1940. (*Bóletin de musicologia y folklore*, January, 1940.)

—— La música en el primitivo teatro español, anterior a Lope de Vega y Calderón. México, A. Salazar, [1942?].

Samson, Ingrid. "Paisiello—*La bella Molinara*," NZfM CXX (1959) 368–71.

Sandberger, Adolf. "Tommaso Traëtta," DTB XIV, No. 1 (1913) xii–xc.

Saracino, Emanuele. Tommaso Traetta (cenni biografico-artistici). Bitonto, A. Amendolagine, [pref. 1954].

Scarlatti, Gli : Alessandro, Francesco, Pietro, Domenico, Giuseppe; note e documenti sulla vita e sulle opere. Siena, Ticci Poligrafico, 1940.

Schatz, Albert. "Giovanni Bertati," VfMw V (1889) 231–71.

Scheibe, Johann Adolf. Critischer Musikus. Leipzig, B. C. Breitkopf, 1745. New ed.

Schenk, Erich. Wolfgang Amadeus Mozart : Eine Biographie. Zurich, Amalthea Verlag, [1955]. Translated as : Mozart and His Times. New York, Alfred A. Knopf, 1959.

Schenk, Johann Baptist. ["Autobiographische Skizze"], SzMw XI (1924) 75–85.

Scherillo, Michele. L'opera buffa napoletana durante il Settecento : Storia letteraria. [Milan], R. Sandron, [1917]. 2d ed. First published as : Storia letteraria dell' opera buffa napolitana dalle origini al principio del secolo XIX. Naples, R. Università, 1883.

—— "La prima commedia musicale a Venezia," *Giornale storico della letteratura italiana* I (1883) 230–59.

Schering, Arnold. "Zwei Singspiele des Sperontes," ZfMw VII (1924–25) 214–20.

Schiedermair, Ludwig. Bayreuther Festspiel im Zeitalter des Absolutismus. Leipzig, C. F. Kahnt, 1908.

—— "Zur Geschichte der frühdeutschen Oper," JMP XVII (1910) 29–43.

Schiedermair, Ludwig, ed. Die Briefe W. A. Mozarts und seiner Familie. Munich, G. Müller, 1914.

Schletterer, Hans Michael. Das deutsche Singspiel von seinen ersten Anfängen bis auf die neueste Zeit. Leipzig, B&H, [1863?].

—— "Giovanni Battista Pergolesi," in Waldersee, *Sammlung musikalischer Vorträge* (Leipzig, B&H, 1879–98) II, 139–78.

—— "Die Opernhäuser Neapels," MfMg XIV (1882) 175–81, 183–89; XV (1883) 12–19.

Schlitzer, Franco. Antonio Sacchini : Schede e appunti per una sua storia teatrale. Siena, [Ticci], 1955.

—— Cimarosa. Milan, Ricciardi, 1950.

Schlitzer, Franco. Goethe e Cimarosa, con un' appendice di note bio-bibliografiche: In occasione della VII Settimana Musicale (16–22 settembre 1950). Siena, Ticci, 1950.

Schlitzer, Franco, ed. Tommaso Traetta, Leonardo Leo, Vincenzo Bellini: Notizie e documenti raccolti in occasione della "IX Settimana Musicale Senese" 16–22 settembre 1952. Siena, Ticci, 1952.

Schmid, Anton. Christoph Willibald Ritter von Gluck. Leipzig, F. Fleischer, 1854.

Schmid, Ernst Fritz. "Mozart und Monsigny," *Mozart-Jahrbuch 1957* (1958) 57–62.

Schmid, Johan Jacob von. *Die Zauberflöte:* Beschouwingen over Mozart's Opera; een Bijdrage tot de Cultuurgeschiedenis en de Geestesweten-schappen. Assen, Van Gorcum, 1956.

Schmid, Otto. Die Heimstätten der sächsischen Landestheater. Dresden, A. Waldheim, [19—?].

—— Das sächsische Königshaus in selbstschöpferischer musikalischer Be-thätigung (Musik am sächsischen Hofe). Leipzig, B&H, 1900.

Schmidt, Heinrich. Johann Mattheson, ein Förderer der deutschen Ton-kunst, im Lichte seiner Werke. Leipzig, B&H, 1897.

Schmitz, Eugen. "Formgesetze in Mozarts *Zauberflöte*," in *Festschrift Max Schneider zum 80. Geburtstage* (Leipzig, Deutscher Verlag für Musik, [1955]) 209–14.

—— "Zu Mozarts *Bastien und Bastienne*," *Hochland* IX, No. 2 (1912) 607–11.

Schneider, Constantin. "Die Oratorien und Schuldramen Anton Cajetan Adlgassers," SzMw XVIII (1931).

Schneider, Ludwig. Geschichte der Oper und des königlichen Opernhauses in Berlin. Berlin, Duncker & Humblot, 1852.

Schneider, Max. "Die Begleitung des Secco-Rezitativs um 1750," *Gluck-Jahrbuch* III (1917) 88–107.

Schnerich, Alfred. "Wie sahen die ersten Vorstellungen von Mozart's *Don Juan* aus?" ZIMG XII (1910–11) 101–8.

Schramm, Erich. "Goethe und Diderots Dialog *Rameaus Neffe*," ZfMw XVI (1934) 294–307.

Schütze, Johann Friedrich. Hamburgische Theatergeschichte. Hamburg, J. P. Treder, 1794.

Schuh, Willi. "Il Flauto magico," in *Festschrift Friedrich Blume* (Kassel, Bärenreiter, 1963) [327]–339.

—— "Über einige frühe Textbücher zur *Zauberflöte*," in *Bericht über den internationalen musikwissenschaftlichen Kongress Wien, Mozartjahr 1956* (Graz, Böhlaus, 1958) 571–78.

Schultz, William Eben. Gay's *Beggar's Opera:* Its Content, History, and Influence. New Haven, Yale University Press, 1923.

—— "The Music of the *Beggar's Opera* in Print, 1728–1923," MTNA XIX (1934) 87–99.

Schwan, Wilhelm Bernhard. Die opernästhetischen Theorien der deutschen klassischen Dichter. Bonn Dissertation, 1928.

Schwartz, Rudolf. "Zur Geschichte der liederlosen Zeit in Deutschland," JMP XX (1913) 13–27.

Schwarz, Max. "Johann Christian Bach," SIMG II (1900–1901) 401–54.

Scudo, Pierre. Le Chevalier Sarti. Paris, Hachette, 1857. (Previously in *Revue des deux mondes*, 1854–56.)

—— "Pergolèse et *La serva padrona*," *Revue des deux mondes* XXXII, No. 41 (September 1, 1862) 226–30.

Sear, H. G. "Charles Dibdin : 1745–1814," M&L XXVI (1945) 61–65.

Segnitz, Eugen. Goethe und die Oper in Weimar. Langensalza, Beyer, 1908.

Seiffert, Max. "J.A.P. Schultz' 'dänische' Oper," AfMw I (1918–19) 422–23.

—— "Zur Biographie Joh. Adolph Hasse's," SIMG VII (1905–6) 129–31.

Seligmann, Herbert Wolff. Beiträge zur Geschichte der Bühne der opera seria. Bonn Dissertation, 1924.

Serauky, Walter. "Das Ballett in G. F. Händels Opern," *Händel-Jahrbuch* VIII (1956) 91–112.

—— Georg Friedrich Händel : Sein Leben, sein Werk. Band 3 : [Von Händels innerer Neuorientierung bis zum Abschluss der *Samson* (1736–1743)] and Band 4 : [Von Händels *Semele* bis zum Abschluss des *Judas Makkabäus* (1743–1746)]. Leipzig, Deutscher Verlag für Musik, 1956–58.

Sharp, Geoffrey. "*Don Giovanni:* Some Observations," MR IV (1943) 45–52.

Sherwin, Oscar. Mr. Gay : Being a Picture of the Life and Times of the Author of the *Beggar's Opera*. New York, John Day, 1929.

Siegmund-Schultze, Walther. Georg Friedrich Händel : Leben und Werk. Leipzig, Deutscher Verlag für Musik, 1954.

—— "Der Gesangsstil der Händel-Oper," MuG IX (1959) 137–41.

Siena Settimane Musicali. B. Galuppi detto "Il Buranello" (1706–1785): Note e documenti, raccolti in occasione della settimana celebrativa, (20–26 settembre 1948). Siena, Ticci, 1948.

Sievers, Heinrich. 250 Jahre Braunschweigisches Staatstheater, 1690–1940. Brunswick, Appelhans, 1941.

Silva, G. Silvestri. Illustri musicisti calabresi : Leonardo Vinci. Genoa, Tip. Nazionale, [1935].

Simon, Alicja. "Grétry au Théâtre national de Varsovie," in *International Society for Musical Research, First Congress, Report* (Burnham, Plainsong and Medieval Music Society, [1930]).

Sittard, Josef. "Reinhard Keiser in Württemberg," MfMg XVIII (1886) 3–12.

Smith, William C. Concerning Handel, His Life and Works : Essays. London, Cassell, [1948].

Smith, William C., compiler. The Italian Opera and Contemporary Ballet in London, 1789–1820 : A Record of Performances and Players with Reports from the Journals of the Time. London, Society for Theatre Research, [1955].

Solar Quintes, Nicolás A. "Nuevas aportaciones a la biografía de Carlos Broschi (Farinelli)," *Anuario musical* III (1948) 187–204.

—— "Nuevos documentos para la biografía del compositor Sebastián Durón," *Anuario musical* X (1955) 137–62.

Soleinne, Martineau de. Bibliothèque dramatique. Paris, Administration de l'Alliance des arts, 1843–45. 7 vols. See also : Tableau générale du catalogue (Paris, Administration de l'Alliance des arts, 1845); and Table des pièces du théâtre décrites dans le catalogue . . . par Charles Brunet publiée par Henri de Rothschild (Paris, D. Morgand, 1914).

Somerset, H. V. F. "Giovanni Paisiello," M&L XVIII (1937) 20–35.

—— "Jean Jacques Rousseau as a Musician," M&L XVII (1936) 37–46, 218–24.

Sommer, Hans. "Die Oper *Ludwig der Fromme* von Georg Caspar Schürmann," MfMg XIV (1882) 48–51, 53–55.

—— "Zur Schürmann'schen Oper *Ludovicus Pius*," MfMg XXIV (1892) 137–39.

Sondheimer, Robert. "Gluck in Paris," ZfMw V (1922–23) 165–75.

Sonette, Jean Jacques, pseud. *See* Goudar, Ange.

Sonneck, Oscar George Theodore. "Ciampi's *Bertoldo, Bertoldino e Cacasenno* and Favart's *Ninette à la cour*," SIMG XII (1911) 525–64.

—— "Die drei Fassungen des Hasse'schen *Artaserse*," SIMG XIV (1912–13) 226–42.

—— "Foot-note to the Bibliographical History of Grétry's Operas," in *Gedenkboek . . . Scheurleer* (The Hague, Nijhoff, 1925) 321–36.

—— "*Il Giocatore*," MA IV (1912–13) 160–74.

—— "La nuova rappresentazione del *D. Giovanni* di Mozart a Monaco," RMI III (1896) 741–55.

Sooper, Frances O. "The Music of Dittersdorf," M&L XI (1930) 141–45.

Specht, Richard. Das Wiener Operntheater : Von Dingelstedt bis Schalk und Strauss. Vienna, P. Knepler, 1919.

Spectator, The (London, 1711–1714). London and Toronto, J. M. Dent, 1919–26. 4 vols.

Speziale, G. "Ancora per Paisiello," RassM IV (1931) 1–16.

Spinelli, Alessandro Giuseppe. Bibliografia goldoniana. Milan, Dumolard, 1884.

Spitta, Philipp. Johann Sebastian Bach. Leipzig, B&H, 1930. 4th ed. 2 vols.

—— "Rinaldo di Capua," VfMw III (1877) 92–121.

Spitz, Charlotte. Antonio Lotti in seiner Bedeutung als Opernkomponist. Borna–Leipzig, Noske, 1918.

—— "Die Opern *Ottone* von G. F. Händel (London 1722) und *Teofane* von A. Lotti (Dresden 1719) : Ein Stilvergleich," in *Festschrift Adolf Sandberger* (Munich, Zierfuss, 1918) 265–71.

Squire, William Barclay. "Gluck's London Operas," MQ I (1915) 397–409.

—— "An Index of Tunes in the Ballad-Operas," MA II (1910–11) 1–17.

Stählin, Karl. Aus den Papieren Jacob von Stählins. Königsberg, Ost-Europa-Verlag, 1926.

Stauder, Wilhelm. "Johann André : Ein Beitrag zur Geschichte des deutschen Singspiels," AfMf I (1936) 318–60. Also separate : Leipzig, B&H, 1936.

Stefan, Paul. Die Zauberflöte: Herkunft, Bedeutung, Geheimnis. Vienna, Reichner, 1937.

Steglich, Rudolf. "Das deutsche Händelfest in Leipzig," ZfMw VII (1924–25) 587–92.

—— "Göttinger Händelfestspiele 1924," Zeitschrift für Musik XCI (1924) 496–98.

—— "Göttinger Händel-Opern Festspiele 1927," Zeitschrift für Musik XCIV (1927) 424–26.

—— "Das Händelfest in Münster (2. bis 5. Dezember 1926)," ZfMw IX (1926–27) 290–93.

—— "Die Händel-Opern-Festspiele in Göttingen," ZfMw III (1920–21) 615–20.

—— "Händels Oper Rodelinde und ihre neue Göttinger Bühnenfassung," ZfMw III (1920–21) 518–34.

—— "Händels Saul in szenischer Darstellung," Zeitschrift für Musik XC (1923) Heft XVII, 15–17.

—— "Händels Xerxes und die Göttinger Händel-Opern-Festspiele 1924," ZfMw VII (1924–25) 21–33.

—— "Händel und die Gegenwart," Zeitschrift für Musik XCII (1925) 333–38.

—— "Die neue Händel-Opern-Bewegung," Händel-Jahrbuch I (1928) 71–158.

—— "Schütz und Händel," Zeitschrift für Musik LXXXIX (1922) 478–80.

—— "Ueber die gegenwärtige Krise der Händelpflege," ZfMw X (1927–28) 632–41.

Steinitzer, Max. Zur Entwicklungsgeschichte des Melodrams und Mimodrams. Leipzig, C. F. W. Siegel, [1919].

Stendhal, pseud. See Beyle, Henri.

Stephenson, Kurt. Hamburgische Oper zwischen Barock und Romantik. Hamburg, J. P. Toth, [1948].

Sternfeld, Frederick W. "The Melodic Sources of Mozart's Most Popular Lied," MQ XLII (1956) 213–22.

Stier, Ernst. "Georg Caspar Schürmann," Die Musik III, No. 2 (1903–4) 107–11.

Strasser, Stefan. "Susanna und die Gräfin," ZfMw X (1927–28) 208–16.

Streatfeild, Richard Alexander. Handel. New York, John Lane, 1909.

Streatfeild, Richard Alexander. "Handel, Rolli, and Italian Opera in London in the Eighteenth Century," MQ III (1917) 428–45.

Strüver, Paul. Die cantata da camera Alessandro Scarlattis. Munich Dissertation, 1924.

Stubenrauch, Herbert, Wilhelm Herrmann, and Claus Helmut Drese. 175 Jahre Nationaltheater Mannheim : Dokumente zur Theatergeschichte, zusammengestellt und erläutert. Mannheim, Nationaltheater, 1954.

Subirá, José. El compositor Iriarte (1750–1791) y el cultivo español del melólogo (melodrama). Madrid, Consejo Superior de Investigaciones Científicas, Instituto Español de Musicología, 1949–50. 2 vols.

—— El gremio de representates españoles y la Cofradia de Nuestra Señora de la Novena. Madrid, Consejo Superior de Investigaciones Científicas, Instituto de Estudios Madrileños, 1960.

—— Historia de la música teatral en España. Barcelona, Editorial Labor, 1945.

—— "Les Influences françaises dans la tonadilla madrilène du XVIIIe siècle," in Mélanges de musicologie (Paris, Droz, 1933) 209–16.

—— Los maestros de la tonadilla escénica. Barcelona, Editorial Labor, 1933.

—— "Un manuscrito musical de principios del siglo XVIII : Contribución a la musica teatral española," Anuario musical IV (1949) 181–91.

—— La música en la casa de Alba. Madrid, ["Sucesores de Rivadeneyra"], 1927.

—— El operista español d. Juan Hidalgo. Madrid, Bermejo, 1934.

—— La participación musical en el antiguo teatro español. Barcelona, Diputación provincial, 1930.

—— "Le Style dans la musique théâtrale espagnole," Acta musicologica IV (1932) 67–75.

—— La tonadilla escénica. Madrid, Tipografía de archivos, 1928–30. 3 vols.

—— Tonadillas teatrales inéditas. Madrid, Tipografía de archivos, 1932.

Supplément aux parodies du théâtre italien. Paris, Duchesne, 1765. New ed.

Szabolcsi, Bence. "Exoticisms in Mozart," M&L XXXVII (1956) 323–32.

—— "Mozart et la comédie populaire," in Studia musicologica I (Budapest, Hungarian Academy of Sciences, 1961) 65–91. Originally published in Hungarian (Budapest, 1957).

Szametz, Ralph. Hat Mozart eine Psychose durchgemacht? Frankfurt Dissertation, 1936.

Tanner, Richard. Johann David Heinichen als dramatischer Komponist. Leipzig, B&H, 1916.

Taut, Kurt. "Verzeichnis des Schrifttums über Georg Friedrich Händel," Händel-Jahrbuch VI (1933).

Taylor, Eric. "William Boyce and the Theatre," MR XIV (1953) 275–87.

Taylor, Sedley. The Indebtedness of Handel to the Works by Other Composers : A Presentation of Evidence. Cambridge, University Press, 1906.

Teneo, Martial. "Les Chefs-d'œuvre du chevalier Gluck à l'Opéra de Paris," RHCM VIII (1908) 109–16.

—— "La Détresse de Niccola Piccinni," RHCM VIII (1908) 237–44, 279–81.

—— "Un Spectacle à la cour en 1763," MM I (1905) 480–86.

Tenschert, Roland. Christoph Willibald Gluck, der grosse Reformator der Oper. Olten & Freiburg i Br., O. Walter AG., [1951].

—— Mozart : Ein Leben für die Oper. Vienna, Frick, 1941.

—— "Die Ouvertüren Mozarts," Mozart-Jahrbuch II (1924).

Terry, Charles Stanford. Johann Christian Bach. London, Oxford University Press, 1929.

Theater-Kalendar auf das Jahr . . . (Reichard). Gotha, Vols. 1–25, 1775–1800.

Thouret, Georg. "Einzug der Musen und Grazien in die Mark," Hohenzollern-Jahrbuch IV (1900) 192–230.

Thrane, Carl. "Sarti in Kopenhagen," SIMG III (1901–2) 528–38.

Tibaldi Chiesa, Mary. Cimarosa e il suo tempo. [Milan], A. Garzanti, [1939].

Tiersot, Julien. "Etude sur Don Juan de Mozart," Le Ménestrel LXII (1896) 399–411 passim; LXIII (1897) 1–139 passim.

—— "Etude sur Orphée de Gluck," Le Ménestrel LXII (1896) 273–386 passim.

—— "Gluck and the Encyclopædists," MQ XVI (1930) 336–57.

—— Histoire de la chanson populaire en France. Paris, Plon, Nourrit, 1889.

—— Jean-Jacques Rousseau. Paris, Alcan, 1912.

—— "La Musique de J.-J. Rousseau," MM VIII, No. 6 (1912) 34–56.

—— "Rameau," MQ XIV (1928) 77–107.

—— "L'ultima opera di Gluck, Eco e Narciso," RMI IX (1902) 264–96.

Tintori, Giampiero. L'opera napoletana. [Milan, Ricordi, 1958.]

Titon du Tillet, [Evrard]. Le Parnasse françois. Paris, J. B. Coignard, 1732–[43]. 2 vols., paged continuously.

Tommasini, Oreste. "Pietro Metastasio e lo svolgimento del melodramma italiano," in Scritti di storia e critica (Rome, E. Loescher, 1891) 153–222.

Tosi, Pietro Francesco. Opinioni de' cantori antichi, e moderni, o sieno Osservazioni sopra il canto figurato. [Bologna, L. dalla Volpe, 1723.] Translated as : Observations on the Florid Song; or, Sentiments on the Ancient and Modern Singers. London, J. Wilcox, 1742. Later English editions : 1743, 1906, 1926.

Tottmann, Albert. Mozart's Zauberflöte. Langensalza, Beyer, 1908. Makes use of C. Grüel's "Aufschlüsse über die Bedeutung des angeblich Schikanederschen Textes zu Mozart's Zauberflöte," Magdeburg, 1868.

Tovey, Donald Francis. "Christopher Willibald Gluck (1714–1787) and the Musical Revolution of the Eighteenth Century," in *The Heritage of Music*, ed. Hubert J. Foss (London, Oxford University Press, 1934) II, 69–117.

Tutenberg, Fritz. "Die *opera-buffa* Sinfonie und ihre Beziehungen zur klassischen Sinfonie," AfMw VIII (1926–27) 452–72.

"Ueber das Rezitativ," *Bibliothek der schönen Wissenschaften* XI, No. 2 (1764) 209; XII, No. 1 (1765) 1; XII, No. 2 (1765) 217.

Uffenbach, Johann Friedrich von. Pharasmen : Ein Singspiel. Berlin, O. Elsner, 1930.

Uhlenbruch, Fritz. Herforder Musikleben bis zur Mitte des 18. Jahrhunderts. Münster Dissertation, 1926.

Ujfalussy, J. "Intonation, Charakterbildung und Typengestaltung in Mozarts Werken," in *Studia musicologica* I (Budapest, Hungarian Academy of Sciences, 1961) 93–145. Originally published in Hungarian (Budapest, 1957).

Ulibishev, Aleksandr Dmitrievich. Mozart's Opern : Kritische Erläuterungen. Leipzig, B&H, 1848. Originally in French.

Ursprung, Otto. "*Celos* usw., Text von Calderón, Musik von Hidalgo,— die älteste erhaltene spanische Oper," in *Festschrift Arnold Schering* (Berlin, A. Glas, 1937) 223–40.

Valdrighi, Luigi Francesco, conte. I Bononcini da Modena. Modena. G. T. Vincenzi, 1882.

Valentin, Erich. Georg Philipp Telemann. Burg b.M., A. Hopfer, [1931].

Vallas, Léon. "Jacques-Simon Mangot," RdM V (1924) 123–26.

Van Vechten, Carl. "Notes on Gluck's *Armide*," MQ III (1917) 539–47.

Vatielli, Francesco. "Le opere comiche di G. B. Martini," RMI XL (1936) 450–76.

—— "Riflessi della lotta Gluckista in Italia," RMI XXI (1914) 639–72.

Veen, J. van der. Le Mélodrame musical de Rousseau au romantisme : Ses aspects historiques et stylistiques. The Hague, Martinus Nijhoff, 1955.

Vené, Ruggero. "The Origin of *Opera Buffa*," MQ XXI (1935) 33–38.

Verlet, Pierre. "L'Opéra de Versailles," *Revue d'histoire du théâtre* IX (1957) 133–54.

Vetter, Walther. Die Arie bei Gluck. Leipzig Dissertation, 1921.

—— "Deutschland und das Formgefühl Italiens : Betrachtungen über die Metastasianische Oper," *Deutsches Jahrbuch der Musikwissenschaft* V (1960) 7–37.

—— "Georg Christoph Wagenseil als Vorläufer . . . Glucks," ZfMw VIII (1925–26) 385–402.

—— "Gluck's Entwicklung zum Opernreformation," AfMw VI (1924) 165–212.

—— "Glucks Stellung zur tragédie lyrique und opéra comique," ZfMw VII (1924–25) 321–55.

—— "Gluck und seine italienischen Zeitgenossen," ZfMw VII (1924-25) 609-46.

—— "Italienische Opernkomponisten um Georg Christoph Wagenseil," in *Festschrift Friedrich Blume* (Kassel, Bärenreiter, 1963) [363]-374.

—— "Mozart im Weltbild Richard Wagners," in *Bericht über den internationalen musikwissenschaftlichen Kongress Wien, Mozartjahr 1956* (Graz, Böhlaus, 1958) 657-60.

—— "Stilkritische Bemerkungen zur Arienmelodik in Glucks *Orfeo*," ZfMw IV (1921-22) 27-49.

—— "Zur Entwicklungsgeschichte der opera seria um 1750 in Wien," ZfMw XIV (1931-32) 2-28.

Villarosa, Carlo Antonio de Rosa, marchese de. Memorie dei compositori di musica del regno di Napoli. Naples, Stamperia reale, 1840.

[Villeneuve, Josse de.] Lettre sur le méchanisme de l'opéra italien. Ni Guelfe, ni Gibelin; ni Wigh, ni Thoris. Paris, Duchesne; Florence and Paris, Lambert, 1756. German translation by R. Haas, ZfMw VII (1924-25) 129-63. *See also* Bédarida, Henri. "L'Opéra italien jugé par un amateur français en 1756," in *Mélanges de musicologie* (Paris, Droz, 1933) 185-200.

Viollier, Renée. "Les Divertissements de J.-J. Mouret pour la 'Comédie italienne' à Paris," RdM XXIII (1939) 65-71.

—— Jean-Joseph Mouret, le musicien des grâces, 1682-1738. Paris, Librairie Floury, 1950.

—— "Un Opéra-ballet au XVIIIe siècle : *Les Festes ou le triomphe de Thalie*," RdM XVI (1935) 78-86.

Vitale, Roberto. Domenico Cimarosa. Aversa, Noviello, 1929.

Vivaldi, Antonio; note e documenti sulla vita e sulle opere. Rome, Sansaini, 1939.

Voigt, F. A. "Reinhard Keiser," VfMw VI (1890) 151-203.

Volbach, Fritz. Die Praxis der Händel-Aufführung, 2. Theil : Das Händel-Orchester . . . I. Das Streichorchester. Charlottenburg, "Gutenberg," 1899.

Volkmann, Hans. "Domenico Terradellas," ZIMG XIII (1911-12) 306-9.

Walker, Frank. "*Orazio:* The History of a Pasticcio," MQ XXXVIII (1952) 369-83.

—— "Pergolesi Legends," MMR LXXXII (1952) 144-48, 180-83.

—— "Some Notes on the Scarlattis," MR XII (1951) 185-203.

Walter, Friedrich. Geschichte des Theaters und der Musik am kurpfälzischen Hofe. Leipzig, B&H, 1898.

Waltershausen, Hermann Wolfgang Karl Sartorius, Freiherr (von). *Die Zauberflöte:* Eine operndramaturgische Studie. Munich, H. Bruckmann, 1920.

Weckerlin, Jean Baptiste. L'Ancienne Chanson populaire en France. Paris, Garnier, 1887.

Weichlein, William J. A Comparative Study of Five Musical Settings of

Metastasio's Libretto of *La Clemenza di Tito*. Ann Arbor, University Microfilms, 1957. 2 vols.

Weil, Rudolf. Das Berliner Theaterpublikum unter A. W. Ifflands Direktion (1746–1814). Berlin, Gesellschaft für Theatergeschichte, 1932.

Wellesz, Egon. "Ein Bühnenfestspiel aus dem 17. Jahrhundert," *Die Musik* LII (1914) Qt. 4, pp. 191–217.

—— "*Don Giovanni* and the 'dramma giocoso,'" MR IV (1943) 121–26.

—— "Francesco Algarotti und seine Stellung zur Musik," SIMG XV (1913–14) 427–39.

—— "Giuseppe Bonno," SIMG XI (1909–10) 395–442.

Welti, Heinrich. "Gluck und Calsabigi," VfMw VII (1891) 26–42.

Wendschuh, Ludwig. Ueber Jos. Haydns Opern. [Halle a. S.], 1896.

Werner, Arno. "Sachsen-Thüringen in der Musikgeschichte," AfMw IV (1922) 322–35.

—— Städtische und fürstliche Musikpflege in Weissenfels bis zum Ende des 18. Jahrhunderts. Leipzig, B&H, 1911.

Werner, Eric. "Leading or Symbolic Formulas in *The Magic Flute*," MR XVIII (1957) 286–93.

Werner, Theodor Wilhelm. "Zum Neudruck von G. Ph. Telemanns *Pimpinone* in den Reichsdenkmalen," AfMf (1936) 361–65.

Westerman, Gerhart von. Giovanni Porta als Opernkomponist. Munich Dissertation, 1921.

Wiel, Taddeo. I teatri musicali di Venezia nel Settecento. Venice, Visentini, 1897.

Wieland, Christoph Martin. Sämmtliche Werke, 26. Band : Singspiele und Abhandlungen. Leipzig, G. J. Göschen, 1796. Contains : "Versuch über das Deutsche Singspiel" (pp. 229–67, 323–42); "Ueber einige ältere Deutsche Singspiele, die den Nahmen Alceste führen" (pp. 269–320).

Winckelmann, Johann Joachim. Sämtliche Werke. Donauöschingen, Im Verlage deutscher Classiker, 1825–29. 12 vols. Contains "Gedanken über die Nachahmung der griechischen Werke in der Malerei und Bildhauerkunst," I, 1–58; "Geschichte der Kunst des Alterthums," III–VI.

Winesanker, Michael. "Musico-Dramatic Criticism of English Comic Opera, 1750–1800," JAMS II (1949) 87–96.

—— The Record of English Musical Drama, 1750–1800. Cornell Dissertation, 1944.

Winterfeld, Carl von. *Alceste*, 1674, 1726, 1769, 1776, von Lulli, Händel und Gluck. Berlin, Bote & Bock, 1851.

Wirth, Helmut. "Johann Christian (Jean Chrétien) Bach," RIdM n.s. No. 8 (Autumn, 1950) 133–42.

—— Joseph Haydn als Dramatiker. Wolfenbüttel, Kallmeyer, 1940.

—— "The Operas of Joseph Haydn before *Orfeo*," in *Joseph Haydn, Orfeo ed Euridice ... Analytical Notes* (Boston, Haydn Society, [1951]) 12–48.

Wörner, Karl. "Die Pflege Glucks an der Berliner Oper von 1795–1841," ZfMw XIII (1930–31) 206–16.

Wolff, Hellmuth Christian. *Agrippina:* Eine italienische Jugendoper von Georg Friedrich Händel. Wolfenbüttel, Kallmeyer, 1943.

—— Die Händel-Oper auf der modernen Bühne : Ein Beitrag zu Geschichte und Praxis der Opern-Bearbeitung und -Inszenierung in der Zeit von 1920 bis 1956. Leipzig, Deutscher Verlag für Musik, 1957.

Wolzogen, Alfred von. Ueber die scenische Darstellung von Mozart's *Don Giovanni.* Breslau, Leuckart, 1860.

Wortsmann, Stephan. Die deutsche Gluckliteratur. Nuremberg, Karl Koch, 1914.

Wotquenne, Alfred. Alphabetisches Verzeichnis der Stücke in Versen aus den dramatischen Werken von Zeno, Metastasio und Goldoni. Leipzig, B&H, 1905.

—— "Baldassare Galuppi (1706–1785) : Etude bibliographique sur ses œuvres dramatiques," RMI VI (1899) 561–79.

—— Catalogue thématique des œuvres de Chr. W. v. Gluck. Leipzig, B&H, 1904. Ergänzung und Nachträge . . . Leipzig, Reinecke, 1911, ed. by Josef Liebeskind. "Ergänzungen und Berichtigungen," *Die Musik* XIII (1913–14), Qt. 1, 288–89, by Max Arend.

Wright, Edward. Some Observations Made in Travelling through France, Italy &c in the Years 1720, 1721, and 1722. London, T. Ward and E. Wicksteed, 1730. 2 vols.

Wyndham, Henry Saxe. The Annals of Covent Garden Theatre from 1732–1897. London, Chatto & Windus, 1906. 2 vols.

Wyzewa, Teodor de. W. A. Mozart : Sa vie musicale et son œuvre de l'enfance à la pleine maturité. Paris, Desclée, [1937]. G. de Saint-Foix is joint author of Vols. I and II and sole author of Vol. III.

Wyzewa, Teodor de, and Georges de Saint-Foix. W.-A. Mozart, sa vie musicale et son œuvre. Paris, Desclée, de Brouwer et Cie., 1912–46. 5 vols.

Yorke-Long, Alan. Music at Court : Four Eighteenth-Century Studies. London, Weidenfeld & Nicolson, [1954].

Zabala, Arturo. La opera en la vida valenciana del siglo XVIII. Valencia, Instituto de literatura y estudios filológicos, 1960.

Zeller, Bernhard. Das recitativo accompagnato in den Opern Johann Adolf Hasses. Halle a. S., Hohmann, 1911.

Zelter, Carl Friedrich. "Ein Aufsatz . . . über Georg Benda und seine Oper *Romeo und Julie,*" AMZ XIV (1879) 645–49.

Zeno, Apostolo. Lettere. Venice, F. Sansoni, 1785. 6 vols.

—— Poesie drammatiche. Orleans, Couret de Villeneuve, 1785–86. 11 vols.

[Zille, Moritz Alexander.] *Die Zauberflöte:* Text-Erläuterung für alle Verehrer Mozarts. Leipzig, T. Lissner, 1866.

Zingerle, Hans. "Musik- und Textform in Opernarien Mozarts," *Mozart-Jahrbuch 1953* (1954) 112–15.

Zuckerkandel, Viktor. Prinzipien und Methoden der Instrumentation in Mozarts dramatischen Werken. Vienna Dissertation, 1927.

V

NINETEENTH CENTURY

A. GENERAL

Abbiati, Franco. Giuseppe Verdi. Milan, Ricordi, 1959. 4 vols.

Abert, Hermann. "Robert Schumann's *Genoveva*," ZIMG XI (1909–10) 277–89.

Abraham, Gerald. "The Best of Spontini," M&L XXIII (1942) 163–71.

—— "*The Flying Dutchman:* Original Version," M&L XX (1939) 412–19.

—— A Hundred Years of Music. London, Duckworth, 1949. 2d ed.

—— "The Leitmotif since Wagner," M&L VI (1925) 175–90.

—— "Nietzsche's Attitude to Wagner: A Fresh View," M&L XIII (1932) 64–74.

—— "Weber as Novelist and Critic," MQ XX (1934) 27–38.

Abraham, Gerald, ed. The Music of Schubert. New York, W. W. Norton, 1947.

—— Schumann: A Symposium. London, New York, Toronto, Oxford University Press, 1952.

Adam, Adolphe. Derniers souvenirs d'un musicien. Paris, Michel Levy frères, 1859.

—— Souvenirs d'un musicien . . . précédés de notes biographiques écrites par lui-même. Paris, Calmann-Lévy, 1884.

Adami, Giuseppe. Il romanzo della vita di Giacomo Puccini. Milan-Rome, Rizzoli, 1944. 3d ed.

Adler, Guido. "*Euryanthe* in neuer Einrichtung [von Gustav Mahler]," ZIMG V (1903–4) 269–75.

—— Richard Wagner, Vorlesungen gehalten an der Universität zu Wien. Munich, Drei Masken Verlag, 1923. 2d ed. (first publ. 1904).

Adorno, Theodor Wiesengrund. Versuch über Wagner. Berlin & Frankfurt/M., Suhrkamp, [1952].

Alberti, C. E. R. Ludwig van Beethoven als dramatischer Tondichter. Stettin, 1859.

Almanach des Spectacles. Paris, Nos. 1–43, 1874–1913.

Altmann, Wilhelm. "Lortzing als dramaturgischer Lehrer," *Die Musik* XIII (1913–14) Qt. 4, 157–58.

—— "Meyerbeer-Forschungen: Archivalische Beiträge aus der Registratur der Generalintendantur der Königlichen Schauspiele zu Berlin," SIMG IV (1902–3) 519–34.

—— "Spontini an der Berliner Oper : Eine archivalische Studie," SIMG IV (1902–3) 244–92.

Amico, Tomasino d'. Francesco Cilèa. Milan, Curci, [1960].

Anheisser, Siegfried. "Das Vorspiel zu *Tristan und Isolde* und seine Motivik," ZfMw III (1921) 257–304.

Annen, Josef. Le versioni italiane rappresentate delle opere di Riccardo Wagner. Muralto-Locarno, Tipografia Moderna Pax, [1943].

Antonini, G. "Un episodio emotivo di Gaetano Donizetti," RMI VII (1900) 518–35.

Appia, Adolphe. La Mise en scène du drame Wagnérien. Paris, L. Chailley, 1895.

Arnaudiès, Fernand. Histoire de l'opéra d'Alger : Episodes de la vie théâtrale algéroise, 1830–1940. Algiers, V. Heintz, [1941].

Atti del primo Congresso Internazionale di Studi Spontiniani. Jesi-Maiolati-Fabriano-Ancona, 6–9 settembre 1951. Relazioni, communicazioni, verbali. Fabriano, Arti Grafiche "Gentile," 1954.

Augé de Lassus, Lucien. Boieldieu . . . : Biographie critique illustrée. Paris, H. Laurens, [1908].

Augé-Laribé, Michel. Messager, musicien de théâtre. Paris, La Colombe, [1951].

Bacchelli, Riccardo. Rossini e esperienze rossiniane. Milan, Mondadori, 1959.

Bätz, Rüdiger. Schauspielmusiken zu Goethes *Faust*. Leipzig Dissertation, 1924.

Bagge, Selmar. "Robert Schumann und seine *Faust*-Scenen," in Waldersee, *Sammlung musikalischer Vorträge* (Leipzig, Graf, 1879) I, 121–40.

Baily, Leslie. The Gilbert & Sullivan Book. London, Cassell & Co., 1956; New York, Coward-McCann, 1957. Revised ed.

"Le Ballet au XIXe siècle," RM II (December, 1921; numéro special) 97–231.

Ballo, Ferdinando. Arrigo Boito. Turin, Edizioni Arione, [1938].

Barblan, Guglielmo. L'opera di Donizetti nell' età romantica. Bergamo, Edizione del Centenario a cura della Banca Mutua Popolare, 1948.

Bardi-Poswiansky, Benno. Flotow als Opernkomponist. Königsberg Dissertation, 1924.

Barford, Peter T. "The Way of Unity : A Study of *Tristan und Isolde*," MR XX (1959) 253–63.

Barini, Giorgio. "Noterelle Belliniane," RMI IX (1902) 62–71.

Barraud, Henry. Hector Berlioz. [Paris], Costard, [1955].

Barrett, William. Balfe : His Life and Work. London, Remington, 1882.

Barricelli, Jean-Pierre, and Leo Weinstein. Ernest Chausson : The Composer's Life and Works. Norman, University of Oklahoma Press, [1955].

Barry, C. A. "Introductory to the Study of Wagner's Comic Opera *Die Meistersinger von Nürnberg*," PMA VII (March 7, 1881) 74–97.

Barzun, Jacques. Berlioz and the Romantic Century. Boston, Little, Brown, 1950. 2 vols.
—— Darwin, Marx, Wagner : Critique of a Heritage. Boston, Little, Brown, 1941. 2d ed. : Garden City, N.Y., Doubleday & Co., 1958.
Batka, Richard. Die alt-italienische Aria : Ida Isori und ihre Kunst des Bel-Canto. Vienna, H. Heller, 1912.
—— Die moderne Oper. Prague, Verlag der Lese- und Redehalle der deutschen Studenten in Prag, 1902.
Bauer, Anton. 150 Jahre Theater an der Wien. Leipzig, Vienna, Amalthea-Verlag, [1952].
Baumann, Ken C. The Change of Style in Verdi's Operatic Work in the Interlude between Aida and Otello. Cornell A.M. Thesis, 1945.
Beaufils, Marcel. Wagner et le wagnérisme. Paris, Ed. Aubier, 1946.
Becker, Heinz. Der Fall Heine-Meyerbeer : neue Dokumente revidieren ein Geschichtsurteil. Berlin, W. de Gruyter, 1958.
—— "Meyerbeers Beziehungen zu Louis Spohr," Mf X (1957) 479–86.
—— "Meyerbeers Ergänzungsarbeit an Webers nachgelassener Oper Die drei Pintos," Mf VII (1954) 300–12.
Becker, Heinz, ed. See Meyerbeer.
Becker, Marta. "Der Einfluss der Philosophie Schellings auf Richard Wagner," ZfMw XIX (1931–32) 433–47.
Beckers, Paul. Die nachwagner'sche Oper bis zum Ausgang des 19. Jahrhunderts im Spiegel der Münchener Presse. Bielefeld, Beyer & Hausknecht, 1936.
Beethoven, Ludwig van. Ludwig van Beethoven : Ein Bekenntnis mit Briefen und Zeitdocumenten. [Hrsg. von Heinz Freiberger.] [Berlin], Verlag der Nation, [1951].
Beetz, Wilhelm. Das Wiener Opernhaus 1869 bis 1945. [Zurich], The Central European Times Verlag, [1949].
Bekker, Paul. Wagner : Das Leben im Werke. Stuttgart, Deutsche Verlags-Anstalt, 1924. Translated as : Richard Wagner : His Life in His Works. New York, W. W. Norton, [1931].
Belardinelli, Alessandro, ed. Documenti Spontiniani inedite. Raccolti, tradotti e annotati. Florence, Ed. Sansoni Antiquariato, 1955. 2 vols.
Bellaigue, Camille. "Les Epoques de la musique: Le grand opéra français," Revue des deux mondes (1906) No. 5, 612–49.
Bellasis, Edward. Cherubini : Memorials Illustrative of His Life. London, Burns & Oates, 1874.
Bellini, Vincenzo. Epistolario, a cura di Luisa Cambi. Verona, Mondadori, 1943.
Berl, Paul. Die Opern Giuseppe Verdis in ihrer Instrumentation. Vienna Dissertation, 1931.
Berlioz, Hector. A Travers Chants : Etudes musicales. Paris, Michel Lévy, 1872. 2d ed.
—— Les Grotesques de la musique. Paris, A. Bourdilliat, 1854.

—— Mémoires. Paris, Michel Lévy, 1870. Translated as : Memoirs of Hector Berlioz. New York, Tudor, [1935]. Annotated and the translation revised by Ernest Newman.

—— Les Musiciens et la musique. Paris, Calmann-Lévy, [1903]. A selection of articles from the *Journal des débats*, 1835–63.

—— New Letters of Berlioz, 1830–1868. With Introduction, Notes and English Translation by Jacques Barzun. New York, Columbia University Press, 1954.

—— Les Soirées de l'orchestre. Paris, Michel Lévy, 1852. Translated as : Evenings in the Orchestra. New York and London, Alfred A. Knopf, 1924.

Besch, Otto. Engelbert Humperdinck. Leipzig, B&H, 1914.

Beyle, Henri. Vie de Rossini, suivi des notes d'un dilettante. Paris, E. Champion, 1922. Preface and annotations by Henry Prunières. Translated as : Memoirs of Rossini. London, T. Hookham, 1824.

Biedenfeld, [Ferdinand, Freiherr von]. Die komische Oper der Italiener, der Franzosen und der Deutschen. Leipzig, Weigl, 1848.

Bienenfeld, Elso. "Verdi and Schiller," MQ XVII (1931) 204–8.

Billeci, A. *La Bohème* di Giacomo Puccini : Studio critico. Palermo, Vesca, 1931.

Bitter, K[arl] H[ermann]. Die Reform der Oper durch Gluck und R. Wagner's Kunstwerk der Zukunft. Brunswick, F. Vieweg, 1884. Critical review by H. Kretzschmar, VfMw I (1885) 227–34.

[Bizet, Georges.] *See* RdM XXII (November, 1938), special number devoted to Bizet.

Bizet, René. Une Heure de musique avec Oscar Straus. Paris, Editions cosmopolites, 1930.

Blum, Klaus. "Bemerkungen Anton Reichas zur Aufführungspraxis der Oper," Mf VII (1954) 429–40.

Bohe, Walter. Die Wiener Presse in der Kriegszeit der Oper. Würzburg, Triltsch, 1933. Published also with the title : Wagner im Spiegel der Wiener Presse.

Boïto, Arrigo. Lettere. Rome, Società editrice "Novissima," [1932].

—— "Pensieri critici giovanili," RMI XXXI (1924) 161–98.

—— Tutti gli scritti, a curo di Piero Nardi. [Milan], A. Mondadori, [1942].

Bollert, Werner. "Hugo Wolfs *Corregidor*," *Musica* XIV (1960) 143–47.

Bonaccorsi, Alfredo. Giacomo Puccini e i suoi antenati musicali. Milan, Curci, [1950].

—— "La sinfonia del *Barbiere* prima del *Barbiere*," RassM XXIV (1954) 210–19.

Bonafé, Félix. Rossini et son oeuvre. [Conférence prononcée à la Fondation Rossini, à Paris, le 25 juin 1955.] Le Puy-en-Velay, Editions la Main de Bronze, 1955.

Bonaventura, Arnaldo. Giacomo Puccini. Leghorn, [1925].

—— Verdi. Paris, F. Alcan, 1923.

Bonavia, Ferrucio. Verdi. London, Oxford University Press, 1930.

Bonnefon, Paul. "Les Métamorphoses d'un opéra (lettres inédites d'Eugène Scribe)," *Revue des deux mondes* (1917) No. 5, 877–99.

Boromé, Joseph A. "Bellini and *Beatrice di Tenda*," M&L XLII (1961) 319–35.

Borrelli, E. "Il Wort-Ton-Drama," RassM VII (1934) 333–43, 433–36.

Borren, Charles van den. L'Oeuvre dramatique de César Franck : *Hulda et Ghiselle*. Brussels, Schott Frères, 1907.

Borriello, A. Mito, poesia e musica nel *Mefistofele* di Arrigo Boito, con prefazione di V. Gui. Naples, Guida, [1950].

Boschot, Adolphe. "A propos du centenaire de *La Damnation de Faust*," RM XXII (February–March, 1946) 11–14.

—— Le Faust de Berlioz : Etude sur la *Damnation de Faust* et sur l'âme romantique. Paris, Librairie Plon, 1945.

—— Hector Berlioz, une vie romantique. Paris, Plon, [1951]. Edition définitive.

—— L'Histoire d'un romantique : Hector Berlioz. I. La Jeunesse d'un romantique . . . 1803–1831. Paris, Plon-Nourrit, 1906. New ed., rev. et cor. [1946]. II. Un Romantique sous Louis-Philippe . . . 1831–1842. Paris, Plon-Nourrit, 1908. Ed. rev. et cor. 1948. III. Le Crépuscule d'un romantique . . . 1842–1869. Paris, Plon-Nourrit, 1913. Ed. rev. et cor. [1950].

—— "Sur Gluck et Wagner," *Revue politique et littéraire* XXXVII (1900) 19–23.

—— La Vie et les œuvres de Alfred Bruneau. Paris, Fasquelle, [1937].

Bossi, Lea. Donizetti. Brescia, Ed. La Scuola, 1956.

Botti, Ferruccio. Giuseppe Verdi. Alba, Istituto Missionario Pia Società S. Paolo, [1941].

Boucher, Maurice. Les Idées politiques de Richard Wagner. Paris, Aubier, 1948. Translated as : The Political Concepts of Richard Wagner. New York, M & H Publications, [1950].

Bouvet, Charles. Spontini. Paris, Rieder, [1930].

Brancour, René. Félicien David. Paris, H. Laurens, [190–].

—— Méhul. Paris, H. Laurens, [1912].

Braunstein, Josef. Beethovens Leonore-Ouvertüren : Eine historisch-stilkritische Untersuchung. Leipzig, B&H, 1927.

—— "Gibt es zwei Fassungen von der Ouvertüre Leonore Nr. 2?" ZfMw IX (1926–27) 349–60.

Brenon, Algernon. "Giuseppe Verdi," MQ II (1916) 130–62.

Bréville, Pierre de, and H. Gauthier-Villars. *Fervaal:* Etude thématique et analytique. Paris, A. Durand, 1897.

Brindejont-Offenbach, Jacques. Offenbach, mon grand-père. Paris, Plon, 1940.

Brion, Marcel. Schumann et l'âme romantique. Paris, A. Michel, [1954].

Brockt, Johannes. "Verdi's Operatic Choruses," M&L XX (1939) 309–12.

Brown, Maurice J. E. Schubert: A Critical Biography. London, Macmillan & Co.; New York, St. Martin's Press, 1958.

Bruneau, Alfred. Massenet. Paris, Delagrave, 1934.

—— Musiques d'hier et de demain. Paris, Bibliothèque Charpentier, 1900.

Brunswick, Mark. "Beethoven's Tribute to Mozart in Fidelio," MQ XXXI (1945) 29–32.

Brusa, Filippo. "Il Nerone di Arrigo Boito," RMI XXXI (1924) 392–443.

Burgmüller, Herbert. Die Musen darben: Ein Lebensbild Albert Lortzings. Düsseldorf, Progress-Verlag, [1956].

Buschkötter, Wilhelm. "Jean François Le Sueur: Eine Biographie," SIMG XIV (1912–13) 58–154.

Bustico, Guido. "Un librettista antiromantico (Angelo Anelli)," RMI XXVIII (1921) 53–81.

—— "Saggio di una bibliografia di libretti musicali di Felice Romani," RMI XIV (1907) 229–84.

—— "Saverio Mercadante a Novara," RMI XXVIII (1921) 361–96.

Butler, E. M. The Fortunes of Faust. Cambridge, The University Press, 1952.

Calvocoressi, Michel D. Vincent d'Indy, L'Etranger: Le poème, analyse thématique de la partition. Paris, Editions du Courrier musical, [1903].

Cametti, Alberto. "Donizetti a Roma: Con lettere e documenti inediti," RMI XI (1904) 761–88; XII (1905) 1–39, 515–54, 689–713; XIII (1906) 50–90, 522–45, 616–55; XIV (1907) 301–32.

—— "Il Guglielmo Tell e le sue prime rappresentazioni in Italia," RMI VI (1899) 580–92.

—— La musica teatrale a Roma cento anni fa: Il Corsaro di Pacini. Rome, Mezzetti, 1931.

—— La musica teatrale a Roma cento anni fa: Olivo e Pasquale di Donizetti. Rome, A. Manuzio, 1928.

—— Un poeta melodrammatico romano . . . Jacopo Ferretti. Milan, Ricordi, [1898].

Cantillon, Arthur. Essai sur les symboles de la tétralogie wagnerienne. Mons, Imprimerie générale, 1911.

Canudo, Ricciotto. "L'Esthétique de Verdi et la culture musicale italienne," MM III (1907) 719–37.

Capri, Antonio. Musica e musicisti d'Europa dal 1800 al 1938. Milan, Hoepli, 1939. 2d ed.

—— Verdi, uomo e artista. Milan, Ed. ufficio concerti, 1939.

Carlez, Jules. Catel. Caen, H. Delesques, 1894.

—— Grimm et la musique de son temps. Caen, Le Blanc-Hardel, 1872.

—— L'Œuvre d'Auber. Caen, Le Blanc-Hardel, 1874.

—— Pacini et l'opéra italien. Caen, H. Delesques, 1888.

Carlyle, Thomas. "The Opera," in Critical and Miscellaneous Essays (New York, Scribner, 1904) IV, 397–403.

Carner, Mosco. "The Exotic Element in Puccini," MQ XXII (1936) 45–67.

—— Puccini: A Critical Biography. London, Duckworth, 1958; New York, Alfred A. Knopf, 1959.

—— "Puccini's Early Operas," M&L XIX (1938) 295–307.

Cattini, Umberto. "Note sul *Roberto Devereux* de Gaetano Donizetti," *Ricordiana* III (1957) 478–88.

Cauchie, Maurice. "The High Lights of French *Opéra Comique*," MQ XXV (1939) 306–12.

Cellamare, Daniele. Mascagni e la *Cavalleria* visti da Cerignola. Rome, Filli Palombi, 1941.

—— Umberto Giordano: La vita e le opere. [Milan], Garzanti, [1949].

Cenzato, Giovanni. Itinerari verdiani: La semplicità di una vita grande di opere, luminosa di gloria. Milan, Casa Editrice Ceschina, [1955]. 2d ed.

Chamberlain, Houston Stewart. Das Drama Richard Wagners. Leipzig, B&H, 1921. 6th ed. First published 1892. Translated as: The Wagnerian Drama. London and New York, John Lane, 1915.

—— Die Grundlagen des neunzehnten Jahrhunderts. Munich, F. Bruckmann, 1912. 10th ed. First published 1900. Translated as: Foundations of the Nineteenth Century. Munich, F. Bruckmann, 1911.

—— Richard Wagner. Munich, F. Bruckmann, [1936]. 9th ed. First published 1896. English translation: London, Dent, 1900.

Chantavoine, Jean. Camille Saint-Saëns. Paris, Richard-Masse, 1947.

Chantavoine, Jean, and Jean Gaudefroy-Demombynes. Le Romantisme dans la musique européenne. Paris, A. Michel, 1955.

Cherbuliez, Antoine Elisée Adolphe. Giuseppe Verdi: Leben und Werk. Rüschliken-Zurich, Albert Müller Verlag, 1949.

Chop, Max. August Bungert. Leipzig, H. Seemann Nachfolger, 1903.

—— E. N. v. Reznicek. Vienna, Leipzig, Universal-Edition, [1920].

Chorley, Henry F. Music and Manners in France and Germany. London, Longmans, 1844.

—— Thirty Years' Musical Recollections. New York, Alfred A. Knopf, 1926.

Chrysander, Friedrich. "Spontini nach Mitteilungen von Caroline Bauer und H. Marschner," AMZ XIV (1879) 259–64, 274–80, 289–93.

—— ". . . über Wagners Tannhäuser," ZIMG V (1903–4) 208–19.

Cinquante Ans de musique française de 1874 à 1925. Paris, Librairie de France, [1925]. Ed. by L. Rohozinski.

Coeuroy, André. La *Tosca* de Puccini. Paris, Mellottée, [1922?].

—— "Wagner et le ballet," RM II (December, 1921) 206–13.

—— Weber. Paris, Denoël, 1953. New ed.

Collet, Henri. Samson et Dalila de C. Saint-Saëns. Paris, Mellottée, [1922].

Colling, Alfred. César Franck, ou le concert spirituel. Paris, R. Julliard, [1951].

Colombani, A. L'opera italiana nel secolo XIX. Milan, Ed. Corriere della Sera, 1900.

Colson, J. B. Manuel dramatique. Bordeaux, chez l'auteur, 1817.

Commons, Jeremy. "[Donizetti's] *Emilia di Liverpool*," M&L XL (1959) 207–28.

Cone, Edward T. "The Old Man's Toys : Verdi's Last Operas," *Perspectives USA*, No. 6 (Winter, 1954) 114–33.

Confalonieri, Giulio. Prigionia di un artista. (Il romanzo di Luigi Cherubini.) [Milan], Genio, [1948]. 2 vols.

Cooley, William Julius, Jr. Music in the Life and Works of Franz Grillparzer. Ann Arbor, University Microfilms, 1954.

Cooper, Martin. "Charles Gounod and His Influence on French Music," M&L XXI (1940) 50–59.

—— French Music : From the Death of Berlioz to the Death of Fauré. London, Oxford University Press, 1951.

—— Georges Bizet. London and New York, Oxford University Press, 1938.

Cornelissen, Thilo. C. M. v. Webers *Freischütz* als Beispiel einer Opernbehandlung. Berlin, Matthiesen, 1940.

Cornelius, Carl Maria. Peter Cornelius, der Wort- und Tondichter. Regensburg, G. Bosse, [1925].

Cornelius, Peter. Literarische Werke. Leipzig, B&H, 1904–5. 4 vols.

Cornet, J. Die Oper in Deutschland und das Theater der Neuzeit. Hamburg, O. Meissner, 1849.

Cortolezis, Fritz. "Gedanken über eine stilgerechte Aufführung des *Fidelio*," *Neues Beethoven Jahrbuch* III (1926) 93–102.

Costa, Alessandro. "Schopenhauer e Wagner," RMI XXXIX (1932) 1–12.

Crosten, William L. French Grand Opera : An Art and a Business. New York, King's Crown Press, 1948.

Curtiss, Mina. Bizet and His World. New York, Alfred A. Knopf, 1958.

—— "Fromental Halévy," MQ XXXIX (1953) 196–214.

—— "Gounod Before *Faust*," MQ XXXVIII (1952) 48–67.

—— "Unpublished Letters by Georges Bizet," MQ XXXVI (1950) 375–409.

Curzon, Henri de. Ernest Reyer. Paris, Perrin, 1924.

—— La Légende de Sigurd. Paris, Fischbacher, [1889].

—— Léo Delibes, Paris, G. Legouix, 1926.

—— "L'Opéra en 1843 : Mémoire du directeur Léon Pillet," RdM II (1920–21) 223–33.

—— "Les Opéras-comiques de Boieldieu," RM XIV (November, 1933) 249–63.

Czech, Stan. Franz Lehár : Weg und Werk. Berlin, Werk-Verlag, 1942.

—— Schön ist die Welt : Franz Lehárs Leben und Werk. Berlin, Argon-Verlag, [1957].

Daffner, Hugo. Friedrich Nietzsches Rundglossen zu Bizets *Carmen*. Regensburg, Bosse. 1938.

Damerini, Adelmo. Amilcare Ponchielli. Turin, Edizioni Arione, [1940].

Dandelot, Arthur. Evolution de la musique de théâtre depuis Meyerbeer jusqu'à nos jours. Paris, Flammarion, 1927.

Daninger, Josef G. Sage und Märchen im Musikdrama : Eine ästhetische Untersuchung an der Sagen- und Märchenoper des 19. Jahrhunderts. Prague, Hoffmanns Witwe, 1916.

Daube, Otto. Siegfried Wagner und die Märchenoper. Leipzig, Deutscher Theater-Verlag, M. Schleppegrell, [1936].

Dauriac, Lionel. "Herbert Spencer et Meyerbeer," ZIMG V (1903–4) 103–9.

—— Meyerbeer. Paris, Alcan, 1913.

—— "Un Problème d'esthétique Wagnérienne," MM IV (1908) 50–55.

Dean, Winton. Bizet. London, J. M. Dent & Sons, Ltd., 1948.

—— "Bizet's Self-Borrowings," M&L XLI (1960) 238–44.

—— "*Carmen:* An Attempt at a True Evaluation," MR VII (1946) 209–20.

—— "An Unfinished Opera by Bizet," M&L XXVIII (1947) 347–63.

De Angelis, Alberto. "Cantanti italiani del secolo XIX : Erminia e Giuseppe Frezzolini," RMI XXXII (1925) 438–54.

Decaux, Alain. Offenbach, roi du second empire. [Paris], P. Amiot, [1958].

Decsey, Ernst. Franz Lehár. Munich, Drei Masken-Verlag, 1930. 2d ed.

—— Hugo Wolf. Berlin, Schuster & Loeffler, [1919]. 3d–6th ed., revised.

—— Johann Strauss. Stuttgart, Berlin, Deutsche Verlags-Anstalt, 1922.

—— Johann Strauss : Ein wiener Buch. Vienna, Paul Neff Verlag, 1948.

De Donno, Alfredo. Mascagni nel 900 musicale. Rome, Casa del libro, [1935].

—— Modernità di Mascagni. Rome, Pinciana, 1931.

De Eisner-Eisenhof, A. "Giuseppe Weigl : Una biografia," RMI XI (1904) 459–83.

Della Corte, Andrea. "La drammaturgia nella *Semiramide* di Rossini," RassM XI (1938) 1–6.

—— Un Italiano all' estero, Antonio Salieri. Turin, G. B. Paravia, [1936].

Delmas, Marc. Gustave Charpentier et le lyrisme français. Paris, Delagrave, 1931.

Demuth, Norman. César Franck. London, Dennis Dobson Ltd.; New York, Philosophical Library, 1949.

De Napoli, Giuseppe de. Amilcare Ponchielli (1834–1886) : La vita, le opera, l'epistolario . . . Cremona, Società Editoriale "Cremona Nuova," 1936.

—— La triade melodrammatica altamurana : Giacomo Tritto, 1733–1824; Vincenzo Lavigna, 1776–1836; Saverio Mercadante, 1795–1870. Milan, Rosio e Fabe, 1932.

Dent, Edward J. "A Best-Seller in Opera [Flotow's *Martha*]," M&L XXII (1941) 139–54.

—— "Italian Opera in London," PMA LXXI (1944–45) 19–42.

—— The Rise of the Romantic Opera. (The Messenger Lectures at Cornell University, 1937–38.) Typescript, 256 pp.

—— "The Romantic Spirit in Music," PMA LIX (1932–33) 85–102.

—— "Translating *Trovatore*," M&L XX (1939) 7–20.

De Rensis, Raffaello. Primo Riccitelli : *I compagnacci;* guida attraverso la commedia e la musica. Milan, Bottega di poesia, 1923.

Destranges, Etienne. *Le Chant de la cloche*, de Vincent d'Indy : Etude analytique. Paris, Tresse et Stock, 1890.

—— *L'Etranger* de M. Vincent d'Indy : Etude analytique et thématique. Paris, Fischbacher, 1904.

—— L'Evolution musicale chez Verdi : *Aida—Othello—Falstaff*. Paris, Fischbacher, 1895.

—— *Fervaal* de Vincent d'Indy : Etude thématique et analytique. Paris, A. Durand, 1896.

—— *Messidor* d'A. Bruneau : Etude analytique et critique. Paris, Fischbacher, 1897.

—— L'Œuvre théâtral de Meyerbeer : Etude critique. Paris, Fischbacher, 1893.

—— *L'Ouragan* d'Alfred Bruneau : Etude analytique et thématique. Paris, Fischbacher, 1902.

—— *Le Rêve* d'Alfred Bruneau : Etude thématique et analytique. Paris, Fischbacher, 1896.

Deutsch, Otto Erich. "*Hoffmann* in Wien," OeM XIII (1958) 16–20.

—— Schubert, a Documentary Biography. Translated by Eric Blom. London, J. M. Dent & Sons, [n.d.].

—— Schubert : Thematic Catalogue of All His Works. New York, W. W. Norton, [1950].

Dickinson, Alan Edgar Frederic. "Berlioz and *The Trojans*. Part I : Forward from Beethoven," *Tempo*, No. 48 (Summer, 1958) 24–28.

—— The Musical Design of *The Ring*. London, Oxford University Press, 1926.

—— "The Structural Methods of *The Ring*," MMR LXXXIV (1954) 87–92, 124–29.

Donati Petteni, Giuliano. Donizetti. Milan, Fratelli Treves, 1930.

Donington, Robert. Wagner's *Ring* and Its Symbols : The Music and the Myth. London, Faber & Faber, [1963].

Dorn, Heinrich. Aus meinem Leben. Berlin, B. Behr, 1870–86. 7 vols.

—— Gesetzgebung und Operntext (eine Schrift für Männer) : Zeitgemässe Betrachtungen. Berlin, Schlesinger, 1879.

Dünnebeil, Hans, ed. Carl Maria von Weber, ein Brevier. Berlin, AFAS-Musikverlag, 1949.

Dünnebeil, Hans, ed. Schrifttum über Carl Maria von Weber mit Schall-plattenverzeichnis. Berlin, Bote und Bock, 1957. 4th ed.

Dufrane, Louis. Gossec. Paris, Fischbacher, 1927.

Duhamel, Raoul. "Eugène Delacroix et la musique," RMI XLIII (1939) 35–54, 333–56.

—— "Ferdinand Herold," RM XIV (November, 1933) 278–90.

—— "Quelques Maîtres de l'opéra-comique au XIXe siècle," RM XIV (November, 1933) 291–302.

Du Moulin-Eckart, Richard Maria Ferdinand. Wahnfried. Leipzig, Kist-ner & Siegel, 1925.

Dunhill, Thomas F. Sullivan's Comic Operas : A Critical Appreciation. New York, Oxford University Press; London, Edw. Arnold, 1928.

Du Tillet, Jacques. "A propos du drame lyrique : Une lettre de M. Camille Saint-Saëns," Revue politique et littéraire (July 3, 1897) 27–30.

Edwards, Henry Sutherland. The Life of Rossini. London, Hurst & Blackett, 1869.

—— Rossini and His School. New York, Scribner & Welford, 1881.

Egert, Paul. Peter Cornelius. Berlin, B. Hahnefeld, [ca. 1940].

Ehinger, Hans. E. T. A. Hoffmann als Musiker und Musikschriftsteller. Olten & Cologne, Walter, [1954].

Ehrenhaus, Martin. Die Operndichtung der deutschen Romantik : Ein Beitrag zur Geschichte der deutschen Oper. Einleitung und I. Teil. Bres-lau, F. Hirt, 1911.

Ehrhard, Auguste. "La Danse à l'opéra en 1834 : Les débuts de Fanny Elssler," Bulletin de la société des amis de l'université de Lyon XIX (1906) 61–81.

Einstein, Alfred. Music in the Romantic Era. New York, W.W. Norton, 1947.

—— "Richard Wagners Liebesverbot: Zur Aufführung am Münchner National-Theater (24. März 1923)," ZfMw V (1922–23) 382–86.

—— "Vincenzo Bellini," M&L XVI (1935) 325–32.

Ellis, William Ashton. "Cyrill Kistner and Kunihild," The Meister VI (1893) 64–79.

—— "Richard Wagner's Prose," PMA XIX (1892) 13–33.

Engel, Carl. "Die Wagnerdämmerung," MQ XIV (1928) 438–55.

Engel, Hans. "Über Richard Wagners Oper 'Das Liebesverbot,'" in Festschrift Friedrich Blume (Kassel, Bärenreiter, 1963) [80]–91.

—— "Versuche einer Sinndeutung von Richard Wagners Ring des Nibelungen," Mf X (1957) 225–41.

—— "Wagner und Spontini," AfMw XII (1955) 167–77.

Engelfred, Abele, "Hulda . . . di Cesare Franck," RMI II (1895) 312–23.

Engländer, Richard. "Paërs Leonora und Beethovens Fidelio," Neues Beethoven Jahrbuch IV (1930) 118–32.

—— "The Struggle between German and Italian Opera at the Time of Weber," MQ XXXI (1945) 479–91.

Engler, Günther. Verdis Anschauung vom Wesen der Oper. Breslau, Stenzel, 1938.

Eösze, László. Az opera útja. Budapest, Zenemükiadó Vállalat, 1960.

Ernst, Alfred. "Les Motifs du *Héros* dans l'œuvre de R. Wagner," RMI I (1894) 657–77.

—— L'Œuvre dramatique de Berlioz. Paris, Levy, 1884.

—— "*Thaïs* . . . de J. Massenet," RMI I (1894) 296–306.

Esbert, C. L. R. "Hans Sachs," M&L XVII (1936) 59–61.

Eschweiler, Hans-Georg. Klara Ziegler : Ein Beitrag zur Theatergeschichte des 19. Jahrhunderts. Rostock Dissertation, 1935.

Ettler, Carl. "Bibliographie des œuvres de Meyerbeer," RHCM IV (1904) 436–44.

Faller, H. Die Gesangskoloratur in Rossinis Opern und ihre Ausführung. Berlin, Triltsch & Huther, 1935.

Fano, Fabio. "*Norma* nella storia del melodramma italiano," RassM VIII (1935) 315–26.

Favre, Georges. "L'Amitié de deux musiciens Boieldieu et Cherubini," RM XXII (1946) 217–25.

—— Boieldieu : Sa vie—son œuvre. Paris, Droz, 1944–45. 2 vols.

Fehr, Max. Richard Wagners Schweitzer Zeit. Aarau and Leipzig/Aarau and Frankfurt/M., H. R. Sauerländer, [1934–53]. 2 vols.

Fellerer, Karl Gustav. "Verdi und Wagner," *Studi italiani* III (1959) 46–55.

Ferchault, Guy. Faust : Une legende et ses musiciens. Paris, Larousse, [1948].

Ferrari, A. Rodigino; le convenienze teatrali; analisi della condizione presente del teatro musicale italiano. Milan, Redaelli, 1843.

Ferrarini, Mario. Parma teatrale ottocentesca. Parma, Casanova, [1946].

Février, Henry. André Messager : Mon maître, mon ami. Paris, Amiot-Dumont, 1948.

Filippi, Joseph de. Parallèle des principaux théâtres modernes de l'Europe et des machines théâtrales françaises, allemandes et anglaises. Paris, Lévy, 1870. 2 vols.

Fischer, Georg. Marschner-Erinnerungen. Hanover and Leipzig, Hahn, 1918.

Fleischer, Oskar. "Napoleon Bonaparte's Musikpolitik," ZIMG III (1901–2) 431–40.

Floch, Siegfried. Die Oper seit Richard Wagner. Cologne, Fulda, 1904.

Flood, W. H. Grattan. William Vincent Wallace : A Memoir. Waterford, "The Waterford News," 1912.

Flotow, Rosa. Friedrich von Flotow's Leben von seiner Witwe. Leipzig, B&H, 1892.

Foerster-Nietzsche, Elizabeth. "Wagner and Nietzsche : The Beginning and End of Their Friendship," MQ IV (1918) 466–89.

Fondi, Enrico. "Il sentimento musicale di Vittorio Alfieri," RMI XI (1904) 484–99.

Fouque, Octave. "Le Sueur comme prédécesseur de Berlioz," in *Les Révolutionnaires de la musique* (Paris, Calmann-Lévy, 1882) 1–183.

Fraccaroli, Arnaldo. Bellini. Verona, A. Mondadori, 1945.

—— Donizetti. Milan, A. Mondadori, 1945.

—— Giacomo Puccini si confida e racconta. [Milan], Ricordi, [1957].

—— Rossini. Milan, Casa Editrice Mondadori, 1944. 4th ed.

—— La vita di Giacomo Puccini. Milan, Ricordi, 1925.

Fragapane, Paolo. Spontini. [Bologna], Sansoni, [1954].

Fraguier, Marguerite-Marie de. Vincent d'Indy : Souvenirs d'une élève. Paris, Jean Naert, 1933.

"The *Freischütz* in London, 1824," ZIMG XI (1909–10) 251–54.

Frensdorf, Victor Egon. Peter Winter als Opernkomponist. Erlangen, Junge, 1908.

Friedländer, Max. "Deutsche Dichtung in Beethovens Musik," JMP XIX (1912) 25–48.

Friedrich, Gerhard. Die deutsche und italienische Gestaltung des Falstaff-Stoffes in der Oper. Habelschwerdt, Groeger, 1941.

Friedrich, Julius. Claus Schall als dramatischer Komponist. Herchenbach, Wanne-Eickel, 1930.

Fries, Othmar. Richard Wagner und die deutsche Romantik : Versuch einer Einordnung. Zurich, Atlantis-Verlag, [1952].

Fröhlich, Willi. Jean Paul's Beziehungen zur Musik. Frankfurt Dissertation, 1922.

Frost, Henry F. "Some Remarks on Richard Wagner's Music Drama *Tristan und Isolde*," PMA VIII (1882) 147–67.

Gaartz, Hans. Die Opern Heinrich Marschners. Leipzig, B&H, 1912.

Gál, Hans. "A Deleted Episode in Verdi's *Falstaff*," MR II (1941) 266–72.

Gallini, Natale. "Inediti donizettiani," RMI LV (1953) 257–75.

Gallusser, Rita. Verdis Frauengestalten. Zurich Dissertation, 1936.

Gandolfi, Riccardo. "Cinque lettere inedite di Giuseppe Verdi," RMI XX (1913) 168–72.

Gatti, Carlo. Catalani : La vita e le opere. [Milan], Garzanti, [1953].

—— Verdi. [Milan], Arnoldo Mondadori Editore, [1951]. "Nuova [i.e., 3d] edizione riveduta," [1953]. Translated as : Verdi, the Man and His Music. New York, G. P. Putnam's Sons, [1955].

Gatti, Guido Maria. Le Barbier de Seville de Rossini : Etude historique et critique, analyse musicale. Paris, P. Mellottée, [1924?].

—— "Boito's *Nero*," MQ X (1924) 596–621.

—— "The Works of Giacomo Puccini," MQ XIV (1928) 16–34.

Gaudier, Charles. Carmen de Bizet : Etude historique et critique, analyse musicale. Paris, P. Mellottée, [1922].

Gautier, Théophile. Les Beautés de l'opéra. Paris, Soulié, 1845.

—— Histoire de l'art dramatique en France depuis vingt-cinq ans. Paris, Magnin, Blanchard, 1858–59. 6 vols.

Gavazzeni, Gianandrea. "Donizetti e l' *Elisir d'amore*," RassM VI (1933) 44–50.

Geddo, Angelo. Donizetti (l'uomo, le musiche). Bergamo, Edizioni della Rotonda, [1956].

George, André. *Tristan et Isolde* de Richard Wagner : Etude historique et critique, analyse musicale. Paris, Mellottée, [1929].

Gerigk, Herbert. "Das alte und das neue Bild Rossinis," ZfMw XVI (1934) 26–32.

Gerlach, L. August Klughardt, sein Leben und seine Werke. Leipzig, Hug, 1902.

Ghislanzoni, Alberto. Gaspare Spontini : Studio storico-critico. Rome, Edizioni dell' Ateneo, 1951.

Giani, Romualdo. "Il *Nerone* di Arrigo Boito," RMI VIII (1901) 861–1006.

Gianoli, Luigi. Verdi. Brescia, La Scuola, [1951].

Gilman, Lawrence. Wagner's Operas. New York, Toronto, Farrar & Rhinehart, [1937].

Girardon, Renée. "Le Don Chabrier à la Bibliothèque Nationale," RdM XXVIIe année, Tome XXIV, nouv. sér. 75–76 (3e–4e trimestre 1945) 69–87; XXVIIIe année, nouv. sér. 77–78 (1e–2e trimestre 1946) 22–28.

Glasenapp, Carl Friedrich. Das Leben Richard Wagners. Leipzig, B&H, 1904–11. 6 vols. 4th ed. Translated as : The Life of Richard Wagner. London, Paul, Trench & Trübner, 1900–1908. 6 vols.

—— Siegfried Wagner und seine Kunst. Leipzig, B&H, 1911.

—— Siegfried Wagner und seine Kunst. Neue Folge. I. Schwartz-schwanenreich (Leipzig, B&H, 1913); II. Sonnenflammen (Leipzig, B&H, 1919).

—— Versuch einer thematischen Analyse der Musik zu Siegfried Wagner's *Kobold*. Leipzig, M. Brockhaus, 1904.

Glaser, G. Franz von Holstein, ein Dichterkomponist des 19. Jahrhunderts. Leipzig Dissertation, 1930.

Gnirs, Anton. Hans Heiling. Carlsbad, Heinich, 1931.

Goldberg, Isaac. The Story of Gilbert and Sullivan. New York, Simon & Schuster, 1928.

Goldmark, Karl. Erinnerungen aus meinem Leben. Vienna, Rikola, 1922. Translated as : Notes from the Life of a Viennese Composer. New York, A. and C. Boni, 1927.

Goldschmit-Jentner, Rudolf Karl. "Wagner und Nietzsche," in *Die Begegnung mit dem Genius: Darstellungen und Betrachtungen.* (Hamburg, Christian Wegner Verlag, [1946].)

Gorer, R. "Weber and the Romantic Movement," M&L XVII (1936) 13–24.

Goslich, Siegfried. Beiträge zur Geschichte der deutschen romantischen

Oper zwischen Spohrs *Faust* und Wagners *Lohengrin.* Leipzig, Kistner & Siegel, 1937.

Gounod, Charles François. Autobiographical Reminiscences, with Family Letters and Notes on Music. London, W. Heinemann, 1896.

—— Mémoires d'un artiste. Paris, Calmann Lévy, 1896. 5th ed. Translated as : Memoirs of an Artist. New York, Rand, McNally, 1895.

Graedener-Hattingberg, Magda von. Hugo Wolf. Vienna, E. Wancura, 1953.

Graf, Herbert. Richard Wagner als Regisseur. Vienna Dissertation, 1925.

Gramisch, Lore. Die Erscheinungsformen des melodramatischen Stils im 19. Jahrhundert. Vienna Dissertation, 1936.

Grattan Flood. *See* Flood, William Henry Grattan.

Gray, Cecil. "Pietro Raimondi," MR I (1940) 25–35.

—— "Vincenzo Bellini," M&L VII (1926) 49–62.

Greeff, Paul. E. T. A. Hoffmann als Musiker und Musikschriftsteller. [Cologne & Krefeld], Staufen-Verlag, 1948.

Grégoir, Edouard. Bibliothèque musicale populaire. Brussels, Schott, 1877–79. 3 vols.

Griepenkerl, Wolfgang Robert. Die Oper der Gegenwart. Leipzig, Hinrich, 1847.

Grosheim, Georg Christoph. Selbstbiographie. Hamburg, Kassel, F. Settnick, 1925.

Gross, Rolf. Joseph Hartmann Stuntz als Opernkomponist. Würzburg, Triltsch, 1936.

Grovlez, Gabriel. "Jacques Offenbach : A Centennial Sketch," MQ V (1919) 329–37.

Grun, Bernard. Prince of Vienna : The Life, the Times and the Melodies of Oscar Straus. London, W. H. Allen, 1955.

Gysi, Fritz. Max Bruch. Zurich, Orell Füssli, [1922].

Haas, Robert M. "Zur Wiener Balletpantomime um den *Prometheus,*" *Neues Beethoven Jahrbuch* II (1925) 84–103.

Hadamowsky, Franz Heinz Otto. Die Wiener Operette : Ihre Theater- und Wirkungsgeschichte. Vienna, Bellaria Verlag, 1947.

Hadow, Sir William Henry. Studies in Modern Music, Second Series. New York, Macmillan, [1923]. 10th ed.

Hänsler, Rolf. Peter Lindpainter als Opernkomponist. Stuttgart-Caunstadt, Kirchoff, [1930].

Halévy, François. Derniers Souvenirs et portraits. Paris, M. Lévy, 1863.

—— Souvenirs et portraits. Paris, M. Lévy, 1861.

Hanslick, Eduard. Die moderne Oper : Kritiken und Studien. Berlin, A. Hofmann, 1875. This is also the title of a series of books by Hanslick, the respective subtitles and dates of which are as follows : I. Die moderne Oper, 1875; II. Musikalische Stationen, 1880; III. Aus dem Opernleben der Gegenwart, 1884; IV. Musikalische Skizzenbuch, 1888; V. Musikalisches und Litterarisches, 1889; VI. Aus dem Tagebuche eines

Musikers, 1892; VII. Fünf Jahre Musik (1891–1895), 1896; VIII. Am Ende des Jahrhunderts (1895–1899), 1899; IX. Aus neuer und neuester Zeit, 1900.

—— Vom Musikalisch-Schönen : Ein Beitrag zur Revision der Aesthetik der Tonkunst. Leipzig, R. Weigel, 1854.

Hardy, Joseph. Rodolphe Kreutzer : Sa jeunesse à Versailles. Paris, Fischbacher, 1910.

Hasse, Max. Der Dichtermusiker Peter Cornelius. Leipzig, B&H, 1922–23. 2 vols.

—— Peter Cornelius und sein *Barbier von Bagdad*. Leipzig, B&H, 1904.

Hasselberg, Felix. *Der Freischütz:* Friedrich Kinds Operndichtung und ihre Quellen. Berlin, Dom Verlag, 1921.

Hausegger, Siegmund von. Alexander Ritter : Ein Bild seines Characters und Schaffens. Berlin, Marquardt, [1907].

Hausswald, Günther, ed. Carl Maria von Weber : Eine Gedenkschrift. Dresden, VVV Dresden Verlag, 1951.

Hédouin, Pierre. Gossec, sa vie et ses ouvrages. Paris, Prignet, 1852.

Heinemann, Franz. "Schillers *Wilhelm Tell* in der Musikgeschichte des 19. Jahrhunderts," *Zeitschrift für Bücherfreunde* XI, No. 2 (1907) 321–38.

Hellberg (-Kupfer), Geerd. Richard Wagner als Regisseur. Berlin, Gesellschaft für Theatergeschichte, 1942.

Hellmer, Elmund, ed. *Der Corregidor* von Hugo Wolf. Vienna, Hugo Wolf Verein; Berlin, S. Fischer, 1900.

Hellouin, Frédéric. Gossec et la musique française à la fin du XVIIIe siècle. Paris, A. Charles, 1903.

—— Un Musicien oublié : Catel. Paris, Fischbacher, 1910.

Henseler, Anton. Jakob Offenbach. Berlin-Schöneberg, M. Hesse, 1930.

Hernried, Robert. "Hugo Wolf's *Corregidor* at Mannheim," MQ XXVI (1940) 19–30.

—— "Hugo Wolfs 'Four Operas,'" MQ XXXI (1945) 89–100.

Herre, Max. Franz Danzi : Ein Beitrag zur Geschichte der deutschen Oper. Munich Dissertation, 1930.

Herzfeld, Friedrich. Königsfreundschaft : Ludwig II. und Richard Wagner. Leipzig, Goldmann, [1939].

Hess, Willy. Beethovens Oper *Fidelio* und ihre drei Fassungen. Zurich, Atlantis Verlag, [1953].

—— "Die künstlerische Dreieinheit in Wagners Tondramen : Einige 'unzeitgemässe' Betrachtungen im Geiste Richard Wagners," Mf XI (1958) 293–306.

Heuberger, Richard. Im Foyer : Gesammelte Essays über das Opernrepertoire der Gegenwart. Leipzig, H. Seemann, 1901.

—— Musikalische Skizzen. Leipzig, H. Seemann, 1901.

Heuss, Alfred. "Verdi als melodischer Charakteristiker," ZIMG XV (1913–14) 63–72.

Hey, Julius. Richard Wagner als Vortragsmeister 1864–1876: Erinnerungen. Leipzig, B&H, 1911.

Heyden, Otto. Das Kölner Theaterwesen im 19. Jahrhundert. Emsdetten, Lechte, 1939.

Himonet, André. *Lohengrin* . . . étude historique et critique, analyse musicale. Paris, Mellottée, [1925].

—— *Louise* de Charpentier: Etude historique et critique, analyse musicale. Paris, Mellottée, [1922].

Hirsch, Hans. Richard Wagner und das deutsche Mittelalter. Vienna, R. M. Rohrer, 1944.

Hirschfeld, Robert. "Oper in Wien [1857–1900]," ZIMG I (1899–1900) 264–67.

Hirt, Giulio C. "Autografi di G. Rossini," RMI II (1895) 23–35.

Hirzel, Bruno. "Der Text Wagner's *Liebesverbot* nach der Handschrift in Washington," SIMG XIII (1911–12) 348–82.

Hodik, Fritz. Das Horn bei Richard Wagner. Innsbruck Dissertation, 1937.

Hoechst, Coit Roscoe. Faust in Music. Gettysburg, Pa., Gettysburg Compiler Print, 1916.

Hoffmann, Ernst Theodor Amadeus. Sämtliche Werke. Leipzig, M. Hesse, 1900. 15 vols.

—— Musikalische Novellen und Aufsätze: Vollständige Gesamtausgabe, hrsg. von Dr. Edgar Istel. Regensburg, G. Bosse, [1921?]. 2 vols.

Hogarth, George. Memoirs of the Musical Drama. London, R. Bentley, 1838. 2 vols. New ed. as: Memoirs of the Opera in Italy, France, Germany, and England. London, R. Bentley, 1851. 2 vols.

Hohenemser, R. Luigi Cherubini. Leipzig, B&H, 1913.

Holde, Artur. "A Little-Known Letter by Berlioz and Unpublished Letters by Cherubini, Leoncavallo, and Hugo Wolf," MQ XXXVII (1951) 340–53.

Hollinrake, Roger. "Nietzsche, Wagner and Ernest Newman," M&L XLI (1960) 245–55.

Hoover, Kathleen O'Donnell. "Gustave Charpentier," MQ XXV (1939) 334–50.

—— "Verdi's *Rocester*," MQ XXVIII (1942) 505–13.

Hughes, Gervase. Composers of Operetta. London, Macmillan, 1962.

—— The Music of Arthur Sullivan. London, Macmillan & Co.; New York, St. Martin's Press, 1960.

Hussey, Dyneley. "Beethoven as a Composer of Opera," M&L VIII (1927) 243–52.

—— Verdi. London, J. M. Dent, 1948.

Hutcheson, Ernest. A Musical Guide to the Richard Wagner *Ring of the Nibelung*. New York, Simon & Schuster, 1940.

Indy, Vincent d'. César Franck. Paris, F. Alcan, 1906. Translated: New York, John Lane, 1910.

—— Richard Wagner et son influence sur l'art musical français. Paris, Delagrave, 1930.

Irvine, David. *Parsifal* and Wagner's Christianity. London, H. Grevel, 1899.

Istel, Edgar. "Act IV of *Les Huguenots*," MQ XXII (1936) 87–97.

—— "Beethoven's *Leonora* and *Fidelio*," MQ VII (1921) 226–51.

—— Bizet und *Carmen*. Stuttgart, J. Engelhorn, 1927.

—— Die Blütezeit der musikalischen Romantik in Deutschland. Leipzig, B. G. Teubner, 1909. 2d ed., 1921.

—— "Fünf Briefe Spohrs an Marschner," in *Festschrift . . . Liliencron* (Leipzig, B&H, 1910) 110–15.

—— "A Genetic Study of the *Aida* Libretto," MQ III (1917) 34–52.

—— "German Opera Since Richard Wagner," MQ I (1915) 260–90.

—— "Hermann Goetz," ZIMG III (1901–2) 177–88.

—— Das Kunstwerk Richard Wagners. Leipzig, B. G. Teubner, 1918.

—— "Meyerbeer's Way to Mastership," MQ XII (1926) 72–109.

—— Die moderne Oper vom Tode Wagners bis zum Weltkrieg. Leipzig, B. G. Teubner, 1915. 2d ed., 1923.

—— "The *Othello* of Verdi and Shakespeare," MQ II (1916) 375–86.

—— "Peter Cornelius," MQ XX (1934) 334–43.

—— "Rossini : A Study," MQ IX (1923) 401–22.

Jacob, Heinrich Eduard. Johann Strauss, Father and Son. [New York], Greystone Press, 1940.

—— Johann Strauss und das neunzehnte Jahrhundert. Amsterdam, Querido Verlag, 1937.

Jacob, Walter. Taten der Musik : Richard Wagner und sein Werk. Regensburg, Bosse, [1952].

Jacob, Walter, ed. Leo Blech : Ein Brevier. Hamburg-Leipzig, Prisman-Verlag, [1931].

Jacobsohn, Fritz. Hans Gregors komische Oper, 1905–1911. Berlin, Oester-held, [1911].

Jähns, Friedrich Wilhelm. Carl Maria von Weber in seinen Werken: Chronologisch-Thematische Verzeichniss seiner sämmtlichen Composi-tionen . . . Berlin, Lienau, 1891.

Janowitzer, Erwin. Peter Cornelius als Opernkomponist. Vienna Disserta-tion, 1921.

Jaspert, Werner. Johann Strauss. Berlin, Werk Verlag, [1939].

Jean-Aubry, G. "A Romantic Dilettante : Emile Deschamps (1791–1871)," M&L XX (1939) 250–65.

Jensen, Wilhelm. Spontini als Opernkomponist. Berlin Dissertation, 1920.

Jeri, Alfredo. Mascagni : Quindici opere, mille episodi. Cernusco sul Naviglio, Grazanti, 1945. 3d ed.

Jones, Arthur E. The Choruses in the Operas of Richard Wagner : A Study of Massed Vocal Ensemble in Music Drama. Ann Arbor, University Microfilms, 1957.

Jouvin, B[enoît Jean Baptiste]. Hérold, sa vie et ses œuvres. Paris, Au Ménestrel, Heugel, 1868.

Jullien, Adolphe. "Ambroise Thomas," RMI III (1896) 358–66.

—— "A Propos de la mort de Charles Gounod," RMI I (1894) 60–67.

—— "Hector Berlioz," RMI I (1894) 454–82.

—— Hector Berlioz, sa vie et ses œuvres. Paris, Librairie de l'Art, 1888.

—— Musiciens d'aujourd'hui. Paris, Librairie de l'Art, 1892–94. 2 vols.

Kalbeck, Max. Opern-Abende. Berlin, "Harmonie," 1898.

Kapp, Julius. Carl Maria von Weber. Berlin, M. Hesse, 1944. 15th ed.

—— Meyerbeer. Berlin, Schuster & Loeffler, [1920]. 8th ed., 1930.

—— Richard Wagner. Berlin, M. Hesse, 1929. 32d ed.

—— Richard Wagner und die Berliner Oper. Berlin-Schöneberg, M. Hesse, 1933.

—— Richard Wagner und die Frauen. Berlin-Halensee, M. Hesse, [1951]. Translated as : The Loves of Richard Wagner. London, W. H. Allen, 1951.

Karsten, Werner. "Harmonische Analyse des Tristan-Akkordes," SchwM XCI (1951) 291–96.

Kastner, Emerich. Bibliotheca Beethoveniana : Versuch einer Beethoven-Bibliographie. Leipzig, B&H, 1913.

—— Die dramatischen Werke R. Wagner's : Chronologisches Verzeichnis der ersten Aufführungen. Leipzig, B&H, 1899. 2d ed.

Keller, Otto. Franz von Suppé. Leipzig, R. Wöpke, 1905.

—— Karl Goldmark. Leipzig, H. Seemann, [1901].

Kenney, Charles Lamb. A Memoir of Michael William Balfe. London, Tinsley, 1875.

Kerman, Joseph. "Verdi's Otello, or Shakespeare Explained," The Hudson Review VI (1953–54) 266–77.

—— "Wagner : Thoughts in Season," The Hudson Review XIII (1960–61) 329–49.

Keys, A. C. "Schiller and Italian Opera," M&L XLI (1960) 223–37.

Kienzl, Wilhelm. Meine Lebenswanderung. Stuttgart, J. Engelhorn, 1926.

Kienzl-Rosegger : Wilhelm Kienzls Lebenswanderung im Auszug . . . . Briefwechsel mit Peter Rosegger. Ed. by Hans Sittner. Zurich & Vienna, Amalthea-Verlag, [1953].

Killer, Hermann. Albert Lortzing. Potsdam, Athenaion, 1938.

Kirby, Percival R. "Washington Irving, Barham Livius and Weber," M&L XXXI (1950) 133–47.

—— "Weber's Operas in London, 1824–1826," MQ XXXII (1946) 333–53.

Klein, John W. "Alfredo Catalani," MQ XXIII (1937) 287–94.

—— "Alfredo Catalani : 1854–93," M&L XXXV (1954) 40–44.

—— "Bizet and Wagner," M&L XXVIII (1947) 50–62.

—— "Bizet's Early Operas," M&L XVIII (1937) 169–75.

—— "Boito and His Two Operas," M&L VII (1926) 73–80.

—— "Catalani and His Operas," MMR LXXXVIII (1958) 67–69, 101–7.

—— "Meyerbeer's Strangest Opera," MMR LXXXIX (1959) 221–26.

—— "Nietzsche and Bizet," MQ XI (1925) 482–505.

—— "Verdi and Boito," MQ XIV (1928) 158–71.

—— "Verdi's Italian Contemporaries and Successors," M&L XV (1934) 37–45.

—— "Wagner and His Operatic Contemporaries," M&L IX (1928) 59–66.

Kling, H. "Goethe et Berlioz," RMI XII (1905) 714–32.

—— "Helmine de Chézy," RMI XIV (1907) 25–39.

Klob, Karl Maria. Die komische Oper seit Lortzing. Berlin, "Harmonie," [1905].

Knappe, Heinrich. Friedrich Klose. Munich, Drei Masken, 1921.

Knopf, Kurt. Die romantische Struktur des Denkens Richard Wagners. Jena, G. Neuenhahn, 1932.

Knudsen, Hans. "Das Posener Theater unter Franz Wallner," Zeitschrift der historischen Gesellschaft für die Provinz Posen XXVI (1911) 225–42.

[Koch, Lajos.] Karl Goldmark. Budapest, Hauptstädtische Hausdruckerei, 1930.

Koch, Max. Richard Wagner. Berlin, E. Hofmann, 1907–18. 3 vols.

Kohut, Adolph. Auber. Leipzig, Reclam, 1895.

Komorzyński, Egon von. "Lortzings Waffenschmied und seine Tradition," Euphorion VIII (1901) 340–50.

Kracauer, Siegfried. Orpheus in Paris. New York, Alfred A. Knopf, 1938. First published as: Jacques Offenbach und das Paris seiner Zeit. Amsterdam, de Lange, 1937.

Kralik, Heinrich. Das Opernhaus am Ring. Vienna, Brüder Rosenbaum, [1955]. Translated as: The Vienna Opera House. Vienna, Verlag Brüder Rosenbaum; [London, Methuen & Co.], [1955].

Kraus, Ludwig. Das deutsche Liederspiel in den Jahren 1800–1830. Halle Dissertation, 1921.

Kretzschmar, Hermann. "Giuseppe Verdi," JMP XX (1913) 43–58.

—— "Die musikgeschichtliche Bedeutung Simon Mayrs," JMP XI (1904) 27–41.

—— "Peter Cornelius," in Waldersee, Sammlung musikalischer Vorträge (Leipzig, B&H, 1879–98) II, 225–60.

—— "Ueber das Wesen, das Wachsen und Wirken Richard Wagners," JMP XIX (1912) 49–64.

—— "Ueber die Bedeutung von Cherubinis Ouvertüren und Hauptopern für die Gegenwart," JMP XIII (1906) 75–91.

Kreuzhage, Eduard. Hermann Goetz. Leipzig, B&H, 1916.

Krienitz, Willy. Richard Wagner's Feen. Munich, G. Müller, 1910.

Krohn, Ilmari. "Puccini: Butterfly," in Gedenkboek D. F. Scheurleer (The Hague, Nijhoff, 1925) 181–90.

Kroll, Erwin. Carl Maria von Weber. Potsdam, Athenaion, [1934].

Kroll, Erwin. Ernst Theodor Amadeus Hoffmann. Leipzig, B&H, 1923.

Krott, Rudolfine. Die Singspiele Schuberts. Vienna Dissertation, 1921.

Kroyer, Theodor. "Die circumpolare Oper," JMP XXVI (1919) 16–33.

Krüger, Viktor. Die Entwicklung Carl Maria von Webers in seinen Jugend-opern *Abu Hassan* und *Silvana*. Vienna Dissertation, 1907.

Krüger-Riebow, Joachim. "Albert Lortzing als politischer Freiheitssänger," MuG I (1951) 10–15.

Kruse, Georg Richard. Albert Lortzing. Berlin, "Harmonie," 1899.

—— Hermann Goetz. Leipzig, Reclam, [1920].

—— "Meyerbeers Jugendopern," ZfMw I (1918–19) 399–413.

—— Otto Nicolai. Berlin, Verlag "Berlin-Wien," [1911].

—— "Otto Nicolai's italienische Opern," SIMG XII (1910–11) 267–96.

Kuckuk, Ludwig. Peter Winter als deutscher Opernkomponist. Heidelberg Dissertation, 1924.

Kufferath, Maurice. "*Fervaal* . . . di V. d'Indy," RMI IV (1897) 313–27.

—— *Fidelio* de L. van Beethoven. Paris, Fischbacher, 1913.

Kuhlmann, Hans. Stil und Form in der Musik von Humperdincks Oper *Hänsel und Gretel*. Borna-Leipzig, Universitätsverlag von Robert Noske, 1930.

Kurth, Ernst. Romantische Harmonik und ihre Krise in Wagners *Tristan*. Berlin, M. Hesse, 1923. 2d ed.

Kuznitzky, Hans. "Weber und Spontini in der musikalischen Anschauung von E. T. A. Hoffmann," ZfMw X (1927–28) 292–99.

Lafontaine, H. C. de. "Richard Wagner," PMA XVI (1890) 63–78.

La Laurencie, Lionel de. "Les Débuts de Viotti comme directeur de l'opéra en 1819," RdM V (1924) 110–22.

Laloy, Louis. "Le Drame musical moderne," MM I (1905) 8–16, 75–84, 169–77, 233–50.

Lamm, Max. Beiträge zur Entwicklung des musikalischen Motivs in den Tondramen Richard Wagners. Vienna Dissertation, 1932.

Lamy, Félix. Jean-François le Sueur. Paris, Fischbacher, 1912.

Landestheater Hannover : 100 Jahre Opernhaus, 1852–1952. Hanover, Städtisches Verkehrs- und Presseamt; Landestheater Hannover, 1952.

Landormy, Paul Charles René. Bizet. [Paris], Gallimard, [1950].

—— *Faust* de Gounod. Paris, P. Mellottée, [1922].

—— *Faust*, de Gounod : Etude et analyse. Paris, Mellottée, 1944.

—— Gounod. Paris, Gallimard, 1942.

—— La Musique française de Franck à Debussy. Paris, Gallimard, [1943].

—— La Musique française de la Marseillaise à la mort de Berlioz. Paris, Gallimard, 1944.

—— "Vincent d'Indy," MQ XVIII (1932) 507–18.

Langlois, Jacques. Camille Saint-Saëns. Moulins, Crépin-Leblond, 1934.

Larousse, Pierre. Grand dictionnaire universel du XIXe siècle. Paris, 1874. 15 vols. and 2 supplements.

Laue, Hellmuth. Die Operndichtung Lortzings. Bonn am Rhein, L. Röhrscheid, 1932.

Lavignac, Albert. Le Voyage artistique à Bayreuth. Paris, C. Delagrave, 1900. 4th ed. Translated as : The Music Dramas of Richard Wagner and His Festival Theatre in Bayreuth. New York, Dodd, Mead, 1904. New French edition : [1951].

Lavoix, H[enri], fils. Histoire de l'instrumentation depuis le seizième siècle jusqu'à nos jours. Paris, Firmin-Didot, 1878.

Lehmann, Lilly. Studien zu Fidelio. Leipzig, B&H, 1904.

Leib, Walter. Joseph Huber : Beitrag zur Geschichte der circumpolaren Oper. Heidelberg Dissertation, 1923.

Leibowitz, René. "Fidelio ou l'amour de l'opéra," Les Temps modernes X (1955) 1505–17.

Leichtentritt, Hugo. "Schubert's Early Operas," MQ XIV (1928) 620–38.

Leo, Sophie Augustine. "Musical Life in Paris (1817–1848)," MQ XVII (1931) 259–71, 389–403.

Leoni, Carlo. Dell' arte e del teatro nuovo di Padova : Racconto anecdotico. Padua, Sacchetto, 1873.

Leroy, L. Archier. Wagner's Music Drama of The Ring. London, N. Douglas, [1925].

Lespês, Léo. Les Mystères du grand-opéra. Paris, Maresq, 1843.

Levi, Vito. "Un grande operista italiano (Antonio Smareglia, 1854–1929)," RMI XXXVI (1929) 600–15.

Lippman, Edward Arthur. "The Esthetic Theories of Richard Wagner," MQ XLIV (1958) 209–20.

Liszt, Franz. Dramaturgische Blätter, I. Abtheilung. Essays über musikalische Bühnenwerke ... Leipzig, B&H, 1881.

—— Gesammelte Schriften. Leipzig, B&H, 1880–83. 6 vols.

Vol. III, Parts 1 and 2 are the "Dramaturgische Blätter."

Loisel, Joseph. Manon de Massenet : Etude historique et critique, analyse musicale. Paris, Mellottée, [1922].

Longyear, Rey Morgan. Daniel-François-Esprit Auber (1782–1871): A Chapter in French Opéra Comique. Ann Arbor, University Microfilms, 1957.

—— " 'Le Livret bien fait' : The Opéra Comique Librettos of Eugène Scribe," The Southern Quarterly I (1963) 169–92.

—— "La Muette de Portici," MR XIX (1958) 37–46.

—— "Notes on the Rescue Opera," MQ XLV (1959) 49–66.

Loomis, Roger Sherman, ed. The Romance of Tristram and Ysolt by Thomas of Britain. New York, Columbia University Press, 1931. Rev. ed.

Loos, Paul Arthur. Richard Wagner : Vollendung und Tragik der deutschen Romantik. Bern, Francke, [1952].

Lorenz, Alfred Ottokar. Das Geheimnis der Form bei Richard Wagner. Berlin, M. Hesse, 1924–33. 4 vols.

Lortzing, Gustav Albert. Gesammelte Briefe. Regensburg, Gustav-Bosse Verlag, [1913]. 3d ed., 1947.

Loschelder, Josef. Das Todesproblem in Verdis Opernschaffen. Stuttgart, Deutsche Verlagsanstalt, 1938.

Lothar, Rudolf, [and Julius Stern]. 50 Jahre Hoftheater : Geschichte der beiden Wiener Hoftheater unter der Regierungszeit des Kaisers Franz Josef I. Vienna, Steyermühl, [1898].

Lualdi, Adriano. "Arrigo Boito, un' anima," RMI XXV (1918) 524–49.

Ludwig II, King of Bavaria. König Ludwig II. und Richard Wagner: Briefwechsel . . . . Karlsruhe i. B., G. Braun, [1936–39]. 5 vols.

Lütge, Wilhelm. "Zu Beethovens Leonoren-Ouvertüre Nr. 2," ZfMw IX (1926–27) 235–36.

Lusson, A. L. Projet d'un théâtre d'opéra définitif pour la ville de Paris en remplacement de l'opéra provisoire. Paris, Gratiot, 1846.

Lynn, Thelma. César Franck : A Bio-bibliography. New York, 1934. Typescript. Available at the New York Public Library.

Lyon, Raymond, and Louis Saguer. Les Contes d'Hoffmann: Etude et analyse. Paris, Editions Mellottée, 1948.

Macchetta, Mrs. Blanche Roosevelt (Tucker). Verdi : Milan and Othello . . . by Blanche Roosevelt. London, Ward & Downey, 1887.

MacCormack, Gilson. "Weber in Paris," M&L IX (1928) 240–48.

Maecklenburg, Albert. "Der Fall Spontini-Weber," ZfMw VI (1923–24) 449–65.

—— "Verdi and Manzoni," MQ XVII (1931) 209–18.

Magnani, Giuseppe. Antonio Salieri. [Legnano], Edito a cura del commune di Legnano e di un comitato cittadino, 1934.

Maione, Italo. Il dramma di Wagner. Naples, Libr. Scientifica, 1959. 2d ed.

Maisch, W. Puccinis musikalische Formgebung, untersucht an der Oper La Bohême. Neustadt a. d. Aisch, Schmidt, 1934.

Malherbe, Charles Théodore. Auber : Biographie critique. Paris, H. Laurens, [1911].

——"Le Centenaire de Donizetti et l'exposition de Bergamo," RMI IV (1897) 707–29.

Malherbe, Henry. Carmen. Paris, Michel, [1951].

Mandalari, M. T. "Gradi della evoluzione drammatica nel Ballo in Maschera di Verdi," RassM XII (1931) 277–87.

Mann, Thomas. Altes und Neues : Kleine Prosa aus 6 Jahrzehnten. Frankfurt/M., S. Fischer Verlag, 1953. Contains : "Briefe Richard Wagners," 575–86; "Wagner und kein Ende," 787–89.

—— Leiden und Grösse der Meister. Berlin, S. Fischer, 1935. A condensed English translation of the essay on Wagner in this volume is found in Mann's Freud, Goethe, Wagner (New York, Alfred A. Knopf, 1937).

Manschunger, Kurt. Ferdinand Kauer. Vienna Dissertation, 1929.

Mapleson, James Henry. The Mapleson Memoirs, 1848–1888. London, Remington, 1888. 2d ed. 2 vols.

Marcello, ——. "La prima rappresentazione del Guglielmo Tell a Parigi," RMI XVI (1909) 664–70.

Marek, George R. Puccini, a Biography. New York, Simon & Schuster, 1951.

Mariani, Renato. "L'ultimo Puccini," RassM IX (1936) 133–40.

Marino, Samuel J. "Giacomo Puccini : A Check List of Works by and about the Composer," Bulletin of the New York Public Library LIX, No. 2 (February, 1955) 62–81.

Marix-Spire, Thérèse. "Gounod and His First Interpreter, Pauline Viardot," MQ XXXI (1945) 193–211, 299–317.

Martens, Frederick H. "Music Mirrors of the Second Empire," MQ XVI (1930) 415–34, 563–87.

Martersteig, Max. Das deutsche Theater im 19. Jahrhundert. Leipzig, B&H, 1924.

Mascagni, Pietro. Mascagni parla : Appunti per le memorie di un grande musicista. Rome, De Carlo, [1945].

Massenet, Jules. Mes Souvenirs. Paris, P. Lafitte, [1912]. Translated as: My Recollections. Boston, Small, Maynard, [1919].

Mayer, Ludwig K. "Eine Vorwebersche 'Preciosa'-Musik," AfMf I (1936) 223–27.

Mayerhofer, Gottfried. Abermals vom Freischützen : Der Münchener Freischütze von 1812 [by Franz Xavier von Caspar]. Regensburg, Bosse, 1959.

Medicus, Lotte. Die Koloratur in der italienischen Oper des 19. Jahrhunderts. Zurich, Wetzikon & Rüti, 1939.

Merbach, Paul Alfred. "Briefwechsel zwischen Eduard Devrient und Julius Rietz," AfMw III (1921) 321–60.

—— "Parodien und Nachwirkungen von Webers Freischütz," ZfMw II (1919–20) 642–55.

Merlo, G. M. "L'arte di Arrigo Boito e il valore di Nerone," RassM VIII (1935) 126–32.

Meyerbeer, Giacomo. Briefwechsel und Tagebücher . . . herausgegeben und kommentiert von Heinz Becker. Band I : Bis 1824. Berlin, de Gruyter, [1960].

Mila, Massimo. Giuseppe Verdi. Bari, Laterza, 1958.

—— Il melodramma di Verdi. Bari, G. Laterza, 1933.

—— "Verdi als Politiker," Melos XVIII (1951) 73–78.

Miragoli, Livia. Il melodramma italiano nell' Ottocento. Rome, P. Maglione & C. Strini, [1924].

Misch, Ludwig. "Fidelio als ethisches Bekenntnis," in Beethoven-Studien (Berlin, de Gruyter, 1950) 143–49.

Monaldi, Gino. "A proposito del centenario di Vincenzo Bellini," RMI IX (1902) 72–78.
—— Verdi : La vita, le opere. Milan, Bocca, 1951.
—— Vincenzo Bellini. Milan, Sonzogno, [1935].
Mondolfi, A. "Appunti donizettiani : Il Belisario," Gazzetta musicale di Napoli (1957) Nos. 1 and 2.
—— "Appunti donizettiani : L'Assedio di Calais," Gazzetta musicale di Napoli (1957) No. 4.
—— "Appunti donizettiani : Pia de' Tolomei e Poliuto," Gazzetta musicale di Napoli (1957) No. 6.
Monographien moderner Musiker, ed. E. Segnitz. Leipzig, C. F. Kahnt, 1906–9. 3 vols.
Monterosso, Raffaello. La musica nel risorgimento. Milan, F. Vallardi, 1948.
Moos, Paul. Richard Wagner als Aesthetiker. Berlin and Leipzig, Schuster & Loeffler, 1906.
Mosel, Ignaz Franz, Edler von. Ueber das Leben und die Werke des Anton Salieri. Vienna, J. B. Wallishausser, 1827.
—— Versuch einer Aesthetik des dramatischen Tonsatzes. Vienna, A. Strauss, 1813. New ed., Munich, Lewy, 1910, with introduction and notes by Eugen Schmidt.
Moser, Hans Joachim. Carl Maria von Weber : Leben und Werk. Leipzig, VEB B&H, 1955. 2d ed.
—— "Giuseppe Verdi," RassM XII (1939) 149–58.
—— "Kleine Beiträge zu Beethovens Liedern und Bühnenwerken," Neues Beethoven Jahrbuch II (1925) 43–65.
Moser, Max. Richard Wagner in der englischen Literatur des 19. Jahrhunderts. Bern, Stämpfli, 1938.
Moss, Arthur, and Evalyn Marvel. Cancan and Barcarolle : The Life and Times of Jacques Offenbach. New York, Exposition Press, [cop. 1954].
Moutoz, A. Rossini et son Guillaume Tell. Paris, A. Pilon, 1872.
Münzer, G. Heinrich Marschner. Berlin, "Harmonie," 1901.
Munter, Friedrich. Ludwig Thuille. Munich, Drei Masken, 1923.
Nacamuli, Guido Davide. Discorso commemorativo su Antonio Smareglia. Trieste, Giuliana, 1930.
Nardi, Piero. Vita di Arrigo Boito. Milan, Casa Editrice Mondadori, 1944. 2d ed.
Nathan, Hans. Das Rezitativ der Frühopern Richard Wagners. Berlin, Dobrin, 1934.
Naylor, Bernard. "Albert Lortzing," PMA LVIII (1931–32) 1–13.
Naylor, Edward Woodall. "Verdi and Wagner," PMA XX (1893) 1–10.
Neretti, Luigi. L'importanza civile della nostra opera in musica. Florence, Tipografia cooperativa, 1902.
Neues Beethoven Jahrbuch. Augsburg, B. Filser, 1924– . Articles relevant to opera will be found separately listed under the names of the following

authors : Cortolezis, Engländer, Haas, Moser, Schiedermair, Unger, Wallner, Waltershausen.

Neumann, Alfred Robert. The Evolution of the Concept Gesamtkunstwerk in German Romanticism. Ann Arbor, University Microfilms, 1951.

Neumann, Egon. Die Operetten von Johann Strauss. Vienna Dissertation, 1919.

Newman, Ernest. Hugo Wolf. London, Methuen, [1907].

—— The Life of Richard Wagner. New York, Alfred A. Knopf, 1933–46. 4 vols.

—— The Wagner Operas. New York, Alfred A. Knopf, 1949.

Nicolai, Otto. Tagebücher. Edited, with biographical notes, by B. Schröder. Leipzig, B&H, 1892. New ed. by Wilhelm Altmann. Regensburg, G. Bosse, 1937.

Nietzsche, Friedrich. Gesammelte Werke. Munich, Musarion, 1920–29. 23 vols. Contains : "Die Geburt der Tragödie," Vol. 3; "Jenseits von Gut und Böse," Vol. 15; "Der Fall Wagner," "Nietzsche contra Wagner," Vol. 17.

Niggli, Arnold. "Giacomo Meyerbeer," in Waldersee, Sammlung musikalischer Vorträge (Leipzig, B&H, 1879–98) V, 287–324.

Nohl, Walther. "Beethovens Opernpläne," Musik XXXI, No. 11 (August, 1939) 741–47.

Nordau, Max. Entartung. Berlin, Duncker, 1893. 2 vols. Translated as : Degeneration. New York, D. Appleton, 1895.

Notarnicola, Biagio. Saverio Mercadante, biografia critica nel 150° dalla nascità (1795–1945). Rome, [Tipi della Poliglotta], 1945.

—— Saverio Mercadante nella gloria e nella luce. Rome, Editrice "Diplomatica," 1948–49.

Nowak, Leopold. "Beethovens Fidelio und die österreichischen Militärsignale," OeM X (1955) 373–75.

Oberdorfer, Aldo. Giuseppe Verdi. [Milan], Mondadori, 1949.

Odendahl, Laurenz. Friedrich Heinrich Himmel. Bonn, P. Rost, 1917.

The Meister : The Quarterly Journal of the London Branch of the Wagner Society. London, George Redway, 1888–94. 7 vols.

Oesterlein, Nikolaus. Katalog einer Wagner-Bibliothek. Leipzig, B&H, 1882–95. 4 vols.

Oesterreicher, Rudolf. Emmerich Kálmán : Der Weg eines Komponisten. Zurich, Leipzig, Vienna, Amalthea Verlag, [1954].

Offenbach, Jacques. Offenbach en Amérique : Notes d'un musicien en voyage. Paris, Calmann Lévy, 1877. English translation : Orpheus in America. Bloomington, Indiana University Press, [1957].

Ollone, Max d'. "Gounod et l'opéra-comique," RM XIV (November, 1933) 303–8.

"L'Opéra-comique au XIXe siècle," RM XIV (November, 1933) 241–312.

Orsini, Giovanni. Pietro Mascagni e il suo Nerone. Milan, A.&G. Carisch, 1935.

Ortigue, Joseph Louis d'. Le Balcon de l'opéra. Paris, Renduel, 1833.

—— De l'école musicale italienne. Paris, Au dépot central des meilleures productions de la presse, 1839. Second edition in 1840 entitled: Du théâtre-italien et son influence sur le goût musical français.

Overhoff, Kurt. Richard Wagners germanisch-christlicher Mythos: Einführungen in den Ring des Nibelungen und Parsifal. Dinkelsbühl/ Mittelfranken, Kronos-Verlag, [1955].

Pagani, Severino. Alfredo Catalani: Ombre e luci nella sua vita e nella sua arte. Milan, Casa Editrice Ceschina, 1957.

Pagano, Luigi. "Arrigo Boito: L' artista," RMI XXXI (1924) 199–234.

Palmer, John. "Gesture and Scenery in Modern Opera," MQ II (1916) 314–30.

Pannain, Guido. Ottocento musicale italiano: Saggi e note. Milan, Curci, [1952].

—— "Rossini nel Guglielmo Tell," RMI XXXI (1924) 473–506.

—— "Saggio sulla musica a Napoli nel secolo XIX," RMI XXXV (1928) 198–208; 331–42; XXXVI (1929) 197–210; XXXVII (1930) 231–42; XXXVIII (1931) 193–206; XXXIX (1932) 51–72.

—— "Vincenzo Bellini," RassM VIII (1935) 1–13, 100–110, 174–88, 237–44.

Pardo Pimentel, Nicolas. La opera italiana. Madrid, Aguado, 1851.

Parker, Douglas C. Bizet. London, Routledge & Kegan Paul, 1951. 2d ed.

—— "A View of Giacomo Puccini," MQ III (1917) 509–16.

Pastura, Francesco. Bellini secondo la storia. Parma, U. Guanda, 1959.

—— "Due frammenti della Beatrice di Tenda di Bellini," RassM VIII (1935) 327–34.

—— Vincenzo Bellini. Turin, Società Editrice Internazionale, 1959.

Paulig, Hans. Peter Cornelius und sein Barbier von Bagdad: Ein stilkritischer Vergleich der Originalpartitur mit der Bearbeitung von Felix Mottl. Cologne Dissertation, 1923.

Pearson, Hesketh. Gilbert and Sullivan: A Biography. New York, Harper, 1935.

Pelicelli, Nestore. "Musicisti in Parma dal 1800 al 1860," Note d'archivio XII (1935) 213–22, 317–63; XIII (1936) 180–97.

Pereira Peixoto d'Almeida Carvalhaes, Manoel. Inês de Castro: Na opera e na choregraphia italianas. Lisbon, Castro Irmão, 1908, 1915. 2 vols.

Perrino, Marcello. Nouvelle Methode de chant . . . précédé . . . de la vie de Benedetto Marcello . . . d'une notice sur les usages du théâtre en Italie. Paris, Ebrard, 1839. Originally published as: Osservazioni sul canto. Naples, Stampa reale, 1810.

Peteani, Maria von. Franz Lehar: Seine Musik, sein Leben. Vienna, London, Glocken Verlag, 1950.

Peterson-Berger, Olof Wilhelm. "The Life Problem in Wagner's Dramas," MQ II (1916) 658–68.

—— Richard Wagner als Kulturerscheinung. Leipzig, B&H, 1917. Review by R. Hohenemser, ZfMw I, 683–84.

—— "The Wagnerian Culture Synthesis," MQ VII (1921) 45–56.

Peyser, Herbert F. "*Tristan*, First-Hand," MQ XI (1925) 418–36.

Pfordten, Hermann, Freiherr von der. Carl Maria von Weber. Leipzig, Quelle & Meyer, [1918].

Pilati, Mario. "Francesco Cilèa," *Bollettino bibliografico musicale* VII, No. 6 (June, 1932) 5–13. Followed by unsigned "Bibliografia delle opere musicali di Francesco Cilèa," 14–16.

Pinetti, Gian Battista. Teatro Donizetti (già Riccardi); la stagione d'opera alla fiera d'agosto; cronistoria illustrata dal 1784 al 1936. Bergamo, Sesa, 1937.

Pirker, Max. *Die Zauberflöte.* Vienna, Wiener literarischer Anstalt, 1920.

Pizzetti, Ildebrando. "L'arte di Verdi : Spiriti e forme," RassM X (1937) 201–6.

—— "Contrappunto e armonia nell' opera di G. Verdi," RassM XXI (1951) 189–200.

—— "Il Faust della leggenda, del poemo e del dramma musicale," RMI XIII (1906) 1–49.

—— La musica di Vincenzo Bellini. Florence, La Voce, [1915?]. Also in his *La musica italiana dell' Ottocento,* 149–228.

—— La musica italiana dell' Ottocento. Turin, Edizioni Palatine, [1947].

Pizzetti, Ildebrando, ed. Vincenzo Bellini. Milan, Fratelli Treves, [1936]. Rev. ed. : Milan, Garzanti, 1940.

Pohl, Richard. "Richard Wagner," in Waldersee, *Sammlung musikalischer Vorträge* (Leipzig, B&H, 1879–98) V, 121–98.

Policastro, Guglielmo. Vincenzo Bellini. Catania, Studio editoriale moderno, 1935.

Pompée, Hélène. Peppino ou enfance et jeunesse de Giuseppe Verdi. Paris, Corrêa, [1940].

Pompei, Edoardo. Pietro Mascagni. Rome, Editrice nazionale, 1912.

Pougin, Arthur. Adolphe Adam. Paris, G. Charpentier, 1877.

—— Auber : Ses commencements, les origines de sa carrière. Paris, Pottier de Lalaine, 1873.

—— Boieldieu. Paris, Charpentier, 1875.

—— "Les Dernières Années de Spontini," RMI XXIX (1922) 54–80, 236–63.

—— F. Halévy, écrivain. Paris, A. Clauden, 1865.

—— "Gounod écrivain," RMI XVII (1910) 590–627; XVIII (1911) 747–68; XIX (1912) 239–85, 637–95; XX (1913) 453–86, 792–820.

—— Herold. Paris, H. Laurens, [1906].

—— "Massenet," RMI XIX (1912) 916–85.

—— Méhul. Paris, Fischbacher, 1893. 2d ed.

—— "Notice sur Méhul par Cherubini," RMI XVI (1909) 750–71.

Pougin, Arthur. "La première Salle Favart et l'opéra-comique 1801–1838," *Le Ménestrel* LX (1894) and LXI (1895), *passim*.

—— William-Vincent Wallace. Paris, A. Ikelmer, 1866.

Pourtalès, Guy de. Wagner : Histoire d'un artiste. Paris, Gallimard, 1942. New ed.

Presser, Diether. "Die Opernbearbeitung des 19. Jahrhunderts," AfMw XII (1955) 228–38.

Pretzsch, Paul. Die Kunst Siegfried Wagners. Leipzig, B&H, 1919.

Prod'homme, Jacques Gabriel. "Les Deux *Benvenuto Cellini* de Berlioz," SIMG XIV (1912–13) 449–60.

—— François-Joseph Gossec, 1734–1829 : La vie, les oeuvres, l'homme et l'artiste. Paris, La Colombe, 1949.

—— Gounod. Paris, Delagrave, [1911]. 2 vols.

—— "*Léonore ou l'amour conjugal*, de Bouilly et Gaveaux," SIMG VII (1905–6) 636–39.

—— "Lettres de G. Verdi à Léon Escudier," *Bulletin de la Société union musicologique* V (1925) 7–28.

—— "Lettres inédites de G. Verdi à Léon Escudier," RMI XXXV (1928) 1–28, 171–97, 519–52.

—— "Miscellaneous Letters by Charles Gounod," MQ IV (1918) 630–53.

—— "Rossini and His Works in France," MQ XVII (1931) 110–37.

—— "Une Source française de l' *Anneau du Nibelung*," RdM XXI (1942) 2–7.

—— "Spontini et Ch. Gounod," ZIMG XI (1909–10) 325–28.

—— "Unpublished Letters from Verdi to Camille du Locle," MQ VII (1921) 73–103.

—— "Wagner and the Paris Opéra : Unpublished Letters (February–March, 1861)," MQ I (1915) 216–31.

—— "Wagner, Berlioz and Monsieur Scribe : Two Collaborations That Miscarried," MQ XII (1926) 359–75.

—— "The Works of Weber in France (1824–1926)," MQ XIV (1928) 366–86.

"Prospetto cronologico delle opere di Gaetano Donizetti," RMI IV (1897) 736–43.

Prunières, Henry. "Stendhal and Rossini," MQ VII (1921) 133–55.

Puccini, Giacomo. Carteggi pucciniani. A cura di Eugenio Gara. [Milan], Ricordi, [1958].

—— Epistolario. Milan, A. Mondadori, 1928. Translated as : Letters of Giacomo Puccini. Philadelphia and London, J. B. Lippincott, 1931.

Pültz, Wilhelm. Die Geburt der deutschen Oper : Roman um Carl Maria v. Weber. Leipzig, v. Hase & Koehler, [1939].

Pugliati, Salvatore. Chopin e Bellini. Messina, Editrice Universitaria, [1952].

Rabich, Franz. Richard Wagner und die Zeit. Langensalza, Beyer, 1925.

Radiciotti, Giuseppe. "Due lettere inedite di G. Rossini e la sua definitiva partenza da Bologna," RMI XXXII (1925) 206–12.

—— "La famosa lettera al Cicognara non fu scritta dal Rossini," RMI XXX (1923) 401–7.

—— Gioacchino Rossini. Tivoli, A. Chicca, 1927. 3 vols.

—— "Primi anni e studi di Gioacchino Rossini," RMI XXIV (1917) 145–72, 418–48.

—— "Il *Signor Bruschino* ed il *Tancredi* di G. Rossini," RMI XXVII (1920) 231–66.

Radius, Emilio. Verdi vivo. Milan, Bompiani, 1951.

Raff, Joachim. Die Wagnerfrage. Brunswick, Vieweg, 1854.

Raimund, Ferdinand. Die Gesänge der Märchendramen in den urspringlichen Vertonungen. Vienna, A. Schrall, 1924. (Vol. VI of his collected works.)

Rauh, Adam. Heinrich Dorn als Opernkomponist. Neustadt a. d. Aisch, Schmidt, 1939.

Rayner, Robert Macey. Wagner and *Die Meistersinger*. London, Oxford University Press, 1940.

Rebois, Henri. La Renaissance de Bayreuth de Richard Wagner à son fils Siegfried. Paris, Fischbacher, 1933.

Refardt, Edgar. Hans Huber : Leben und Werk eines Schweizer Musikers. Zurich, Atlantis-Verlag, [1944].

Regli, Francesco. Dizionario biografico dei più celebri poeti ed artisti melodrammatici ... in Italia dal 1800 al 1860. Turin, E. Dalmazzo, 1860.

Reiber, Kurt. Volk und Oper : Das Volkstümliche in der deutschen romantischen Oper. Würzburg, Triltsch, 1942.

Reich, Willi. "Dokument eines Gesprächs : (Zur Wiener Erstaufführung von Wolfs *Corregidor*)," *Musica* XIV (1960) 148–50.

Reicha, Antoine. Art du compositeur dramatique. Paris, A. Farrenc, 1832. 2 vols.

Reina, Calcedonio. Il cigno catanese : Bellini. Catania, "Etna," 1935.

Reipschläger, Erich. Schubaur, Danzi und Poissl als Opernkomponisten. Berlin-Mariendorf, H. Wegner, 1911.

Rellstab, Ludwig. "Die Gestaltung der Oper seit Mozart," *Die Wissenschaft im 19. Jahrhundert* II (1856) 361.

Rensis, Raffaello de. Arrigo Boito. Florence, Sansoni, 1942.

Revue Wagnérienne. Paris, 1885–88.

Reyer, i.e., Louis Etienne Ernest Rey. Notes de musique. Paris, Charpentier, 1875. 2d ed.

—— Quarante Ans de musique. Paris, Calmann Lévy, [1909].

Ricca, Vincenzo. Il centenario della *Norma:* Vincenzo Bellini. Catania, N. Gianotta, 1932.

Ricci, Luigi. Puccini interprete di se stesso. [Milan], Ricordi, [1954].

Ricci des Ferres-Cancani, Gabriella. Francesco Morlacchi (1784–1841): Un maestro italiano alla corte di Sassonia. Florence, Olschki, 1958.

Riedel, Fridolin. Richard Wagner : *Der Ring des Nibelungen*. Leipzig, Max Beck, 1942. 3d ed.

Rieger, Erwin. Offenbach und seine Wiener Schule. Vienna, Wiener literarischer Anstalt, 1920.

Riehl, Wilhelm Heinrich. Musikalische Charakterköpfe. Stuttgart, Cotta, 1899. 2 vols.

—— Zur Geschichte der romantischen Oper. Berlin, Weltgeist-Bücher, [1928].

Rinaldi, Mario. Musica e verismo. Rome, Fratelli de Santis, [1932].

—— "Valori drammatici e musicali del *Simon Boccanegra* di Verdi," RassM VIII (1935) 42–53.

—— Verdi critico : I suoi giudizi, la sua estetica. Rome, Ergo, 1951.

Rinuccini, Giovanni Battista. Sulla musica e sulla poesia melodrammatica italiana del secolo XIX. Lucca, L. Guidotti, 1843.

Robert, Paul-Louis. "Correspondance de Boieldieu," RMI XIX (1912) 75–107; XXII (1915) 520–59.

Röder, Erich. Felix Draeseke : Der Lebens- und Leidensweg eines deutschen Meisters. Dresden, W. Limpert, [1932–37]. 2 vols.

Roethe, Gustav. "Zum dramatischen Aufbau der Wagnerschen *Meistersinger*," *Akademie der Wissenschaften, Berlin: Sitzungsberichte* (Jahrgang 1919) 673–708.

Rogers, Francis. "Adolphe Nourrit," MQ XXV (1939) 11–25.

—— "Victor Maurel," MQ XII (1926) 580–601.

Rognoni, Luigi. Rossini : Con un' appendice comprendente lettere, documenti, testimonianze. [Modena], Guanda, [1956].

Rolandi, Ulderico. Quattro poeti ed un compositore alle prese . . . per un libretto d'opera (*Il bravo* di S. Mercadante). Rome, A. Marchesi, 1931.

Rolland, Romain. "*L'Etranger* de Vincent d'Indy," RMI XI (1904) 129–39.

Roncaglia, Gino. "L'abbozzo del *Rigoletto* di Verdi," RMI XLVIII (1946) 112–29.

—— L'ascensione creatrice di Giuseppe Verdi. [Florence], Sansoni, [1951].

—— L'Otello di Giuseppe Verdi. Florence, Fussi, [1946].

—— Rossini, l'olimpico. Milan, Fratelli Bocca, [1953]. 2d ed.

—— "Il 'temo-cardine' nell' opera di Giuseppe Verdi," RMI XLVII (1943) 220–29.

—— "Vincenzo Bellini, il musicista, quale appare dal suo epistolario," RMI L (1948) 159–77.

Roosevelt, Blanche. *See* Macchetta.

[Rossini, Gioacchino.] Articles in *La Rassegna musicale* XXIV, No. 3 (July–September, 1954).

Rossmayer, Richard. Konradin Kreutzer als dramatischer Komponist. Vienna Dissertation, 1928.

Royer, Louis. Bibliographie stendhalienne. Paris, Champion, 1931.

Rubsamen, Walter H. "Music and Politics in the 'Risorgimento,' " *Italian Quarterly* V (1961–62) 100–120.

Rühlmann, Franz. Richard Wagner und die deutsche Opernbuehne. Kiel Dissertation, 1925.

Rusca, Paolo. "Studi critici sul *Tristano e Isotta*," RMI XIX (1912) 286–314.

—— "Il *Tannhäuser* nella vita e nell' arte di Riccardo Wagner," RMI XXI (1914) 675–98.

Sachs, Curt. "The Road to Major," MQ XXIX (1943).

Sachs, Edwin O., and E. A. E. Woodrow. Modern Opera Houses and Theatres. London, B. T. Batsford, 1896–98. 3 vols.

St. John-Brenon, Algernon. "Giuseppe Verdi," MQ II (1916) 130–62.

Saint-Saëns, Charles Camille. Portraits et souvenirs. Paris, Société d'édition artistique, [1900]. Translated as : Musical Memoirs. Boston, Small, Maynard, [1919].

Saitschick, Robert. Götter und Menschen in Richard Wagners *Ring des Nibelungen:* Eine Lebensdeutung. Tübingen, Katzmann, [1957]. 3d ed.

Salburg, Edith, Gräfin. Ludwig Spohr. Leipzig, Koehler & Amelang, [1936].

Salerno, F. Le donne Pucciniane. Palermo, A. Trimarchi, 1929.

[Salvioli, Giovanni.] Saggio bibliografico relativo ai melodrammi di Felice Romani [per] Luigi Lianovosani [pseud.]. Milan, Ricordi, [1878].

[——] Serie cronologica delle opere teatrali, cantate, ed oratori del maestro Giovanni Comm. Pacini. Milan, Ricordi, 1875.

Sandberger, Adolf. "Rossiniana," ZIMG IX (1907–8) 336–45.

—— "Zu den literarischen Quellen von Richard Wagners *Tannhäuser*," in *Gedenkboek* . . . *Scheurleer* (The Hague, Nijhoff, 1925) 267–69.

Sanders, Ernest. "*Oberon* and *Zar und Zimmermann*," MQ XL (1954) 521–32.

Santi, Piero. "Senso comune e vocalità nel melodramma pucciniano," RassM XXVIII (1958) 109–21.

Sartori, Claudio. "Franco Faccio e venti anni di spettacoli di fiera al Teatro Grande di Brescia," RMI XLII (1938) 64–77, 188–203, 350–62.

—— Puccini. [Milan], Nuova Accademia Editrice, [1958].

—— "Lo *Zeffiretto* di Angelo Tarchi," RMI LVI (1954) 233–40.

Sartori, Claudio, ed. Giacomo Puccini. Milan, Ricordi, 1959.

Sassi, Ramualdo. "Lettere inedite di Gaspare Spontini," *Note d'archivio* XII (1935) 165–83.

Saussine, Henri de. "L'Harmonie Bellinienne," RMI XXVII (1920) 477–82.

Schäfer, Karl. Das Opernschaffen Siegfried Wagners. Vienna Dissertation, 1936.

Schall, Heinrich. Beiträge zur Entwicklungsgeschichte der Oper mit besonderer Berücksichtigung der deutschen in neuerer Zeit. Bonn, J. Bach, 1898.

Schemann, Ludwig. Cherubini. Stuttgart, Deutsche Verlags-Anstalt, 1925.

Schemann, Ludwig. "Cherubinis dramatisches Erstlingsschaffen," *Die Musik* XVII (June, 1925) 641–47.

Schenk, Erich. Johann Strauss. Potsdam, Athenaion, 1940.

Schiedermair, Ludwig. "Eine Autobiographie Pietro Generalis," in *Festschrift Liliencron* (Leipzig, B&H, 1910) 250–53.

—— Beiträge zur Geschichte der Oper um die Wende des 18. und 19. Jahrhunderts. Leipzig, B&H, 1907–10. 2 vols.

—— "Briefe . . . an Simon Mayr," SIMG VIII (1906–7) 615–29.

—— *"I sensali del teatro,"* SIMG VI (1904–5) 589–94.

—— "Ueber Beethovens *Leonore*," ZIMG VIII (1906–7) 115–26.

—— "Ein unbekannter Opernentwurf für Beethoven," *Neues Beethoven Jahrbuch* VII (1937) 32–36.

Schletterer, Hans Michael. "Ludwig Spohr," in Waldersee, *Sammlung musikalischer Vorträge* (Leipzig, B&H, 1879–98) III, 127–62.

Schlitzer, Franco. "Curiosità epistolari inedite nella vita teatrale di G. Donizetti," RMI L (1948) 273–83.

—— L'eredità de Gaetano Donizetti: Da carteggi e documenti del l'archivio dell' Accademia Chigiana. Siena, Ticci, 1954.

—— Frammenti biografici di Gaspare Spontini con lettere inedite. Siena, [Tip. Ticci], 1955. 2 vols.

—— Inediti verdiani nell' archivio dell' Accademia Chigiana. Siena, Ticci, 1953.

—— Mondo teatrale dell' Ottocento: Episodi, testimonianze, musiche e lettere inedite. Naples, F. Fiorentino, [1954].

—— L'ultima pagina della vita di Gaetano Donizetti, da un carteggio inedito dell' Accademia Chigiana. Siena, [Ticci], 1953.

Schmid, Otto. Carl Maria von Weber und seine Opern in Dresden. [Dresden?, Selbstverlag des Verfassers, 1922.]

—— Richard Wagner: Gedanken über seine Ideale und seine Sendung. Langensalza, Beyer, 1920.

Schmidt, Friedrich. Das Musikleben der bürgerlichen Gesellschaft Leipzigs im Vormärz (1815–1848). Langensalza, Beyer, 1912.

Schmidt, Leopold. Zur Geschichte der Märchenoper. Halle an der Saale, O. Hendel, 1895.

Schmidt, Ludwig. "Briefe von und über Carl Maria von Weber," ZIMG III (1901–2) 93–99.

Schmieder, Wolfgang. "Lortzing privat: Drei unveröffentlichte Briefe des Meisters," M V (1951) 7–12.

Schmitz, Eugen. "Louis Spohr's Jugendoper *Alruna*," ZIMG XIII (1911–12) 293–99.

—— "Zur Geschichte des Leitmotivs in der romantischen Oper," *Hochland* IV, No. 2 (1907) 329–43.

Schnapp, Friedrich. "E. T. A. Hoffmanns letzte Oper," SchwM LXXXVIII (1948) 339–45.

—— "Robert Schumann's Plan for a Tristan-Opera," MQ X (1924) 485–91.

Schneider, Louis. Hervé. Charles Lecocq. Paris, Perrin, 1924.

—— Massenet. Paris, L. Carteret, 1908. Revised ed., without illustrations and documents, Paris, Charpentier, 1926.

—— Offenbach. Paris, Perrin, 1923.

Schnoor, Hans. Weber auf dem Welttheater : Ein Freischützbuch. Dresden, Deutscher Literatur-Verlag Otto Melchert, 1942.

—— Weber : Gestalt und Schöpfung. Dresden, VEB Verlag der Kunst, 1953.

Scholes, Percy A. The Mirror of Music, 1844–1944 : A Century of Musical Life in Britain as Reflected in the Pages of the Musical Times. London, Novello & Co., Ltd., and Oxford University Press, 1947. 2 vols.

Scholz, Hans. "Hektor Berlioz zum 50. Todestage," ZfMw I (1918–19) 328–51.

Schopenhauer, Arthur. Sämmtliche Werke. Leipzig, Brockhaus, 1922–23. 6 vols.

Schubert, Karl. Spontinis italienische Schule. Strasbourg, Heitz, [1932].

Schünemann, Georg. "Mendelssohns Jugendopern," ZfMw V (1922–23) 506–45.

—— "Eine neue Tristan-Handschrift zu Richard Wagners 125. Geburtstag," AfMf III (1938) 129–37.

Schuller, Kenneth Gustave. Verismo Opera and the Verists. Washington University Dissertation, 1960.

Segnitz, Eugen. "Anselmo Feuerbach e Riccardo Wagner," RMI XIII (1906) 437–50.

—— "La musica nel romanticismo tedesco," RMI XV (1908) 500–18.

Selden, Margery Stomne. "Napoleon and Cherubini," JAMS VIII (1955) 110–15.

—— See also Stomne, Margery.

Serafin, Tullio, and Alceo Toni. Stile, tradizioni e convenzioni del melodramma italiano del Settecento e dell' Ottocento. [Milan], Ricordi, [1958].

Serauky, Walter. "Die Todesverkündigungsszene in Richard Wagners Walküre als musikalisch-geistige Achse des Werkes," Mf XII (1959) 143–51.

Servières, Georges. La Musique française moderne. Paris, G. Havard, 1897.

—— "Le 'Wagnerisme' de C. Saint-Saëns," RMI XXX (1923) 223–44.

Shaw, George Bernard. The Perfect Wagnerite. New York, Brentano's, 1909.

Shedlock, J. S. "The Correspondence between Wagner and Liszt," PMA XIV (1888) 119–43.

Simon, James. Faust in der Musik. Leipzig, C. F. W. Siegel, [1906].

Sincero, Dino. "Da Tannhäuser a Parsifal," RMI XXI (1914) 122–26.

Sittard, Josef. "Gioachimo Antonio Rossini," in Waldersee, *Sammlung musikalischer Vorträge* (Leipzig, B&H, 1879–98) IV, 385–433.

Slanina, Ernst Alfred. Die Sakralszenen der deutschen Oper des frühen 19. Jahrhunderts. Bochum-Langendreer, Pöppinghaus, 1935.

Slawik, Friedrich. Die Jugendopern Richard Wagners und ihre Beziehungen zu den späteren Meisterwerken. Vienna Dissertation, 1928.

Smareglia, Ariberto. Vita ed arte di Antonio Smareglia. [Lugano, C. Mazzuconi, 1932.]

Smareglia, Mario, compiler. Antonio Smareglia nella storia del teatro melodrammatico italiano dell' Ottocento attraverso critiche e scritti raccolti da Mario Smareglia. Pola, Smareglia, [1934].

Solar Quintes, Nicolás A. "Saverio Mercadante en España y Portugal," *Anuario musical* VII (1952) 201–8.

Somiglio, Carlo. "Del teatro reale d'opera in Monaco di Baviera e del suo repertorio," RMI V (1898) 721–53.

Sonneck, Oscar George Theodore. "Heinrich Heine's Musical Feuilletons," MQ VIII (1923) 119–59, 273–95, 435–68.

Soubies, Albert. Histoire de l'opéra-comique : La seconde Salle Favart, 1840–[1887]. Paris, E. Flammarion, 1892–93. 2 vols.

—— Histoire du théâtre-lyrique, 1851–1870. Paris, Fischbacher, 1899.

—— Le Théâtre-italien de 1801 à 1913. Paris, Fischbacher, 1913.

Soubies, Albert, and Henri de Curzon. Documents inédits sur le *Faust* de Gounod. Paris, Fischbacher, 1912.

Specht, Richard. E. N. v. Reznicek. Leipzig, E. P. Tal, 1923.

—— Giacomo Puccini. Berlin-Schöneberg, M. Hesse, [1931]. English translation : New York, Alfred A. Knopf, 1933.

—— Julius Bittner. Munich, Drei Masken, 1921.

Spencer, H. "Meyerbeer," RMI X (1903) 126–28.

Spinner, Leopold. Das Rezitativ in der romantischen Oper bis Wagner. Vienna Dissertation, 1931.

Spitta, Philipp. "Die älteste Faust-Oper und Goethe's Stellung zur Musik," in his *Zur Musik* (Berlin, Paetel, 1892) 199–234.

—— "Jessonda," in his *Zur Musik* (Berlin, Paetel, 1892) 237–66.

Spohr, Louis. Louis Spohr's Selbstbiographie. Kassel and Göttingen, Wigand, 1860–61. 2 vols. English translation : London, Reeves & Turner, 1878. New German ed. : Kassel & Basel, Bärenreiter, 1954–55. 2 vols.

Spontini, G. "Lettere inedite," *Note d'archivio* IX (1932) 23–40.

Stebbins, Lucy Poate, and Richard Poate Stebbins. Enchanted Wanderer: The Life of Carl Maria von Weber. New York, G. P. Putnam, [1940].

Stefan, Paul. Das neue Haus : Ein Halbjahrhundert Wiener-Opernspiel und was voranging. Vienna and Leipzig, E. Strache, 1919.

Stefan-Gruenfeldt, Paul. Georges Bizet. Zurich, Atlantis-Verlag, [1952].

Stefani, Giuseppe. Verdi e Trieste. Trieste, Il Comune, 1951.

Steglich, Rudolf. "Das melodische Hauptmotiv in Beethovens *Fidelio*," AfMw IX (1952) 51–67.

Steigman, B. M. " 'Nicht mehr Tristan,' " MQ VII (1921) 57–67.

Stein, Jack M. Richard Wagner and the Synthesis of the Arts. Detroit, Wayne State University Press, 1960.

Stein, Leon. The Racial Thinking of Richard Wagner. New York, Philosophical Library, [1950].

Stendhal, pseud. *See* Beyle, Henri.

Stier-Somlo, Helene. Das Grimmsche Märchen als Text für Opern und Spiele. Berlin and Leipzig, de Gruyter, 1926.

Stock, Richard Wilhelm. Richard Wagner und seine Meistersinger. Nuremberg, Verlag Karl Ulrich & Co., 1938.

Stomne, Margery. The French Operas of Luigi Cherubini. Yale Dissertation, 1951.

Stoullig, E. Les Annales du théâtre et de la musique. Paris, Ollendorf, 1899.

Strecker, Ludwig. Richard Wagner als Verlagsgefährte : Eine Darstellung mit Briefen und Dokumenten. Mainz, B. Schott's Söhne, 1951.

Strelitzer, Hugo. Meyerbeers deutsche Jugend-Opern. Münster Dissertation, 1922.

Strobel, Heinrich. "Die Opern von E. N. Méhul," ZfMw VI (1923–24) 362–402.

Strobel, Otto. Richard Wagner. Leben und Schaffen. Eine Zeittafel. Bayreuth, Verlag der Festspielleitung, 1952.

Sullivan, Herbert, and Newman Flower. Sir Arthur Sullivan : His Life, Letters & Diaries. London, Cassell & Co., [1950]. New and rev. ed.

Tabanelli, Nicola. "Oriani e la musica," RMI XLII (1938) 325–43, 495–505.

Tebaldini, Giovanni. "Giuseppe Persiani e Fanny Tacchinardi : Memorie ed appunti," RMI XII (1905) 579–91.

Teneo, Martial. "Le Chevalier de Malte ou la reine de Chypre," ZIMG VIII (1906–7) 352–54.

—— "Jacques Offenbach d'après des documents inédits," MM VII, No. 12 (1911) 1–35.

—— "Jacques Offenbach : His Centenary," MQ VI (1920) 98–117.

—— "Pierre Montan Berton," RHCM VIII (1908) 389–97, 416–24, 493.

Thayer, Alexander Wheelock. The Life of Ludwig van Beethoven. Ed. by H. E. Krehbiel. New York, The Beethoven Association, [1921].

Thiess, Frank. Puccini : Versuch einer Psychologie seiner Musik. Vienna, P. Zsolnay, 1947.

Thomas of Britain. The Romance of Tristram and Ysolt. *See* Loomis, Roger Sherman, ed.

Thomas, Eugen. Die Instrumentation der *Meistersinger von Nürnberg* von Richard Wagner. Vienna, Universal, [1907]. 2 vols. 2d ed.

Thompson, Herbert. Wagner and Wagenseil. London, Oxford University Press, 1927.

Thompson, Oscar. "If Beethoven Had Written *Faust*," MQ X (1924) 13–20.

Tiersot, Julien. "Auber," RM XIV (November, 1933) 265–78.

—— "Bizet and Spanish Music," MQ XIII (1927) 566–81.

—— "Charles Gounod : A Centennial Tribute," MQ IV (1918) 409–39.

—— Un Demi-siècle de musique française. Paris, Alcan, 1918.

—— "Gounod's Letters," MQ V (1919) 40–61.

—— "Hector Berlioz and Richard Wagner," MQ III (1917) 453–92.

Till, Theodor. Die Entwicklung der musikalischen Form in Richard Wagners Opern und Musikdramen, von der Ouvertüre (Vorspiel) und deren Funktionsvertretern aus betrachtet. Vienna Dissertation, 1930.

Tommasini, Vincenzo. "L'opera di Riccardo Wagner e la sua importanza nella storia dell' arte e delle cultura," RMI IX (1902) 113–47, 422–41, 694–716.

Torchi, Luigi. "*Consuelo* di A. Rendano," RMI X (1903) 564–80.

—— "*Germania*, dramma lirico in un prologo, due quadri ed un epilogo di Luigi Illica. Musica di Alberto Franchetti," RMI IX (1902) 377–421.

—— "*Guglielmo Ratcliff* . . . di Pietro Mascagni," RMI II (1895) 287–311.

—— "*Iris*... di Pietro Mascagni," RMI VI (1899) 71–118.

—— "*Oceana* di A. Smareglia," RMI X (1903) 309–66.

—— "L'opera di Giuseppe Verdi e i suoi caratteri principali," RMI VIII (1901) 279–325.

—— "R. Schumann e le sue 'Scene tratte dal *Faust* di Goethe,'" RMI II (1895) 381–419, 629–65.

—— "The Realistic Italian Operas," in *Famous Composers and Their Works, New Series* (Boston, J. B. Millet, [1900]) I, 183.

—— "Studi di orchestrazione : L' *Anello del Nibelunge* di Riccardo Wagner," RMI XX (1913) 347–53; XXI (1914) 509–12, 768–75.

—— "*Tosca*, di G. Puccini," RMI VII (1900) 78–114.

Torrefranca, Fausto. "Arrigo Boito," MQ VI (1920) 532–52.

Torri, Luigi. "Saggio di bibliografia verdiana," RMI VIII (1901) 379–407.

Tovey, Donald Francis. "Dungeon Scene from *Fidelio*," in *Essays in Musical Analysis*. V : *Vocal Music* (London, Oxford University Press, 1937) 185–93.

Toye, Francis. Giuseppe Verdi. London, W. Heinemann; New York, Alfred A. Knopf, 1931.

—— Rossini : A Study in Tragi-Comedy. London, Barker, [1954]. New ed.

—— "Verdi," PMA LVI (1929–30) 37–53.

Unger, Max. "Beethoven und das Wiener Hoftheater im Jahre 1807," *Neues Beethoven Jahrbuch* II (1925) 76–83.

—— Ein Faustopernplan Beethovens und Goethes. Regensburg, G. Bosse, [1952].

Unterholzner, Ludwig. Giuseppe Verdis Opern-typus. Hanover, A. Madsack, [1933].

Vajro, Massimiliano. Arrigo Boito. Brescia, La Scuola, [1955].

Valentin, Caroline. " 'Ach wie ist's möglich dann' von H. von Chézy und seine erste Melodie," in Festschrift Liliencron (Leipzig, B&H, 1910) 358–86.

Valentin, Erich. Hans Sommer : Weg, Werk und Tat eines deutschen Meisters. Brunswick, H. Litolff, 1939.

Vallas, Léon. "The Discovery of Musical Germany by Vincent d'Indy in 1873," MQ XXV (1939) 176–94.

—— La Véritable Histoire de César Franck (1822–1890). Paris, Flammarion, [1955]. Translated as : César Franck. London, Harrap; New York, Oxford University Press, 1951.

—— Vincent d'Indy. Paris, Editions Albin Michel, [1946–50]. 2 vols.

Van Vechten, Carl. "Back to Delibes," MQ VIII (1922) 605–10.

—— "Shall We Realize Wagner's Ideals?" MQ II (1916) 387–401.

Vautier, Gabriel. "Le Jury de lecture et l'opéra sous la restauration," RHCM X (1910) 13–25, 44–49, 75–78.

Verdi : Bolletino quadrimestrale dell' Istituto di Studi Verdiani. Parma-Busseto. Vol. I (1960). Articles on Un ballo in maschera, with bibliography.

[Verdi, Giuseppe.] Comitato nazionale per le onoranze a Giuseppe Verdi nel cinquantenario della morte. Mostra degli autografi musicali di Giuseppe Verdi. Ridotto del Teatro alla Scala. [Milan, Unione Tipografica, 1951.]

—— I copialettere. [Milan, Stucchi Ceretti, 1913.] Ed. by G. Cesari and A. Luzio, preface by M. Scherillo.

[——] Giuseppe Verdi. Scritti di S. A. M. Bottenheim, Matteo Glinski, Augusto Hermet, Dyneley Hussey, Pierre Petit, Ulderico Rolandi, Franco Schlitzer, Bence Szabolcsi, Albert van der Linden, Frank Walker; raccolti in occasione delle Celebrazione Verdiane . . . 1951. Siena, Ticci, [Printed for the Accademia Musicale Chigiana], 1951.

Viardot-Garcia, Pauline. "Pauline Viardot-Garcia to Julius Rietz (Letters of Friendship)," MQ I (1915) 350–80, 526–59; II (1916) 32–60.

Vetter, Walther. "Richard Wagner und die Griechen," Mf VI (1953) 111–26.

Vienna. Internationale Ausstellung für Musik- und Theaterwesen, 1892. Fach-Katalog der Abtheilung des Königreiches Italien. Vienna, [J. N. Vernoy], 1892.

Viereck, Peter. Metapolitics from the Romantics to Hitler. New York, Alfred A. Knopf, 1941.

Viotta, H. A. "Richard Wagner's verhouding tot die muziekgeschiedenis," in Gedenkboek . . . Scheurleer (The Hague, Nijhoff, 1925) 359–65.

Visetti, Albert. "Tendencies on the Operatic Stage in the Nineteenth Century," PMA XXII (1896) 141–51.

Vittadini, Stefano. Il primo libretto del *Mefistofele* di Arrigo Boito. Milan, Gli amici del museo teatrale alla scala, 1938.

Vlad, Roman. "Anticipazioni nel linguaggio armonico verdiano," RassM XXI (1951) 237–46.

Wagner, Richard. Briefe in Originalausgaben. Leipzig, B&H, [1911–13]. 17 vols.

—— Gesammelte Schriften und Dichtungen. Leipzig, B&H, n.d. 12 vols. 5th ed.

—— Letters : The Burrell Collection, Edited with Notes by John N. Burk. New York, Macmillan, 1950. See also review by Thomas Mann in his *Altes und Neues* (Frankfurt/M., S. Fischer Verlag, 1953) 575–86.

—— Mein Leben : Volks-Ausgabe. Munich, Bruckmann, 1914.

—— Opera and Drama. New York, C. Scribner; London, W. Reeves, [1913]. Translated by Edwin Evans.

Wagner, Siegfried. Erinnerungen. Stuttgart, J. Engelhorn, 1923.

Wahl, Eduard. Nicolo Isouard. Munich, C. Wolf, 1906.

Wahle, Werner. Richard Wagners szenische Visionen und ihre Ausführung im Bühnenbild. Munich Dissertation, 1937.

Waldersee, Paul. "Robert Schumann's *Manfred*," in Waldersee, *Sammlung musikalischer Vorträge* (Leipzig, B&H, 1879–98) II, 1–20.

Walker, Frank. "Donizetti, Verdi and Mme. Appiani," M&L XXXII (1951) 1–18.

—— Hugo Wolf, a Biography. London, Dent, [1951]; New York, Alfred A. Knopf, 1952.

—— "The Librettist of *Don Pasquale*," MMR LXXXVIII (1958) 219–23.

—— The Man Verdi. New York, Alfred A. Knopf, 1962.

—— "Mercadante and Verdi," M&L XXXIII (1952) 311–21; XXXIV (1953) 33–38.

—— "Verdi's Ideas on the Production of His Shakespearean Operas," PMA LXXVI (1951) 11–21.

Wallner, Bertha Antonia. "Fidelio in Gotik und Barock," *Neues Beethoven-Jahrbuch* X (1942) 78–103.

Waltershausen, Hermann Wolfgang Karl Sartorius, Freiherr (von). Der Freischütz : Ein Versuch über die musikalische Romantik. Munich, Bruckmann, 1920.

—— Das Siegfried-Idyll, oder, Die Rückkehr zur Natur. Munich, H. Bruckmann, 1920.

—— "Zur Dramaturgie des *Fidelio*," Neues Beethoven Jahrbuch I (1924) 142–58.

Wassermann, Rudolf. Ludwig Spohr als Opernkomponist. Munich, Huber, 1909.

Weber, Carl Maria, Freiherr von. Sämtliche Schriften, ed. Georg Kaiser. Berlin and Leipzig, Schuster & Loeffler, 1908.

Weber, Max Maria von. Carl Maria von Weber. Leipzig, E. Keil, 1864–66. 3 vols.

Weingartner, Felix. Bayreuth (1876–1896). Leipzig, B&H, 1904.
—— Lebenserinnerungen. Zurich and Leipzig, Orell Füssli, [1928–29]. 2 vols. Translated as : Buffets and Rewards. London, Hutchinson, [1937].
—— Die Lehre von der Wiedergeburt des musikalischen Dramas. Kiel and Leipzig, Lipsius & Fischer, 1895.
Weinstock, Herbert. Donizetti and the World of Opera in Italy, Paris, and Vienna in the First Half of the Nineteenth Century. New York, Pantheon Books, [1963].
Weissmann, Adolph. "Richard Wagner : Constructive and Destructive," MQ XI (1925) 138–56.
Werfel, Franz. Verdi : Roman der Oper. Berlin, Zsolnay, [1924]. Translated as : Verdi : A Novel of the Opera. New York, Simon & Schuster, 1926.
—— Verdi : The Man in His Letters. New York, L. B. Fischer, [1942]. Edited by Franz Werfel and Paul Stefan, translated by Edward Downes.
Werneck-Brueggemann, Fritz. Ueber E. T. A. Hoffmanns Oper Aurora: Anlässlich der 3. Funk-Aufführung. Rudolstadt, Edda-Verlag, 1936.
Westernhagen, Curt von. Richard Wagner : Sein Werk, sein Wesen, sein Welt. [Zurich], Atlantis-Verlag, [1956].
—— Vom Holländer zum Parsifal : Neue Wagner-Studien. [Freiburg i. Br. and Zurich], Atlantis-Verlag, [1962].
White, Terence. "The Last Scene of Götterdämmerung : A New Production," M&L XVII (1936) 62–64.
Wiessner, Georg Gustav. Richard Wagner, der Theater-Reformer vom Werden des deutschen Nationaltheaters im Geiste des Jahres 1848. Emsdetten (Westf.), Lechte, 1951.
Williamson, Audrey. Gilbert & Sullivan Opera : A New Assessment. London, Rockliff, 1955. 2d ed.
Wimmersdorf, W. Oper oder Drama? Die Notwendigkeit des Niederganges der Oper. Rostock i. M., C. J. E. Volckmann, 1905.
Winternitz, Giorgio F. "I cimeli belliniani della R. Academia Filarmonica di Bologna," RMI XL (1936) 104–18.
Wirth, Helmut. "Natur und Märchen in Webers Oberon, Mendelssohns Ein Sommernachtstraum und Nicolais Die lustigen Weiber von Windsor," in Festschrift Friedrich Blume (Kassel, Bärenreiter, 1963) [389]–397.
Wörner, Karl. "Beiträge zur Geschichte des Leitmotivs in der Oper [Teil I]," ZfMw XIV (1931–32) 151–72.
—— Beiträge zur Geschichte des Leitmotivs in der Oper (Teil 2, 3). Bayreuth, Ellwanger, 1932.
—— Robert Schumann. [Zurich], Atlantis-Verlag, [1949].
Wolzogen, Alfred von. Ueber Theater und Musik : Historisch-kritische Studien. Breslau, Trewendt, 1860.
—— "Wagners Siegfried," in Waldersee, Sammlung musikalischer Vorträge (Leipzig, B&H, 1879–98) I, 59–80.

Wolzogen und Neuhaus, Hans Paul, Freiherr von. Lebensbilder. Regensburg, Bosse, [1923].
—— Thematischer Leitfaden durch die Musik zu Richard Wagners Festspiel *Der Ring des Nibelungen*. Leipzig, E. Schloemp, 1876.
Würz, Anton. Franz Lachner als dramatischer Komponist. Munich, Knorr & Hirth, 1928.
Zademack, Franz. Die Meistersinger von Nürnberg: Richard Wagners Dichtung und ihre Quellen. Berlin, Dom-Verlag, 1921.
Zadig (pseud.?). "Ludovic Halévy," *Revue politique et littéraire* (1899) No. 2, p. 705.
Zambiasi, G. "Le date (a proposito de G. Verdi): Bibliografia," RMI VIII (1901) 408–12.
Zavadini, Guido. Donizetti: Vita, musiche, epistolario. Bergamo, Istituto Italiano d'Arti Grafiche, 1948.
Zoref, Fritz. Wesen und Entwicklung des musikalischen Erinnerungsgedankens in der deutschen romantischen Oper. Vienna Dissertation, 1919.
Zur Nedden, Otto. Die Opern und Oratorien Felix Draesekes. Marburg Dissertation, 1926.

VI

NINETEETH CENTURY

B. NATIONALISM

Abascal Brunet, Manuel. Apuntes para la historia del teatro en Chile: La zarzuela grande. Santiago de Chile, Imprenta universitaria, 1940–51. 2 vols.
Abascal Brunet, Manuel, and Eugenio Pereira Salas. Pepe Vila: La Zarzuela chica en Chile. Santiago de Chile, Imprenta universitaria, 1952.
Abraham, Gerald. Borodin, the Composer and His Music. London, Wm. Reeves, [1927].
—— "The Genesis of *The Bartered Bride*," M&L XXVIII (1947) 36–49.
—— "Moussorgsky's *Boris* and Pushkin's," M&L XXVI (1945) 31–38.
—— On Russian Music. New York, Scribner, 1939.
—— "*Prince Igor:* An Experiment in Lyrical Opera," MQ XVII (1931) 74–83.
—— Rimsky-Korsakov. London, Gerald Duckworth, [1949].
—— Studies in Russian Music. New York, Scribner, 1936.
—— *See also* Calvocoressi.
Abraham, Gerald, ed. Tchaikovsky: A Symposium. London, Lindsay Drummond, 1945.
Ábrányi, Kormél. Erkel Ferenc élete és müködése. Budapest, 1895.
Acquarone, Francisco. História da música brasileira. Rio de Janeiro, Editora Paulo de Azevedo Ltda., [n. d.].
Adaiewsky, E. "Glinka: Etudes analytiques," RMI XI (1904) 725–60; XVII (1910) 113–29.

Adorján, Andor. "L'Opérette hongroise," *Revue de Hongrie* VI (1910) 269–80.

Akademiia Nauk SSSR. Institut istorii iskusstv. Istoriia russkoĭ sovetskoĭ muzyki. Moscow, Muzgiz, 1956–59. 3 vols.; vol. 4 in preparation.

—— Institut istorii iskusstv. Pamiati Glinki, 1857–1957 : Issledovaniia i materialy. Moscow, Akademiia Nauk, 1958.

Alarcón, Esperanza. "La ópera en México, sus comienzos y los mexicanos autores de óperas," *Boletín del instituto mexicano de musicología y folklore* I (1940) 5–9.

Almeida, Renato. História da música brasileira. Rio de Janeiro, F. Briguiet, 1942. 2d ed.

Al'shvang, Arnol'd Aleksandrovich. P. I. Chaĭkovskiĭ. Moscow, Gos. muzykal'noe izd-vo, 1959.

Andrade, Mário de. Carlos Gomez. Rio de Janeiro, Pongetti, 1939.

Arkhymovych, Lidiia Borysivna. Ukraïns'ka klasychna opera. Kiev, Derzh. vyd-vo obrazotvorchoho mystetstva i muzychnoĭ lit-ry, 1957.

Armitage, Merle. George Gershwin, Man and Legend. New York, Duell, Sloan & Pearce, [1958].

Asaf'ev, Boris Vladimirovich. Izbrannye trudy. Moscow, Akademiia Nauk SSSR, 1952–54. 5 vols. (Vol. 1 : Glinka; Vol. 2 : Tchaikovsky, Rubinstein, Rachmaninov, Dargomyshsky, Serov, . . . ; Vol. 3 : The "Mighty Five"; Vol. 4 : On Russian Musical Culture; Vol. 5 : On Soviet Music.)

—— Russkaia muzyka ot nachala XIX stoletiia. Moscow-Leningrad, Akademiia Nauk SSSR, 1930. Translated as : Russian Music from the Beginning of the 19th Century. Ann Arbor, J. W. Edwards, [1953].

Ayesterán, Lauro. Crónica de una temporada musical en el Montevideo de 1830. Montevideo, Ediciones Ceibo, 1943.

Badalbeĭli, Afrasiiab. Azerbaĭdzhanskiĭ gosudarstvennyĭ ordena Lenina teatr opery i baleta im. M. F. Akhundova : Kratkiĭ ocherk. Moscow, 1959.

Barros Sierra, José. "*Tata Vasco* y su partitura," *Romance* II, No. 23 (April [1941]).

Batka, Richard. Aus der Opernwelt : Prager Kritiken und Skizzen. Munich, Callwey, 1907.

Béha, Paul-Emile. "De l'inédit sur l'édition originale de *Boris Godounof*," SchwM XCVIII (1958) 200–202.

Beliaev, Viktor Mikhaĭlovich. Musorgsky's *Boris Godunov* and Its New Version. London, Oxford University Press, 1928.

Benestad, Finn. Waldemar Thrane : En Pionér i norsk Musikliv. Oslo, Universitetsforlag, 1961.

Berkov, Pavel Naumovich, ed. Russkaia komediia i komicheskaia opera XVIII veka. Moscow, Iskusstvo, 1950.

Berliand-Chernaia, E. S. Pushkin i Chaĭkovskiĭ. [Moscow], Muzgiz, 1950.

Bernacki, Ludwik. Teatr, dramat i muzyka za Stanisława Augusta. Lvov, Zakład Narodowy imienia Ossolińskich, 1925. 2 vols.

728   BIBLIOGRAPHY: NATIONALISM

Bernandt, Grigoriĭ Borisovich. Slovar' oper. Moscow, Sovetskiĭ Kompozitor, 1962.

Bernstein, Nikolaĭ Davidovich. Russland's Theater und Musik zur Zeit Peters des Grossen. Riga, Giżycki; Leipzig, Pabst, [1904].

Bertensson, Serge. "Ludmila Ivanovna Shestakova—Handmaid to Russian Music," MQ XXXI (1945) 331–38.

Bilbao, José. Teatro Real : Recuerdos de las cinco temporadas del empresario Arana. Madrid, Editorial Norma, 1936.

Blockx, Frank. Jan Blockx, 1851–1912. Brussels, Uitgeversmij. A. Manteau, [1943].

Boelza, Igor' Fedorovich. Cheshskaia opernaia klassika. Moscow, Iskusstvo, 1951.

Boelza, Igor' Fedorovich, ed. S. V. Rakhmaninov i russkaia opera : Sbornik stateĭ. Moscow, Vserossiĭskoe Teatral'noe Obshchestvo, 1947.

Boladeres Ibern, Guillermo de. Enrique Granados. Barcelona, Editorial Arte y letras, [1921].

Bónis, Ferenc. Mosonyi Mihály. Budapest, 1960.

Borren, Charles van den. Peter Benoit. Antwerp, De Nederlandsche Boekhandel, 1943.

Bosch, Mariano. Historia de la ópera en Buenos Aires. Buenos Aires, El Comercio, 1905.

Bottenheim, S. A. M. De Opera in Nederland. Amsterdam, P. N. Van Kampen & Zoon, 1946.

Bowen, Catherine D. Free Artist. New York, Random House, [1939].

Bowen, Catherine D., and Barbara von Meck. "Beloved Friend." New York, Random House, 1937.

Brabec, Ernst. Richard Wagner und Friedrich Smetana. Prague Dissertation, 1937.

Braga, Theophilo. Historia do theatro portuguez [Vol. III] : A baixa comedia e a opera, secolo XVIII. Oporto, Impr. portugueza-editora, 1870–71.

Braudo, Evgeniĭ Maksimovich. "Concerts, Opera, Ballet in Russia Today," MMus X, No. 4 (May–June, 1933) 213–19.

—— "The Russian Panorama," MMus X, No. 2 (January–February, 1933) 79–86.

Bravo, F. Suarez. "La Musique à Barcelone : Los Pireneos de F. Pedrell," ZIMG III (1901–2) 231–39.

Brazil. Ministerio da educação e saude. Relação das opéras de autores brasileiros por Luiz Heitor Corrêa de Azevedo. Rio de Janeiro, Serviço gráfico do Ministerio da educação e saude, 1938.

Broeckx, Jan L. Lodewijk Mortelmans. Antwerp, Uitgeversmij. N. v. Standaard-Boekhandel, 1945.

Calvocoressi, Michel D. "Boris Goudonov," MM IV (1908) 61–78.

—— Glinka. Paris, H. Laurens, [1911?].

—— "Le Mariage, par Moussorgsky," MM IV (1908) 1284–90.

—— Modest Mussorgsky : His Life and Works. Fair Lawn, N.J., Essential Books, 1956.

—— "Moussorgsky's Musical Style," MQ XVIII (1932) 530–46.

—— "L'orchestrazione autentica dal *Boris Godunof*," RassM I (1928) 633–39.

—— "La vera *Kovanscina* di Mussorgski," RassM V (1932) 166–75.

—— "Il vero e completo *Boris Godunof*," RassM I (1928) 217–25.

Calvocoressi, Michel D., and Gerald Abraham. Masters of Russian Music. New York, Alfred A. Knopf, 1936.

Carlberg, Bertil. Peterson-Berger. Stockholm, Bonnier, [1950].

Carlsen, Irina Margaret. A Russian Opera Reader. Vancouver, B.C., [Dept. of Slavonic Studies, University of British Columbia], 1956.

Carson, Wm. G. B. St. Louis Goes to the Opera, 1837–1941. St. Louis, The Missouri Historical Society, 1946.

Cernicchiaro, Vincenzo. Storia della musica nel Brasile dai tempi coloniali sino ai nostri giorni. Milan, Fratelli Riccioni, 1926.

Chaĭkovskiĭ, Modest Il'ich. The Life and Letters of Peter Ilich Tchaikovsky. London, J. Lane, 1906. Ed. from the Russian by Rosa Newmarch.

Chaĭkovskiĭ, Petr Il'ich. Diaries : Translated from the Russian with Notes by Wladimir Lakond [pseud.]. New York, W. W. Norton, 1945.

Chase, Gilbert. America's Music, from the Pilgrims to the Present. New York, Toronto, London, McGraw-Hill Book Co., [1954].

—— A Guide to the Music of Latin America, 2d ed., revised and enlarged. Washington, Pan American Union, 1962.

—— The Music of Spain. New York, Dover Publications, [1958]. 2d ed.

—— "Origins of the Lyric Theater in Spain," MQ XXV (1939) 292–305.

—— "Some Notes on Afro-Cuban Music and Dancing," *Inter-American Monthly* I, No. 8 (December, 1942) 32–33.

Cheshikhin, Vsevolod. Istoriia russkoĭ opery (1674–1903). St. Petersburg, Jurgenson, 1905.

Chybiński, A. "Zygmunt Noskowski," *Przegląd Powszechny* CIV (1909) 130–36.

Clapham, John. "The Operas of Antonín Dvořák," PMA LXXXIV (1957–58) 55–69.

Closson, Ernest, and Charles Van den Borren, eds. La Musique en Belgique du Moyen Age à nos jours. Brussels, La Renaissance du Livre, [1950].

Collet, Henri. Albeniz et Granados. Paris, Librairie Plon, 1948. New ed.

Cooper, Martin. Russian Opera. London, Max Parrish & Co., [1951].

Corbet, August, ed. De vlaamse Muziek sedert Benoit. Met de medewerking van F. van der Mueren, [and others]. Antwerp, Vlaams Economisch Verbond, 1951.

Corrêa de Azevedo, L. H. "Carlos Gomes : Sua verdadeira posição no quadro da ópera italiana no sec. XIX e na evolução da musica brasileira," *Boletin latino-americano de música* III (1937) 83–87.

Corrêa de Azevedo, L. H. 150 anos de música no Brasil (1800–1950). Rio de Janeiro, Libraria José Olympio, 1956.

Cowen, Sir Frederic Hymen. My Art and My Friends. London, E. Arnold, 1913.

Cui, César. Izbrannye stat'i. Leningrad, Gos. muzykal'noe izd-vo, 1952.

—— La Musique en Russie. Paris, Fischbacher, 1880.

Curzon, Henri de. Felipe Pedrell et *Les Pyrénées*. Paris, Fischbacher, 1902.

Cvetko, Dragotin. Davorin Jenko : Doba, življenje, delo. Ljubljana, Slovenski knjižni zavod, 1955.

Czerwiński, B. "Henryk Jarecki," EMTA (1886) 31–32, 34–37.

Dale, William H. A Study of the Musico-Psychological Dramas of Vladimir Ivanovich Rebikov. University of Southern California Dissertation, 1955.

Damrosch, Walter. My Musical Life. New York, Scribner, 1923.

David, Ernest. Les Opéras du juif Antonio José da Silva. Paris, A. Wittersheim, 1880.

Davis, Ronald L. A History of Resident Opera in the American West. Ann Arbor, University Microfilms, 1961.

Dianin, Sergeĭ Aleksandrovich. Borodin : Zhizneopisanie, materialy i dokumenty. Moscow, Gos. muzykal'noe izd-vo, 1960. 2d ed.

Dieckmann, Karin. *Die Braut von Messina* auf der Bühne im Wandel der Zeit. Helsingfors Dissertation, 1935.

Dmitriev, A. N. Muzykal'naia dramaturgiia orkestra M. I. Glinki. Leningrad, 1957.

Dobronić, A. "A Study of Jugoslav Music," MQ XII (1926) 56–71.

Dolleris, Ludwig. Carl Nielsen, en Musikografi. Odense, Fyns Boghandels Forlag, 1949.

Dovzhenko, Valerian D. Narysy z istorii ukraïns'koï radians'koï muzyky. Kiev, Derzh. vid-vo obrazotvorchoho mystetstva i muz. lit-ry URSR, 1957. Vol. I.

Dresden, Sem. Het Muziekleven in Nederland sinds 1880. Amsterdam, Uitgeversmaatschappij "Elsevier," 1923.

Druskin, Mikhail Semenovich. Ocherki po istorii russkoĭ muzyki, 1790–1825. Leningrad, Gos. muzykal'noe izd-vo, 1956.

—— Voprosy muzykal'noĭ dramaturgii opery. Leningrad, Gos. muzykal'noe izd-vo, 1952.

Durham, Frank. DuBose Heyward : The Man Who Wrote Porgy. Columbia, University of South Carolina Press, 1954.

Elson, Louis C. The History of American Music. New York, Macmillan, 1925. Revised to 1925 by Arthur Elson.

Engländer, Richard. "Die Gustavianische Oper," AfMw XVI (1959) 314–27.

Evans, Edwin. Tchaikovsky. New York, Pellegrini & Cudahy, 1949.

Ewen, David. Complete Book of the American Musical Theater : A Guide to More Than 300 Productions of the American Musical Theater from *The Black Crook* (1866) to the Present, with Plot, Production History, Stars, Composers, Librettists, and Lyricists. New York, Henry Holt & Co., [1959]. Rev. ed.

—— A Journey to Greatness : The Life and Music of George Gershwin. New York, Henry Holt & Co., [1956].

Fédorov, V. "Le Voyage de M. I. Glinka en Italie," *Collectanea historiae musicae* II (1957) 179–92.

Ferrari Nicolay, Mauricio. "En torno a *Las Vírgenes del Sol,* la nueva opera argentina," *Estudios* (Buenos Aires) Año 29, tomo 62 (1939) 29–46.

Fétis, Edouard. Les Musiciens belges, tome premier. Brussels, Ajamar, n.d.

Findeisen, Nikolaï Fedorovich. "The Earliest Russian Operas," MQ XIX (1933) 331–40.

—— "Die Entwicklung der Tonkunst in Russland in der ersten Hälfte des 19. Jahrhunderts," SIMG II (1900–1901) 279–302.

—— Ocherki po istorii muzyki v Rossii . . . do kontsa XVIII veka. Moscow, Leningrad, Gosudarstvennoe izdatel'stvo, Muzsektor, 1928–29.

—— "Die Oper in Russland," ZIMG I (1899–1900) 367–75.

Fiorda Kelly, Alfredo. Cronología de las óperas, dramas líricos, oratorios, himnos, etc. cantados en Buenos Aires. Buenos Aires, Riera, 1934.

Fischl, Viktor, ed. Antonin Dvořák, His Achievement. London, L. Drummond, [1943].

Foerster, Josef Bohuslav. Der Pilger : Erinnerungen eines Musikers. Einleitende Studie und Auswahl für die deutsche Ausgabe von F. Pala. Prague, Artia, 1955.

[——] J. B. Foerster : Jeho životní pouť a tvorba, 1859–1949. [Prague], Orbis, [1949].

Fonseco Benevides, Francisco da. O real theatro de S. Carlos de Lisboa, desde a sua funação em 1793 até á actualidade. Lisbon, Castro Irmão, [1883].

Fuller-Maitland, John Alexander. The Music of Parry and Stanford. Cambridge, W. Heffer, 1934.

Gagey, Edmond McAdoo. The San Francisco Stage : A History. New York, Columbia University Press, 1950.

Galindo, Miguel. Nociones de historia de la música mejicana, tomo 1. Colima, Tip. de "El dragón," 1933.

Gettel, William D. "Arthur Clifton's *Enterprise,*" JAMS II (1949) 23–35.

Gettemann, H. "*Sniégourotchka* opéra de M. Rimsky-Korsakoff," RHCM VIII (1908) 137–43, 179–87, 213–16.

Gilse van der Pals, Nikolai van. N. A. Rimsky-Korssakow : Opernschaffen nebst Skizze über Leben und Wirken. Paris-Leipzig, W. Bessel, 1929.

Ginzburg, Semen L'vovich, ed. Russkiĭ muzykal'nyĭ teatr 1700–1835. Moscow, "Iskusstvo," 1941.

Glinka, Mikhail Ivanovich. Literaturnoe nasledie. [Leningrad], Gos. muzykal'noe izd-vo, 1952–53. 2 vols.

—— Zapiski. Leningrad, Gos. muzykal'noe izd-vo, 1953.

Glowacki, John M. The History of Polish Opera. Boston University Dissertation, 1952.

Goddard, Scott. "Editions of Boris Goudonov," M&L X (1929) 278–86.

Godet, Robert. En Marge de Boris Godounof: Notes sur les documents iconographiques de l'édition Chester. Paris, F. Alcan, 1926.

Gomes Vaz de Carvalho, Itala. Vida de Carlos Gomes. Rio de Janeiro, A. Noite, 1946. 3d ed.

Gozenpud, Abram Akimovich. Muzykal'nyĭ teatr v Rossii : Ot istokov do Glinki. Leningrad, Gos. muzykal'noe izd-vo, 1959.

—— N. A. Rimskiĭ-Korsakov : Temy i idei ego opernogo tvorchestva. Moscow, Gos. muzykal'noe izd-vo, 1957.

Graf, Herbert. The Opera and Its Future in America. New York, W. W. Norton, [1941].

—— Producing Opera for America. Zurich, New York, Atlantis Books, [1961].

Green, Stanley. The World of Musical Comedy : The Story of the American Musical Stage as Told through the Careers of Its Foremost Composers and Lyricists. New York, Ziff-Davis, [1960].

Greene, Harry Plunket. Charles Villiers Stanford. London, E. Arnold, [1935].

Habets, Alfred. Alexandre Borodine, d'après la biographie et la correspondance publiées par M. Wladimir Stassof. Paris, Fischbacher, 1893. Translated as : Borodin and Liszt. London, Digby, Long, [1895].

Hackett, Karleton. "The Possibilities of Opera in America," MTNA IV (1909) 52–60.

Handbook of Latin American Studies. Cambridge, Mass., Harvard University Press, 1936–.

Harászti, Emil. La Musique hongroise. Paris, Laurens, 1933.

Hebanowski, S. "Trzydziestolecie opery Poznanskiej," Kronika miasta Poznania (1949) 201–18.

Helfert, Vladimír. Geschichte der Musik in der tschechoslovakischen Republik. Prague, Orbis-Verlag, 1936.

Hipsher, Edward E. American Opera and Its Composers. Philadelphia, T. Presser, [1927].

Hitchcock, H. Wiley. "An Early American Melodrama : The Indian Princess of J. N. Barker and John Bray," MLA Notes, 2d ser., XII, No. 3 (1954–55) 375–88.

Hnilička, Alois. Kontury vývoje hudby poklasické v Čechách. Prague, 1935.

Hoffmann-Erbrecht, Lothar. "Grundlagen der Melodiebildung bei Mussorgski," in Bericht über den internationalen musikwissenschaft-

lichen Kongress Bamberg 1953 (Kassel & Basel, Bärenreiter, [1954]) 262–66.

Hoffmeister, Karel. Antonín Dvořák. London, John Lane, 1928. Ed. and translated by Rosa Newmarch.

Hofmann, Rostislav. Moussorgski. Paris, Editions du Coudrier, [1952].

—— Rimski-Korsakov : Sa vie, son oeuvre. Paris, Flammarion, 1958.

—— Un Siècle d'opéra russe (de Glinka à Stravinsky). Paris, Corrêa, [1946].

Holbrooke, Josef. Contemporary British Composers. London, C. Palmer, [1925].

[——] Josef Holbrooke : Various Appreciations by Many Authors. London, R. Carte & Co., 1937.

Hostinský, Otakar. Die Musik in Böhmen. Vienna, Hof- u. Staatsdruckerei, 1894.

Howard, John Tasker. "The Hewitt Family in America," MQ XVII (1931) 25–39.

—— Our American Music : Three Hundred Years of It. With Supplementary Chapters by James Lyons. New York, Thomas Y. Crowell Co., [1954]. 3d ed.

—— Studies of Contemporary American Composers : Deems Taylor. New York, J. Fischer, 1927.

Hoza, Stefan. Opera na Slovensku. Martin, Osveta, 1953–54. 2 vols.

Hussey, Dyneley. "Nationalism and Opera," M&L VII (1926) 3–16.

Huygens, Constantijn. Correspondance et œuvre musical. Leiden, W. J. A. Jonckbloet, 1882.

Iakovlev, Vasiliĭ Vasil'evich. Pushkin i muzyka. Moscow, Gos. muzykal'noe izd-vo, 1949.

Iarustovskiĭ, B. M. Dramaturgiia russkoĭ opernoĭ klassiki. Moscow, Muzgiz, 1953. Translated as : Die Dramaturgie der klassischen russischen Oper. Berlin, Henschelverlag, 1957.

—— Opernaia dramaturgiia Chaĭkovskogo. Moscow, Gos. muz. izd-vo, 1947.

Iastrebtsev, Vasiliĭ Vasil'evich. Nikolaĭ Andreevich Rimskiĭ-Korsakov : Vospominaniia, 1886–1908. [Leningrad, Gos. muzykal'noe izd-vo, 1959.]

Iglesias, Ignasi. Enric Morera : Estudi biografie. Barcelona, Artis, [1921].

Inch, Herbert Reynolds. A Bibliography of Glinka. [New York, 1935.] Typewritten; available in the Music Division of the New York Public Library.

Istel, Edgar. "Felipe Pedrell," MQ XI (1925) 164–91.

—— "Isaac Albeniz," MQ XV (1929) 117–48.

Jachimecki, Zdzisław. "Dwie opery polskie o Napoleonie," *Muzyka* (1929) No. 1, 5–13.

—— Historia muzyki polskiej w zarysie. Warsaw, Gebethner i Wolff, [1920].

Jachimecki, Zdzisław. Muzyka polska w rozwoju historycznym. Cracow, S. Kamiński, [1948–51]. 2 vols.
—— "Stanislaus Moniuszko," MQ XIV (1928) 54–62.
—— Stanisław Moniuszko. Warsaw, Gebethner i Wolff, [1921].
—— Władysław Żeleński. Cracow, Polskie Wyd. Muzyczne, 1952.
Kann-Novikova, E. M. I. Glinka. Moscow, Muzgiz, 1950–55. 3 vols.
Karasowski, Maurycy. "Jan Stefani," Ruch Muzyczny (1857) 210–14, 217–19, 226–29, 237–39.
—— "Moniuszko jako kompozytor dramatyczny," Biblioteka Warszawska (1861) vol. 82 (i.e., vol. 2 of n.[3]s. [1861–65], vol. II of 1861), 261–81.
—— Rys historyczny opery polskiej, poprzedzony szczegółowym poglądem na dzieje muzyki dramatycznej powszechnej. Warsaw, M. Glücksberg, 1859.
—— "Rys historyczny opery polskiej z końca epoki panowania Stanisława Augusta aż do dni naszych," Biblioteka Warszawska (1858) vol. 70 (i.e., vol. 6 of n.[2]s., vol. II of 1858), 94–122, 276–312.
Karysheva, T. P. P. Sokal's'kiĭ : Narys pro zhyttia i tvorchist'. Kiev, Derzh. vid-vo obrazotvorchoho mystetstva i muzychnoï lit-ri URSR, 1959.
Keefer, Lubov. "Opera in the Soviet," MLA Notes, 2d ser., II, No. 2 (March, 1945) 110–17.
Keeton, A. E. "Elgar's Music for The Starlight Express," M&L XXVI (1945) 43–46.
Keldysh, Iurii Vsevoldovich. Istoriia russkoĭ muzyki. Moscow, Muzgiz, 1947, 1954. Vols. 2 and 3.
Kelly, Alfredo. See Fiorda Kelly, Alfredo.
Kindem, Ingeborg Eckhoff. Den norske Operas Historie. Oslo, E. G. Mortensen, 1941.
Kleczyński, J. "Opera polska przed i po Halce," EMTA (1885) 224–25.
Klein, Herman. "Albéniz's Opera Pepita Jiménez," The Musical Times LIX (March, 1918) 116–17.
Kling, H. "Le Centenaire d'un compositeur suisse célèbre : Louis Niedermeyer," RMI IX (1902) 830–59.
Kolodin, Irving. The Story of the Metropolitan Opera, 1883–1950 : A Candid History. New York, Alfred A. Knopf, 1953.
Kulikovich, Mikola. Belaruskaia savetskaia opera. Munich, 1957.
Lange, Francisco Curt. "Leon Ribeiro," Boletin latino-americano de musica III (1937) 519–36.
Laplane, Gabriel. Albeniz : Sa vie, son oeuvre. [n.p.], Editions du Milieu du Monde, [1956].
Latoszewski, Z. "Opera w Polsce pryedrozbiorowej," Wiadomości Muzyczne (1925) 45–47; Muzyk Wojskowy (1926) No. 3.
Layton, Robert. Berwald. London, publ. under the auspices of the Anglo-Swedish Literary Foundation [by] Blond, [1959].
Lehmann, Dieter. Russlands Oper und Singspiel in der zweiten Hälfte des 18. Jahrhunderts. Leipzig, B&H, 1958.

Leonard, Richard Anthony. A History of Russian Music. London, Jarrolds, [1956].

Leyda, Jay, and Sergei Bertensson, eds. The Musorgsky Reader : The Life of Modeste Petrovich Musorgsky in Letters and Documents. New York, W. W. Norton, 1947.

Lindström, Sven. "Vårt första nationalla Sångspel," STM XXIV (1942) 68–83.

Livanova, Tamara Nikolaevna. Ocherki i materialy po istorii ruskoĭ muzykal'noĭ kultury. Moscow, "Iskusstvo," 1938.

—— Russkaia muzykal'naia kul'tura XVIII veka v ee sviaziakh s literaturoĭ, teatrom i bytom. Moscow, Gos. muzykal'noe izd-vo, 1952–53. 2 vols.

—— Stasov i russkaia klassicheskaia opera. Moscow, Gos. muzykal'noe izd-vo, 1957.

Livanova, Tamara Nikolaevna, ed. M. I. Glinka : Sbornik materialov i stateĭ. Moscow, Gos. muzykal'noe izd-vo, 1950.

Lloyd-Jones, David. "[Borodin's] The Bogatyrs: Russia's First Operetta," MMR LXXXIX (1959) 123–30.

Loëb, Harry Brunswick. "The Opera in New Orleans," Louisiana Historical Society, Proceedings and Reports IX (1916) 29–41. .

Loft, Abram, translator. "Excerpts from the Memoirs of J. W. Tomaschek," MQ XXXII (1946) 244–64.

Lowe, George. Josef Holbrooke and His Work. London, K. Paul [etc.]; New York, E. P. Dutton, 1920.

Lualdi, Adriano. "Il Principe Igor de Borodine," RMI XXIII (1916) 115–39.

Maine, Basil. "Don Juan de Mañara: Goossens' New Opera," The Chesterian XVI (1935–36) 5–10.

Marchant, Annie d'Armond. "Carlos Gomes, Great Brazilian Composer," Bulletin of the Pan American Union LXX (1936) 767–76.

Maria y Campos, Armando de. Una temporada de opera italiana en Oaxaca. Mexico, Ediciones populaires, 1939.

Martineau, René. Emmanuel Chabrier. Paris, Dorbon, [1910].

Mates, Julian. The American Musical Stage before 1800. New Brunswick, Rutgers University Press, [cop. 1962].

Mattfeld, Julius. A Hundred Years of Grand Opera in New York, 1825–1925 : A Record of Performances. New York, The New York Public Library, 1927.

Mayer-Serra, Otto. Panorama de la música mexicana desde la independencia hasta la actualidad. [México], El Colegio de México, [1941].

Mellers, Wilfrid. "Music, Theatre and Commerce : A Note on Gershwin, Menotti and Marc Blitzstein," The Score No. 12 (June, 1955) 69–76.

Meyer, Torben. Carl Nielsen, Kunstneren og Mennesket : En Biografi. Gennemgang af Vaerkerne : Frede Shanford Petersen. Copenhagen, Nyt Nordisk Forlag, 1947–48. 2 vols.

Michałowski, Kornel. Opery Polski. [Cracow], Polskie Wydawnictwo Muzycne, [1954].

Mitjana y Gordón, Rafael. "La Musique en Espagne," in Lavignac, Encyclopédie de la musique (Paris, Delagrave, 1920) Part I, Vol. IV, 1913–2351.

Moberg, Carl Allan. "Essais d'opéras en Suède, sous Charles XII," in Mélanges de musicologie (Paris, Droz, 1933) 123–32.

Montagu-Nathan, Montagu. Glinka. London, Constable, 1916.

—— A History of Russian Music. London, W. Reeves, [1914]. 2d ed., 1918.

—— Moussorgsky. London, Constable, 1916.

—— "The Origin of The Golden Cockerel," MR XV (1954) 33–38.

—— Rimsky-Korsakof. London, Constable, 1916.

Moore, Edward C. Forty Years of Opera in Chicago. New York, H. Liveright, 1930.

Mooser, Robert Aloys. Annales de la musique et des musiciens en Russie au XVIIIe siècle. Geneva, Mont-Blanc, 1948–51. 3 vols.

—— Contribution à l'histoire de le musique russe : L'Opéra-comique français en Russie au XVIIIe siècle. Geneva, L'auteur, 1932.

—— "Un Musicien espagnol en Russie à la fin du XVIIIe siècle [Martin i Soler]," RMI XL (1936) 432–49.

—— L'Opéra-comique français en Russie au XVIIIe siècle. Geneva-Monaco, Editions René Kistner, 1954. 2d ed.

—— Opéras, intermezzos, ballets, cantates, oratorios joués en Russie durant le 18e siècle. Avec l'indication des oeuvres de compositeurs russes parues en Occident, à la même époque. Essai d'un répertoire alphabétique et chronologique. Geneva, R. Kistner; Monaco, Union Européene d'Editions, 1955. 2d ed.

Morgan, James O. French Comic Opera in New York, 1855–1890. Ann Arbor, University Microfilms, 1959.

Moscow. Gosudarstvennaia konservatoriia. Kafedra istorii russkoĭ muzyki. Istoriia russkoĭ muzyki. Moscow, Gos. muzykal'noe izd-vo, 1957–60. 3 vols.

Muñoz, Matilde. Historia de la zarzuela y el género chico. Madrid, Editorial Tesoro, [1946].

Muzyka : Monografje muzyczne. Warsaw, [1934]. Mateusz Gliński, ed. Tom 10 (incorrectly called tom 9), also called rok 11, nr. 8–9.

Muzykal'noe nasledie Chaĭkovskogo : Iz istorii ego proizvedeniĭ. Moscow, Akademiia Nauk SSSR, 1958.

Nejedlý, Zdeněk. Bedřich Smetana. [Prague], Orbis, 1950–54. 2d ed. 7 vols.

—— Dějiny opery Národního divadla. [Prague], Práce, 1949. 2d ed.

—— Frederick Smetana. London, G. Bles, [1924].

—— J. B. Foerster. Prague, M. Urbánek, 1910.

—— Zpěvohry Smetanovy. Prague, Státní nakl. politické literatury, 1954. 2d ed.

Newmarch, Rosa. The Music of Czechoslovakia. London, Oxford University Press, 1942.

—— The Russian Opera. New York, E. P. Dutton, [1914].

—— Tchaikovsky, His Life and Works. New York, J. Lane, 1900.

—— "Tchaikovsky's Early Lyrical Operas," ZIMG VI (1904–5) 29–34.

Niewiadomski, S. "Manru [of Paderewski]," Biblioteka Warszawska (1901) vol. 243 (i.e., vol. 143 of n.[4]s., vol. III of 1901) 87–104.

—— "O pierwszej muzyce do Fausta i o jej twórcy Antonim [-ie?] Radziwille," Muzyka (1929) Nos. 3–4.

—— "W. Zeleński i jego Goplana," EMTA (1897) 64.

—— "Z przeszłości opery polskiej," Muzyka (1931) 65–68.

Nilsson, Kurt. Die Rimsky-Korssakoffsche Bearbeitung des Boris Godunoff von Mussorgskii als Objekt der vergleichenden Musikwissenschaft. Münster, Buschmann, 1937.

Nosek, Vladimir. The Spirit of Bohemia : A Survey of Czechoslovak History, Music, and Literature. London, G. Allen & Unwin, [1926].

Noskowski, W. "Damy i huzary Łucjana Kamieńskiego," Muzyka Polska (1938) No. 10, 452–55.

Nowak-Romanowicz, Alina. Jósef Elsner. Cracow, Polskie Wydawn. Muzyczne, [1957].

Opieński, Henryk. La Musique polonaise. Paris, Gebethner & Wolff, 1929.

—— "Les Premiers Opéras polonais considérés dans leur rapports avec la musique de Chopin," RdM X (1929) 92–98.

—— Stanisław Moniuszko, życie i dzieła. Lvov-Poznan, Nakładem Wydawn. Polskiego, 1924.

Paderewski, I. J. "Konrad Wallenrod," Tygodnik Illustrowany I (1885) 175–76.

Panov, Petŭr. "Der nationale Stil N. A. Rimsky-Korsakows," AfMw VIII (1926) 78–117.

Paris, Luis. Museo-archivo teatral (Madrid) : Catálogo provisional. Madrid, Yagües, 1932.

Patterson, Frank. "Fifty Years of Opera in America," MTNA XXIII (1928) 176–85.

Pedrell, Felipe. Cancionero musical popular español. Valls, E. Castells, [1918–22]. 4 vols.

—— Jornadas de arte (1841–1891). Paris, Ollendorf, 1911.

—— "La Musique indigène dans le théâtre espagnol du XVIIe siècle," SIMG V (1903) 46–90.

—— Orientaciones (1892–1902) : Continuaciò de Jornadas de arte. Paris, Ollendorf, 1911.

—— Por nuestra música : Algunas observaciones sobre la magna cuestión de una escuela lírico nacional. Barcelona, Heurich, 1891.

Pekelis, Mikhail Samoĭlovich. Dargomyzhskiĭ i narodnaia pesnia. Moscow, Muzgiz, 1951.

Pekelis, Mikhail Samoĭlovich, ed. Istoriia russkoĭ muzyki. Moscow, Muzgiz, 1940. Vol. II.

Peña y Goñi, Antonio. La ópera española y la música dramática en España en el siglo XIX. Madrid, El Liberal, 1881.

Pereira Peixoto d'Almeida Carvalhaes, Manoel. Marcos Portugal na sua musica dramatica. Lisbon, Castro Irmão, 1910.

Pereira Salas, Eugenio. História de la música en Chile (1850–1900). [Santiago], Universidad de Chile, 1957.

—— See also Abascal Brunet.

Peterson-Berger, Olof Wilhelm. Peterson-Berger Recensioner : Glimtar och Skuggor ur Stockholms musik Värld 1896–1923. Stockholm, Ahlén & Åkerlund, 1923.

Pisk, Paul A. "Lazare Saminsky," The Chesterian XX (1938–39) 74–78.

Poliński, A. Pierwszi tworcy oper polskich," Kurjer Warszawski (1905) No. 1.

Pols, André M. Vijftig Jaar vlaamsche Opera. Antwerp, Drukkerij Pierre Dirix, [1943].

Pomorska, Hanna. Karol Kurpiński. [Warsaw], Czytelnik, 1948.

Poźniak, W. "Niezrealizowane projekty operowe Moniuszki," Kwartalnik Muzyczny (1948) Nos. 21–22, 234–51.

—— "Opera polska przed Moniuszka : Szkic historyczny," Muzyka (1951) No. 12 (21), 30–37.

Pražák, Přemysl. Smetanovy zpěvohry. Prague, Za svobodu, 1948. 4 vols.

Prod'homme, Jacques Gabriel. "Chabrier in His Letters," MQ XXI (1935) 451–65.

Protopopov, Vladimir Vasil'evich. Ivan Susanin Glinki : Muzykal'no-tvorcheskoe issledovanie. Moscow, Izd-vo Akademii Nauk SSSR, 1961.

—— Opernoe tvorchestvo Chaĭkovskogo. Moscow, Akademiia Nauk SSSR, 1957.

Rabinovich, Aleksandr Semenovich. Russkaia opera do Glinki. [Moscow], Muzgiz, 1948.

Raux Deledicque, Michel. Albéniz, su vida inquieta y ardorosa. [Buenos Aires], Ediciones Peuser, [1950].

Reeser, Eduard. Een Eeuw nederlandse Muziek [1815–1915]. Amsterdam, Querido, 1950.

Reiff, A. "Ein Katalog zu den Werken von Felipe Pedrell," AfMw III (1921) 86–97.

Reiss, J[ósef]. W[ładysław]. "Koryfeusz muzyki polskiej, Karol Kurpiński," Wiedza i Życie (1949) 1061–69.

—— Muzyka w Krakowie w XIX wieku. Cracow, W. L. Anczyc, 1931.

—— Najpiękniejsza ze wszystkich jest muzyka polska. Cracow, T. Gieszczykiewicz, 1946; Warsaw, Polskie Wydawnictwo Muzyczne, [1958].

Rektorys, Artuš, ed. Zdeněk Fibich : Sborník dokumentů a studií o jeho životé a díle. [Prague], Orbis, 1951–52. 2 vols.

Richter, Carl Ludwig. Zdenko Fibich. Prague, F. A. Urbánek, 1900.

Riesemann, Oskar von. Monographien zur russischen Musik. Munich, Drei Masken, 1923–26. 2 vols. Vol. II, Modest Petrowitsch Mussorgski, translated as : Moussorgsky. New York, Tudor, 1935.

Rimskiĭ-Korsakov, Andreĭ Nikolaevich. N. A. Rimskiĭ-Korsakov : Zhizn' i tvorchestvo. Moscow, Ogiz-Muzgiz, 1933–46. 5 vols.

Rimskiĭ-Korsakov, Nikolaĭ Andreevich. Letopis' moeĭ muzykal'noĭ zhizni. Moscow, Gos. muzykal'noe izd-vo, 1955. 7th ed. English translation of 5th ed. (1935) as : My Musical Life. New York, Alfred A. Knopf, 1942.

—— My Musical Life. New York, Alfred A. Knopf, 1923. Translated from the revised second Russian edition.

[——] USSR, Tsentral'nyĭ gosudarstvennyĭ literaturnyĭ arkhiv. N. A. Rimskiĭ-Korsakov : Sbornik dokumentov. Moscow, Gos. muzykal'noe izd-vo, 1951.

Ritter, Frédéric Louis. Music in America. New York, Scribner, 1883.

Robertson, Alec. Dvořák. New York, Pellegrini & Cudahy, 1949.

Rogers, Francis. "America's First Grand Opera Season," MQ I (1915) 93–101.

—— "Henriette Sontag in New York," MQ XXVIII (1942) 100–104.

Rogge, Hendrik Cornelis. "De Opera te Amsterdam," Oud Holland V (1887) 177, 241–62.

—— "De Opvoeringen van Mozarts Don Juan in Nederland," Tijdschrift der Vereeniging voor Noord-Nederlands Muziekgeschiedenis II (1887) 237–77.

Romero, Jésus C. La ópera en Yucatán. Mexico, Ediciones "Guion de América," 1947.

Rubinstein, Anton. Erinnerungen aus fünfzig Jahren, 1839–1889. Leipzig, B. Senff, 1895. Translated from the Russian.

Rudziński, Witold. "Szkice Moniuszkowskie. IV. Śpiewak domowy," Muzyka (1952) No. 9/10 (30–31) 65–76.

Sabaneev, Leonid Leonidovitch. Geschichte der russischen Musik. Leipzig, B&H, 1926.

—— Modern Russian Composers. Translated by Joffe. New York, International Publishers, [1927].

Sáez, Antonia. El teatro en Puerto Rico (notas para su historia). [San Juan], Editorial Universitaria, Universidad de Puerto Rico, 1950.

Salas, Carlos, and Eduardo Feo Calcaño. Sesquicentenario de la opera en Caracas : Relato histórico de ciento años de opera 1808–1958. Caracas, Tip. Vargas, 1960.

Salazar, Adolfo. La música contemporánea en España. Madrid, Ediciones La Nave, [1930].

Salcedo, Angel S. Tomás Bretón. Madrid, Imprenta clásica española, 1924.

Saldívar, Gabriel. História de la música en México (épocas precortesiana y colonial). Mexico, "Cvltvra," 1934.

Saldoni, Baltasar. Diccionario biográfico-bibliográfico de efemérides de músicos españoles. Madrid, D. Antonio Perez Dubrull, 1868–81. 4 vols.

Sanders, Paul F. Moderne nederlandsche Componisten. The Hague, Kruseman, [1930].

Saunders, William. "The American Opera," M&L XIII (1932) 147–55.

—— "National Opera, Comparatively Considered," MQ XIII (1927) 72–84.

Seaman, Gerald. "The National Element in Early Russian Opera, 1779–1800," M&L XLII (1961) 252–62.

Seidl, Roberto. Carlos Gomes. Rio de Janeiro, [Imprensa moderna], 1935.

Seilhamer, George Overcash. History of the American Theatre. Philadelphia, Globe Printing House, 1888–91. 3 vols.

Selden, Margery Stomne. "Early Roots of Russian Opera," JAMS XV (1962) 206–11; see also ibid. XVI (1963) 257–60.

Seroff, Victor I. The Mighty Five. New York, Allen, Towne and Heath, [1948].

—— Rachmaninoff. New York, Simon & Schuster, 1950.

Serov, Aleksandr Nikolaevich. Rusalka, opera A. S. Dargomyzhskogo. Moscow, Gos. muzykal'noe izd-vo, 1953.

Servières, Georges. Emmanuel Chabrier. Paris, F. Alcan, 1912.

Shaw, George Bernard. London Music in 1888–89 as Heard by Corno di Bassetto. New York, Dodd, Mead, 1937.

Silva, Lafayette. Historia do teatro brasileiro. Rio de Janeiro, Ministério da educaçiõ e saude, 1938.

Sincero, Dino. "Boris Godounow al teatro Alla Scala di Milano," RMI XVI (1909) 385–94.

Sixto Prieto, Juan. "El Perú en la música escénica," Fenix No. 9 (1953) 278–351.

Skilton, Charles Sanford. "American Opera," MTNA XX (1925) 112–18.

Slonimsky, Nicolas. Music of Latin America. New York, Thomas Y. Crowell, 1945.

Smetana, Bedřich. Smetana in Briefen und Erinnerungen. Hrsg. und eingeleitet von František Bartoš. Prague, Artia, 1954. English translation : Letters and Reminiscences. Prague, Artia, [1955].

Smith, Cecil. Musical Comedy in America. New York, Theatre Arts Books, [1950].

Solvay, Lucien. Notice sur Jean Blockx. Brussels, Hayez, 1920.

Sonneck, Oscar George Theodore. A Bibliography of Early Secular American Music (Eighteenth Century). Washington, D.C., The Library of Congress, Music Division, 1945.

—— Early Concert Life in America. Leipzig, B&H, 1907.

—— Early Opera in America. New York, G. Schirmer, [1915].

—— Francis Hopkinson, the First American Poet-Composer. Washington, D.C., Printed for the Author by H. L. McQueen, 1905.

Soriano Fuertes, Mariano. História de la música española. Madrid, Martin y Salazar; Barcelona, Narciso Ramírez, 1856–59. 4 vols.

Soubies, Albert. Histoire de la musique en Bohême. Paris, E. Flammarion, 1898.

Šourek, Otakar. Antonín Dvořák : His Life and Works. Prague, Orbis, 1952; New York, Philosophical Library, [1954].

—— Život a dílo Antonína Dvořáka. Prague, Hudební matice umělecké besedy, 1922–33. 4 vols.

Sovetskaia muzyka. [Moscow], Gos. muzykal'noe izd-vo, 1933–

Stals, Georgs. Das lettische Ballett der Rigaer Oper. Riga, Kadilis, 1943.

Stasov, Vladimir Vasil'evich. Izbrannye stat'i o M. I. Glinke. Moscow, Gos. muzykal'noe izd-vo, 1955.

—— Mikhail Ivanovich Glinka. Moscow, Gos. muzykal'noe izd-vo, 1953.

—— Russkiia i inostrannyia opery ispolniavshiasia na Imperatorskikh Teatrakh v Rosii v XVIII-m'i XIX-m stoletiiakh. St. Petersburg, 1898.

—— Sobranie sochineniĭ. Vols. 1–3 (works of 1847–86) : St. Petersburg, M. M. Stasiulevich, 1894. Vol. 4 (works of 1886–1904) published separately in 1905.

Stefan, Paul. Anton Dvořák. New York, Greystone, [1941]. Translated and rearranged from the German edition, which was based on the authoritative four-volume biography by Otakar Šourek.

Steigman, B. M. "The Great American Opera," M&L VI (1925) 359–67.

Štěpán, Václav. Novák a Suk. Prague, Hudební matice umělecké besedy, 1945.

Stevenson, Robert. Music in Mexico, a Historical Survey. New York, Thomas Y. Crowell Co., [1952].

—— The Music of Peru : Aboriginal and Viceroyal Epochs. Washington, Pan American Union, [1960].

—— "Opera Beginnings in the New World," MQ XLV (1959) 8–25.

Streatfeild, Richard Alexander. Musiciens anglais contemporains. Paris, Editions du temps présent, 1913.

Stromenger, K. "Jan Stefani," Lódź Teatralna (1946–47) No. 3, 15–19.

Subirá, José. Enrique Granados. Madrid, [Z. Ascasíbar], 1926.

—— Historia y anecdotario del Teatro Real. Madrid, Editorial Plus Ultra, [1949].

—— El Teatro del Real Palacio (1849–1851), con un bosquejo preliminar sobre la música palatina desde Felipe V hasta Isabel II. Madrid, Consejo Superior de Investigaciones Científicas, Instituto Español de Musicología, 1950.

Sundström, Einar. "Franz Berwalds Operor," STM XXIX (1947) 16–62.

Suomalainen, Yrjö. Oskar Merikanto : Suomen kotien jäveltäjä. Helsinki, Kustannusosakeyhtiö Otava, [1950].

Swan, Alfred J. "Moussorgsky and Modern Music," MQ XI (1925) 271–80.

Szabolcsi, Bence. Bausteine zu einer Geschichte der Melodie. Budapest, Corviva, [1959].

Szabolcsi, Bence, ed. Az opera történetéből. Budapest, Akadémiai Kiadó, 1961.

Szopski, Felicjan. Władysław Żeleński. Warsaw, Gebethner i Wolff, [1928].

Szyfman, Arnold. "Problem opery polskiej," Muzyka (1951) No. 9 (18), 18–21.

Tebaldini, Giovanni. "Felipe Pedrell ed il dramma lirico spagnuolo," RMI IV (1897) 267–98, 494–524. Also separate : Turin, Bocca, 1897.

Teuber, Oscar. Geschichte des Prager Theaters. Prague, Haase, 1883–87. 3 vols.

Theatro comico portuguez, ou Collecção das operas portuguezas, que se representárão na casa do theatro público do Bairro Alto di Lisboa. Lisbon, S. T. Ferreira, 1787–92. 4 vols.

Thomson, Virgil. "George Gershwin," MMus XIII, No. 1 (November–December, 1935) 13–19.

—— "Most Melodious Tears," MMus XI, No. 1 (November–December, 1933) 13–17.

Tigranov, Georgiĭ. Armianskiĭ muzykal'nyĭ teatr. Erevan, Armianskoe gos. izd-vo, 1956, 1960. 2 vols. Vol. II has imprint : Erevan, Aipetrat, 1960.

Törnblom, Folke H. "Opera [in Sweden]," Theatre Arts XXIV (1940) 597–600.

Tolón, Edwin T., and Jorge A. González. Operas cubanas y sus autores. Havana, [Imprenta Ucar, García], 1943.

Trend, John Brande. A Picture of Modern Spain. New York, Houghton Mifflin, 1921.

Trilogia Los Pireneos y la critica, La. Barcelona, Oliva, 1901.

Trocki, Ladislas von. Die Entwickelung der Oper in Polen. Leipzig, Voigt, 1867.

Tsukkerman, Viktor Abramovich. Sadko: Opera-bylina N. A. Rimskogo-Korsakovo. Moscow, Muzgiz, 1936.

Tutenberg, Fritz. "Moderne schwedische Musik und Musiker im Umriss, II : Die schwedische Oper," Zeitschrift für Musik CVI (1939) 930–34.

Upton, William Treat. "Max and Agathe vs. Rodolph and Agnes, et al.," MLA Notes, 2d ser., IV, No. 2 (March, 1947) 217–24.

—— "Secular Music in the United States 150 Years Ago," in Papers of the American Musicological Society, Annual Meeting, 1941 . . . Edited by Gustave Reese (Printed by the Society [cop. 1946]) 105–11.

—— William Henry Fry : American Journalist and Composer-Critic. New York, Thomas Y. Crowell Co., 1954.

USSR. Tsentral'nyĭ gosudarstvennyĭ literaturnyĭ arkhiv. N. A. Rimskiĭ-Korsakov : Sbornik dokumentov. Moscow, Gos. muzykal'noe izd-vo, 1951.

Vieira, Ernesto. Diccionario biographico de musicos portuguezes : Historia e bibliographia da musica em Portugal. Lisbon, M. Moreira & Pinheiro, 1900. 2 vols.

Villalba, L. "La cuestión de la ópera española : Carta abierta," *La Ciudad de Dios* XXXIII, No. 2 (1913) 204–11.

Virella Cassañes, Francisco. La ópera en Barcelona. Barcelona, Redondo y Zumetra, 1888.

Virgilio, Rudolph. Development of Italian Opera in New York. New York, Italian Library of Information, 1938.

Walicki, Aleksandr. Stanisław Moniuszko. Warsaw, Nakład autora, Skład główny w księgarni Gebethnera i Wolffa, 1873.

Walsh, T. J. Opera in Old Dublin, 1819–1839. [Wexford, Ireland], Wexford Festival, 1952.

Waters, Edward N. Victor Herbert : A Life in Music. New York, Macmillan Co., 1955.

Wegelin, Oscar. Early American Plays, 1714–1830. New York, The Dunlap Society, 1900.

—— Micah Hawkins and the Saw-Mill : A Sketch of the First Successful American Opera and Its Author. New York, privately printed, 1917.

White, Richard Grant. "Opera in New York," *Century Magazine* I (1881) 686–703, 865–82; II (1882) 31–43, 193–210.

Wierzbicka, Karyna. Źródła do historii teatru warszawskiego od roku 1762 do roku 1833. Wrocław, Zakład narodowy imienia Ossolińskich, 1951. Cz. 1.

Wilson, Charles. "The Two Versions of *Goyescas*," MMR LXXXI (1951) 203–7.

Winkelmann, Johann. Josef Myslivecek als Opernkomponist. Vienna Dissertation, 1905.

Winter, Marian Hannah. "American Theatrical Dancing from 1750–1800," MQ XXIV (1938) 58–73.

Yellin, Victor. The Life and Operatic Works of George Whitefield Chadwick. Harvard Dissertation, 1957.

Zagiba, Franz. Tschaikovskij : Leben und Werk. Zurich, Leipzig, Vienna, Amalthea-Verlag, [1953].

Zawiłowski, Konrad. Stanislaus Moniuszko. Vienna Dissertation, 1902.

Zetlin, Mikhail. The Five : The Evolution of the Russian School of Music. New York, International Universities Press, [cop. 1959].

Zetowski, S. "Teoria polskiej opery narodowej z końca XVIII i początku XIX wieku," *Muzyka Polska* (1937) 274–80.

Zichy, Géza. Aus meinem Leben. Stuttgart, Deutsche Verlags-Anstalt, 1911–13. 2 vols.

Zurita, Marciano. Historia del género chico. Madrid, Prensa popular, 1920.

VII

TWENTIETH CENTURY

Abendroth, Walter. Hans Pfitzner. Munich, A. Lagen & G. Müller, 1935.

Abert, Anna Amalie. "Stefan Zweigs Bedeutung für das Alterswerk von Richard Strauss," in *Festschrift Friedrich Blume* (Kassel, Bärenreiter, 1963) [7]–15.

Abraham, Gerald. Eight Soviet Composers. London, New York, Toronto, Oxford University Press, [1943].

Ackere, Jules van. Maurice Ravel. [Brussels], Elsevier, [1957].

—— *Pelléas et Mélisande*, ou la recontre miraculeuse d'une poésie et d'une musique. Brussels, Librairie Encyclopédique, 1952.

Almanach der deutschen Musikbücherei auf das Jahr 1924/25. Regensburg, Gustav Bosse, 1924.

Altmann, Wilhelm. "Ur- und Erstaufführungen von Opernwerken auf deutschen Bühnen in den letzten Spielzeiten 1899/1900 bis 1924/25," in *Jahrbuch der Universal-Edition* (1926).

American Composers Alliance Bulletin. New York, 1938, 1952– .

Amico, Fedele d', and Guido M. Gatti, eds. Alfredo Casella. [Collected essays by various authors.] [Milan], Ricordi, [1958].

Annuario del teatro lirico italiano, 1940– . [Milan], Edizioni Corbaccio, [1940–   ].

Antcliffe, Herbert. "A British School of Music-Drama : The Work of Rutland Boughton," MQ IV (1918) 117–27.

Antheil, George. "Opera—a Way Out," MMus XI, No. 2 (January–February, 1934) 89–94.

—— "Wanted—Opera by and for Americans," MMus VII, No. 4 (June–July, 1930) 11–16.

Archibald, Bruce. "Ulysses in Tone," *Opera News* XXIII, No. 19 (March 9, 1959) 12–13, 28.

Armitage, Merle, ed. Arnold Schoenberg. New York, G. Schirmer, 1937.

—— ed. Igor Stravinsky : Articles and Critiques. New York, G. Schirmer, 1936.

Arnold, Denis. "Strauss and Wilde's *Salome*," MMR LXXXIX (1959) 44–49.

Arundell, Dennis. "Arthur Benjamin's Operas," *Tempo* No. 15 (Spring, 1950) 15–18.

Aubry, Georges Jean. La Musique française d'aujourd'hui. Paris, Perrin, 1916. Translated as : French Music of Today. London, K. Paul [etc.], 1919.

Babbitt, Milton. "An Introduction to the Music [of Schoenberg's *Moses und Aron*]," in brochure accompanying the recording of the opera: Columbia K 3 L –241.

Bachmann, Claus-Henning. "Oper in entzauberter Welt," *Musica* XIV (1960) 75–80.

Bahle, Julius. Hans Pfitzner und der geniale Mensch : Eine psychologische Kulturkritik. Constance, C. Weller, [1949].

Barblan, Guglielmo. "*L'oro*, ultima opera di Pizzetti alla 'Scala,'" RMI XLIX (1947) 57–68.

Barlow, Samuel. "Blitzstein's Answer," MMus XVIII, No. 2 (January–February, 1941) 81–83.

Bauer, Marion. "Darius Milhaud," MQ XXVIII (1942) 139–59.

Beck, Georges. Darius Milhaud. (Etude suivie du catalogue chronologique complet de son oeuvre.) Paris, Heugel & Cie., 1949.

—— Darius Milhaud; catalogue chronologique complet de son oeuvre (supplément) : oeuvres composées de novembre 1949 à avril 1956. Paris, Heugel et Cie., [1956?].

Beecham, Sir Thomas. Frederick Delius. New York, Alfred A. Knopf, 1960.

Beer, Otto Fritz. "Egon Wellesz und die Oper," *Die Musik* XXIII (1931) 909–12.

Bekker, Paul. Franz Schreker : Studie zur Kritik der modernen Oper. Berlin, Schuster & Loeffler, 1919.

—— Das Musikdrama der Gegenwart. Stuttgart, Strecker & Schröder, 1909.

—— Neue Musik. Berlin, E. Reiss, 1920. 5th ed.

—— "The Opera Walks New Paths," MQ XXI (1935) 266–78.

Béla Bartók : A Memorial Review including Articles on His Life and Works, Reprinted from Tempo, the Quarterly Review of Contemporary Music; a Chronological Listing of Works [and] Bartók on Records. New York, Boosey & Hawkes, [1950].

Benjamin Britten : Das Opernwerk. Bonn, Boosey & Hawkes, [1955].

Bennett, Howard G. "Opera in Modern Germany," MTNA XXIX (1934) 65–73.

Berg, Alban. "A Word about *Wozzek*," MMus V, No. 1 (November–December, 1927) 22–24.

Bernet Kempers, Karel Philippus. Inleiding tot de Opera *Halewijn* van Willem Pijper. Rotterdam, Brusse, [1948?].

Berrsche, Alexander. Kurze Einführung in Hans Pfitzners Musikdrama *Der arme Heinrich*. Leipzig, [1910].

Berthoud, Paul B. The Musical Works of Dr. Henry Hadley. New York, National Association for American Composers and Conductors, 1942.

Bibliographie für Theatergeschichte 1905–1910, bearbeitet von Paul Alfred Merbach. Berlin, Selbstverlag der Gesellschaft für Theatregeschichte, 1913.

Bie, Oscar. "Stand der Oper," *Die Neue Rundschau* XLIII, No. 2 (July–December, 1932) 124–31.

Bitter, Werner. Die deutsche komische Oper der Gegenwart : Studien zu ihrer Entwicklung. Leipzig, Kistner & Siegel, 1932.

Blaukopf, Kurt. "Autobiographische Elemente in Alban Bergs *Wozzeck*," OeM IX (1954) 155–58.

Blitzstein, Marc. *"Hin und Zurück* in Philadelphia," MMus V, No. 4 (May–June, 1928) 34–36.

—— "On *Mahagonny*," *The Score* No. 23 (July, 1958) 11–13.

—— "The Phenomenon of Stravinsky," MQ XXI (1935) 330–47.

Boardman, Herbert Russell. Henry Hadley, Ambassador of Harmony. Emory University, Georgia, Banner Press, [1932].

Boll, André. Marcel Delannoy. Paris, Ventadour, [1957].

—— "Marcel Delannoy, musicien de théâtre," RM XXV, No. 209 (1949) 22–29.

Bonajuti Tarquini, Vittoria. Riccardo Zandonai, nel ricordo dei suoi intimi. Milan, Ricordi, 1951.

Bontempelli, Massimo. Gian Francesco Malipiero. Milan, Bompiani, [1942].

Boughton, Rutland. The Death and Resurrection of the Music Festival. London, W. Reeves, [1913].

—— The Glastonbury Festival Movement. London, [Somerset Press], 1922. Reprinted from *Somerset and the Drama* [by S. R. Littlewood and others].

—— Music Drama of the Future : *Uther and Igraine*, Choral Drama . . . with Essays by the Collaborators. London, W. Reeves, 1911.

—— "A National Music Drama : The Glastonbury Festival," PMA XLIV (1917–18) 19–35.

Brand, Max. " 'Mechanische' Musik und das Problem der Oper," *Musikblätter des Anbruch* VIII (1926) 356–59.

Brecht, Bertolt. "Two Essays," *The Score* No. 23 (July, 1958) 14–26.

Bréville, Pierre de. Un Grand Musicien français : Marie-Joseph Erb, sa vie et son oeuvre. Strasbourg, F. X. Le Roux, 1948.

Briner, Andres. "Eine Bekenntnisoper Paul Hindemith : Zu seiner oper *Die Harmonie der Welt*," SchwM XCIX (1959) 1–5, 50–56.

Britten, Benjamin, and others. The Rape of Lucretia: A Symposium by Benjamin Britten, Eric Crozier, John Piper, Henry Boys. London, John Lane, 1948.

Brod, Max. Leoš Janáček. Vienna, [etc.], Universal Edition, [1956].

Bruneau, Alfred. La Vie et les œuvres de Gabriel Fauré. Paris, Charpentier & Fasquelle, 1925.

Burkhard, Willy. "Zu meiner Oper *Die schwarze Spinne*," M III (1949) 126–28.

Busne, Henry de. *"Ariane et Barbe-bleue* de M. Paul Dukas," MM III (1907) 465–71.

Busoni, Ferruccio. Entwurf einer neuen Aesthetik der Tonkunst. Leipzig, Insel-Verlag, [19—]. Translated as : Sketch of a New Esthetic of Music. New York, G. Schirmer, 1911.

[——] "Nota bio-bibliografica su Ferruccio Busoni," RassM XIII (1940) 82–88.

—— Über die Möglichkeiten der Oper und über die Partitur des *Doktor Faust*. Leipzig, B&H, 1926.

—— Von der Einheit der Musik. Berlin, M. Hesse, [1923].

—— Wesen und Einheit der Musik. Revidiert, ergänzt und mit Nachwort versammelt von J. Herrmann. Berlin, Wunsiedel, Hesse, 1956. Translated as : The Essence of Music and Other Papers. London, Rockliff, 1957.

Busser, Henri. De *Pelléas* aux *Indes galantes*, de la flûte au tambour. Paris, A. Fayard, [1955]. 4th ed.

Campogalliani, Ettore. Luigi Ferrari-Trecate operista : Tema e variazioni. Verona, Edizioni di "Vita Veronese," 1955.

Canudo, Ricciotto. "Le Drame musical contemporain," MM III (1907) 1185–92; IV (1908) 56–60.

Capell, Richard. "Dame Ethel Smyth's Operas at Covent Garden," MMR LIII (1923) 197–98.

Casella, Alfredo. I segreti della giara. Florence, Sansoni, 1941. Translated as : Music in My Time. Norman, University of Oklahoma Press, [1955].

Cecil, George. "Impressions of Opera in France," MQ VII (1921) 314–30.

—— "Monte Carlo : Opéra de Luxe," MQ IX (1923) 65–71.

Chadwick, George. Horatio Parker. New Haven, Yale University Press, 1921.

Chailley, Jacques. "Le Symbolisme des thèmes dans *Pelléas et Mélisande*," *L'Information musicale*, No. 64, 2e année (April 3, 1942) 889–90.

Challis, Bennett. "Opera Publics of Europe : Impressions and Reminiscences," MQ XII (1926) 564–79.

Cherbuliez, Antoine-Elisée. "Kleine Monographie der Schweizer Oper," M I (1947) 96–99.

Chybiński, A. "L. Różycki jako twórca dramatu muzycznego *Bolesław Smiały*," *Młoda Muzyka* (1909) No. 7–8.

Cinquanta anni di opera e balletto in Italia. [A cura di Guido M. Gatti.] Rome, Carlo Bestetti, Edizioni d'Arte, [1954].

Clapham, John. *"The Whirlpool:* A Slovak Opera," MR XIX (1958) 47–51.

Coeuroy, André. La Musique française moderne. Paris, Delagrave, 1922.

Cohen, Alex. "Ernest Bloch's *Macbeth*," M&L XIX (1938) 143–48.

Collaer, Paul. Darius Milhaud. Paris, Richard-Masse, Editeurs, 1947.

—— La Musique moderne, 1905–1955. Paris-Brussels, Elsevier, 1955.

Colles, H. C. "Philip Napier Miles," M&L XVII (1936) 357–67.

Cooke, Deryck. *"The Rake* and the 18th Century," *The Musical Times* CIII (1962) 20–23.

Copland, Aaron. Our New Music. New York, Whittlesey, [1941].

Corrodi, Hans. Othmar Schoeck : Bild eines Schaffens. Frauenfeld, Huber, [1956]. 3d ed.

—— "Othmar Schoeck's *Massimilla Doni*," M&L XVIII (1937) 391–97.

Cortese, Louis. Alfredo Casella. Genoa, Orfini, [1935].

Craft, Robert. "Reflections on *The Rake's Progress*," *The Score* No. 9 (September, 1954) 24–30.

Crozier, Eric. "Foreword to *Albert Herring*," *Tempo* No. 4 (Summer, 1947) 10–14.

Dallapiccola, Luigi. "The Genesis of the *Canti di prigionia* and *Il prigioniero:* An Autobiographical Fragment," MQ XXXIX (1953) 355–72.

Danckert, Werner. Claude Debussy. Berlin, de Gruyter, 1950.

Deane, Basil. Albert Roussel. London, Barrie and Rockliff, [1961].

De Angelis, Alberto. "Musica e musicisti nell' opera di G. d'Annunzio," RMI XLIII (1939) 275–301.

Debussy, Claude. Monsieur Croche, anti-dilettante. Paris, Dorbon-aîné, 1921.

Delannoy, Marcel. Honegger. Paris, Flore, P. Horay, [1953].

Della Corte, Andrea. "*The Rake's Progress* di I. Strawinsky," RMI LIII (1951) 262–68.

—— Rittrato di Franco Alfano. Turin, G. B. Paravia, [1935].

Demuth, Norman. Albert Roussel. [London], United Music Publishers, [n.d.].

Dent, Edward J. "Busoni's *Doctor Faust*," M&L VII (1926) 196–208.

—— Ferrucio Busoni : A Biography. London, Oxford University Press, 1933.

—— "Hans Pfitzner," M&L IV (1923) 119–32.

De' Paoli, Domenico. "Italy's New Music of the Theatre," MMus VIII, No. 1 (November–December, 1930) 21–26.

—— "*Orfeo* and *Pelléas*," M&L XX (1939) 381–98.

—— "Pizzetti's *Fra Gherardo*," MMus VI, No. 2 (January–February, 1929) 39–42.

De Rensis, Raffaello. Ermanno Wolf-Ferrari, la sua vita d'artista. Milan, Fratelli Treves, 1937.

—— Ottorino Respighi. Turin, Paravia, [1935].

Desderi, Ettore. "Le tendenze attuali della musica : Il teatro," RMI XXXVIII (1931) 247–77.

D'Estrade-Guerra, O. "Les Manuscrits de *Pelléas et Mélisande*," RM No. sp. 235 (1957) 5–24.

Deutsch, Max. "*Phèdre*, de Marcel Mihalovici," RIdM No. 12 (Spring, 1952) 66–74.

Dickinson, A. E. F. "Round about *The Midsummer Marriage*," M&L XXXVII (1956) 50–60.

Dioli, Arrigo, and Maria Fernanda Nobili. La vita e l'arte di Amilcare Zanella. Bergamo, Edizioni Orobiche, [1941].

Drew, David. "Brecht versus Opera," *The Score* No. 23 (July, 1958) 7–10.

—— "Topicality and the Universal : The Strange Case of Weill's *Die Bürgschaft*," M&L XXIX (1958) 242–55.

Du Bled, Victor. "Le Ballet de l'opéra," RM II (December, 1921) 191–205.

[Dukas, Paul.] RM numéro spécial (May–June, 1936) contains articles on Dukas's operas.

Dumesnil, Maurice. Claude Debussy, Master of Dreams. New York, Ives Washburn, [1940].

—— "Gabriel Dupont, Musician of Normandy," MQ XXX (1944) 441–47.

Egk, Werner. "Irische Legende," OeM X (1955) 125–30.

—— Musik, Wort, Bild. Texte und Anmerkungen : Betrachtungen und Gedanken. Munich, A. Langen, G. Müller, [1960].

Einem, Gottfried von. "Der Prozess," OeM VIII (1953) 198–200.

Einstein, Alfred. "L'opera tedesca d'oggi," RassM V (1932) 26–37.

Emmanuel, Maurice. Pelléas et Mélisande de Debussy : Etude et analyse. Paris, Mellottée, [1925?]. New ed., 1950.

Engelfred, Abele. "Enoch Arden di Riccardo Strauss," RMI VI (1899) 176–84.

Eősze, László. Kodály Zoltán, élete és munkássága. Budapest, Zeneműkiadó Vállalat, 1956. In English : Zoltan Kodaly, His Life and Work. London, Collet, 1962.

Epstein, Peter. "Paul Hindemiths Theatermusik," Die Musik XXIII (May, 1931) 582–87.

Erhardt, Otto. "The Later Operatic Works of Richard Strauss," Tempo No. 12 (Summer, 1949) 23–31.

—— Richard Strauss : Leben, Wirken, Schaffen. Olten & Freiburg i. B., O. Walter AG., [1953].

Evans, Peter. "Britten's New Opera [A Midsummer Night's Dream] : A Preview," Tempo No. 53–54 (1960) 34–48.

Everett, Horace. "Notes on The Tender Land," Tempo No. 31 (Spring, 1954) 13–16.

Eyer, Ronald. "Carlisle Floyd's Susannah," Tempo No. 42 (Winter, 1956–57) 7–11.

Fähnrich, Hermann. "Das 'Mozart-Wagner-Element' im Schaffen von Richard Strauss," SchwM LXXXIX (1959) 311–16.

—— "Richard Strauss über das Verhältnis von Dichtung und Musik (Wort und Ton) in seinem Opernschaffen," Mf XIV (1961) 22–35.

Falle, G. "Canadian Opera," Canadian Forum XXXVI (1956) 206–7.

[Fauré, Gabriel Urbain.] See RM, numéro spécial (October, 1922).

[——] "Gabriel Fauré : Note biografiche," Bollettino bibliografico musicale V, No. 3 (March, 1930) 5–[17].

—— Lettres intimes. Présentées par Philippe Fauré-Fremiet. Paris, La Colombe, [1951].

Fauré-Frémiet, Philippe. Gabriel Fauré. Nouvelle éd., suivie de Réflexions sur la confiance Fauréenne et de Notes sur l'interprétation des oeuvres. Paris, A. Michel, [1957].

Favre, Georges. Paul Dukas : Sa vie, son oeuvre. Paris, La Colombe, [1948].

Ferchault, Guy. "A propos de Mélisande," *L'Information musicale*, No. 60, 2e année (March 7, 1942) 819–21; No. 62, 2e année (March 20, 1942) 874.

Fickler, August. "Oper und Operette in Rundfunk und Fernsehen 1957," NZfM CXIX (1958) 282–88.

Finck, Henry T. Richard Strauss. Boston, Little, Brown, 1917.

Foerster, Lilian A. *"Peter Grimes* in Score and Performance," *Musicology* I (1947) 221–41.

Forneberg, Erich. "Das Volkslied als expressionistisches Symbol in Alban Bergs *Wozzeck*," NZfM CXX (1959) 261–65.

Fortner, Wolfgang. "Bluthochzeit nach Federico Garcia Lora," *Melos* XXIV (1957) 71–73.

Gardner, John. *"The Duenna* [by Roberto Gerhard] (1945–47)," *The Score* No. 17 (September, 1956) 20–26.

Gatti, Guido Maria. "Franco Alfano," MQ IX (1923) 556–77.

—— "Gabriele D'Annunzio and the Italian Opera Composers," MQ X (1924) 263–88.

—— Ildebrando Pizzetti. Turin, G. B. Paravia, [1934]; 2d ed., Milan, Ricordi, [1955]. English translation : London, Dennis Dobson, 1951.

—— "Ildebrando Pizzetti," MQ IX (1923) 96–121, 271–86.

—— "Malipiero and Pirandello at the Opera," MMus XI, No. 4 (May–June, 1934) 213–16.

—— Musicisti moderni d'Italia e di fuori. Bologna, Pizzi, 1920.

—— "Opernkomponist Ferruccio Busoni," *Melos* XXV (1958) 189–94.

—— "Recent Italian Operas," MQ XXIII (1937) 77–88.

—— "The Stage Works of Ferruccio Busoni," MQ XX (1934) 267–77.

—— Il Teatro alla Scala rinnovato : Le prime quattro stagioni. Milan, Fratelli Treves, 1926.

—— "Two *Macbeths:* Verdi—Bloch," MQ XII (1926) 22–31.

Gatti, Guido M., ed. L'opera di Gian Francesco Malipiero : Saggi di scrittori italiani e stranieri . . . seguiti dal catalogo delle opere con annotazioni dell' autore e da ricordi e pensieri dello stesso. [Bologna], Edizioni di Treviso, 1952.

Gatti-Casazza, Giulio. Memories of the Opera. New York, Charles Scribner's Sons, 1941.

Gavazzeni, Gianandrea. Altri studi pizzettiani. Bergamo, Stamperia Conti, [1956].

—— "Karol Szymanowski e il *Re Ruggero*," RassM X (1937) 409–15.

—— Tre studi su Pizzetti. Como, E. Cavalleri, 1937.

George, André. Arthur Honegger. Paris, C. Aveline, 1926.

Giazotto, Remo. Busoni : La vita nell' opera. [Milan], Genio, [1947].

Gilman, Lawrence. Aspects of Modern Opera. London, John Lane; New York, Dodd, Mead, 1924.

—— Debussy's *Pelléas et Mélisande*, a Guide to the Opera. New York, G. Schirmer, 1907.

Glanville-Hicks, P[eggy]. "Some Reflections on Opera : Rolf Liebermann, a Man of the Theatre," *American Composers Alliance Bulletin* VI, No. 4 (1957) 12–15, 22.

"*Gloriana:* A Synopsis," *Tempo* No. 28 (Summer, 1953) 8–13.

Golachowski, Stanisław. Karol Szymanowski. [Wyd. 1 Cracow], Polskie Wydawnictwo Muzyczne, [1956].

Goldovsky, Boris. "*Mavra*, a Lyric Masterpiece," *Chrysalis* IV (1951) 3–4.

Goléa, Antoine. Pelléas et Mélisande : Analyse poétique et musicale. Paris, [Impr. du Château-Rouge], 1952.

Gordon, Diane Kestin. Folklore in Modern English Opera. University of California, Los Angeles Dissertation, 1959. 2 vols.

Goslich, Siegfried. "Das Wandbild : Othmar Schoeck und Ferruccio Busoni," M XI (1957) 322–25.

Graf, Max. "*Der Prozess* von Gottfried von Einem," OeM VIII (1953) 259–64.

Gregor, Joseph. Richard Strauss. Munich, R. Piper, [1939].

—— "Typen der Regie der Oper im 20. Jahrhundert," in *Bericht über den internationalen musikwissenschaftlichen Kongress Wien, Mozart-jahr 1956* (Graz, Böhlaus, 1958), 253–60.

Grisson, Alexandra Carola. Ermanno Wolf-Ferrari. Regensburg, Bosse, 1941; 2d ed., Zurich, Amalthea-Verlag, [1958].

Guerrini, Guido. Ferruccio Busoni : La vita, la figura, l'opera. Florence, Casa Editrice Monsalvato, 1944.

Gui, Vittorio. "Arlecchino," RassM XIII (1940) 30–37.

Gutman, Hans. "*Mahagonny* and Other Novelties," MMus VII, No. 4 (June–July, 1930) 32–36.

—— "Tabloid Hindemith," MMus VII, No. 1 (December, 1929–January, 1930) 34–37.

Hall, Raymond. "The *Macbeth* of Bloch," MMus XV, No. 4 (May–June, 1938) 209–15.

Halusa, Karl. Hans Pfitzners musikdramatisches Schaffen. Vienna Dissertation, 1929.

Hamburg, Nordwestdeutscher Rundfunk. Zur Uraufführung von Arnold Schönbergs nachgelassener Oper *Moses und Aron* : Die Uraufführung fand am 12. März 1954 in der Hamburger Musikhalle statt. [Hamburg, 1954(?).]

Hammerschmidt, Wolfgang. 10 Jahre Komische Oper. (Berlin 1947–1957.) Berlin, Komische Oper, [1958].

Handschin, Jacques. Igor Stravinsky. Zurich and Leipzig, Hug, 1933.

Harászti, Emil. Béla Bartók, His Life and Works. Paris, The Lyrebird Press, [1938].

—— "Le Problème du Leit-motiv," RM IV (August, 1923) 35–37.

Harcourt, Eugène d'. La Musique actuelle en Allemagne et Autriche-Hongrie. Paris, Durdilly, [1908].

—— La Musique actuelle en Italie. Paris, Durdilly, [1907].

Harth, Walther. "Oper zwischen Montage und Breitwand," *Melos* XXIV (1957) 4–8.

Hartung, Günther. "Zur epischen Oper Brechts und Weills," *Wissenschaftliche Zeitschrift des Martin-Luther-Universität Halle-Wittenberg* VIII (1959) 659–73.

Hausswald, Günter. "Antiker Mythos bei Richard Strauss," M XII (1958) 323–26.

Heinsheimer, H. W. "Opera in America Today," MQ XXXVII (1951) 315–29.

—— "Die Umgestaltung des Operntheaters in Deutschland," *Anbruch* XV (August–September, 1933) 107–13.

Hell, Henri. Francis Poulenc, musicien français. Paris, Plon, [1958]. English translation : London, Calder, [1959].

Helm, Everett. "Carl Orff," MQ XLI (1955) 285–304.

—— "Virgil Thomson's *Four Saints in Three Acts*," MR XV (1954) 127–32.

Henze, Hans Werner. "Neue Aspekte in der Musik," NZfM CXXI (1960) 3–9.

[Heseltine, Philip.] Frederick Delius. Reprinted with Additions, Annotations and Comments by Hubert Foss. New York, Oxford University Press, 1952.

Hill, Edward Burlingame. Modern French Music. Boston and New York, Houghton Mifflin, 1924.

Hill, Richard S. "Concert Life in Berlin, Season 1943–44," *MLA Notes*, 2d ser. I, No. 3 (June, 1944) 13–33.

—— "Schoenberg's Tone-Rows and the Tonal System of the Future," MQ XXII (1936) 14–37.

Hindemith, Paul. A Composer's World : Horizons and Limitations. Cambridge, Mass., Harvard University Press, 1952.

Hirtler, Franz. Hans Pfitzners *Armer Heinrich* in seiner Stellung zur Musik des ausgehenden 19. Jahrhunderts. Würzburg, K. Triltsch, 1940.

Hoérée, Arthur. Albert Roussel. Paris, Rieder, 1938.

Hoffman, Rudolf Stephan. Franz Schreker. Leipzig, E. P. Tal, 1921.

Hofmannsthal, Hugo von. "Ce que nous avons voulu en écrivant *Ariane à Naxos* et *Le Bourgeois Gentilhomme*," MM VIII, Nos. 9–10 (1912) 1–3.

Hohlfeld, Charlotte. "Wieder eine neue Oper : *Kolumbus* von Karl-Rudi Griesbach," MuG IX (1959) 80–82.

Holländer, Hans. "Hugo von Hofmannsthal als Opernlibrettist," *Zeitschrift für Musik* XCVI (1929) 551–54.

—— "Leoš Janáček and His Operas," MQ XV (1929) 29–36.

—— "Leoš Janáček in seinen Opern," NZfM CXIX (1958) 425–27.

—— "The Music of Leos Janacek—Its Origin in Folklore," MQ XLI (1955) 171–76.

Holst, Imogen. "Britten's *Let's Make an Opera!*," *Tempo* No. 18 (Winter, 1950–51) 12–16.

—— Gustav Holst. London, Oxford University Press, 1938.

—— The Music of Ralph Vaughan Williams. London, New York, To- University Press, 1951.

Honolka, Kurt. Das vielstimmige Jahrhundert : Musik in unserer Zeit. Stuttgart, Cotta, [1960].

Hoover, Kathleen O'Donnell, and John Cage. Virgil Thomson : His Life and Music. New York, Thomas Yoseloff, [1959].

Howard, John Tasker. Our Contemporary Composers : American Music in the Twentieth Century. New York, Thomas Y. Crowell Co., 1941.

Howes, Frank. The Dramatic Works of Ralph Vaughan Williams. London, Oxford University Press, 1937.

—— The Music of Ralph Vaughan Williams. London, New York, To- ronto, Oxford University Press, 1954.

Hübner, O. Richard Strauss und das Musikdrama. Leipzig, [Pabst], 1910. 2d ed.

Hurd, Michael. Immortal Hour, the Life and Period of Rutland Bough- ton. London, Routledge and Kegan Paul, [1962].

Husssey, Dyneley. "Walton's *Troilus and Cressida*," M&L XXXVI (1955) 139–45.

Hutchings, Arthur. "Delius's Operas," *Tempo* No. 26 (Winter, 1952–53) 22–29.

Huth, Arno. "Forbidden Opus—Protestant," MMus XVI, No. 1 (Novem- ber–December, 1938) 38–41.

Inghelbrecht, Germaine, and D. E. Inghelbrecht. Claude Debussy. [Paris], Costard, [1953].

Internationale Richard-Strauss-Gesellschaft, *Mitteilungen*. Berlin, No. 1– (October, 1952–).

Istel, Edgar. "For a Reversion to Opera," MQ X (1924) 405–37.

Iwaszkiewicz, J. "Dzieje *Króla Rogera*," *Muzyka* (1926) 271–72.

Jachimecki, Zdzisław. Karol Szymanowski. Cracow, Skład gł. w Księgarni Jagiellońskiej (Druk. "Czasu"), 1927.

—— "Karol Szymanowski," MQ VIII (1922) 23–37.

—— "Karol Szymanowski," *Slavonic and East European Review* XVII (July, 1938) 174–85.

—— "Operetka Karola Szymanowskiego," *Muzyka* (1952) Nos. 3–4 (24– 25), 27–39.

Jahn, Renate. "Vom *Spieler* zur *Erzählung vom wahren Menschen*," MuG XI (1961) 232–38.

Janáček, Leoš. Korespondence Leoše Janáčka s libretisty Výletü Broučko- vých. Prague, Hudebni Matice, 1950.

Janáček, Leoš. Korespondence Leoše Janáčka s Marié Calmou a MUDr. Frant. Veselým. Prague, Orbis, 1951.

—— Leoš Janáček in Briefen und Erinnerungen, ausgewählt, mit Beiträgen und Anmerkungen versehen von Bohumír Štědroň. [Prague], Artia, [1955]. Translated as : Letters and Reminiscences. Prague, Artia, 1955.

Jardillier, Robert. Pelléas. Paris, C. Aveline, 1927.

Jones, John Kester. The *Elektra* of Strauss : The Relation of the Music to the Drama. University of California, Berkeley A.M. Thesis, 1955.

Jouve, Pierre Jean, and Michel Fano. *Wozzeck* ou le nouvel opéra. Paris, Plon, [1953].

Kalisch, Alfred. "Impressions of Strauss's *Elektra*," ZIMG X (1908–9) 198–202.

Kamieński, Ł. "[Nowowiejski's] *Legenda Bałtyku*," *Muzyka* (1924) No. 2, 64–68.

Kamiński, M. Ludomir Różycki, the Jubilee Concert : Biographical Notes. Katowice, 1951.

Kapp, Julius. Franz Schreker. Munich, Drei Masken, 1921.

—— Die Staatsoper Berlin 1919 bis 1925. Stuttgart, Deutsche Verlags-Anstalt, [1925].

Keller, Hans. "Britten and Mozart," M&L XXIX (1948) 17–30.

—— "Britten's *Beggar's Opera*," *Tempo* No. 10 (Winter, 1948–49) 7–13.

—— "Schoenberg's Comic Opera [*Von Heute auf Morgen*]," *The Score* No. 23 (July, 1958) 27–36.

—— "Schoenberg's *Moses and Aron*," *The Score* No. 21 (October, 1957) 30–45.

Keller, Wilhelm. Karl Orff's *Antigonae:* Versuch einer Einführung. Mainz, Schott, [1950].

Kerman, Joseph. "Grimes and Lucretia," *The Hudson Review* II (1949–50) 277–84.

—— "Opera à la mode. [Stravinsky's *The Rake's Progress*]," *The Hudson Review* VI (1953–54) 560–77.

—— "Terror and Self-Pity : Alban Berg's *Wozzeck*," *The Hudson Review* V (1952–53) 409–19.

Kiekert, Ingeborg. Die musikalische Form in den Werken Carl Orff's. Regensburg, Gustav-Bosse Verlag, 1957.

Klebe, Giselher. "Meine Oper *Alkmene*," *Melos* XXVIII (1961) 272–75.

—— "Uber meine Oper *Die Räuber*," *Melos* XXIV (1957) 73–76.

Klein, John W. "Delius as a Musical Dramatist," MR XXII (1961) 294–301.

—— "Some Reflexions on *Gloriana*," *Tempo* No. 29 (Autumn, 1953) 16–21.

—— "*Wozzeck*—a Summing-up," M&L XLIV (1963) 132–39.

Klein, Rudolf. "Frank Martins erste Oper [*Der Sturm*]," OeM XI (1956) 50–56.

—— "Molière auf der Opernbühne : Zur Salzburger Uraufführung von Liebermanns *Schule der Frauen*," OeM XII (1957) 151–54.

—— "Rolf Liebermann als dramatischer Komponist," *Melos* XXI (1954) 275–80.

—— "Rolf Liebermanns Opera semiseria *Penelope*," SchwM XCIV (1954) 271–76.

—— "Style et technique musicale de l'opéra *La Tempête* de Frank Martin," SchwM XCVI (1956) 240–44.

Koechlin, Charles Louis Eugène. Gabriel Fauré : Avec citations musicales dans le texte. Paris, Plon, [1949]. New ed.

Koegler, Horst. "Opernkomponisten heute : Eine Rundfrage des Internationalen Theaterinstituts der UNESCO," *Melos* XX (1953) 316–18.

Korngold, Julius. Deutsches Opernschaffen der Gegenwart. Vienna, Rikola, 1922.

—— Die romanische Oper der Gegenwart. Vienna, Rikola, 1922.

Kornprobst, Louis. J. Guy Ropartz : Etude biographique et musicale. Strasbourg, Editions Musicales d'Alsace, [1949].

Krause, Ernst. "*Penelope* und der neue Kurs," MuG V (1955) 125–27.

—— Richard Strauss : Gestalt und Werk. Leipzig, B&H, 1955.

Krenek, Ernst. Music Here and Now. New York, W. W. Norton, [1939]. Originally in German, 1937.

—— "The New Music and Today's Theatre," MMus XIV, No. 4 (May–June, 1937) 200–203.

—— "Opera between the Wars," MMus XX, No. 2 (January–February, 1943) 102–111.

—— "Problemi di stile nell' opera," RassM VII (1934) 199–202.

—— Selbstdarstellung. Zurich, Atlantis-Verlag, [1948].

—— Zur Sprache gebracht : Essays über Musik. Munich, Langen/ Müller, [1958].

Krieger, Erhard. "Heinrich Kaminski's Drama *Jürg Jenatsch*," *Zeitschrift für Musik* C (1933) 992–95.

Kroó, György. Bartók Béla szinpadi müvei. Budapest, 1962.

Krüger, Karl Joachim. Hugo von Hofmannsthal und Richard Strauss. Berlin, Junker und Dünnhaupt, 1935.

Kulikovich, Mikola. Sovetskaia opera na sluzhbe partii i pravitel'stva. Munich, 1955.

Labroca, Mario. "The Rebirth of Italian Opera," MMus IV, No. 4 (May–June, 1927) 8–14.

La Maestre, André Espiau de. "Francis Poulenc und seine Bernanos-Oper," OeM XIV (1959) 4–9.

—— "Milhauds *Christophe Colomb*," OeM XII (1957) 9–12.

La Morgia, Manlio, ed. La città dannunziana di Ildebrando Pizzetti : Saggi e note. [Pescara, Comitato Centrale Abruzzese per le Onoranze a I. Pizzetti; Milan, Ricordi], 1958.

Lamy, Fernand. J. Guy Ropartz : L'homme et l'œuvre. Paris, Durand et Cie., [1948].

Landormy, Paul Charles René. "Gabriel Fauré," MQ XVII (1931) 293–301.

—— "Maurice Ravel," MQ XXV (1939) 430–41.

Landowski, Marcel. Honegger. [Paris], Editions du Seuil, [1957].

Landowski, Wanda Alice L. Maurice Ravel : Sa vie, son oeuvre. Paris, Les Editions Ouvrières, [1950].

Lang, Paul Henry. "Background Music for *Mein Kampf*," *Saturday Review of Literature* XXVIII, No. 3 (January 20, 1945) 5–9.

Laux, Karl. Joseph Haas. Berlin, Henschelverlag, 1954.

—— Die Musik in Russland und der Sowjetunion. Berlin, Henschelverlag, 1958.

—— "Oper aus Ost und West," MuG IX (1959) 153–58.

Leibowitz, René. "Alban Berg et l'essence de l'opéra : Réflexions sur la musique dramatique 'sub una specie,'" *L'Arche* No. 13, 3e année (February, 1946) 130–34; No. 13, 4e année (March, 1946) 158–66.

—— "Renaissance de l'opéra," *Les Temps modernes* XII, No. 134 (1957) 1599–1607.

Lendvai, Ernö. "A kékszakállu herceg vára," *Magyar Zene* I (1961) 339–87.

Lepel, Felix von. Die Dresdner Oper als Weltkulturstätte. Dresden, Spohr, 1942.

—— Max von Schillings und seine Oper *Mona Lisa:* Ein Ruhmesblatt für die Städtische Oper in Berlin-Charlottenburg. Berlin-Charlottenburg, Selbstverlag, 1954.

Lesznai, Lajos. Béla Bartók, sein Leben—seine Werke. Leipzig, Deutscher Verlag für Musik, 1961.

Lewinski, Wolf-Eberhard von. "Der Dramatiker Giselher Klebe," *Melos* XXVIII (1961) 4–7.

Liess, Andreas. Carl Orff : Idee und Werk. [Zurich], Atlantis-Verlag, [1955].

—— Franz Schmidt, Leben und Schaffen. Graz, H. Böhlaus Nachf., 1951.

—— "Die musiké techné Carl Orffs," M IX (1955) 305–9.

Lindner, Dolf. Richard Strauss/Joseph Gregor : *Die Liebe der Danae;* Herkunft, Inhalt und Gestaltung eines Opernwerkes. Vienna, Oesterreichischer Diana Verlag, [1952].

Lissa, Z. "Pierwsza opera w Polsce Ludowej. (*Bunt żaków*)," *Muzyka* (1951) No. 10 (19), 3–29.

List, Kurt. "*Lulu*, after the Premiere," MMus XV, No. 1 (November–December, 1937) 8–12.

Łobaczewska, Stefanja. Karol Szymanowski : Życie i twórczość. Cracow, Polskie Wydawnictwo Muzyczne, [1950].

Lockspeiser, Edward. Debussy. New York, Pellegrini & Cudahy, 1949 [i.e., 1952]. 3rd ed.

—— "Musorgsky and Debussy," MQ XXIII (1937) 421–27.

Lopatnikoff, Nikolai. *"Christophe Colomb* [by Milhaud]," MMus VII, No. 4 (June–July, 1930) 36–38.

Louis, Rudolf. Die deutsche Musik der Gegenwart. Munich, G. Müller, 1909. 3d ed., 1912.

—— Hans Pfitzners *Die Rose vom Liebesgarten.* Munich, C. A. Seyfried, 1904.

Lualdi, Adriano. "Claudio Debussy, la sua arte e la sua parabola," RMI XXV (1918) 271–305.

McCredie, Andrew. "Contemporary Swedish Opera," *Sweden in Music* (*Musikrevy International*) XV (1960) No. 3 extra, 34–38.

Machlis, Joseph. Introduction to Contemporary Music. New York, W. W. Norton, [1961].

Maclean, Charles. *"La Princesse Osra* [by Herbert Bunning] and *Der Wald* [by Ethel Smyth]," ZIMG III (1901–2) 482–88.

Malipiero, Gian Francesco. "Orchestra e orchestrazione," RMI XXIII (1916) 559–69; XXIV (1917) 89–114.

Mann, Thomas. Pfitzners *Palestrina.* Berlin, S. Fischer, 1919.

Manuel, Roland. *See* Roland-Manuel.

Marangoni, Guido, and Carlo Vanbianchi. "La Scala," studie e ricerche : Note storiche e statistiche (1906–20). Bergamo, Istituto italiano d'arti grafiche, 1922.

Martynov, Ivan I. Dmitri Shostakovich, the Man and His Work. New York, Philosophical Library, [cop. 1947]. Trans. from the Russian by T. Guralsky.

Mason, Colin. "Stravinsky's Opera [*The Rake's Progress*]," M&L XXXIII (1952) 1–9.

Mason, Ronald. "Herman Melville and *Billy Budd,*" *Tempo* No. 21 (Autumn, 1951) 6–8.

Mathis, Alfred. "Stefan Zweig as Librettist and Richard Strauss," M&L XXV (1944) 163–76, 226–45.

Matthes, Wilhelm. "Paul von Klenau," *Blätter der Staatsoper* XX (1940) 5–14.

Mila, Massimo. "Ascoltando *La figlia de Jorio* di Pizzetti," RassM XXV (1955) 103–7.

—— *"Il prigioniero* di L. Dallapiccola," RassM XX (1950) 303–11.

—— *"The Turn of the Screw,"* The Score No. 10 (December, 1954) 73–76.

Milhaud, Darius. Notes sans musique. Paris, Juilliard, 1949. Translated as : Notes without Music : An Autobiography. London, Dennis Dobson, 1952. American edition with final chapter especially written for it : New York, Alfred A. Knopf, 1953.

Milner, Anthony. *"Billy Budd,"* The Score No. 6 (May, 1952) 59–61.

Mitchell, Donald. "The Character of Lulu," MR XV (1954) 268–74.

Mitchell, Donald. "Prokofieff's *Three Oranges:* A Note on Its Musical-Dramatic Organisation," *Tempo* No. 41 (Autumn, 1956) 20–24.

—— "*The Turn of the Screw:* A Note on Its Thematic Organization," MMR LXXXV (1955) 95–100.

Mitchell, Donald, and Hans Keller, eds. Benjamin Britten : A Commentary on His Works, from a Group of Specialists. London, Rockliff, [1952].

Moisenco, Rena. Realist Music : 25 Soviet Composers. London, Meridian Books, 1949.

Moreux, Serge. Béla Bartók. Paris, Richard-Masse, 1955. Rev. ed.

Morton, Lawrence. "Stravinsky," in *Encyclopédie de la musique* III (Paris, Fasquelle, 1961) 740–52.

Müller-Blattau, Joseph. Hans Pfitzner. Potsdam, Athenaion, 1940.

Muller, Daniel. Leoš Janáček. Paris, Rieder, [1930].

Murrill, Herbert. "*The Rake's Progress,*" *The Score* No. 6 (May, 1952) 55–58.

Nathan, Hans. "The Twelve-Tone Compositions of Luigi Dallapiccola," MQ XLIV (1958) 289–310.

Nest'ev, Izrail' Vladimirovich. Prokof'ev. Moscow, Gos muzykal'noe izd-vo, 1957. English translation : Stanford, California, Stanford University Press, 1960.

Nest'ev, Izrail' Vladimirovich, ed. Sergeĭ Prokof'ev, 1953–1963 : Stat'i i materialy. Moscow, Sovetskiĭ Kompozitor, 1962.

Newman, Ernest. Richard Strauss. London and New York, J. Lane, 1908.

Newmarch, Rosa. "New Works in Czechoslovakia : Janáček and Novák," *The Chesterian* XII (July, 1931) 213–19.

Oboussier, Robert. "Randbemerkungen zu meiner Oper *Amphitryon,*" M IV (1950) 458–60.

Oeser, Fritz. "Janáčeks Oper *Schicksal,*" M XII (1958) 586–92.

Ohrmann, Fritz. "Max Brands Oper *Maschinist Hopkins,*" *Signale für die musikalische Welt* LXXXVIII (1930) 395–99.

Oláh, Gustav. "Bartók and the Theatre," *Tempo* No. 14 (Winter, 1949–50) 4–8. Reprinted in *Béla Bartók: A Memorial Review*, 54–60.

Olkhovsky, Audrey. Music under the Soviets : The Agony of an Art. New York, F. A. Praeger, 1955.

Olsen, Derrick. "Souvenirs et réflexions d'un interprète à propos de la création de *Léonore 40–45,*" SchwM XCIV (1954) 277–78.

Opera Annual. Edited by Harold Rosenthal. London, John Calder, 1954– .

"Opera As It Is—and May Be," general title of several articles in M&L IV (1923) 85 ff.

Opera News. New York, Metropolitan Opera Guild, [December] 1936– .

Oper im Bild : Ein Querschnitt durch das deutsche Opernschaffen seit 1945. Berlin-Halensee, M. Hesse, [1961].

Oper im XX. Jahrhundert. Bonn, Boosey & Hawkes, [1954].

Oper in neuer Gestalt. *Musica* XIII (April, 1959) No. 4.

Orel, Alfred. "Ein unbekanntes Szenar zu Hans Pfitzners *Palestrina*," SchwM LXXXIX (1949) 132–38.

Osthoff, Helmuth. "Mozarts Einfluss auf Richard Strauss," SchwM XCVIII (1958) 409–17.

Othmar Schoeck im Wort : Äusserungen des Komponisten mit einer Auswahl zeitgenössischer Bekenntnisse. St. Gall, Tschudy, 1957.

Pagano, Luigi. "*Débora e Jaéle* di Ildebrando Pizzetti," RMI XXX (1923) 47–108.

Pahissa, Jaime. Vida y obra de Manuel de Falla. Buenos Aires, Ricordi Americana, 1947. Translated as : Manuel de Falla, His Life and Works. London, Museum Press, [1954].

Pahlen, Kurt. Manuel de Falla und die Musik in Spanien. Olten & Freiburg i. B., Walter, [1953].

Pannain, Guido. "Il *Dottor Faust*," RassM XIII (1940) 20–29.

Parente, Alfredo. "Note sull' estetica musicale contemporanea in Italia," RassM III (1930) 289–310.

Perle, George. "*Lulu:* The Formal Design," JAMS XVII (1964) 179–92.

—— "The Music of *Lulu:* A New Analysis," JAMS XII (1959) 185–200. Corrections : *ibid.* XIV (1961) 96.

Petzet, Walter. "*Maschinist Hopkins*," *Signale für die musikalische Welt* LXXXVII (1929) 1363–65.

Peyser, Herbert F. "Some Fallacies of Modern Anti-Wagnerism," MQ XII (1926) 175–89.

Pfannkuch, Wilhelm. Das Opernschaffen Ermanno Wolf-Ferraris. Kiel Dissertation, 1952.

Pfitzner, Hans Erich. Gesammelte Schriften. Augsburg, B. Filser, 1926. 3 vols.

—— Reden, Schriften, Briefe. Unveröffenlichtes und bisher Verstreutes. Hrsg. von Walter Abendroth. [Berlin-Frohnau & Neuwied/Rhein], Luchterhand, [1955].

—— Vom musikalischen Drama : Gesammelte Aufsätze. Munich and Leipzig, Süddeutsche Monatshefte, 1915.

Pincherle, Marc. Albert Roussel. Geneva, Kister, [1957].

Pintacuda, Salvatore. Renzo Bossi. Milan, M. Gastaldi, 1955.

Pisk, Paul A. "Schönberg's Twelve-Tone Opera," MMus VII, No. 3 (April–May, 1930) 18–21.

Pizzetti, Ildebrando, "*Ariadne et Barbebleue* . . . de Paul Dukas," RMI XV (1908) 73–112.

—— "*Pelléas et Mélisande* . . . Debussy," RMI XV (1908) 350–63.

Plomer, William. "Notes on the Libretto of *Gloriana*," *Tempo* No. 28 (Summer, 1953) 5–7.

Pollatschek, Walter. Hofmannsthal und die Bühne. Frankfurt Dissertation, 1924.

Polyakova, Lyudmila. Soviet Music. Moscow, Foreign Languages Publishing House, [1961].

Ponz de Leon, Giuseppe. "Il dramma lirico nell' arte di Pizzetti," RMI XLIII (1939) 539–44.

Porter, Andrew. "Britten's *Billy Budd*," M&L XXXIII (1952) 111–18.

—— "Britten's *Gloriana*," M&L XXXIV (1953) 277–87.

Poulenc, Francis. "Comment j'ai composé les *Dialogues des Carmélites*," *L'Opéra de Paris* No. XIV (1957?) 15–17.

—— Entretiens avec Claude Rostand. Paris, R. Julliard, [1954].

Pound, Ezra Loomis. Antheil and the Treatise of Harmony. Chicago, P. Covici, 1927.

Previtali, F. "*Turandot* [Busoni]," RassM XIII (1940) 38–46.

Prod'homme, Jacques Gabriel. "The Recent Fiftieth Anniversary of the 'New Opera,'" MQ XII (1926) 13–21.

Prokof'ev, Sergeĭ Sergeevich. Autobiography, Articles, Reminiscences. [Compiled, edited, and annotated by S. Shlifstein; translated by Rose Prokofieva.] Moscow, Foreign Languages Publishing House, [1959?]. Translation of : S. S. Prokof'ev : Materialy, documenty, vospominaniia. Moscow, Gos. muzykal'noe izd-vo, 1956. 2d ed., 1961.

—— "The War Years," MQ XXX (1944) 421–27.

Prunières, Henry. "Honegger's *Judith*," MMus III, No. 4 (May–June, 1926) 30–33.

Raabe, Peter. Die Musik im dritten Reich. Regensburg, G. Bosse, [1935].

Rabinovich, D. Dmitry Shostakovich, Composer. Moscow, Foreign Languages Publishing House, 1959.

Racek, Jan. "Der Dramatiker Janáček," *Deutsches Jahrbuch der Musikwissenschaft* V (1961) 39–57.

——Leoš Janáček. Leipzig, Reclam, [1962?].

Ramuz, Charles Ferdinand. Souvenirs sur Igor Stravinsky. Paris, Gallimard, Editions de la Nouvelle Revue Française, [1929].

La Rassegna Musicale XXXII, Nos. 2, 3, 4 (1962). (Special number containing articles and bibliographies on opera in the twentieth century.)

Raupp, Wilhelm. Eugen d'Albert. Leipzig, Koehler & Amelang, [1930].

—— Max von Schillings. Hamburg, Hanseatische Verlagsanstalt, [1935].

[Ravel, Maurice.] *See* the two special issues of RM : April, 1925; December, 1938.

Rebatet, Lucien. "L'Enregistrement de *Pelléas et Mélisande*," *L'Information musicale* II (1942) No. 54.

Redlich, Hans Ferdinand. Alban Berg : The Man and His Music. London, Calder; New York, Abelard-Schuman, [1957].

—— Alban Berg : Versuch einer Würdigung. Vienna, Universal Edition, 1957.

—— "Egon Wellesz," MQ XXVI (1940) 65–75.

—— "A New Welsh Folk Opera [Parrott's *The Black Ram*]," M&L XXXVII (1956) 101–6.

—— "The Significance of Britten's Operatic Style," *Music Survey* II (1950) 240–45.

—— "Unveröffentlichte Briefe Alban Bergs an Arnold Schönberg," in *Festschrift Friedrich Blume* (Kassel, Bärenreiter, 1963) [272]–280.

Reich, Willi. Alban Berg. Vienna, H. Reichner, [1937].

—— "Alban Berg's *Lulu*," MQ XXII (1936) 383–401.

—— "Alban Bergs Oper *Lulu*," *Melos* XIX (1952) 337–42.

—— A Guide to Alban Berg's *Wozzek*. [New York, League of Composers, 1931.]

—— "A Guide to *Wozzeck*," MQ XXXVIII (1952) 1–21.

——"*Lulu*—the Text and Music," MMus XII, No. 3 (March–April, 1935) 103–11.

—— "Paul Hindemith," MQ XVII (1931) 486–96.

Reizenstein, Franz. "Walton's *Troilus and Cressida*," *Tempo* No. 34 (Winter, 1954–55) 16–27.

Respighi, Elsa. Ottorino Respighi: Dati biografici ordinati. [Milan], Ricordi, [1954].

Richard Strauss Jahrbuch. Bonn, 1954–1959/60. 2 vols.

Riemer, Otto, "Johannes Driessler als Opernkomponist," M VI (1952) 398–406.

Riesenfeld, Paul. "Die Romantik der neuen Sachlichkeit," *Signale für die musikalische Welt* LXXXVII (1929) 1075–78.

Riezler, Walter. Hans Pfitzner und die deutsche Bühne. Munich, Piper, 1917.

—— "Neue Horizonte: Bemerkungen zu Carl Orffs *Antigonae*," in *Gestalt und Gedanke, ein Jahrbuch* ([Munich], Oldenbourg, [1951]) 103–16.

Rimkus, Günter. "*Der arme Konrad:* Eine Oper von Jean Kurt Forest," MuG IX (1959) 198–202.

Rinaldi, Mario. Lo *Straniero* de Ildebrando Pizzetti. Florence, Casa Editrice Monsalvato, 1943.

Rochberg, George. "Hugo Weisgall," *American Composers Alliance Bulletin* VII, No. 2 (1958) 2–7.

Röttger, Heinz. Das Formproblem bei Richard Strauss. Berlin, Junker & Dünnhaupt, 1937.

Roland-Manuel. Manuel de Falla, "Cahiers d'art," 1930.

—— Maurice Ravel. London, Dennis Dobson, 1947.

—— Maurice Ravel et son œuvre dramatique. Paris, Librairie de France, 1928.

Rolland, Romain. Musiciens d'aujourd'hui. Paris, Hachette, 1912. 5th ed. Translated as: Musicians of Today. New York, Holt, 1915. 2d ed.

Roseberry, Eric. "The Music of *Noye's Fludde*," *Tempo* No. 49 (Autumn, 1958) 2–11.

Rosenzweig, Alfred. Zur Entwicklungsgeschichte des Strauss'schen Musikdramas. Vienna Dissertation, 1923.

Rossi-Doria, Gastone. "Il teatro musicale di G. F. Malipiero," RassM II (1929) 354–64.

Rostand, Claude. La Musique française contemporaine. Paris, Presses Universitaires, 1952. Translated as : French Music Today. New York, Merlin Press, [1957].

—— "The Operas of Darius Milhaud," Tempo No. 19 (Spring, 1951) 23–28.

Roth, Ernst, ed. Richard Strauss, Bühnenwerke : Dokumente der Uraufführungen. Stage Works, Documents of the First Performances. London, Boosey & Hawkes, 1954.

Różycki, L. "Dzieje Erosa i Psyche," Muzyka (1930) No. 2, 82–85.

—— "Kilka słów o mojej Beatrix Cenci," Muzyka (1927) 69–70.

—— "O mojej operze Casanova," Muzyka (1925) 129–30.

Rutz, Hans. Hans Pfitzner : Musik zwischen den Zeiten. [Vienna], Humboldt-Verlag, [1949].

—— Neue Oper : Gottfried Einem und seine Oper Dantons Tod. Vienna, Universal Edition, [1947].

—— "Strawinsky und die Zukunft der Oper : Versuch einer geschichtlichen Perspektive," OeM VII (1952) 213–18.

Sabaneev, Leonid Leonidovitch. "Remarks on the Leitmotif," M&L XIII (1932) 200–206.

Sabin, Robert. "Carlisle Floyd's Wuthering Heights," Tempo No. 59 (Autumn, 1961) 23–26.

Šafránek, Miloš. Bohuslav Martinů, the Man and His Music. New York, Alfred A. Knopf, 1944.

—— "Bohuslav Martinů und das musikalische Theater," Musica XIII (1959) 550–54.

Sailer, Rudolf. Waltershausen und die Oper. Cologne Dissertation, 1957.

Saint-Cyr, Mario. Musicisti italiani contemporanei . . . prima serie. Rome, De Santis, [1932 ?].

St. John, Christopher. Ethel Smyth : A Biography. With Additional Chapters by V. Sackville-West and Kathleen Dale. [London, New York, Toronto], Longmans, Green & Co., [1959].

Salazar, Adolfo. La música moderna : Las corrientes directrices en el arte musical contemporáneo. Buenos Aires, Editorial Losada, 1944. Translated as : Music in Our Time : Trends in Music Since the Romantic Era. New York, W. W. Norton, 1946.

Samazeuilh, Gustave. Paul Dukas. Paris, A. Durand, 1913.

Saminsky, Lazare. "Jürg Jenatch," MMus VII, No. 1 (December, 1929–January, 1930) 37–39.

—— "More about Faustus," MMus V, No. 1 (November–December, 1927) 38–39.

—— Music of Our Day. New York, T. Y. Crowell, [1939]. New ed.

"Sampiero Corso et Henri Tomasi," RM No. 230 (1956).

Sargent, Winthrop. "Orlando in Mount Kisco" [Gian Carlo Menotti], *The New Yorker* XXXIX, No. 11 (May 4, 1963) 49 ff.

Sartori, Claudio. Riccardo Malipiero. Milan, Edizioni Suvini Zerboni, 1957. In English.

Schaal, Richard. Hugo Kaun : Leben und Werk (1863–1932). Ein Beitrag zur Musik der Jahrhundertwende. Regensburg, J. Habbel, [1946?].

Schaeffner, André. Igor Stravinsky. Paris, Rieder, [1931].

Schloezer, Boris Fedorovich. Igor Stravinsky. Paris, C. Aveline, 1929.

—— "The Operatic Paradox," MMus IV, No. 1 (November–December, 1926) 3–8.

Schmitz, Eugen. "Eugen d'Albert als Opernkomponist," *Hochland* VI, No. 2 (1909) 464–71.

—— Richard Strauss als Musikdramatiker. Munich, Lewy, 1907.

Schreiber, Flora Rheta, and Vincent Persichetti. William Schuman. New York, G. Schirmer, [1954].

Schuch, Friedrich von. Richard Strauss, Ernst von Schuch und Dresdens Oper. Dresden, Verlag der Kunst in Arbeitsgemeinschaft mit dem Dresdner Verlag, [1952].

Schuh, Willi. Das Bühnenwerk von Richard Strauss in den unter Mitwirkung des Komponisten geschaffenen letzten Münchner Inszenierungen : Ein Bildwerk. . . . Zurich, Atlantis-Verlag; London & New York, Boosey & Hawkes, 1954.

—— Othmar Schoeck. Zurich, Hug, [1934].

—— "*Tristan und Isolde* im Leben und Wirken Richard Strauss," in *Beyreuther Festspielbuch, 1952.*

—— Über Opern von Richard Strauss. (Kritiken und Essays, Band I.) Zurich, Atlantis-Verlag, [1947].

—— Von Neuer Musik. Zurich, Freiburg i. B., Atlantis-Verlag, [1955].

—— "Zur Harmonik Igor Strawinskys unter besonderer Berücksichtigung von *The Rake's Progress*," in *Internationaler Musik-Kongress Wien 1952, Bericht* (Vienna, Österreichischer Bundesverlag, 1953) 127–34.

Schumacher, Ernst. Die dramatischen Versuche Bertolt Brechts, 1918–1933. Berlin, Rütten & Loening, 1955.

Schwerké, I. "Paul Dukas : A Brief Appreciation," MQ XIV (1928) 403–12.

Seldes, Gilbert. "Delight in the Theatre," MMus XI, No. 3 (March–April, 1934) 138–41.

—— "Jazz Opera or Ballet?" MMus III, No. 2 (January–February, 1926) 10–16.

Selva, Blanche. Déodat de Séverac. Paris, Delagrave, 1930.

Semler, Isabel Parker. Horatio Parker : A Memoir for His Grandchildren Compiled from Letters and Papers. New York, G. P. Putnam's Sons, 1942.

Seré, Octave. Musiciens français d'aujourd'hui. Paris, Mercure de France, 1911.

Seroff, Victor I. Debussy : Musician of France. New York, G. P. Putnam's Sons, [1956].

—— Dmitri Shostakovitch. New York, Alfred A. Knopf, 1943.

Servières, Georges. Edouard Lalo. Paris, H. Laurens, [1925].

—— Gabriel Fauré. Paris, H. Laurens, 1930.

Shawe-Taylor, Desmond. "The Operas of Leoš Janáček," PMA LXXXV (1958–59) 49–64.

Shlifstein, S. "On *War and Peace,*" MMus XX, No. 3 (March–April, 1943) 185–87.

Shostakovich, Dmitriĭ. "My Opera, *Lady Macbeth of Mtzensk,*" MMus XII, No. 1 (November–December, 1934) 23–30.

Slonimsky, Nicolas. Music Since 1900. New York, Coleman-Ross Co., Inc., 1949. 3d ed.

—— "Sergei Prokofiev : His Status in Soviet Music," *American Quarterly on the Soviet Union* II, No. 1 (1939) 37–44.

Smith, David Stanley. "A Study of Horatio Parker," MQ XVI (1930) 153–69.

Smith, Julia Frances. Aaron Copland, His Work and Contribution to American Music. New York, E. P. Dutton, 1955.

Smyth, Dame Ethel. Impressions That Remained : Memoirs. New York, Alfred A. Knopf, 1946. First published London, New York [etc.], Longmans, Green, 1919. 2 vols.

Sovetskaia opera : Sbornik kriticheskikh stateĭ. Moscow, Gos. muzykal'noe izd-vo, 1953.

Die sowjetische Musik im Aufstieg : Eine Sammlung von Aufsätzen. Hrsg. vom Sowj. Komponistenverband d. UdSSR Red. Kollegium, E. A. Groschewa. Halle-Saale, Mitteldeutscher Verlag, 1952.

Specht, Richard. Richard Strauss, *Die Frau ohne Schatten:* Thematische Einführung. Berlin, Fürstner, 1919.

—— Richard Strauss und sein Werk. Leipzig, P. Tal, 1921. 2 vols.

Squire, W. H. Haddon. "The Aesthetic Hypothesis and *The Rape of Lucretia,*" *Tempo,* New ser., No. 1 (September, 1946) 1–9.

Stäblein, Bruno. "Schöpferische Tonalität : Zum Grossaufbau von Orffs *Antigonae,*" M VI (1952) 145–48.

Stefan, Paul. "Schoenberg's Operas," MMus II, No. 1 (January, 1925) 12–15.

—— "Schönberg's Operas," MMus VII, No. 1 (December, 1929–January, 1930) 24–28.

Stein, Erwin. "*The Turn of the Screw* and Its Musical Idiom," *Tempo* No. 34 (Winter, 1954–55) 6–14.

Stephan, Rudolf. "Zur jüngsten Geschichte des Melodrams," AfMw XVII (1960) 183–92.

Sternfeld, Frederick W. "Some Russian Folk Songs in Stravinsky's *Petrouchka,*" *MLA Notes,* 2d ser. II, No. 2 (March, 1945) 95–107.

Stevens, Halsey. The Life and Music of Béla Bartók. New York, Oxford University Press, 1953.

Strauss, Franz, ed. Richard Strauss Briefwechsel mit Hugo von Hofmannsthal. Vienna, Zsolnay, 1926. Translated as : Correspondence between Richard Strauss and Hugo von Hofmannsthal, 1907–1918. New York, Alfred A. Knopf, 1927.

Strauss, Richard. "The Artistic Testament of Richard Strauss. Translated and with an Introduction by Alfred Mann," MQ XXXVI (1950) 1–8.

—— Betrachtungen und Erinnerungen. Zurich, Atlantis-Verlag, [1957]. 2d ed.

[——] Richard Strauss et Romain Rolland : Correspondance, fragments de journal. Paris, A. Michel, [1951].

Strauss, Richard, and Hugo von Hofmannsthal. Briefwechsel. Gesamtausgabe. Hrsg. von Franz Strauss und Alice Strauss, bearb. von Willi Schuh. 2d ed. Translated as : A Working Friendship : The Correspondence between Richard Strauss and Hugo von Hofmannsthal. New York, Random House, [1961].

Strauss, Richard, and Joseph Gregor. Briefwechsel, 1934–1949 : Im Auftrag der Wiener Philharmoniker, hrsg. von Roland Tenschert. Salzburg, O. Müller, [1955].

Strauss, Richard, and Stefan Zweig. Briefwechsel. [Hrsg. von Willi Schuh.] [Frankfurt/M.], S. Fischer, 1957.

Stravinsky, Igor Fedorovich. Chroniques de ma vie. Paris, Denoël & Steele, [1935]. Translated as : Chronicles of My Life. London, V. Gollancz, 1936.

—— Memories and Commentaries. Garden City, N.Y., Doubleday, 1960.

—— "On Oedipus Rex," Encounter XVIII (1962) 29–35.

—— Poetics. New York, Vintage, 1956.

—— Poétique musicale sous forme de six leçons. Cambridge, Mass., Harvard University Press, 1942.

—— See RM, numéro spécial (May–June, 1939).

Stravinsky, Igor, and Robert Craft. Conversations with Igor Stravinsky. Garden City, N.Y., Doubleday, 1959.

—— Expositions and Developments. Garden City, N.Y., Doubleday, 1962.

Strobel, Heinrich. Paul Hindemith. Mainz, B. Schott's Söhne, [1948]. 3d ed.

—— "The Rake's Example," Melos XIX (1952) 7–9.

Stuart, Charles. "Katya Kabanova Reconsidered," MR XII (1951) 289–95.

Stuckenschmidt, Hans Heinz. Arnold Schönberg. Zurich & Freiburg i. B., Atlantis-Verlag, [1951]. 2d ed., 1957. English translation : New York, Grove Press, [1959].

—— "Ernst Křenek," MMus XVI, No. 1 (November–December, 1938) 41–44.

—— "Hellenic Jazz," MMus VII, No. 3 (April–May, 1930) 22–25.

Stuckenschmidt, Hans Heinz. "Opera in Germany Today," MMus XIII, No. 1 (November–December, 1935) 32–37.

—— "Rede über Busonis *Doktor Faust*," SchwM XCVI (1956) 3–9.

Suckling, Norman. Fauré. London, Dent, 1946.

Swarsenski, Hans. "Sergeii Prokofieff : *The Flaming Angel*," *Tempo* No. 39 (Spring, 1956) 16–27.

Szabolcsi, Bence, and Dénes Bartha, eds. Bartók Béla emlékére. Budapest, Akadémiai Kiadó, 1962. Series : Zenetudományi tanulmányok, X.

Tappolet, Willy. Arthur Honegger. Zurich, Atlantis-Verlag, [1954].

Tebaldini, Giovanni. "Telepatia musicale : A proposito dell' *Elettra* di Richard Strauss," RMI XVI (1909) 400–412.

Tenschert, Roland. *"Die Frau ohne Schatten:* Ihre Stellung und Bedeutung innerhalb von Richard Strauss' Opernschaffen," OeM VIII (1953) 139–43.

—— "A 'Gay Myth' : The Story of *Die Liebe der Danae*," *Tempo* No. 24 (Summer, 1952) 5–11.

—— "Die Kadenzbehandlung bei Richard Strauss," ZfMw VIII (1925–26) 161–82.

—— "Richard Strauss' Opernfassung der deutschen Übersetzung von Oscar Wildes *Salome*," *Richard Strauss Jahrbuch* (1959–60) 99–106.

—— Richard Strauss und Wien : Eine Wesensverwandtschaft. Vienna, Verlag Brüder Hollinek, 1949.

—— "Das Sonett in Richard Strauss' Oper *Capriccio*," SchwM XCVIII (1958) 1–5.

——"Versuch einer Typologie der Richard Strausschen Melodik," ZfMw XVI (1934) 274–93.

Thomas, Juan Maria. Manuel de Falla en la isla. [n.p.], Ediciones Capella Classica, [n.d.].

Thompson, Oscar. Debussy, Man and Artist. New York, Dodd, Mead, 1937.

—— "Fly-Wheel Opera," MMus VII, No. 1 (December, 1929–January, 1930) 39–42.

Thompson, Randall. "George Antheil," MMus VIII, No. 4 (May–June, 1931) 17–27.

Thomson, Virgil. The Musical Scene. New York, Alfred A. Knopf, 1945.

—— The State of Music. New York, W. Morrow, 1939.

Tiersot, Julien. "Edouard Lalo," MQ XI (1925) 8–35.

Tolksdorf, Cäcilie. John Gays *Beggar's Opera* und Bert Brechts *Dreigroschenoper*. Rheinberg, Rhl., Sattler & Koss, 1934.

Torchi, Luigi. "L'esito del concorso Sonzogno : Le tre opere rappresentate al 'Teatro Lirico' di Milano," RMI XI (1904) 516–49.

—— "*Ghismonda*, opera in tre atti di Eugenio D'Albert," RMI III (1896) 526–61.

—— "*Salome* di Riccardo Strauss," RMI XIV (1907) 113–56.

—— "*La vita nuova* di E. Wolf-Ferrari," RMI X (1903) 712–36.

Torrefranca, Fausto. "La nuova opera di Riccardo Strauss," RMI XIX (1912) 986–1031.

—— "*Il Rosencavalier* di R. Strauss," RMI XVIII (1911) 147–79.

—— "R. Strauss e l' *Elektra*," RMI XVI (1909) 335–84.

Trenner, Franz, ed. Richard Strauss : Dokumente seines Lebens und Schaffens. Munich, Verlag C. H. Beck, [1954].

Tretti, Luigi, and Leonello Fiumi, eds. Omaggio a Italo Montemezzi. Verona, Tip. Ghidini e Fiorini, [1952].

Tuthill, Burnet C. "Howard Hanson," MQ XXII (1936) 140–53.

Vaillat, Léandre. La Danse à l'Opéra de Paris. Paris, Amiot-Dumont, [1951].

Valentin, Erich. Hans Pfitzner. Regensburg, G. Bosse, 1939.

Vallas, Léon. Claude Debussy et son temps. Paris, F. Alcan, 1932; Paris, A. Michel, [1958]. Translated as : Claude Debussy, His Life and Works. London, Oxford University Press, 1933.

Veress, Sandor. "*Bluebeard's Castle*," *Tempo* No. 13 (Autumn, 1949) 32–37; No. 14 (Winter, 1949–50) 25–35. Reprinted in *Béla Bartók: A Memorial Review*, 36–53.

Viu, Vicente Salas. "The Mystery of Manel de Falla's *La Atlántida*," *Inter-American Music Bulletin* No. 33 (January, 1963) 1–6.

Vlad, Roman. "Dallapiccola 1948–1955," *The Score* No. 15 (March, 1956) 39–52.

—— Strawinsky. [Turin], Giulio Einaudi, 1958. English translation : London, New York, Oxford University Press, 1960.

Vogel, Jaroslav. Leoš Janáček, dramatik. Prague, Nákl. Hudební matice Umělecké besedy, 1948.

—— Leoš Janáček : Leben und Werk. Prague, Artia, [cop. 1958].

Vogel, Werner. Thematisches Verzeichnis der Werke von Othmar Schoeck. Zurich, Atlantis-Verlag, 1956.

Wachten, Edmund. "Der einheitliche Grundzug der Straussschen Formgestaltung," ZfMw XVI (1934) 257–74.

Wade, Carroll D. "A Selected Bibliography of Igor Stravinsky," MQ XLVIII (1962) 372–84.

Warlock, Peter, pseud. *See* Heseltine.

Weissmann, Adolph. "Germany's Latest Music Dramas," MMus IV, No. 4 (May–June, 1927) 20–26.

Wellesz, Egon. "Hofmannsthal and Strauss," M&L XXXIII (1952) 239–42.

—— "The Return to the Stage," MMus IV, No. 1 (November–December, 1926) 19–24.

Werba, Erik. "Musik der freien Entscheidung : Werner Egks *Irische Legende*," OeM X (1955) 231–36.

Werker, Gerard. "Oper *Katja Kabanowa* van Leos Janacek," *Mens en Melodie* XIV (1959) 178–82.

Westphal, Kurt. Die moderne Musik. Leipzig and Berlin, B. G. Teubner, 1928.

Westphal, Kurt. "Das musikdramatische Prinzip bei Richard Strauss," *Die Musik* (September, 1927) 859–64.

White, Eric Walter. Benjamin Britten : A Sketch of His Life and Works. London, Boosey & Hawkes, 1948. New ed., 1954.

—— "The Rake's Progress," *Tempo* No. 20 (Summer, 1951) 10–18.

White, John S. The Salome Motive. New York, Eloquent Press Corp., N. Morgillo, n.d. [*ca.* 1947].

Wieke, Johannes. "Paul Kurzbachs Oper *Thyl Claas,*" MuG VIII (1958) 626–28.

Wieniawski, Adam. Ludomir Różycki. Warsaw, Gebethner i Wolff, [1928].

Wiesengrund-Adorno, Theodor. "Transatlantic," MMus VII, No. 4 (June–July, 1930) 38–41.

Willms, Franz. Führer zur Oper *Cardillac* von Paul Hindemith. Mainz, B. Schott, [1926].

—— "Paul Hindemith : Ein Versuch," *Von neuer Musik* I (1925) 78–123.

Witherspoon, Herbert. "Grand Opera and Its Immediate Problems," MTNA XXVII (1932) 148–49.

Wörner, Karl H. "Arnold Schoenberg and the Theater," MQ XLVIII (1962) 444–60.

—— "Egk and Orff : Representatives of Contemporary German Opera," MR XIV (1953) 186–204.

—— Gotteswort und Magie : Die Oper *Moses und Aron* von Arnold Schönberg. Heidelberg, Schneider, 1959.

—— "Katjas Tod, die Schlussszene der Oper *Katja Kabanowa* von Leoš Janáček," SchwM XCIV (1959) 91–96.

—— Neue Musik in der Entscheidung. Mainz, B. Schott's Söhne, [1956]. 2d ed.

[Wolf-Ferrari, Ermanno.] *See* special number of *Zeitschrift für Musik* CVIII, No. 1 (January, 1941).

Wolff, Stéphane. Un demi-siècle d'opéra comique (1900–1950). [Paris], A. Bonne, [1953].

Young, Percy M. Vaughan Williams. London, Dennis Dobson, 1953.

MODERN EDITIONS

OF OPERAS OR EXCERPTS FROM OPERAS COMPOSED BEFORE *1800*

Including Pre-operatic Works of the Sixteenth Century

ABBREVIATIONS

B&H	Breitkopf & Härtel
C.E.	Collected Edition (Gesamtausgabe)
C.F.	*Les Chefs d'œuvre classiques de l'opéra français* (Leipzig, B&H, 1880)
DdT	*Denkmäler deutscher Tonkunst* (Leipzig, B&H, 1892–1931)
DTB	*Denkmäler deutscher Tonkunst: Denkmäler der Tonkunst in Bayern* (Braunschweig, H. Litolff's Verlag, 1900–1938)
DTOe	*Denkmäler der Tonkunst in Oesterreich* (Vienna, Artaria, 1894–)
EDM	*Das Erbe Deutscher Musik*. Erste Reihe, Reichsdenkmale (Leipzig, B&H, 1935–)
EP	R. Eitner, ed., *Publikationen älterer praktischer und theoretischer Musikwerke, vorzugsweise des XV. und XVI. Jahrhunderts* (Berlin, Bahn; Leipzig, B&H, 1873–1905)
HAM	Archibald T. Davison and Willi Apel, eds., *Historical Anthology of Music* (Cambridge, Mass., Harvard, 1950) II
JF	Knud Jeppesen, ed., *La Flora, arie &c. antiche italiane* (Copenhagen, Hansen, 1949) 3 vols.
LAM	Ludwig Landshoff, ed., *Alte Meister des Bel Canto* (Frankfurt, New York, C. F. Peters, 1912–27) 5 vols.
MM	Carl Parrish and John F. Ohl, eds., *Masterpieces of Music before 1750* (New York, Norton, 1951)

OHM   *The Oxford History of Music.* 2d edition (London, Oxford, 1929–38)

RB   Hugo Riemann, ed., *Musikgeschichte in Beispielen* (Leipzig, B&H, 1921)

SB   Arnold Schering, ed., *Geschichte der Musik in Beispielen* (Leipzig, B&H, 1931; reprint, New York, Broude Bros., 1950)

SCA   *Smith College Archives* (Northampton, Mass., Smith College, 1933–   )

TEM   Carl Parrish, ed., *A Treasury of Early Music* (New York, Norton, 1958)

SHORT TITLES (see also bibliography)

Abert: Anna Amalie Abert, ed., *Die Oper von den Anfängen bis zum Beginn des 19. Jahrhunderts* (Cologne, A. Volk, 1953)

Bücken: Ernst Bücken, *Die Musik des Rokokos und der Klassik* (Wildpark-Potsdam, Akademische Verlagsgesellschaft Athenaion, 1927)

Burney: Charles Burney, *A General History of Music from the Earliest Ages to the Present Period* (London, Printed for the Author, 1776)

Bush: Geoffrey Bush, ed., *Songs from the Ballad Operas* (London, Elkin; New York, Galaxy, 1956) 3 vols.

I classici: I classici della musica italiana. Raccolta diretta da Gabriele d'Annunzio (Milan, Società Anonima Notari La Santa, 1919–21) 36 vols.

—— (Milan, Istituto Editorale Italiano, 1918–20) 307 Quaderni.

Deldevez: Edouard Deldevez, ed., *Fondation de l'opéra en France* (Paris, Richault, *ca.* 1875)

Della Corte: Andrea della Corte, ed., *Piccola antologia settecentesca* (Milan, Ricordi, 1925)

Delsarte: François Delsarte, ed., *Archives du chant* (Paris, Choudens, ca. 1900) 7 vols.

Einstein: Alfred Einstein, *A Short History of Music* (New York, Knopf, 1947), supplement of music examples

Gevaert: François Auguste Gevaert, *Les Gloires d'Italie* (Paris, Heugel, 1868) 2 vols.

Goldschmidt: Hugo Goldschmidt, *Studien zur Geschichte der italienischen Oper im 17. Jahrhundert* (Leipzig, B&H, 1901–4) 2 vols.

Krehbiel: Henry E. Krehbiel, ed., *Voices from the Golden Age of Bel Canto* (New York, G. Schirmer, 1910)

Leichtentritt: Hugo Leichtentritt, ed., *Deutsche Hausmusik aus vier Jahrhunderten* (Berlin, Hesse, 1905)

Mantica: Francesco Mantica, ed., *Prime fioriture del melodramma Italiano* (Rome, Casa editrice Claudio Monteverdi, 1912–30) 2 vols.

Mortari: Francesco Cavalli, *Tre frammenti di opere.* Elaborazione di Virgilio Mortari (Milan, Carisch, 1942)

Musica Britannica (London, Stainer and Bell, 1951–   )

Nagels Musik Archiv (Hanover, Adolph Nagel, 1927–   )

Prosnak: Jan Prosnak, *Kultura muzyczna Warszawy XVIII w.* (Cracow, Polskie Wydawn. Muzyczne, 1955) 2 vols.

Prunières: Henry Prunières, *Maîtres du chant* (Paris, Heugel, [1924–27]) 6 vols. in one

Riemann: Hugo Riemann, *Handbuch der Musikgeschichte* (Leipzig, B&H, 1919–22) 2 vols. in 5 parts

Sabol: A. J. Sabol, ed., *Songs and Dances for the Stuart Masque* (Providence, R.I., Brown University Press, 1959)

Sondheimer: Robert Sondheimer, ed., *Werke aus dem 18. Jahrhundert* (Berlin-Basel, Edition Bernoulli, 1922–39) 52 Hefte

Torchi: Luigi Torchi, ed., *L'arte musicale in Italia* (Milan, Ricordi, 1897–1908?)

Wolff BoHg: Hellmuth C. Wolff, *Die Barockoper in Hamburg, 1678–1738* (Wolfenbüttel, Möseler, 1957) 2 vols.

Wolff DBa: Hellmuth C. Wolff, ed., *Deutsche Barockarien* (Kassel, Bärenreiter, n.d.) 2 vols.

Worsthorne: S. Towneley Worsthorne, *Venetian Opera in the 17th Century* (Oxford, Clarendon, 1954)

Zanon: Maffeo Zanon, *30 Arie Antiche* (Milan, Ricordi, 1922)

Abbatini, Antonio (1597–1680)
  La comica del cielo : LAM I
  Dal male il bene : see Marazzoli
Aranaz, Pedro (1742–1821)
  La maja limonera : Subirá, *Tonadilla escénica* III
Ariosti, Attilio (1666–*ca.* 1740)
  Lucio vero : LAM II
Arne, Thomas Augustine (1710–78)
  Achilles in Petticoats : Bush
  Alfred : *Three Songs*, ed. A. Carse (London, Augener, 1928)
  Artaxerxes : Overture, ed. G. Warrack (London, Hawkes and Son, *ca.* 1941)
  Comus : *Musica Britannica* III; Dances, ed. Whittaker (London, Oxford, 1938)
  The Guardian Outwitted : Bush
  The Judgment of Paris : Overture, ed. A. Carse (London, Augener, 1939)
Bach, Johann Christian (1735–82)
  Amadis des Gaules : Geiringer, *Music of the Bach Family* (New York, 1954)
  Carattaco : LAM II
Banchieri, Adriano (1568–1634)
  Il festino nella sera : complete, ed. B. Somma, De Santis (Rome, 1939); ed. F. Vatielli, *I classici* I (Quad. 1–3); translation, *The Animals Improvise Counterpoint* (New York, 1937)
  La pazzia senile : ed. Torchi IV; ed. F. Vatielli, *I classici* I (Quad. 1–3)
  La saviezza giovanile : ed. R. Allorto, *Le Chant du Monde* (Milan, 1956)

Beaulieu, Lambert de
> *Circe, ou le Ballet comique de la reine* : complete, ed. J. B. Weckerlin, C.F.; Deldevez

Benda, Georg (1722–95)
> *Ariadne auf Naxos* : complete, ed. Einstein (Leipzig, C. W. F. Siegel, 1920)
>
> *Der Jahrmarkt* : complete, ed. Th. W. Werner, DdT 64; complete, newly ed. and rev. H. J. Moser, DdT, Neuauflage, 64 (1959)

Bernasconi, Andrea (1706–84)
> *Adriano* : Krehbiel

Bianchi, Francesco (1752–1810)
> *L'orfano della China* : Krehbiel; Della Corte
>
> *La villanella rapita* : Della Corte

Blow, John (1649–1708)
> *Venus and Adonis* : complete, ed. G. P. E. Arkwright, Old English Edition, No. 25 (London, J. Williams, 1902); complete, ed. A. Lewis (Paris, Oiseau-Lyre, 1939); HAM 243

Bononcini, Giovanni Battista (1670–1747)
> *Astianatte* : HAM 262
>
> *Erminia* : LAM I
>
> *Mario fuggitivo* : LAM I
>
> *Polifemo* : complete, ed. Gerd Kärnbach (Berlin, Fürstner, 1938)

Bontempi, Giovanni Andrea Angelini (1624–1705)
> *Dafne* : RB 105; Engländer, "Zur Frage der *Dafne*," *Acta musicologica* XIII (1941) 61 ff.
>
> *Il Paride* : Burney *History*, Book IV

Bustos, Mariano
> *La Necedad* : Subirá, *Tonadilla escénica* III

Caccini, Francesca (1588–*ca.* 1640)
> *La liberazione di Ruggiero* : complete, ed. Doris Silbert, SCA VII (1945); LAM I; Goldschmidt I, 174–79

Caccini, Giulio (*ca.* 1546–1618)
> *Euridice* : EP X; RB
>
> *Le nuove musiche* : Facsimile, ed. Mantica, *Prime fioriture* II; *I classici* IV (Quad. 9–12); Deldevez; SB 172, 173; HAM 184; JF I, III; Prunières, III

Caldara, Antonio (1670–1736)
> *La costanza in amor vince l'inganno* : LAM II
>
> *Dafne* : DTOe 91

Cambert, Robert (*ca.* 1628–77)
> *Les Peines et les plaisirs d'amour* : complete, C.F.
>
> *Pomone* : complete, C.F.; SB 222; HAM 223; Deldevez

Campra, André (1660–1744)
> *L'Europe galante* : complete, C.F.
>
> *Les Festes vénitiennes* : complete, C.F.; SB 261; TEM 45

Iphigénie en Tauride : Deldevez
Tancrède : complete, C.F.
Carnicer, Ramón (1789–1855)
    Los maestros de la Raboso : Subirá, *Tonadilla escénica* III
Castel, José
    La gitanilla en el coliseo : Subirá, *Tonadilla escénica* III
Cavalieri, Emilio de (*ca.* 1550–1602)
    Rappresentazione di anima e di corpo : Facsimile, ed. Mantica, *Prime fioriture* I; *I classici* X (Quad. 35–36); SB 169; HAM 183; OHM III; TEM 37; Deldevez; ed. Fr. Vatielli (Leipzig, 1906); ed. G. Tebaldini (1915); ed. E. Gubitosi (Milan and New York, Ricordi, *ca.* 1956); Goldschmidt I, 153–54
Cavalli, Francesco (1602–76)
    Alcibiade : SIMG, Jg. 2 (1900); Goldschmidt I, 389–90
    Elena rapita da Teseo : JF III
    Ercole amante : HAM 206; Mortari
    Erismena : JF III
    Eritrea : Deldevez
    Giasone : Prologue and Act I, EP XII; JF III; RB 101; SB 201; Mortari
    Le nozze di Teti e Peleo : Goldschmidt I, 391–402
    Ormindo : Sinfonia, SIMG, Jg. 4 (1903); SB 200
    Serse : HAM 206
    See also : *Venti arie tratte dai drammi musicali di Francesco Cavalli*, ed. Zanon (Vienna-Trieste, Vlg. Schmiedel, 1909)
Cesti, Pietro Antonio (1623–69)
    Argia : SB 203
    Le Disgrazie d'amore : EP XII
    La Dori : EP XII; OHM III; RB 103; Wolff, BoHg II
    La magnanimità d'Alessandro : EP XII
    l'Orontea : Gevaert; LAM I
    Il pomo d'oro : Acts I, II, IV only, DTOe III^2, IV^2; SB 202; HAM 221
    Semiramide : EP XII
Charpentier, Marc-Antoine (1634–1704)
    C.E. : *Oeuvres*, ed. G. Lambert (Paris, Editions de la Lyre d'Or, 1948–53) 15 vols.
    La Couronne de fleurs : ed. H. Busser (Paris, 1907)
    Le Malade imaginaire : ed. Saint-Saëns (Paris, Durand, 1894); first intermedio, ed. J. Tiersot (Paris, Heugel, 1925)
    Médée : Three airs, ed. Guy-Lambert (Paris, Editions de la Lyre d'Or, 1950–51)
Cimarosa, Domenico (1749–1801)
    Le astuzie femminili : ed. Respighi (Milan, Ricordi, n.d.)
    Convito : Zanon
    Credulo : Zanon
    Le donne rivali : Zanon

Giannina e Bernardone : ed. Respighi (Milan, Ricordi, n.d.); ed. F.
 d'Arcais (Milan, Ricordi, 1870?)
Il matrimonio segreto : (Leipzig, Peters, 1871); (Mainz, Schott, n.d.)
I traci amanti : Della Corte
La vergine del sole : LAM II
Colasse, Pascal (1649–1709)
 Les Saisons (with Lully) : complete, C.F.; Delsarte
 Thétis et Pélée : complete, C.F.
Conti, Francesco (1681–1732)
 Griselda : SB 274
Cornacchioli, Giacinto (17th century)
 Diana schernita : Goldschmidt I, 185–87
Corteccia, Francesco (16th century)
 Intermedi of 1539 : SB 99
Cousser, Johann Sigismund
 See Kusser, Johann Sigismund
Della Viola, Alfonso
 Il Sacrificio d'Abramo : Solerti, "Precedenti del melodramma"; Solerti,
 Gli albori
Destouches, André-Cardinal (1672–1749)
 Les Eléments : complete, C.F.; Prunières VI
 Issé : complete, C.F.
 Omphale : complete, C.F.
 See also Lacôme, ed. *Les Fondateurs de l'opéra français* (Paris, Enoch,
 1878)
Dibdin, Charles (1754–1814)
 Lionel and Clarissa : ed. A. Reynolds (London, Elkin, 1926)
 The Quaker : ed. F. Pascal (1904)
Dittersdorf, Karl Ditters von (1739–99)
 Der Betrug durch Aberglauben (Leipzig, Peters, n.d.)
 Doktor und Apotheker : complete, ed. Kleinmichel in Senff's *Opernbib-
 liothek*; ed. E. Fischer and F. Gessner (Berlin, R. Birnbach, *ca.* 1943);
 ed. H. Burkhard (Vienna, Universal, 1935); HAM 305; Abert
 Hieronymus Knicker : Kleinmichel in Senff's *Opernbibliothek*
Draghi, Giovanni Baptista (1657–1712)
 Creso : Wolff, BoHg II
 La pazienza di Socrate : SB 226
 Psiche : RB 116
 See also Neuhaus, "Antonio Draghi," SzMw I (1913) 104–92
Duni, Egidio Romoaldo (1709–75)
 La Clochette : Delsarte VI
 La Fée Urgèle : Delsarte VI
 Les Moissonneurs : Delsarte VI
Durante, Francesco (1684–1755)
 Arlecchino : ed. G. L. Tocchi (Milan, Carisch, 1937)

Esteve y Grimau, Pablo (d. 1794)
  El desvalido : Pedrell, *Cancionero* IV
  Garrido enfermo y su testamento : Subirá, *Tonadilla escénica* III
  El juicio del año : Subirá, *Tonadilla escénica* III; Subirá, *Maestros* I
  Los novios y la maja : Pedrell, *Cancionero* IV
  El pretendiente : Pedrell, *Cancionero* IV
  Los signos del año : Subirá, *Inéditas*

Ferandiere, Fernando
  La consulta : Subirá, *Tonadilla escénica* III; Subirá, *Maestros* I

Flecha, Mateo (1530–1604)
  Las ensaladas (1581) : ed. H. Anglès (Barcelona, Diputación Provincial, 1954)

Förtsch, Johann Philipp (1652–1732)
  See Zelle, *J. P. Förtsch*; Wolff, BoHg II

Franck, Johann Wolfgang (1644–*ca.* 1710)
  Die drey Töchter Cecrops : complete, EDM II (DTB XXXVIII)
  See also Zelle, *J. W. Franck*; Wolff, BoHg II

Fux, Johann Josef (1660–1741)
  C.E., Serie V—Opern (Kassel, Bärenreiter, 1962–   )
  Costanza e fortezza : complete, ed. E. Wellesz, DTOe 34–35 (Jg. XVII); incomplete, ed. G. Smith, SCA II; SB 272
  La decima fatica d'Hercole : aria in A. Liess, *Wiener Barockmusik* (Vienna, 1946)

Gabrieli, Andrea (*ca.* 1510–86)
  Edipo tiranno : ed. L. Schrade (Paris, 1960)

Gabrieli, Domenico (*ca.* 1640–90)
  Clearco in Negroponte : LAM III
  Flavio Cuniberto : LAM III

Gagliano, Marco da (*ca.* 1575–1642)
  Dafne : incomplete, EP X; SB 175; RB 69; Einstein 24; Krehbiel
  La Flora : Goldschmidt I, 180–84; LAM I
  See also Krehbiel

Galuppi, Baldassare (1706–85)
  Adriano in Siria : Krehbiel
  Il filosofo di campagna : complete, ed. V. Mortari (Milan, Carisch, 1938); complete, ed. Wolf-Ferrari (Milan, Ricordi, *ca.* 1954); HAM 285; *I classici* XIII (Quad. 54–58); Zanon
  L'inimico delle donne : Gevaert

Galván, Ventura
  Los vagamundos y ciegos fingidos : Subriá, *Tonadilla escénica* III; Subirá, *Maestros* II

García, Manuel
  El majo y la maja : Subirá, *Tonadilla escénica III*

Gassmann, Florian Leopold (1729–74)

La contessina : DTOe, XLII–XLIV (Jg. 21[1])

See Donath, "Gassmann als Opernkomponist," SzMw II (1914) 34–211

Gluck, Christoph Willibald (1714–87)

C.E. : *Werke*, ed. Pelletan and others (Leipzig, B&H, 1873–96); contains *Alceste, Armida, Echo und Narziss, Iphigenie in Aulis, Iphigenie auf Tauris, Orpheus und Euridice; Sämtliche Werke*, ed. R. Gerber (Kassel and Basel, Bärenreiter–Vlg., 1951–)

Armide : SB 313

Don Juan : complete, ed. A. Einstein, DTOe 82 (Jg. XXX[2])

L'innocenza giustificata : complete, ed. A. Einstein, DTOe 60 (Jg. XLIV)

Iphigénie en Tauride : complete, ed. H. Abert (Leipzig, Eulenburg, 1927); Einstein 39

Le nozze d'Ercole e d'Ebe : complete, ed. H. Abert, DTB 14[2]

Orfeo ed Euridice : complete, DTOe 44a (Jg. XXI[2]); HAM 292

La Rencontre imprévue : complete (Leipzig, B&H, 1923; Paris, Legouix, 1923); as *Die Pilger von Mecca* (Leipzig, Gluckgesellschaft, 1931); Abert

Il trionfo di Clelia : LAM II

Grabu, Louis

Albion and Albanius : Dent, *Foundations*

Graun, Karl Heinrich (1704–59)

Montezuma: complete, ed. A. Meyer-Reinach, DdT 15; ed. H. J. Moser, DdT, Neuauflage, 15; HAM 282

Graupner, Christoph (1683–1760)

See Wolff BoHg II

Grétry, André Ernest Modeste (1741–1813)

C.E. : *Collection complète des oeuvres de Grétry* (Leipzig, B&H, 1884–1923) 44 vols. in 39

La Caravane du Caire : complete, C.F.

Céphale et Procris : complete, C.F.

Les Deux Avares : ed. R. Kleinmichel (Vienna, Universal, 1911)

Richard Coeur-de-Lion : HAM 306

Guerrero, Antonio

Los señores fingidos : Subirá, *Tonadilla escénica* III

Guglielmi, Pietro (1728–1804)

I finti amori : Della Corte

L'inganno amoroso : Della Corte

Handel, George Frideric (1685–1759)

C.E. : *Georg Friedrich Händels Werke*. Herausgegeben von Friedrich Chrysander (Leipzig, B&H, 1858–94, 1902); *Hallische Händel-Ausgabe* . . . Herausgegeben von Max Schneider und Rudolf Steglich (Kassel, Bärenreiter–Vlg., 1955—)

Alcina : JF I, III

Rinaldo : SB 278; JF I, III; MM 44
Serse : JF I, II
Tamerlano : JF II, III
Hasse, Johann Adolph (1699–1783)
    Arminio : complete, EDM 27–28; Abert
    Euristeo : LAM II; A. Schering, *Perlen alter Kammermusik* (Leipzig,
    C. F. Kahnt Nachf.)
    Leucippo : Bücken
    Piramo e Tisbe : Bücken
    See also Otto Schmid, *Musik am sächsischen Hofe* I, II
Haydn, Franz Joseph (1732–1809)
    C.E. : Hrsg. vom Joseph-Haydn-Institut, Cologne (Munich-Duisberg,
    G. Henle, 1958—)
    L'infedeltà delusa : ed. H. C. Robbins Landon (Salzburg, Haydn-Mozart
    Presse, 1961)
    Lo speziale : German translation, *Der Apotheker*, ed. R. Hirschfeld
    Vienna, Universal, 19??)
Heubel, Johann Georg
    Triumph der Freundschaft : DTOe 64 (Jg. XXXIII[1])
Hidalgo, Juan (*ca.* 1600–1685)
    Celos aun del aire matan : ed. Subirá (Barcelona, Biblioteca de Cata-
    lunya, 1933)
    Empezo la noche toda : Pedrell, *Teatro* III
    Ni amor se libra de amor : Pedrell, *Cancionero* IV
    See also Pedrell, *Teatro* IV, V
Hiller, Johann Adam (1728–1804)
    Der Erntekranz : SB 309b
    Die Jagd : complete, ed. Kleinmichel (Leipzig, Senff, 1890); complete,
    ed. Lortzing (Leipzig, 1904)
    Die Liebe auf dem Lande : M. Friedlaender, *Das deutsche Lied im 18.
    Jahrhundert* (Stuttgart and Berlin, Cotta, 1902)
    Lisuart und Dariolette : HAM 301
    Die verwandelten Weiber : Friedlaender (see above, *Die Liebe*)
Holzbauer, Ignaz (1711–83)
    Günther von Schwarzburg : complete, ed. H. Kretzschmar, DdT 8–9
    (1902); complete, ed. H. J. Moser, DdT, Neuauflage, 8–9 (1957)
Huber, Josef Karl
    Etwas wider Vermuten : DTOe 64 (Jg. XXXIII[1])
Intermedi of 1589
    *Les Fêtes de Florence (1589), Vol. I. Musique des Intermèdes de "La
    Pellegrina,"* ed. D. P. Walker (Paris, Editions du Centre national de la
    recherche scientifique, 1963)
Jommelli, Niccolò (1714–74)
    Fetonte : complete, ed. H. Abert, DdT 32–33 (1907); complete, rev. and
    ed. H. J. Moser, DdT, Neuauflage, 32–33

Joseph I, Holy Roman Emperor (1678–1711)

   See G. Adler, *Musikalische Werke der Kaiser Ferdinand III, Leopold I, und Joseph I* (Vienna, Artaria, 1892–93) II

Kamieński, Mathias (1734–1821)

   See Prosnak, supplement

Keiser, Reinhard (1674–1739)

   Adonis : HAM 267; RB 197

   Croesus : complete, ed. M. Schneider, DdT 37–38 (1912); complete, rev. and ed. H. J. Moser, DdT, Neuauflage, 37–38 (1958); SB 269; TEM 46; Leichtentritt

   La forza della virtù : SB 268

   L'inganno fedele : incomplete, ed. M. Schneider, DdT 37–38 (1912); incomplete, rev. and ed. H. J. Moser, DdT, Neuauflage, 37–38; RB 127; Leichtentritt

   Der lächerliche Prinz Jodelet; EP XVIII (Jg. 21–22)

   Octavia : Handel, C.E., ed. Chrysander, Supplement, VI

   Pomona : E. O. Lindner, *Die erste stehende deutsche Oper* II

   See also R. Eitner in MfMg XVI (1883), supplement; H. Unger, ed., *Althamburgische Opernsuiten . . .* (Berlin, Bote und Bock, 1933); Wolff, BoHg II

Krieger, Johann Philipp (1649–1725)

   Flora : SB 236b

   Procris : SB 236a

   See also H. J. Moser, ed., *Vierundzwanzig Lieder und Arien* (Nagels Musik Archiv, 174–75)

Kurz, Joseph Felix (1715–86)

   Der auf das neue begeisterte und beliebte Bernardon : DTOe 64 (Jg. XXXIII[1])

   Bernardon auf der Gelseninsel : DTOe 64

   Die glückliche Verbindung des Bernardon : DTOe 64

Kusser, Johann Sigismund (1660–1727)

   Erindo : incomplete, ed. H. Osthoff, *Das Erbe deutscher Musik, Landschaftsdenkmale, Schleswig-Holstein*, 3; SB 250

Landi, Stefano (*ca.* 1581–1650)

   La morte d'Orfeo : Goldschmidt I, 188–201

   Il Sant' Alessio : Goldschmidt I, 202–57; HAM 208, 209; Riemann II, Part 2, 255–61; Torchi V

Lanier, Nicolas (1588–1666)

   Luminalia : OHM III, 200

   See also Sabol

Laserna, Blas de (1741–1816)

   El majo y la italiana fingida : Subirá, *Tonadilla escénica* III

   El trueque de los amantes : Subirá, *Inéditas*

   See also Nin, *Sept Chansons picaresques* and *Sept Chants lyriques*; Pedrell, *Cancionero* IV; Pedrell, *Teatro lírico* II

Latilla, Gaetano (1711–91)
  Siroë : Krehbiel
  See also Prunières I
Lawes, Henry (1596–1662)
  Comus : ed. E. H. Visiak (Bloomsbury, Nonesuch Press, 1937); Sabol; HAM 204
  The Triumphs of the Prince d'Amour : Sabol
Legrenzi, Giovanni (1626–90)
  Eteocle e Polinice : RB 106–7
  Il Giustino : SB 231
  Totila : ed. G. Tebaldini (Milan, Ricordi, 1937); Wolff, *Die venezianische Oper*; Heuss . . . *die venetianischen Opern-Sinfonien*; ed. Prunières, RM Supplément I, July, 1923; OHM III, 177
Leo, Leonardo (1694–1744)
  Amor vuol sollerenze : Sondheimer 46–47
  Olimpiade : LAM II
  S. Elena al Calvario : Sondheimer 46–47
  See also Marx, *Gluck und die Oper*, No. 3; Gevaert I, II; Prunières I; Zanon
Leopold I, Holy Roman Emperor (reigned 1658–1705)
  See G. Adler, *Musikalische Werke der Kaiser Ferdinand III, Leopold I, und Joseph I* (Vienna, Artaria, 1892–93) II
Linley, Thomas, Sr. (1733–95)
  The Duenna : complete, ed. A. Reynolds (London, Boosey and Co., 1925); Bush
Locke, Matthew (*ca.* 1630–77)
  Cupid and Death : complete, ed. Dent, *Musica Britannica* II; OHM III, 213–18; Dent, *Foundations*
  Macbeth (incidental music) : Dent, *Foundations*
  Psyche : OHM III, 291–93; Dent, *Foundations*
  The Tempest (incidental music) : complete, ed. W. G. Whittaker (London, Oxford, 1934); OHM III, 289–90
Löhner, Johann (1645–1705)
  Theseus : Sandberger, "Zur Geschichte der Oper in Nürnberg," AfMw I (1918) 84–107; same ed. (Munich, Drei Masken Vlg., 1921)
  Triumphierende Treue : Sandberger, see above
Lotti, Antonio (1667–1740)
  Alessandro Severo : SB 270
  Ascanio : Schmid, *Musik am sächsischen Hofe* I
  See also Gevaert
Lully, Jean-Baptiste (1632–87)
  C.E. : *Oeuvres complètes de J.-B. Lully . . . publiées sous la direction de Henry Prunières . . .* (Paris, Editions de la Revue musicale, 1930–39) 10 vols. (Contains the following operas : *Alceste, Amadis de Gaule, Cadmus et Hermione*)

Alceste : complete, ed. Prunières, C.F.; HAM 224, 225

Armide et Renaud : EP XIV; complete, C.F.; ed. R. Lalande (Paris, H. Lemoine, *ca.* 1957); SB 234; MM 36

Isis : complete, C.F.; Abert

Persée : complete, C.F.; SB 232

Roland : SB 233

In addition to the above, C.F. contains the following complete editions: *Atys, Bellérophon, Cadmus et Hermione, Phaëton, Proserpine, Psyché, Les Saisons* (finished by Colasse), *Thésée*

Majo, Gian Francesco di (1732–70)

Alessandro : Bücken 115

Ifigenia in Tauride : LAM II

See also Marx, *Gluck und die Oper*, Musical Supplement Nos. 5 and 6

Malvezzi, Christoforo (1547–97)

Intermedi of 1589 (with Marenzio, Cavalieri, *et al.*) : Goldschmidt I, 374–80

Marais, Marin (1656–1728)

Semele : suite, ed. L. Boulay (Paris, Sofirad, 1958)

Marazzoli, Marco (*ca.* 1602–62)

Chi soffre, speri : Goldschmidt I, 312–24

Dal male il bene : Goldschmidt I, 325–48

See also L. Torri, *Quattro arie tratte da melodrammi italiani del secolo XVII* (Padua, Zanibon, n.d.); LAM III

Marcello, Benedetto (1686–1739)

Arianna : ed. O. Chilesotti, *Biblioteca di rarità musicale* (Milan, Ricordi, 1884–1915) 4; LAM II

Marcolini, Juan

Naranjera, petimetre y extranjero : Subirà, *Tonadilla escénica* III

Marenzio, Luca (1553–99)

Intermedi of 1589 (with Cavalieri, Malvezzi, *et al.*) : Schneider, *Die Anfänge des Basso Continuo*, pp. 116–57

Mattheson, Johann (1681–1764)

See Wolff BoHg; Wolff DBa I

Mayberg, Johann Wilhelm (18th century)

Der Kaufmann zu London : DTOe 64 (Jg XXXIII[1])

Mazzocchi, Domenico (1592–1665)

La catena d'Adone : Goldschmidt I, 155–73; LAM I; Prunières III

Mazzocchi, Virgilio (1597–1646)

Chi soffre, speri : see Marazzoli

See also Torchi V

Melani, Jacopo (1623–76)

Il girello : LAM I

La Tancia, overo il podestà di Colognole : Goldschmidt I, 349–73; *Atti dell' Accademia del R. Istituto musicale di Firenze, Anno XXXIII* (1895) Supplement 3; Riemann II, Part 2, 240 ff.

Misón, Luis (d. 1766)
  Los ciegos : Subirá, *Inéditas*
  Una mesonera y un arriero : Subirá, *Maestros* I; Subirá, *Tonadilla escénica* III
  Los jardineros : ed. M. N. Hamilton, in *Music in Eighteenth Century Spain*
Monsigny, Pierre-Alexandre (1729–1817)
  Le Déserteur : complete (Paris, A. Leduc, No. 5204)
  See Delsarte VI
Monteverdi, Claudio (1567–1643)
  C.E. : *Tutte le opere. Nuovamente date in luce da G. Francesco Malipiero* (Asola, G. F. Malipiero; Vienna, Universal, 1926–42) 16 vols.
  Arianna (Lament) : SB 177; JF II; Prunières III
  Il ballo delle ingrate : ed. D. Stevens (London, Schott; New York, Associated, 1960); Torchi VI
  Il combattimento di Tancredi e di Clorinda : *I classici* XIX
  L'incoronazione di Poppea : complete, Goldschmidt II; ed. Ghedini (Milan, Ricordi, 1953); Abert; RB 91, 92
  Orfeo : facsimile of 1609 edition, ed. A. Sandberger (Augsburg, 1927); SB 176; HAM 187; MM 31
  Il ritorno d'Ulisse in patria : complete, ed. R. Haas, DTOe 57 (Jg. XXIX¹); SB 178; Prunières III
  This list supplements the list of editions in *Grove's Dictionary*, 5th ed. (1954) V, 846–47. See also *Die Musik in Geschichte und Gegenwart* IX, 528–29
Moral, Pablo del
  La ópera casera : Subirá, *Tonadilla escénica* III
  La tia burlada : Subirá, *Inéditas*
Mouret, Jean-Joseph (1682–1738)
  Triomphe des sens : Prunières VI
Mozart, Wolfgang Amadeus (1756–91)
  C.E. : *Werke*. Hrsg. von J. Brahms, F. Espagne, [et al.] (Leipzig, B&H, 1876–86); *idem*, reprinted (Ann Arbor, Mich., J. W. Edwards, 1951–56); *Neue Ausgabe sämtlicher Werke*. . . . hrsg. von der Internationalen Stiftung Mozarteum Salzburg (Kassel, Bärenreiter, 1955—)
Müller, Wenzel (1767–1835)
  Die Schwestern von Prag : ed. R. Kleinmichel (Leipzig, Senff, 1890); ed. Czarniawski (Vienna, Universal, 1935)
Naumann, Johann Gottlieb (1741–1801)
  Medea : Sondheimer, 30/31
  Protesilao : Sondheimer, 30/31
Paisiello, Giovanni (1740–1816)
  Il barbiere di Siviglia : full score (Milan, Ricordi, 1868); piano-vocal score (Milan, Ricordi, *ca.* 1879, 1903)
  Nina : *I classici* XX (Quad. 80–81)

La bella molinara (*Die schöne Müllerin*) : complete (Leipzig, Senff, 1890); Della Corte
La serva padrona : Della Corte
Socrate immaginario : complete, ed. G. Barini (Florence, 1939)

Pallavicino, Carlo (1630–88)
L'amazone corsara : Heuss, . . . *die ventianischen Opern- Sinfonien*
Le amazoni nelle isole fortunate : Goldschmidt I, 403 f.; Worsthorne
Antiope : RB 120; Riemann II, Part 2, 469 f.
Diocletiano : SB 224; Wolff BoHg II
Gallieno : Worsthorne
Gerusalemme liberata : complete, ed. H. Abert, DdT 55; rev. and ed., H. J. Moser, DdT, Neuauflage, 55
Messalina : Wolff, *Die venezianische Oper*, Anhang, No. 67

Palomino, José
El canapé : Subirá, *Tonadilla escénica* III

Pepusch, John Christopher (1667–1752)
The Beggar's Opera : facsimile of 1729 edition (Larchmont, N.Y., Argonaut, 1961); complete, ed. F. Austin (London, Boosey and Co., 1920); SB 281; HAM 264; for a complete list of modern editions see *Die Musik in Geschichte und Gegenwart* X, 1029–30

Peranda, Marco Giuseppe (*ca.* 1600–1675)
See Bontempi, *Dafne*

Pergolesi, Giovanni Battista (1710–36)
C.E. : *Opera omnia*, ed. F. Caffarelli (Rome, Gli amici della musica da camera, 1939–42); *idem*, republished by Bärenreiter (Kassel, 1943)
Lo frate 'nnammorato : Della Corte
Olimpiade : LAM II; Gevaert; Krehbiel
La serva padrona : complete, ed. K. Geiringer (Vienna, Universal, 1953); *I classici* XXIII (Quad. 89–90); HAM 287; Einstein 36

Peri, Jacopo (1561–1633)
Dafne : Ghisi, *Alle fonti della monodia* (Milan, 1940); Schneider, *Die Anfänge*, 109
Euridice : facsimile (Rome, R. Accademia d'Italia, 1934); Torchi VI; *I classici* XXIV (Quad. 95–96); SB 171; HAM 182; RB 56; Deldevez
Flora (with Gagliano) : see Gagliano, *Flora*
La sole lusinghiera : Solerti, *Gli albori* (1904)

Pez, Johann Christoph (1664–1716)
Trajano : ed. B. A. Wallner, DTB 27–28

Philidor, François-André Danican (1726–95)
Ernelinde : complete, C.F.
Le Maréchal ferrant : Delsarte VI
Sancho Pança : Delsarte VI; Prunières VI
Le Sorcier : Delsarte VI
Tom Jones : Delsarte VI

Piccinni, Niccolò (1728–1800)
  Alessandro nelle Indie : LAM II; Gevaert; Zanon
  La buona figliuola : *I classici musicali italiani* (Milan, 1941–43) 7;
    Eistein 31; Della Corte
  Le contadine bizzarre : Della Corte
  Didon : complete, C.F.
  Le Faux Lord : HAM 300
  La molinarella : Della Corte
  Roland : complete, C.F.
  Le vicende della sorte : Della Corte
  La villeggiatura : Della Corte
Porpora, Nicola (1686–1768)
  See Zanon
Provenzale, Francesco (1627–1704)
  Il schiavo di sua moglie : *HAM* 222
  La stellidaura vendicata : LAM I
  See also Rolland, *Histoire de l'opéra en Europe*, Supplement
Purcell, Henry (*ca.* 1659–95)
  C.E. : *Works.* Published by the Purcell Society (London, Novello, Ewer
    and Co., 1878–1928; 1958?–   )
  Dido and Aeneas : complete, ed. Dent (London, Oxford, 1925); HAM
    255
  King Arthur : SB 247
Quagliati, Paolo (*ca.* 1555–1628)
  Il carro di fedeltà d'amore : ed. V. Gotwals and P. Keppler (1957) SCA
    13
Rameau, Jean-Philippe (1683–1764)
  C.E. : *Oeuvres complètes.* Publiées sous la direction de C. Saint-Saëns
    (Paris, A. Durand, 1896–1924); contains *Castor et Pollux, Dardanus,
    Les Festes d'Hébé ou les talents lyriques* (opéra-ballet), *Hippolyte et
    Aricie, Les Indes galantes* (opéra-ballet), *Platée* (comédie lyrique),
    Zaïs (pastorale héroique), *Zoroastre*
  Castor et Pollux : SB 296, 297a; MM 41
  Dardanus : SB 297b; HAM 277
  Le Temple de la gloire : HAM 276
  See also C.F.—contains editions of all works noted above in the C.E.
    except *Zaïs*
Reichardt, Johann Friedrich (1752–1814)
  See H. J. Moser, *Alte Meister des deutschen Liedes* (Leipzig, Peters,
    1912) 28, 29
Rinaldo da Capua (fl. 1737–78)
  Vologeso : Krehbiel
  La zingara : Della Corte
Rosales, Antonio
  El recitado : Subirá, *Tonadilla escénica* III; Subirá, *Maestros* II

Rossi, Luigi (*ca.* 1598–1653)
 Orfeo : Goldschmidt I, 295–311; SB 199; Prunières III
 Il palazzo incantato : Goldschmidt I, 385–88; LAM I; SIMG, Jg. 1
   (1900) 56–59
Rossi, Michelangelo (fl. 1620–60)
 Erminia sul Giordano : Goldschmidt I, 258–72; Prunières III; H.
   Botstiber, *Geschichte der Ouvertüre*, Beilage 2.
Rousseau, Jean-Jacques (1712–78)
 Le Devin du village : HAM 291
Sacchini, Antonio (1730–86)
 Chimène ou Le Cid : complete, C.F.
 Montezuma : Gevaert
 Oedipe à Colone : Delsarte III
 Renaud : complete, C.F.
 Tamerlano : Zanon
Salieri, Antonio (1750–1825)
 Les Danaïdes : complete, ed. G. Lefèvre, C.F.
 La grotta di Trofonio : Della Corte
 Tarare : complete, C.F.; *Kleine Harlekinade, komisches Intermezzo aus
   der Oper Axur, König von Ormus* [German title of *Tarare*], ed. F.
   Schröder (Mainz, Schott, 1951)
Sarri, Domenico (1679–1744)
 Didone abbandonata : LAM II
 Vespasiano : Zanon
Sarti, Giuseppe (1729–1802)
 Armida e Rinaldo : *A Giuseppe Sarti nel 2º centenario di sua nascità
   (1729–1929)* (Faenza, Soc. tipografica faentina, 1929)
 Fra due litiganti il terzo gode : Della Corte
 See also Gevaert
Sartorio, Antonio (*ca.* 1620–81)
 Adelaide : SB 223; *Nagels Musik Archiv* 141
Scarlatti, Alessandro (1660–1725)
 La caduta de decem viri : TEM 44; Bücken 38 f.
 Il Clearco in Negroponte : LAM III
 La donna ancora è fedele : LAM III
 Eraclea : Haas, *Die Musik des Barocks*, 297 f.
 Griselda : SB 259; HAM 259
 Gl'inganni felici : SB 258
 La Rosaura : EP XIV; RB 119; Krehbiel
 Il trionfo dell' onore : ed. V. Mortari (Milan, Carisch, 1941)
 See also Dent, *Scarlatti*
Schenk, Johann (1753–1836)
 Der Dorfbarbier : ed. R. Haas (1927) DTOe 66 (Jg. XXXIV); ed. R.
   Kleinmichel (Vienna, Universal, 1914)
 Le nymphe di Rheno : EDM 44

Schiassi, Gaetano Maria (d. 1754)
  Alessandro nell' Indie : Krehbiel
Schürmann, Georg Caspar (*ca.* 1672–1751)
  Die getreue Alceste : Abert
  Heinrich der Vogler : MfMg XVII (1885) Beilage, 148–60
  Ludwig der Fromme : incomplete, EP XVII; SB 293
Staden, Sigmund Theophil (1607–55)
  Seelewig : Eitner, MfMg XIII (1881)
Standfuss, J. C. (d. 1756?)
  Die verwandelten Weiber : SB 309a
Steffani, Agostino (1654–1728)
  Alarico : DTB 11 ²
  Henrico Leone : ed. Th. Werner, *Musikalische Denkwürdigkeiten* (Hanover, 1926) I; LAM III; HAM 244; *Nagels Musik Archiv* 141
  Niobe : RB 117
  Orlando generoso : Einstein 30
  Tassilone : ed. G. Croll, *Denkmäler Rheinischer Musik* (Kassel, Bärenreiter, 1958)
  See also DTB 6², 12¹
Storace, Stephen (1763–96)
  No Song, No Supper : ed. R. Fiske (1959) *Musica Britannica* XVI
  The Siege of Belgrad : Thouret, *Musik am preussischen Hofe* (Leipzig, B&H, 1892–97) 9
Stradella, Alessandro (1644–82)
  Il Corispero : HAM 241
  Il Floridoro : LAM I
  La forza d'amor paterno : ed. Gentili (Milan, Ricordi, 1930)
  Giasone : aria from an intermezzo, LAM III
  Orazio : JF I
  See also Deldevez
Striggio, Alessandro (*ca.* 1535–*ca.* 1595)
  Il cicalamento delle donne al bucato : ed. E. Mucci (Rome, de Santis, 1947)
Strungk, Nikolaus Adam (1640–1700)
  Esther : Wolff BoHg II
Telemann, Georg Philipp (1681–1767)
  Pimpinone : ed. Th. Werner (1936), EDM 6; rev. and ed. W. Bergmann (1955), EDM 6; SB 266
Terradellas, Domingo (1713–51)
  Merope : ed. R. Gerhard (Barcelona, Diputación Provincial : Biblioteca Central, 1951); SB 298
  See also Carreras y Bulbena, *Domenech Terradellas*
Theatrical chansons, 15th and 16th centuries
  Theatrical Chansons of the Fifteenth and Early Sixteenth Centuries, ed.

Howard Mayer Brown (Cambridge, Mass., Harvard University Press, 1963)

Theile, Johann (1646–1724)
Orontes : Wolf BoHg II

Torelli, Gaspare
I fidi amanti : Torchi IV

Traetta, Tommaso (1727–79)
See DTB 14^1, 17

Umlauf, Ignaz (1746–96)
Die Bergknappen : ed. R. Haas (1911) DTOe 36 (Jg. XVIII ^{1})

Valledor, Jacinto
See Subirá, *Tonadilla escénica* III

Vecchi, Orazio (1550–1605)
Amfiparnaso : EP XXVI; Torchi IV; ed. C. Perinello (Milan, 1938); SB 164

Vinci, Leonardo (1690–1730)
Artaserse : Zanon
See also Gevaert; Bücken 36

Vitali, Filippo (ca. 1600–1653)
See JF II, III; Gevaert

Vittori, Loreto (1604–70)
La Galatea : Goldschmidt I, 273–94

Vivaldi, Antonio (?1678–1741)
See Prunières I

Ziani, Marc' Antonio (1653–1715)
See Heuss, . . . *die venetianischen Opern- Sinfonien*

SOURCES OF EXAMPLES
AND TRANSLATIONS

1. Coussemaker, ed. *Oeuvres complètes du trouvère Adam de la Halle.*
   Translation : Robin : Yes, and you shall be my love, you shall have
   my belt, my purse, and my buckle. Shepherdess, sweet girl, give me
   your rosary. Marion : Gladly, my sweet friend.
2. *Ballet comique de la reine* (1582) p. 31.
3. Schneider, *Die Anfänge des Basso Continuo*, pp. 147–48.
   Translation : Rejoice, ye mortal throng, happily and gladly rejoice
   at such a gift, and with music and song allay the fatigue of your toil.
4. Solerti, *Gli albori del melodramma.*
   Translation : Thou with heavenward-pointing horns fixed in thy
   broad and spacious forehead : O Lycian Pan !
5. *L'Euridice composta in musica in stile rappresentativo da Giulio
   Caccini Romano* (Florence, G. Marescotti, 1600), p. 15.
   Translation : And raising her eyes toward heaven, her lovely face
   pale and colorless, all her great beauty remained immobile, frozen.
6. Kretzschmar, *Geschichte der Oper*, p. 38. Realization omitted.
   Translation : Alas ! How my heart turns cold in my breast with
   horror and pity; O miserable beauty, how in an instant, ah ! thou
   art brought low.
7. Caccini, *L'Euridice*, 1600.
   Translation : To song, to dance, to the shade, to the flower-decked
   meadows, to the happy streams run singing, O shepherds, on this
   blessed day.
8. *La Dafne di Marco da Gagliano . . . rappresentata in Mantova*
   (Florence, G. Marescotti, 1608), pp. 3–4.
   Translation : If a heart can find mercy above in the golden cloisters,
   hear our lamentations and prayers, O monarch and king of Heaven.
9. *L'Orfeo favola in musica da Claudio Monteverdi rappresentata in
   Mantova l'anno 1607 & novamente data in luce* (Venice, R.
   Amadino, 1609), p. 1.
10. Monteverdi, C.E. XI, 31. Note values halved, bar lines twice as
    frequent.
    Translation : Remember, O shady thickets, my long and bitter
    torments.

11. Monteverdi, *Orfeo*, facsimile of first ed. Figures in brackets correspond to Malipiero's realization, C.E. XI, 59.
    Translation : Messenger : To you I come, Orpheus, unhappy messenger of most unhappy and baneful news. Thy lovely Euridice—Orpheus : Alas, what do I hear? Messenger : Thy beloved wife is dead. Orpheus : Alas!

12. Monteverdi, *Orfeo*, facsimile of first ed. Last two accidentals under bass notes correspond to Malipiero's realization, C.E. XI, 61.
    Translation : Calling to thee, Orpheus! Orpheus! after a deep sigh she breathed her last in my arms and I remained, my heart filled with pity and horror.

13. *La catena d'Adone posta in musica da Domenico Mazzocchi* (Venice, A. Vincenti, 1627), p. 23. Rome, Bibl. Santa Cecilia, G.C.S. 2. C.6
    Translation : The breeze smiles to the fair sky of your divine countenance, and amid dances and songs is revealed to you a smiling new heaven, a new earth, and a new world.

14. *Il S. Alessio, dramma musicale . . . posto in musica da Stefano Landi Romano* (Rome, P. Masotti, 1634), p. 107.
    Translation : Brief shall be the delay; rest and take hope. And when thou art come to the last hour, do not fear death. Contemplate the dark pass, full of hope to all who have suffered pain.

15. *Il S. Alessio . . .* , p. 1.

16. *Il S. Alessio . . .* , pp. 1–2.

17. *La Galatea, dramma del Cav.ᵉ Loreto Vittori da Spoleti, dal medesimo posto in musica* (Rome, V. Bianchi, 1639), pp. 112–13.
    Translation : Weep, O fields and flowers, for the vanished splendors; and thou, O earth, wrap thy breast in a dark mantle and sadly keep company to our plaints.

18. Rossi, *Orfeo* (Rome, Biblioteca Apostolica Vaticana, MS Chigi Q. V 58, f. 189).
    Translation : Kill me, O sorrows : and while I go with desperate pace amidst these savage rocks seeking how I may die, to you more than to a serpent or a wild beast is due that despicable glory. Kill me : since death knew that Euridice alone was my life, and he does not remember that I still live. Kill me, O sorrows.

19. Mazzocchi, *Chi soffre, speri* (Rome, Biblioteca Apostolica Vaticana, MS Barb. lat. 4376, ff. 49ᵛ–50).
    Translation : Let each one follow his pleasure, as long as I may live happily on this shady bank where my father, near to death, promised me (may the prophecy be true!) an unexpected outcome of fortunate happenings.

20. Abbatini, *Dal male il bene* (Rome, Biblioteca Apostolica Vaticana, MS Barb. lat. 4376, ff. 49ᵛ–50).
    Translation : What is the good of searching forever so anxiously to

know what others do? Of fretting my brain in my own craze to understand what may be outside of this and that?

21. Montervedi, C.E. XIII, 80–81. Realization omitted.
Translation : Seneca : Reason is the ruler of man and gods. Nero : You—you—you drive me to frenzy!

22. Monteverdi C.E. XIII, 136. Signature changed from one flat; flat omitted under bass C in measures 1, 4, 8.
Translation : When I am with you my heart beats, when you are away I am dull; I long for and constantly think about your beauty.

23. Monteverdi, C.E. XIII, 85–86. Realization omitted.
Translation : O my adored one, still in my arms I held thee. Poppea, I hardly breathe; I gaze upon thy lips and, gazing, recover with my eyes the fiery spirit which, embracing thee, O dear one, I diffused into thee.

24. Cavalli, *Egisto* (Venice, Biblioteca Nazionale di San Marco, MS It. IV–411, ff. 84–85ᵛ). Time values halved; original time signature C$\frac{3}{2}$, no accidentals in signature.
Translation : Rejoice with me, beloved trees; resound with glad harmonies, ye songsters; Lidio returns and leaves Clori.

25. Cavalli, *Egisto* (Venice, Biblioteca Nazionale di San Marco, MS It. IV–411, f. 50ᵛ). Time values halved; original signature $\frac{3}{2}$. Bar lines added before measures 5, 9, 16.
Translation : Weep, sorrowing eyes, and let the fountain and river weep to my tearful plaint.

26. Cavalli, *Giasone* (Venice, Biblioteca Nazionale di San Marco, MS It. IV–363, ff. 58ᵛ–59). Original time signature $\frac{3}{2}$; time values halved.
Translation : Open to me the creaking hinges of the magic cave and admit me among the shades of the black abode.

27. Venice, Biblioteca Nazionale di San Marco, MS It. IV–41, ff. 30–30ᵛ.
Translation : If perfidious Love pierce thee with his arrows . . .

28. DTOe VI, 108. Continuo omitted.
Translation : These are the tricks used by madmen and mountebanks.

29. Venice, Biblioteca Nazionale di San Marco, MS It. IV–41, f. 33ᵛ.
Translation : The sweet sighs and afflictions are precious to me.

30. Rolland, *Histoire de l'opéra en Europe*, Supplément musical, p. 9. Reduced from four staves.
Translation : Let me die, cruel stars.

31. H. Hess, *Die Opern Alessandro Stradellas*, pp. 88–89. Introduction omitted (six measures of two parts over continuo).
Translation : What are you thinking of, my heart? Your beloved is lost, and lost is all hope of ever having him back.

32. DdT LV, 102. Bass and realization omitted.
Translation : Victory! victory! etc.

33. DdT LV, 74. Realization and German text (translation) omitted. Translation: Cruel lady, you laugh at me but I shall laugh at you. I shall pray to Jupiter that he someday burn with his lightnings the one who has outraged me.

34. DTB XII², 119–20. Condensed from five staves; realization omitted. Translation: Cease, O fate, to make me suffer.

35. DTB XII², 159. Accompaniment (three-part strings) omitted. Translation: I tremble, and mortal cold runs through my veins.

36. DTB XII², 163–64. Condensed from five staves; realization omitted. Translation: The trumpet calls me here.

37. MfMg XIII (1881). Translation: Ah, omnipotent God, worker of miracles, who has led me mercifully through many a plight! Neither in misery nor in happiness would I know what to do without you.

38. Franck, *Cara Mustapha*; H. C. Wolff, *Die Barockoper in Hamburg* (Möseler Verlag, Wolfenbüttel and Zurich) II, 40–41. Translation: Parting, sad parting, forever; ah, how my heart is torn by suffering, all too heavy.

39. *Das Erbe deutscher Musik*, ser. 2, II, 147. Realization omitted. Translation: When one has achieved his goal he should not let any misgivings trouble his happiness, which will be gone before he knows it.

40. Kusser, *Erindo*; H. C. Wolff, *Die Barockoper in Hamburg* II, 68–69. Translation: Thus, in this longed-for sanctuary, may remembrance and pledge both flourish together.

41. SB ex. 232. Accompaniment omitted. Translation: O death, come and put an end to my sad lot.

42A. *Atys, Tragédie mise en musique par Monsieur de Lully* . . . A Paris, Par Christopher Ballard . . . M.DC.LXXXIX, pp. 58–59. Translation: When danger is pleasant, how can one be fearful of it? Is it so wrong to love overmuch that which we find lovable?

42B. *Atys, Tragédie mise en musique par Monsieur de Lully* . . . , 2d ed., Oeuvre VI, [Paris] Christopher Ballard . . . M.DCCXX, pp. 42–43.

43. Lully, *Amadis*. Prunières ed. *Opéras* III, 95–96. Condensed from five staves; flat added before last bass note of measure 8. Translation: Thick woods, redouble your shade; you will never be dark enough, you will never conceal deeply enough my unhappy love.

44. Lully, *Phaëton* (1683).

45. *Old English Edition* XXV, 110. Slurs omitted.

46. *Old English Edition* XXV, 21. Reduced from three staves; realization omitted.

47. *Old English Edition* XXV, 130–31. Realization omitted.

48. Purcell, C.E. XXVI, 41.

49. Purcell, C.E. IX, 17–18. Reduced from four staves; realization omitted.
50. Purcell, C.E. XIX, 49. Reduced from two staves; realization omitted.
51. Händel, C.E. Supplement VI, 104. Reduced from four staves; names of instruments changed from "violino e flauto dolce"; "(Bassi)" changed to "[Continuo]."
   Translation : Babble not so loud, O crystal-silver brook.
52. Händel, C. E. Supplement VI, 26.
   Translation : Ormena! Ormena, thou settest me on fire !
53. DdT XXXVII/XXXVIII, 38. Reduced from five staves; realization omitted; stage direction translated.
   Translation : . . . and lovest no other?
54. DdT XXXVII/XXXVIII, 202. Reduced from five staves.
   Translation : Gods, show pity.
55. Händel, C. E. LVII, 72. Accompaniment omitted.
   Translation : Let the world fall.
56. Händel, C.E. LXVIII, 82–83. Recitative reduced from five staves, aria from six staves.
   Translation : (Recitative) What do I hear? O God ! Cleopatra will yet die. Vile soul, when wilt thou depart? But still ! To avenge myself I shall have . . . . (Aria) If you do not feel pity for me, just Heaven, I shall die.
57. Rameau, C.E. X, *Appendice*, p. 26.
   Translation : Mournful spot, where everything breathes shame and sorrow; dark and cruel realm of despair.
58. A. Scarlatti, *Mitridate Eupatore* (Library of Congress M 1500 .S28M5 case. f. 45–46ᵛ).
   Translation : Kind Gods of our fathers, graciously hear my sorrow; as you favored with your help the undertakings of my ancestors, give strength to him who is preparing to punish a traitor.
59. Dent, *Alessandro Scarlatti*, p. 110. Realization omitted; figure and accidentals in brackets correspond to Dent's realization.
   Translation : O vain hope ! O broken faith ! O brief, alluring, dolorous, impious happiness ! From whom now can I seek aid or consolation? In heaven, on the sea or the earth, in the abyss? Ah! Mithridates is dead !
60. Händel, C.E. XCII. Three string parts omitted; ornamented version of melody by Dr. Putnam Aldrich.
   Translation : Never was shade of plant so dear, precious, and kindly.
61. Haas, *Aufführungspraxis*, p. 186. Signature changed from two flats.
   Translation : . . . explains the cruelty of fate.
62. Vinci, *Artaserse* (Library of Congress M 1500 .V6A6), pp. 17 ff.
   Translation : The wave of the sea bathes the valley and the mountain, goes by in the river, is imprisoned in the fountain, murmurs and groans always until it returns to the sea.

63. Pergolesi, *L'Olimpiade* (MS copy, Library of Congress M 1500 .P42O6 case).
Translation : While you sleep, Love increases the pleasure of your dreams with the thought of my pleasure.

64. Gerber, *Der Operntypus Hasses*, pp. 77–78. Slurs added, other slight changes in notation.
Translation : I will be silent if you desire it, but you are wronging my faithfulness if you call me betrayer.

65. DdT XV, 166. Accompaniment reduced from four staves.
Translation : Without regret I leave a greatness which I have known to be all too fragile and fleeting, and which I have possessed without being overcome by pride. A great and strong soul should always be ready to quit those goods from which death one day will separate him. But thou, O faithful wife !

66. DTB XIV^1, 146–47. Accompaniment (first and second violins, viola, continuo) omitted; realization and reduction omitted.
Translation : Do not weep for my misfortunes, do not be distressed at my torments.

67. DTB XIV^2, 144. Accompaniment (four string parts) omitted.
Translation : As your beautiful flame is lighted in your natal star, so will it shine resplendent.

68. DTOe LX, 46–47. Reduced from nine staves.

69. *I classici della musica italiana* XXIII, Quaderno 89–90, p. 11.
Translation : And yes and no, and no and yes, and here and there, and up and down—now enough of this : let's have an end of it !

70. *I classici della musica italiana* XX, Quaderno 80, pp. 6–7. Reduced from three staves.
Translation : But if Lindoro comes, then, ah ! then all is joy, all is well. When I shall see my love . . .

71. *Théâtre de la Foire*, Vol. I.

72. Monsigny, *Le Déserteur*. Piano-vocal score, Paris, Alphonse Leduc, no. A.L. 5204, pp. 10–11.
Translation : Can one give pain to the one he loves? Why try to annoy him? It is just like being spiteful toward oneself.

73. Grétry, C.E. I, 43–44. Orchestra parts condensed from seven staves.
Translation : O Richard, O my king ! All the world abandons you; only I in all the earth am concerned about you; I alone want to break your chains, and all the rest abandon you.

74. *The Beggar's Opera*, 2d ed. (1728), p. [45]. Repeat marks after first double bar omitted to conform with text.

75. Hiller, *Die Jagd* (Leipzig, 1772).
Translation : O, that his heart loved me as my heart loves him !

76. Dittersdorf, *Das rote Käppchen*. MS Vienna Nationalbibliothek.
Translation : 1. Why, in a word, does Mr. Schulz stay at home and not appear at today's meal? 2. I thank you for the food and drink,

when drunken men fall off their chairs. (Refrain) It might go bad with the women, but if one stays at home nothing can happen.

77. Subirá, *La tonadilla escénica* III, [16–17].
Translation : Let us go to the market, my dear.

78. Cherubini, *Lodoïska* (Paris, s.d. [1791 ?]), pp. 180–83.
Translation : Alas, in this cruel refuge, there was enough of my misfortune. . . . the end of the woes which I have suffered.

79. Cherubini, *Les Deux Journées.* Piano-vocal score, Universal Ed. 3157, p. 14. Text underlaid from another ed., Braunschweig, Meyer, [before 1862].
Translation : Good Frenchman, may God reward you; a good deed is never in vain.

80. Spontini, *Fernand Cortez.* Leipzig, Hofmeister, plate no. 1135, p. 282. Condensed from three staves.
Translation : Sorrowful presentiments, you do not deceive me; my fate is decided.

81. Auber, *La Muette de Portici.* Novello piano-vocal score, p. 137.
Translation : Holy love for our country, give us boldness and pride; to my country I owe life and it owes me liberty.

82. Meyerbeer, *L'Africaine.* Edition Peters No. 2773, piano-vocal score, p. 127. Reduced from three staves; indication of instruments omitted.
Translation : How pale she is ! What cold runs in my veins !

83. Berlioz, *Les Troyens.* Piano-vocal score, Choudens, p. 420. Names of instruments translated; flat added before bass D in measure 11; first eighth rest added in measure 15.
Translation : Farewell, proud city, which generous striving has so quickly built and made to flourish; my loving sister, follower in all my wanderings; farewell, my people, farewell !

84. Boieldieu, *Jean de Paris.* Piano-vocal score, Brussels, E. Loweryns, s.d., [ca. 1830?], pp. 60–61.
Translation : Remain faithful to Glory, cherish the beauty of ladies : that is the way to act like a true French cavalier.

86. Translation : Return, my protectress, help your poor servant; turn from me the rigor of a fate whose caprice I fear.

87. Herold, *Le Pré aux clercs.* Piano score, Paris, Léon Grus, plate no. 1746, pp. 72–73.

88. Mercadante, *La Vestale.* Piano-vocal score, [183–?] plate no. v. 12212 v, pp. 155–62.
Translation : Vestal & chorus : Through my being courses the horrid cold of death; surely a God whom the Tiber abhors today gave a sign in Heaven; he has crushed a father's heart, has changed joy into lamentation, glad songs of triumph into silence and terror.
Emilia : Chaste goddess, if our love is such a horrible crime, let one victim be enough to satisfy your anger; I pray for the hero : O save Decio's life and give me a hundred fearful and terrible deaths.

Decio : She did not know that I had penetrated this sanctuary forbidden to all men. I profaned the place sacred to the goddess. If heaven demands vengeance, if it awaits a victim, cut off this head, still girt with laurels.

89. Rossini, *Tancredi*. Piano-vocal score, Paris, Launer, plate no. 3237, pp. 50–51.

90. Donizetti, *Linda di Chamounix*. Piano-vocal score, Paris, Schonenberger, s.d. [184–?] plate no. S–975, p. 157.
    Translation : If our love is so hateful to men, let us break the hard tie of this bitter life : in Heaven above our struggle will be ended.

91. Bellini, *La sonnambula*. Novello octavo piano-vocal score.
    Translation : Ah, I will not look upon thee, O flower so soon withered; thou hast passed away even as love, which endured but a single day.

92. Verdi, *Ernani*. Piano-vocal score, Novello, plate no. 8063, pp. 174–75. Condensed from six staves.
    Translation : So thou didst laugh, Lion of Castile, and every mountain of Iberia; every glad echo produced a great roar as once against the oppressing Moor.

93. Verdi, *La Traviata*. Piano-vocal score, G. Schirmer, p. 108.
    Translation : Love me, Alfredo, love me as I love you.

94. Verdi, *Otello*. Piano-vocal score, Ricordi, plate no. 52105, p. 361.
    Translation : And thou, how pale thou art! and motionless, and mute, and lovely, blessed creature born under an evil star.

95. Wagner, *Das Liebesverbot*. Piano-vocal score. B&H, plate no. E. B. 4520, p. 396.
    Translation : Ah, what a death for love and honor; to it I dedicate my youthful strength.

96. Wagner, *Tannhäuser*. Eulenburg small score, plate no. E.E. 4850, pp. 648–49. Reduced from six staves.
    Translation : With fervor in my heart such as no sinner has ever felt, I sought the road to Rome.

97. Wagner, *Lohengrin*. B&H, plate no. 25700, p. 140.
    Translation : Never shalt thou ask me, never trouble to know whence I came, nor my name and state.

100. D'Indy, *L'Etranger*. Piano-vocal score, Durand (1902), pp. 149–50. Some notes enharmonically altered.
    Translation : O sea ! Sinister sea, seductive in thy raging.

101. Puccini, *Tosca*. Piano-vocal score, G. Ricordi & Co., plate no. q 109916 q, p. 1. By kind permission of G. Ricordi & Co., Milan.

102. Puccini, *Madama Butterfly*. Piano score, Ricordi, plate no. 110001, p. 123.

103. Giordano, *Andrea Chénier*. Piano-vocal score, Sonzogno (1896), plate no. 929, pp. 88–89.

Translation : I have often heard her say with her ardent voice : have faith in love, Chénier! thou art loved !

104. Kienzl, *Der Evangelimann*. Bote & Bock, piano-vocal score (1894), plate no. 14035, pp. 66–67. Upper staff of accompaniment omitted. Translation : You're not hitting anything any more. The bowling ball is too heavy for you.

105. Glinka, *A Life for the Tsar*. Piano-vocal score, Moscow, n.d., p. 212. Alto voice and accompaniment omitted.

106. Glinka, *Ruslan and Ludmila*. Piano-vocal score, Moscow, P. Jurgenson, s.d., plate no. 30087, pp. 269–70.

107. Mussorgsky, *Boris Godunov*. Piano-vocal score, London, J. & W. Chester, plate no. J.W.C. 9722, p. 154. Reproduced by permission of J. & W. Chester, Ltd., London. Translation : Phew! Give me air! This suffocates my soul! I felt blood surging upward to my face, then down again like a torrent. O conscience, thou art cruel, merciless thy vengeance !

108. Rimsky-Korsakov, *Sadko*. Piano-vocal score, Leipzig, M. P. Balaieff, [1906?] plate no. 1434–1643, pp. 82–83. Translation : Come out from the blue sea, come out to the green fields; come out, prophetic sisters.

109. Pedrell, *Los Pirineos*. Piano-vocal score, J. B. Pujol, plate no. P.25C., pp. 239–40. Time signature, tempo mark, and first "pp" inserted from previous directions.

110. Debussy, *Pelléas et Mélisande*. Piano-vocal score, Durand (1907), p. 236. Translation : Mélisande : Pelléas! Pelléas : Mélisande! Is it thou, Mélisande? Mélisande : Yes. Pelléas : Come here.

111. Dukas, *Ariane et Barbe-Bleue*. Piano-vocal score, Durand (1906), pp. 72–74. Reduced from three or five staves to show only essential harmonic outline; recitatives (two soloists) omitted. Translation : The five daughters of Orlamonde (the black fairy is dead) have sought the gates, have lighted their five lamps, have opened the towers, have traversed three hundred rooms without finding daylight, have opened a well . . .

112. Montemezzi, *L'amore dei tre re*. Piano-vocal score, Ricordi, plate no. 114651, pp. 126–27. Reduced from four staves; first two measures notated with signature of three flats instead of three sharps. Translation : Take, take her; there thou art, Fiora.

113. Pfitzner, *Palestrina*. Piano-vocal score cop. 1916 by Adolph Fürstner (A.7403, 7415, 7418F), p. 5.

114. Richard Strauss, *Capriccio*. Piano-vocal score, Boosey & Hawkes, plate no. 8453, pp. 80–81. Copyright 1942 by Richard Strauss. Reprinted by permission of Boosey & Hawkes Inc., Sole Agents. Translation of Pierre de Ronsard's Sonnet XXVIII from his *Continuation des Amours* (Paris, 1555). Pierre de Ronsard, *Oeuvres*

complètes, Vol. VII, ed. Paul Laumonier (Paris, Droz, 1934), pp. 145–46.

> Je ne saurois aimer autre que vous,
> Non, Dame, non, je ne saurois le faire :
> Autre que vous ne me sauroit complaire,
> Et fust Venus descendue entre nous.
>
> Vos yeus me sont si gracieus & dous,
> Que d'un seul clin ils me peuvent defaire,
> D'un autre clin tout soudain me refaire,
> Me faisant vivre ou mourir en deux cous.
>
> Quand je serois cinq cens mille ans en vie,
> Autre que vous, ma mignonne m'amie,
> Ne me feroit amoureus devenir.
>
> Il me faudroit refaire d'autres venes,
> Les miennes sont de vostre amour si plenes,
> Qu'un autre amour n'y sauroit plus tenir.

115. Szymanowski, *König Roger.* Piano-vocal score, Universal Ed., plate no. U.E. 7750, pp. 23–26. Used by permission of Universal Editions, A.G., Vienna.
Translation : See, there he is! There he comes! Seize the wretch, kill the blasphemer, stone him, stone him!

116. Bartók, *Herzog Blaubarts Burg.* Piano-vocal score, Universal Ed., plate no. U.E. 7026, p. 11. Copyright 1921 by Universal Edition. Renewed 1948. Copyright and renewal assigned to Boosey & Hawkes Inc. Reprinted by permission.
Translation : The walls are wet! What moisture is this on my hands? Do the rocks and dungeons weep?—Ah, Judith, better were the bright days of our betrothal, when white walls enclosed the garden of roses and sunshine gilded the gables.

117. Poulenc, *Les Dialogues des Carmélites.* Piano-vocal score, Ricordi, plate no. R.1471, pp. 80–81. By kind permission of G. Ricordi & Co., Milan.
Translation : . . . like the child of one's old age, and also the most risky, the most threatened. To turn away this threat I would gladly have given my poor life.

118. Prokofiev, *War and Peace* (Moscow, 1958, plate no. M 26793ª), pp. 77–79.
Translation : . . . when from the gold-drenched hills the herds are flocking down to the river, and the clamor of their lowing thunders melodiously across the waters; and, his nets hauled in, the fisherman in his boat is shore-bound, sailing alone, framed by bushes . . .

119. Janáček, *Katja Kabanowa.* Piano-vocal score, Universal Ed., plate no. U.E. 7103, pp. 143–45. Used by permission of Universal Editions, A.G., Vienna.
Translation : How kindly my Boris spoke to me, how tenderly! I

know no more. The nights are full of terror; everyone goes to rest, but for me it is like sinking into the grave. This fear of the dark! And such a noise!—That is like singing!

120. Honegger, *Antigone*. Piano-vocal score, Senart, plate no. EMS7297, pp. 51–52.
   Translation : Neither does justice impose laws of this sort, and I did not believe that your decree could make the caprice of a man prevail over the rule of the immortals, over the laws which are not written.

121. Milhaud, *Le Pauvre Matelot*. Piano-vocal score, Paris, Heugel, [no plate no.] pp. 38–40.
   Translation : His wife : Come in! The sailor : I come to bring you news, Madame. His wife : Of my husband? The sailor : Yes, indeed, Madame, news of your husband. His wife : He is dead . . . The sailor : No, Madame, he is alive, I saw him three weeks ago.

122. Hindemith, *Die Harmonie der Welt*. Piano-vocal score, Mainz, B. Schott's Söhne, ed. no. 4925.

123. Stravinsky, *The Rake's Progress*. Piano-vocal score, Boosey & Hawkes, plate no. B&H 17088, p. 222. Copyright 1949, 1950, 1951 by Boosey & Hawkes Inc. Reprinted by permission.

124. Berg, *Wozzeck*. Universal Ed., plate nos. U.E. 7379/U.E. 121000, p. 29. Used by permission of Universal Editions, A.G., Vienna.
   Translation : We poor folk! See, Captain : money, money! Those who have no money!

125. Dallapiccola, *Il Prigionero*. Piano-vocal score, S. Zerboni, plate no. S. 4464 Z., pp. 61–62. By kind permission of Edizioni Suvini Zerboni, Milan.
   Translation : I cannot control [myself]. Surprised here, at night, I could not avoid renewed, atrocious sufferings. What to do? Return to my dark cell and wait still, always in vain?

126. Orff, *Oedipus der Tyrann*. Piano-vocal score, Mainz, B. Schott's Söhne, ed. no. 4996, p. 234. © 1959 by B. Schott's Soehne, Mainz. Reprinted by permission of the original copyright owners and their U.S. representatives, Associated Music Publishers, Inc., New York.
   Translation : Perish the man, whoe'er he was, that loosed me from the cruel fetters on my feet and rescued me from death and saved my life, conferring no kindness thereby! For had I then died, I had not been so sore a woe to my friends or mine own self. (Chorus :) I too could have wished it thus. (E. P. Coleridge's translation)

127. Janáček, *Das schlaue Füchslein*. Piano-vocal score, Universal Ed., plate no. U.E. 7564, pp. 176–78. Used by permission of Universal Editions, A.G., Vienna.

INDEX

Numbers in italic type under titles or names of persons represent
entries of special importance

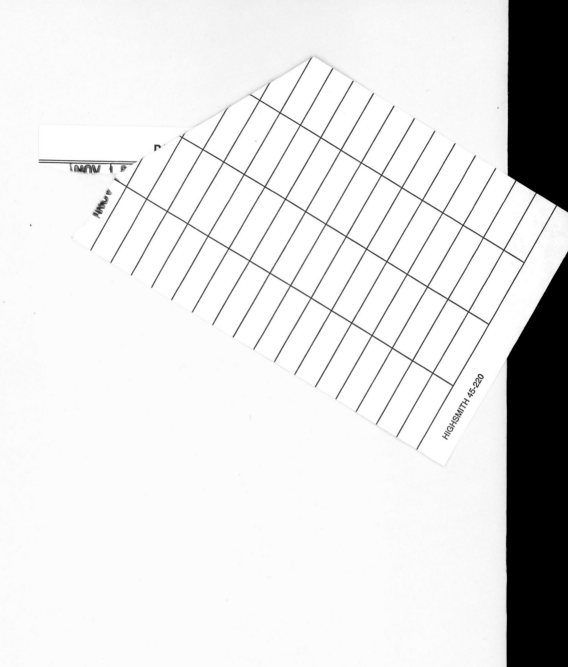

HIGHSMITH 45-220